Strategic
Newspaper
Management

Strategic Newspaper Management

Conrad C. Fink

Henry W. Grady School of Journalism and Mass Communication
University of Georgia

RANDOM HOUSE • NEW YORK

This book is for Sue, my companion on
the trek toward distant horizons, and for
Gar and Stevie, who joined the march
along the way with their special laughter
and love.

McGraw Hill
1-800-338-3987

Library of Congress Cataloging-in-Publication Data

Fink, Conrad C.
  Strategic newspaper management.

  Bibliography: p.
  Includes index.
  1. Newspaper publishing—Management.   I. Title.
PN4734.F54   1987   070.5′068   87-20815
ISBN 0-394-33961-4

Manufactured in the United States of America

Permission to reprint throughout this book materials
credited to the following sources is hereby gratefully
acknowledged: *Advertising Age*, American Newspaper
Publishers Association, Audit Bureau of Circulations,
National Newspaper Association, Newspaper Advertising
Bureau, A. C. Nielsen Co., and Television Bureau of
Advertising.

Foreword

Never has the U.S. newspaper industry been stronger or offered young people such exciting, rewarding careers in so many areas of news and general management.

Advertising and circulation revenues nationwide are at all-time highs. Much of the journalism being produced today is of outstanding quality. And each day newspapers play a truly crucial role in delivering information the citizens of our democratic society need for informed decision making.

At the same time, there has never been a more pressing need for young people both idealistically motivated and professionally prepared to provide leadership for our industry.

The challenges ahead require managers skilled in pragmatic business techniques who also possess the necessary vision and commitment to protect the important role that newspapers play in the cultural and political life of American society.

Future managers will have to work effectively in dealing with the nuts and bolts of sound, profitable management and in assuming community leadership in defense of the First Amendment and the people's right to know.

New competitors will flood into the marketplace, demanding a share of our readers' time and our advertisers' dollars. Newspapers of the future will need innovative leadership from men and women who are not afraid of competition.

Exciting new technology will become available. Our managers will need to be able to implement these new tools efficiently and profitably.

The needs of our readers and advertisers will continue to change as they always have. Our managers will require a sensitive feel for research and marketing techniques to keep their newspapers in touch with the marketplace.

All of this suggests rewarding management careers in an industry that plays a key role in the American way of life. But the tasks ahead

will not be easy and those who want to participate as managers must prepare carefully and methodically.

Where is the best place to start? One proven way is to develop an entry-level specialty in reporting, writing, and editing or in advertising, circulation, or production and simultaneously begin building a strong background in the principles of management.

Three areas can contribute to useful career preparation: First, students can benefit greatly from a broad liberal arts background that can help to formulate a breadth of vision that future managers will clearly need. Second, journalism students should work hard on mastering the basics of getting out a newspaper each day. Those in news–editorial, for example, need to learn how to report the news, write it, and put a headline on it. Those in advertising need to study the basics of selling, layout, and mapping campaigns. Thirdly, students serious about management careers will find it useful to learn the principles of managing people, money, time, and other assets in newspaper production. Conrad Fink's book is designed to give students a start in that direction.

Aspiring managers should know that the concept of integrated management is becoming deeply seated in newspapering. Disruptive internal competition between departments is not only frustrating but counterproductive. Each department—and each employee within those departments—must work in efficient tandem with others, working together toward common goals. Each aspiring manager must have a complete overview of all departmental functions in the newspaper and, whatever his or her own career specialty, be supportive of the mutual effort to succeed. That, too, is a theme of this book.

Some students may not aspire to general management or top leadership. Many will aspire to more narrowly focused as well as fulfilling careers in the newsroom, advertising, or other departments. But even for those not seeking top leadership roles, a total overview—and complete understanding—of all departmental functions can contribute to career success. No editor today, for example, can successfully manage a newsroom and its human and financial resources without understanding the newspaper's other functions and overall strategic corporate goals. That is a major theme of *Strategic Newspaper Management*.

Mr. Fink has made an excellent start in the process of explaining the basics of newspaper management. Not unlike a book on how to play golf or tennis, this book provides a preliminary but comprehensive look at techniques and fundamentals of our business that generally take most of a career to learn and perfect.

Alvah H. Chapman, Jr.
Chairman and Chief Executive Officer
Knight-Ridder, Inc.

Preface

Many U.S. daily newspapers are flourishing as never before. Record profits are flowing from diversified media groups. In rural and smalltown America, many weekly newspapers are yielding bottom line results undreamed of by country editors just a generation ago.

International standards of journalistic excellence are being established by *The New York Times, Wall Street Journal, Philadelphia Inquirer, Washington Post, Los Angeles Times*, and others. And nothing—not Dan Rather broadcasting via satellite, not fancy new national magazines—loosens the hold weekly newspapers and their neighborhood news have on millions of readers.

Simultaneously, however, some once-great newspapers have folded, dismal failures littering the publishing landscape with broken mastheads—*The Philadelphia Bulletin, Washington Star, Cleveland Press, Minneapolis Star, Buffalo Courier-Express*, to name a few big-city examples. And, some small dailies and weeklies are in financial trouble despite their industry's general prosperity. The weekly *Georgia Gazette* in Savannah, for example, failed financially the same year it won a Pulitzer Prize.

How to explain this to students, we who teach in schools of journalism and mass communication? Why unprecedented prosperity and influence on one hand, failure on the other?

Those were among questions I faced when, in 1982, after twenty-five years in news and management ranks in the newspaper industry, I stood for the first time before students at the University of Georgia's Henry W. Grady School of Journalism and Mass Communication. This book is the result of my search for answers, and I place it before my students, fellow teachers, and industry colleagues with a central conclusion: *It is, I think, in long-range planning and in daily operating methodology—in, simply, the professionalism of management at all levels— that is to be found much of the reason for success or failure in publishing newspapers, large or small.*

In search of that professionalism, *Strategic Newspaper Management* first examines the theory of business planning and management and how it enters the success or failure of some major newspapers. But this book also examines more than 200 newspapers and media organizations, small as well as large, for practical "how-to-do-it" operating techniques used every day, at all levels of management, by beginning as well as experienced managers. A successful publishing strategy is possible only if every member of the management team, junior as well as senior, completes his or her assigned task, no matter how seemingly minor. Thus the reader will find in these pages hints on how to strengthen the news columns of a small daily and lay out an ad, as well as the views of the industry's most influential strategists on the sweep of things to come in communications in the decades ahead.

Clearly, a combination of management theory with pragmatic, nuts-and-bolts techniques is necessary in our examination of why, in an era of unrivaled journalistic and financial success, some managers and their newspapers fail. In search for causes of failure, it is not enough to point an accusing finger, as some do, at television, unions, newsprint costs, or the American public's changing lifestyles.

After all, the *Cleveland Plain Dealer* survived the same market disruptions and escalating costs blamed for the death of the *Cleveland Press*. The *Philadelphia Inquirer* came from a distant No. 2 position to vanquish the *Philadelphia Bulletin, the* establishment paper for generations, and in doing so overcame the same unions and lifestyle obstacles blamed for the *Bulletin's* death. And, in smalltown journalism, the pattern repeats: solid journalistic and business success is present alongside shoddy news coverage and financial failure.

So, for both students and aspiring managers already in the industry, *Strategic Newspaper Management* attempts to answer these types of questions:

- Why do some newspapers alertly change news and business strategies to meet marketplace changes, while others do not? When confronted by changing reader lifestyles, why do some editors succeed in moving quickly to meet readers on new lifestyle ground while others continue putting out old-fashioned newspapers for audiences long gone?

- Why, if that Pulitzer Prize-winning weekly failed in Savannah, Georgia, should a weekly in Cobleskill, New York, which never even aspired to a Pulitzer, flourish?

- Why does *The New York Times* evolve brilliantly, developing high-quality special-interest reporting for demographically attractive readers so desired by major advertisers, while *The New York Daily News*, a few blocks away, flounders economically and journalistically?

- Why do suburban weeklies and small dailies prosper around St. Louis while a venerable downtown metro daily dies?

- Why did the family-owned *Los Angeles Times* diversify so profitably, becoming a publicly-owned, multi-billion dollar conglomerate, while the *Washington (D.C.) Star*'s family owners sat on an eroding revenue base until their paper, once among America's greatest, could not be saved even in a last-minute, multi-million dollar rescue effort by Time, Inc.?

And *how*? *How* did the successful managers pull it off? I use numerous case studies and examples, plus many "how-to-do-it" lists, to illustrate the paths successful managers followed to success.

This book is not a pessimistic "survival manual" for newspaper managers or students. It is optimistic for the future of newspapers and those who seek careers in them. An underlying theme of the book, in fact, is that newspapers may be headed for unprecedented influence and prosperity—and responsibility as major influences on how our society works. Competing media are fractionalizing rapidly, which could leave many large and small newspapers the dominant medium in their cities, the single most important vehicle for news and advertising aimed at the general public.

The book illustrates how the marketplace agrees newspapers have profitable futures. Prices paid for newspapers have escalated rapidly. Gannett Co. paid $717 million *cash* in 1985 for the *Detroit News*, four smaller dailies, four weeklies, five TV stations, and one radio station. In 1986, Gannett paid $305 million for the *Louisville (Ky.) Courier-Journal and Times*. Hearst bought the *Houston Chronicle* for $415 million in 1987. Smaller papers commanded premium prices, too. Tribune Co. of Chicago paid $120 million for the *Newport News (Va.) Daily Press*, 62,000 morning and 108,000 Sunday circulation, and the *Times-Herald*, 36,500 afternoon circulation.

This book, then, is about a flourishing industry that offers immense opportunities for bright, aggressive men and women skilled in basic operating methods and newspaper strategy. But the book promises no easy successes. Our students—tomorrow's managers— will not enjoy as many "quick kill" opportunities as did their predecessors. More than one publishing hero was made in the 1970s by new technology that offered unprecedented cost reductions while a booming economy poured in new sales revenue. More than one group executive won fame as a brilliant expansionist by acquiring inefficiently run family newspapers and turning them into cash cows—ruthlessly squeezing costs and editorial content and taking years to pay for the acquisition with discounted dollars heavily eroded by the raging inflation of the time.

So, yes, this book is optimistic. But it is

realistic, too. Teachers, for example, will note throughout my warnings that the "rising tide of shareholder expectations" will put severe pressure on future newspaper managers. John Morton, a leading newspaper analyst, calculates pretax profits of fourteen publicly-owned diversified communications companies averaged 18 percent of gross operating revenues in the period 1974–1984; their newspaper divisions *averaged* 20 percent. In the author's experience, some newspapers do 40 percent or more. Those percentages create envy throughout corporate America and are heady stuff for shareholders, some of whom know nothing about newspapers or care little about their role in our society. Those shareholders simply will demand future managers continue the extraordinary payoff for investing in communications companies.

This book, then, has three basic teaching themes:

- First, newspapers have higher ideals than just making money, responsibilities beyond simply keeping shareholders happy. But newspapers *are* businesses that must be managed efficiently and profitably. A financially failing newspaper cannot shine light in dark corners; a newspaper out of business is no defender of the people's right to know.

- Second, business as well as journalistic success of a newspaper is a responsibility of all who work for it, not just its publisher or business manager. An integrated management team drawn from all departments must administer the complex news and business affairs of a modern newspaper if it is to discharge properly its business *and* First Amendment responsibilities.

- A third teaching theme important to this book: We who teach must help students strive for professional balance as editors and managers with a true sense of journalistic and societal as well as business and managerial responsibilities. If we do that,

if we help create managers skilled in business but also sensitive to news and societal responsibilities, we will accomplish much.

ORGANIZATION

This book has three parts and fifteen chapters. For teachers of stand-alone courses in newspaper management and strategy, assigning front-to-back reading will permit smooth progression from basic "foundation" material in early chapters to increasingly sophisticated treatment in later chapters of more complicated management subjects. However, each chapter is written as a self-contained unit so individual chapters can be assigned students in other courses, such as introduction to mass communications, media and society, ethics, reporting, and writing.

Part I—"The Foundations"—helps teachers lay theoretical groundwork for later discussion of management specifics. Central theme of its five chapters: a manager first must study the newspaper's market, competition, and how its own news and advertising relate to them—then plan carefully.

Chapter One presents the status of the U.S. daily and weekly newspaper industry, how it is positioned against competitors, where its opportunities—and serious problems—lie.

Chapter Two outlines the theory of management, leadership, and corporate organization. It emphasizes—as does *Strategic Newspaper Management* throughout—the principles and techniques managers can use whether leading a workforce of two persons or two thousand, whether managing a small weekly in the first job after school or, later, a metropolitan daily.

Chapter Three is one of the book's most important. It points out that no manager should make any substantive decision without first thoroughly studying the market, competition, and the newspaper's own strengths and weaknesses as a product of news and advertising. How to do this is laid out step by step.

Chapter Four introduces short-term and

long-range planning, a major responsibility of any manager. Here, we take a first look at financial statements and the role they have, along with Management by Objectives, in planning.

Chapter Five combines theory and a "how-to-do-it" approach to personnel ("human resources") management. We run the range of critical tasks—from hiring and firing, to working with (or against) unions. There are suggestions how newspapers can overcome their generally dismal failure to hire and promote minorities and women.

Part II—"Marketing the Newspaper"—has seven chapters with this central teaching theme: Fierce external competition and internal cost pressures force newspapers to adopt a focused marketing thrust that integrates all departments, including news, in a team effort to reach planned goals.

Chapter Six introduces the theory of marketing, including use of research into consumer behavior by modern newspaper marketing departments.

Chapter Seven deals with how managers design efficient, high-quality news organizations and make best possible use of newsroom resources—time, people, money, newshole.

Chapter Eight turns to circulation strategy and the crucial effort to get the newspaper delivered, at acceptable cost, to sufficient numbers of those consumers the marketing function identifies as primary targets.

Chapter Nine describes how to design and manage the advertising effort, which brings in about 80 percent of most newspapers' total revenue. Each advertising category—national, local/retail, classified, legal—is treated in depth.

Chapter Ten treats a crucial subject often overlooked in newspaper management—promotion. We study, first, the newspaper industry's image, then how to organize a newspaper's effort to improve its image, increase circulation, and boost advertising sales.

Chapter Eleven deals with production—the "manufacturing" sector in newspaper man-

agement—and new technology, such as computerized editing and pagination. Joint operating agreements are treated in detail.

Chapter Twelve covers libel, invasion of privacy, and other issues of newsroom law, plus legal problems in circulation (particularly antitrust) and advertising.

Part III—"Those Extra Dimensions"—has three chapters dealing with areas of managerial activity often ignored. Central teaching themes: Ownership opportunities exist, particularly in weekly newspapers, if you know how to spot an opening in the market; and, ethical, socially responsible corporate conduct is required in all management functions.

Chapter Thirteen illustrates how—and why—newspapers diversify and expand into media conglomerates. This is a crucial subject for aspiring managers because, with independent newspapers disappearing rapidly, chances are they eventually will work for a group.

Chapter Fourteen is largely a how-to-do-it case study on finding, acquiring, and managing a weekly newspaper. This chapter is written for (1) those students who will start their careers in the weekly field, and (2) those who, at this point in the book, may feel entrepreneurial stirrings.

Chapter Fifteen recognizes that although this book necessarily focuses on the *business* of newspapering, a manager also has unique historic and societal responsibilities beyond keeping shareholders happy. Thus, we conclude with the ethics of sound journalism, social responsibility, and the manager's public trust.

INSTRUCTOR AIDS

Strategic Newspaper Management combines theoretical background and scholarly references with practical, timely methods and advice drawn from hundreds of newspaper executives who manage newspapers ranging in size from small, family-owned weeklies to metropolitan dailies owned by huge communications conglomerates.

Scores of case studies and real-life examples are used to make the book readable and illustrate concepts and principles students can use in their first job after graduation or years later when they reach significant management levels.

For each chapter, an opening "window" introduces central themes to be discussed. Within each chapter, footnotes are designed to draw students into further reading in both scholarly works and topical journals. Each chapter concludes with a summary, designed to encourage classroom discussion, and a "Recommended Reading" note that lists journals, books, and industry associations (with addresses) where further information may be obtained.

I make a major effort to weave into the text an explanation of each new term or concept as it is encountered. Glossaries follow chapters on circulation, advertising, and production for readers unfamiliar with some terms.

Wherever possible, I use lists and a basic "how-to-do-it" approach that I hope will assist teachers in illustrating immediate application of management techniques in a first job with, say, a weekly newspaper or small daily.

I use "boxed" personality sketches to illustrate for aspiring managers how important figures reached the top in the industry—and the management concepts and methods they used to get there. Many principles of sound management also are "boxed" to highlight their importance. Numerous organizational charts and illustrations are used.

I have written two indexes—one for names, another for subjects—to facilitate efficient search by teachers and students alike for leading personalities and newspapers in the industry and important managerial principles.

ACKNOWLEDGMENTS

As a cub on the nightside in Chicago, a correspondent new to Asian battlefields, as a business executive in many parts of the world, I have been blessed with countless interesting, highly professional colleagues. I cannot acknowledge, here, the assistance of each. But to all I say, many thanks.

More than any others, two are my inspiration, and what giants they are: Wes Gallagher and Paul Miller, retired president and chairman, respectively, of The Associated Press.

In my turn to academia, William S. Morris III, chairman and chief executive officer of Morris Communications, Inc., has been a strong supporter. At the University of Georgia, Warren Agee, Scott Cutlip, Al Hester, George Hough, Kent Middleton, and Tom Russell have been friendly guides.

My special thanks go to Samuel V. Kennedy III, chair of the Newspaper Department at Syracuse University's S. I. Newhouse School of Public Communications, and to Professor Roy Halverson of the University of Oregon's School of Journalism for their several critiques of this book in manuscript form. My thanks also to other reviewers who contributed their time and thoughts: the late Cortland Anderson, Ohio University; Phil Angelo, The Ohio State University; Raymond H. Boone, Howard University; William A. Bray, University of Missouri; William Bridges, Franklin College; James K. Gentry, University of Missouri; E. A. Jerome, Brigham Young University; John M. Lavine, University of Minnesota; Robert H. McGaughey III, Murray State University; Bill Thorn, Marquette University.

At Random House, priceless assistance came from Roth Wilkofsky, executive editor for humanities, and Kathleen Domenig, a superb editor instrumental in shaping this book.

The nimble fingers and good cheer of typist Vera Penn have been most helpful.

Conrad C. Fink
Alta Vista Farm
Cherry Valley, New York

Contents

PART I

THE FOUNDATIONS

Part I of this book will introduce aspiring young managers to the sweep of the industry—its problems as well as its triumphs—and then discuss the foundations of management in each major department of a newspaper.

The author's purpose is to illustrate principles of management through the discussion of well-known newspapers. The reader is urged to remember that entry-level managers at newspapers large and small, daily or weekly, face the same challenges and opportunities faced on the *New York Times*, the *Philadelphia Inquirer*, or any other large newspaper. Only the scale is different.

The five chapters of Part I, in order, are The Status of the Newspaper Industry, The Theoretical Framework, Preface to Planning, The Planning Stage, and The Human Element.

The Status of the Newspaper Industry

CHAPTER
ONE

Many of Napoleon's foot soldiers, it is said, carried marshal's batons in their knapsacks, such was the French leader's reputation for spotting and promoting talent from the ranks. So too should aspiring young newspaper men and women carry dreams of climbing to positions of authority in news, advertising, circulation, production—or, indeed, of "commanding" their own newspapers.

Anyone entering newspapering should keep open the option of assuming greater responsibility one day. Covering cops for a large metro daily or selling ads for your hometown weekly may now seem to be the ultimate career. But there will likely come a day when the challenge of becoming a manager—a leader—will look inviting. Start preparing now for that day. Keep slogging ahead one step at a time, yet also build a wider, strategic view of the total newspaper, its overall mission, its place in society, and how it must be managed.

For the young newspaper person, we begin the march in Chapter 1 by examining the status of the U.S. newspaper industry, its positioning against competitors, some of its opportunities, and some of its problems.

THE STRONG POSITION OF NEWSPAPERS

The American daily and weekly newspaper industry stands on firm economic foundations and, given a reasonably sound general economy, may be headed toward unprecedented prosperity in the decades ahead. Many newspapers are enjoying record-breaking profits and are striving to become the most effective vehicles for the dissemination of news and advertising in their cities. This will not be accomplished without challenge. *Externally*, newspapers face an increasing number of vigorous competitors fighting for reader time and advertiser dollars, the source of any newspaper's strength. *Internally*, complex business problems and rising costs are testing each manager's skill and resolve. Newspaper enthusiasts, however, see golden opportunities in the rampant fractionalization now under way among competing media.

Where will the information seeker turn in the decade ahead for news—to the thirty, forty, or perhaps even one hundred TV channels available? To network TV—to ABC, NBC, CBS? Multichannel cable TV is seriously eroding the time viewers spend with network TV. Will the information seeker turn to magazines and, if so, to which of the 11,000 or more titles offered in the United States? Is it not possible that the professionally edited, high-quality newspaper can look forward to standing out in its marketplace as a manageable, reliable, single-source news medium and thus to competing successfully against the increasingly loud electronic babble—against a blizzard of magazines and other news sources?

And, newspaper optimists ask, where will advertisers put their money in coming decades to reach prospective customers? On which of the thirty, forty, or more TV channels will they place their bets? Or will they go with radio? If so, with which of the fifteen or twenty stations in large cities or the five or six now available in even small towns? Will they go to direct mail, tossing their messages into the flood of adver-

tising mailed each year to the American home? Will advertisers risk parceling out their advertising dollar—dimes to TV, nickels to radio, pennies to direct mail? Or, as seems likely in many cities, couldn't the newspaper stand out as the single most attractive advertising medium?

Newspaper optimists, then, hold that for both the advertiser and the seeker of news, the proliferation of competing media could well diminish the effectiveness of any single one and correspondingly enhance the single-source value of the newspaper.

Dramatic communications changes are promised for the years ahead, and perhaps only nimble editors, shrewd publishers, and alert professional managers at every level will pull newspapers through the predicted revolution in the way news and advertising is sped electronically around this country. But the newspaper survives—indeed flourishes—despite past communications revolutions, and is strongly positioned to meet new challenges.

Growth of Advertising and Circulation

The American Newspaper Publishers' Association (ANPA) calculates that in 1950 there were 1,772 daily newspapers of paid circulation in the United States; in 1985, there were 1,676—a

Table 1.1   Number of Daily Newspapers

Year	Morning	Evening	Total M&E*	Sunday
1960	312	1,459	1,763	563
1965	320	1,444	1,751	562
1970	334	1,429	1,748	586
1975	339	1,436	1,756	639
1980	387	1,388	1,745	735
1985	482	1,220	1,676	798

* In 1985, twenty-six "all-day" newspapers published in both morning and afternoon cycles. They are listed in both morning and evening columns above but only once in the total.

Source: American Newspaper Publishers' Association.

Table 1.2   Daily Newspapers by Circulation Groups

Year	Total	Under 50,000	50,001– 100,000	100,001– 250,000	Over 250,000
1960	1,763	1,540	96	83	44
1965	1,751	1,510	111	88	42
1970	1,748	1,491	127	92	38
1975	1,756	1,504	135	81	36
1980	1,745	1,479	145	86	35
1985	1,676	1,419	140	82	35

Source: American Newspaper Publishers' Association.

drop of just 5.3 percent in a thirty-five-year period that included the birth and explosive growth of network TV. (See Tables 1.1 and 1.2.)

In those thirty-five years, paid daily circulation grew to 62.7 million, up 8.9 million or 16.5 percent. Per-copy readership grew as well until today an average of 2.7 persons read each copy of some newspapers. Even at the more conservative figure of 2.5 readers per copy, about 156.7 million Americans turn to newspapers daily. (See Table 1.3.) Sunday paid circulation hit 58.8 million in 1985, up 12.3 million or 26.4 percent from 1950 (See Table 1.4.)[1]

---

[1] *Facts About Newspapers '86*, Washington, D.C.: American Newspaper Publishers' Association, April 1986, pp. 2–3.

Yes, some metropolitan dailies disappear, often following highly publicized rescue attempts by prestigious communications companies or shrewd private entrepreneurs who succeed in everything else they try but who, despite the investment of millions of dollars and enormous managerial genius, fail to revive wounded metro dailies.

Yes, gone are newsboys who dashed about great cities, hawking multiedition, mass-circulation papers with cries of "Extra" ("Wuxtry," say some purists).

But in suburbs like Hackensack, N.J., and on Long Island, newspapers grow. Such communities—"markets," in trade lingo—are exploding with new population, new wealth—the

Table 1.3   Daily Newspaper Circulation

Year	Morning	Evening	Total M&E	Sunday
1960	24,028,788	34,852,958	58,881,746	47,698,651
1965	24,106,776	36,250,787	60,357,563	48,600,090
1970	25,933,783	36,173,744	62,107,527	49,216,602
1975	25,490,186	36,165,245	60,655,431	51,096,393
1980	29,414,036	32,787,804	62,201,840	54,671,755
1981	30,552,316	30,878,429	61,430,745	55,180,004
1982	33,174,087	29,313,090	62,487,077	56,260,764
1983	33,510,242	29,041,494	62,611,741	56,714,895
1984	35,424,418	27,657,322	63,081,740	57,511,975
1985	36,361,561	26,404,671	62,766,232	58,825,978

Source: American Newspaper Publishers' Association.

Table 1.4   Largest U.S. Dailies

	Circulation
Wall Street Journal (morning)	1,985,559
New York Daily News (morning)	1,275,268
USA Today (morning)	1,168,222
Los Angeles Times (morning)	1,088,155
New York Times (morning)	1,035,426
New York Post (all day)	803,995
Washington Post (all day)	781,371
Chicago Tribune (morning)	760,031
Detroit News (all day)	650,445
Detroit Free Press (afternoon)	645,266

Top Sunday Papers

New York Daily News	1,676,858
New York Times	1,625,649
Los Angeles Times	1,353,376
Chicago Tribune	1,163,083
Washington Post	1,091,307
Philadelphia Inquirer	984,569
Detroit News	832,365
Boston Globe	811,149
Detroit Free Press	744,494
San Francisco Examiner/Chronicle	711,560

Source: Audit Bureau of Circulation, March 31, 1986.

Table 1.5   How U.S. Advertising Is Shared*

	Daily Newspapers	Television	Radio	Magazines
1970	29.2%	18.4%	6.7%	6.6%
1975	30.0	18.7	7.0	5.2
1980	28.5	20.8	6.9	5.8
1985	26.8	21.7	6.8	5.5

* Newspapers enjoy the largest single share of U.S. advertising. Television is the largest single competitor.

Growth in Ad Revenue (in millions)

	Newspapers	Television	Radio	Magazines
1970	$ 5,704	$ 3,596	$1,308	$1,292
1975	8,442	5,263	1,980	1,465
1980	15,541	11,366	3,777	3,149
1985	25,170	20,770	6,490	5,155

Source: American Newspaper Publishers' Association.

spillover from neighboring large cities agonized by traumatic socioeconomic change. Cries of "Wuxtry" are stilled, all right, but—despite the prophets of doom—the "thunk" of community newspapers landing on suburban front porches grows louder.

Paid weekly newspapers, meanwhile, are enjoying rapid growth, thanks largely to population expansion in suburbs and many small towns. By 1987, there were 7,600 weeklies, each with an average circulation of 6,262 and all with a total circulation of 47.5 million. Estimated readership was several times that.[2]

The advertising revenue enjoyed by U.S. dailies is growing rapidly. ANPA says it hit $25.1

billion in 1985, up from $5.7 billion in 1970.[3] Newspapers' share of total advertising revenue was 26.5 percent in 1985, the largest share of any single medium. As in circulation, there is a redistribution of advertising share from failed metros to burgeoning smaller papers. (See Table 1.5.) The newspaper industry is huge, with 453,000 employees in 1985 (41 percent of them women, according to ANPA), and it is certainly both profitable and fundamentally healthy.

Prosperity for Competitors as Well

Competitors, meanwhile, enjoy rapid growth, also. Although total TV revenue, for example, was insignificant in 1950, it hit $20.7 billion in 1985 and registered 12.2 percent annual compound growth in the 1970s. Radio revenue in 1985 reached $6.4 billion, after 11.2 percent compound growth in that decade. Magazines took in $5.1 billion ad revenue after 10.2 percent compound growth in the 1970s.[4]

[2] Ibid, p. 14.

[3] Ibid, p. 7.
[4] Ibid, p. 8.

Table 1.6   Television Household Penetration, 1950–1981 (as of January 1)

Year	TV Households* (thousands)	Total Households* (thousands)	Percent with TV
1950	3,880	43,000	9.0%
1955	30,700	47,620	64.5
1960	45,750	52,500	87.1
1965	52,700	65,900	92.6
1970	58,500	61,410	95.3
1975	68,500	70,520	97.1
1980	76,300	77,900	97.9
1985	86,000	87,500	98.1

* Excludes Alaska and Hawaii.
Source: Television Bureau of Advertising.

TV—ubiquitous TV—is the primary challenger. Born as a commercial medium in the 1950s, it is a fixture in 98.1 percent of all American homes and a seeming obsession of millions. (See Table 1.6.) Can newspapers survive when survey after survey shows that the average TV set is turned on five, six or more than seven hours daily? (See Table 1.7.) In fact, newspaper editors generally react well to TV— so well, perhaps, that their relative success in adjusting to fight TV obscures the much more fundamental threat from changes in the way Americans live and the cities they live in.

The Impact of Changes in Life-Style

American newspapers are much more affected by changes in life-style than from any competing medium, including TV. Let us consider three of the most important life-style changes that present you, the aspiring newspaper manager, with a "shifting scene" in the 1990s:

1. Rapid growth of suburban journalism. Print competition in most large and medium-size markets now pits a single surviving city paper against encircling suburban dailies and weeklies. Rarely do two or more papers of like circulation and characteristics slug it out in the

same "field," morning or afternoon. A manager has new opportunities for meaningful, community-oriented newspapering in suburbs and small towns prospering in the shadow of neighboring metro dailies. For metro daily managers, the challenge of the 1990s will be formidable competition in their own suburban backyards—now markets of primary importance to major advertisers.

2. Visible weakening of afternoon papers. Many, particularly in large cities, approach the 1990s in deep trouble. Afternoon circulation and influence are dropping. In 1982, nationwide morning circulation for the first time surged past afternoon circulation. It's that life-style thing. Cutting deeply into the afternoon metro's perceived relevance and reader appeal are shifts in American work and play habits, along with socioeconomic deterioration in city cores. Some once-dominant afternoon metros die; others shrink almost unrecognizably. Afternoon papers continue strong in many small towns. But life-style changes now strike small afternoon papers too.

Table 1.7   Hours of TV Usage per TV Home per Day (yearly average)

1950	4:35
1955	4:51
1960	5:06
1965	5:29
1970	5:56
1975	6:07
1976	6:18
1977	6:10
1978	6:17
1979	6:28
1980	6:36
1981	6:40
1982	6:48
1983	6:55
1984	7:08
1985	7:07

Source: A. C. Nielsen Co.

The Long Island edition of *Newsday*, which serves a suburb of New York City, is one example of the suburban papers which represent a major advertising medium.

3. The "silent crisis" of shallow household penetration by many newspapers. This means that paid circulation is static, even dropping in relation to household growth, for many papers. And, everywhere, advertisers flee to direct mail and free-circulation papers promising to reach 80 to 90 percent of a market's households. Metro circulation declined 13 percent in the nation's top fifty markets in 1961–1981, while households grew by 41 percent. Newspapers must create new techniques to identify primary markets, geographic and demographic, and then reach them to the advertisers' satisfaction.

By 1980, there were about 80.3 million U.S. households. With 62.2 million paid circulation that year, dailies sold 77 copies for each

100 households—compared with 124 per 100 in 1950. One cause is that the two-newspaper household seems almost a thing of the past—except for those that add to their local newspaper a nearby metro daily or a national newspaper—the *New York Times*, *Wall Street Journal*, *USA Today*. In the 1970s, two-a-day readership dropped to 14 percent of total population, down from 26 percent. And many households simply do without any newspaper. Even great newspapers have penetration problems. For example, the *Los Angeles Times*, reputedly the world's most profitable paper, penetrates only about 24.5 percent of Los Angeles County households.

In advertising, handsome annual increases in revenue mask the critical fact that newspapers' share of the total ad market is deteriorating. Leo Bogart, executive vice president of the Newspaper Advertising Bureau (NAB), sounded alarms in 1985: newspapers' share of local retail advertising, the industry's single most important revenue source, had slipped to 40 percent from 50 percent in 1960. Their share of national advertising had dropped to 11 percent in 1984 from 21 percent in 1960. Both television and direct mail steadily enlarge their share of the total ad dollars available.

CHALLENGES AND FAILURES

Advertisers increasingly demand deeper household penetration—and the newspaper's print competitors are listening.

K Mart wants up to 75 percent penetration; Sears seeks distribution programs promising 80 percent. Says James F. Boynton, supervisor of J. C. Penney's $270 million (1983) local media budget: "If 50% or more of our households are not getting the Penney advertising message through the newspaper, then we have a serious problem, and so does the publisher."[5]

---

[5] "How J. C. Penney Uses Newspaper Audit Reports," *Audit Bureau of Circulations Case Book*, Schaumburg, Ill.: Audit Bureau of Circulation, 1983, p. 5.

Responding to such talk, the "shopper" or free-distribution advertising paper is expanding rapidly, offering Total Market Coverage (TMC). It is relatively shallow penetration by paid dailies and weeklies that permits shoppers to emerge as significant forces in many markets. Direct mail is another competitor exploiting shallow newspaper penetration. Using the U.S. Post Office to flood American homes with advertising, direct mail companies hit $15.5 billion annual revenue in 1985. And if postal rates are too high for single users, several can share the same envelope, allowing "marriage" or "shared" direct mail to come into vogue.

The success of shoppers and direct mail in the hands of skilled marketing organizations reveals that newspapers are guilty of structural failures in two crucial areas:

First, some newspaper editors fail journalistically in not making their packages of news, information, and entertainment attractive enough to ensure widening reader acceptance. Newspapers are no longer a necessity in many homes. Millions of Americans feel no need to read newspapers, perceiving TV as an acceptable substitute.

Second, the growth of shoppers and direct mail clearly signals a marketing failure—the failure of newspaper managers to position their paid circulation newspapers in enough homes with advertising strategies and rates sufficiently attractive to elicit maximum advertising support.

How managers react to changes is crucial. For example, on the problems of afternoon papers, Helen K. Copley, chairman and chief executive officer of the privately held, diversified Copley Newspapers, says:

> Some . . . great afternoon newspapers were, undeniably, victims of economic forces and reading habits changed by television. But, who knows? Perhaps owners of the deceased papers simply failed to make the correct adaptive decisions to a changing environment while [it was] still possible to do so.[6]

[6] Helen K. Copley, speech to the Los Angeles Rotary Club, May 7, 1982.

Socioeconomic change is easily misinterpreted while it is under way and, ironically, those who in the past missed its meaning include the managers of some metropolitan newspapers with the most to lose. On their front pages, they print news of changing life-styles, the horrors of deteriorating city cores, the stampedes of the affluent to the suburbs. But some fail to crank all that into their business strategy.

In some board rooms and publishers' executive suites—and down the managerial ladder—nothing changes. It is business as usual in a newspaper world that is no longer usual. Some continue publishing true "dinosaurs," newspapers designed for audiences that no longer exist and which now reach audiences that have exchanged inner-city blue collars for suburban white collars. And readers now preoccupied with small community school boards and suburban politics no longer see relevance in the same old diet that metropolitan editors have served up for generations.

Inevitably, then, newspapers fail—including metro giants whose demise convinces some observers that *all* newspapers are finished. But is this really a failure of the newspaper as an institution or a failure of individual managers to sense changes in their publishing environment and make appropriate adjustments?

A "new breed" of managers will be needed—men and women who are schooled in traditional journalistic skills and committed to the First Amendment responsibilities of a free press, on the one hand, but who, on the other, also are at ease with profit-and-loss statements, balance sheets, operating budgets and long-range planning.

SUMMARY

The U.S. newspaper industry is stronger than ever. With 62.7 million circulation (1985), the nation's 1,676 daily papers are well positioned for future growth. Weeklies are burgeoning. Total daily newspaper advertising revenue hit

$25.1 billion, or 26.8 percent of all U.S. advertising, in 1985.

The rampant fractionalization of competing media offers great opportunity for newspapers. Cable TV threatens network TV, today the largest single competitor for newspaper ad revenue. Specialty magazines and direct mail, while competing, of course, against general-interest newspapers, may so divide the market that many a newspaper can become the dominant single-source news medium in its market and the most cost-effective advertising vehicle.

But there are major negatives. Newspapers don't penetrate enough households to satisfy advertisers who want 80 percent or more reached with their commercial messages. Consequently, newspapers are losing share of market to television, radio, direct mail, and other media.

RECOMMENDED READING

Scholarly publications that can be helpful in maintaining a continuing overview of the newspaper industry include *Journalism Quarterly*, *Newspaper Research Journal*, *Journal of Communication*, *Mass Media Research*, *Public Opinion Quarterly*, *Communication Research Trends*, and *Nieman Reports*.

Extremely helpful periodicals include *Washington Journalism Review*, *Columbia Journalism Review*, *Quill*, *Editor & Publisher*, *Advertising Age*, *presstime*, and *The Gannetteer*.

For newspaper coverage of the industry, note particularly the *New York Times*, *Wall Street Journal*, and *Los Angeles Times*.

These industry groups (and their publications) cover important developments: American Newspaper Publishers' Association (*presstime*), The Newspaper Center, Box 17407 Dulles International Airport, Washington, DC 20041; Associated Press Managing Editors' Association (*APME Red Book*), 50 Rockefeller Plaza, New York, NY 10020; American Society of Newspaper Editors (*ASNE Bulletin*), The Newspaper Center, Box 17004 Dulles International Airport, Washington, DC 20041; Newspaper Advertising Bureau (excellent periodic research reports), 1180 Avenue of the Americas, New York, NY 10036.

A useful overview is *Readers: How to Gain and Retain Them*, published by the Newspaper Advertising Bureau in 1986.

CHAPTER TWO

The Theoretical Framework

Let's say it has been eighteen months since your graduation and you are happily covering cops for a daily or selling advertising for a country weekly. Suddenly you, the reporter, are asked to supervise two fellow reporters on a team investigating a political scandal at City Hall. Or you, the salesperson, are asked to direct the weekly's two-person ad staff.

Congratulations; you have become a manager. The moment you start supervising the performance of another person, you are a manager. But you don't become a *leader* until you prove it. Where to turn? Where to start?

We start, here in Chapter 2, by considering the theory of newspaper management and the skill—call it the "art"—of leadership. The principles are applicable to the challenge ahead of you, whether on a metro daily or country weekly, whether you supervise one person or a thousand.

Effective newspaper management is efficient use of all resources at every level to move the newspaper toward planned organizational goals. Resources include people, money, time, the goodwill of readers and advertisers, and—increasingly these days—the new production technology that is revolutionizing the industry.

To succeed as a manager, you must coordinate efforts of individual employees and groups of employees primarily in two time frames: in short-range or day-to-day operations and over the long-range, to achieve strategic goals.

This must be done in continually changing environments. A state of flux exists in any newspaper's external environment, in the socioeconomic dimensions of its marketplace, among its competitors and customers, and in the law and society's values

11

and expectations. Change also is under way constantly in a newspaper's internal environment, in human relationships, cost/revenue patterns, and many operational areas.

Making correct decisions in such shifting sand is each manager's key responsibility. At every level, the challenge is to ensure that, despite unforeseen trials and tribulations along the way, the newspaper ultimately reaches planned goals.

And that is the bottom line of being a manager—getting it done and done properly, no matter what. To accomplish this, each manager at every level engages in continual planning, decision making, goal setting, organizing, leading and motivating employees, disseminating information, monitoring and controlling employee performance, and then adjusting operations as necessary to make sure that goals are met.[1]

MANAGEMENT: THE BEGINNINGS

Today's students of newspaper management may understandably reject early management theories, seeing them as narrow philosophically and unduly dependent on the harsh regimentation of both managers and employees. Yet, those early theories influence, for better or worse, many of today's management practices. To understand what is being done today, let's look briefly at yesteryear.

In the beginning, there was Adam Smith (1723–1790), who originated the theory that human work performance is motivated almost exclusively by monetary reward. Smith paid scant attention to the whole human being—to workers' real needs, beyond pay, for fulfillment and recognition. Such a one-dimensional approach to motivating newspaper employees can be disastrous. A wide range of human needs must be satisfied if employees are to be motivated effectively. Yet even today some newspaper managers try to motivate employees in

the erroneous belief that money alone answers all personnel problems.[2]

Frederick W. Taylor (1856–1915) and colleagues of his era, notably Henry Gantt and Frank and Lillian Gilbreth, advanced a theory known as *scientific management*. It, though widely discredited, persists in some newspaper departments. Taylor, working at U.S. Steel and Ford Motor Co., attacked production inefficiency with a scientific approach featuring incentive pay for workers in what amounted to piecework assignments. This advanced the assembly-line approach to mass production. Taylor, however, like Smith, saw economic reward as the primary motivation for work performance; he underestimated a manager's obligation to help employees fulfill other, psychological needs. The impersonal treatment of employees as assembly-line automatons is not effective in the newspaper business.

Max Weber (1864–1920) saw greater efficiency flowing from an organizational structure that clearly communicates work procedures, clearly outlining the flow—the "hierarchy"—of

[1] For helpful overviews of management theory, see James H. Donnelly Jr., James L. Gibson, and John M. Ivancevich, *Fundamentals of Management*, Dallas, Business Publications, 1978; and James A. F. Stoner, *Management*, Englewood Cliffs, N.J., Prentice-Hall, 1978.

[2] For a concise view of the development of management theory, see W. Jack Duncan, *Management*, New York, Random House, 1983.

authority mandating highly specialized work roles for employees. Weber and other theorists of his time created the *administrative* or *bureaucratic* school of management thought, expecting that a corporate bureauracy operating under firmly established rules would be even-handed—even impersonal—in selecting, promoting, and disciplining employees. Meritorious performance, nothing else, is what counts. Today, Weber's concept influences the tables of organization drawn by many newspapers. The assignment of employees to narrowly specialized work in, say, circulation or production smacks of Weber's theory that specialized work roles lead to efficiency. Today's managers must not let Weber's approach become distorted in practice, creating an inflexible organization whose employees are coldly, impersonally fitted into slots. Rigid tables of organization can lead to barriers between departments, an obstacle to the totally integrated management thrust so necessary in an effectively run newspaper.

Extremely important breakthroughs toward modern management technique occurred in the 1920s. Theorists became aware that human relationships in a work force are as important to efficiency as are, for example, physical surroundings, and that those relationships are not restricted to the connecting lines on a table of organization. It became clear that numerous unofficial groups and subgroups form in any company and that a manager must understand them. Perhaps most important, it became obvious that more than money is needed to motivate employees. Thus was born the *human relations* theory of management. Seminal research was done by George Mayo (1880–1949) and others at Western Electric Co. in Hawthorne, New Jersey; this became known as the "Hawthorne Study." Mayo and fellow theorists, including Abraham Maslow (1908–1970) and Chester Barnard (1886–1961), contributed heavily to the philosophy that each employee is unique in personality and attitudes and that no single motivational program, particularly one relying solely on economic reward, will be

uniformly successful with large numbers of employees. Successful management flows from understanding each worker as an individual—truly a key concept for the manager of, say, highly imaginative and creative writers in a newsroom!

The Modern Way

In the 1940s, new influences were felt in management theory; these remain central to progressive thinking today.

Behaviorial scientists studied worker attitudes and how to motivate better performance. As a result, many leading newspapers today employ psychologists to help design their internal organization and personnel policies. A scientific approach to motivating employees—whether ten or a thousand—helps create a work environment free of rigid guidelines, encouraging each worker to develop a sense of responsibility and to participate in decision making.

In contrast with the absolutism of early management theories, the "contingency theory" came into vogue in later times and is used today by many newspapers to create flexibility in management practice. The key is taking a situational approach, with managers adjusting their methods as the newspaper's external and internal situation changes. For example, the newspaper's market or competition may change, and so must its journalistic and business responses.

The "systems theory" holds that managers must ensure an integrated effort by all departments. Neither a problem nor an opportunity arises from a single cause, this theory holds, and neither does a solution. This approach is applicable particularly to newspapers because managers must overcome a tradition of permitting barriers between departments to stand. This prevents many newspapers from instituting the integrated-management team effort so necessary in today's marketplace. Applied to newspapers, the systems theory holds that managers must be alert to any internal development in, say, one department that will affect the paper's overall performance—and to ensure appropriate responses by all departments concerned.[3]

Where the Manager's Role Starts

There is a newspaper tradition of promotion from within, and it can open great opportunities for young staff members. Entry-level jobs in advertising and news traditionally led to the top. In recent years, however, marketing, circulation, and—to a lesser degree—production began contributing men and women who worked up through the ranks.

Whatever the route upward, top executives must be experienced in both of the broad dimensions of newspaper management—*operations* and *strategy*. Ideally, this exposes an individual to three levels of managerial responsibility.

First, the management role starts far down the line, when you become responsible for supervising the performance of even one other employee. That is at the operating level, where supervisors are *first-level managers*, working face-to-face with employees every day. First-level supervisors must motivate individuals and groups of employees, providing leadership and using strong communication skills to pass down management's policies and elicit feedback, to be sent back up the ladder, from subordinates. Key here is the ability to build the teamwork needed to get the job done. Higher management will ignore at its peril the importance of first-level supervisory functions performed, for example, by a desk editor or a carrier supervisor in circulation. Final implementation of policy is in the hands of these first-line supervisors, yet they often are the youngest, most inexperienced, and least trained of all managers.

Middle managers—heads of news, advertising, and circulation departments, for example—communicate top management's policies

to supervisors and coordinate between departments to solve conflicts that arise. At this level, the significant power and authority of management truly come into play.

Top management includes the president, the publisher, and the executive staff responsible for overall direction of the newspaper. The individual alone responsible for the total management function and for planning the newspaper's basic direction is the *chief executive officer* (CEO). Top management must ensure that the newspaper makes effective use of all internal resources so as to adjust to its changing external environment—answering both the needs of the marketplace and threats from the competition.

Peter Drucker, one of America's foremost management commentators, describes top management's functions as constructing master strategy; setting standards for the organization; building and maintaining the "human organization"; conducting relations with outside groups such as banks, government bodies, and so on; serving at "ceremonial" functions; and, simply put, pitching in with leadership when things go wrong.

Owners direct top management. A single individual can hold 100 percent of the newspaper company's stock and run it as a private enterprise. Or there can be a partnership or small group of individuals holding stock in the company. Many small newspapers owned by individuals or families are being acquired by large communications conglomerates. Of the fifteen largest (in media revenues) companies in the country, twelve are publicly owned—their stock traded on exchanges across the country. The three exceptions are Advance Publications, controlled by the Newhouse family and owner of large papers such as the *Cleveland Plain Dealer;* Hearst Corp. (*Los Angeles Herald Examiner, San Francisco Examiner*, and many other media properties); and Cox Enterprises (*Atlanta Journal and Constitution* and many others). A few newpapers, such as the *St. Petersburg (Fla.) Times & Independent*, are owned by trusts; its late owner, Nelson Poynter, gave his stock to a

[3] See Michael Hitt, R. Dennis Middlemist, and Robert L. Mathis, *Effective Management*, St. Paul, Minn., West, 1979.

Effective newspaper management at all level requires teamwork. (Dan Chidester/ The Image Works)

nonprofit trust charged with keeping the paper independent of group control. But most newspapers are run as businesses charged not only with covering the news and serving community but also with making a profit for their owners.

Often, owners serve in management. Katharine Graham is chairman of the Washington Post Co.; her son, Donald, is publisher of the *Washington Post*. Their family owns enough stock to control the publicly owned company. Otis Chandler held important management jobs much of his adult life at Times Mirror Corp., which is also publicly owned but controlled by his family. Increasingly, however, media companies are managed by professionals hired from outside. Policy is set by a board of directors whose members can include owners but also outside experts with skills needed in newspapering.

For publicly owned companies, boards are, in theory, composed of individuals selected not only to guide management but also to represent the interests of each shareholder. And, again in theory, even a shareholder owning just one share can rise on the floor of the company's annual meeting to ask a question, make a speech, or nominate someone to the board and thus influence the conduct of company affairs. In fact, however, boards are most often composed of a relatively few individuals who own large number of shares or of people selected by these individuals. In corporate newspapering, if you have large shareholdings, you have the votes.

If a professional manager is a strong personality with a solid track record, he or she can have strong influence on the makeup of the board and policy it lays down. At Gannett, whose shareholders have enjoyed more than seventy consecutive quarters of increased dividends, Al Neuharth served as chairman of the board and, until 1987, also as CEO. At many companies, board members and professional managers similarly mesh in a hierarchy of command. Those most important on the board control the board's inner circle, sometimes designated as the "executive committee."

Policy, then, is transmitted to the CEO, who must translate policy directives into results; this is frequently done through yet another inner circle in the hierarchy of the newspaper itself, often called the "management committee." This inner circle is made up of executives who exercise leadership within the individual departments. Without effective leadership down the ladder, the newspaper will fail to perform well.

LEADERSHIP: HOW TO INFLUENCE OTHERS TO ACHIEVE

Al Neuharth virtually lives in his private jet, restlessly darting about the Gannett communications empire, a chairman who inhales details, who pushes, prods, punishes, rewards. He is a showman, always impeccably groomed, always expensively dressed in specially tailored clothing (only in black, white, or gray). Al Neuharth is a leader people talk about.

Robert Marbut, a low-profile leader, completely transformed Harte-Hanks Communications into a mirror image of his expansion strategy, his operating techniques. As president, his method is that of the business school: a heavily staffed solution for each problem, a form to fill out, a computer to monitor progress. People talk about Marbut's management systems.

No communications company has a deeper management team than the one Alvah Chapman built at Knight-Ridder, Inc.; few can match its sheer professionalism. But the talk at Knight-Ridder papers is rarely about Chairman Chapman's system for bucking up a faltering group newspaper; instead, it's about how Chapman can personally descend to the ranks with an inquisitional force that makes grown men cry.

Some industries may toy with faddish Japanese-style consensus management, or leadership by committee. However, lesson one for young newspaper managers is that in newspapering, *strong personal leadership* is exercised widely.

Lesson two is that a variety of personal styles and egos drive the overachievers who lead America's influential newspapers and multimillion dollar communications conglomerates. Some operate quietly, in low profile; others do so with flair and showmanship. There is one commonality—each shows deep commitment to making a difference, to putting a personal stamp on the way things are done each day.

Tom Vail, the publisher and editor of the *Cleveland (Ohio) Plain Dealer*, sees it like this:

> I would say that no institution in our society so reflects the personalities of the people who run them as do the nation's newspapers. If a newspaper management team is interesting, or boring, or aggressive, or really doesn't care at all, it shows up immediately in the newspaper. If there is just a formula established to make money and little else it is all too obvious to the people who are reading your newspaper. There is just no way out. If you do a good or bad job everybody knows about it.[4]

Leadership at any level means influencing others, one way or another, to achieve in accordance with plan.

Are Leaders Born?

Some leaders, it is said, are born to the task. And certainly there have arisen, from time to time, individuals who, despite lack of training and experience, somehow prove able to step into a leadership role. But that's no answer for the student who is aiming for a management career in newspapering.

Where, then, are leadership qualities found? Can their origin be traced? Is their appearance

---

[4] Thomas Vail, letter to author, April 8, 1983.

in some, but not in others, predictable? Nobody can be completely sure.

Until the 1950s, the *traitist school* dominated general research in this area. Some suggested, for example, that a man's height was a determinant; a man who was less than 5'8" tall had reduced prospects, it was said. Many researchers, notably Ralph M. Stogdill (1904–1978), took the broader view that successful leaders have certain *behavorial traits* in common:

- Clarity of purpose, the ability to act decisively, persistence

- A strong need to succeed, to achieve on the job

- A desire for responsibility and the wish to supervise others

- Confidence in oneself; a high regard for one's own abilities

- Sound judgment and verbal intelligence, flexibility in thinking, a willingness to try new ideas and methods

Ranked as less important were traits such as the need for job security and financial reward—also masculinity or feminity.

The *situational theory* holds that there is no universally applicable list of traits predicting success in leadership and that, in fact, the *situation* in which leadership is exercised can be a determinant of success. For example, this theory holds that leadership traits leading to success in one situation may be of no help in another. In other words, to be effective, leadership must vary in style and approach to the situation at hand.[5]

Leadership is a complex subject, obviously, and no single theory explains its origins or how to exercise it. In any newspaper, however, it takes two broad forms:

- *Formal* or *legitimate* leadership, flowing from position or rank in the company's management hierarchy. The president of a communications company exercises legitimate leadership.

- *Informal* leadership, which develops spontaneously in work groups that form outside the newspaper's table of organization or formal work structure. Thus a reporter may assume a leadership role among a group of colleagues assigned to investigate a given story.

Gaining the "right" to lead through promotion to rank or title does not guarantee effective leadership. In addition, each manager must learn to recognize—and harness—the often invaluable leadership support that can come informally from below.

Well, then, how should a beginning leader behave?

Developing Leadership Values

A starting point is leader (or manager) views of followers (or employees.)

One theory, enunciated by Douglas McGregor, is that leaders traditionally take one of two basic attitudes:

- That people are lazy, dislike work and responsibility, and are effective only if they are tightly controlled and punished when necessary. This essentially pessimistic view is known as "Theory X."

- That people who are properly motivated, encouraged, and rewarded will perform well because they are eager to express themselves at work in a creative manner and to assume responsibility—that work is natural and can be enjoyed. This optimistic view is called "Theory Y."

Leaders will seldom find well-defined situations covered entirely by either Theory X or Y. This is certainly true on a newspaper, where

[5] See Fred E. Fiedler, *A Story of Leadership Effectiveness*, New York, McGraw-Hill, 1967; and W. J. Reddin, *Managerial Effectiveness*, New York, McGraw-Hill, 1970.

a widely diverse work force under a single roof ranges from highly creative reporters and writers to the lowliest manual laborers, and where jobs range from the daily production of a news and advertising package to making newspaper deliveries.

Before attempting to assume a leadership style, consider your own personal strengths and weaknesses, the overall managerial situation at hand, and the type of employee to be dealt with. Research at the University of Michigan, led by Rensis Likert, found leaders taking two broad views:

- The "job-centered" or "task-oriented" view that personal interest in workers should be avoided and that demanding attitudes and goals, all tightly controlled and with performance closely monitored, are necessary. Decisions are made only by managers, and leaders get intimately involved in worker performance.

- The "employee-centered" view that leaders must take a personal interest in workers and be supportive, not punitive.

The "Ohio State Leadership Studies" probed employee perceptions of leaders; this research uncovered two general views of leader values and behavior:

- "Initiating structure," or leadership perceived by employees as reliant on highly structured organizational lines and methods

- The "consideration" approach, perceived from below as relying on friendship with employees, with support and recognition for their contributions in the form of respect and warmth (see box).

Such neatly defined approaches to leadership presume the ideal leader in the ideal situation—and that does not often happen. So each leader must affect a style to fit each situation, keeping in mind both the employees' interests and the corporation's goals. The type of individuals or group to be led, along with nature of the task to be performed, must be considered. The "contingency theory" holds that leadership success depends on achieving the proper mix of leader behavior and style *plus* organizational or environmental factors. In other words, adapt to the situation.

The nature of newspaper work and the creative, independent people it attracts make it

---

PERCEPTIONS OF LEADERSHIP

Staff psychologists at Knight-Ridder, Inc., report that in years of methodically searching for effective leaders for their $1.9 billion (1986) company, they identified these characteristics essential to a manager's success:

General intelligence
Verbal reasoning
Quantitative reasoning
Analytical thinking
Supervisory knowledge
Practical judgment
Energy
Seriousness

Social aggressiveness (a willingness to stand for what is right)
Sociability
Emotional stability
Objectivity
Friendliness
Thoughtfulness

A study of twenty-eight Knight-Ridder editors and forty reporters reveals that *they* perceive these characteristics as essential:

Leadership
Problem solving and judgment
Planning and organizing
Decisiveness
Creativity
Sensitivity

Flexibility
Delegation/control
Personal motivation
Tenacity
Stress tolerance
Energy
Oral/written communications skills

Source: Douglas C. Harris, vice president and corporate secretary, Knight-Ridder.

imperative that the aspiring manager use a leadership style featuring the "employee-centered" and "consideration" approach. But, the student might rightly ask, how does the leader make it all happen? How do I make sure my direction and commands will be accepted? Where does the power come from?

The Source of Power

Leadership power at every level in a newspaper flows from various sources under a variety of labels:

- *Legitimate* power—granted by a newspaper when it appoints a leader. Appointment as, say, a special project editor would give you a certain amount of power in the hierarchy.

- *Expert* power—flowing from the leader's own special skills or experience (as in the case of an editor who has a track record as a great reporter).

- *Referent* power—granted by followers who admire the leader or want to identify with his or her charismatic personality or style.

- *Coercive* power—which flows from the leader's ability to punish and thus is based essentially on fear.

- *Reward* power—or the power to recognize good performance and give something in return.[6]

Of course, a newspaper manager can possess power flowing from all five factors. The key is when and how to use each type of power or in what mix—and that requires careful situational analyses of the individuals or groups involved and the tasks to be performed.

Note a basic theme: the need for flexibility and careful adaptation to the challenge at hand.

It is nowhere more important than in the effort to make effective use of power.

One noted researcher, Fred E. Fiedler, suggests that a leader's effectiveness depends primarily on three factors:[7]

- *Leader-group relations*, or the leader's ability to engender support and respect from subordinates, to build confidence and loyalty in the work group

- *Task structure*, or whether or not jobs are simple and routine

- *Position power*, or the leader's ability, granted by the organization, to reward and punish

The "path-goal" theory of leadership seeks predictors of success in a leader's *behavior* (not traits or characteristics) and ability to motivate subordinates. As a leader, you must determine what rewards will motivate employees and set a motivational example through your own activities; then, you are likely to be perceived by subordinates as charting a course that will satisfy their needs. The path-goal approach—how the leader affects the subordinates' paths to their goals—requires the leader to communicate clearly that ambitious goals are being set and then, using rewards, to stimulate performance required to meet them. It is crucial to carefully match employees and their skills to the tasks and then provide strong, considerate support to eliminate barriers to their success. A key is making each subordinate's assignment as meaningful and personally satisfying as possible.

What Today's Leaders Say

Against this theoretical backdrop, what lessons can students of leadership draw from leaders in the newspaper industry? These ideas come from interviews and correspondence with corporate leaders and publishers:

---

[6] Note John R. P. French and Bertram Roven, "The Bases of Social Power," in Darwin Cartwright and A. F. Zander, eds., *Group Dynamics*, ed. 2, Evanston, Ill., Row, Peterson, 1960.

[7] Fiedler, op. cit.

1. *Be well informed.* Know what is happening inside *and* outside the company. An ill-informed leader necessarily is a poor leader. Warning: Avoid being swamped by information. Create a communications system that brings you the right information at the right time in clear, concise, and manageable form. This requires building a favorable environment for the exchange of information. Deal openly with subordinates; be receptive to their ideas—*LISTEN.*

Richard Capen, chairman and publisher of the *Miami (Fla.) Herald,* held more than a hundred meetings with some 4,400 employees in groups of twenty to forty for two-hour discussions of "their problems and my goals."[8] He instituted a "think tank" for a three-month study by thirty-six senior editors of the paper's performance. Capen meets regularly with members of the public. Capen is an informed leader.

2. *Know your purpose.* The successful leader sees the goal, understands how to get there, and builds effective communications to transmit the vision to subordinates.

In the words of Chairman Warren Phillips of Dow Jones Co., Inc.: "I have worked consciously on this, through repeated conversations with our executives and staff members, through increased communications via such devices as the employee newsletter and by other means . . . and of course standards also are set via example." The vision, he says, is primarily one of "maintaining and raising standards—standards of editorial excellence, of efficient service to readers, of ethics, of independence in news coverage. . . ."[9]

3. *Delegate and share.* To clear time for top-priority tasks, a leader must delegate duties to subordinates. That requires training subordinates to accept more work, giving them responsibility to act, then motivating them to do well. Be honest and fair with subordinates. Give them public credit and reward for success; consistently unsatisfactory performance—or fail-

ure—must be dealt with decisively and privately. Successful leaders demonstrate a knack for selecting and motivating subordinates. Says Knight-Ridder's Chapman: ". . . the most important part of my job (is) insuring we have the best possible people in our key jobs. . . . I think that must be a prime responsibility of any CEO."[10]

4. *Work hard.* There is no substitute for disciplined, effectively organized hard work. Organize your workday (and evening) for maximum efficiency. Waste no time, yours or others'. Meet deadlines and carry your share (and more) of the work load. Set this example for subordinates and insist that they follow it.

The rewards of hard work can be immense. So can the penalties. Al Neuharth's cash compensation from Gannett was $1,250,000 in 1985.[11] By that time, he had been through two marriages, had virtually no private life and, at age 62, wore on his face the etchings of perpetual fatigue.

5. *Study the options.* "Instinct" may help spot a problem or opportunity, but it is not operative in the decision-making process used by effective managers. Repeatedly, today's leaders demonstrate that they favor, instead, solid, methodical research plus careful study of possible risks and benefits in any important move. Today, even for relatively small papers, a single decision can put a great deal of money at risk, and no manager should approach significant risk without carefully calculating the odds for success.

6. *Act.* Nothing happens until you act. If you've done your homework, consulted your subordinates, carefully calculated the odds, you have a high probability of deciding correctly. But you must make a move; you must take action. Committees pass resolutions; strong leaders act.

7. *Seek opportunity.* Only in fairy tales

[8] Richard Capen, letter to author, May 27, 1983.
[9] Warren Phillips, letter to author, March 18, 1983.

[10] Alvah Chapman, letter to author, March 16, 1983.
[11] 1986 Notice of Annual Meeting of Shareholders, Arlington, Va., Gannett Co., Inc.

does opportunity arrive unsummoned, in the nick of time, on your doorstep. Successful leaders *make* their luck and search out opportunity in its many guises. Learn to recognize it, then boldly commit the necessary resources—money and manpower—to exploit it.

Examples: Dow Jones deliberately set out in the early 1970s to diversify from its narrow base—comprising essentially the *Wall Street Journal, Barron's,* and "Ticker" services for business clients. At that time, activities other than the *Journal* accounted for 6 percent of the company's net income; by 1980, they contributed over 40 percent.[12] Company leaders sought out acquisitions such as Ottaway Newspapers, a group of small community papers that fit nicely—and profitably—into today's expanded Dow Jones. Gannett leaders sought out opportunities to diversify their company and built it into a conglomerate that by 1985 was a $2.2 billion enterprise.[13]

8. *Lead with integrity.* Acting with courage and integrity is essential to successful leadership. It can bring great pain and expose you to risks. But beware the expedient solution to matters of professional conscience. Leaders set the "tone" for subordinates, and a failure of courage or integrity can hurt morale internally and damage a newspaper's public image.

In decades of high-caliber reporting of public affairs, the *New York Times* resisted heavy pressure from presidents and kings many times. Katharine Graham, chairman of the *Washington Post,* withstood the Nixon administration's ire and, at great risk to her company, refused to halt the *Post's* Watergate investigation. The *Wall Street Journal* has risked millions of dollars in revenue by spurning advertiser efforts to influence news coverage.

For all three newspapers, courageous stands on matters of integrity inspired staff members

as little else could, won public acclaim—and were translated into long-term business strength. For the young manager, a display of integrity can, like few other techniques, win the support of subordinates.

9. *Develop command presence.* It's a learned skill. Work at it. Exude success, be affirmative and positive. Be visible. *Act like a leader.* Sell yourself. Use imagination, flair and, yes, showmanship. Dramatize what you do (but don't get too far out of character; that won't work). Successful leaders develop a sense of when to intervene and when not to; a sense of when to praise and when to punish.

10. *Smile.* It's hard work, leading others. At times, it is a crisis a minute in management. Don't get too gloomy; don't forget to be human through it all. People perform better for leaders with a streak of humor, a glimmer of sensitivity. Relax once in a while, have fun. If you can't do that, you can't be effective—and maybe you belong in another line of work.

DESIGNING THE ORGANIZATION

Jim Copley was a newspaper owner known for, among other things, remembering friends. Not only did he remember them; he hired many for his executive staff at Copley Newspapers, Inc., and built the company's organizational structure around them.

Copley Newspapers then owned fifteen small or medium-size dailies and one bimonthly in California and Illinois, twenty-nine weeklies or "shoppers," one radio station, a small news service and other businesses. To run that group—not large as media conglomerates go—Jim Copley put together an executive staff made up in part of retired admirals and generals whose friendship he enjoyed. It ran into considerable numbers: a chairman, a president, fourteen vice presidents, a secretary, treasurer, a senior management group of other top executives, plus several standing committees, made up of executives from both inside and outside the com-

---

[12] *Annual Report to Shareholders,* New York, Dow Jones Co., Inc., 1980.
[13] *Annual Report to Shareholders,* Arlington, Va., Gannett Co. Inc., 1985.

pany, to do studies for the board of directors. The company later added four senior vice presidents.

Jim Copley died in 1973 and his widow, Helen, took control of the privately held company. She became a capable, tough manager who pared down the elaborate, topheavy executive staff built at San Diego headquarters. Her view:

> We now have a corporate structure with a chairman and chief executive officer; a president; an assistant to the president; vice presidents in charge of finance, marketing and planning, and vice presidents who are publishers or general managers of newspapers. We also have a secretary-treasurer, a smaller board of directors (50% outside personnel), some standing committees, a senior management board and a few department directorships.
>
> As you can envision by the previous descriptions, it is obvious that I believe a small tight corporate structure is probably the best direction for our group. In my estimation, there is no stereotype perfect staff structure because each corporation has its own requirements and staff should be watchfully tailored to those requirements.[14]

By 1985, Copley Newspapers was the nation's thirty-eighth largest media company with eleven daily newspaper among its holding and an annual revenue of about $308 million. Yet it was being run with an executive organization greatly reduced in numbers.

How to Design for Efficiency

Efficiency, systematic management, coordination—all are goals in organizational design. In the design of overall corporate structure and each departmental structure, a manager should keep some key principles in mind.[15]

It is important to design so that managers

can delegate and conserve time and energy for crucial functions. These are *conceptualizing and planning strategy, representing the newspaper in its external environment, and organizing the newspaper internally.* Managers must be free to balance the competing goals and needs of departments; to motivate individuals and lead the entire group toward planned objectives; to establish performance standards; to control, measure, and evaluate performance; and to make adjustments when performance is unsatisfactory.

Importantly, when tasks are delegated, *authority* must also be handed down. No first-level editor should be asked to improve journalistic quality without being given authority to hire and fire in order to build a staff capable of producing quality. Of course, significant *responsibility* for success goes to any subordinate who is delegated task and authority.

"Unity of command" is another objective in organizational design. It means making sure that each employee receives orders from only one supervisor at a time and reports to that supervisor. This is elusive in newspaper organizational design because of the interdependence of news, circulation, advertising, and other departments. But unless straight-line flow in authority and reporting relationships is achieved, conflict and confusion will result.

"Span of control" (or "span of management") is the concept of assigning each supervisor the ideal number of subordinates to achieve optimum performance and efficiency. Many variables exist, including the abilities of the leader, the complexity of the task, and the skills of the individuals being supervised. Careful experimentation can determine the optimum number of employees each supervisor can handle effectively.

"Division of labor" or specialization is a concept developed in U.S. manufacturing firms seeking maximum efficiency by assigning workers exclusively to certain tasks, thus obtaining full benefit of their skills. But the concept calls for the uninterrupted concentration of employees' efforts on a narrowly defined task, and this

---

[14] Helen Copley, letter to author, March 31, 1983.
[15] See Hitt, Middlemist, and Mathis, op. cit., and Duncan, op. cit.

can create boredom and low morale. Newspaper managers should approach the concept warily, particularly in newsrooms where highly individualistic, self-motivated people are required. Rotating employees to other jobs or enriching their jobs with new responsibility can help avoid boredom.

Decentralization in design, giving more authority to subordinate managers, frees managers to do more things or, in effect, be in more places at once. But many managers find decentralization difficult, for it relaxes their control and increases chance for error at lower levels. And although a manager may delegate authority, he or she can never delegate responsibility—thus the very human tendency to resist decentralization.

The "profit-center" concept in organizational design gives a subordinate, department, or subsidiary unit a high degree of independent authority. It is a goal sought by many newspapers today. Individual newspapers and communications conglomerates try to create autonomy, which carries with it decision-making authority (and also, of course, responsibility).

THE EXECUTIVE STAFF

The design of the executive staff is particularly important in newspapers, where strong personalities traditionally served as semiautonomous department heads. They are often at odds with each other, a condition that certainly does not contribute to a team effort or move the newspaper toward corporate goals.

Manager disunity—at any level—is inefficient, cumbersome, and costly, a form of management neglect that cannot be tolerated in this era of intense competition, rising costs, and rapidly evolving new technology. An executive staff must organize cooperation between departments. The staff must focus all its energies toward common goals through action-oriented planning and supervision

Publisher and executive staff together will set the tone for a newspaper's operation. If they are alert, aggressive managers, the newspaper will be alert and aggressive. Conversely, no newspaper will rise above the limitations of its managers for long.

The Formal and Informal Structures

The newspaper's basic structure is represented in the organizational chart, whose purpose is to schematically outline, usually vertically, the formal relationships between the organization's people and their tasks. Theoretically, the chart shows lines along which flow authority (the "chain of command"), internal communications, and reporting responsibility. But the word "theoretically" is important here, since newspaper work also includes informal relationships—sometimes horizontal, not vertical—and enormous amounts of information may flow outside official channels. An aspiring manager must pick up on these informal arrangements quickly—particularly on the "grapevine," along which much information, both accurate and inaccurate, is likely to travel.

Tables of organization vary widely. Each must reflect the newspaper's size, its own unique organizational needs and, importantly, the availability of talented executives. See Figures 2.1 and 2.2 for examples. Note that the *Lexington (Ky.) Herald-Leader*, a medium-size paper, has both a chairman-publisher and a president-general manager. In such configurations, the chairman-publisher retains direct authority for news and directs the newspaper's business activity through the president-general manager. At the *Athens (Ga.) Daily News* and *Banner-Herald*, small papers of 9,900 morning and 12,700 afternoon circulation, respectively, the publisher also serves as general manager and directly supervises all major departments. Managers of small papers get involved in every department.

Danger: the executive staff can become an end in itself, swelling in numbers and simply grinding out more studies, exchanging more paper. It can also be expensive. (See box.)

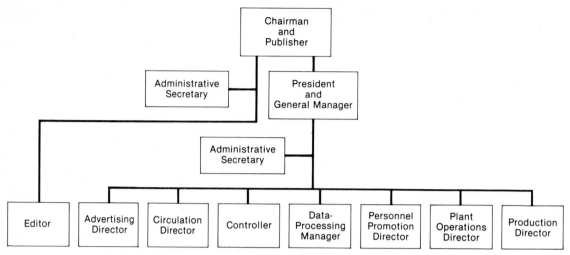

Figure 2.1 *Lexington (Ky.) Herald-Leader* **General Management and Divisional Heads**
Source: Frank N. Hawkins, Jr., vice president, corporate relations/planning, Knight-Ridder, owning group.

Another danger is that conflicts can arise between staff executives and line supervisors. *Line supervisors* are responsible for meeting the primary organizational mission through the direct supervision of employees and discharge of daily activities. One example is a desk editor with responsibility for the performance of copy editors. *Staff executives* should make expert knowledge available and serve in advisory capacities, but they should *not* directly supervise line activities. A vice president in charge of marketing, an important staff executive, would

not directly supervise a clerk taking classified advertisements by telephone. Conflict often arises if staff executives maneuver in ways likely to reduce the authority of line supervisors.

Aspire to the Top Jobs

At each newspaper, an aspiring manager can aim for these slots:

Publisher and CEO. This single individual is responsible for overall performance of the news-

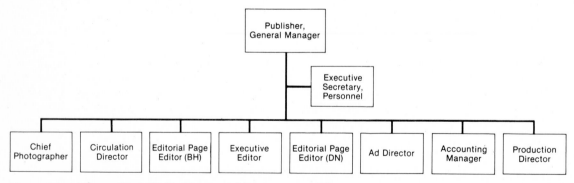

Figure 2.2 **Athens (Ga.) Daily News and** *Banner-Herald*
Source: Publisher Mark Smith

HOW THEY ARE PAID

Leaders of U.S. communications companies are compensated well for their efforts.

For directing diversified Gannett Co., Inc., the top five executives in 1984 drew the following cash compensation:

Allen H. Neuharth, chairman and chief executive officer $1,250,000
John E. Heselden, deputy chairman 587,500

John J. Curley, president/chief operating officer 560,000
Douglas H. McCorkindale, vice chairman/chief financial officer 548,750
John C. Quinn, executive vice president and chief news executive, president of Gannett News Service and editor of *USA Today* 465,000

Source: Gannett Notice of Annual Meeting of Shareholders, April 1, 1985.

---

paper, having primary responsibility for the newspaper's relations with its community, advertisers, and readers. Internally, the publisher must coordinate the efforts of all departments and oversee the allocation of resources to each. In most newspapers, this is a position of great responsibility, prestige, and potential reward.

General manager. The GM runs daily *business* (as contrasted with *news*) operations, supervising at most newspapers the advertising, circulation, promotion, production, and personnel departments. The GM reports to the CEO (who should avoid daily operational control, so that his or her time and energy are reserved for broader questions of strategy and relations with the external environment). At smaller papers, where the CEO takes a more active role in daily operations, there may be no GM or perhaps one with authority in only some aspects of operations. Then, the title is often business manager. Whatever the title, the job calls for the ability to coordinate interdepartmental efforts.

Chief financial officer. The CFO maintains outside relations with bankers and the financial public—important for any newspaper that borrows, as most do, for acquisition and expansion or capital improvements. Internally, the CFO is responsible for financial planning and projections, cost control, and providing each depart-

ment with the detailed financial information necessary for efficient management.

Editor. Depending on the newspaper's size and tradition, the chief news executive carries the title of editor, executive editor, or managing editor. On some papers, the editor writes editorials; the executive editor or managing editor supervises the daily production of news. Whatever the title, the individual in daily control of news coverage must be highly competent, capable of independent action, and closely attuned to the market's news needs and desires.

Marketing director. At larger newspapers, this executive coordinates efforts to analyze the market and its changing needs, to design new products, and then to price, promote, sell, and distribute them. The advertising, promotion, and circulation departments report to the marketing director, who reports, in turn, to the publisher. The marketing director is often active in supervising shoppers, direct-mail efforts, and commercial printing facilities—all within a comprehensive marketing plan. On smaller papers, the publisher or ad director serve as marketing director.

Advertising director. With 80 percent or more of most newspapers' total revenue coming from advertising, this executive must be a strong administrator who can coordinate sale of local/

retail, national, and classified advertising. He or she is often among the highest paid executives.

Personnel or "human resources" director. Few individuals have greater impact on a newspaper's character than the executive in charge of hiring, firing, and motivating employees, for quality of staff determines quality of newspaper. This executive must build a staff whose quality and productivity continually improve and do it within increasingly restrictive legal and societal guidelines. A danger is that this position will be ignored by top management or will go to an individual able and willing to fight unions and hold down wages when the true need is for creative, sensitive personnel techniques.

Circulation director. This executive's responsibility involves everything from marketing and sales strategy at the highest level to making sure that the newspaper has enough thirteen-year-olds on bicycles to make the day's deliveries. (*Newsday,* the dominant afternoon paper on Long Island, N.Y., has 10,000 carriers.) This job's importance is shown by the fact that, of frequent newspaper readers responding to one national survey, 35 percent said they had problems getting their papers delivered and 22 percent of nonsubscribers cited service problems as one reason for not taking a newspaper.[16]

Production chief. In another industry, this executive might be called the director of manufacturing. Taking news and advertising copy on the one hand and raw materials—newsprint and ink—on the other, the production chief manufactures the daily newspaper. Extraordinary capital investments are necessary to give this person the tools: The *Los Angeles Times* spent $215 million on press expansion, and even small papers spend hundreds of thousands of dollars on presses. Profound technical skills are

needed by the production chief. Computers and technically complex editing terminals are used widely; operating costs are high. It takes a talented executive to keep it all running—and running on time.

With the growth of publicly owned communications conglomerates and their large staffs, the student of newspaper organization must become familiar with the corporate-level executive staff. This staff deals with all aspects of the conglomerate's business activity, which often includes managing television and radio stations, cable TV, direct mail efforts, or magazines and other business activities as well as newspapers. See Figure 2.3 for a table of organization that charts relationships between corporate executives at Knight-Ridder headquarters in Miami. This staff has nationwide responsibilities for managing newspapers as well as broadcast and business information services, such as commodity news wires for brokers and traders. If Knight-Ridder's chairman wanted to pass instructions to the chairman-publisher of the group's *Lexington Herald-Leader* (see, again, Figure 2.1), he could contact Lexington directly, of course. But that would bypass his own immediate subordinates in Miami, so instructions more likely would follow the table of organization through the group president, Jim Batten, and the president of the newspaper division, then onward to Lexington.

The two-tier approach leads to inefficient proliferation of staff jobs at many companies. Peter Drucker, widely recognized expert on management systems, estimates that staff employment grew five to ten times faster than the number of operating people in production, engineering, accounting, research, sales, and customer service in major U.S. manufacturing after 1950. Drucker quotes foreign critics, including some Japanese, as blaming bloated staffs for many of corporate America's ills.[17] (See box for another view of staff management.)

---

[16] Celeste Huenergard, "Newspapers Must Hustle For More Readers: Bogart," quoting Leo Bogart, executive vice president, Newspaper Advertising Bureau, *Editor & Publisher,* June 25, 1983, p. 8a.

[17] Peter Drucker, "Getting Control of Corporate Staff Work," *The Wall Street Journal,* April 28, 1982, p. 19.

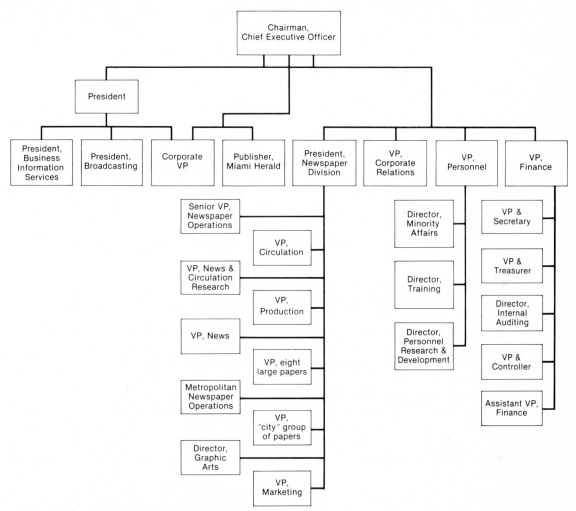

Figure 2.3 Knight-Ridder, Inc. Corporate Staff
Source: Frank N. Hawkins, Jr., vice president, corporate relations/planning, May 13, 1986.

Harte-Hanks' Marbut cautions that executive staffs must be kept small at the corporate level and must concentrate on vital functions:

Philosophically, we have always been line (operations) oriented. Our staff structure is aimed at being lean and as close to the field as possible. . . . we have continued to try to move the staff role away from the corporate office. Thus, we have within the newspaper area of business a human resources department, a financial institution, an editorial consulting function, a sales function, a training function and ultimately we will have a marketing function. All of these are considered to be crucial to make newspaper operations effective.

There is need, Marbut says, for these *corporate* staff functions:

Human resources—"to find and develop people, to improve the organizational structure and climate."

A CONTRARY VIEW

While newspapers around him draw formal tables of organization, an elaborately unstructured approach to management is taken by Bob Haring, executive editor of the Tulsa (Okla.) World, *a paper of 120,000 morning and 205,000 Sunday circulation:*

Most observers would probably think this newsroom is not managed at all. Which is exactly the style of management we seek. We're very low key, informal. We let the organization evolve out of the people in it, rather than build an organization chart and try to cram the folks into those little boxes.

Our formal flow chart is non-existent. Much of our organization is horizontal, relying on interdepartmental communications below the supervisor level. The current buzzword for this approach, I believe, is "networking."

We also strive for lots of communication. My office door is never closed. We take three to five staffers from various areas to lunch each week. Senior executives meet outside the office every few weeks. And all department heads, etc., meet several times a year, both in the office and outside. We also have periodic group meetings (not full formal staff meetings) to present ideas, exchange thoughts, introduce new technology, etc. Sometimes top management (i.e., me) sits in, sometimes staffers are left to talk among themselves.

We also practice a lot of what some "experts" call "management by walking around"—that is, by having me and other senior managers out in the newsroom, sitting at the copy desk, etc. And, of course, we do the routine stuff of sponsoring softball and basketball games, buying drinks at Press Club parties, etc. Anybody in this place who feels he can't communicate with the management is not trying very hard.

Letter to author, March 2, 1983.

Marketing—"to perform research and help with product development and pricing strategies and the like."

Financial—"to help understand what had happened and why certain variances have occurred."

Planning—"to be the keeper of the planning system—not do the planning but make sure that the system works."

Capital investment—"we call it systems and engineering. . . . [it] is helpful in ferreting out which of the new technologies is most important, which can be standardized, etc."

Marbut adds:

The key to long-term efficiency is getting an individual employee to be more productive. This is more important in the long run than investing in the right equipment or in having various training programs or sending people off to school. This ultimately is a management function, but the human resources department can play a key role here.[18]

Arguments for Flexibility

Some executives reject formal tables of organization, rigid staff assignments, and stylized executive conferences. Like their more tightly organized brethren, however, they fashion, perhaps unwittingly, a management style featuring many characteristics of the formal approach. Among those are goal setting—if only scribbled on the back of an envelope—and a well-developed internal communications system that makes sure each manager understands corporate goals and what other managers are doing to help reach them.

Thomas Vail, publisher of the *Cleveland (Ohio) Plain Dealer*, who engineered that pa-

---

[18] Robert Marbut, letter to author, March 3, 1983.

per's victory over the *Cleveland Press* (which folded on June 17, 1982), puts his philosophy this way:

> I used to make up notes for myself about objectives for the coming year and had consultations with all of our management team at the end of the year to see how we did. The overall goal was always to maintain editorial leadership followed by circulation leadership, to be followed by advertising leadership and, of course, we participated aggressively with the unions to fully automate the *Plain Dealer* and take part in the technological revolution in the printing industry.
>
> In the day-to-day operation of the paper there was no formal long-range strategy except the ones I have stated above. I never passed around any written statements or memos on the subject, although I often made speeches inside and outside the office about what we were trying to achieve. I do not have any committees and I seldom have a lot of meetings, although some department heads do meet daily or weekly just to see how reporters, salesmen and others are getting along.
>
> We do not have any budgets although we keep a very close tab on all cost increases. We will do special studies of individual departments of the paper to see if over a period of time we need more or less of certain activities or certain personnel.

Despite his informal approach, Vail clearly manages to engender interdepartmental cooperation, a prime mission of any executive staff, saying:

> I should state that when you establish an aggressive series of goals for a newspaper that it must involve all of the departments of the paper. . . . I do not subscribe at all to the notion that editorial, advertising and other departments should not cooperate with each other. Each department should have the final authority in [its] field of responsibility, but I have tried to create both an understanding and cooperation between all areas of the newspaper and I have encouraged department heads to make comments about other departments. Circulation, for example, is very sensitive to sports coverage, and as we have 5,000 carriers and four or five hundred other people in the circulation department, I see no reason why this vast source of information cannot be passed on to our editorial and sports departments. In addition, advertising salesmen get all kinds of interesting information, and this can be useful.[19]

Many newspapers promote to staff duty only those men and women who have proven themselves in operating roles. Exceptions might be, say, outside legal or accounting experts whose skills can be inserted into an organization at the staff level. Whether drawn from inside or outside, executives considered for staff duty should be of proven competence, having demonstrated that they are leaders with general management abilities. Care should be taken to select executives of varying backgrounds and opinions. Staff diversity is essential to effective attack on the high-priority tasks of running a newspaper.

SUMMARY

Newspaper managers at any level must make efficient use of people, money, time, and other resources to make sure that the newspaper, large or small, reaches planned organizational goals.

The manager—of no matter how many or few employees—must coordinate efforts over both the short and long term, adjusting to continual change in the newspaper's external environment (marketplace, law, society's values, and so on) and change in the internal environment (relations between employees, costs, revenue and so forth).

Getting the job done properly, regardless of obstacles, is the manager's responsibility. It requires continual decision making, planning, goal setting, the organization of resources, leading and motivating, the monitoring and controlling of performance.

---

[19] Thomas Vail letter, op. cit.

Management at the first level directly supervises employees; middle managers communicate policy to supervisors and coordinate between departments; top management (which includes the chief executive officer) is responsible for the entire management function.

Leadership is a complex function that can be exercised in many ways to meet many situations. The nature of newspaper work is that leaders who take a personal interest in employees and who are supportive often get best results.

At every level, the newspaper organization must be designed for efficiency, systematic management, and coordination of efforts. A traditional vertical organizational chart presents such organization schematically, but an informal flow of authority and information often exists outside the chart.

The executive staff must be constructed carefully, for no publisher can manage even a small paper single-handedly. And along with the publisher, the executive staff will set the tone for the newspaper organization and its effectiveness.

RECOMMENDED READING

Important sources on the theory of management and leadership are listed in the footnotes. Also see William Fallon, ed., *Management Handbook*, New York, American Management Association, 1983; James MacGregor Burns, *Leadership*, New York, Harper & Row, 1978; William F. Christopher, *Management for the Nineteen Eighties*, Englewood Cliffs, N.J., Prentice-Hall, 1980; Peter Drucker, *Managing in Turbulent Times*, New York, Harper & Row, 1980; George Odiorne, *How Managers Make Things Happen*, Englewood Cliffs, N.J., Prentice-Hall, 1982; Joseph H. Reitz, *Behavior in Organizations*, Homewood, Ill., Richard W. Irwin, 1981.

In newspaper structure/management, see Jon Udell, *The Economics of the American Newspaper*, New York, Hastings House, 1978; Herbert L. Williams, *Newspaper Organization and Management*, Ames, Iowa, Iowa State University Press, 1978.

CHAPTER THREE | Preface to Planning

Consider for a moment the discussion of management and leadership theories in Chapter 2. Does anything strike you about the successful newspaper managers that were mentioned? For one thing, each obviously had mapped out precisely where a given newspaper (and career) was to go. Each had a plan.

Ah, the plan! Here you are, headed for a career as, say, a reporter or advertising salesperson—and you have *no* plan? Well, let's get started—no, not yet on the plan itself, but rather on what precedes it. For to plan properly where you want to go you must first understand where you are. In the newspaper business, it all starts with understanding your newspaper's market, its competitors, and its current strengths and weaknesses as a "product" of news and advertising.

Look at it this way: The core of a newspaper's *business* responsibility is to be profitable. It has other, social responsibilities that we will discuss later. But on the business side, extracting appropriate economic reward from the market—from readers and advertisers—comes first. That can be done only if the newspaper meets the needs of its market and can beat off competitors. Managing a newspaper, then, is a process of continually "tuning" the product—its news, advertising, promotion, and overall strategy—to meet those needs.

But, understanding market, competition, and your own product is necessary at *all* career levels for a newspaper man or woman. For example:

- If you seek an entry-level job, find a newspaper in an economically strong market that is well positioned against competitors and is thus able to support you in the style to which you would love to become accustomed. Bluntly, a weak paper in a deteriorating market won't be—cannot be—free and easy with raises.
- If you have first-level management responsibility, you won't keep it unless your performance is consistent with the demands of the market you are serving. You cannot

produce, as news editor of a small midwestern daily, a news diet fit for New Yorkers; if you want to make it in New York City, study *that* market and the news needs and desires of *its* residents.

- If you want to go into business for yourself, don't think about buying or launching a *newspaper;* rather, think how you can "buy" an economically vigorous market, free of direct competition, in which you can get started.

And all that, again, takes you back to starting, whatever your career interest, with analysis of market, competition, and the type product called for. So we turn, in this chapter, to a three-part look at market analysis, product analysis, and competitive analysis.

A manager's first function is planning. At the top, that means laying down *long-range strategy* to achieve, in years ahead, the newspaper's overall mission. For junior managers, planning involves primarily detailed *short-term operating plans* for, say, twelve months ahead. At both levels, planning attempts to map coming events, so that the smallest country weekly or largest metro daily can get the best possible fix on the future, plan for it, and adjust so goals are met. But first, to ensure planning validity, there must be comprehensive audits of those factors in the newspaper's external and internal environments that will influence the direction of planning and, eventually, its chances of success.

Externally, analysis must cover current economic conditions in the newspaper's market and attempt to predict its future: whether it will be stable and growing or unstable and shrinking, whether favorable or hostile economic times will be ahead. The newspaper's competition, present and future, must be analyzed, along with technology and the law, government, and society's values and expectations. All have enormous bearing on the newspaper's prospects.

Internally, analysis must cover the newspaper itself as a product of news and advertising and how it fits into present and future needs of the market. There must be a careful audit of financing, production capabilities, personnel, executive talent, time, and other resources crucial to the newspaper's ability to perform.[1]

---

[1] For more detailed treatment, see Michael Hitt, R. Dennis Middlemist, and Robert L. Mathis, *Effective Management*, St. Paul, Minn., West, 1979; and George A. Steiner and John B. Miner, *Management Policy and Strategy*, New York, Macmillan, 1977. Also note Francis Joseph Aguilar, *Scanning The Business Environment*, New York, Macmillan, 1967; William F. Glueck, *Business Policy: Strategy Formation and Management Action*, New York, McGraw-Hill, 1976.

MARKET ANALYSIS

Understanding the newspaper's market is the first step in preplanning. The market can be a geographic unit—a five-county area, for example. Or, it can be defined as a group of persons with shared interests or characteristics—say potential readers who are interested in business and enjoy annual incomes of $50,000 or more. In newspaper operations today, the market sought is frequently a combination: high-income people with shared news interests living in a geographic area that the newspaper can reach and serve.

However the market is defined, understanding it is crucial to effective performance by every manager in the newspaper. If your first management job is, say, supervising county news correspondents, you cannot determine what type coverage is needed unless you understand your readers and what they want and need to know. If your management career begins in advertising, you must understand everything in the market that influences retail sales, because your job will be to convince retailers that advertising in your newspaper will improve their business.

Few managers have displayed a better grasp of this than Harte-Hanks' President Marbut (see box). Marbut led his company on a nationwide diversification effort that was unusually rapid even in the go-go 1970s and early 1980s, when many communications companies expanded rapidly.

Harte-Hanks bought daily and weekly newspapers, shoppers, free circulation papers, radio and TV stations, and research companies; it also diversified into direct-mail operations and other areas. After a decade of carefully choosing properties that made his company prosper, Marbut looked back and said, "The market is the most important thing."[2]

The lesson is that a newspaper can be purchased or created, a building erected, a staff hired and trained—but all to no avail if there is no market in which the newspaper can flourish. Journalistic genius and money can be poured into a newspaper—but also to no avail unless every manager at each level understands the market's needs and demands and how the newspaper's operation must be "tuned" to fulfill them.

What Makes a Market

The market must be geographically coherent, with "lay of the land" permitting the newspaper to serve reader and advertiser, to establish a "franchise" and hold it against competitors, and then to achieve maximum economic reward for its efforts.

For most newspapers, this means a city plus surrounding counties that have a sense of community. There will be commonality of news interests in such a market, enabling the newspaper to fashion a news-and-feature product of wide appeal. Common economic interests—employment, shopping—give the newspaper another frame of reference for news and business operations.

Unlike many industrial companies, a newspaper must conduct operations within its geographic market. A manufacturer of hair driers can move to Singapore in search of cheap labor and still sell its product in California. Not so a newspaper. Its product—news and advertising—is perishable and must be collected, manufactured, and sold in its primary market.

The market must be economically appealing, offering a fundamental business strength attractive to the advertisers who, in large measure, support the newspaper. Just as the newspaper is tied to market geography, so is it inextricably linked with the size, location, and economic quality of its readership and the general strength of its market.

Residents in the market—readers and potential readers—must be demographically appealing, offering educational and income levels and other characteristics sought by advertisers.

---

[2] Robert G. Marbut, letter to author, March 3, 1983.

ROBERT GORDON MARBUT

What career is a man fit for after taking an industrial engineering degree from Georgia Tech, an MBA (with distinction) from Harvard, and then working as a Standard Oil engineer? Why, a career in newspapering, of course.

Bob Marbut followed that route before breaking in as a Copley Newspaper management trainee in 1963, then in 1970 joining the small, family-owned Harte-Hanks newspaper company in Texas. In 1971, he became president and chief executive officer and began the classic expansion of Harte-Hanks into a nationwide media conglomerate of (in 1985) $500 million annual revenue.

For engineer Marbut, corporate life—perhaps life itself—is a blueprint to be followed with precision; a newspaper is a marketing-oriented "community information center" that must meet every reader and advertiser need, and it is all done under a comprehensive planning/control system.

Marbut was born in 1935, undoubtedly in a hurry. He travels constantly, is a frequent guest speaker, and stalks civic and industry responsibilities like a big-game hunter, serving on numerous boards and committees.

The population's psychographic qualities—attitudes, spending habits—must be attractive to advertisers.

National newspapers, of course, pursue demographic and psychographic targets regardless of where they are located geographically. The *Wall Street Journal* and *New York Times*, for example, seek high-income, heavy-spending readers anywhere in the United States and, often, abroad.

Standard Market Designations

Basic geographic delineations commonly used throughout the industry are charted by the Audit Bureau of Circulations. ABC is a nonprofit organization created by newspapers in 1914 to offer independent audit of circulation figures and thus inject some order (and objective reliability) into what historically had been a chaotic jumble of circulation claims and counterclaims aimed at bewildered and suspicious advertisers. Under ABC rules, publishers may record circulation in three areas:

City Zone (CZ). This normally comprises a city's corporate limits but sometimes includes more when the term is used to describe the target area for circulation efforts.

Primary Market Area (PMA). This is the area in which the newspaper is judged to provide primary journalistic and advertising service.

Retail Trading Zone (RTZ). This is that area beyond the CZ whose residents regularly trade to an important degree with retail merchants in the CZ.

Government designations are as follows:

Primary Metropolitan Statistical Area (PMSA). Essentially, a county or counties of at least 50,000 population in an urban area. The 1980 U.S. Census designated 323 PMSAs (until 1983 termed *Standard* Metropolitan Statistical Areas) in the United States and Puerto Rico.

Consolidated Metropolitan Statistical Area (CMSA). (Until 1983 termed *Standard* Consolidated Statistical Area). CMSAs are formed of two or more contiguous PMSAs, one having at least 1 million population or being 75 percent urban. The largest, the New York-New Jersey-Connecticut CMSA, includes nine PMSAs.

A TV market designation widely used in newspaper marketing is

Area of Dominant Influence (ADI). Each market's ADI consists of all counties in which the home-market TV stations receive a preponderance of viewing. Each county is assigned to just one ADI; there is no overlap.

Market analysis must include transportation facilities and commuter or shopper flow, natural barriers (rivers, mountains) that might split a market, and even weather conditions. Trucking tons of newspapers around dry Sun Belt streets is one thing; distribution in a Minnesota blizzard is another.

How to Check Appeal to Advertisers

In assessing a market's demographic attraction, managers must remember that advertisers, who provide 80 percent or more of a newspaper's revenue, want to reach an audience of sufficient size in the right location (near the retail outlets) that is able and willing to purchase their products.

Consider, therefore:

Population size. U.S. Census Bureau figures, updated annually with ABC estimates, are available in *Editor & Publisher International Year Book* for newspaper markets.[3] Of course, current figures are available from local authorities such as the chamber of commerce.

Households. Most U.S. newspapers are delivered to households, not sold singly to individuals. Household delivery, penetrating the household with the advertising message, most attracts advertisers. The term "house-

hold" covers all individuals living in a housing unit and should not be confused with "family." Household estimates from ABC are available in *Editor & Publisher International Year Book* or from a local authority.

Income. Crucial in analyzing the appeal of those households to advertisers and, thus, to the newspaper itself is income. Commonly accepted measurements are Effective Buying Income (EBI) and Average Household Income (AHI). County totals are available from *Editor & Publisher Market Guide.*[4]

Retail Sales. This valuable indicator of a market's demographic attractiveness should be broken down: food sales (single most important source of ad revenue for most newspapers), eating/drinking, general merchandise, furniture/appliances, automotive, drug sales. U.S. Census findings and updated estimates are available in *Editor & Publisher Market Guide.*

Other indicators of a market's economic potential include character of local industry and business or any educational or governmental institutions that promise payroll stability. Note the number of construction permits issued for new commercial or residential buildings—or installations by telephone, gas, water, and electric companies. Asset levels at local banks and savings and loan associations, reported by *Editor & Publisher Market Guide*, often indicate market growth patterns. Valuable "feel" of market trends comes from interviews with bankers, realtors, leading retailers, and, of course, local government and chamber of commerce officials.

In sum, before entering the planning stage or making *any* important decision on newspaper operations, a manager should carefully analyze the market. Downward trends for any indicator mean trouble ahead, for no newspaper can run for long counter to a decline in its market's economic health. A "down" market inevitably

---

[3] *Editor & Publisher International Years Book.* Also, annually, the *Statistical Abstract of the United States* is available from the Bureau of Census, U.S. Department of Commerce, Washington, D.C. Also available from the Bureau of Census are the *Census of Population* and *Census of Housing,* revised every ten years. Important *monthly* publications are the *Monthly Catalog of U.S. Government Publications,* available from Superintendent of Documents, U.S. Government Printing Office, Washington, D.C. From the same address, the *Monthly Checklist of State Publications* and *Economic Indicators* are available.

[4] *Editor & Publisher Market Guide.*

means a "down" newspaper. This is true for the largest metro or the smallest weekly.

Harte-Hanks's Marbut cautions that market research must penetrate deeply beneath surface considerations:

> Over the years, this has become more complicated. Earlier on, the market was primarily a geographic area around a city. More and more in the communications industry, the market is determined by demographic and psychographic profiles within a geographic area. Some of these may transcend a city or even a region. Therefore, it has become more and more challenging to really identify the market and be sure that we know what can be done.[5]

He counsels these steps:

1. Clearly try to identify the market the current newspaper product (or products) serves.

2. Try to understand where the future marketplace will be.

3. Identify related markets not yet tapped. (Marbut acquired for Harte-Hanks the *Hamilton (Ohio) Journal-News*, noting that it did not publish a Sunday edition. Harte-Hanks successfully launched a Sunday paper after taking over.)

4. Carefully analyze the market's retail structure and determine what new retailers will enter it within the subsequent five years, then estimate their economic impact on the market.

5. Establish a "feel" for the market's competitive nature and its overall nature—whether it is better than average, average, or worse.

Advertisers Want Research, Too

This type research really is aimed at determining the market's attractiveness to advertisers. For

newspapers sell news to readers—then sell readers to advertisers. Advertisers want to know the economic quality—the buying power—of the market's residents and the newspaper's readers. The newspaper needs an economically vigorous market because that is what advertisers need, and within that market the newspaper must collect readers ready and willing to purchase the advertisers' goods and services. The newspaper must serve advertisers by being a credible, persuasive medium that elicits a buy response from prospective customers; merely to expose mass numbers of readers to an advertising message is not enough.

James Duffy, vice president of sales promotion for 521 Allied Stores Corp. retail outlets, calls for newspapers to provide advertisers with detailed information on readers' life-styles, ages, and median incomes: "More than just having copious numbers of subscribers," Duffy says, "we need to know who these subscribers are and where in the market they reside. . . ."[6]

Armed with demographic and psychographic profiles of prospective customers, a retailer can design advertising and promotion campaigns to maximize sales. It is in the newspaper's self-interest to assist. A number of research firms specialize in such newspaper projects. One, Belden Associates, Inc., has fifty or more market studies under way for newspapers in any given year. The advertiser orientation of much preplanning research is revealed by these promotional theses directed by newspapers at advertisers and ad agencies:

> *Harrisburg (Pa.) Patriot-News:* "Harrisburg was the fastest-growing metro in Per Capita Income . . . stable economy . . . over 48,000 state and federal jobs and a strong retailing base. . . ."[7]

[5] Marbut, op. cit.

[6] *"Where Is Newspaper Advertising Going in the Next Five Years?"* speech reprint, Audit Bureau of Circulations, Nov. 9, 1982, p. 11.
[7] Advertisement, "Metro Harrisburg Cited," *Editor & Publisher Magazine*, Aug. 22, 1981, p. 8.

Newark (N.J.) Star-Ledger: ". . . In the Greater New Jersey market, more people in households with incomes of $25,000+ read the *Star-Ledger* than the *New York News* and *New York Times* combined. . . ."[8]

The *New York Times:* "In both city and suburbs, *The New York Times* alone provides substantial coverage of primary target groups . . . college graduates, post graduates, household income $50,000+, individual income of $35,000+. . . ."[9]

Springfield (Mass.) Union and News: ". . . our [market's] 1981 food sales were $746,900,000. . . ."[10]

Beware of Market Changes

Change in a market can occur with little warning. *Short-term change,* involving, for example, the arrival or departure of a single factory, can shift a small town's employment picture radically in just weeks. One-industry towns are particularly vulnerable, as many midwestern towns that have lost auto or steel manufacturing plants can testify. Such market change has a dramatic, immediate impact on a newspaper's spending and operations. In such a town, a newspaper manager at any level must have a finger on the market's economic pulse.

Long-term change often is less obvious and can be overlooked unless management is alert. Some newspapers were trapped in the 1960s and 1970s by marketplace changes whose radical nature was masked by their subtle, evolutionary character. It took a full decade, but in 1970–80, Cleveland lost 23.6 percent of its population. In the same ten years, Detroit lost 20.5 percent (and an additional 3.7 percent in 1980–1984). There was no visible daily exodus. No bands

played. But one by one, thousands of families left those cities. Decade's end was too late for newspapers in either city to start adjusting their operations. Adjustments in management philosophy were required throughout that period, but by the time the need became obvious, it was too late. The *Cleveland Press,* for one, didn't change enough, quickly enough. It died on June 17, 1982.

N. S. (Buddy) Hayden, appointed last-minute publisher of the *Philadelphia Bulletin* before it folded on Jan. 29, 1982, says, ". . . I was hired as a cardiac surgeon to do a heart transplant and when I opened the patient I found cancer."[11] (In fact, the patient was dead already, and Hayden was hired as an undertaker to perform what turned out to be a very expensive funeral. See Chapter 4.)

Allied Stores' Duffy warns publishers that retailers also need quick advisories on such change:

. . . America is on the move, and any six-month period can mean considerable shifting of what you call subscribers and what we call customers, or potential customers. Therefore, the demographics (which newspapers report to retailers) could change considerably in six months, let alone an entire year.[12]

Changes in the newspaper's external environment can affect psychographic and attitudinal considerations, such as the public's view of press credibility. Society's values—and political and legal trends that reflect those values—are changing. For example, the harsh penalties that juries sometimes hand down against newspapers in libel cases are a sure reflection of public attitudes on press credibility.[13]

---

[8] Advertisement, "New Jersey's Got It All . . .," *Editor & Publisher Magazine,* March 13, 1982, p. 10.
[9] Advertisement, "Times Like These Demand An Audience Like This," *New York Times,* Feb. 21, 1982, p. 12.
[10] Advertisement, "A ¾ Billion Dollar Market," *Editor & Publisher Magazine,* Aug. 29, 1981, p. 6.
[11] N. S. Hayden, letter to author, April 6, 1983.
[12] Audit Bureau of Circulations reprint, op. cit.
[13] Societal implications will be discussed in a later chapter, but readers who want to forage on their own should note Steiner and Miner, op. cit.; W. Jack Duncan, *Management,* New York, Random House, 1983; and S. Benjamin Prasad, *Policy, Strategy and Implementation,* New York, Random House, 1983.

In sum, careful, ongoing geographic, demographic, and psychographic research must be part of the newspaper manager's daily operating habits. At all levels, managers must be intellectually and professionally prepared to shift news and business planning to meet change. Managers must be certain every day that the newspaper is ready to meet tomorrow's needs.

PRODUCT ANALYSIS

The preplanning *internal* appraisal must cover all newspaper operations, probing for weaknesses as well as strengths, weighing assets against liabilities. It must consider employee skills and attitudes, availability of management talent and financing, and condition of physical plant, such as buildings and equipment. As a manager, you must audit human, financial, technological, and time resources on which to build basic strategy.

The nature of the newspaper dictates that analysis quickly turns to the newspaper product in two critical areas—news and advertising—and how both fit the marketplace's needs and demands.

Consider News First

Newspaper managers constantly argue whether publishing success in a given marketplace is tied inextricably to journalistic excellence—whether expensive, high-quality news, information, and entertainment are essential to high profits. Argued that way, the question is unanswerable and the evidence hopelessly confusing. Newspaper casualties in recent years include some of the finest journalistic products ever created in this country, while other papers flourish with content that is shoddy by any definition.

In its simplistic form, the argument has a faulty premise: that there is universal argument on the definition of "journalistic excellence." There is no such agreement among newspaper managers or readers. Nor do advertisers in different markets agree on the content they require of a newspaper as a medium for their messages.

The quality vs. success argument, though certainly entertaining and in its own way constructive, can divert a newspaper manager from the true issue facing each newspaper today: Is *this* newspaper and its content right for *this* market at *this* time?

Markets and Responses Differ

No two newspaper markets are exactly alike, so the question of what journalistic response is correct can yield quite different answers. Example:

Rupert Murdoch, an Australian with great media victories under his belt (see box), spotted in 1976 what he thought was an opening in the alluring New York City market. He bought the *New York Post*, a faltering tabloid filled with liberal editorials, countless opinion columns, and mixed political and sports news seemingly shot blindly into print in hopes of striking a market segment not already occupied by the *New York Times* or *New York Daily News*.

Murdoch analyzed his new product, his market, and the times—and plunged headlong into a news diet of murder and mayhem. The *Post* became a daily screamer, full of ax slayings, fires, and other disasters. Like a journalistic thumb in the eye, it catches reader attention. For many, the *Post* is vastly entertaining. It carries deftly written columns, excellent sports coverage, amusing cartoons. Its "Page Six," a collection of human-interest stories, New York City gossip, and one-liners, has caught the fancy of editors across the country, many of whom introduced its fast pace and style to their own papers. New York readers liked the *Post*. Circulation doubled in the first six years of Murdoch's ownership, hitting 960,000. But then circulation plunged to 752,000 in 1986, making the paper's image—and the demographics of its readers—less appealing to New York City ad-

KEITH RUPERT MURDOCH

Rupert Murdoch is probably his era's most criticized newspaper executive, and one of the shrewdest. He was born in 1931, in Australia. His family owned a small newspaper company which Murdoch built into a communications empire in Australia and Britain. He moved on to America in 1974. In 1985, News America Publishing, the U.S. arm of his international News Corporation, Ltd., became America's twenty-first largest media company, with annual revenues estimated at $636 million.

Murdoch theorizes that U.S. newspapers, driving for "upscale" readers attractive to sophisticated advertisers, are leaving behind a vast potential audience: the subway riders, the beer drinkers, the "average" man. His news diet of racy gossip, crime, and "human interest" copy, much criticized as sensational and shallow by his fellow publishers and editors, is designed to entertain and pull in that "forgotten" audience for his *New York Post, Boston Herald, San Antonio (Tex.) Express and News,* the *Star* (a national weekly), and other publications. Murdoch's editorial approach often brought huge increases in circulation, but some advertisers, desiring a higher-quality environment for their ads, have shunned his newspapers.

Conversation with the author.

vertisers. As a result, the *Post* lost a great deal of money—reportedly $10 to $14 million in 1986.[14]

In sum, Murdoch's analysis of *news* interests correctly spotted an opening for his type of newspaper; he misjudged, however, the *advertising* support that this type paper would draw.

A fundamentally opposite approach to news "quality" is taken by Knight-Ridder, widely admired among newspeople for its willingness

to spend heavily to produce excellent newspapers. The group's management team has always featured strong personalities—first, founding brothers Jack and Jim Knight; then Bernard H. Ridder, Jr., who merged his family newspapers with the Knights in 1974; and Lee Hills, often acclaimed as one of his era's greatest metropolitan news strategists. These men were succeeded by Alvah H. Chapman, Jr., a Georgian relentless in his drive for corporate excellence (see box).

In 1961, the year after Chapman became president, the company owned newspapers in Detroit, Miami, Akron, and Charlotte, N.C.

---

[14] "Post Has The Numbers, But Lineage Trails," *Advertising Age,* Nov. 29, 1985, p. 62.

ALVAH HERMAN CHAPMAN, JR.

Alvah Chapman's career is on the business side. However, since his appointment as chairman of Knight-Ridder, Inc., in 1982, he has become as well known for building journalistic quality in the group's newspapers as for his business acumen.

"Our newspapers are living organisms that reflect the times we live in and the communities they serve," he writes. "But that implied flexibility does not apply to the basic principles of fairness and excellence which, along with a fierce devotion to the truth, form the basis of quality journalism."*

Chapman, born in 1921, was a 1942 graduate of The Citadel and a highly decorated bomber pilot in World War II. He became president of Knight Newspapers in 1960. Thereafter, he guided the company from $82.6 million revenue in 1961 to a merger with Ridder Publications in 1974 and onward to Knight-Ridder revenue in 1986 of $1.9 billion and a net income of $140 million.

For all this, Knight-Ridder's board of directors paid Chapman well. His compensation in 1985 was $813,473.

* Alvah Chapman, letter to author, March 16, 1983.

Knight-Ridder staff members meet regularly in quality circles to work out strategies and solve problems. Alvah Chapman, chairman of Knight-Ridder, attributes the success of Knight-Ridder to a staff-wide "deeply felt commitment to quality in everything we do." (Courtesy of Knight-Ridder)

Revenues were $82.6 million; net income was $3.6 million. By 1986, with Chapman as chairman and chief executive officer, the company owned thirty-two daily newspapers (and part of two more), seven weeklies, eight TV stations, a worldwide business information services group, and a book publishing company; it was also active in cable TV and newsprint production. Total revenues were $1.9 billion; net income was $140 million.

Chapman says many factors contributed to this success, adding:

At the bottom line, however, I think much of this translates into our deeply felt commitment to quality in everything we do. This theme has been

a dominating factor in all the progress we have made. . . . we have placed emphasis on producing the best journalism possible. Knight-Ridder's Pulitzer Prizes are a testament to that commitment. . . . [The total hit 37 in 1986.] The issue of whether we have placed too much stress on product quality to the detriment of earnings is a question that has arisen before and probably will again. There is no question we could have produced higher quarterly earnings in the past by shaving amounts spent on product quality. But at what longer-term costs? The graveyards of American publishing and business are filled with the tombstones of companies that compromised on the issue of product quality for the sake of adding a few cents a share to quarterly earnings. It's an addictive habit that once begun can eventually be fatal. Ultimately, I believe, the commitment to quality pays off and will continue to pay off on the bottom line. . . .[15]

Newspaper managers devise varying responses to market needs. For Knight-Ridder, the response is a news strategy widely regarded as producing—in the group's *Philadelphia Inquirer, Miami Herald,* and other papers—some of the finest and most profitable metropolitan journalism ever seen in this country.

For Murdoch, squeezed by The *New York Times* and *New York Daily News,* the *Post's* response elicited circulation support but failed to win advertiser support.

Small Papers Face the Same Problem

The delicate problem of matching product quality with market needs and demands is not limited to metropolitan newspapers. Managers of smaller papers face it too. For example, John M. McClelland, Jr., then publisher of the family-owned *Longview (Wash.) Daily News* (26,000 afternoon circulation), took his small company on the expansion trail and, through careful market research, found an opening in suburban Seattle. McClelland purchased two weeklies on the east side of Lake Washington and merged them into the twice-weekly *Journal-American.* The *Journal-American,* now owned by Persis Corp., is a successful afternoon daily and Sunday paper of 28,000 circulation with a companion shopper of 80,000 twice-weekly distribution. It is a profitable operation, tucked tightly under the shadow of the *Seattle Times* (partially owned by Knight-Ridder) and Hearst's *Post-Intelligencer.*

McClelland's analysis of market, product, and timing indicated that his attack against his big-city neighbors on his own home ground should begin with high-quality and detailed *local* news coverage. In his words:

The *Journal-American* is an excellent journalistic product. So, if there is any reason why we have been able to do as well as we have in the face of competition from two metropolitan newspapers that are aggressively competing with us, it has to do with the way we cover the local news and the general content of the newspaper. This means we have to have a news staff far larger than a non-metropolitan newspaper ordinarily has . . . 55 on our news staff.

We have columnists and arts directors and religion editors and specialists of that kind not ordinarily found on non-metropolitan news staffs. . . . We are always aware that the only thing we can offer that the metropolitan papers cannot is the detailed coverage of the local news on the East Side, so we concentrate on doing a good job there, especially in the area of sports and school activities. . . .[16]

This is a striking example of how a competitive opening in a demographically attractive market was found by a thorough, painstaking market analysis and how that was followed up by the careful product analysis and custom design for that market of a quality newspaper.

Some small newspapers take the low-cost, low-quality approach and still prosper. The Thomson, Park, Ingersoll, and Donrey newspaper companies are enormously successful financially with small papers in one-newspaper towns, but they publish journalistically undistinguished papers. Such companies, seeking only short-term profits, spurn McClelland's high-cost approach to journalistic content. Their strategy is to carefully gauge the minimum quality needed to extract maximum economic reward from the market.

How to Approach Research

Large newspapers often hire survey firms to help match product and market. Smaller papers sometimes rely on staff-generated interviews,

---

[15] Alvah Chapman, Jr., letter to author, March 16, 1983.

[16] John M. McClelland, Jr., March 17, 1983.

"editor's instinct," and groups of readers ("focus groups") who are invited to critique the paper.

Until 1985, Thomas Winship was editor of the *Boston Globe*; he was the one who guided its climb onto most ten-best newspaper lists. His approach in his own words:

> In terms of reader research, we try to do two types on a regular basis. One, I would call "attitudinal" research, where we try to find reasons for people's likes and dislikes about the *Globe*. The second is what we call "habit" research. A recent study, where we measured people's actual reading of a specific issue of the Sunday *Globe*, is an example of this kind of research.
>
> We do periodic reader surveys of the entire contents of the paper. We pay serious attention to the results. We do this about once every five years.
>
> For the advertiser we are also, on a regular basis, attempting to identify who the *Globe* audience is and what their characteristics might be.[17]

Analysis of a market and the newspaper's journalistic validity in it sometimes yields obvious answers:

- Will a flashy morning tabloid designed for New York City subway riders appeal to small-town residents in the Midwest whose news interests are local, with lots of local names, delivered on front porches at 4 P.M.? Probably not.

- Should a small-town paper whose audience has an average household income of $9,000 devote four pages daily to detailed stock and commodities exchange coverage? Certainly not.

- Should a sports columnist in a small town obsessed with high school basketball spend time writing about the Super Bowl and World Series? Definitely not.

---

[17] Thomas Winship, letter to author, March 11, 1983.

To be effective, however, product research must probe deeper than that.

A Manager's News Checklist

An analysis of how the newspaper "fits" its market should include:

- Quality of writing and reporting. Do both meet the market's educational levels and interests? Do they match the newspaper's overall marketing strategy? If a goal is, say, penetration of upper-income homes in a cosmopolitan university town, is the writing pitched at the appropriate level?

- Geographic spread of datelines. Is the newspaper covering news throughout its *total* market area? Are the retail trading zone and city zone well covered regularly?

- Age groups. Does the newspaper have sufficiently wide appeal to all age groups, particularly young readers (tomorrow's primary audience)? Does it appeal to all age groups that are attractive to advertisers?

- Income groups. Is the newspaper's appeal to income groups consistent with overall market strategy? If advertisers demand high-income readers in a certain neighborhood, will the news content attract such readers?

- Balance. Is there proper balance between international, national, state, and local news? What is "proper"? Check the market. John McClelland's market surveys in suburban Seattle showed that his newspaper should concentrate on local, not international, news. And that's what it did.

The analysis of news content, writing, graphics, and layout is subjective, often imprecise, and always crucial to sound management strategy. Says Knight-Ridder's Chapman:

> Basically, the question is, how do we determine what quality is? How do we measure good

writing? How do we determine whether readers really want quality? Admittedly, much of this is subjective.

Instinct, training and readership surveys are all important. By recruiting, developing and retaining the highest caliber people possible, we attempt to insure that we make the soundest judgments possible. We have been using focus groups and reader panels and have found them helpful. Many of our publishers and editors participate in community reach-out meetings. We also have found it useful for top editors to knock on doors with circulation sales teams to hear at the grass roots levels what people feel about our newspapers. As you can imagine, that has been an eye opener for a number of our people, but it's the kind of reaching out we feel pays real dividends.[18]

How to Analyze Advertising

Analyzing advertising content is more objective than analyzing news. The primary question is whether there is sufficient content of advertising from enough of the market's quality advertisers at rates consistent with profitable operation.

ANPA found that morning papers averaged 60.7 percent ad content in 1984; evening papers, 61.2 percent; Sunday papers, 68.8 percent. For all papers, ad content was 63 percent.

The ad-to-news ratios in Table 3.1 are drawn from a Newspaper Advertising Bureau survey of 164 newspapers, accounting for 56 percent of total U.S. circulation.

A newspaper with ad content dramatically lower than those averages may be in financial trouble. One with ad content much higher than average might not be carrying sufficient news to fulfill its journalistic responsibility—and the long-range implications of that could involve a loss of readership.

In *qualitative* analysis of advertising content, caution flags should go up if only a few of the market's leading food stores or retailers are found in the newspaper's pages. Where do top

---

[18] Chapman letter, op. cit.

Table 3.1   Ad-to-News Ratios

	Weekday	Sunday
Advertising content		
Display	23.7%	30.6%
Classified	19.2	17.7
House ads	3.1	2.1
Preprints	17.6	19.7
Editorial content	36.4	29.9
Total pages	75.5	265.0

Source: Leo Bogart, "Both News and Advertising Expand As The Newspaper Gets Fatter," *presstime,* March 1985, p. 8.

stores advertise if not in the newspaper? With a print competitor? TV or radio? Direct mail? Is a boycott of the paper under way?

A careful census of the market's leading stores must be compared against published advertising. *Editor & Publisher Market Guide* is one source for names of shopping centers, major food stores, and retailers; the Chamber of Commerce is another.

Advertising will be discussed later, but initial analysis in this preplanning phase should determine whether the newspaper is its market's dominant advertising medium. Some industry standards:

Newspapers in 1985 received 53 percent of all *local* advertising and were overwhelmingly dominant in *classified* ads. In 1984, classified generated on average 31.4 percent of the daily newspaper's total ad revenue; in 1930, 18.2 percent.

Legal—or "public notice"—advertising yields relatively little revenue for most papers; in smaller towns, however, its absence might indicate that the paper is at odds with those governmental jurisdictions which place such advertising.

Preprinted inserts can be an indicator of the newspaper's competitive position. They are important sources of revenue; well over $2 billion is spent annually by advertisers seeking distribution of their messages via preprints. Competition for inserts is rising. Newspapers had 89 percent of the business in 1979 but only 62 percent in 1985. Direct mail is the big threat.

A manager's analysis must turn quickly to whether appropriate rates are charged for advertising. A great deal of ad lineage from the market's leading stores won't do a newspaper much good if rates are not consistent with profitable operation.

Rate analysis will be discussed later, but initial study must revolve around the newspaper's own costs and profit goals, rates offered by competing media (all competitors, not just other newspapers), and what the market will bear.

In sum, preplanning product analysis must consider the market's competitive nature. *News-content analysis* must include the study of news and information offered by other newspapers, radio, and TV—all competitors. *Advertising-content analysis* must include the competitors already mentioned plus shoppers, direct mail, and others. For even a seemingly healthy newspaper with large circulation can slide quickly into difficulty if it occupies the number-two position behind vigorous advertising competitors.

COMPETITIVE ANALYSIS

The Los Angeles metropolitan market, with 7.7 million population, more than 2.8 million households, and well over $84 billion Effective Buying Income (in 1986) is second in size only to the New York-New Jersey market. It is second to none in number of vigorous print competitors battling each other. In Los Angeles County alone, twenty-four dailies circulate to a measurable degree; they range from the *Los Angeles Times*, with a morning circulation of 682,000, to the *San Francisco Examiner*, with afternoon sales of about 100. Further, the market is split many ways by scores of weekly and twice-weekly newspapers of paid or free circulation.

Yet onto the battleground in December 1973 stepped the Tribune Co. of Chicago, a media conglomerate with an eye for "hot" markets. Tribune Co. purchased for $24 million the *Green Sheet*, a "voluntary pay" publication distributed four days weekly primarily in the San Fernando Valley, on the south side of Los Angeles. About 278,000 copies of the *Green Sheet* were distributed but only some 50,000 recipients volunteered to pay for it—$1.50 per month.

The publication, renamed the *Daily News*, is now a seven-day morning paper with a fully paid circulation of 147,000 daily, 195,000 on Sunday. It is generating huge revenue and is profitable ($95 million revenue and $15 million cash flow in 1984). How could the *Daily News* prosper in such a competitive market? Tribune Co. commissioned painstaking market research by outside survey firms which showed that the *Green Sheet*, an almost entirely local paper, had to be restructured to present readers a broader offering. The emphasis on local news had to be continued, but the paper also had to offer enough international, national, and state news to make it a "complete read." Research pointed toward expansion into a regional paper which at the same time had to "zone," that is, to present narrowly focused editions with news and ad content tailored to specific slices of that regional market. Above all, research warned against competing head-on against the *Los Angeles Times*—journalistically superb, financially strong, and the area's dominant paper. Says J. Scott Schmidt, then publisher:

We prosper, I believe, by coming in underneath the [Los Angeles] *Times* and above the local dailies and weeklies. We consider ourselves a regional newspaper with emphasis on local news, but a complete daily. In addition, we zone seven ways every day.

Generally, I believe *we have succeeded because we have identified clearly where we fit in the marketplace* [author's emphasis], developed a solid editorial newspaper, and have worked hard to build a solid circulation department that offers prompt, reliable service.

Most importantly, we do not try to be something we cannot be—a miniature *Los Angeles Times.*

I believe that if newspapers clearly define their roles, they should continue to prosper.[19]

Tribune Co.'s lesson is that painstaking analysis of competition is necessary *before* a manager constructs a newspaper's approach to its marketplace. When *Daily News* managers entered planning, they knew precisely where to insert the paper in the competitive jungle known as Los Angeles County. A large crowd of media doesn't necessarily fill a market. There may still be room for smart managers to find an opening and design a newspaper product to fit it—and be rewarded for the effort. (In 1985, Tribune Co. agreed to sell the *Daily News* to Jack Kent Cooke, owner of the Washington Redskins football team, for $176 million—7.3 times the $24 million it paid for the paper in 1973! Tribune Co. had to sell because it bought KTLA-TV in Los Angeles, and the Federal Communications Commission, which regulates broadcast licensing, has banned since 1975 "cross-ownership" acquisitions that would give a single owner control of both a newspaper and a TV or radio station in the same market.)

Study Competitors Real and Perceived

To fight competition aggressively, a manager must learn everything possible about each competing medium—and the *public's perception* of who the players are. Perceptions can be as important as realities in newspaper fights, and if the public perceives television, radio, or free-circulation papers as strong competitors for reader time and advertiser dollars, those media *are* competitors. Learn how the competition operates. How many reporters and editors does a

competing paper have? Where are its bureaus? What are its news coverage areas? Its production schedules? How does it structure ad rates and selling campaigns? The competitive fight is *not* limited to newspapers or the struggle for dominance in news. It covers all media and their total capabilities to identify consumer needs and fulfill them.

Few Markets Support Two Dailies

The presence of two newspapers of like size and characteristics in the same market today spells financial difficulty for at least one and perhaps both. Increasingly, therefore, newspaper groups seeking new markets refuse to acquire newspapers in or near markets occupied by other papers of similar nature. All markets are competitive, occupied by radio, TV, direct-mail companies, city magazines, shoppers—competitors of all kinds. Against them, many daily newspaper companies willingly compete; those same companies often simply walk away from head-to-head confrontations with other dailies. Recent newspaper history indicates that is the intelligent thing to do.

By 1987, only twenty-nine U.S. cities had two or more separately owned daily newspapers. In twenty-one other cities, newspapers maintained separate newsrooms and competed journalistically, but they shared advertising, circulation, and production facilities under "joint operating agreements" (see Chapter 11). As recently as 1954, eighty-eight cities had newspaper competing across the board in news, advertising, and circulation.

The number of crosstown competitors—almost all in large cities—is sure to be reduced. One problem plaguing two-newspaper markets is the growing tendency among advertisers to throw all their advertising to the market leader, no matter how narrow its lead in circulation or advertising lineage or how sound journalistically the market's number-two paper may be. Number two is thus starved for ad dollars, even if

---

[19] J. Scott Schmidt, letter to author, March 18, 1983.

its circulation approaches that of number one. This creates a journalistic "Catch-22": the number-two paper has the heavy costs of maintaining high circulation, but its advertising revenue does not cover the costs.

Shortly before it folded in 1982, the *Cleveland Press* claimed a daily circulation of 316,000, representing 45.1 percent of city circulation. At best, the *Press* had 35.5 percent of the market's ad lineage daily; its new (and very costly) Sunday paper had 19 percent of Sunday lineage. Loss of advertisers—not readers—was the *Press's* problem.

Worsening the *Press's* condition was competitive pressure that forced its published rates as much as 14 percent below those of the *Cleveland Plain Dealer*. The *Press* got less advertising—and had to cut rates to get it.

Similar circulation and lineage disparities developed in Detroit. Knight-Ridder's *Free Press*, battling the *Detroit News*, had 46.8 percent of metro circulation, 40 percent of its lineage. The Detroit battle escalated into an enormously costly fight for survival. In 1980–85, the *News* lost $20 million and the *Free Press*, $35 million. *News* owners sold to Gannett in 1986. With the papers hemorrhaging losses totalling $450,000 *weekly*, Gannett and Knight-Ridder announced they would seek to establish a joint operating agreement as the only way to assure profitability.

The balance was shifting in other highly competitive markets, even some previously strong enough economically to support two large dailies. In Baltimore, for example, Hearst closed its *News-American* in 1986, after decades of struggle for advertiser and reader support against the *Sun*. (The *Sun* was purchased that year by Times Mirror in a $600 million package deal that included TV stations and other properties.) Even in Dallas, once one of the nation's strongest newspaper markets, there was upheaval. Times Mirror, publisher of journalistically outstanding newspapers, could not extract from Dallas sufficient support to maintain its *Times Herald* in even a close number-two position behind Belo Corp.'s *Morning News*. The *Times Herald's*

share of total daily newspaper advertising in Dallas plummeted to about 42 percent, circulation fell to 244,000 daily and 348,000 Sunday—against the *News's* 390,000 daily, 521,000 Sunday. In 1986, in a move that shocked the newspaper world, Times Mirror gave up on Dallas. It sold the *Times Herald* for a relatively paltry $110 million to a group of investors headed by William Dean Singleton.[20]

Once the competitive balance shifts significantly in favor of one paper, the other seems doomed—even though number-two newspapers often hang on for years. Examples:

The *Cleveland Press* lasted decades even while it was a financial basket case. It was owned by Scripps-Howard, a group financially capable of subsidizing the paper but completely out of ideas on what to do about the basic problem. By 1980, the balance had shifted to the *Plain Dealer*, and the *Press* suffered operating losses that were reportedly near $8 million annually. Scripps-Howard sold out. In the eighteen months he owned the paper, Joe Cole, an entrepreneur of varied and, until then, profitable business background (but with no newspaper experience), pumped in about $12.6 million. He introduced the use of editorial color, launched a Sunday paper, tried to develop suburban circulation and advertising—all too late. The tide had turned and Joe Cole's millions couldn't sweep it back.

Time Inc., focused enormous staff and financial resources on saving the *Washington Star*, which it bought in 1976 from family owners who had run out of both ideas and managerial steam. Time folded the *Star* in 1981, after losing a reported $85 million. Ben Bradlee, executive

---

[20] Among better analyses of the Detroit situation is one dated April 30, 1986, by John Morton, a media analyst with Lynch, Jones & Ryan in Washington, D.C. Also see "The Detroit News Is A Heavy Hitter in The Big Leagues of Newspapers," *Gannetteer*, March/April 1986, and James E. Roper, "Detroit Papers Claim Heavy Losses," *Editor & Publisher*, Sept. 6, 1986, p. 11. For background on Baltimore, see Alex Jones, "213-year-old Baltimore Daily Is Closed," *New York Times*, May 28, 1986, p. 7, and George Garneau, "Good-bye Baltimore," *Editor & Publisher*, May 31, 1986, p. 16.

BENJAMIN ("Ben") CROWNINSHIELD BRADLEE

Colorful, daring, highly professional — the stuff movies are made of — Ben Bradlee runs one of the nation's outstanding newsrooms. His *Washington Post* staff reached greatness in the 1970s and broke the Watergate story.

Backed by courageous management (Publisher Katharine Graham withstood Nixon's ire during Watergate) that spends heavily on news coverage, Bradlee has made the *Post* a newspaper regarded by some as second only to the *New York Times*.

Born in 1921, expensively educated (St. Mark's School, Harvard), thrice-married, a World War II Navy combat veteran, former *Newsweek* foreign correspondent, confidant of President Jack Kennedy, Bradlee says:

> I speak uncomfortably about myself. . . . I'm an overachiever. What you see is absolutely all there is, and you don't know anyone who operates closer to a hundred percent of his talent than I do. I work hard, I have a lot of energy, and I like what I do.*

* Benjamin Bradlee, letter to author, June 20, 1983.

---

editor of the competing *Washington Post* and acknowledged architect of its journalistic greatness (see box), says the competitive tide turned in Washington way back in 1954, twenty-seven years before the *Star* died. That year, the *Post* acquired a third Washington paper, the *Times Herald.*

"I think the *Post* survived, when the *Star* didn't," Bradlee writes, "because the *Post* was hungrier, because the *Post* bought the *Times Herald* (when the *Star* could have), and because the *Post* locked up the morning field. *Time* had plenty of money but it was too late. It had been too late for the *Star* since 1954."[21]

Many Competitors Appear

Disappearance of a head-to-head competitor rarely relieves pressure on a surviving paper. View competitive markets as flights of stairs, with print competitors stacked thusly: free-circulation shoppers on the first step, small-town or neighborhood weeklies of paid circulation one step up, then small dailies, and, on the top step, metro dailies. Atop all that are the national dailies—the *Wall Street Journal, New York Times, USA Today.* On each step, print

publications carve out reader and advertiser support which is somewhat unique to their level.

Newspaper battles across the country indicate that, in the future, competitive relationships within single markets will be arranged along such stair-step or vertical lines. This will offer competitors room as long as each finds a stair step that is not overly crowded.

Ingenious measures are taken in some competitive markets, against all odds, to turn the tide of battle. For example, in Los Angeles, where the *Times* firmly occupies the top stair step, Hearst's *Herald Examiner* first tried a fruitless head-to-head attack from its distant number-two position, then spent the 1970s dodging up and down, trying to find a niche on an increasingly competitive staircase. In mid-1981, the *Herald Examiner* blinked in its confrontation with the *Times* and moved outside its downtown market to acquire twenty-eight weekly and two daily community newspapers ringing Los Angeles. The *Herald Examiner* hoped to entice advertisers with a "package buy" of advertising in the *Herald Examiner* plus one or more—or all—of the community papers. But that failed, too, and Hearst sold most of its community papers.

Competitive analysis must include the suburbs, where small dailies and weeklies compete fiercely these days. We will discuss the details in Chapter 7, but the trade group Suburban

---

[21] Benjamin C. Bradlee, letter to author, July 11, 1983.

Newspapers of America classifies as "suburban" 1,700 daily and weekly newspapers with a combined paid, voluntary paid, or free circulation of nearly 22 million. The association reports that most suburban papers were once-weekly a decade earlier, but at least one-third are now published daily or twice or more times weekly.

Assessing Other Competitors

Preplanning analysis must answer important questions about electronic competitors:

- Does local TV possess more than the national average of a 13.6 percent share (in 1985) of the market's local advertising? If so, why? And, what must the newspaper do to counter it—at what cost?

- Does radio hold more than the average 11 percent share of local advertising? If so, how must the newspaper react?

- How active is direct mail in the market? Does it include locally originated mail campaigns and, importantly, are local merchants cooperating in "marriage mail" and thus spurning the newspaper's distribution role?

No competitive analysis can ignore the burgeoning growth of *free-circulation shoppers.* By some counts, 10,000 or more distribute 15 million copies weekly and provide the total market coverage (TMC) that advertisers demand. By 1985, most dailies had their own TMC publications; six years earlier, only 40 percent did.

Special-interest magazines are proliferating as "market" is redefined to mean something other than a geographic entity. Such publications appeal to narrowly focused interest groups— motorcycle fans, airplane buffs, collectors of antique guns, and so on, regardless of where they live. Other special-interest publications aim at narrow interest groups *within* a traditional geographic market. City magazines—numbering 147 in 1984—are published within the shadows of dailies; state and regional magazines compete for ad dollars.

Some special business news publications, despite stiff newspaper competition, are expertly edited and successful in delivering to the advertiser demographically attractive audiences. For example, Crain Communications, Inc., publisher of twenty-five trade journals, launched *Crain's Chicago Business* in June 1978 with a $3 million investment. In 1981, its advertising and subscription revenue totalled $4.3 million annually and the publication turned profitable; in 1984, revenue hit $9.2 million and paid circulation was 46,551—solid success for a weekly operating in a market dominated by the *Chicago Tribune* and *Chicago Sun-Times* and ringed by scores of general-interest weeklies and small dailies.

Outdoor advertising, with nearly $1 billion revenue in 1985, also fights for advertiser dollars. An estimated 500,000 outdoor boards are offered to advertisers across the nation. In sum, a manager's audit of competition must estimate the marketplace impact of all competitors. Dollars spent with a city magazine, on a business weekly, or on outdoor advertising are dollars the newspaper will not get.

Dailies' Counterattacks Vary

Analysis of competition is designed, of course, to lay the groundwork for devising a strategy for the newspaper. We will discuss this in subsequent chapters, but let us take a quick look here at how competition draws varying reactions from managers.

Bob Haring, executive editor of the *Tulsa (Okla.) World,* says:

> Our general attitude toward local dailies and weeklies is to ignore them, [assuming that] most of our readers in Okemah or Jay [communities near Tulsa] or wherever take the local paper, too.

ABRAHAM ("Abe") MICHAEL ROSENTHAL

When he was made *New York Times* executive editor in 1977, Abe Rosenthal had already done it all as a reporter and managing editor—and better than most reporters and editors then on the U.S. newspaper scene.

Born in Canada in 1922, Rosenthal was taken by his parents in 1926 to the Bronx. This led to a love affair with New York City and, later, with its premier paper, the *Times*. Rosenthal was *Times* campus correspondent at City College of New York, then a brilliant correspondent based at the United Nations, in Warsaw, New Delhi, and Tokyo. He won a Pulitzer Prize in 1960 for international reporting.

Although he was widely acclaimed for implementing dramatic improvements in the *Times*, Rosenthal, who retired as executive editor in 1986 and became a columnist, writes

> . . . perhaps the most important single thing in the success of a newspaper is the willingness of a publisher to invest his mind and money to improve the quality of the newspaper. Not just promotion, not just circulation, not just advertising, but quality. When in trouble, you can either put more water in the soup or more tomatoes—the *Times's* publishing tradition has been to add tomatoes.*

* A. M. Rosenthal, letter to author, March 28, 1983.

But we want to deliver the best possible paper to that area, so that the readers cannot do without us, too.[22]

Nationwide, a reaction to suburban competition is the zoned edition or tabloid neighborhood insert, normally published once weekly, to cover local news in detail. Such editions require additional staff and other expensive moves—adding to costs already much too heavy for many papers. But for many metro papers, it is zone or perish, produce detailed local coverage and ad rates commensurate with a smaller circulation or, very simply, abrogate the plush suburban markets.

The *New York Times*, in one of the nation's most competitive markets (fourteen neighborhood weeklies in the borough of Brooklyn alone), employs a strategy of some geographically zoned editions, but it aims primarily at producing a first-rate journalistic package of special sections designed to gather readers—regardless of where they live—so demographically attractive that advertisers will find them irresistible. The strategy was implemented just in time, for the *Times* had long ignored many of the competitive factors

mentioned in this chapter and, by the early 1970s, was facing a cloudy financial future. Says A. M. Rosenthal, the executive editor who, until 1986, led the *Times's* counterattack (see box): "The fact is that a decade or so ago we had some real problems, and we seem to have pulled out of them. . . . what makes me proud is that we did this without changing the character of the paper. . . ."[23] (The *Times* indeed achieved a turnaround. It now is the flagship of a communications conglomerate with, in 1985, over $1.4 billion in annual revenue.)

At Dow Jones's headquarters in New York City, Chairman Phillips sees the *Wall Street Journal's* print competitors as no competition at all.

> . . . the rise of business journalism competition— improved newspaper business sections, improvements at *Business Week* and *Forbes*, improved TV coverage—contributed to broadening the public interest in business news and, rather than eating into our market, it has enlarged our market, with our greatest growth in recent years coinciding with this new "competition."[24]

---

[22] Bob Haring, letter to author, March 8, 1983.

[23] A.M. Rosenthal, letter to author, March 28, 1983.
[24] Warren H. Phillips, letter to author, March 18, 1983.

The *Journal*, the nation's largest-circulation newspaper, sells about 2 million papers Mondays through Fridays. Phillips says this represents "far from the limits of our opportunities. . . ."

Not many papers can take the *Journal's* attitude toward print or, certainly, nonprint competitors. For most, competition is anyone or anything that contests for the readers' time or advertisers' dollars. This is as true today in small towns as it is in one-newspaper metro markets.

Says Knight-Ridder's Chapman:

> . . . the concept of the daily newspaper monopoly is now practically a myth. The national phenomenon of slippage in newspaper household penetration rates is the most telling evidence of the real competition that so-called monopoly newspapers face in today's exacting marketplace. Television, movies, radio, national newspapers, home computers, video games and cable television all compete with our metropolitan and community newspapers for our readers' time and attention. Only with the highest quality product can we compete effectively.[25]

SUMMARY

Planning is a manager's first function. Comprehensive audits of the newspaper's external and internal environments must precede strategic planning, the decision-making phase of implementation or detailed operational planning. Many factors must be appraised. Three are crucial:

First, the market itself—who lives there and what their life-styles, interests, and needs are. To succeed, a newspaper must have a *geographically definable* market that it can dominate in circulation and advertising sales. The market must be *demographically appealing*, offering fundamental economic strength, and must have *psychographic quality* in reader life-style and buying habits that advertisers want.

Second, the newspaper's relevance to the market. No two markets are exactly alike; neither

should newspapers be identical. The *product analysis* must determine whether the newspaper meets the needs of its readers and advertisers in reporting and writing, news coverage of its geographic market, and subject diversity. Is content structured to the needs and desires of targeted readers, whatever their ages, incomes, or demographic profiles?

Third, the market's *competitive structure*—what other media are present, how they fit in, and how the newspaper can position itself against them. Anyone or anything competing for reader time or advertiser dollars is a competitor.

These three variables in the publishing equation—market, product, and competition—must be thoroughly analyzed before long-term strategy or operating policy for the near term is drafted.

RECOMMENDED READING

Important market research is issued periodically by Audit Bureau of Circulations, 900 N. Meacham Road, Schaumburg, IL 60195; International Circulation Managers Association, The Newspaper Center, Box 17420, Dulles International Airport, Washington, DC 20041; and International Newspaper Advertising and Marketing Executives, The Newspaper Center, P.O. Box 17210, Dulles International Airport, Washington, DC 20041. ABC provides specifics on individual newspaper markets on request.

Also see Leo Bogart, *Press and Public: Who Reads What, Where and Why in American Newspapers*, Hillsdale, N.J., L. Erlbaum Associates, 1981; Benjamin Compaine, *The Newspaper Industry in the Nineteen Eighties: An Assessment of Economics and Technology*, White Plains, N.Y., Knowledge Publishing, 1980; John Mauro, ed., *Newspaper Research Primer*, ed. 2, Reston, Va., International Newspaper Promotion Association, 1978; Michael E. Porter, *Competitive Strategy: Techniques for Analyzing Industries and Competitors*, New York, The Free Press, 1980.

---

[25] Chapman letter, op. cit.

CHAPTER FOUR | The Planning Stage

If your newspaper career progresses beyond the rudimentary stage, much of your time will be devoted to planning. If you assume any significant managerial responsibility, planning will be your most important function.

Even the young reporter supervising only a two-man investigative reporting team must plan how to dig out the story and plan the team's use of time, money, and other resources. The young director of a weekly newspaper's two-person ad sales staff similarly must plan for achieving maximum results with available resources.

Planning extends through all levels of newspaper operations, culminating at the publisher level, where the newspaper's overall strategic mission is designed.

Chapter 4 introduces you to short- and long-range planning functions. Mastering them is essential for anyone aspiring to management careers; understanding them is important for those who don't aspire to leadership but hope to work effectively at other levels. Whether you help make them or just follow them, plans will be integral to your newspaper career.

This chapter will also touch on two top-priority areas tied to planning: cost control and decision making. Let's start by looking at a competitive battle where planning triumphed.

A CASE IN POINT

In Philadelphia, it truly seemed, nearly everybody read the *Bulletin*. But that was in the 1950s and 1960s, before Philadelphia, with many other U.S. cities, felt the full impact of socioeconomic change revolutionizing city life. It was before many afternoon papers such as the *Bulletin* encountered financial difficulty, due largely to changes in life-style. And it was before a determined group of tough professionals from Knight Newspapers (now Knight-Ridder, Inc.) landed in town with a long-range strategy for taking over the newspaper scene. It was a scene dominated by the *Philadelphia Bulletin*, once the country's largest evening newspaper, with more than 700,000 circulation daily. That meant perhaps 1.7 million or so readers for a newspaper employing 2,300 persons and enjoying annual revenue of nearly $90 million at its peak.[1]

To general amusement, the *Bulletin* deliberately understated its strength with a promotional slogan that became famous: "In Philadelphia, *nearly* everybody reads the Bulletin." The *Bulletin* was a political, social, and economic power, an integral part of Philadelphia's civic woodwork, and *everybody*—not *nearly* everybody—knew it. In those days, when the *Bulletin* spoke, Philadelphia listened.

In retrospect, it is amazing that any newspaper group would pick a toe-to-toe fight with the *Bulletin*. But Knight did, acquiring in late 1969 the morning *Philadelphia Inquirer* and afternoon *Daily News* from Walter Annenberg (owner of *TV Guide*) for $55 million. Some, including *Bulletin* executives, thought Knight wanted only a slice of the pie. Not so. Subsequent developments revealed that Knight clearly intended, early on, to dominate and eventually occupy the market exclusively—and it had a plan for doing so.

In those days, the *Bulletin* and *Inquirer* represented opposite planning and management styles.[2] *Bulletin* managers, led (but not aggressively so) by McLean family members, seemed uncertain of what next step to take and what character the *Bulletin* should assume. With Philadelphia's inner city rapidly changing, management knew that its business there was jeopardized. But where to take the paper? How to get there? The paper hesitated, uncertain what to do; then it plunged heavily into zoned coverage for scores of communities ringing Philadelphia. This significantly weakened its influence as a regional and national newspaper, yet the *Bulletin* never really bested the highly detailed local coverage in the numerous small dailies and weeklies located in those communities.

At the *Inquirer*, there was an aggressive spirit and confidence that belied Knight's position, then still very much that of the underdog. The *Inquirer* had been less than a distinguished newspaper under Annenberg; it was a limping, old-fashioned city paper that never had been anywhere, and here it was trying a comeback! Yet, at every level of *Inquirer* management there was optimism and a plan—a plan for today, tomorrow, and five years ahead.

Years later, Sam S. McKeel, *Inquirer* president, said: "Despite what seemed to be *Bulletin* strength, we felt as early as 1974 there would be major changes in the Philadelphia newspaper publishing scene. *At that time, we were losing money and the* Bulletin *was slightly more than breaking even* [author's emphasis]."[3]

Knight-Ridder's planning, that is, projected victory even while its *Inquirer* was a losing number two to the profitable *Bulletin*. It is not accurate to say, as some do, that a big, rich communications company simply was throwing money at the *Inquirer*'s problems, buying success. In fact, there was a plan.

Enormous drive, aggressiveness, and attention to detail, in strict accord with priorities,

---

[1] Sam S. McKeel, president, Philadelphia Newspapers, Inc., speech to Philadelphia Rotary Club, Dec. 15, 1982.

---

[2] The author, then vice president of the Associated Press, visited both newspapers frequently for conversations with executives.

[3] McKeel speech, op. cit.

characterized the *Inquirer* plan. In the words of John Brown, then *Inquirer* senior vice president of circulation:

> Our first years in Philadelphia were devoted to learning about the market, and developing a strong editorial product to satisfy our readers' needs. . . . In a few years we began to see the impact of our changes. . . . *Philadelphia Magazine*, a long-time critic, in 1973 changed its mind and called the *Inquirer* the best paper in Philadelphia. National and regional prizes began to flow in, culminating in 1975 with the *Inquirer's* first Pulitzer. Five more would follow. [Author's note: By 1987, it was ten.] Pulitzer Prize stories don't sell papers in the sense of a next day ad or more voluntary starts, but they are an important symbol of a newspaper's commitment to excellence and to the community. . . . By 1975, we felt confident enough in our position in the market to begin establishing aggressive, long-range circulation and advertising goals.

Among other things, Philadelphia life-styles were surveyed. Brown says:

> We wanted to determine how we were viewed . . . our perceived strengths and weaknesses, and those of our competitors. We wanted to know more about the lifestyles of our readers, and any ways in which they differed dramatically from those of readers of other local papers—ways we could take advantage of in terms of future editorial improvements, and targeted promotional strategies.[4]

The *Inquirer's* journalistic architect is Executive Editor Gene Roberts, a North Carolinian hired from the *New York Times*, where he had built a national reputation as an extremely skilled editor. Roberts, though affecting a "laid back" down-home style complete with quiet drawl, is a hard-hitting editor with great drive and instinct for a news story. And he is a man renowned for detailed planning.

One observer describes him as "a consummate and careful planner . . . a devoted student of newspaper detail, right down to the agate lines of the high school sports scores. . . . The *Inquirer* under Roberts is like the Russian economy: always on some sort of multi-year plan. . . ."[5]

Inquirer executives analyzed their market, their own newspaper's journalistic and advertising strengths and weaknesses, the competitive picture, and—having methodically done their homework—laid down long-range strategy that, with their concurrent day-to-day operational plan, guides the *Inquirer's* every move.

Under such heavy pressure, the *Bulletin's* family owners gave up in 1980, selling to Charter Co. of Jacksonville, Fla. Charter invested millions of dollars in a game fight. But nothing worked, and on Jan. 29, 1982, the 134-year-old *Bulletin*, by then a wizened shadow of the *Bulletin* nearly everybody used to read, closed its doors. It was losing $20 million annually at the end.

Inquirer executives quickly shifted to another plan: "Plan Alpha," laid down several years earlier to ensure that the *Bulletin's* predictable death would be followed immediately by an aggressive *Inquirer* campaign to pick up *Bulletin* readers and advertisers. Plan Alpha included hiring *Bulletin* circulation managers, who, in turn, hired former *Bulletin* boy and girl carriers to deliver the *Inquirer* or its sister, the *Daily News*, to former *Bulletin* readers. Plan Alpha even provided for the precise number of new telephone lines (twenty) needed to handle calls from ex-*Bulletin* readers seeking *Inquirer* subscriptions.

Says the *Inquirer's* Brown, modestly,

> We were satisfied with Alpha's success. While the *Bulletin* was declaring audited circulation of just over 400,000, by the time of their demise,

---

[4] John Brown, senior vice president, Philadelphia Newspapers, Inc., speech, April 25, 1983.

[5] Paul Taylor, "Gene Roberts, Down-Home Editor of the *Philadelphia Inquirer*," *Washington Journalism Review*, April 1983, p. 35.

we estimated their net sale to be closer to 360,000—about one-third of which was duplicated with the *Inquirer* or *Daily News*. Of the 250,000 circulation available to us, the *Inquirer* and *News* quickly achieved over 200,000, or 80%.[6]

That increased the *Inquirer's* daily circulation 33 percent, to 540,000 in the months following the *Bulletin's* death. Sunday circulation jumped 22 percent, to 1,050,000. The afternoon circulation of the *Daily News* increased 33 percent to 300,000 (the *Daily News*, however, never became as successful financially as the *Inquirer;* in 1981–1986, the afternoon tabloid lost about $5 million annually, company officials said, and its mission essentially was to prevent an outside competitor from entering the city against the highly profitable *Inquirer*.)

In sum, Philadelphia offers a classic example of alert professionals fusing short-range operating plans with long-term strategy, all soundly based in research, to seize every advantage in a changing marketplace and achieve a stunning victory. Tomorrow's manager must, similarly, be able to construct successful short-term plans for effective day-to-day operations while simultaneously planning long-range strategy.

THE THEORY OF PLANNING

Planning should establish, at all levels of newspaper operations, specific goals and should assign a priority to each activity necessary to reach them. Whether you are managing the newspaper's mail room or, as publisher, are responsible for all operations, your planning must spur present and future action. It must be flexible, so you can adjust course as needed in what inevitably will be changing external and internal conditions.[7]

[6] Brown speech, op. cit.
[7] Readers seeking more detailed approaches to planning should see George A. Steiner and John B. Miner, *Management Policy and Strategy*, New York, Macmillan, 1977; also, Kenneth R. Andrews, *The Concept of Corporate Strategy*, Homewood, Ill., Dow Jones-Irwin, 1971. Also see James A.F. Stoner, *Management*, Englewood Cliffs, N.J., Prentice-

As discussed in Chapter 3, planning follows careful external audits of the newspaper's market and competition; it keeps abreast of how both are met by the newspaper's own news and advertising product. Internally, preplanning includes a detailed audit of the resources—people, talent, money, time—available to take the paper to its goals. Such an internal audit requires *internal communications systems* to give managers guidance on which decisions can be made: information on how the newspaper performed in each sector in the past and precisely how it is situated today, as well as valid forecasts of what future conditions likely will be. Managers then must make fundamental assumptions about the future and plan to position the newspaper effectively for whatever the future brings.

The Three Parts of Planning

Planning comes in three parts:

- *Strategic planning* is long range, stating the newspaper's overall mission and major goals. It lays down policy guidelines for reaching those goals, which can be five, ten, or more years distant. Strategic planning *always* questions fundamental assumptions and provides alternate avenues for reaching corporate goals. This planning is continuous, changing constantly as external and internal conditions change. Flexibility is key.

- *Intermediate* or *medium-range planning* initiates the refinement of specific activities necessary to reach strategic goals. Managers evaluate the approach most likely to succeed, set the time frame, and, importantly, inform employees of goals to be achieved.

- *Short-range planning* for most newspapers covers one year. It is highly detailed and

Hall, 1978, and Michael Hitt, R. Dennis Middlemist, and Robert L. Mathis, *Effective Management*, St. Paul, West, 1979.

specifies the allocation of resources to be used. Tools include the budget and "management by objectives."[8]

Strategic planning is in top management's hands. Only executives at that level have the information and experience required to take the broad view that is needed in long-range planning (although, as we will see later, even top planners depend heavily on cooperation and "feedback" from subordinates).

Intermediate planning must include middle-level executives charged with implementing departmental activities over the next few years so the newspaper moves toward strategic goals. Interdepartmental coordination—true team effort—is crucial in this planning.

Managers at the lowest levels participate in short-range planning, for they are responsible for the operating methods that will move the paper through the next twelve-month cycle.

Planning to Coordinate Efforts

In planning, managers, whatever their level, must strive for unmistakably clear statements of the newspaper's mission. Plans must coordinate activity by all departments and set standards, against which results will be measured, for each individual performance.

After planning come three broad efforts (these will be discussed in greater detail later on):

- *Implementation* of plans

- *Control and evaluation* of results and comparison against standards

- *Adjustment* of operations to make sure that, however conditions shift, long-term goals and short-range objectives will be met

---

[8] For a strong exploration of the three stages of planning see W. Jack Duncan, *Management*, New York, Random House, 1983. Also see Hitt, Middlemist, and Mathis, op. cit.

Without planning, in this era of rapid change, a newspaper is a corporate wanderer doomed to drift into disarray. Without a plan, individual managers can only react to developments, often in the most expedient manner, without due regard for long-term implications. This is *crisis management*—simply reacting to problems, not anticipating them.

The stress of getting the newspaper on the street each day (the "daily agony," some call it, or "daily miracle") creates a pragmatic, short-range outlook in many newspaper departments. "Old ways" are comfortable; being forced to meet planned goals often is not. There is threat of failure in having to live up to standards in a planned approach. Planning is costly in time and money. It is extra work, means more paper being passed around, and sometimes takes years to smooth out—so pragmatists often cannot see the point of it all.

To overcome such barriers, managers must emphasize planning's advantages—pointing out that for each employee it provides consistent guidelines plus the advantages of working for a newspaper that, instead of simply reacting to circumstances, anticipates challenges. If planning strengthens the newspaper over the long haul, everybody wins.

STRATEGY: THE REALITIES OF LONG-RANGE PLANNING

For centuries, it all went Johannes Gutenberg's way. For hundreds of years after he popularized movable type in the 1400s, printers made no substantive changes in the way Gutenberg had done things.

Yet after about 1950, it took scarcely a decade for television to leap from birth as a commercial medium to enormous economic and social influence in America.

The electronic editing of newspapers, a chancy experiment in 1970, went through three completely new generations of editing terminals in its first eighteen months, so explosive was the new technology. In just a few years, this new technique transformed the methods and economics of newspaper production.

For newspaper strategists today, the first reality is that rapid, traumatic change is a fact of life and that newspapers ignore it at their peril. In their long-range planning, newspapers will anticipate change and adapt to it, or perish.

A second reality is that newspaper strategists must consider as central to their planning certain external factors that were previously only marginally important. For example:

- Planners must prepare—as always—to achieve the profits required to meet the newspaper's internal needs and finance its expansion. What is new is that many leading newspapers now are held by publicly owned groups which means that thousands of shareholders, many seeking only return on investment and having no particular attachment to the newspaper business, now assume unprecedented importance for newspaper strategists. Much of the managerial genius in American newspapering today is preoccupied with anticipating the "rising tide of shareholder expectation."

- As always, society and its values are factors in newspaper planning. But never before has society pressured the media as strongly as today in areas such as ethics, social responsibility, and general conduct of business. Thus, a "social audit" of the newspaper's external environment is mandatory. (This will be covered in a subsequent chapter.)

- The general legal climate has always been an important external influence on planning. But never before has the law intruded so deeply into the newsroom, personnel management, and the daily operations of a newspaper. And that, too, must be factored into strategic planning. (See Chapter 12, "The Law and You.")

A third reality of long-range strategy is that new technology transforms internal newspaper operations and externally opens new opportunities for competitors. Rapid change in the way information and advertising can be transmitted has created new competitors, particularly those using electronic means.

Planning That Challenges Basic Assumptions

Strategic planning for newspapers, then, must deal with such basic questions as whether in twenty years there will be markets for newspapers as we know them. Planning must look ahead and ask what business the newspaper should be in, who its customers will be, who will be competitors, and how the newspaper can use its resources—both internal and external—to ensure its future strength.

With such basic reassessments in mind, Harte-Hanks executives, while planning how to position their media conglomerate strategically, track developments in eight areas:

- The national/international political scene

- The general economy

- Work-force trends

- Consumer attitudes and changing values

- New technology's impact

- The role of government and regulatory agencies

- Advertising trends

- Competitive developments

Long-range assumptions are made about these areas, and any error in assumptions is detected by ongoing monitoring that "signals a red flag to either change our strategy or programs, or even change our goals," in the words of President Marbut.[9]

---

[9] Robert Marbut, letter to author, March 1, 1983.

Planning for the Information Center Concept

In positioning newspapers to meet change, whatever its form, some strategists suggest converting the traditional stand-alone community paper into a widely diversified *information and advertising center* of completely different character. They suggest using not only newsprint to meet reader and advertiser needs but *any* means, including direct mail and electronic delivery (such as cable TV). This concept presumes not merely positioning a newspaper to sell space to advertisers but, rather, accepting the advertiser's business problem, whatever it is, and solving it through a variety of means.

Technological breakthroughs in the 1970s and 1980s permit managers to rethink basic ways of doing things, to make radical adjustments in their competitive stance against other media, and to plan services perhaps unfettered by the severe technical limitations imposed by printing presses, newsprint, and thirteen-year-olds on bicycles delivering the final product. Newspaper strategy, then, must develop options for diversification, looking far afield for new areas of service and profit.

In the 1970s and 1980s, newspapers broadened their revenue bases with moves into other forms of print, such as free-circulation publications, or they widened their geographic base by acquiring newspapers in other markets. But some struck out adventurously into completely new fields. For example, the Tribune Co. of Chicago ranges wide afield—into left field, some think—by owning the Chicago Cubs baseball team as well as seven newspapers, two newsprint mills, four TV stations, and a large cable TV operation. Other newspaper-based companies have entered the entertainment industry, auto auctions, equipment manufacturing—endeavors not even close to their main thrust. But there is renewed interest in strategic planning that emphasizes staying closer to traditional business. Paul S. Hirt, after years as senior vice president of the *Chicago Sun-Times*, says:

Through current literature describing the outstanding companies of Europe, Asia and America, many of the same ideas recur: Get back to basics, stick to your knitting, concentrate on value, service and excellence, and the profits will follow; beware of overemphasis on short-term profit to the neglect of future survival; avoid fostering internal bureauracies; encourage "networking" [internal communications among peers] and entrepreneurial thinking throughout the organization. Each of these ideas is applicable to newspapers. . . .[10]

Leading communications companies are committed to such long-range planning. Dow Jones, generally recognized as among the industry's best-managed firms, is one. Sterling E. Soderlind, Dow Jones vice president/planning, says:

We have had systematic long-range planning on a corporate-wide basis since 1975. We have gone through the planning cycle annually, sometimes for three-year periods but most often for five-year spans. The plans contain written statements on corporate objectives and strategies to achieve these goals during the plan period. There are similar sections giving details on objectives and strategies for each of our products, services and subsidiaries. These include *The Wall Street Journal, Barron's*, our Information Services Group, the Community Newspapers Group (Ottaway Newspapers) and Richard D. Irwin, Inc., the subsidiary that publishes college textbooks and professional business books.

To help our managers in their planning, the Planning Department provides analysis on demographic, economic and lifestyle trends, in some cases looking ahead 10 years or more.

Soderlind speaks directly to Dow Jones's successful drive for improved profits:

One corporate long-range objective is to increase net earnings at a rate that equals or exceeds

---

[10] Paul S. Hirt, *Newspaper Marketing: A Time For Reappraisal?* pamphlet, International Newspaper Promotion Association, 1983.

WARREN HENRY PHILLIPS

How do you work your way up the executive staff ladder at Dow Jones & Co., Inc., and gain the business experience necessary to become chairman and chief executive officer? (Dow Jones was the nation's seventeenth largest media company in 1985, with $1 billion revenue.) It was up through the newsroom, not the business office, for Warren Phillips.

Born in 1926 and educated at Queens College, Phillips joined the *Wall Street Journal* in 1947 (circulation then 150,000) as a copy reader, then worked as foreign correspondent in Germany, bureau chief in London, foreign editor in New York, news editor, managing editor of the

Midwest edition, managing editor in New York, executive editor of all Dow Jones publications, general manager, editorial director, and executive vice president. He was named president in 1972, chief executive officer in 1975, and chairman in 1978.

By 1987, the *Wall Street Journal* had just under 2 million circulation, Dow Jones was widely regarded as one of the nation's best-managed media companies, and former copy reader Phillips, at age fifty-seven, enjoyed a comfortable income as his reward (total compensation: $1,107,252).

---

the growth of the economy, including inflation. In the case of some of our divisions, this also is part of their financial objective. But other yardsticks also are used. Thus, some publications and services aim to meet or surpass a certain level in their operating profit margin. A new venture may aim at achieving a specific annual growth rate in revenues during a plan period—and also may set a time period during which the venture is expected to achieve profitability.[11]

Planning for Profits

Future profits must be a centerpiece of long-range planning. A newspaper must generate profits to attract investors with capital necessary for expansion and improvement. The industry, long regarded as "people-intensive," has also become capital-intensive. Further, only profitable newspapers attract talented staff and executives; only profitable newspapers can afford the journalistic quality so necessary in today's highly competitive communications world.

Varying routes can lead to profitability. One is a strategy of holding down costs by delivering low-quality service to readers or communities and counting on high profits over the short run.

All questions of social responsibility and professional ethics aside, this fast route to profit can bleed a newspaper of self-respect and public regard. Except in unusual cases, it can also lead to loss of market share, disaffected readers, and competitive disadvantage. Nevertheless, the technique is practiced by many newspaper planners.

Another plan involves investing more in the newspaper, guaranteeing high-quality service, and projecting over the long haul for greater profit to flow from a satisfied, demographically attractive readership that, in turn, attracts a greater number of advertisers willing to pay higher rates.

Chairman Phillips of Dow Jones (see box) casts his company's long-range planning for profit against the wider background of service to reader, advertiser and community, saying, ". . . our number one objective, our primary objective, is to serve the public exceedingly well—i.e., to raise further the standards of editorial content and of service."[12]

In sum, long-range strategy demands immediate action to accomplish change in three, five, or more years. Only with a clearly defined

---

[11] Sterling E. Soderlind, letter to author, March 1, 1983.

[12] Warren Phillips, letter to author, March 18, 1983.

strategy can management turn to intermediate and short-range planning and thus move the paper pragmatically toward its overall goals.

INTERMEDIATE PLANNING: FOCUSING EFFORTS, SETTING TIME FRAME

In this second broad area of planning, managers focus operational methods necessary to accomplish long-range goals. For many newspapers, this involves establishing the time frames and most appropriate methods in these areas:

- Improving journalistic quality to levels that will be demanded in the 1990s by a more sophisticated, discerning audience

- Upgrading staff quality, including hiring and promoting women and minorities

- Increasing advertising quantity and quality

- Deepening circulation penetration of households and raising reader demographics

- Strengthening the newspaper's competitive posture

- Constructing production facilities to meet future needs

- Diversifying in a manner appropriate to the company's main thrust

- Improving profit levels

Intermediate planning means expediting information to all employees on what the plan entails. This is essential, for success depends on everyone's complete grasp of what is expected and the time frame for each task.

An upward flow of information—a "feedback loop"—is also necessary, so that comments and suggestions from first-level supervisors and employees are available to higher managers. By informing employees, management invites will-ing, creative participation. And the feeling of being part of an important planning project as well as the sense that management is interested in comments from below can work wonders for employee morale.

Planning for Three Constituencies

Planners must stay tuned to the needs of *reader*, *advertiser*, and *community*, a newspaper's three constituencies.

Conditions change rapidly and no single individual can track developments in all three constituencies or fashion comprehensive strategy. A planning committee of specialists must be formed. All key departments must be represented—finance, news, circulation, advertising, production, personnel, promotion. The chair must be occupied by top management. Each specialist should watch specific subject areas for the entire committee. The following industry organizations do excellent long-range analysis and should be monitored closely.

American Newspaper Publishers' Association. ANPA is the largest trade group and maintains strong research efforts at its headquarters (The Newspaper Center, Box 17047, Dulles International Airport, Washington, DC 20041). Standing committees of newspaper executives from around the country keep members current on new developments in all areas of newspaper operations.

American Society of Newspaper Editors. Members of ASNE (11600 Sunrise Valley Drive, Reston, VA 20091) are editors of papers large and small. The society is active in news and editorial issues, freedom of the press, and ethical/legal issues.

Associated Press Managing Editors' Association. APME (50 Rockefeller Plaza, New York, NY 10020) is an organization of managing editors from Associated Press member newspapers; however, it is independent of AP control. It does excellent research in reader attitudes and newsroom management.

Regional and state press associations are valuable to newspaper managers. Notable are the Southern Newspaper Publishers' Association (P.O. Box 28875, Atlanta, GA 30328) and Inland Daily Press Association (Suite 802-W, 840 North Lake Shore Drive, Chicago, IL 60611). Both hold seminars and training sessions for middle-level managers.

SHORT-TERM PLANNING: PROFITS, GROWTH, AND MARKET SHARE

Ben Bradlee became executive editor of the *Washington Post* on the strength of proven talent as a reporter, jugular-slashing competitive instincts, and leadership flair—and the ability to handle huge sums of money.

Handle money? Bradlee, an editor, handling money? Yes, for Ben Bradlee, flashiest metropolitan editor of his era, captain of the *Post's* Watergate team, is charged with effectively and wisely spending huge sums of money. Bradlee's newsroom budget grew rapidly from about $4 million when he joined the *Post* from *Newsweek* in 1965 to $38 million in 1983 and almost $50 million in 1986.[13]

At the *Los Angeles Times,* Editor William Thomas had $45 million in 1982, $68.6 million in 1986.[14] The *New York Times,* probably biggest newsroom spender of all, keeps its budget confidential but reportedly spent $53 million in 1980, $80 million in 1986.

Because of the huge sums being spent, newsrooms and other departments that once operated with an informality approaching fiscal anarchy now have disciplined short-term plans that specify priority projects for the year ahead and ensure careful, efficient handling of money.

The One-Year Plan

By contrast with the long view of strategic planning, short-term planning states each manager's goals only for the coming year.

Managing under such a plan requires creative and tightly disciplined managerial skill at all levels. The short-term plan cannot be a rigid list of performance demands laid down unilaterally by top management for subordinate managers. Rather, team goals must be drawn jointly and sensitively by top management *and* each manager who must meet the goals. Properly implemented, short-range planning can elicit enthusiastic participation from every level and move the newspaper ahead on all fronts. However, a plan that is improperly drawn or arbitrarily presented is worse than no plan; it can harm staff morale and operations.

Precision short-term planning touches many employees who are otherwise only vaguely aware of corporate planning. So, particularly in newsrooms, it often stirs resentment as yet another administrative burden—or even fear that the new program will threaten job security. A careful, advance explanation of planning goals can head off complaints. But planning must proceed despite almost inevitable grousing. Publisher Capen of Knight-Ridder's *Miami (Fla.) Herald* says, "Planning is essential. It is a difficult discipline and often an unpleasant one, but it is critical that a communications organizations have its goals clearly in mind and that they be understood and accepted by the management team."[15]

Short-term planning specifies, among other objectives, what the newspaper must achieve in profits, growth, and market share. Two primary tools are used:

- *Budgets* specifying how a manager will employ resources—particularly money and personnel—to meet given objectives. Importantly, budgets also set goals for indi-

[13] Benjamin Bradlee, letter to author, July 11, 1983; also see David Shaw, "Foreign Correspondents: It's on-the-Job Training," the *Los Angeles Times,* July 2, 1986, p.7.

[14] "Coast Paper Feeling Pinch of Recession," the *New York Times,* Aug. 15, 1982, p. 13; also see Shaw, "Foreign Correspondents: It's on-the-Job Training," Ibid.

[15] Richard G. Capen, Jr., letter to author, May 27, 1983.

viduals and measure and evaluate perform-ance. Thus, budgets are motivational and control mechanisms. They inform the en-tire management team of goals and coor-dinate efforts to achieve them.

- *Management by Objectives* (MBO), a proc-ess popularized by management theorist Peter Drucker. Under MBO, employees and managers collaborate in establishing goals that are not easily reduced to the statistical representations of a budget, such as improving journalistic quality or upgrad-ing staff talent.

Before you can implement short-range plan-ning, you must understand your newspaper's basic financial position. Two instruments, the balance sheet and profit-and-loss statement, help you do that.

How the Balance Sheet Works

Accounting is for experts. But even nonfinancial managers with "math fright" must learn to keep score in the business of newspapering. Here are a few tips:

The *balance sheet* represents financial con-ditions on a certain date. Conditions change rapidly, so note that the balance sheet reflects your newspaper's assets and liabilities only on that date. *Assets* are things of value owned by a business. *Current assets* can be turned into cash within one year; they include cash in the bank, marketable securities, inventory (such as newsprint), and accounts receivable, or sums owed by subscribers or advertisers in the next twelve months. *Fixed assets* are such things as land and equipment. *Intangible assets* may not show on the balance sheet but can be extremely valuable. They include franchises, licenses, trademarks, and goodwill. In accounting usage, goodwill is the difference between the actual book value of assets and the higher price a buyer would pay for those assets because the news-paper has a strong reputation in its market and with its customers.

Balance sheet *liabilities* include: *current liabilities*, those due in the coming twelve months; *accounts payable*, or amounts the paper owes creditors; *notes payable*, such as promissory notes held by banks; *accruals*, such as wages, pension contributions, and taxes owed but not yet paid. *Long-term liabilities* are debts such as mortgages due after the current year. The bal-ance sheet will also show *shareholder equity*, or the owners' share of the business. It is computed by subtracting liabilities from assets.

In sum, the balance sheet represents things of value the newspaper owns (assets). On the other side are what it owes (liabilities) and the owners' share of the company.

The two sides—assets and liabilities—must balance; every entry into or out of one side must be balanced by a corresponding entry on the other side. To illustrate, let's assume you are P. Anthony and, along with a former classmate, B. Stone, you start a newspaper. Relatively inexpensive equipment permits low-cost entry into small-paper publishing, so you each put up $500,000. You divide fifty-fifty the stock in the new company, Risk Publishing, Inc. Your first balance sheet entry is shown in Table 4.1.

The $1 million put into Risk Publishing's bank account is carried on the balance sheet as cash; the value of your stock in the company is carried on the liabilities and capital side.

Now, things look a little tight in start-up. You need newsprint and ink and other supplies. So, you borrow $50,000 from the local bank on a six-month note. Again, entries are made on both sides, as shown in Table 4.2.

Your first purchase is $12,000 in production equipment and $5,000 in newsprint. Delivery is completed, but you have thirty days to pay. Meanwhile, your partner has leased a small building and paid one month's rent, $250, in advance. You record those transactions as in Table 4.3.

Note several things about the entries in Table 4.3: All cash is still on the balance sheet except the $250 paid in advance rent. That is listed as prepaid expense. Your $12,000 in

Table 4.1

Risk Publishing, Inc.
Balance Sheet

Assets		Liabilities and Capital	
Cash	$1,000,000	*Liabilities*	$_____
		Capital	
		Common stock	
		P. Anthony	500,000
		R. Stone	500,000
Total assets	$1,000,000	Total liabilities and capital	$1,000,000

production equipment is a fixed asset. The $5,000 in newsprint is listed under inventory. On the liabilities side, the $12,000 you owe for equipment and $5,000 for newsprint are represented as accounts payable of $17,000. The $50,000 note payable, of course, is your bank loan. Capital is still $1 million in common stock.

Each subsequent transaction, as Risk Publishing gets under way, is similarly recorded on both sides, so assets and liabilities always stay in balance. Transactions are actually recorded in journals, or chronological records of transactions, and ledgers, or records of transactions segregated by area or account—such as cash, accounts payable, and so on. At the end of an accounting period—six months, one year, or whatever period you choose—entries from journals and ledgers are transferred to a balance sheet.

Table 4.4 shows the balance sheet used by an actual small paper of 10,500 circulation.

Understanding the P&L

The *profit and loss statement,* or "P&L"— variously called "earnings report" or "income statement"—summarizes the newspaper's operations for any period but usually for a calendar year or "fiscal" year (which begins and ends on dates other than January 1 and December 31). In your early years as a manager, you may never work with a balance sheet; indeed, few managers

Table 4.2

Risk Publishing, Inc.
Balance Sheet

Assets		Liabilities and Capital	
Cash	$1,050,000	*Liabilities*	
		Note payable	$50,000
		Capital	
		Common stock	
		P. Anthony	500,000
		R. Stone	500,000
Total assets	$1,050,000	Total liabilities and capital	$1,050,000

Table 4.3

Risk Publishing, Inc.
Balance Sheet

Assets		Liabilities and Capital	
Cash	$1,049,750	*Liabilities*	
Inventory	5,000	Accounts payable	$17,000
Prepaid expense	250	Note payable	50,000
Fixed assets	12,000		
		Total liabilities	$67,000
		Capital	
		Common stock	
		P. Anthony	500,000
		R. Stone	500,000
Total assets	$1,067,000	Total liabilities and capital	$1,067,000

in daily operations are concerned with it. For them, the P&L is most important because it shows the newspaper's revenue from advertising, circulation, and other sources; it shows expenses and, on the "bottom line," the result of operations—profit or loss.

Table 4.5 shows the form *Small Daily* uses.

Note that the P&L has four main sections—sales, expenses, taxes, profit—and that performance is measured against last year in each. The P&L format is the basic form for budgeting; when you, for the first time as a manager, become responsible for revenue and expense, you will learn very quickly to spot any entries that may vary from what you are budgeted to produce. In sum, your job is to increase revenue and decrease, or hold to minimum, expenses. Doing that consistently yields improved profits.

We will discuss how to analyze a balance sheet and P&L in more detail in a later chapter. But to give you an idea of what numbers are involved, let's look at revenue and expense for one year at two typical dailies. *Small Daily*, at 10,500 circulation, would be classed as "small" indeed; the other, at 50,000, ranks as "medium size."

Table 4.6, *Small Daily*'s operating highlights, shows that this enterprise is extremely profitable—46.6 percent of operating revenue is converted to operating profit. Not many newspaper managers serious about journalistic quality have operating margins that high; they spend more on their product in order to better serve readers and advertisers and insure a strong competitive posture in their marketplaces in future years. Experienced managers studying those highlights would guess *Small Daily* is weak journalistically—and it is.

Operating highlights for the medium-size paper were put together by Inland Daily Press Association after a national survey of "typical" newspapers. (See Table 4.7.)

Note that the 50,000-circulation daily didn't have a good 1982. Operating profit fell $81,100 to $1,844,400 and operating margin slipped to 15.9 percent from 17.2 percent. Strong steps were required to ensure a revenue increase for the next year and containment of costs. Owners won't long entertain slipping profits. If you were managing this paper, much of your plan for improvement would be embodied in next year's *budget*.

Table 4.4

Small Daily Publishing Co.

Assets	September 30	
	This Year	*Last Year*
Current Assets		
Cash (in bank or readily available elsewhere)	_____	_____
Accounts receivable (amounts owed by customers, less reserve for those unlikely to be paid)	_____	_____
Inventory (newsprint, ink)	_____	_____
Prepaid expenses (rent or insurance paid in advance, for example)	_____	_____
Fixed Assets		
(building, press, etc., less depreciation—that portion of the fixed assets' original cost used up since purchase)	_____	_____
Other Assets		
(includes goodwill)	_____	_____

Liabilities		
Current Liabilities		
Bank note payable (amount due within twelve months on a loan)	_____	_____
Accounts payable (what the newspaper owes its suppliers)	_____	_____
Accruals (salaries, taxes owed but not yet paid)	_____	_____
Long-Term Liabilities		
(mortgage payments and bank debt due after current twelve-month period)	_____	_____
Stockholders' Equity		
Capital stock (amount investors put in to buy *Small Daily*)	_____	_____
Retained earnings (net profits after taxes, less any dividends paid stockholders)	_____	_____

BUDGETING

Budgeting is a complex subject that requires its own book. For our purposes, it can be broken into three types:

- *The master budget*, forecast budget, or earnings plan. This is a projection of earnings and maps the newspaper's overall financial goals.

- *The capital budget*, which covers expenditures for land, buildings, equipment, and similar assets which will benefit the newspaper over a longer period than the one-year, short-term planning period.

- *The control budget*, which deals with revenue and costs and measures operating performance by individuals or departments. Here, in the generation of revenue

Table 4.5

Small Daily Publishing Co.
Statement of Income
Twelve Months Ended September 30

	This Year	Last Year	Increase (Decrease)
Sales			
Newspaper (advertising and circulation revenue)	_____	_____	_____
Commercial printing (from doing invitations, business cards, etc.)	_____	_____	_____
Less discounts (given large advertisers)	_____	_____	_____
Cost of Sales			
(Salaries, newsprint, payroll taxes, etc.)	_____	_____	_____
Operating Expenses			
(Officers' salaries, property taxes, bank interest)	_____	_____	_____
Operating income (sales minus cost of sales and operating expenses)	_____	_____	_____
Other Income			
(Rental income, interest on cash in bank, sales of waste paper)	_____	_____	_____
Other Deductions			
(Includes payment to former owner acting as consultant)	_____	_____	_____
Net income (loss) before taxes	_____	_____	_____
Income Taxes			
Federal	_____	_____	_____
State	_____	_____	_____
Net income (loss)	_____	_____	_____

and control of costs, aspiring newspaper managers must first win their spurs; we will concentrate on this area of management responsibility.[16]

Looking Backward and Ahead

Cost/revenue budgets are normally broken into twelve one-month segments. They guide managers toward the future but are based largely on the past plus best estimates of what is ahead. So in budgeting for any newspaper, daily or weekly, large or small, first determine cost/revenue patterns of previous years and months. There must be a historical perspective against which the budget for the forthcoming year is constructed. This can be difficult. Some small papers are lax in expense control or in applying the kind of business methodology that was implemented much earlier by other industries; it sometimes takes years to develop reliable cost/revenue patterns against which to compare current budget performance.

[16] Many accounting texts cover types of budgeting; the author found one particularly helpful: R. F. Salmonson, Roger H. Hermanson, and James Don Edwards, *A Survey of Basic Accounting*, Homewood, Ill., Dow Jones-Irwin, 1977.

Table 4.6

Small Daily
Operating Highlights

Operating Revenues		Operating Expenses	
Local advertising	$1,219,499	Total salaries	439,363
National ad	73,527	Circulation delivery	41,028
Classified ad	277,428	Circulation postage	29,100
Legal ad	—	Newsprint	212,867
Preprints	88,500	Other	90,468
Weekly free shopper	171,024	Total Significant Expense	812,826
Circulation	429,670	Total Operating Expense	1,207,710
Commercial printing	—		
Other	2,100	Operating profit	1,054,038
		Operating margin	46.6%
Total	2,261,748		

Table 4.7   Typical 50,000 Circulation Newspapers* ($000 omitted)

	1981	1982	1982 Percent of Total
Revenue			
Advertising			
Local	$ 4,984.0	$ 5,160.5	44.8%
National	594.4	612.5	5.3
Classified	1,823.8	1,723.8	14.9
Preprint	847.0	922.6	8.0
Total	8,536.1	8,804.3	76.5
Circulation	2,307.6	2,463.8	21.4
Total Revenue	11,075.3	11,507.0	
Expense			
News-Editorial	1,246.9	$ 1,311.8	13.5%
Circulation-Distribution	1,169.3	1,271.9	13.1
Advertising	730.7	779.6	8.0
Production	1,142.3	1,177.2	12.1
Newsprint	2,024.1	2,051.4	21.1
General/Administrative	2,617.3	2,844.2	29.3
Total Expense	$ 9,169.8	$ 9,682.6	
Operating profit	1,905.5	1,824.4	
Operating margin	17.2%	15.9%	

* Inland's "typical" figures will not yield precisely 100% totals in either expense or revenue.
Reprinted with permission from the Inland Daily Press Association, Inc., 777 Busse Highway, Park Ridge, Ill. 60068.

But before you proceed, decide precisely what type newspaper you want to publish—a function of long-range strategic planning. The key question is whether *this* budget is correct for *this* newspaper at *this* time in *this* market against *this* competition. For example, high-quality news is costly; if you want it, the newsroom must budget accordingly. But how many news staffers are enough? Some editors say one per thousand circulation; most larger papers get by with fewer. How much must be spent? An APME poll indicates that newspapers under 20,000 circulation have newsroom expense equal to about 18 percent of total advertising and circulation revenue; papers over 100,000 circulation spend about 12.5 percent. The swing is equally wide if newsroom expenditures are expressed in percentages of total costs. Nationwide, newsrooms spend from 7 to 20 percent of the newsroom's total budget.

But there is no truly valid industrywide standard, and managers must adjust to local conditions to achieve operating efficiency consistent with overall strategy. Managers, in other words, must decide where the newspaper is to go in the years ahead and adjust spending to get it there.

Avoid Budgeting "Gamesmanship"

Each manager must dovetail twelve-month operating goals into the overall plan, then project accurately the resources—the share of total expense—needed to reach those goals. Each manager, in effect, competes with others for an allocation of corporate resources to do the job in the coming year. Each cost must be the responsibility of an individual (who, of course, must also have the authority to control it).

The budgeting process easily degenerates into a contest of wills with, say, an operating head hiding a "fat factor" of 25 percent or so in the budget proposal and hoping top management will not catch it. Or, management plays the game by automatically rejecting as too high each executive's first or second budget proposal,

however fat or lean. Avoid such gamesmanship and avoid arbitrarily constructing a budget without in-depth prior consultation between operating executives. A budget drawn without consultation is likely to be just plain wrong, missing by a country mile the cost/revenue precision essential to planning. And it is only human for operating executives to treat cavalierly, in the year ahead, any budget they did not help construct.

Make sure that the budget process is disciplined and assigns *accountability*, so that each executive has measureable responsibility for meeting budget goals. Delineating precisely which executive is responsible for which goals is the fabric of planning in any communications company. Nowhere is it more important than in budgeting.

Particularly among news executives, it is often felt that newspaper budgets cannot be drawn with quite the inflexible finality of budgets in other industries. It is argued that news is not predictable, and what looks like a quiet news year ahead could be one of famine, strife, and rising creeks—all expensive to cover.

Charles Hauser, vice president and executive editor of the *Providence (R.I.) Journal/Bulletin*, says editors need more flexibility in how news departments spend money. Editors, he says, must be able to shift funds to cover unexpected news developments and "meet changes in the competitive situation."[17]

New York Times editors, whose spending on news coverage is envied by editors around the world, today operate under tight budgets. Not long ago, *Times* editors spent as needed to cover the news, then asked the business office for more. Not today. If news-coverage emergencies require unusual spending, *Times* editors must shift funds from elsewhere in their budgets. ". . . we usually are able to cover unexpected news events by tightening up here and there,"

[17] Charles Hauser, speech to Institute of Newspaper Controllers and Finance Officers, quoted in *Southern Newspaper Publishers' Association Bulletin*, July 7, 1983, p. 3.

said A. M. Rosenthal, when he was *Times* executive editor.[18]

Start by Forecasting Revenue

A budget can run to scores of pages, with hundreds of individual revenue and cost items, so we cannot reproduce one here. But let's discuss how *Small Daily* goes about getting its financial house in order for the twelve months ahead.

Detailed budgets are drawn for seven departments: editorial, advertising, composing, press room, circulation, general and administration, and commercial printing.

The beginning point is a revenue forecast for the next year. Advertising must project its sales first, because the amount of ad space sold will determine the number of pages the other departments must create. Circulation must project how many papers will be sold, so accurate estimates for newsprint and ink needed, transportation costs, and so forth can be made.

Forecasting sales is tricky, of course. Understanding past sales trends is important, but there will be many variables in the months ahead: Will local business flourish, giving merchants more money to spend on advertising? Or will it slump? Difficulty at a single local factory—a strike, bankruptcy—could create havoc with *Small Daily*'s projections. So could the appearance of a new competitor—a free-circulation shopper, for example—or one that suddenly cuts advertising rates. Some variables will lie in the paper's overall plan. For example, if the plan is to put more salespeople on the streets and promote sales more heavily, new costs will occur.

Small Daily's ad manager asks individual salespersons for their thinking on what lies ahead. For major accounts, particularly food and department stores, careful month-by-month estimates are made. For each advertising category (we'll discuss them in a later chapter), the

manager projects column inches that will be sold and the rate for each. The two multiplied represent expected revenue. *Small Daily* makes its projections as shown in Table 4.8.

Variables affecting such month-by-month projections include *Small Daily*'s own rate structure; rates in each category will be raised at least once each year. Exactly when to increase rates, and how much, is crucial. Also, there are seasonal fluctuations in advertising. Stores advertise more just before Christmas; other months—January and February, for example—are less active. Both variables will be discussed in a later chapter.

Many variables influence projections of circulation revenue. We'll discuss circulation fully in a subsequent chapter, but among the fundamental issues of market economics a circulation manager must consider are these: If the market's population is expanding, circulation expansion is possible; if tough economic times are ahead, circulation may drop. And what sales implications are in the newspaper's overall plan for the year ahead? If the newsroom plans to begin covering a new suburb, circulation salespeople will have something to sell to prospective subscribers living there. Expected sales must be projected. Then, the circulation manager must project new revenue to be raised through rate increases. *Small Daily* is in a city which isn't expanding in population. Several nearby competitors have vigorous journalistic and marketing strategies that limit *Small Daily*'s circulation growth. For the year ahead, any growth in circulation revenue must come from an increase in per-copy price or subscription rate—or both.

Estimate Expenses Next

With circulation and advertising revenue projections in hand, *Small Daily*'s managers turn to the second major task in budgeting—estimating costs. Each department head must project costs within the context of the paper's overall plan.

Editorial, for example, must calculate the

---

[18] A. M. Rosenthal, letter to author, April 11, 1983.

Table 4.8   Revenue Patterns 1986 (dollars)

	Local Adv.	Local Color	National Adv.	Contract Classified	Transient Classified	Legal Adv.	Preprint Adv.	Total
Jan.	——	——	——	——	——	——	——	——
Feb.	——	——	——	——	——	——	——	——
Mar.	——	——	——	——	——	——	——	——
April	——	——	——	——	——	——	——	——
May	——	——	——	——	——	——	——	——
(etc.)								
TOTAL								

	Present Rate (per inch)	Proposed Increase (%) and Date	New Rate
Local	————	————	————
National	————	————	————
Contract classified	————	————	————
(etc.)			

cost of assigning reporters to the new suburb where the paper plans to expand. Circulation must estimate the cost of putting salespeople into the suburb to sell subscriptions. The production manager must project the number of pages to be produced in the twelve-month period. The pattern over past years must be reviewed, along with the circulation department's estimate of how many copies will be sold next year and the advertising department's projection of how much advertising will be placed. From that, the production manager must project how many employees will be needed, and at what costs. Adequate newsprint and ink must be ordered for the next year. Expert production managers know at all times their costs for each page produced, how much newsprint is in storage, and what their presses and other production facilities can produce.

Each significant cost must be isolated for examination. Most attention must be paid "big ticket" expenses—salaries and benefits, often 46 to 48 percent of a paper's total, and newsprint and ink, often 24 to 26 percent.

Table 4.9 shows how *Small Daily* budgets salaries.

Note that the advertising manager (and all other departmental managers) must decide in advance what salary increases will be granted in the forthcoming year. Each month's salary costs then are calculated before the new year begins—and if the budget is closely followed, an employee scheduled for a raise on September 1, as B. Brown is, will get it on that date and not a day earlier.

Similarly detailed projections are made for other costs. Table 4.10 shows how *Small Daily* does it for the editorial department.

General & Administration has the most departmental cost categories in *Small Daily*'s budget: thirty-nine, covering such things as payroll taxes for all departments, rent, insurance, electricity, water, and telephone. The newspaper is working on a new budgeting system that will allocate portions of such costs to each department. A new telephone switching system, for example, will ensure that each department is charged appropriately for its usage.

Table 4.9   Advertising Department—1986*

Name	Position	Hired	Last Raise	Current Salary	Proposed Increase	Jan.	Feb.	Mar.	(etc.)
J. Jones	Ad mgr.	9/'84	$50 6/85	$475	$40 1 Feb.	$475	$515	$515	
B. Brown	Sales	6/'85	$25 12/85	$250	$30 1 Sept.	$250	$250	$250	
C. Wells	Clerk	3/'83	$15 1/85	$190	$15 1 Jan.	$205	$205	$205	
(etc.)									

* Number of staffers this budget, 11.
Number of staffers last budget, 10.

Monitoring Performance

With cost and revenue estimates from department heads, the newspaper's chief financial officer projects an *operating statement*, outlining what the financial picture should be at year's end. If projections do not satisfy top management (or its board of directors), each department must lower projected costs or increase revenue—or both.

Once the budget year begins, management must monitor closely—at least monthly—ongoing budget performance by each operating section. Year end is too late to discover cost overruns or revenue shortfall. Off-budget performance has a crack-the-whip effect: seemingly minor variances up front snap fiercely at year's end. There must be control, with each variance from budget caught quickly and corrected.

Control, a major duty of each manager,

Table 4.10   Editorial Department, Year 1985/1986

	January 1985	January 1986	February 1985	February 1986	March 1985	March 1986	(etc.)
Salaries	____	____	____	____	____	____	
Overtime	____	____	____	____	____	____	
Operating supplies	____	____	____	____	____	____	
Associated Press	____	____	____	____	____	____	
Feature syndicates	____	____	____	____	____	____	
Correspondents (local)	____	____	____	____	____	____	
Travel/entertainment	____	____	____	____	____	____	
Motor vehicles							
company	____	____	____	____	____	____	
employee mileage	____	____	____	____	____	____	
Dues/subscriptions	____	____	____	____	____	____	
Misc.	____	____	____	____	____	____	
TOTAL	____	____	____	____	____	____	

must ensure that results match or exceed those planned. Basic to the control function are the following:

- *Standards* for performance established by the budget.

- *Information* to alert a manager immediately when performance deviates from standards.

- *Action* by a manager to correct substandard performance.

Small Daily's managers receive a printout of each month's expense and of revenue in their department within days following the close of business for each month. The publisher and a few key executives get printouts on all departments. But analyzing that vast amount of infor-

mation takes time, so the publisher gets two "quick read" documents that give an immediate picture of how the newspaper is performing.

One is a "budget summary" that reports revenue and expense performance in major categories, including a free-circulation shopper published by *Small Daily*. Table 4.11 shows how it looks.

Note that the budget summary lists each category with an "actual" figure—the precise total of revenue or expense in the month just ended. Alongside that is "this year's budget" figure. Any variance is expressed both in dollars and percentages. Learn to watch both. A $500 increase in an expense might not look significant, but if that is a 100 percent increase, investigate. Note that the budget summary presents the operating profit and conversion ratio. That is

Table 4.11 Budget Summary

	Actual	This Year's Budget	Dollar Variance	Percent Variance
Revenue				
Local				
National				
Classified				
Legal				
Preprint				
Weekly/shopper				
Total advertising				
Circulation				
Commercial printing				
Other				
Total Revenue				
Expenses				
Editorial				
Advertising				
Production				
Circulation				
General & Administration				
Depreciation				
Total Expense				
Operating profit				
Conversion ratio				

Table 4.12 Weekly Summary

Significant Expenses	Actual	Budget	Dollar Increase (decrease)	Percent Increase (decrease)
Total Salaries				
Circ. delivery costs				
Circulation postage				
Newsprint				
Overtime				
Total significant expense				
Total operating expense				
Statistical Summary				
Inches	**Actual**	**Budget**	**Increase**	**Decrease**
Local				
National				
Classified				
Legal				
Shopper				
Total				
Circulation	**Actual**	**Budget**	**Increase**	**Decrease**
Daily				
Shopper				

the bottom line, so important to *Small Daily's* owner.

The publisher's second "quick read" document is a *weekly summary* of significant expenses. (See Table 4.12.)

The weekly summary lists total salaries, cost of newsprint, overtime, and other large costs. Note that the publisher is informed weekly on performance in advertising as expressed in column inches and in circulation totals.

For any progressive newspaper, the budget is but one step in short-range planning. Says Harte-Hanks's Marbut:

> As a matter of corporate policy the budgeting process is merely part of the ongoing operational planning process. While everything tends to come out dollar signs, the dollar signs come as a result of programs and strategies being developed to accomplish specific goals. The operational planning

side of our system is a 12-month calendar year look ahead. . . .[19]

MANAGEMENT BY OBJECTIVES

Many newspapers employ management techniques beyond budgeting to establish order, predictability, and accountability in operating sectors where those conditions have not always existed. These are programs for participatory goals within a twelve-month framework, but they are wider in scope than the budget.

Managers use these techniques to make themselves more visible at all operating levels, to reach down into lower ranks with programs that touch individuals and thus create a sense

---

[19] Robert Marbut, letter to author, March 3, 1983.

of corporate direction at levels previously untouched by top-level planning. Another aim is to measure progress—or lack of it—in areas not easily quantified, such as quality of reporting and writing or effectiveness of corporate promotion. These areas are not regarded by some newspaper people as fertile for business methodology. The new techniques smack of corporate discipline, a condition studiously avoided by some newspaper people. Objections are that planning takes too much time and work or that the future is so unpredictable that planning is useless. But the need for more orderly management is too great, and *management by objectives (MBO)* has joined budgeting as a way of life in progressive communications companies. The industry's leading companies are deeply committed to formal MBO programs.

Why The MBO Approach?

In the words of Harte-Hanks's Marbut:

> Management by Objectives is part of the whole planning process and certainly part of our culture. . . . it is done for financial planning, for human resources planning, for organizational planning, for facilities and capital investment planning, for product development planning and the like. It covers a lot of areas that are hard to measure, such as editorial quality and staff quality. However, we do feel that there are ways to get your arms around even those esoteric things. It is based on the idea that we ought to know on the front end how we are going to measure our results—that way, everyone is happier and tends to be in greater agreement as to where we are.

> If the goal is just to have a "better product," how do we measure it at the end of a year? But if we say that a better product means more local editorials, more local photographs, a higher rating on the part of readers in the next readership survey, a larger percentage of the total news given to local news, etc., then we can measure what we mean by this.

> The same is true with people development. If we set a goal to have people improve certain technical skills, we can identify what they are and then measure at least on some related basis—such

as "better than/about the same as/less effective" than last year. The same is true about a lot of other areas. . . .[20]

Knight-Ridder, in the vanguard of innovative management, has more than three hundred managers in MBO programs. Chairman Chapman says that the program "enables us to define company-wide goals that keep us all moving in the same direction and take advantage of our collective wisdom and experience without stifling individual initiative."[21]

Publisher Capen of Knight-Ridder's *Miami Herald* says: "Our goals program applies equally to business-side people as well as to news and editorial executives. We have proven that it is possible to put together goals programs—measured objectively—within the newsroom as well as the rest of the operation."[22]

Increasingly, editors are becoming committed to goals programs, though many find it difficult to measure newsroom performance. Says Burl Osborne, president and editor of the *Dallas Morning News:*

> We do have a goals program for the news department that we are trying to implement in some form at every management level. It is related to an improved budgeting system that pushes accountability and control down to every subdepartment supervisor.

> In general, the goals are combinations of quantifiable matters, budget being chief, and less tangible elements such as writing and editing quality. It is a matter of stated practice that any (staff) replacement must raise the level of the given position, and that, along with other intangibles such as design improvement, better packaging, stronger headlines and the like, are subjective judgments, arrived at by the supervisor and the person with the goal.

> It is an imperfect system . . . but we think it can serve the purpose of achieving improvements of which all parties can be proud.[23]

---

[20] Ibid.
[21] Alvah H. Chapman, Jr., letter to author, March 16, 1983.
[22] Capen letter, op. cit.
[23] Burl Osborne, letter to author, April 11, 1983.

Constructing Your Program

Any successful MBO program features clear statement of corporate goals and short-term objectives, commitment by top management, and enthusiastic follow-through by all managers along the chain of command.

Detailed discussion is required of what each individual or unit must accomplish in the year ahead, specific improvement to be made, and target dates. Each individual is often given flexibility in determining precisely how goals will be met. That can elicit imaginative efforts from individuals and is a morale booster.

As in budgeting, there must be interim reporting dates for monitoring and controlling progress. Each manager's goals must be reasonably attainable; goals patently beyond reach simply turn off operating managers and create serious morale problems. Yet goals must be "far enough out" to make each manager stretch to unusual lengths.

Early drafting, say two or three months before the year opens, permits discussion, so a manager can sense how employees regard goals being assigned them. "Feedback" from lower echelons is extremely valuable, and a manager must listen carefully. Responsive adjustment in goals can launch a finely turned program with full staff support.

A manager should *never* stifle questioning or even dissent. Both can create synergism essential to progress.

All managers should have uniform reporting dates—say, the first of March, May, July, September, and November. This permits control of performance and allows for adjustments during the year, which, in turn, makes possible a companywide survey of progress in a meaningful manner.

Benefits and Dangers

One benefit of an MBO program is the sense of participation—opportunity for creative contribution—it gives junior employees. To make that happen, each manager must delegate significant goals responsibilities to younger subordinates. More than one MBO program encounters difficulty, however, when managers, misunderstanding the program or feeling threatened by it, refuse to delegate authority as long as they retain responsibility for performance. Directors of the program must explain thoroughly what MBO is all about and understand any uneasiness among those with responsibility for making it work.

An MBO program can fail if it becomes an end in itself, creating mountains of paperwork and degenerating into meaningless bureaucratic exercises. Keep the program *results-oriented*, keep paper to a minimum, state goals briefly and precisely. An Associated Press MBO program assigned the executive editor just five goals and required only seven progress reports to higher management during the year. Goals included improving writing and editing, generating monthly sports news projects of substance, invigorating reporting by specialist reporters—and other news projects.[24]

In sum, an MBO program improves planning and communication with each individual on overall goals and on what is expected. As a control mechanism, periodic review of each participant's progress permits operating adjustments as the year progresses. Weaknesses include the time and effort needed to make the program succeed plus difficulty in framing challenging yet realistic goals.

Properly directed, MBO can aid the top-priority tasks of cost control and decision making. And to those we now turn.

TOP PRIORITY: COST CONTROL

Many factors forced Publisher N. S. Hayden, with Executive Editor Craig Ammerman at his

---

[24] Additional readings in MBO are Duncan, op. cit., and Stoner, op. cit. Very useful, of course, is Peter Drucker, *The Practice of Management*, New York, Harper & Row, 1954.

side, to walk into the *Philadelphia Bulletin* newsroom and tell the assembled staff that their famous old newspaper was closing on January 29, 1982. These factors included competitive patterns established before either man arrived in Philadelphia, plus socioeconomic changes of an even earlier era—and neither Hayden, an aggressive and sales-oriented executive, nor Ammerman, a creative and dynamic editor, could do anything about them.

When they joined the *Bulletin* after its sale to Charter Co. in April 1980, both understood the historic evolution of newspapering in Philadelphia had thrown up a stronger, more capable species in the *Philadelphia Inquirer*. But both hoped they could find a quick fix that would give them breathing space while they worked on long-range survival strategy.

All the top-priority tasks of newspaper management came crashing down on Hayden and Ammerman—circulation, advertising, news, the competition, unions. But there is now no question in Hayden's mind about what top-priority challenge ruined his effort to achieve a short-term turnaround and return the *Bulletin* to profitability:

> As to why the *Bulletin* was terminal in May 1980 [when Hayden took control], that in itself is a book. For a myriad of reasons, management decisions, etc., another simple way to state it is that the cost base was simply too high and could not be reduced. The paper died by suffocation under a cost load that couldn't be lightened quickly enough.[25]

The cost load. Like a giant tumor, it can grow almost unseen, spread through a newspaper, sap its strength, and, if ignored too long, finally defeat last-minute efforts by even the most skilled management surgeon. Cost control—getting firm grip on every dollar spent—might well be first priority for every manager. For while other newspaper operations often change slowly, costs are volatile and can zoom quickly out of control. And that negates the most innovative circulation and advertising expansion programs.

An Inland Daily Press Association study of a "typical" 50,000-circulation daily newspaper shows that in 1979–1982, total revenue increased 21 percent *but expenses increased 24 percent.*[26] A typical 20,000-circulation daily had to run hard in 1959–1980 to stay ahead of costs. Revenue increased 22 percent in that period; expenses climbed 20 percent.[27]

Newspaper managers of the next generation will also face strong upward pressure on costs. And competition from other media plus resistance from advertisers and readers will prevent newspapers from instituting, willy-nilly, rate increases to cover higher costs. Managers at all levels of the newspaper must consider cost control a priority.

Avoid, Control, Monitor, Reexamine

The first and best way to handle costs is to avoid them. Question every new expense proposal and insist on a cost/benefit study to, simply, prove what benefit will be derived. It is difficult, obviously, to judge exactly the contribution of, say, a syndicated column to overall journalistic quality. If it demonstrably assists the newspaper in reaching its overall goal, add the new cost to the budget. If it doesn't improve quality or profitability, reject it.

The second step in controlling costs, if they prove unavoidable, is to make sure they are kept as low as possible. Shop around, compare; *think.* Is there a cheaper way?

Third, constantly monitor all costs against last year's actual costs and this year's expense budget. Correct any overrun immediately.

Fourth, never stop reexamining all costs,

---

[25] N. S. Hayden, letter to author, March 8, 1983.

[26] B. E. Wright, "Study Shows Inflation's Bite on Papers," *presstime*, July 1983, p. 59.
[27] "Soaring Expenses Reduce Profits of Typical Daily," *Editor & Publisher*, July 24, 1982, p. 11.

repeatedly weighing the cost/benefit balance. Because somebody's grandfather justified a cost in 1940 does not mean it is acceptable today. And, many newspapers are burdened with costs dating back to about 1940 or so. Arthur Ochs (Punch) Sulzberger is fond of describing how, shortly after he became publisher of the *New York Times,* a study of production costs uncovered highly paid back-shop employees without duties or job descriptions—and neither management nor union knew what they were supposed to be doing.[28] At one point, Sulzberger told shareholders, the *Times* employed 50 percent more production workers than did competing papers. He said this was one reason the *Times,* for years, contributed only 24 percent of the parent corporation's profit, although it contributed 66 percent of total revenue.

Watch costs such as staff additions that could become fixed expenses forever. A one-time cost of $35,000 for new equipment is one thing; a new copy editor at $35,000 annually for an indefinite time is quite another.

Plan for Smooth Cost Control

Every manager must motivate the full staff to think cost control. To manage otherwise risks being forced, as were Messrs. Hayden and Ammerman, to explain to the staff that costs have outrun revenue and that profitability has disappeared—along with their jobs.

Absent ongoing cost control implemented calmly and smoothly, with the staff educated to regard this as a part of newspaper life, even a minor business downturn can force management to slash costs suddenly and drastically. The shock of such cuts can cause discontent dangerous to staff morale. This occurred in Minneapolis in 1982, as Cowles Media Co. attempted to recover from several years of poor acquisitions and questionable management decisions. Profits plunged, and the company's *Buffalo (N.Y.) Courier-Express* was forced to close (after losing $26 million in three years). The afternoon *Min-*

neapolis Star* was forced to merge with its morning sister, *The Tribune,* and the stability of the new flagship, the combined *Minneapolis Star and Tribune,* was threatened. Management jumped into cost cutting, a shocking departure for a company known for paternalism. It suddenly announced that two hundred previously secure jobs would be cut.

Top management had not convinced Editor Charles W. Bailey, a respected journalist whose reputation was wider than his Upper Midwest base, to support the economy campaign. That was mistake number one. Mistake number two was that management had not convinced Bailey to limit his objections to the inner, private councils of war. Bailey went public in a very big way, resigning in a newsroom packed with staff members invited to hear why he quit. The staff cut, he said, was "a very serious mistake and one that will have grave consequences for the newspaper."[29]

The doubt thus publicly cast on management's leadership did not stop there. Because of Bailey's nationwide reputation, the Minneapolis fracas quickly became somewhat notorious throughout the industry, hardly building confidence in Cowles Media. Then Christopher Burns, vice president and associate publisher, resigned in public disagreement with Publisher Donald R. Dwight. Next, Dwight, a former lieutenant governor of Massachusetts and also a man with a national reputation, was fired suddenly by John Cowles, Jr., president of the parent company. That caught national attention. Two months later, Cowles Media's board of directors summoned President Cowles to a room in the Hilton Hotel at Chicago's O'Hare International Airport, and suddenly *he* was out of a job.

Cowles Media's troubles were complicated and many factors contributed to the bloodletting. This much is clear: In economic boom times, Cowles Media might have been able to solve

---

[28] Arthur Sulzberger, conversation with author, 1973.

[29] Jonathan Friendly, "Minneapolis Newspaper Editor Quits in Protest Over New Staff Cuts," *New York Times,* Oct. 8, 1982, p. 22.

COST CONTROL IS CRUCIAL

Increasing revenue is key in any newspaper's strategy. But the smart manager turns quickly and decisively to cost control in an economic downturn. Says W. J. Pennington, *Seattle (Wash.) Times* publisher and president:

> Cost containment is the basic and most effective method to remain profitable under difficult economic conditions because one dollar of cost savings equals one dollar of profit improvement. Increased sales are important, too, but with incremental costs of 70% or higher in a typical manufacturing operation, only 30 cents of each new dollar of revenue is retained for profit improvement. *One dollar of cost savings is worth more than three dollars of additional sales!*
>
> . . . cost containment must not be implemented blindly. We fully recognize the importance of containing and reducing costs to improve profitability. However, we make every possible effort to maintain our news and editorial product quality. Cost containment at the expense of product quality can produce short-term benefits but longer-term problems for any organization.

its problems without mass firings. Unfortunately, the problems erupted in recessionary times—or because of them—and management, with revenue weakening, sought solutions in drastic cost reductions. The firings unleashed a round of emotional moves that included the O'Hare drama. Lesson: Do not accept costs in economic boom times just because revenue is flowing in to cover them. The costs will still be with you in bad times, even if the revenue is not (see box).

Labor Biggest Cost

Labor is a newspaper's largest single cost, and every manager is responsible for keeping it at a level that is sustainable in the newspaper's market.

Cowles Media accepted (indeed, in its paternalism helped create) costs—and staff expectations—far too high for the basic economic strength of its marketplace. For years, it paid reporters salaries second only to those paid in New York City, the nation's largest market in population and disposable personal income. Minneapolis was the fifteenth largest market. Salaries paid by the *Star* and *Tribune* were not only out of line with the market's basic economic strength but also too high for the financial performance of the two papers. In the early 1980s, the papers were only marginally profitable.

Cowles Media was also out of step with the industry: About 49 percent of its total expense was for labor, compared with 46.1 percent for Harte-Hanks and 45.3 percent for Knight-Ridder. The Inland Daily Press Association says a 20,000-circulation daily allocates 36.9 percent of costs to payroll; payroll represents 42.3 percent of costs for the "typical" 50,000-circulation paper. (Those figures illustrate the competitive advantage that lower labor costs give to smaller papers. They also underline how "labor-intensive" the newspaper industry is. Labor costs are about 6 percent of total costs in the petroleum industry, 14 percent in auto manufacturing, and 22 percent in steel.)

A newspaper's greatest cost inefficiency lies in the very nature of its business: staff must be sufficiently large to produce a fat paper on the biggest advertising day in the busiest month of the year. And that means sometimes dramatic *overstaffing* on days in slow months when thin papers are produced.

An auto manufacturer counts inventory and projects sales, and then, if necessary, lays off relatively unskilled workers for months. Not so a newspaper. It takes years to assemble and train a skilled staff for news and other departments, and this staff must be kept at full complement or it withers. And, of course, even if nothing is happening now, big news might break in five minutes.

NEWSPRINT PRICES
(per metric ton)

Zooming newsprint prices force newspapers into crash programs to control waste. Consumption, meanwhile, is jumping sharply upward as well. A combination of both factors puts newspapers in a tight cost squeeze.

YEAR	PRICE
1970	$179
1971	188
1972	194
1973	235
1974	259
1975	287

YEAR	PRICE
1976	336
1977	336
1978	353
1979	413
1980	440
1981	500
1982	469
1983	500
1984	535
1985	535
1986	570
1987	610

It is not only basic salaries that managers must watch. Benefits or "fringes" in printing and publishing in 1984 averaged 36.5 percent of basic payroll. That covers the employer's contribution to Social Security, unemployment insurance, workers' compensation, pensions, vacations, and so on. Therefore a Minneapolis reporter who is paid $33,124 salary annually costs the newspaper at least $12,090 more, or about $45,214. A cost-control program must look at each department's requests for staff additions in those *total-dollar* terms.

Cut Newsprint Costs to Increase Profits

Newsprint costs are the second largest expense for newspapers, often 15 to 16 percent of total costs for small dailies and 32 to 33 percent or more for large papers.

U.S. dailies use about 76 percent of all the newsprint consumed each year—8.8 million metric tons in 1985. The price jumped to $610 per metric ton in 1987 and no end was in sight (see box).

Edward E. Beckley, consultant for Copley Press, Inc., estimates that a 1 percent reduction in newsprint usage or waste can increase profits up to 14 percent for a typical paper.[30] Beckley warns managers to calculate the cost-effectiveness of producing sample copies of the newspaper for sales promotion, a widespread practice, and to reconsider the cost/benefit of selling and distributing newspapers in "fringe areas," those circulation areas that are not particularly appealing to advertisers. Revenue may not justify costs, he says.

Lloyd E. Foss, newsprint coordinator for Hearst Newspapers, Inc., warns that sound newsprint management must start the moment delivery contracts are negotiated with suppliers. Then, there must be close monitoring of shipping damage, loss in storage due to poor housekeeping, and production waste in the press room.[31] Foss estimates that a single web break—a tear as newsprint rolls through the press, forcing a shutdown—can cost $25 to $100 in wasted newsprint and lost production.

Charles W. Carroll, manager of press and

---

[30] Edward E. Beckley, "The Care and Feeding of Newsprint; Reducing Waste," *Editor & Publisher*, July 9, 1983, p. 30.
[31] Lloyd E. Foss, "Sound Newsprint Management Opens Several 'Avenues Of Opportunity,'" *Editor & Publisher*, July 9, 1983, p. 31.

distribution for the *Orlando (Fla.) Sentinel*, says intensive employee training at his 196,000-circulation paper reduced waste to 2.9 percent. That compares with 4.7 percent for newspapers surveyed by the American Newspaper Publishers' Association and using over 20,000 tons annually. In ten months, Carroll's pressroom crew reduced costs by $400,000—and shared in the savings through a bonus system he established to encourage careful handling of newsprint.[32]

Times Mirror Corp. turned to rigid cost control, as well as revenue expansion, when it acquired the *Denver Post* and vigorously attacked its crosstown rival, the *Rocky Mountain News*. Times Mirror stripped $3 million out of the *Post*'s operating costs, including $1 million by simply reducing the width of its newsprint web by 2 inches. The readers got a somewhat narrower paper; the *Post* got a return to "moderately profitable" status.[33]

A Few Tips

Make sure you have an efficient *purchasing system* to seek competitive bids on supplies and negotiate the best possible prices, particularly for any commodity (like newsprint) that is purchased in bulk. Purchasing should be headed by a tenacious man or woman who is skilled in narrowing the gap between asking price and what the vendor will take when pressed.

Contingency plans should be made for cost cutting if business turns suddenly sour. Planning in advance gives each manager at every level the opportunity, without the pressure of a crash effort, to target cost pruning methodically yet avoid slicing too deeply into crucial operational areas and journalistic quality.

Cost reduction goals should be assigned to each manager in dollar or percentage terms; managers should then strip costs out in a manner

they feel will least disturb operations. This preserves accountability—making every manager responsible for his or her operation. It can also motivate each manager to make sure that fat, not muscle, comes out of costs.

Although they represent large shares of total expense, labor and newsprint costs should not dominate any cost-control program. Substantial savings can be achieved with disciplined control of variables such as vehicle use, overtime, travel/entertainment, telephone, stringers, postage, electricity, and so on.

Cost control programs must encourage imaginative solutions. The *Atlanta Journal* and *Constitution* extracts for salvage more than 4,000 troy ounces of silver annually from fixer solutions in film and paper processors—an imaginative way to save money.[34]

And beware seemingly insignificant percentage increases. A 5 percent increase in newsroom costs might not sound like much, but applied to Ben Bradlee's $50 million (1986) budget at the *Washington Post*, it would add $2.5 million to costs in the first year.[35]

TOP PRIORITY: MANAGEMENT INFORMATION AND DECISION MAKING

Effectiveness of operations management—actual production of the newspaper—depends on the quality and timeliness of information available to managers and on the decisions that result.[36]

---

[32] Charles W. Carroll, "Have Newsprint Waste Problems?" *Editor & Publisher*, July 23, 1983, p. 30.

[33] "Shoot-Out in the Rockies," *Time*, June 7, 1982, p. 77.

[34] "Atlanta Newspapers' Silver Recovery System Nets 4,000 Troy Ounces," *Southern Newspaper Publishers' Association Bulletin, Technology*, July 7, 1983, p. 1.

[35] For fuller discussion of management's control function, see J. C. Emery, *Organizational Planning and Control Systems: Theories and Technology*, New York, Macmillan, 1969; also, T. G. Rose and D. E. Farr, *Higher Management Control*, New York, McGraw-Hill, 1957.

[36] See Billy M. Thornton and Paul Preston, *Introduction to Management Science*, Columbus, Ohio, Merrill, 1977; Hitt, Middlemist, and Mathis, op. cit., are strong on decision-making theory. On management information systems, see James H. Donnelly, Jr., James L. Gibson, and John M. Ivancevich, *Fundamentals of Management*, Dallas, Business Publications, Inc., 1978.

Newspaper managers increasingly rely on computer systems to analyze information about all aspects of newspaper management and production. (Courtesy of Digital Equipment Corporation)

Management information systems (MIS) must be constructed for the efficient collection, coordination, and distribution of *internal* and *external* information. Budgeting and MBO are key in the internal information system. Managers increasingly use sophisticated computer systems—"decision support systems"—to analyze information from marketing, finance, production, and other departments by comparing it with decision models. External information crucial to decision making includes reader, advertiser, and marketplace data plus socioeconomic input of a wider nature—and government information, as well.

Management information systems employed by newspapers take many forms. To be effective, they must provide information in the correct quantity (enough but not too much), of high quality (as accurate as possible), in usable form, at the right time (when needed, not the next day). Much of the needed information is scattered throughout operating departments and is hard to collect.

Management information systems must assist managers in evaluating pertinent information, then in rationally and unemotionally identifying problems and alternative solutions. Picking alternatives to follow, then implementing them and monitoring progress complete the process. And that's not simple.

Decision making is a complex matter requiring managers to have a high degree of social skills as well as wide experience and the right attitudes and abilities. Conflict and inability to arrive logically at decisions that will best move the newspaper toward its goals and then to implement them are prime causes of disarray in newspaper managerial suites today. Theorists identify many approaches to decision making, ranging from techniques that are useful when managers possess accurate and plentiful information to others that help when managers have little or no information and thus cannot reliably predict the outcome.

Computers and *simulation techniques* make it possible to run problems in abstract form and to study alternatives; *linear programming* allows for mathematical approaches to problems, particularly those involving money, time, and people. But it's still fashionable in the newspaper industry for managers to draw on the expertise and opinions of their executive staffs, audit the newspaper's external and internal environments, then personally match decisions with existing conditions—the *"contingency approach."*

SUMMARY

Having studied the market, the competition, and the relevance of its newspaper to both, the management team turns to planning. Two stages are essential:

Long-range strategy is designed to position the newspaper for journalistically effective and profitable operation three, five, or more years hence, whatever the socioeconomic environment may be. Looking externally, long-range planners should question basic assumptions—even whether newspapers will continue to exist in their present form. Internally, managers must plan improved performance by each department over the long haul with action-oriented programs that begin now. Planning for profit is key to long-range strategy; for without profit, newspapers will not attract quality personnel and staff strength will diminish.

Short-range planning, for the year immediately ahead, is designed to move the newspaper step by step toward its long-range goal. Budgeting, followed with precision and discipline, is crucial. It sets dollar goals that each revenue-generating department must meet if the newspaper is to reach overall goals. It assigns expense limits for all departments. Thus, accountability is assigned to each manager and department. MBO programs are handy in short-range planning for establishing order, predictability and accountability in operational areas that are not easily controllable by budgeting. Goals such as improved writing and reporting are assigned.

Cost control might well be the first priority for every manager. Costs can zoom out of control quickly, negating the most innovative advertising and circulation expansion programs.

Costs should be avoided or controlled, monitored and reexamined in a methodical, disciplined manner. Cost control must be a way of life for the entire management team—and employees, too.

Labor is a newspaper's largest single cost—as much as 45 to 49 percent of total costs. Newsprint can represent 15 to 16 percent of total costs for small dailies, 32 to 33 percent for large papers.

RECOMMENDED READING

For nonaccountant managers, Merrill Lynch Pierce Fenner & Smith, Inc., One Liberty Plaza, 165 Broadway, New York, NY 10080, published *How to Read A Financial Report,* a superb step-by-step analysis of a balance sheet and profit and loss statement. Also note Charles Horngren, *Introduction to Management Accounting,* Englewood Cliffs, N.J., Prentice-Hall, 1978; George Odiorne, *Executive Skills: A Management-by-Objectives Approach,* Dubuque, Iowa, Brown, 1980; and George Odiorne, *MBO II: A System of Managerial Leadership for the 80s,* Belmont, Calif., Fearon Pitman, 1979.

CHAPTER FIVE

The Human Element

If you've ever led a Boy Scout troop or coordinated fellow students working on a class project, you have already been introduced to one of a manager's greatest responsibilities: supervising the human element.

People, not machines, produce newspapers. People are any newspaper's greatest asset—and its largest single cost. Aspiring managers who cannot effectively motivate people will have short careers. There is no room, even at the lowest managerial level, for those who are indifferent to or unable to deal effectively with the human element.

In this chapter, we will discuss the theory and basic tasks of personnel ("human resources") management, including motivating and controlling the performance of others according to plan. Then, we'll discuss challenges ahead in newspaper management, such as the much-needed hiring of minorities and caring for employees who are displaced by new technology. We'll spend considerable time on how to avoid unions or, if they can't be avoided, how to work with them.

But, let's first look at how a couple of highly regarded newspaper professionals gave top priority to the human element in a hotly competitive fight in Denver—how they made improving staff quality their first and single most important step once battle had been joined.

THE POWER OF PERSONNEL

Having paid $95 million to acquire the afternoon *Denver Post* in 1981, the giant Times Mirror Corp. launched an old-fashioned newspaper war in the Mile High City by vigorously attacking the *Rocky Mountain News*, a morning paper owned by Scripps-Howard Newspapers. Times Mirror sent for Lee Guittar, publisher of the company's *Dallas Times Herald* (and later a Hearst executive), to direct the attack. Guittar took with him Will Jarrett to serve as executive editor.

Although they were facing a multitude of "top priority" tasks, Guittar and Jarrett turned quickly to improving the quality of the *Post*'s news staff. For starters, they raided the *Rocky Mountain News* for Woodrow Paige, Jr., the city's best-known sports columnist, paying him $75,000 a year to jump to the *Post*. At that time, top minimum for reporters at both newspapers was $28,600 annually.

Was it sound personnel policy to pay Paige 2.6 times the going rate? Well, at minimum, Guittar and Jarrett got this for their $75,000: first, a fast talent transfusion for the *Post*'s sports pages, important in sports-crazy Denver; second, proportionate weakening of the *Rocky Mountain News*'s sports pages; and third, fully $75,000 worth of public relations advantage by demonstrating to reader and advertiser alike that Times Mirror had landed in town and was serious indeed about dominating the newspaper scene.

Guittar and Jarrett then raided the *New York Daily News* for Buddy Martin, its sports editor, and made similar moves to strengthen the *Post*'s general news staff. The *Rocky Mountain News* launched raids of its own, and both companies began improvements in all aspects of operations for what promised to be a lengthy war.

Guittar and Jarrett, be it noted, decided that they could achieve quicker return on investment in personnel management than in perhaps any other sector of newspaper operations. It is a lesson for your first step into management, when you become responsible for the performance of one other person; all the way up the management ladder, the principle remains unchanged. Weak news coverage can be improved quickly with the addition of talented reporters and columnists. If they are hired from a competitor, who thereby is weakened, so much the better. A production department that fails to meet its press schedules can be turned around overnight by a new production director who makes the system work; hiring the right sales director can improve ad sales. It is in personnel that managers put their own stamp on a newspaper's long-range character. The newspaper of the future will be a mirror image of the people hired today.

Conversely, manager failures surface quickly in personnel matters and can actually prevent the next edition from getting out or cause a sudden exodus of talented staff to other newspapers. Over the long term, management failures—by first-level supervisors as well as top-level strategists—can contribute mightily to the decline of a newspaper. A newspaper cannot rise above the quality of its employees—their morale, their sense of mission, their productivity.

For even first-level supervisors, personnel management today is "human resources management"; it can involve helping employees deal with personal problems, alcoholism or drug abuse, or stress in the workplace. And personnel management must be accomplished within a demanding and shifting social and legal framework that increasingly dictates the relationship between manager and employee. For example, the *newspaper*'s needs are just one dimension of the complex requirements that managers must meet. The *work force* and its needs, desires, and demands are changing, and newspapers face unprecedented pressure for a better work environment, job satisfaction, and personal fulfillment as well as better wages and benefits. And *government*, with its move into equal opportunity in employment, health and safety, and pensions, is also creating new standards that newspapers must meet.

PERSONNEL MANAGEMENT'S BASIC TASK

The basic task in personnel management is to obtain the best available talent at a cost the newspaper can afford and then to establish an environment that will create and motivate a staff of high morale to move the newspaper toward goals of improved quality, productivity, and profitability.[1]

In the following section, we will look at key steps in the basic task: *Auditing* the newspaper's personnel needs and resources, *planning* effective development and use of personnel, *hiring* and *motivating, controlling* performance, and *disciplining*.

Auditing Needs and Resources

As in any kind of planning, auditing is a manager's first step. This means forecasting the human resources the newspaper's operating departments must have to meet their short, intermediate, and long-range goals. The next step is to assess which resources are available in-house and which must be obtained outside.

Forecasting for the *short term* is relatively

easy. The budget and operating plan for the year ahead will authorize certain numbers and types of employees; the audit determines how many are already on staff and how many will probably be lost (through termination, promotion, transfer, etc.); thus, a manager determines how many must be hired, trained, and put in place. For example, if retirements will create two openings on the sports desk, two sports reporters must be hired. Simple enough.

However, over the *intermediate term*, forecasting becomes much more difficult. Looking two to five years ahead, forecasters must decide who is needed, when, where, with what type skills, and at what cost. Let us say your intermediate planning calls for a general improvement in the quality of the entire sports staff and creation of new coverage in, say, prep sports over the next three years. To forecast personnel resources needed for such a general overhaul of an entire department is much more difficult, so the personnel manager and sports editor must plan precisely where and how to obtain the needed resources. This could involve, for example, a stipulation that each new sportswriter must be more experienced and demonstrably abler than the employee being replaced—and that the new employee be hired from among the outstanding sports reporters working for competing newspapers.

Human resources forecasting for the *long range*, say five years or more, brings into play a manager's best analytical skills. The challenge is to assess probable changes in the environment and then to fashion the appropriate human resources strategy. For example, long-range forecasting should anticipate such trends as societal pressure for hiring and promoting women and minorities. Many newspapers that failed to do so in the 1970s and early 1980s are now hurrying, at inordinate cost, to catch up.[2]

---

[1] A number of authors have produced extremely valuable overviews of the personnel function. Among them are the following: Paul Pigors and Charles A. Myers, *Personnel Administration*, New York, McGraw-Hill, 1977; Rensis Likert, *The Human Organization: Its Management and Value*, New York, McGraw-Hill, 1967; Peter Drucker, *Management Tasks, Responsibilities, Practices*, New York, Harper & Row, 1974; Lyman W. Porter and Edward E. Lawler III, *Managerial Attitudes and Performance*, Homewood, Ill., Irwin, 1968; F. E. Fiedler, *A Theory of Leadership Effectiveness*, New York, McGraw-Hill, 1967; Douglas McGregor, *The Human Side of Enterprise*, New York, McGraw-Hill, 1960; A. H. Maslow, *Motivation and Personality*, New York, Harper & Row, 1954; Dale S. Beach, *Personnel: The Management of People at Work*, New York, Macmillan, 1975.

---

[2] Particularly helpful in forecasting are Pigors and Myers, op. cit.

THE HANDBOOK CONTROVERSY

Sharp controversy exists over whether newspapers should provide employees with handbooks explaining corporate policy and, if so, how they should be written.

Some managers feel improving corporate communications requires that employees be given written explanations of policy, pension plans, health programs, and so on. Yet handbooks and written guidelines are interpreted by some courts to be work contracts, and employees have used them in suits against newspapers.

One major difficulty is handbook language referring to the "permanent employee" or in some way implying guaranteed employment, promotion, or wage increases. Newspapers that discharge an individual even for incompetence or to reduce workforces in an economic slump are vulnerable to lawsuit if such a "contract" exists.

Another problem is with handbooks—or even oral statements during hiring—that precisely define work rules or conditions of employment in a manner deemed contractual. A newspaper that changes rules or conditions by, say, transferring a reporter to night work in contravention of an implied contract is also vulnerable.

Some newspapers are withdrawing policy handbooks from circulation; many seek legal advice in writing them. One remedy is including a handbook disclaimer stating that no contract is implied and asking employees to sign it.

Making Plans and Stating Policy

Having audited existing resources and forecast needs, management must establish its human resources policy and clearly communicate it through every supervisory level to each employee.

The policy statement should cover the newspaper's attitudes and intentions in dealing with people. It can be a highly detailed handbook covering, say, a newspaper's determination to hire and promote strictly on merit, as well as such minutiae as how to join the company softball team. Or a manager can express the *spirit* of the policy rather simply. Chairman Al Neuharth of Gannett tells his managers to pay close attention to employees because they account for "50 percent of our costs and 100 percent of our accomplishments." That is a clear signal to every Gannett manager that the company regards its people as its most valuable resource.[3]

Increasingly, newspapers are swinging away from traditional, tightly-centralized authoritarianism based on the "Theory X" concept (see Chapter 2, "Leadership"), that human beings instinctively dislike work and must be forced to perform. The theme in policy statements is the "Theory Y" approach, that each employee is an individual with special needs who wants to perform well—and *will* do so if properly motivated.[4]

However expressed, communication on personnel policy should elicit suggestions and feedback from all managers, including first-line supervisors. There is controversy over whether the policy should be stated in writing (see box).

Personnel policy should enlist employee initiative in the drive to achieve the newspaper's goal. A reporter who is a self-starter in developing story ideas and pursuing them should be rewarded with bonuses, raises, or public recognition and compliments. An advertising salesperson should be rewarded for digging up new business. Policy must inspire teamwork, creating an atmosphere in which news and photo

---

[3] Andrew Radolf, "More Hiring of Women and Minorities Urged," *Editor & Publisher*, July 2, 1983, p. 10.

[4] For a concise view of these theories, see W. Jack Duncan, *Management*, New York, Random House, 1983.

Three staff members of the *Miami Herald* won Pulitzer prizes in 1986. Recruiting the best possible employees is a key factor in the quality and success of any newspaper. (UPI/ Bettmann Newsphotos)

departments automatically cooperate in coverage and in which production and circulation cooperate to get papers on the street on time. Importantly, personnel policy must assign each manager the task of *listening* to employees with sensitivity and empathy as well as *talking* to them. Employees must be able to express their views as well as receive orders; two-way communication is essential.[5]

Recruiting the Best, Wherever They Are

Managers can prepare for the newspaper's future personnel needs in two broad ways:

- Insert qualified employees into the training pipeline so they will be promotable when

needed. We will cover this in a later section on appraising employee performance to locate the talent already on a newspaper staff.

- Hire experienced talent from the outside.

Most papers use a combination approach. For now, let's concentrate on how you get involved in locating and pursuing outside talent when you join management. There are three important points to keep in mind:

First, competition for talent is fierce. It won't come to you; you must launch an aggressive search program—and keep it going.

Second, the greatest single attraction for talent in the newspaper business is reputation— yours as a fair and professional manager, the newspaper's as a "hot" paper offering journalistic excellence and sharp competitive instincts. Such papers often attract top talent even with wage patterns behind those of other newspapers. For example, the *Washington Post* was sixteenth on a Newspaper Guild list of U.S. newspapers ranked in order of minimum salaries for reporters in 1985. The *Philadelphia Inquirer* was tenth. (The *Post* paid a minimum of $640.75 weekly for reporters with five years' experience, the *Inquirer*, $671.94; the *New York Times* was highest, with $885.) Yet because both the *Post* and *Inquirer* set standards of excellence in news reporting and writing, they are regarded as meccas by thousands of talented journalists across the country and can pick the best and brightest.

Third, a newspaper's personnel needs today are diverse, and you should seek talent outside journalism schools and other media. Get your recruiting lines open to nonmedia schools and industries where you can find talent with background in data processing, accounting, the law, science, engineering—the specialized skills needed in newsrooms and other departments of your newspaper.

When recruiting beginning reporters and editors, concentrate on journalism school stu-

---

[5] Particularly helpful in this area are Michael Hitt, R. Dennis Middlemist, and Robert L. Mathis, *Effective Management*, St. Paul, West, 1979.

dents and majors from other disciplines working on university newspapers. Insist that all candidates have some newsroom experience from a college paper or summer job. Ask faculty members to prescreen for you, selecting the best available for your interview. Frequently visit schools in your region; establish for your newspaper and yourself a reputation among the students by participating in class projects and occasionally lecturing.

Establish "talent banks" of files on prospective employees currently working on other papers. Monitor their progress and follow their careers. Let them learn the basics on somebody else's payroll, then hire when they are ready to work for you. Watch competing newspapers. The bylines of star reporters will be on front pages regularly; the work of talented photo editors is there for you to see; energetic advertising salespeople advertise their own presence through the ads they sell and publish; if you need pressroom talent, which newspaper is well printed?

Be as liberal as your budget permits in offering summer internships for college students—and not just in the newsroom, either. Establish programs for students interested in all departments—particularly advertising, circulation and production, where your needs will probably be great. Students working under daily supervision, either yours or a colleague's, will be forced to reveal whether they have the required talent. Whenever possible, offer paid tryouts for experienced workers you are considering hiring. A two-week stint on your copy desk or in your circulation department will tell you a great deal about the candidates.

Promoting from within is generally less expensive than recruiting outside and can create loyalty to your newspaper, but it also can lead to insular thinking and a "comfortable" atmosphere that permits substandard performance. By recruiting outside, you get a double dividend: talent with fresh views that also can shake things up a bit in your shop.

Selecting and Hiring with Care

The newspaper hiring process is dominated by three broad considerations:

First, greater talent is needed in every department. Competitive and marketplace demands for improved journalistic quality are increasing; complex business and technical problems require highly specialized workers. Simply put, you must make sure that *each* new hire is a qualitative improvement in staff professionalism. New reporters, for example, must be better educated and more experienced than those they replace.

Second, severe legal and societal constraints cover each step of the hiring and employment process, and expert legal advice is necessary. Be aware that, because you cannot easily fire a bad selection, the hiring process has become more critical in recent years.

Third, most newspapers today employ experts specially trained in sophisticated testing and interview techniques. But as a manager, *you* must be intimately involved in the hiring process.

Throughout the process, you should work from two documents: a *job description* that specifies duties and responsibilities for the position in question and a *job specification* that lists qualifications—education, experience, and so on—the job applicant must have. See box for how one newspaper writes both.

Follow these steps:

- *Completion of application form.* Get all relevant personal data, a resume, and references. For reporters, editors, and photographers, obtain samples of work.

- *Initial screening and interviewing.* Those patently unqualified should be put aside immediately. For the others, there is *no* substitute for a detailed interview by you or the supervisor involved. Use all the time you can spare. Let applicants talk at will. Ask what they read and about skills ob-

COURIER-JOURNAL JOB DESCRIPTION

The Louisville (Ky.) Courier-Journal *issued the following "employment opportunity" when an assistant managing editor's slot became vacant. Note the detailed job description and outline of qualifications needed.*

Job Description

Will be responsible for overall planning, co-ordination and critique of news gathering, processing and presentation, within the context of the goals and standards established by the managing editor.

Will work with the city, state, Indiana and business editors, providing direction and problem-solving on a day-to-day basis, and will insure that the activities of all departments are coordinated in the best interests of the total product.

Will serve as liaison with photo, news art, production, circulation, advertising, and research and analysis departments, in order to accomplish daily and long-range planning.

Will assume the first-echelon responsibility for preparation of the annual departmental expense and newsprint budget, coordinating the work of each desk and department. Will work with the managing editor's administrative secretary in preparation of budget documents.

Will monitor and evaluate each edition of the newspaper, in order to assist the managing editor in assessing the content of each and the performance of staff members.

Will advise the managing editor on staff needs, recruitment and training, personnel administration, departmental management, research and marketing, and news policy.

Will take charge of the newspaper's various operations in the absence of the managing editor, and will assume such other duties in the areas of policy and planning as the managing editor may dictate.

Qualifications

College degree most desirable. Advanced study desirable.

Extensive, varied experience as a daily newspaper reporter and/or copy editor most desirable. Previous experience in news administration most desirable.

Ability to communicate effectively, in writing and in person, essential.

Ability to work with other news administrators and staff.

---

viously needed—language skills for newsroom applicants, an intimate understanding of equipment for pressroom applicants, and so forth. But in all applicants look for enthusiasm, commitment, and determination. You can train employees in skills; they must light in their own bellies the fire you need.

• *Testing.* This is a high art, and you need tests professionally drawn up and evaluated.

• *Detailed checking of background.* Sadly, resumes and letters of reference cannot always be trusted. One study showed that

26 percent of firms surveyed found that new employees had falsified their resumes. Check academic credentials and talk with former employers.

• *Second interview.* On an important new hire, this will require a commitment of considerable time by you. Interview over a relaxed dinner and a drink; then, do it again in the formal, somewhat stressful surroundings of your office. Ask pointed questions—precisely what did the applicant do in his or her last job? Then, ask broad questions that force the applicant to take a wider view, such as "Tell me about your strengths." "What are your weaknesses?" "What job do you want ten years from now?"

Dos and Don'ts of Interviewing

We will discuss the law and human resources in Chapter 12, but for now we must stress the fact that there are severe legal constraints on the questions you may ask in interviews. Attorneys advise the following:

- Do not ask a prospective employee about race, creed, color, national origin, sex, marital status, or handicaps *unless* there is justifiable occupational reason.

- Do not ask about height, weight, plans to have children, number of children, arrangements for child care, a spouse's salary, previous arrest records, type of military discharge received.

- Do not outline a specific career path or promise promotions or special benefits.

- Do not speak of benefits, salary or employment being possible in general terms, such as "you've got a job here as long as you do a good job."

Two additional points of caution:

First, does this applicant possess potential for growth? Always strive to fill even an entry-level vacancy with a person talented enough to qualify for promotion. *Hire today for tomorrow.*

Second, have you, in your excessive eagerness to obtain the best talent, oversold the job? Is this an overqualified individual who will not be able to use his or her full abilities? If so, serious and disruptive morale problems could arise after employment.

You can never be completely certain you have matched a properly qualified individual with the proper job despite painstaking recruiting and hiring efforts. So accept the applicant only on the condition that a six-month probationary period is completed successfully.

Now comes motivating the new hire to perform in a desired manner that helps you and the newspaper reach your goals. Let us turn to motivation as a crucial role for every manager.

MOTIVATION: ITS THEORY AND PRACTICE

The importance of properly motivating each individual employee and thus the entire newspaper staff cannot be overestimated. It is central to each manager's personal career success and to the newspaper's ability to achieve its objectives. Luckily, the aspiring manager has a great deal of scholarly research from which to draw in learning how to motivate people.[6]

The Theoretical Background

Progressive motivational attitudes in newspaper management (as in other industries) are strongly influenced by Abraham Maslow (1908–1970), a psychologist who developed a theory of human needs as an explanation of behavior. Maslow developed the idea of a *hierarchy of needs*, suggesting that as individuals satisfy their needs on a lower level they will move on to a higher one and an ever-enlarging range of needs. The manager's challenge is to understand the employee's shifting view of his or her needs and respond appropriately in the interests of both the employee and the newspaper.

For example, Maslow's theory holds that each individual has basic *physiological needs* such as food, clothing, and shelter. In a newspaper, these needs are served by wages, which enable the employee to purchase the minimum

---

[6] A number of excellent books are available on motivation, among them Abraham H. Maslow, *Motivation and Personality*, New York, Harper & Row, 1954; Frederick Herzberg, Bernard Mausner, and Barbara Snyderman, *The Motivation to Work*, New York, Wiley, 1983; Victor H. Vroom, *Work and Motivation*, New York, Wiley, 1964; B. F. Skinner, *Contingencies of Reinforcement*, New York, Appleton Century Crofts, 1969.

necessities of life. But, Maslow theorized, once such minimum needs are met, each individual expresses *safety and security needs.* These would be met by job security, health insurance, and other fringe benefits.

Meanwhile, however, employees also develop *social needs*, which Maslow defined as need for group belonging and companionship. If an employee's work environment doesn't permit satisfaction of those needs, an unhappy employee could look elsewhere, perhaps joining a union to satisfy them. Gannett executives speak of "the Gannett family" to give employees a feeling of belonging to a group.

Maslow's *esteem needs* represent an individual's desire for self-confidence and wish to be considered important by others. The smart manager will bolster employees' self-confidence by giving them authority to act independently and will demonstrate how important they are. Corporate status symbols—a title on the door and a rug on the floor—are efforts to meet esteem needs among top executives; a reporter's might be fulfilled with a byline on an important front-page story.

Self-actualization needs, according to Maslow, are those all human beings feel to realize their potential, to be creative, to achieve.[7] Simply put, if you assign a highly creative writer to handling routine obituaries you will soon have an unhappy employee on your hands; an advertising salesperson capable of achieving success with major accounts will become restive if assigned only to minor accounts.

Note that the Maslow theory is directed at explaining the *individual's* needs. A manager's challenge is to help employees fulfill those personal needs, but within the context of meeting the newspaper's overall corporate objectives. The manager's goal is to produce not simply a happy employee but one who is happily and productively contributing to the newspaper's overall effort.

A manager does not have to make sure that *each* need is fully satisfied—indeed, Maslow's theory holds this to be almost impossible, since human beings, once satisfied on one level, will move on to the next and expand the range of needs yet to be satisfied. Rather, the manager should be on the lookout for those *unsatisfied needs* that create frustration, *constructive behavior* (seeking fulfillment outside the job), or *defensive behavior* (anger, withdrawal, or bitterness.)

Building an effective personnel policy within the context of Maslow's theoretical framework is a complex challenge. Obviously, pay alone will not do it. Newspaper employees (like those in other industries) increasingly point to a complex equation for job satisfaction. Playing a meaningful role in a worthwhile task and being appreciated for it are prime demands these days.

Knowing that the newspaper is a meaningful force in the community and that they play key roles in getting it published can be extremely important to employees. From newsroom to circulation loading dock, a manager should demonstrate to all employees how essential they are to the overall operation. Helping employees with personal problems is extremely important. Helping a working mother find a day-care center for her children or a new employee to obtain a home mortgage can pay huge dividends for a manager.

There are many avenues for a manager seeking to elicit from each employee the desired performance. Researcher Frederick Herzberg and others developed the so-called "two-factor" theory, according to which employees obtain *satisfaction* from "motivation factors" such as the job and its opportunities for promotion, personal growth, responsibility, and status but that *dissatisfaction* results from "maintenance factors" such as pay, company policies, managers, relationships with others. For example, a job perceived as important and prestigious will help create a satisfied employee. Pay—even high pay—does not in itself guarantee a satisfied effective employee. But if pay is too low, dis-

---

[7] For a fuller account, see Abraham Maslow, op. cit.

satisfaction and ineffective performance may result. This led Herzberg to conclude that people are motivated by *job enrichment*.[8]

This concept holds that an employee's sense of recognition and achievement can be more important than pay or working conditions and that managers must therefore design jobs to be challenging and meaningful. The theory does *not* suggest mere rotation of jobs, each as boring as the other. Rather, it points to *task identity*—making sure that each employee has an entire piece of work to complete and that it be significant. That is, avoid whenever possible job assignments smacking of assembly-line work—putting nuts on bolts all day long. Give a copy editor, for example, total responsibility for a series of stories on one subject; let an advertising salesperson completely design and implement a campaign for a major retailer. The sense of both starting and finishing something is important.

It comes down to managers determining, first, what performance is needed, then what rewards are valued by employees and linking rewards to performance. People respond differently to rewards.

Pay, obviously, is important, but it is just one motivational tool at a manager's disposal. The floor for pay levels is set by the federal minimum wage law, but most of a newspaper's work force is paid above that. For most, pay is based on these factors:

- *The newspaper's ability to pay*. Obviously, financially strong newspapers can pay more.

- *What competitors pay*. This means not just other newspapers of like size and characteristics but all employers who compete for the talented people needed in newspapering. If pay is too low, talent will move to broadcasting, public relations, advertising, and a number of other industries.

Pay policy must clearly demonstrate a relationship between each job and the pay for it. That link must be discernible to employees and be perceived as satisfactory. That is, an employee loading newspaper bundles into circulation trucks must understand that there is only so much pay available for moving bundles, and that higher pay requires promotion to a more responsible job. In advertising and circulation sales, incentives should be built into the pay structure: more pay, quickly, for more, better work. If employees expect pay to be linked to good performance, pay can be an effective motivational tool in a reward environment involving other, nonmonetary rewards as well.

Care must be taken in distributing rewards. If pay and other rewards are perceived as being unfairly distributed—and there are few secrets in newspapers on such matters—great dissatisfaction can result.

One researcher into motivation, B. F. Skinner, a psychologist, fashioned the theory of "operant conditioning" (or "reinforcement theory"), which holds that individuals perform to be rewarded and that their behavior is shaped by reinforcement. Skinner's theory is that *positive reinforcement* is most effective in shaping desired behavior. That is, a newspaper manager can be much more effective by patting someone on the back, granting public recognition, or paying a bonus than by using *negative reinforcement* like criticism or punishment.[9]

Now the next step is to decide where, how, when, and in what measure to use motivational tools. For a discussion of that we turn to *control*, a major responsibility of every manager.

CONTROL: A MAJOR RESPONSIBILITY OF ALL MANAGERS

To reach desired objectives, the manager must *control* employees in the workplace. This re-

---

[8] See Herzberg, Mausner, and Snyderman, op. cit.

[9] Skinner, op. cit.

ESTABLISHING PERFORMANCE STANDARDS

A prime responsibility of management is to issue clear guidelines for employees on what is expected of them. Can there be any doubt about these standards, which the Louisville (Ky.) Courier-Journal *has established for reporters and copy editors?*

Reporters

Writing ability—Grammar and spelling; ability to tell a good story well; use of quotes, anecdotes and descriptive detail; use of active voice and strong verbs; ability to write leads that are inviting and that hit the point of the story; ability to write tightly and to organize information in logical, compelling sequence.

Reporting ability—Pursuit, digging, enterprise, diligence; ability and eagerness to see and pursue promising angles; ability to seek and obtain anecdotes, detail and quotations that provide documentation and add liveliness to copy; ability to see the need for and to get both sides of the story; ability to cultivate good sources.

Speed, productivity and efficiency—Speed on deadline; speed and efficiency in completing non-deadline assignments; ability and willingness to manage more than one assignment at a time; ability and willingness to make frequent, substantive contributions to the content of the paper.

Accuracy—Skill with basic factual information such as names, addresses, dates and figures; ability to identify and make use of the best sources, whether they are documents, references or people.

Work habits—Punctuality, reliability, readiness to go beyond the minimum requirements of the job; interest in assuming and ability to assume more than minimum responsibility; ability and willingness to anticipate and fulfill the demands of an assignment without prompting; ability to deal even-handedly with peers and supervisors, to accept constructive criticism and offer constructive suggestions; interest in all areas of the news operation; knowledge of community, regional, national and international events; regular and thorough reader of the newspaper.

Judgment—Commitment to fairness and balance; ability to recognize and assess possible adverse consequences of actions; knowledge of, respect for and observance of the news department's policies.

Potential—Likelihood that the reporter is a candidate for a more challenging reporting assignment; for a supervisory position; evidence that

quires establishing performance standards, measuring each employee's performance and, through supervision, correcting shortcomings. The control function will be key to your career success at every level of management.

As a *first-level* manager, directly supervising employees each day, you will need strong technical skills. As, say, a copy-desk supervisor, you must know how to edit; if you become a first-level foreman in the pressroom, you'll have to know the nuts and bolts of presses. First-level managers must be skilled in explaining in clear, understandable terms what must be done and how to do it. (See the first box for how one newspaper explicitly spells out performance standards; see the second box for a personnel

director's view of how a first-level supervisor should operate.)

Middle-level managers—heads of circulation or advertising, for example—must shift their supervisory emphasis from controlling day-to-day performance by individuals to controlling interdepartmental efforts. Working smoothly and effectively with other middle-level managers is crucial.

Top-level managers—publishers—must be strong on the conceptual approaches necessary in controlling the newspaper's overall strategic performance. They must motivate others to view the newspaper as an integrated whole that needs strong teamwork to accomplish its mission.

At all levels, successful control requires

he or she possesses the characteristics of leadership and supervisory ability expected of supervising editors.

Copy Editors

Editing ability—Grammar and spelling; ability to trim excess verbiage, clarify confusing or contradictory language, improve a story without robbing it of the writer's style; ability to identify and give proper emphasis to important news angles; ability to spot and correct holes in stories; ability to spot and correct errors, libel, unfairness and imbalances; ability to condense stories for use in digests and round-ups; knowledge of and adherence to style.

Headlines—Accuracy; ability to convey the essence of the story; ability to write inviting feature heads; knowledge of headline orders and style.

Accuracy—Skill with basic factual information such as names, addresses, dates and figures; ability to identify and make use of the best sources, whether they are documents, references or people.

Work habits—Punctuality, reliability, readiness to go beyond the minimum requirements of the job; interest in assuming and ability to assume

more than minimum responsibility; ability and willingness to anticipate and fulfill the demands of an assignment without prompting; ability to deal even-handedly with peers and supervisors, to accept constructive criticism and offer constructive suggestions; interest in all areas of the news operation; knowledge of community, regional, national and international events; regular and thorough reader of the newspaper.

Potential—Likelihood that the copy editor is a candidate for a more challenging editing assignment; for a supervisory position; evidence that he or she possesses the characteristics of leadership and supervisory ability expected of supervising editors.

Versatility—Ability and willingness to learn and perform a variety of jobs on the news desk and copy desks.

Judgment—Commitment to fairness and balance; ability to recognize and assess possible adverse consequences of actions; knowledge of, respect for and observance of the news department's policies.

Design skills (where appropriate)—Mastery of layout and design skill; of typesetting techniques; of the use of photographs; of the development and use of graphic devices such as charts, graphs and maps.

continual, systematic, and detailed appraisal of each employee's current effectiveness. Appraisals must spot weak areas that need correcting and help select employees suitable for promotion. Performance is appraised in many ways, depending on the employee's job. For example, reporters should be appraised on initiative in pursuing stories, ability to write clearly and well, reliability in handling facts. Reporters—and other employees—should also be appraised for ability to use time wisely, solve problems, make speedy decisions, and work well with peers. Appraisals normally rank employees on a wide scale. Knight-Ridder asks supervisors to rank each employee on whether performance is low, below average, average, above average, or

outstanding. An employee consistently ranked outstanding obviously could be considered for promotion.

At least annually, a supervisor must discuss performance with each employee: pointing out not only that person's shortcomings but also suggesting how performance can be improved. If training is required, the supervisor should suggest on-the-job help from a more experienced employee or recommend outside assistance, perhaps at a local college, technical school, of one of the many formal seminars and training programs run by ANPA, Southern Newspaper Publishers' Association, or other industry groups.

Most newspapers require supervisors to give each employee a written appraisal, which

THE ROLE OF THE SUPERVISOR

Bobby Reid, corporate personnel director for Morris Communications Corp., a privately held group with (in 1985) about $284 million annual revenue, says the successful supervisor:

1. Is firm but always fair with every employee.
2. Understands that a supervisor's conduct often determines an employee's motivation.
3. Recognizes that some problems always exist in every group of employees.
4. Uses two-way communications effectively and is available for individual discussions of problems.
5. Brings problems to the attention of the company and pursues solutions.
6. Explains company policy effectively.
7. Sells the company and its policies to employees.
8. Knows employees—their backgrounds and goals—and is interested in them.
9. Uses constructive criticism to help employees prepare for promotion; promotes the qualified.
10. Is impartial and consistent in enforcing rules; plays no favorites.
11. Views employees gripes as an opportunity to solve a problem.
12. Cultivates leadership among employees.
13. Supervises people, not machines.
14. Keeps employees informed of their progress; praises in public, criticizes privately.
15. Talks with employees, not to them; is a good listener.
16. Terminates poor employees and chronic complainers.
17. Answers questions and seeks answers to those he or she doesn't know.
18. Can clearly explain what is required of an employee and provides the information necessary for doing the job.
19. Backs employees when they are right.

the employee is asked to read and sign, attaching comments if desired.

James D. Boswell, vice president for employee relations at the *Los Angeles Times*, says appraisals must be made of all employees, from lowest salary level to highest. He says such measurements meet various needs. *For the employee*, they answer questions like: How am I doing in my job? What are my strengths? Weaknesses? How can I improve? Where is my career going? *For management*, appraisals help spot employees who are not doing well and who may need training or, if that won't help, transfer from the job. Consecutively poor appraisals may suggest dismissal. Appraisals of below-par performers serve as documentation for discipline. Importantly, appraisals also help spot talented employees worthy of promotion.

For both employee and management, appraisals are agreements on what each employee's job objectives must be and when and how to reach them. They also provide recognition for employees. Many workers feel proud of consistently being appraised as outstanding performers. Appraisals help determine whether—and when—wage changes are to be made. Being ranked low across the board should be explained as a clear signal that merit increases will be mighty slow in coming; an outstanding employee *should* get increases. Used properly, then, appraisals are an effective communications medium between supervisor and employee.[10]

The more detail covered in an appraisal, the better. See Figure 5.1 for how Knight-Ridder, an industry leader in efficient personnel practices, uses appraisals to draw detailed pictures of each of its (in 1986) 22,000 employees.

Ideally, appraisals lead employees to adjust

---

[10] James D. Boswell, speech before Operations Management Conference and Exposition, Las Vegas, Nev., June 13, 1983.

Knight Ridder, Inc.
INDIVIDUAL DEVELOPMENTAL PROGRAM

NAME _____   NEWSPAPER/COMPANY _____

POSITION _____   SUPERVISOR _____

A. PERFORMANCE (See Manager's Guide for Definitions)

Rating	Low	Below Average	Average	Above Average	Outstanding	N/A*
1. Utilization of Resources:						
• Personnel						
• Capital						
• Budget						
• Facilities						
• Time						
• Professional Knowledge						
2. Reaction to Unforeseen Events						
3. Planning — Objective Setting						
4. Problem Solving						
• Identification						
• Analysis						
• Creativity						
5. Decision Making						
• Basis						
• Speed						
• Quality						
• Follow-through						
6. Attitude Concerning						
• Subordinates						
• Peers						
• Immediate Supervisor						
• Your Newspaper/Company						
7. Dependability						
8. Personal Effectiveness						
9. Overall Evaluation						

*N.A — Not applicable

B. EVALUATION OF PROMOTABILITY

1. Short Term Promotability

a. Employee is promotable and ready now ☐

b. Employee is promotable with additional experience and training. ☐
Specify additional experience and training needed; then specify positions.

		WHEN	
		Now	# Mos.
Recommended Position(s)	Current Department		
Recommended Position(s)	Other Department(s)		

If this employee exhibits exceptional potential for development at an accelerated rate, please comment:

Figure 5.1   Evaluating and Appraising in Detail
With 22,000 employees, Knight-Ridder, Inc., has a mammoth task in evaluating the performance and promotability of its staff. This detailed appraisal form is one step in that process.   (continued)

Figure 5.1　continued

Is employee satisfied with present career direction and rate of development?

Is this employee willing to relocate?

2. Not Promotable: Well placed now ☐ In wrong position, needs transfer ☐ Over his/her head ☐
   Should be replaced in job but kept in company ☐ Should be terminated ☐ Too soon to tell ☐

3. Near Retirement (Within 5 Years): Promotable as indicated above ☐ Better utilization could be made ☐
   Performance is slipping ☐ Valuable where placed ☐ Should consider early retirement ☐

C. LONG TERM CAREER ASPIRATIONS AND POTENTIAL

1. What are the employee's career aspirations?

2. How realistic are the individual's goals and are they compatible with your views of his or her capabilities?

D. DEVELOPMENTAL RECOMMENDATIONS

1. Ideally, what should be done to assist employee in achieving ultimate potential?
   (Skill training and experience; management training and experience; experience outside present area.)

2. What specific actions will be taken? Specify when action will be taken and who will be responsible.

E. BACK-UP IDENTIFICATIONS

Considering the employee's present position, identify persons by name and title who might fill the job should the employee move.

Signature of preparer _____　Date prepared _____

their performance to the standards expected of them and become productive workers. But ideal conditions do not always exist, so managers must be prepared to take firm—sometimes distasteful—steps.

Discipline: The Distasteful Task

The hiring and training of talented personnel are often a manager's most creative and enjoyable tasks. However, one of the most distasteful—disciplining and, sometimes, firing people—can be just as important in constructing and controlling a professionally capable staff.

Unfortunately, mistakes—by an unfit person in applying for a job and by a manager in providing one—sometimes land unsuitable men and women on a newspaper staff. Job counseling or reassignment can sometimes set things right. A writer who doesn't improve as expected may be suited for an editing job; an editor who is impatient with working on somebody else's writing might make a superb reporter. But there are occasions when consistently poor performance or disruptive behavior leave a manager with no alternative but harsh discipline or discharge.

Discipline and when and how it is applied must be fair and even-handed. You should follow these steps:

- Obtain all pertinent facts about the alleged infraction (and it *is* alleged until proven). That means taking a dispassionate view from the employee's side as well as management's. For example, a supervisor who complains that an ad salesperson is unproductive may in fact be giving that person only dormant, unrewarding clients to visit; your job is to look at the employee's side of the story.

- Consider union implications, if any. Under some union contracts, you may be obliged to inform the union that disciplinary action is contemplated. Some contracts require a union representative to be present during discussions with the employee.

- Talk with the employee whenever possible in a low-key, informal way; ask for his or her views. Often, a chat over coffee is helpful.[11]

- If facts dictate a warning, consider whether you can keep it oral and still make sure your point is taken without a written complaint that becomes part of the employee's permanent record.

- However, if the situation calls for more forceful treatment, issue a written warning that states management's view in detail. Ask for the employee's written response. Both become part of the permanent record. In the case of, say, a reporter, the warning should include specific examples of factual errors committed or other lapses.

- If punishment is required, a pay increase or promotion can be denied or, in extreme cases, the employee must be fired. Note: If an employee is genuinely surprised at being fired, management has not done its job properly. The newspaper's statement of personnel policy should spell out infractions that can lead to discharge. If the issue is, say, gradual deterioration of performance rather than a single incident, supervisors should be on record as having warned the employee that discharge was inevitable unless performance improved.

Throughout the entire process, from day of hiring onward, there should be a fully documented, written record of the employee's work performance, *including* copies of any written warnings or criticisms by supervisors. Keeping voluminous records, alas, is part of personnel management in the 1980s, because numerous

---

[11] Pigors and Myers, op. cit., presents an excellent approach to employee interviewing.

lawsuits crop up. Often, the question is whether a contract for employment exists. Courts sometimes rule that even an implied promise of continued employment can constitute a contract which, if broken, opens the newspaper to damages. To discuss an "annual" salary in a hiring interview, for example, might be viewed as promising a one-year contract. Speak only of a "weekly wage." A pattern of raises, promotions, and favorable critiques by supervisors can be held as strengthening the implied contract, particularly if the record shows no warnings or criticisms for substandard performance. Neglecting such legalisms could mean years and thousands of dollars spent in litigation over charges of breaking a contract or failing to deal in good faith with an employee. There is under way a steady erosion of the tradition that American newspapers—or corporations of any type—have the right to "employ at will" or fire without reason or notice. Employees gain rights, of course, under any union contract that might exist or under certain laws, such as the Civil Rights Act of 1964, that restrict employers in hiring and firing. But beyond this, ANPA estimates that courts in about thirty states have defined circumstances (in addition to those spelled out in contracts or in federal law) which restrict your right to "employ at will." For example, the right to serve in the National Guard or on a jury or to refuse a lie detector test is protected by law. A manager who fires an employee for exercising such a right may face a jury. And as in libel cases, juries are often sympathetic to plaintiffs. ANPA finds in that California, for example, the average award in such cases has been about $400,000.

Sometimes you do employees a favor by suggesting they move on. One of life's great frustrations is to hold a job beyond one's capabilities, and a wise personnel manager will find ways of bringing that reality to the attention of employees who are not suited for newspaper work. Many young reporters have moved on to other fields when gently informed that their writing ability was not good enough for newspaper work.

SPECIAL PROBLEMS: NEW TECHNOLOGY AND MINORITY HIRING

Two special problems complicate human resources management:

New technology eliminates thousands of newspaper jobs and forces radical change in the work skills and habits of many employees.

Legal and societal pressure is increasing to hire more minorities and women and promote those qualified to responsible positions. The industry in general has not succeeded in this—but it must in coming decades.

Job Displacement by Technology Ahead

One of a manager's most difficult problems is dealing sensitively and fairly with employees displaced by technology, yet protecting the newspaper's best interests by pursuing the economies and efficiencies the technology offers.

Employees whose jobs vanish through no fault of their own often suffer great trauma. This was apparent as displacement by technology hit "back shop" production jobs, from the 1960s onward, with the switch to offset printing and photocomposition. In 1969, there were 162 offset plants among ANPA newspapers; by 1987, 82 percent of all U.S. newspapers were offset. Letterpress-stereotype plants went from 696 to zero in the same period—and each conversion eliminated jobs.

The 1970s brought another wave of job eliminations as computerized electronic writing and editing swept the industry. There were no video display terminals at ANPA member newspapers in 1969; in 1981, there were 40,651. Production workers represented 38.2 percent of the total newspaper work force in 1981, down from 43.4 percent in 1976—and a great many stereotypers, composing room workers, and others in back shops possessed skills that were no longer needed.[12]

---

[12] Clark Newsom, "Retraining: Workers in Superfluous Jobs Get New Opportunities," *presstime*, March 1983, p. 4.

A third large job displacement will occur when pagination—the makeup of a newspaper page through computerized means—comes into its own. Portent of things to come: In 1974, before it introduced a pioneering pagination system, the *Pasadena (Calif.) Star-News* had a composing room staff of a hundred. It was down to thirty-three workers in 1981 and, by 1983, to nine.[13]

Various means are used to deal with displaced workers. Some newspapers, particularly those with unions, make expensive "buyouts," providing early retirement or cash incentives for displaced workers. In 1982, the *New York Times* agreed to spend about $11.5 million to buy out 127 printers—about $90,550 per person. Many newspapers retrain employees for new jobs with the same company. Gannett's Westchester (N.Y.) Rockland Newspapers, a group of community dailies north of New York City, transferred sixty-six displaced composing room workers into almost every other department, including advertising and editorial. Eleven were trained as electronics technicians to service the very machines that had displaced them.[14] Retraining employees familiar with general operations proves easier, in many cases, than hiring outsiders and substantially cheaper than a buyout.

Betty A. Duval, for years vice president for staff development of Dow Jones & Co., cautions managers to be particularly sensitive to staff worries when making technological changes. Because managers initiate change, it is rational and understandable to them, she says; but change can be perceived negatively by employees who feel no control over developments that can threaten them. She cautions managers to:

1. Explain company goals and what other newspapers are doing.

2. Seek employee input on proposed changes and offer options if possible.

3. Provide training when new equipment is introduced.

4. Realize that cost-cutting measures or new equipment may mean fewer people doing more work, and consider lightening the load.

5. Listen to employee concerns and suggestions; watch for boredom and loneliness due to the introduction of new technology.

6. Implement major changes in stages, involving employees in this and discussing any problems along the way.[15]

The Need to Hire More Minorities and Women

Industrywide, the record of hiring blacks and other minorities is dismal; and although some reporter staffs are 30 to 40 percent female, the top jobs are generally held by men. ANPA reported in 1987 just 7 percent of all U.S. daily newspaper publishers and general managers were women.

Societal demands for change are reflected in a wide range of legislation aimed at ensuring equal opportunity in the workplace. Seminal legislation was the 1964 Civil Rights Act. Under Title VII of that act, the Equal Employment Opportunity Commission (EEOC), a federal body, was formed to investigate charges of discrimination.

Law aside, however, it makes *business* sense for a newspaper, which must mirror its marketplace, to build a staff representative of the people who live there. Chairman Neuharth of Gannett, a long-time leader in this area, says that the "major unconquered challenge" facing newspapers is hiring of minorities and women.[16] "Promoting and practicing equal opportunity is not only the right thing to do," he says; "it's the

---

[13] Ibid.
[14] Ibid.

[15] Ibid.
[16] Gannett Co. management report to annual meeting of shareholders, reported in special supplement to *USA Today*, May 25, 1983.

smart thing to do . . . no newspaper can cover all of the community unless it employs all of the community."[17]

Gannett moves minorities and women onto its board of directors, into publisher slots and corporate staff jobs; women constitute 35 percent of its top four job categories of officials and managers, professionals, technicians, and sales persons; 12 percent are minorities. Gannett says that at *USA Today*, 43 percent of the staff are women and 23 percent are minorities. Not many newspaper companies match Gannett's record in this regard. A 1985 survey for ASNE of 948 general circulation dailies (58 percent of the total) found that:

- 60.1 percent employed no minority journalists, compared with 61 percent in 1984.

- Minority journalists increased to 3,080, up just 176 from the previous year. The pollsters estimate that about 53,800 persons were employed in the newsroom job categories covered by the survey—reporters, copy editors, photographers, artists, and news executives.

- Minorities were 5.72 percent of all newspaper journalists, down marginally from 5.76 percent. (The 1980 U.S. census put minorities at 20 percent of the total U.S. population and projects that they will be 25 percent of the total in 1990.)

The survey showed that 89 percent of the newspapers had no minority news executives.

Importantly, smaller papers—where newsroom jobs are more frequently open to beginners—have the weakest minority representation.[18]

A clear signal of what can happen to newspapers that lag in hiring women and minorities is a $2 million settlement forced on the Associated Press by the EEOC and seven women, former AP employees, who sued on grounds of sex discrimination. The AP, a cooperative of 1,300 U.S. newspapers and 5,700 TV and radio stations, must operate under a consent decree, paying $500,000 in legal costs plus $1.5 million in back pay for the seven and establishing training and affirmative action programs for women and blacks. It is the deepest, most meaningful government intrusion into hiring and promotion policies experienced by any major news organization. Because of AP's links with its thousands of newspapers and broadcast members, the case could set standards for the industry.[19]

Minority hiring requires aggressive recruiting and training programs. Many newspapers conduct special intern programs for university minority students, striving to *create* black or Hispanic journalists in an industry where too few exist. The *Atlanta (Ga.) Journal & Constitution* recruits minority interns, offering paid summer jobs as reporters and writers under direction of experienced editors. The *Los Angeles Times* has a year-long program that exposes black students to intensive training in all phases of reporting, writing, and editing. Other newspapers, the *Macon (Ga.) Telegraph and News*, for example, start even earlier, with junior high and high school students. The Macon paper also sponsors a Journalism Explorer Post under the auspices of the Georgia Boy Scouts. (See box for organizations that assist newspapers in hiring and training minorities.)

MEASURING YOUR SUCCESS

Now, let's see where you are as a manager of human resources. You develop a positive ("Y") attitude toward employees. You study motivational theory and try to open honest, sensitive

---

[17] Radolf, op. cit.

[18] "1985 Census of Minority Employment in U. S. Daily Newspapers," American Society of Newspaper Editors, April 8, 1985.

[19] "AP Settlement Called Precedent for Newspapers," *Editor & Publisher*, July 2, 1983, p. 13.

FOR HELP IN HIRING MINORITIES

These organizations assist newspapers in minority hiring:

- American Society of Newspaper Editors, P.O. Box 17004, Washington, DC 20041, provides information on existing minority programs at newspapers.
- School of Communications, Howard University, Washington, DC 20059, holds an annual minority journalists conference and operates a placement bureau for minority graduates of any college or university.
- Institute for Journalism Education, located at School of Journalism, Northgate Hall, University of California, Berkeley, CA 94720, operates minority training programs and placement services.
- Asian American Journalists Association, Japanese American Cultural & Community Center, Room 411, 244 S. San Pedro Street, Los Angeles, CA 90012, coordinates placement of Asian American journalists.
- National Association of Hispanic Journalists, C/O *Tucson (Ariz.) Citizen*, Box 26767, Tucson, AZ 85726, locates jobs for Hispanics.
- Indian journalists and publishers can be reached through Native American Press Association, C/O School of Journalism, Pennsylvania State University, 215 Carnegie Building, University Park, PA 16802.
- American Newspaper Publishers' Association, The Newspaper Center, Box 17407, Dulles International Airport, Washington, DC 20041, is an excellent source for general information on human resources planning.

communications with each of them. Is it working?

You better find out. Because if it isn't you are failing to elicit optimum performance from the newspaper's most important and costly asset, its people. And that, as a manager, is what you are paid to do. You may even be unwittingly contributing to worsening morale, which can defeat your best efforts to achieve your goals or cause union organizers to be summoned by disgruntled employees. You must measure your effectiveness in human resources management, whether you are responsible for the performance of one person or thousands.

Watch Important Indicators

Watch for signs that may indicate whether your management has gone awry:

Excessive turnover. This is disruptive, harms morale, and is costly, because new hires must be found, trained, and put in place—with inevitable loss of productivity. When employees stalk out the door, much expensive training and experience goes along. And before they stalk out, there is a great deal of complaining and grousing to fellow workers, and their morale suffers, too. Of course, some turnover is good. It gives you an opportunity to hire new blood— perhaps better-qualified replacements. How much turnover is excessive? Smaller newspaper, traditionally serving as training grounds for nearby metros, will have high turnover; some, in fact, serve as "farm clubs," hiring new college graduates with the knowledge that these people will move to the "big leagues" in a few years. It's not uncommon for small-town editors to promise new hires, "Do the job for me for a couple years and I'll introduce you to my friend, the metro editor." Papers renowned for journalistic quality, good working conditions, and high pay will naturally have low turnover. But whatever your paper's size, if turnover exceeds 15 percent annually, you have serious problems.

Deteriorating job performance. This is often a prime indicator of morale problems. Watch carefully, for example, the journalistic quality of the paper; a sudden slump demands investigation. The performance of individual employees should be monitored carefully.

Absenteeism and tardiness. Among the staff in general, this can signal widespread difficulties; in the case of individuals, it may mean serious personal problems such as alcoholism or drug usage.

Complaints. Complaints delivered through your own grievance system if you don't have a union or formally through the union if you do have one are prime measurements of employee sentiment.

The grapevine. Speedily transmitting information and misinformation outside the formal chain of command, the grapevine is a barometer of mood. If you are a first-level supervisor in direct contact with employees, they will often discuss what is on the grapevine; if you have moved up to middle or top management, they won't, so make sure your supervisors are tuned in.

Formal Audits of Employee Morale

Simply keeping an ear cocked to the grapevine is hardly an adequate method of auditing employee attitudes. Therefore you should develop scientific, formal measurements.[20] Written questionnaires and in-depth personal interviews can be effective. Both can be employed as the newspaper's pocketbook permits—small papers can conduct homemade surveys at low cost; large papers can call in professional consultants.

Some newspapers use questionnaire surveys every eighteen to twenty-four months, letting employees, anonymously, answer questions ranging from whether restrooms are kept

clean to how well the newspaper is managed. In-depth personal interviews can add greatly to measurements of employee attitudes if the interviewer keeps in mind that it takes planning to elicit the desired information. A few hints:

- Go into the interview well prepared with personal background and job performance data on the interviewee and the subject to be discussed. Have a plan and stick to it, gently pulling the conversation back on track if it strays.

- Establish a relaxed atmosphere by interviewing in private and without interruptions. Set a friendly tone by opening informally, chatting easily and reassuring the interviewee (who may be alarmed by the whole process).

- Listen; don't monopolize the talk. Let the conversation follow leads the interviewees may give you; they may have been waiting to tell you what's bothering them. But ask questions to probe for the information you want. Take notes to signal the importance of the occasion as much as to record information you want to remember.

- *Always* be courteous. And if you can handle it, use humor, too! Nothing shuts employees up as effectively as brusque, humorless treatment. If you want information, you should relax.

Warning: employees are often reluctant to respond frankly in attitude surveys. Some fear that doing so will jeopardize their position or anger a supervisor. In interviews, some employees are inacapable of expressing themselves on complex problems. You must create an atmosphere of trust that will embolden employees to speak frankly, without fear of retribution.

Follow Through

One key to effective audits of employee attitudes is careful record keeping. Whether you are

[20] Particularly helpful in employee attitude surveys are Pigors and Myers, op. cit.

auditing one employee or a thousand, you must *gather* information through surveys and interviews and *verify* it by cross-checking through additional contacts with the staff, asking the same question another way or running more surveys. Then, *correlate* it and pull it all together for *interpretation*. Detailed record keeping permits you to chart staff behavior, establish norms, and then spot future variances from the norm that might signal changes in employee attitudes. For example, suppose that absenteeism, charted over a period of years, comes to an average of six days per year per employee. If that figure should suddenly jump to ten days, you would have to determine why.

It is essential for you to *act* whenever possible on the information gathered. If you ask an employee what is wrong, you have raised the expectation that what is wrong will be fixed. If it isn't, the letdown can cause even greater morale problems. If you ask a circulation truck driver how his job is going and he says the brakes on the truck are no good—and you don't get the brakes fixed—you have destroyed your credibility with that employee.

Sometimes, a departing employee can be a valuable source of information for you to follow through on. The *Athens (Ga.) Banner-Herald and The Daily News* asks outgoing employees these questions in interviews conducted by appropriate department heads:

- What did you like most about your job?

- What did you like least?

- What did you like most about the company?

- What did you like least about the company?

- Was your job training adequate?

- What problems did you encounter on your job?

- Further comments or observations?

Such "exit interviews" can provide meaningful views of the newspaper's workplace efficiency and morale. Of course, their validity is limited if an employee is leaving under pressure or is reluctant to be frank for fear of jeopardizing references for future jobs.

In your follow through, don't hesitate to adjust your performance on what you learn. Look at it this way: As a supervisor, you establish standards for your employees, you monitor their performance—and you ask them to make adjustments if performance falls short. So isn't it only fair (and logical) that you should adjust *your* performance if employee (and ex-employee) attitude surveys so dictate? If you don't act openly and responsively, you may find yourself no longer dealing one on one with individual employees but rather with groups of employees that have coalesced against you. Let's look at dealing with groups.

Groups: Learn to Work with Them

As you will learn quickly in your first supervisory job, the influence you exert on an employee is just one of many influences. One of the most important among these is *group pressure*.[21] It's human nature. People form groups. There are many kinds, not just the *formal groups*—the work sections, the departments—represented by your newspaper's table of organization.

You must learn to recognize and work with the *informal groups* that evolve naturally and inevitably in any work situation. They may be groups of employees who see economic benefit in sticking together (this, of course, can lead to unionization) or who seek socio-psychological benefits, such as a feeling of security, and who may select one member to come forward and tell you that the air conditioning is inadequate. Or a group may form out of the purely *social desire* to form friendships.

Group formation can have either positive or negative effects on a manager's efforts to achieve goals. On the negative side, for example,

---

[21] See Duncan, op. cit., also James H. Donnelly, Jr., James L. Gibson, John M. Ivancevich, *Fundamentals of Management*, Dallas, Business Publications, Inc.,1978, and Hitt, Middlemist, and Mathis, op. cit.

groups can pressure individual members to reduce production, to write fewer stories per day, and thus to create a slower, more comfortable pace for all reporters. As a manager, you make a mistake if you attempt to ignore the reality of such disruptive group behavior. On the positive side, the thoughtful manager will recognize that the desire for group membership is very human and that the dynamics of group behavior can be turned to good effect. Behavioral scientists have found that group members derive satisfaction from certain activities. For example:

- Membership in an elite, highly regarded group helps meet the individual's need for self-esteem and self-actualization. Creating a special team of investigative reporters can fulfill this need for members of the team; so can membership on a select task force assigned to reducing the waste of newsprint in the pressroom.

- Group membership gives the individual the perception of being part of the decision-making process, of participating in judgments that affect his or her own life. This leads to a feeling of being valued. Assigning employees to help design a new electronic editing system they will use or lay out new circulation routes they will service are examples of how managers can turn group activity to advantage.

Working through groups has other advantages. It brings into play the expertise of the group and uses the natural strengths of group activity to generate ideas and collect and disseminate information.

But working through groups has its dangers. Group members tend to rally together when pressured by management, and a wrong move can turn an informal, loosely structured group into a disciplined, antimanagement force. Also, if improperly directed, groups can indulge in "groupthink," the tendency to avoid any controversy that might destroy group unity. That can lead individual members to subordinate their own judgments—or reservations—to the group. And group membership can mean, for some individuals, opportunity to slip comfortably into a group to avoid full effort on the job or to avoid any decision making at all.

The aspiring manager, then, must use groups to best advantage, which some newspapers—both large and small—are doing through *quality circles*.

The Quality Circle Concept

This concept originated in Japan and was imported to the United States in 1971 by Lockheed Aircraft. Some newspaper managers view it as an excellent tool for improving job performance by harnessing the positive strengths of group interaction and avoiding the negatives that groups sometimes create.

Quality circles are small groups of ten or so employees doing similar work who meet on a voluntary basis for an hour or so each week to discuss and try to solve problems in their workplace. This is usually done on company time and a member of management is usually present. The group's leaders are selected by the members, and any subject except the personal affairs of other employees is open to discussion. Quality circles at some newspapers have discussed, for example, how to arrange electronic editing terminals in the newsroom for most efficient use by the staff. Others have dealt with lighting in the workplace, how group members will share the workload, even when best to take a coffee break. Anything goes.

The aim is to improve relations between managers and employees, give employees an opportunity to participate in decisions affecting them and the newspaper, and elicit from individuals the valuable suggestions many would make if only they were asked. Quality circles give managers an opportunity to recognize and reward achievement, spot rising talent, and consider for promotion the most capable.[22]

---

[22] See Duncan, op. cit.

Newspapers using quality circles include Tribune Co. of Chicago, McClatchy Newspapers (owner of dailies in California, Washington State, and Alaska), and Knight-Ridder, which by 1985 had a hundred quality circles at work among its 22,000 employees.

Knight-Ridder tells employees frankly why it uses the circles. Circle members, it says, will get:

- Training in problem-solving techniques

- An opportunity to identify/solve problems "no one seems to care about"

- A chance to "make your department and newspaper a better place to work"

- Recognition "as an expert in your work area"

- An opportunity to present recommended solutions directly to management

Knight-Ridder states that its objectives are to increase productivity, improve quality and employee relations, and reduce operating costs. Knight-Ridder encourages each quality circle to present management formally with recommendations for change. The company says it has approved more than 95 percent.[23]

Not all group relations are smooth. Some result in conflict, and to that we now turn.

Group Conflict: Causes and Remedies

Because a manager's job includes coordinating the activities of groups as well as individuals, an understanding of the sources of conflict within and between groups is crucial.

Within a group, conflict is likely to arise if there is lack of clarity on what task must be performed and when. This underlines the importance of, say, a first-level supervisor in retail advertising being crystal clear in laying out each salesperson's client list or territory. Conflict also

erupts when group members have difficulty communicating with each other; hence the same supervisor should hold regular staff conferences to give sales people an opportunity to discuss their problems—to let off steam with each other. Conflict within a group is certain to arise if the members have widely differing interests and attitudes. A group of pressmen will erupt in conflict if half are serious about high-quality printing and half couldn't care less. Supervisors in both instances must weed out the unenthusiastic. Conflict frequently arises over competition for limited resources. Supervisors make a grievous mistake if, for example, they distribute pay increases that are dramatically uneven for members of the same group. Giving some members better tools than others can create serious conflict, too.

Conflict *between* groups can arise, also. Competitive patterns often develop when two groups strive for third-party recognition or favor. For example, if two investigative reporting teams in the same newsroom strive for the editor's favor (or most of the travel budget), a competitive condition exists. Some newspaper managers strive to create this condition. Ben Bradlee, executive editor of the *Washington Post*, sometimes pits groups against each other, expecting that this will improve efficiency and quality. Thus, two newsroom teams are urged to outperform each other in producing important front-page stories. It's called building "dynamic tension," a sense of controlled competition.

However, *conflict*—outright hostility—can develop between groups if competition gets so hot that one sets out not only to outperform the other but also to destroy it. In many newsrooms, for example, the quarrel between different desks to get news into the paper can become downright vicious. The wire desk competes with the local news desk and both compete with sports for the limited space available. Also, if "dynamic tension" creates too much pressure on employees, mistakes can occur. Because of such pressure at the *Washington Post*, reporter Janet Cooke was able to get past editing-desk safeguards and into

---

[23] Knight-Ridder Newspapers, Inc.

print with a gripping—and entirely false—story about a child heroin addict.

Some management theorists say conflict between groups is inevitable. A manager's task, they say, is to control the conflict as well as possible and channel it in creative directions. Thus, a newsroom supervisor should permit group conflict as long as it truly creates superior reporting and writing; but if the conflict begins detracting from the newsroom's overall mission, the supervisor should halt it.

Other theorists say that conflict between groups can and must be avoided entirely if the newspaper is to move efficiently toward its goals. Three broad paths are suggested for solving conflict:

Domination. This is a solution that leaves one group satisfied but the other dissatisfied—an outcome that is not normally acceptable at any newspaper. A group of reporters who feel shunted aside in favor of another group can lose effectiveness or, worse, openly rebel.

Compromise. This is a supervisor's effort to arrive at a resolution that, although it doesn't completely satisfy everybody, doesn't leave anybody terribly dissatisfied, either. Compromise, too, falls short of the ideal solution if it leaves *two* groups of people smoldering with dissatisfaction.

Integration. The attempt to make everybody happy, admittedly a difficult thing, is known as integration. This calls out the best in any supervisor, requiring the creative resolution of competing demands. Perhaps, for example, the local news desk can be given its day in the sun—major front-page display—for an important series on a compelling local story, while the wire desk is given equally prominent display at a later date for a major series on a national or international story.

One very real danger of uncontrolled group conflict is that it can create such ill will that employees turn to an outside party—a union—

for solutions. And that brings us to an extremely important aspect of any manager's function—union relations.

UNIONS: AVOID THEM IF YOU CAN, WORK WITH THEM IF YOU CAN'T

If you accept any significant management responsibility, you implicitly agree to support management attitudes and efforts. That can mean going to the ramparts to help management avoid unions or, if they are unavoidable, help fashion a relationship with them that will ensure that management attitudes prevail.

The fundamental management attitude is that unions insert a third party—a union lawyer or organizer—between manager and employee and thus reduce the manager's ability to make decisions unilaterally—to run things. Unions are costly because they force higher wages and benefits and can even threaten a newspaper's financial stability with economic demands or strikes. In many newspapers, even first-level supervisors are expected to reject union membership for themselves and to support such management attitudes. If you cannot accept that, a manager's career is not for you, because few areas of management require such deep commitment by each manager.

Despite occasional past instances of cooperation, union-management attitudes in the U.S. newspaper industry come essentially from a history of tension and struggle. The history of management's stance is primarily one of strong-willed owners who dominated the American newspaper scene until, in the 1960s, they rapidly began selling to publicly owned communications groups. Those often highly individualistic owners built a tradition of fighting to protect profits and management prerogatives. With similar—but perhaps more subtle and realistic—determination, managers of publicly owned companies, in turn, strive today to prevent union interference in those same profits and prerogatives.

Early union patterns were set in picket-line confrontations; there won't soon be any fundamental change in the basic union attitude that the way to deal with management is to build membership in an adversarial context and bargain hard—to strike, if necessary.

Metropolitan papers, with their large staffs and high wages, draw special attention from unions. Many have ten or more. Unions are weaker in small towns and suburban areas, however, and only about 19.2 percent of the newspaper industry's 453,600 employees in 1986 were union members—as compared to 21.4 percent in 1979, according to ANPA.

Unions to Watch

The following unions, in this order, are most important to a newspaper manager because of their size and history of newspaper involvement:

The *International Typographical Union* (ITU) represents primarily composing room workers and mailers and has (in 1986) about 34,000 active members at 369 U.S. papers. ITU is losing many members to automation, which it bitterly resisted, and seeks new strength by pairing with other unions. It tried but failed to link with several, including the Teamsters Union. Then, in 1987, it merged with the Communications Workers of America (see below). The ITU also seeks a wider membership base by organizing newsroom workers.

The *Newspaper Guild* was organized in 1933 by reporters and copy editors but increasingly represents clerical and advertising employees as well. It has (1986) about 32,500 members at 121 newspapers. Of them, 55 percent are employees in departments other than news.

The *Graphics Communications International Union* was created in a merger of two independent unions in 1983. It has about 200,000 members, of whom 27,500 are newspaper production employees such as pressmen, lithographers, photoengravers, stereotypers, and paper handlers.

The *International Brotherhood of Teamsters* is a powerful union of 1.9 million members whose leaders are vigorously attempting to expand Teamster influence in the industry. About 8,000 newsprint and newspaper delivery drivers are members, which gives the Teamsters power to shut down some newspapers.

The *Communications Workers of America* has 650,000 members in other industries and seeks to expand in newspapers.

The *International Association of Machinists* and *International Brotherhood of Electrical Workers* are active in the industry to a lesser degree.

The pioneering newspaper union was the ITU. Clark Newsom, labor writer for ANPA's *presstime*, quotes former ITU President Joe Bingle as follows:

> The benefits enjoyed by today's graphic arts and newspaper employees are not by and large the results of [the] employer's benevolence and magnanimity. They exist today because of hard work, tenacity and aggressiveness by the ITU's nationwide efforts in connection with the struggle beginning in 1906 for the eight-hour workday.

David J. Eisen, Guild director of research and information, says that when the Guild was formed in 1933, the five-day week was unheard of and the seven-day week was not unusual. The Guild worked to change that, he says, and "pioneered severance pay in 1937," along with higher wages. Nonunion papers raised wages "to match what we've gained elsewhere."[24]

The Weakening Union Power Base

Newspaper unions approach the 1990s with weakening power bases. Membership is dropping dramatically due to newspaper shutdowns, displacement of workers through automation, and management success in throwing out unions.

The ITU calculated that its membership

---

[24] Newsom, op. cit.

had dropped by 49 percent between 1967 and 1982 due to failures of newspapers and computerization of production functions.[25]

The Guild, in 1980–1981 alone, lost 1,400 members when fourteen dailies folded. Under President Charles A. Perlik, the Guild sought new strength through merger with other unions, but without success. Larger unions feel that Guild units are too small to be administered effectively.[26]

Withdrawal of labor—the strike—is the primary weapon of any organized work force, but even here newspaper unions are losing strength. The strike, traditionally, was effective against newspapers. Advertising lost during a strike is lost forever, and a newspaper's "inventory" of news and advertising cannot be built up in anticipation of a strike, as can inventory in many industries. Also, producing newspapers requires a major dependence on labor, and a high percentage—perhaps 75 percent—of the work force could, at one time, shut down or severely impair operations. These included production and maintenance workers, typically about 48 percent of the total work force; news, 15 percent; and circulation, 12 percent. (Others are advertising, 10 percent; and business and administration, 15 percent.)

However, rapidly developing technology weakens—in some cases, destroys—the ability of unions to shut down newspapers because managers and nonunion personnel can maintain operations. For example:

- The ITU felt compelled to appeal for public support in a quarrel with the *Kansas City Star*, which refused for five years to sign a contract covering 140 ITU workers. The ITU set up a Fair Contract Committee and advertised its complaint nationally. Not too many years earlier, the ITU could have shut down the *Star* instantly to get what it wanted.

- Capital Cities Communications, owner of the *Star*, also published its *Wilkes-Barre (Pa.) Times Leader*, despite a bitter strike that for years was supported by nonnewspaper unions in coal districts around Wilkes-Barre.

- As far back as 1975, the *Washington (D.C.) Post* published regularly despite a violent strike by pressroom workers in which presses were set afire and employees beaten (tactics that cost the union public support).

For both the ITU and the Guild, the problem is electronic editing and automated production processes that don't need union members to operate them. Electronic editing terminals—VDTs or video display terminals—"capture" in a computer a reporter's keystroke as he or she writes a story, and that same keystroke is later used in electronic editing, makeup, and production without the once-mandatory "rekeystroking" by unionized back-shop workers. In precedent-setting arbitration in the early 1970s, the Associated Press won the right to use them without union interference—and, except where jurisdiction is won by unions in bargaining—they are used today by newspapers without union interference.

Sometimes, however, even small unions shut down newspapers. In 1985, eighty-one janitors struck the *Philadelphia Inquirer* for seventeen hours. Because Teamster Union drivers refused to cross the janitors' picket lines, the *Inquirer* couldn't distribute one Sunday edition and had to rebate advertiser's payments—$1 million. A later strike that year shut down the *Inquirer* for more than a month, causing losses the company put at $48 million.

Unions: Cause, Prevention, Treatment

A union's basic appeal to employees, of course, is that although they are virtually powerless to

[25] "Two ITU Officers Balk at Merger With Guild," *Editor & Publisher*, Dec. 11, 1982, pp. 9–10; also see "GCIO-ITU Merger Collapses," *presstime*, April 1985, p. 46.
[26] "Two ITU Officers Balk," op. cit.

influence management individually they can, by combining forces—in a union—protect and improve their lot. Unless managers address employees' fears and meet their nonmonetary but very real needs, unions can grow strong even at newspapers that pay high wages and provide ample benefits.

Although high wages will not always *prevent* union activity, low wages and inadequate benefits can create morale problems that lead employees to invite unions. This is true particularly if wages are perceived as being unfairly distributed or if managers don't communicate well and employees see inequity in their manager's treatment of employees.

Historically, American newspaper unions grew out of unfair, even harsh treatment in the workplace; there, they struggled almost exclusively to improve wages and working conditions. For the most part, employees didn't organize for ideological purposes. However, some unions have broadened their demands. In the early 1970s, for example, the Wire Service Guild began demanding, albeit perfunctorily, a seat on the Associated Press board of directors. In 1985, the Newspaper Guild demanded legislation to limit the number of newspapers a single company can own.

ANPA's analysis of 198 labor agreements reveals these features:

- 74 contracts call for a forty-hour, five-day week; most for fewer than forty hours—17 contracts call for thirty-five-hour weeks.

- 158 contracts prohibit discrimination in hiring or promotion on the basis of race, color, religion, sex, age, or national origin; 17 contracts require active recruitment of women, minorities, and the hard-core unemployed.

- 113 contracts require a reporter's permission to use his or her byline, 32 require that a reporter be consulted before corrections or retractions are published; 16 call for employees to be notified before criticisms (e.g., letters to the editor) of their work are published.

- 13 contracts contain codes of ethics; 106 prohibit employees from taking outside work or engaging in activity that could embarrass the paper.

When union activity erupts, three factors frequently are behind discontent:

- Poor communications between managers and employees, preventing the work force from gaining any idea of where the newspaper is going, what its plans are, and what goals are to be achieved. The communications breakdown prevents employees from expressing their views to management or gaining any voice in the way things are run.

- Management neglects—or is perceived as neglecting—adequate and fair pay, or there is a feeling that unhealthy or unpleasant working conditions exist. Management is perceived as neglecting the dignity of the individual, job security, and quality of life—things that are highly important to men and women working on newspapers today.

- There is poor, uninformed supervision, often by young, inexperienced first-level managers.

Because of the large economic stakes involved and the tricky legal environment, specialized management skills are needed if the newspaper is unionized or threatened by unionization. Some newspapers with unions establish a separate labor relations department whose executives are experienced in union relations.

Unless a manager is alert, seemingly insignificant problems can fester, with tension among employees then overriding even good pay, benefits, and working conditions. This is proven repeatedly in newspapers that paternalistically pay some of the highest salaries in the nation yet have unending labor unrest because there is no responsive communication directly between management and staff. Quality circles can create communication by giving units of co-workers who are interested in their work direct, frequent contact with a responsive management.

A common error is for managers to feel that because *they* take an enlightened attitude toward employee needs and desires, the newspaper's personnel policy is automatically being communicated correctly to the staff. But for most employees, "management" is the immediate supervisor—and if that supervisor cannot skillfully represent corporate policy in daily contact with the staff, the most carefully drawn personnel program will fail. Detailed training of supervisors must ensure that top management's policies are implemented and that management, in turn, receives an upward flow of employee feedback. Let the first-level supervisor, not a union official, be the "lightning rod" to hear out employees on their problems and the instrument of correcting those problems.

To keep its communications lines open, the *Roanoke (Va.) Times World-News*, a morning-afternoon combination of 115,000 circulation owned by Landmark Communications Co., requires department heads to meet individually with each employee at least annually. The publisher and personnel manager, additionally, meet monthly with small groups of employees for open discussion of any topic except other employees and their salaries. Personnel Director Vaughn Porter says he and Publisher Walter Rugaber want to obtain a feel for employee problems and give everyone opportunity to talk to top management without fear of retribution. The *Norfolk (Va.) Virginian-Pilot and Ledger Star*, Landmark's flagship, hired an outside training firm to develop an educational program designed to help supervisors better understand their managerial role and communicate more effectively with subordinates.[27]

---

[27] "Norfolk Papers Hire Training Firm to Develop Program For Supervisors," *Southern Newspaper Publishers' Association Bulletin*, Oct. 25, 1982, p. 3.

Every manager must understand that avoiding unions is a daily priority. If a strategy for dealing with unions is formulated only when union organizers arrive in the publisher's office, it may be too late. Each manager must create a work environment that makes it unnecessary for employees to join unions. The entire human resources program—from hiring to firing—must be constructed with avoiding unions as a prime objective.

Some newspapers encourage independent—or "company"—unions because they are often less militant than international unions. The *Wall Street Journal*, for example, has negotiated for years with an "Independent Association of Publishers' Employees."

Smaller newspapers often avoid organization because the relevant bargaining unit, say, a newsroom of five or six persons, is too small for an international union. But metros sometimes operate without unions, too. Both the *Los Angeles Times* and *Miami Herald* have fought off unions by offering attractive personnel policies and high wages and benefits.

In sum, union *avoidance*—using preventive labor relations—is an acceptable management technique. But managers cannot try to defeat a union's organizing attempts illegally or discriminate against prounion employees. Both have legal rights, and we now turn to that area of your managerial responsibilities.

When Union Organizers Arrive

Union organizers are often invited in by disgruntled employees. They then establish local organizing committees to win support in the targeted "bargaining unit" or department. They try to win majority backing before management even learns they are at work.

Legal and often very effective steps can be taken to beat back organizing efforts. But your first step has to be consulting an expert labor lawyer to explain the legalities of fighting unions, because union-management relations must be conducted within an elaborate, highly technical legal framework.

The *National Labor Relations Act of 1935*—also known as the Wagner Act—provides legal protection for the right of employees to join unions and bargain collectively. The *Taft-Hartley Act of 1947* protects management's rights to campaign against unions and urge employees not to join as long as certain guidelines are followed. The *National Labor Relations Board (NLRB)*, a federal agency, watches over the relationship—or, if it comes to that, the battleground. The rules are precisely defined, and the NLRB has major powers.

The NLRB zealously protects labor's basic right to organize and bargain collectively and will monitor unions' attempts to organize a newspaper, ensuring fair elections and making certain that management does not interfere illegally. Managers cannot infringe on labor's rights without risking NLRB action. Those rights include being able to contact and talk with individual employees in private, free of management interference. Unions are permitted to post bulletin boards on the newspaper's premises. Names of employees must be given to union organizers. Infringing on those rights can be costly in both money and lost management prerogatives. For example, the NLRB can force a newspaper to rehire an employee illegally discharged, fine newspapers for unfair labor practices, and influence every area of personnel policy.

By law, a union can petition the NLRB to schedule an employee election on union representation if 30 percent of the targeted unit's employees sign authorization cards designating the union as their collective bargaining representative. Organizers normally seek signatures from substantially more than 50 percent of employees, however, to ensure sufficient support in any election that follows.

Managers may react vigorously (and legally), *before* the NLRB is petitioned, by raising wages or changing working conditions—provided that they act for proper business reasons and without discrimination for or against any employee on grounds of his or her union sentiments. Once a union has petitioned the NLRB with sufficient authorization cards, there are severe legal restrictions on what management can say and do.

Management Must Counterattack

When an election is scheduled under NLRB guidance, management must launch a vigorous campaign to win. Even if union organizers have been long at work, even if managers have been laggard in communicating effectively with employees in the past, management now must confront and solve the problems that inspired the organizing effort.

Campaigning by both sides often gets heated. Expect union charges that management neglected employees—underpaid and overworked them. Management must have a program to respond effectively to even the wildest charge and each complaint raised. Sometimes a single vote can swing a union representation election, and management should keep close count on how employee sentiment is moving. Even a seemingly minor complaint raised by the union can be important to an individual employee. Let no complaint go unanswered.

One crucial element of the battle is precisely which employees belong in the relevant bargaining unit. The union will attempt to include as many employees as possible, even some who might be regarded as managers: desk editors with supervisory duties, for example, or circulation employees directing other employees and handling money. Management's goal is to hold to a minimum the number of employees permitted to vote—and concentrate on persuading them to reject the union at the NLRB ballot box.

Managers should emphasize, in daily conversations and bulletin board announcements, their desire to deal fairly and directly with individual employees, not through an outside third party. Managers should inform workers about the union, its financial strength, salaries of paid officers, and, importantly, dues and fees that would be charged each member. Such information can be obtained from the forms designated IM-2 or IM-3 that each union is obliged to file in Washington with the Department of Labor. The facts about a union often reveal quite a different picture than the one organizers have been painting for employees.

Managers *cannot* discharge union supporters or threaten them in any way. Raises or preferential treatment *cannot* be promised for an antiunion vote. But managers can and must react quickly and vigorously in the early stages of any organizing effort.

What to Do if the Union Wins

If a union wins the right to represent employees, management has lost only the first skirmish, not the battle. The law forces management to negotiate in good faith, but not to accept union demands blindly.

Unquestionably, however, a dangerous new element has been introduced: the threat of an organized strike is now very real. Each manager, therefore, must immediately prepare to continue publication if a strike occurs. That means training supervisors or outsiders to replace employees who might strike. Assume that all union employees will walk out in the event of a strike. The more detailed strike preparations are and the more obvious it is that publication can be continued, the less the danger of a strike will be.

The next step, with advice of legal counsel, is for the management team to construct a bargaining strategy. Supervisors should be consulted on staff feelings toward the union and the union's likely objectives. A bargaining team, normally three or four experienced, strong-willed executives, then prepares to go to the table with the union. Bargaining often is heated, lengthy, and tiring. So management's strategy must be developed in detail and followed carefully and coolly. Intemperate, careless moves in negotiations must be avoided.

The Prebargaining Audit

Before talks open, management must audit external and internal factors likely to affect bargaining.

Internally, management must audit its strengths and weaknesses. What is the newspaper's true bargaining power? Is it financially capable of taking a strike, or if it must reach accommodation with the union, how rich a contract can it afford? Each manager, particularly first-level supervisors, should review attitude surveys, past grievances, and other indicators of how strongly employees will back union negotiators. Are employees prepared to walk out, or are they likely to press for a reasonable settlement short of a strike? All department heads should be consulted even if only one department has been slated for organization. The implications of, say, a Guild attempt to organize the news department are meaningful to other departments.

Externally, managers should audit public attitudes, which cannot be ignored by any newspaper. Preparing for money talks, management must forecast future business conditions, inflation, and unemployment so as to get a fix on the economic context in which any contract will be enforced.

Carefully study the union, its general attitudes and strategy. What agenda did it push forward in negotiations with other newspapers? What is the union's bargaining power? Is the international union present and supportive with negotiating expertise and money? Is there a strike fund established? Valuable background on comparable contracts and settlements is available from ANPA and the Southern Newspaper Publishers' Association.[28]

---

[28] ANPA's address is P. O. Box 17407, Dulles International Airport, Washington, DC 20041; SNPA's is P. O. Box 28875, Atlanta, GA 30328.

A Few Negotiating Hints

Bargaining strategy should be firmly fixed before negotiations open.[29] Parameters must be set for all *economic* discussions likely to occur: how much is management willing to offer in pay increases, fringe benefits, and other dollars-and-cents areas?

Beware of what many union negotiators call *noneconomic* issues. They ostensibly deal with such things as workplace rules and not with money, but they can end up costing the newspaper a great deal. For example, a "noneconomic" request for two coffee breaks, not one, in the composing room means that management has to pay somebody extra to work during the second break. Calculate the dollar cost of that.

Pin down timing. Negotiating is fatiguing and stressful, so plan to start and end talks at reasonable hours. When should management put forward each proposal? What does management want to achieve and, frankly, what is it likely to attain?

A spokesperson must be selected (and only he or she should speak for management). Some newspapers prefer the spokesperson be an insider; others call in labor lawyers or professional negotiators. The CEO may direct negotiations from behind the scenes, but he or she stays fresh and clear-headed by keeping out of the talks and avoiding the long hours of often highly emotional confrontation with union negotiators. And by staying out, the CEO reserves flexibility to move in at the last minute with an offer for settlement. The negotiating team can vary in composition, but it must include a person thoroughly acquainted with labor law and a financial expert who can calculate the costs of various union and management proposals. Other team members can include managers who are familiar with the operational matters being discussed or,

simply, an executive who can keep talks going while other management negotiators get a rest.

There are countless approaches to negotiating, ranging from "take it or leave it" to the more widely used "bid and ask." The former is just that: an offer dropped on the table without negotiation. This, of course, can create political problems for union negotiators with their own members, who expect tough bargaining for advantage; it often leads to impasse and strike. "Bid and ask" involves making an offer (which everybody recognizes as being preliminary and, thus, low), then negotiating a series of offers and counteroffers until a mutually acceptable agreement is reached.

The management team must tailor its approach to its own objectives, strengths, and weaknesses. A few things to keep in mind throughout the bid and ask process are as follows:

- Always protect management's right to manage, protect profitability, hire and fire for cause, change and improve operations, control size and composition of the staff. Unions cannot be permitted to chip away at these prerogatives and responsibilities that management carries.

- Beware of union demands for a voice in work rules. They limit management's ability to decide who works where and can lead to underutilization of employees.

- Never assume that existing wage and benefit levels are a base and that the whole exercise is how far upward they will be negotiated. When a union takes management to the table, an entire new package of wages and benefits must be negotiated.

- Avoid automatic "escalators" in wages or benefits tied to increases in the cost of living or other external indexes. They can take your costs *up* at a time when your profits are going *down*.

- Resist attempts to win union seats on your board of directors or jointly administer

---

[29] For a thorough review of the bargaining process see Charles S. Loughran's detailed *Negotiating a Labor Contract*, Washington, D. C., Bureau of National Affairs, Inc.

pension and health plans. Both would admit the union to management's inner council and reveal its innermost secrets, destroying flexibility in policymaking.

- Never make a concession without getting something in return. A management proposal that is greeted with a simple "no" from the union should stay on the table until the union responds in good faith with a counterproposal.

- *Never* open with your best offer. If a wage increase of $18 per week over a three-year contract is your goal, don't open with $18. Try $10.

- Keep proposals in writing and take detailed minutes of the meeting, so as to prepare a record for any lawsuit or arbitration arising out of negotiations.

- Prepare package offers with, say, wages and benefits tied to other negotiating goals. Offer, for example, the $18 weekly *if* the union gives ground by, say, dropping demands for another vacation day. Union rejection of any single element invalidates the entire proposal and management is free to withdraw it and make another approach.

- Be alert for the cumulative or "rollup" effect of fringe benefits, pay differentials for working different shifts, and so on. In total, they can add substantially, easily 30 to 50 percent, to the cost of the contract, even though each in itself may appear insignificant.

- Signal the union's chief negotiator where management will go in negotiations and where it won't go. Step out to the corridor for off-the-record talks, particularly if the negotiator is a professional from the international union. Often he or she will want to get on to other things and will help management find a reasonable settlement.

- If settlement is reached, insist that union negotiators recommend acceptance to their membership. Too often, union leadership throws management's offer before its members without a recommendation for approval, hoping that the members will reject it and give union negotiators greater clout in a second round of bargaining.

If There Is An Impasse

If settlement is not reached, management's negotiators must tune in to the words and actions, even the body language, of their counterparts. Signals of readiness to settle may be coming across the table. A casual comment such as, "We sure hate to walk away from this table . . ." can be a signal to try once more for settlement.

Absent such signals, management can try to break the logjam by stating it will make a "final offer"—maybe another dollar in wages or an extra holiday. Management must truly mean that it will offer no more inducements, and the union must understand that.

Sometimes, management's total offer, economic and noneconomic, can be restructured to make it more attractive to the union yet no more expensive to the newspaper. For example, if management has made an offer of, say, a 10 percent pay increase over two years, perhaps each year's increase can be juggled or their effective date changed. One technique is to switch some of management's total money offer to fringe benefits from pay, thus giving union negotiators, in other words, something they can take back with pride to their members.

If all else fails, the dispute can be given to a mediator from the Federal Mediation and Conciliation Service, a similar state body, or a private expert in labor affairs. These professionals frequently engage directly in negotiations, shuttling back and forth between union and management hotel rooms, suggesting compromises, and pointing out ways to break deadlocks. Often, their mere presence as dispassionate outsiders is enough to cool negotiations and speed solutions. Mediation is not binding by law, however, and it still is up to unions and management to agree on a solution. If a true impasse exists and mediation doesn't work, both parties can agree to arbitration which *is* binding. Arbitration is used less frequently than mediation because in arbitration both sides must agree to abide by the ruling handed down.

Sometimes, if negotiations break down, management's choices are either to take a strike or give in. The prebargaining audit should have answered the question, but if not, this is the time for management to decide whether the newspaper can afford a strike.

Living with the Union

Once signed, a union contract must be followed. Departures from it can leave the newspaper vulnerable to lawsuit or NLRB action—and both are expensive to defend against.

Even seemingly insignificant departures can be dangerous because if, for example, a supervisor agrees independently with a handful of employees to change even slightly the work rules spelled out in the contract, a "past practice" can be created. This is a practice permitted to exist over a period of time that thereby can become an accepted contract change.

Any departure from contract should be made only after consultation with counsel and deep thought about its long-range implications. Management then should have a letter exchange with the union, spelling out the change and whether or not it is permanent.

Once under contract, management must set the tone for living with the union. Will it be a cat-and-dog fight all the way? If so, the newspaper will be a tense place to work. Will there be an armed truce, with both sides seeing a basic incompatibility of interests? This generally leads to all-out war.

Some unionized newspapers strive for a harmonious relationship in which the interests of both sides are recognized. Management can sometimes use the union structure to communicate with employees. Sometimes, though in-frequently, there can be true cooperation, with both sides working together to achieve the same goals. Recent U. S. newspaper history provides examples of both extremes.

On September 16, 1982, after five days of intense talks with nine unions, a team of Rupert Murdoch's negotiators pushed back from the bargaining table in Buffalo, N.Y., and walked from the room. The Australian-born entrepreneur had offered to buy and try to save the tottering *Buffalo Courier-Express*—but only if he could eliminate 400 of its 1,100 jobs and gain unchallenged management control of the paper. Newspaper Guild members balked. They did not get a second chance. The 148-year-old *Courier-Express* published its last edition on September 19.[30]

In New York City, ten days later, after all-night negotiations, representatives of New York's *Daily News* and eleven unions shook hands over an agreement almost unique in the city's strife-ridden newspaper history. They had *cooperated* to save the nation's largest general-circulation daily. The *Daily News*, plagued by high costs and loss of advertising share, took the unusual step of opening its books to the unions, showing that it had lost $12.6 million in 1981 and projected 1982 losses of $30 million. The unions granted concessions, including elimination of more than a thousand jobs (the *Daily News*'s one-time buyout cost was estimated at $50 million). In return, the *Daily News* agreed to a contract guaranteeing, for the first time, a share to employees in any future profits. It was, in Buffalo and New York City, the best and worst of management-union relations.

In Buffalo, it was old-fashioned, table-thumping negotiations, with both sides standing fast on what they considered inalienable principle until everybody lost. Murdoch's men said they would keep 70 of 157 newsroom employees and demanded sole right to say who went and

---

[30] *"Courier-Express* Folds In Buffalo After 148 Years," *Editor & Publisher*, Sept. 25, 1982, p. 11.

who stayed. Full severance plus $5,000 would be paid to those terminated. Says Robert Page, then chief negotiator for Murdoch's News America Publishing:

> We proposed to the unions what we felt had to be done in order to save the paper. . . . We look at a newspaper somewhat differently than many other publishers. We want control of the newsroom. We want to determine the quality of the staff. We want to put out the type of newspaper we want.[31]

The unions rejected the offer. William N. Buil, Buffalo Guild president, described the moment Murdoch's men walked out in these words: "Everyone on our side was frozen in his chair. We knew that was it. We knew we had to go out and face the public. The saddest part is we really wanted to save the paper."[32]

In New York City, few would have predicted the outcome at the *Daily News*. New York newspapers and unions had long histories of bitter confrontation. Hard-line union attitudes, management failures, and socioeconomic change had helped kill, since the mid-1960s, four major papers (leaving the *Times*, *Post*, and *Daily News*); management and unions bitterly charged each other with causing the failures. Nothing in the city's newspaper tradition suggested that the *Daily News* and its eleven unions—representing reporters, printers, pressmen, drivers, paper handlers, electricians, machinists, and others—could work things out. The *Daily News* had been a union battleground in the 1970s, in fact. The paper fought the ITU for the right to reduce its work force through attrition, severely weakening the union in the process. It would be comforting to suggest that a new era of sweet reason had arrived. But unions and management got together only be-

cause they had to or the *Daily News* would die. Tribune Co. started the round of union talks by announcing it would sell the paper. Revenues were falling, costs skyrocketing, and the *Daily News* was in the red. But not even the nation's largest communications companies would risk the mountainous losses the *Daily News* was accumulating. Frequently, prospective buyers mentioned labor difficulties as the reason for their lack of interest.

Tribune Co. faced highly unpalatable options: continue operating the newspaper as it hemorrhaged money or shut it down at a cost of up to $200 million for severance and other termination expenses.[33] Those stunning statistics sent Tribune Co. back to the drawing board with its unions, now concerned that they could lose all five thousand *Daily News* jobs.

Tribune Co. finally won agreement to cut 1,340 jobs (with severance pay) for a $50 million annual reduction in operating costs. Tribune Co. agreed to pump in more than $44 million to revitalize the paper. The unions got a three-year contract with pay increases ($110 weekly per employee over the three-year period, with adjustments tied to the Consumer Price Index) and, importantly, employee profit-sharing of 25 percent of operating profit margins above 6 percent.

The financial picture quickly brightened. The *Daily News*'s 1982 loss, projected at $30 million, actually came in at $14 million; and in July 1983, the paper announced that it was in the black.[34] Art Wible, then executive vice president, said of the union-management cooperation: "It may be one of the largest bottom-line turnarounds a newspaper has ever made."[35]

The *Daily News*, however, still had not solved its fundamental problems of advertising

---

[31] Ibid.
[32] "Closing in Buffalo Centered Around Newsroom Staffing," *Southern Newspaper Publishers' Association Bulletin*, Personnel/Labor, Oct. 25, 1982, p. 3.

[33] "Keeping The *New York Daily News* Alive May Cost Its Owners Less Than Closing It," *Wall Street Journal*, May 5, 1982, p. 56.
[34] "News Works Miracle On 42nd Street," *Advertising Age*, July 11, 1983, p. 1.
[35] Ibid.

loss and reader flight to the suburbs. In 1986, Tribune Co. again turned to the unions for huge economic concessions on grounds that the paper was once more in deep financial trouble. Union–management cooperation well into the 1990s obviously was needed to save the paper.

Although it was the most dramatic, the 1982 *Daily News* agreement is not the only one in which hard-line unions granted concessions to a newspaper in financial difficulty. In the early 1980s, many U. S. newspapers won "give-backs"— wages and benefit freezes or elimination of procedural rules favoring unions.[36] These concessions generally resulted from the 1980–1983 recession and highly publicized newspaper failures in Washington, Minneapolis, Cleveland, and elsewhere. It cannot be said that precedent was established for all future bargaining patterns, since the basic relationship between union and management remains adversarial. And newspaper managers are increasingly going on the offensive, trying to get rid of unions, even those that have been in place for years.

Unions Can Be Thrown Out

Living with a union need not be forever. In addition to monitoring employee organizing efforts, the NLRB oversees decertification of unions when at least 30 percent of the bargaining unit's employees no longer desire union affiliation. By law, it is not management but employees who must file with the NLRB for decertification. Management must stay out of the matter until decertification is under way and, even then, must avoid any offers or threats in campaigning for it. Decertification proceedings frequently start when employees decide the union is not making gains for them. Union dues are expensive, and employees may decide that they can do better for themselves by negotiating with management individually.

In the early 1980s, decertification cost newspaper unions dearly. In the NLRB's fiscal year ending September 30, 1981, decertification elections cost unions 27,527 members, the largest setback ever for newspaper unions in one year. There has been a sharp drop, also, in the number of union representation elections conducted by the NLRB. In 1985, for example, 17 were held (compared with 64 in 1975), and unions lost 9. Strikes dropped sharply, too. Throughout the 1960s and 1970s, more than twenty on average were launched annually against newspapers. By the early 1980s, the average was about three; in 1986, no strikes were started— the first time that had happened since ANPA began keeping records more than fifty years earlier.

Those bad years for unions were caused in part by economic recession; union organizing efforts are less successful when employees fear for their jobs. But in great part, newspaper management teams are creating their own successes against unions through professional personnel policies that make it more difficult for unions to find enough employee dissatisfaction to support their efforts. And newspaper managers are simply negotiating more aggressively, denying unions clear-cut victories at the negotiating table that justify, in their members' eyes, the unions' continued existence.

SUMMARY

A top priority for every young manager is learning how to manage the human element effectively. It is a core function at every level of management and at every newspaper, large or small.

Expert personnel management can achieve fast improvement that quickly infuses a newspaper with new, winning talent. And because tomorrow's newspaper will be a mirror image of today's new hires, it is in personnel that a manager can put a stamp on the newspaper's long-range character.

---

[36] Clark Newsom, "Some Unions Make Concessions During Tough Economic Times," *presstime*, April 1983, p. 44.

The challenge in managing human resources, by far the newspaper's most important and costly assets, is *auditing* the newspaper's personnel needs, *planning* their effective development and use, *establishing policy, recruiting* and *hiring*, and then *motivating*. Then there is the *control* of performance and, at times, the distasteful but necessary job of *disciplining* or firing.

Motivating employees to perform according to plan, thus helping to move the newspaper toward its overall goals, is a function of every manager. Its key is understanding the employees' often shifting view of their needs, then helping each individual satisfy them in a manner that will benefit both the individual and newspaper.

Challenges ahead include increasing minority hiring and promotion (an area in which many newspapers fail), and preparing for the inevitable displacement of many jobs due to automation.

A priority for management is union strategy—how to avoid unions or how to work with them if you must. Despite recent signs of accommodation by unions, relationships with management are based on a history of tension and struggle. The National Labor Relations Board tightly supervises union-management relations, and newspaper managers are wise to seek legal advice on how to work within the guidelines.

RECOMMENDED READING

The Newspaper Personnel Relations Association, The Newspaper Center, Box 17407 Dulles International Airport, Washington, DC 20041, issues research in newspaper human relations. Also note, *Newsroom Management Handbook*, American Society of Newspaper Editors, The Newspaper Center, Box 17004 Dulles International Airport, Washington, DC 20041; The Associated Press Managing Editors' Association, 50 Rockefeller Plaza, New York, NY 10020, has extensive guidance available for managing newsroom personnel. The Newspaper Advertising Bureau, 1180 Avenue of the Americas, New York, NY 10036, has researched extensively the training and motivation of salespeople. Also see Paul Hersey and Kenneth Blanchard, *Management of Organizational Behavior*, Englewood Cliffs, N. J., Prentice-Hall, 1982; and Raymond Hilgert, Sterling Schoen, and Joseph Towle, *Cases and Policies in Personnel/Human Resources Management*, Boston, Houghton Mifflin, 1982.

MARKETING THE NEWSPAPER: A CONCEPT WHOSE TIME HAS ARRIVED

PART
II

Once upon a time, newspaper editors dutifully surveyed each day's news, then published what *they* thought was important or interesting, and that was that. This is no fairy tale. It happened that way. Advertising sales forces made themselves available to sell space in the paper, take it or leave it. Circulation employees sold as many papers as possible—where and to whom didn't really matter; only total numbers counted.

Newspaper production was so cumbersome, costly, and time-consuming that all newspaper operations were production-dominated. Weekly editors weren't really editors; most spent their time in the back shop, just getting the paper out. Promotion? Did newspapers actively promote themselves with society at large, as must any consumer-oriented business? Mostly, that simply wasn't done. Well, times have changed.

Today, the *marketing concept* is upon us, and your generation of newspaper managers must become marketing experts, skilled in discovering scientifically what customers want and need, then focusing the newspaper's resources on satisfying those wants and needs.

In Part II we will discuss the newspaper's operating departments—news, advertising, circulation, production—and how they must be integrated into an organizational whole. The marketing concept holds that you must learn to harness each department in a *customer-oriented team* whose purpose is to identify and satisfy customer needs.

We will start, in Chapter 6, with the theory of marketing. This relatively short chapter is designed primarily to highlight for you the principles of marketing. Then, we'll turn to fuller discussion in subsequent chapters of how those principles are applied to each department.

CHAPTER SIX

The Theory of Marketing

Sorry, but unless good ol' Dad owns the place, there isn't much chance of you jumping directly into the top management of your favorite newspaper. You must start at the bottom, pick up experience and prove yourself. But *where* at the bottom? *What* experience? A couple of clues:

First, today's industry leaders rose by varying routes. Many started in advertising, some in circulation. News was the starting point for Chairman Neuharth of Gannett and Chairman Phillips of Dow Jones. Bob Marbut, president of Harte-Hanks, and Stan Cook, chairman of the Tribune Co., started in production.

Second, although these and other winners followed various career routes, they all arrived at the same point; as general managers, publishers, or presidents, they managed a newspaper as a customer-oriented, truly integrated organization with all resources, human and other, coordinated in a focused marketing thrust.

If their experience means anything, it is that marketing is a concept you must learn to employ effectively, whether your origin or primary career interest is news, advertising, circulation, or another department.

The central thrust of marketing is to identify consumer wants and needs and to satisfy them. If you think about it, that seems an obviously ideal business approach for a newspaper. A newspaper's business, after all, is to sell news to readers, then sell those readers to advertisers. In pursuit of that goal, daily newspapers manufacture and sell nearly 63 million units of their product each weekday; weeklies, 47.5 million each week. The dailies alone, in 1985, sold $25.1 billion in advertising.

Surely, any industry with such sales volume and which serves two consumer constituencies—readers and advertisers— would naturally be *consumer oriented* in the true sense of

121

marketing. But that's not true. Newspapers traditionally have been *production oriented,* burdened with a complex manufacturing process that led to business strategies revolving around the newspaper and its problems, not around consumers and their needs. Contrast that with, for example, Pillsbury Company, which acknowledges that it was production-oriented when it was formed, way back in 1869, but which became sales-oriented in the 1930s, took on full marketing orientation in the 1960s, and quickly evolved into what today is a marketing, not production, company.[1]

Only now, decades behind many other industries, are newspapers switching to the marketing concept, looking upon themselves as products that must be tailored to satisfy consumer needs and which must be sold in a competitive marketplace, just like any other product. Only now are newspaper tables of organization being redrawn to insert "marketing director" into the hierarchy at senior level.

WHY NEWSPAPERS ARE FORCED INTO MARKETING

There are three broad reasons why newspapers must now plunge into the marketing concept. Each will be covered in detail in subsequent chapters discussing marketing in news, advertising, circulation and other departments. But briefly, to open our discussion of marketing, they are:

1. *Competition,* which is forcing newspapers to change, to react creatively. In the fight for advertisers, stiff challenge comes from direct mail, shoppers, broadcast media, and so on. Competition for readers comes from television, magazines, leisure-time activity, and simple public apathy over old-fashioned editorial products.

2. *Weaknesses in newspaper performance.* Neither reader nor advertiser is being served well enough by many papers. For the advertiser, many newspapers fail to achieve deep enough penetration of households or to provide selective targeting that delivers enough of the highly attractive readers desired by those selling goods or services. Advertising rates rise rapidly because the cost of producing the traditional mass-circulation newspaper is leaping ahead; share of advertising market thus is lost to less costly media.

3. Newspapers, however, have *strengths* that open new areas of business opportunity if they are exploited by consumer-oriented marketing techniques. Improved marketing research enables newspapers to identify reader needs as never before. New technology makes it possible to satisfy them with news tailored in zoned editions for special interests. New production methods permit faster, better printing and distribution.

A journalistically outstanding, even superior product will not automatically bring success in the marketplace. Some of your predecessor managers who believed that worked for the *New York Herald Tribune, Washington Star,* and *Philadelphia Bulletin,* all once great papers that are now dead. Something else is needed: profes-

---

[1] For a fascinating summary of the Pillsbury story, see Eugene J. Kelley, ed., *Marketing: Strategy and Functions,* Englewood Cliffs, N.J., Prentice-Hall, 1965.

sional, realistic marketing and dedication to the proposition that a newspaper need not be resigned to whatever fate brings but rather that its long-range future can be guided in large part through planned effort, and that specific short-term goals can be achieved with planning.

The marketing concept means you'll have to create a *consumer-oriented* newspaper whose business philosophy is one of creating customer satisfaction. Here are some other core characteristics of the marketing approach:

- You'll have to create *total company focus* on spotting marketplace demand, analyzing how it can be met, planning to meet it, then meeting it. In the past, that was what the sales arm of a newspaper did; today, it's what every department—including news—must do.

- *Research* to identify and measure customer wants and needs must be continual. Whether you buy professional assistance from outside or develop in-house capability, research must guide every department's daily operations and long-range strategy. News wants to add three columnists? Does research say they are needed? Circulation wants to start a push in the northwest suburbs? What does research say about the potential readers there—and whether advertisers would find them attractive?

- *Profit*, not volume, is the goal under the marketing concept. Producing and selling more newspapers each day is not necessarily better. Are they being sold to the right readers, those attractive to advertisers?

Whatever your management role, you will be helping the newspaper fashion a correct *marketing mix:* creating a product that satisfies consumer needs; pricing it to cover costs, ensure profit, and meet competitive prices; distributing it to the right customers, at the right time, in the right locations; and promoting it in a manner

consistent with the newspaper's overall objectives.[2]

For clues on how to arrive at the correct marketing mix, you must look outward, to the newspaper's external environment.

Monitor the External Environment

Newspapers operate in a marketing environment, and their success, or lack of it, is influenced heavily by external factors. Let's look at four broad areas that will influence your marketing stance:

Society's needs and expectations. They are historic. Since colonial days, newspapers have been expected by their public to do more than make a profit; they are expected to educate, uplift, and serve the public interest. Yet society's attitudes constantly shift, and newspapers simultaneously can be under public attack on many fronts. No significant marketing move can be made without considering society's perceptions of the press. Newspapers must also work to improve their public image. We will cover this in detail later, but for now, briefly, the industry in general suffers from an image problem. Research by Ruth Clark for ASNE shows, for example, that three-fourths of the adults surveyed in 1985 doubt the credibility of the news media; one-fifth deeply distrust the media; three-fourths say reporters want only a good story and don't worry about hurting people. Studies by Clark and others, which will be discussed later, also show that the public can rapidly shift its demands on newspapers—from requiring "soft" or featurish approaches to news, for example, to seeking "hard" or spot news on timely events that delivers the facts and lets

---

[2] Readers interested in detailed looks at marketing theory will be rewarded by Harry A. Lipson and John R. Darling, *Introduction to Marketing*, New York, Wiley, 1971, and David L. Kurtz and Louis E. Boone, *Marketing*, New York, Dryden, 1981. Also see Kelley, op. cit.

readers make up their own minds on how to interpret them.

Government and legal. Like it or not, as a newspaper manager—or manager of any business—you have a partner: the government. It influences every aspect of newspapering. The law today carries unprecedented importance in newspaper operations. We'll discuss this in Chapter 12.

Competitive. Newspapers large and small compete for readers and advertisers against a growing multitude of competitors, new and old. Careful analysis of this influence in the external environment must precede every marketing decision.

Economic. Both the broad national economic picture and the specific economic character of the local market and audience are crucial influences in marketing. In all newspaper operations, what to do, when to do it—indeed, whether to do it—will depend on your analysis of economic influences. Launching a costly Sunday magazine to attract national advertising makes no sense if the national economy is headed into recession; trying to sell subscriptions in a distant area of the state makes no economic sense if advertisers don't care about readers who live there.

The only constant in the external marketing environment is change. Be alert for shifting influences.

Audit the Internal Environment

Important internal considerations influence the newspaper's marketing concept heavily; you must monitor them carefully.

Resources available. If external research identifies a need, can you meet it with the money, time, management, and staff talent available to you? New methods in management and research can stretch resources: the marketing concept *does* give us bigger sales bang for every buck;

research *does* show us where to spend for greatest effect in, say, producing new circulation and advertising revenue. But the parameters of your marketing effort will be limited by the availability of resources.

Financial goals. Your marketing direction will be established in large part by your owner's financial goals. Publicly owned newspapers must meet the rising tide of shareholder expectations and produce ever-improved dividends. If you could listen to some of the most secret strategy sessions at large communications companies, you would hear executives first establishing financial goals, then working back from that to set the marketing and operational objectives required to yield those financial results.

Social goals and ethical standards. What public image do you want for the newspaper? Your answer will greatly influence the type and quality paper you produce. What ethical stance is to be taken? Should the newspaper get involved in community boosterism or limit its role to that of observer?

Technology. Whatever research indicates you should do, whatever marketing goals you establish, your newspaper's ability to perform depends heavily on its technology. Elaborate marketing strategy can be devised to, say, blanket a distant county with your circulation, but all to no avail if your presses cannot produce papers on time or your distribution technology cannot get them there.

Steps in the Marketing Process

To ensure effective results, you should follow discrete steps. They are *organizing* the marketing structure, *analyzing* the newspaper's present and future situation, *setting goals, planning* and assigning resources, *creating the product, controlling* performance, and *adjusting* operations to make sure that objectives are met.

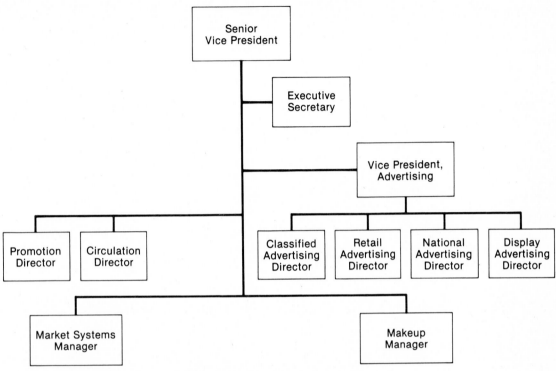

Figure 6.1 *Dallas (Tex.) Times Herald* **Sales & Marketing Division**

Source: John A. Wolf, *Times Herald* senior vice president.

1. Organizing the marketing structure. Drawing a new table of organization that creates a "marketing director" will announce that the marketing era has arrived. See Figure 6.1 for how that is done. But the new chart won't convince anyone. Your task will be to change old ways of thinking and overturn age-old work habits.

Be prepared for conflict. The marketing approach involves new basic tasks for individuals, perhaps new employees. The hierarchy must be realigned, new lines of authority and responsibility established—and that will upset many people. Advertising and circulation executives who formerly reported directly to the publisher will now report to the marketing director. A status symbol in newspaper management is reporting directly to the top boss. The removal of that is seen by many as a demotion.

The marketing director must be a person of outstanding talent who can create and effectively lead a department that serves as the primary link between the newspaper and its two important customer constituencies, readers and advertisers. Ability to motivate others, externally and internally, is required. The accompanying box outlines the career background required of its marketing director by one major newspaper.

Because advertising represents about 80 percent of total revenue for most newspapers, marketing directors are often selected from ad department ranks. In the new job, however, the director must take a broad view that includes strategic planning, market analysis, and leadership of a widely diverse group of employees; normally, he or she is also responsible for the performance of both the advertising and circu-

THE MARKETING DIRECTOR

To focus all sales-related functions in a marketing thrust, a high-level executive must have authority over the newspaper's total marketplace position—everything from research to circulation, advertising, and promotion.

Traditional tables of organization must be redrawn to make sure that all sales-related departments are under the unified command of that single individual—the marketing director—who, in turn, must be a key member of top management.

John A. Wolf, *Dallas (Tex.) Times Herald* senior vice president and marketing director, exemplifies the professional salesperson and marketing executive increasingly rising to the top in newspaper management. After finishing school (Northwestern University), Wolf joined Branham Co., a newspaper "rep" firm that sells client newspaper space to national advertisers, and became Branham's Minneapolis office manager. He joined the *Times Herald* in 1965 and served successively as national ad representative, national ad manager, ad director, vice president of sales and marketing, vice president of marketing. In 1982, at age fifty-four and after thirty-four years in sales, he became senior vice president. Wolf writes:

As senior vice president, I am, responsible for all matters relating to circulation, advertising, research, promotion, and marketing services. . . . As an officer of the company, I participate on a day-to-day basis with the publisher and other officers of the *Times Herald* in establishing our total corporate position in the marketplace. . . . We all work together to produce a product each day which is of value to our readers and advertisers. With this basic philosophy, there are no artificial walls between the departments to inhibit progressive thinking.*

There is a newspaper tradition of autonomous circulation and advertising departments reporting directly to the publisher, and tradition—not to say, "territorial imperative"—dies hard. Such autonomy can create strong-willed leaders zealously protecting departmental prerogatives, often to the detriment of overall operating efficiency.

The *Chicago Sun-Times* moved decisively to remedy its problem, appointing an executive vice president over both advertising and circulation. Increasingly, popular titles are "director of sales and marketing" or, at other papers, "vice president and director of sales."

* John A. Wolf, letter to author.

---

lation departments. Close coordination with production, news, and promotion departments is required.

Organizing the marketing effort also includes providing for top management's total—and visible—commitment to the marketing concept. It is crucial to success, no matter how efficient the marketing organization itself may be.

2. *Analyzing the newspaper's present and future position.* Get visionary. Think big. Take nothing for granted. If you think newspapers have a heavenly mandate for continued prosperity, remember the railroads. They were once one of America's greatest industries. What should the marketing department recommend to top management as long-range strategy? Where are

today's customers and markets? Where will they be tomorrow? How should the newspaper compete for them, with what product, where, and when? Should you stay in the *newspaper* business or branch off into magazines, shoppers, television, cable? Where is there potential reward—in profit or market share—and what investment is necessary to unlock it? Where do competitors, present and future, fit into the picture? What are their strengths and weaknesses?[3]

---

[3] See Wroe Alderson and Paul E. Green, *Planning and Problem Solving in Marketing*, Homewood, Ill., Irwin, 1964; Paul E. Green and Donald S. Tull, *Research for Marketing Decisions*, Englewood Cliffs, N.J., Prentice-Hall, 1966; Mark E. Stern, *Marketing Planning*, New York, McGraw-Hill, 1966.

3. Setting goals. What must be achieved in the short and long term to fulfill strategic objectives or exploit opportunities revealed in market analysis? Precisely what must the newspaper accomplish in profit, market share, social objectives, image? Where in the market must the newspaper be positioned and when—at what cost and for what reward? If your strategic objective in, say, five years is to be the dominant news and advertising medium in a five-county area north of the city, what must be done immediately to improve journalistic quality and advertising and circulation operations to achieve that objective?

4. Planning and assigning resources. What financing is required? What is needed in personnel, management talent, time, plant and equipment, newsprint, and other supplies? Then, *commit them.* Management sets the tone, creating a climate for creative development of ideas, products, services—solutions to customers' needs and wants. Anything less than total commitment—hedging on resources, for example—can ruin the venture.

5. Creating the product. The "product" can be a generally improved newspaper, a Sunday magazine, an overhauled business section—or an entirely new venture into, say, free-circulation shoppers or direct mail. New products create great excitement in a newspaper staff. If everything clicks, the rewards can be enormous. Conversely, failure can be costly in money, market share, competitive position, and public image. We will discuss this later in detail, but creating a product requires intimate understanding of the intended market, likely competition, probable short-term costs and revenue, and long-term potential. Dry runs and test marketing will help gauge reader and advertiser reaction to the new product and suggest how it can be priced. Your goal is the highest possible price consistent with other objectives. (If, for example, circulation is your primary objective, a lower subscription price might be warranted, at least initially.) In pricing, know what your own costs will be, what test marketing indicates customers are likely to pay willingly, what competitors charge, and what profit levels are required by your corporate policy. In assessing competitors' prices, study their *costs* as well. How far can they drop their prices to meet your entry into the market?[4]

6. Monitoring, controlling, adjusting. This critical function involves setting standards, evaluating performance, and making changes if standards are not met. For a new product, this means determining, for example, whether quality and cost standards are being upheld. Are profits, market share, and public reception (image) as planned? If not, move boldly and quickly to improve the performance—or scrap the new product. Don't carry a loser if your evaluation shows its prospects are poor. Knowing when to kill a new product can be as important as knowing when to launch one. Stay flexible to meet constant change in external and internal environments. New opportunities open, old products wither, fresh competitors appear. Marketing requires continual examination of all variables in the marketing mix.

In sum, you must employ the "systems concept" of management—identify opportunities, plan to exploit them, set goals for an integrated effort by all departments, and then control and adjust the effort. Those procedures are crucial to your management career as your company and its products evolve through definite life cycles.

THE COMPANY AND THE PRODUCT: THEIR LIFE CYCLES

Companies and their products go through distinct life cycles. From birth to decline, each stage presents its own opportunities and problems. For each, the manager must organize the appropriate marketing response.

---

[4] For a detailed look at product planning, see A. Edward Spitz, ed., *Product Planning*, New York, Aeurbach, 1972.

Company Life Cycles

In the *development* stage, a company is created to win a new market, or an existing company undergoes radical overhaul and is repositioned to gain a new lease on life. Many new companies are being created in weekly newspaper publishing. Most major daily newspaper corporations are being repositioned as communications conglomerates. Times Mirror Corp., the Washington Post Co., The New York Times Co., Tribune Co.—all grew from a single-newspaper base and are thrusting into other related areas such as broadcast, cable, and magazines.[5]

The *maintenance* or *balancing stage* involves retaining existing market position and carefully controlling existing operations rather than launching new major products. Many newspapers are in this stage, "tuning up" their existing product, improving it here and there, but not moving boldly into radically new areas.

In the *growth* stage, a newspaper enters a new market or introduces a new product similar to existing markets or products. For example, a daily newspaper launches a weekly shopper in a nearby town. That is close to the newspaper's main business thrust but still offers new growth potential.

In a *new venture*, a company often takes high risk in stretching for potentially great reward in an entirely new field. Many large, cash-rich newspaper companies are in this stage today, diversifying into entertainment, forest products and newsprint manufacturing, or communications systems such as mobile telephone service.

Product Life Cycles

For most young managers, firsthand experience in life and death cycles will come with individual products. The newspaper's overall strategy will be in place when you hire on, and you won't get your hands on that for some years. But you will probably be directly involved in product strategy, for we are in a highly innovative era in American newspapering and new products are being launched continually.

For any product, the *birth* stage is the expensive one. Creating the product and introducing it to consumers—promoting it to create consumer demand—is costly. And production and distribution must continue even if initial consumer demand is low. Gannett lost hundreds of millions of dollars in launching its national paper, *USA Today*. Reader demand was substantial, but in the early years, advertiser support was insufficient.

The second stage in the product life cycle is *growth*—if introduction is successful. The growth period often yields substantial profits and market share. But the product's success will attract attention, so competitors will probably enter the market. Rapidly growing city magazines offer examples of competitors flocking to share the profit potential that daily and weekly newspapers uncovered in highly affluent areas.

In *maturity*, a product saturates its potential and sales level off. Competitors force costly adjustments or carve out their share of the market, and profits drop. This is not necessarily the end. In fact, innovative marketing can find new customers and adjust the product to give it new thrust. Many long-established newspapers are in this stage, vigorously adding new journalistic dimensions (business news sections, for example, or new "life-style" pages) and thus attracting entirely new categories of readers and advertisers.

The *decline and death* of a product can result from fundamental changes in environment or consumer desires. Changing American lifestyles put afternoon newspapers under heavy pressure and the flight of affluent residents from cities to suburbs helped kill some.

SEGMENTING THE MARKET AND FORECASTING PROFITABILITY

Two important steps remain as you move toward laying down marketing strategy. First, target

---

[5] Company life cycles are further explained by Kelley, op. cit.

Many newspapers include a number of sections designed to appeal to a wide variety of readers and advertisers. (Courtesy of *The Orlando Sentinel*)

the market segment you are after precisely. Most newspapers have more than one product; thus, more than one marketing segment must be selected. Second, forecast whether your endeavor will be profitable.

Segmenting the Market

No newspaper product will succeed if it is distributed indiscriminately. *Target marketing* is required. This means sorting through the broad geographic, demographic, and psychographic characteristics of a newspaper's market for market segments of smaller, more homogeneous groups or areas that can be targeted. Look for a target audience with similar product interests, people willing and able to buy the product and who are also attractive to your advertisers.

For example, an appealing segment could be a particularly wealthy suburb—a *geographic slice* within your larger market—that you plan to serve with a weekly suburban news section and, in turn, offer to advertisers as a vehicle for reaching an especially attractive audience. Or you could target, within your general readership, a *bloc of readers* particularly interested in

money matters—stock, bonds, investments—and serve them with a once-weekly insert on personal investments. The insert, in turn, could be offered to banks, brokerage houses, realtors, and others as an attractive advertising medium.

The trend in newspaper marketing clearly is away from *undifferentiated marketing* (the creation of a single product and marketing mix for an entire market) and toward *differentiated marketing* (or creation of several products, each with its own marketing mix) aimed at small, discrete segments of the larger market.

For generations, undifferentiated marketing succeeded by bringing all market segments into the same journalistic tent and thus offering advertisers mass distribution of their messages at a relatively low per-subscriber cost. Two developments today limit the success of that strategy:

- Numerous competitors—shoppers, direct mail, and others—are segmenting the market and delivering those narrow slices advertisers have come to desire. Shoppers and direct-mail companies can offer a food store, for example, a distribution scheme covering only homes in the immediate vicinity where the store's primary customers live.

- The costs of the mass-circulation newspaper, especially in labor, newsprint, and distribution, are so high that more narrowly based competitors with lower costs have the significant advantage of being able to price their advertising below the newspaper's rates.

Concentrated marketing in a narrow market segment with high profit potential is the strategy for some newspapers today. The *New York Times*, for example, avoids widespread circulation among readers of low income and educational level; rather, it seeks elitist circulation among highly affluent readers valued by advertisers. This will be the strategy for many profit-oriented newspapers in the future. Costs are simply too high to profitably serve mass audiences that are geographically dispersed and demographically and psychographically diverse because advertisers don't want dispersed, diverse audiences.

Forecasting Product Profitability

New-product ideas spring from all corners of a newspaper. Some managers set up new-product committees ("skunk works") to develop ideas. Each should be analyzed for how it fits into overall strategy, whether it would be unique or face stiff competition, whether it would achieve desired goals in image or community perception.

Then, you calculate profitability. New-product failure rates can be extremely high, so proceed cautiously. If profit is your primary goal (as contrasted, for example, with image or community service), drop the project unless a sound profit margin is indicated. Analysis of data on similar products launched in the past provides the most reliable basis for forecasts. A new zoned edition, the fourth launched in two years, will probably perform predictably. Launching entirely new products in new markets can be hazardous due to lack of previous experience.

The measurement most often used in evaluating profitability is *return on investment*. This measures new product performance on the basis of invested resources, as follows:

$$\text{ROI} = \frac{\text{net profit}}{\text{sales}} \times \frac{\text{sales}}{\text{investment}}$$

To illustrate, let us say a newspaper must invest $400,000 in the first year to launch a free-circulation shopper. First-year advertising sales are expected to hit $1 million; net profit, $80,000.

$$\text{ROI} = \frac{\$80,000}{\$1,000,000} \times \frac{\$1,000,000}{\$400,000}$$
$$= 0.08 \times 2.5 = 20\%$$

Though extremely valuable to the manager, ROI cannot be the only tool in new-product evaluation. The new shopper, for example, may have other and more important goals—achieving market share, protecting the paid circulation newspaper against competing shoppers, and so forth.

And in using ROI, managers must decide what return is appropriate. Within the context of its other goals, a shopper returning 20 percent might be projected a winner. If ROI is the only goal, the 20 percent must be evaluated in light of what ROI is offered from similar investments elsewhere. Perhaps you should invest in a television station if you seek higher ROI (although $400,000 probably would not be enough for a down payment).[6]

CONSUMER BEHAVIOR AND YOUR MARKETING STRATEGY

Throughout our discussion of marketing, we have headed toward this question: How will

---

[6] The author found helpful guidance on financial dimensions in R. F. Salmonson, Roger H. Hermanson, and James Don Ewards, *A Survey of Basic Accounting*, Homewood, Ill., Irwin, 1977.

readers and advertisers—the newspaper's consumers—react? Will they buy the new product, support the strategy?

As a manager in a consumer-oriented business, you must know a great deal about consumer behavior. We will discuss, in Chapters 7, 8, and 9, how to analyze the consumer in relation to news, advertising, and circulation. First, however, let's briefly look at *theory* of consumer behavior.[7]

Determining Who Your Consumers Are

The questions are basic but crucial—and often difficult to answer. In auditing readers and nonreaders, we ask: *Who* buys (or doesn't buy) newspapers? *Why* do or don't they? *When* do they buy and "consume"? Precisely *what* do they seek? Note that we refer to "consumers" of newspapers, not simply "buyers." We must get beyond the "buy" decision into how and why newspapers—or parts of them—are consumed or used and by how many people other than the buyer. Your editors want to know so they can tailor the product; advertisers want to know so they can position their ads.

In auditing advertisers as consumers, managers ask the same questions—who, why, where, when, and what? The newspaper's life blood, its ad revenue, is at stake.

Many behavioral scientists agree that true understanding of consumer behavior lies in a knowledge of basic human needs and perceptions plus the environmental influences that act on them. Needs were discussed in Chapter 5; they include the *physiological* or primary needs for food, shelter, clothing; *safety* needs, or the need for security; the *social* need to belong;

esteem needs, or the desire for status; *self-actualization* needs, involving the realization of one's full potential. As an example of how important it is to understand human needs, let's match them with newspaper promotional slogans:

- Check your local newspaper for food store ads and where to rent an apartment; both are primary *physiological* needs.

- Keep up on the news and don't be surprised by what happens in the world around you; its events often reflect *safety* needs, or the wish for security.

- Join your friends—fulfill your *social* need to belong—by reading the sports pages daily; read the society pages and join the social elite.

- Gain *status* by reading the *New York Times;* all the intelligent, wealthy people in town do.

- *Realize your potential* in the business world by reading the *Wall Street Journal;* all successful business people do.

Note that the reality of needs is one thing; perceptions of them are quite another. For example, a newspaper in reality is a medium of news, information, and advertising. But what it can really do for readers and advertisers is perceived through their eyes, not those of editors and publishers. Thus, to understand consumer behavior you must first understand consumers' perceptions—what they *want* to believe—about the newspaper. We'll discuss details in the next chapter, but editors obviously must understand not only how their product covers the news but also how that coverage is perceived by readers.

Like all human conduct, consumer behavior can be either rational or emotional. The rational approach involves a reasoned, deliberate evaluation of, for example, the newspaper's usefulness—whether it is reliable and worth its price.

[7] For further reading in the marketing implications of consumer behavior, see Philip Kotler, *Marketing Management*, Englewood Cliffs, N.J., Prentice-Hall, 1980; Lipson and Darling, op. cit., and Kurtz and Boone, op. cit. Also see Wroe Alderson and Michael H. Halbert, *Men, Motives and Markets*, Englewood Cliffs, N.J., Prentice-Hall, 1968. For a detailed treatment of the "hierarchy of needs" concept, see Abraham H. Maslow, *Motivation and Personality*, New York, Harper & Row, 1954.

Emotional evaluation can lead to hardened attitudes: "The paper is no good and I'll not buy it regardless of the improvements those editors try to make." Many influences tug and pull at consumers making such judgments.

Environmental Influences on Behavior

Environmental factors strongly influence consumer behavior toward your newspaper. For example, family or other *social* groups and the individual's *status* within a group influence behavior. An individual has a *role* within a group, and that signals what behavior is expected.

Behavioral scientists find individuals identifying with a *reference group* and conforming to the group's behavioral standards; they are also influenced by *social class* (family background, residential area, source of income, and so forth). The *Boston Globe, Chicago Tribune, Los Angeles Times,* and other "establishment" papers have a strong appeal to wealthy, socially powerful readers; readers of the *Bloomington (Ill.) Daily Pantagraph* tell how their fathers and grandfathers read the paper, too. Newspapers large and small can appeal to reference groups or social classes, and simple readership surveys will help to identify them.

Equally important but harder to identify are changes under way in broader *cultural influences* and the effect they have on newspaper operations. For example, dramatic changes are under way in the American family, in its role and the way it is structured. Change is also under way in social mobility, pace of living, attitudes toward work and leisure time, and other values and ideas. For example, one researcher, Philip Kotler, notes that the attitudes of many Americans are changing from self-reliance to reliance on government, from respect for hard work to the search for an easy life. The implications are obvious for, say, a newspaper editor trying to put together an appealing news product, a circulation executive trying to create promotion for a subscription campaign, or an advertising executive trying to formulate winning sales promotion themes.[8]

Let's check how the consumer, influenced by such changing values, makes decisions, and how you, as a newspaper manager, must influence the outcome.

Consumer Decisions and How to Influence Them

Consumers move through identifiable steps in their decision making, and newspaper marketing is aimed at influencing each step.

First, the consumer becomes aware of a need or problem. Perhaps, for example, the consumer recognizes that existing information sources—other newspapers, TV, radio—are inadequate, or an advertiser realizes the ad medium being used isn't doing the job. Your marketing mission is to understand the other media's weaknesses and position your newspaper, in reality and consumer perception, as a viable alternative. Your newspaper's content and promotional themes, then, would emphasize "all the news—not just bits and pieces offered by TV"; you would sell advertisers on the idea that your paper gets into attractive households and, unlike a competing shopper, delivers results.

Second, the consumer takes action, gathering information on what could be done about the need or problem. Here, your promotion must be strong and visible, making every potential reader aware that your news coverage is superior, making certain every nonadvertiser has detailed information on your newspaper's strengths in hand.

Third, the consumer appraises alternative solutions. Does your newspaper cover local news better than TV or the other papers available? At this point, your product must prove itself; your local coverage must indeed be superior.

Fourth, the decision is made. The consumer

---

[8] Kotler, op. cit.

buys. Perhaps an introductory offer—six months at a reduced subscription rate—will help swing the decision your way.

Fifth, there is ongoing appraisal of the choice. Now that your paper has been read for six months, is it still superior to TV or that other paper? In other words, once you have the readers, you must keep them, with coverage that meets their continuing needs.

The consumer may not be aware of a need that is dormant and can be roused only by stimulation. We'll discuss this in Chapter 10, "Newspaper Image and Promotion"; for now, suffice it to say that much of your marketing effort must be aimed at stimulating consumers to recognize that they need your newspaper and must start that five-step process toward becoming your loyal readers.

HOW TO AUDIT THE MARKETING EFFORT

As in all your managerial responsibilities, it is essential that you evaluate your performance in marketing. Measure effectiveness in these areas:

Corporate tone. Has the newspaper, from executive staff to employee ranks, accepted the marketing concept? Is the idea of "consumer first" truly motivating each department? Is the newsroom carefully researching reader needs and wants, then constructing a news package accordingly? Or are editors still putting out what *they* think is important, blind to reader desires? Do the advertising and circulation departments launch forth aggressively each day to satisfy consumer needs, or are they simply out there trying to sell more space or more subscriptions?

People performance. Use budget performance and management by objectives as evaluation tools. Concepts are fine; but without superior performance by each individual, they will not work.

Management's performance. And that includes yours. Have you pitched in to help, made resources (people, financing, and time) available? Go back over the basic marketing steps: organizing the marketing structure, analyzing the market, setting goals, planning and assigning resources, creating the product, monitoring and controlling, adjusting with flexibility. Have you assisted at every step?

Bottom-line results. The marketing effort must deliver results. There must be measurable progress in sales, profit, market share, community image. What precisely has been accomplished? There also must be long-term advantage. Has there been improvement in formulating strategic objectives, planning, and steps taken to achieve them?

The adjustment phase. You won't be pleased with answers to all those questions. Completely satisfactory performance would be a miracle. So you now enter the next phase of your management responsibility—adjustment. This will involve primarily five departments: news, advertising, circulation, production and promotion, and tuning each to respond properly to the demands of the newspaper's overall marketing strategy.

To operations in the first of these, news, we shall turn in the following chapter.

SUMMARY

Although it is far behind many other industries, the newspaper industry is moving vigorously into the marketing concept.

The next generation of managers must be adept at organizing systems and motivating people to orient newspaper operations toward the wants and needs of readers and advertisers.

For generations, newspapers as a business were production-oriented, not consumer-oriented. But thinking changed with the entry of new competitors for readers and advertising dollars—as well as growing awareness of newspapers' general inability to achieve household penetration at the levels demanded by advertisers. However, newspapers' strengths also have opened new opportunities that marketing efforts can exploit.

Marketing theory requires the total commitment of the entire company to satisfying consumer needs. The marketing mix creates a product, prices it, distributes it, and promotes it.

The marketing process includes organizing the marketing structure, analyzing the market, setting goals, planning and assigning resources, creating the product, monitoring and controlling performance, and adjusting as internal and external variables change.

An understanding of consumer behavior is essential for any newspaper manager. This implies a grasp of consumer *needs* that the newspaper can meet and consumer *perceptions* of how well it meets them.

Throughout runs one theme: fundamental changes are under way in the newspaper's environment and one aim of marketing is adjusting to them.

The manager must audit the marketing effort, evaluate its results, and adjust accordingly. The manager must evaluate the entire organization's performance—and his or her own, too.

RECOMMENDED READING

The International Newspaper Advertising and Marketing Executives' Association, Box 17210, Dulles International Airport, Washington, DC 20041, publishes the monthly *INAME News*, an excellent rundown on current developments in newspaper marketing. In addition to sources listed in the preceding footnotes, see Stewart Henry Rewoldt, James Dacon Scott, and Martin Warshaw, *Introduction to Marketing Management*, Homewood, Ill., Irwin, 1981.

CHAPTER SEVEN | News

We have dealt with theories of management, planning, motivation of employees, marketing, and consumer behavior. As a manager, you must turn theory into efficient daily operating techniques in five important areas: news, circulation, advertising, production, and promotion.

Let's start our study of how to do this with news, because in a very real sense news is the soul of a newspaper, its historic rationale. The newspaper's unique status in our society flows from its role in collecting and disseminating the news and information needed to keep our democracy viable.

From the business perspective, a newspaper's financial foundations rest on news—the quantity and quality of news sold to readers who, in turn, are sold to advertisers. If you think this suggests that the marketing concept be applied to the news department, you are correct. Marketing has arrived in the news department, as in other departments.

Regardless of where in newspaper operations your career starts and whatever your future responsibilities may be, an understanding of the news process is crucial to your success. You need not be a great reporter or editor to be a newspaper manager; you *do* need to understand news and how men and women who dedicate their careers to it make the news process work.

In this chapter, we will deal with designing the news organization, researching and planning news content, and managing newsroom resources. We will conclude with hints on monitoring and controlling newsroom performance.

Let's first look at some examples of newspapers that allowed their news content get off track, in a marketing sense, and for that paid the extreme penalty.

HOW NOT TO DO IT

The reading public regards substantive news and information—in volume and detail, quality, topicality, and pertinence—as the core of a newspaper's strength and appeal. That signal comes clearly from marketing research into reader habits. It shows that newspapers *should* be entertaining and colorful, *should* be esthetically pleasing, but *must* be newsy and informative. Nothing underlines this better than recent newspaper experience.

In its death throes, the *Cleveland Press* was fundamentally weak in news content and tried to camouflage that with racy layout and handsomely packaged sections. The *Press* blossomed, splashing color on its front pages. The *Press*, its critics say, became a colorful "daily comic book." But bright hues did not disguise the lack of basic news-gathering resources. The *Press* died in 1982.

In Minneapolis, Cowles Media Co. experimented, sometimes wildly, for five years to save its afternoon *Star*, dropping standard hard-news coverage of the city council's activities, speeches, and news conferences and, instead, substituting magazine-style feature "takeouts" that sometimes ran to many thousands of words. Readers seeking *news* gradually turned away from the *Star*; even loyal readers had not much to give up when it folded in 1982.

Newspapers die for various complicated reasons, and "stunting" with layouts and features was not the cause of death for the *Press* or *Star*. Rather, it was a symptom of frantic last-minute efforts to find a new lease on life. But both papers failed to do the basic job of a newspaper: to inform.

It is not enough, however, simply to produce a newsy, informative newspaper. The *Washington Star* was full of strong reporting and editing right up to its death; so was the *Philadelphia Bulletin* in its decades of gradual decline. The weekly *Georgia Gazette* in Savannah died in 1984, the year it won a Pulitzer Prize. A newspaper, even one that is strong

journalistically, must be marketed properly if it is to succeed.

THE MARKETING CONCEPT IN NEWS

Journalistic excellence must be fashioned within an overall marketing scheme to fulfill reader needs. Marketing must exploit superior news coverage by obtaining appropriate reward—advertising and circulation revenue—for the newspaper's investment. Content must do more than discharge the newspaper's historic responsibility to cover the news and inform the public; it must do more than meet the professional standards of editors and publishers. It must also meet standards set by the marketplace to ensure the newspaper's commercial viability.

Robert Marbut, president of Harte-Hanks, is a leading proponent of sophisticated marketing in newsrooms. He says:

> The need for information is alive and well and strong and appetites for information are growing. But we have to go beyond the basics. The ball game is different than it used to be. We can't define our business in terms of the products we produce; it has to be in terms of the needs we meet. Other media are seeking to meet the same needs—and we have to do it better.[1]

Some argue that marketing in news reduces the newspaper business to something akin to marketing soap—searching for a market opening, then designing a product with a special aroma to fit it—when, say these critics, newspapers should react to *news*, not passing whims of readers, and should let professional editors design news packages that in their eyes cover the news validly.

This argument need never occur. First,

---

[1] "Publishers Discuss Improvements in Marketing, Management, Quality," *Southern Newspaper Publishers' Association Bulletin*, July 13, 1983.

editors and publishers sometimes lose touch with readers and need modern marketing methods and surveys to regain contact. Second, newspaper editors need not let marketing experts take over the newsroom. Marketing technique is one tool, old-fashioned journalistic instinct and method another.

Let's look at two newspapers using that combination in a bitter competitive battle. Note throughout that news is at the tip of the marketing spear for both.

The Importance of News Superiority

Predictably, it was *Time* magazine that dubbed it "Shootout in the Big D," triggering a spasm of western analogy on copy desks across the country. "Shootout at the Lone Star Corral," headlined the *Washington Journalism Review*. "Texas-style Shootout at the Dallas Corral," said *Editor & Publisher Magazine*.[2]

The "shootout" was a rip-roaring fight in Dallas, one of few head-on newspaper confrontations of such intensity anywhere in the United States and, without doubt, the liveliest. The fight was instructive for aspiring managers because it involved two wealthy, marketing-oriented communications companies that assign high priority to news quality in the fight for market supremacy.

On one side of the corral was the *Dallas Morning News*, flagship of A. H. Belo Corp., a communications conglomerate (twenty-seventh largest in the country with $385 million revenue in 1985) owned mainly by Texas families. On the other was the *Dallas Times Herald*, owned by Times Mirror Corp., the nation's fifth-largest media company ($2.9 billion revenue in 1985) with headquarters in Los Angeles. The shooting was over the rich Dallas market, second nationwide only to Houston in growth in the late 1970s and early 1980s.

Times Mirror acquired the *Times Herald* in 1970 (for $91 million) and threw into the fight much executive talent and money, lots of money. In just five years, 1975–80, the paper's newsroom budget was increased 157 percent. In one six-year period, all but about 50 of 203 news staffers were replaced.[3]

Belo Corp. did not react until 1980 and then brought in, at age twenty-nine, Robert Decherd, son of a former Belo chairman, as executive vice president (and, later, as president). One of his first moves was raiding the Associated Press, hiring Burl Osborne, its managing editor, then forty-three, as executive editor (and later as president of the newspaper).

The battle was fought as classic newspaper battles should be fought—over circulation and advertising turf, with superior news coverage the primary marketing weapon. Both newspapers spent heavily to hire more and better staff talent, open bureaus, assign correspondents to far-off places, launch new sections. Both scrambled for features.

Why all the fuss? Both papers, after all, were profitable; why not relax, minimize costs and maximize profits? Well, newspaper marketing experts suspected that even rich Dallas, like most U.S. cities, would one day support only one vigorous metro daily. Osborne says:

> I believe the economy of the Dallas market can support two metropolitan dailies for a long time. Eventually, though, the economy will mature and no longer will have the rapid growth rates that have characterized the past two decades. When that might happen is hard to say. . . . I do wonder, though, whether the basic character of the business is any different here than in Philadelphia or Washington or Cleveland [where metro papers failed]. An interesting question to explore is whether, in fact, metropolitan newspapers are natural monopolies and that, left in a free market, will eliminate all but one by natural selection. Further, I wonder if those conditions exist in

---

[2] *Time*, Sept. 7, 1981, p. 58; *Washington Journalism Review*, April 1982, p. 25; *Editor & Publisher*, April 24, 1982, p. 42.

[3] *Time*, ibid.

Dallas as elsewhere, and are merely masked by the rapid growth of the economy.

I also question whether it is possible for two newspapers to compete vigorously and remain in equilibrium at more or less parity. I think one will emerge as dominant and the other as clearly in a second position. I don't think that means No. 2 must go out of business but rather that it will have to pick its market segment and concentrate on it, forgetting about trying to achieve overall superiority. . . .[4]

To the Dallas combatants, then, long-term stakes were survival, no less, and success could be achieved only through the production of a superior news product that would increase circulation and advertising. Simply put, *News* executives did a better job of that than did their *Times Herald* counterparts and, importantly, they marketed their product more shrewdly in consonance with Dallas and its times. By 1986, the *News* had 390,275 daily circulation, 521,727 on Sunday—and leads of 145,646 and 173,643, respectively, over the *Times Herald*. The *Times Herald's* ad share dropped to 42.7 percent and Times Mirror, which doesn't lose many fights, sold out (for $110 million) and left town, licked.

For all newspapers—metro dailies, small dailies, country weeklies—the survival imperatives are the same. Readers desired by advertisers will be won from competitors only with superior news content.

We will discuss how to create a winning news organization capable of accomplishing that. But first we must look at two major changes under way in the newspaper industry that affect news strategy. They are rapid growth of suburban journalism and deepening difficulties for afternoon papers.

CHANGING TIMES

The *Atlanta Journal* and *Atlanta Constitution* are two grand old southern newspapers that once were regional powers (the *Journal* still

claims it "Covers Dixie Like the Dew"). The two dominated Atlanta journalism without challenge and extended their influence throughout Georgia.

Then in the 1980s came what might be called the "Second Battle of Atlanta." Here is the background: *Journal* and *Constitution* legions had achieved considerable success in fighting distant circulation wars. By 1964, circulation had penetrated 5 percent or more of households in 142 of Georgia's 159 counties. It was 30 percent or more in 43 counties, some 170 miles from Atlanta. Then came forced withdrawal as distant circulation became increasingly unattractive to Atlanta advertisers and thus too expensive to maintain. By 1979, 5 percent or more penetration was holding in only 103 counties; it was 30 percent or more in just 11 counties, all within 40 miles of Atlanta.[5]

Meanwhile, back home, knocking on Atlanta's suburban gates, were invaders of an entirely new competitive force. They were personified by Otis Brumby, heir to his family's *Marietta Daily Journal* (an afternoon paper of 27,590 paid circulation 15 miles northwest of Atlanta) and a man with new visions of publishing success. Brumby launched Neighbor Newspapers in the mid-1960s and now has seventeen small free-circulation weekly papers ringing Atlanta. (See Table 7.1.) They reach 416,403 metro area households each week. (Figure 7.1 shows their distribution.) Revenue is high—reportedly $20 million in 1983—and so is profit.[6]

Brumby's journalistic formula is classic for small suburban papers: concentrate on limited local news and leave to others the "big picture" role—and expense—of covering world, nation, and state. His advertising strategy: do what advertisers want: dedicate up to 75 percent of total content to ads (the post office maximum for preferential mailing rates) and expand dis-

[4] Burl Osborne, letter to author, April 11, 1983.

[5] Judith F. Russell and William H. Berentsen, "Urban Regions in Georgia: 1964–1979," *Southeastern Geographer*, November 1981, p. 84.
[6] Donna Ellingson, "Suburban Newspapers Challenge Leaders," *Atlanta Business Chronicle*, Nov. 28, 1983, p. 7.

Table 7.1   Neighbor Newspapers

NNI Unit No.	Market	Neighbor Newspapers in Market Buy	Circulation
1	Marietta-Cobb County	The Marietta Daily Journal Sunday	27,590
2	North Cobb	The Kennesaw Neighbor The Acworth Neighbor The South Cherokee Neighbor	26,626
3	East Cobb	The East Cobb Neighbor	32,468
4	Smyrna	The Smyrna Neighbor	10,508
5	South Cobb	The Mableton Neighbor The Austell Neighbor The Powder Springs Neighbor	17,222
6	Douglas	The Douglas Neighbor	18,929
7	Paulding	The Paulding Neighbor	9,382
8	North DeKalb	The Dunwoody-DeKalb Neighbor The Chamblee-DeKalb Neighbor The Doraville-DeKalb Neighbor	24,589
9	Mid DeKalb	The Decatur-DeKalb Neighbor The Tucker-DeKalb Neighbor Stone Mountain-DeKalb Neighbor	45,392
10	South DeKalb	The South DeKalb Neighbor	28,281
11	Rockdale	The Rockdale Neighbor	11,621
12	North Fulton	The Roswell Neighbor The Alpharetta Neighbor	24,584
13	Northside/Atlanta Sandy Springs	The Northside Neighbor The Sandy Springs Neighbor The Vinings Neighbor	23,405
14	South Fulton	The South Fulton Neighbor	24,385
15	Clayton	The Clayton Neighbor	39,883
16	Fayette	The Fayette Neighbor	14,850
17	Henry	The Henry Neighbor	18,076
18	Bartow	The Bartow Neighbor	18,612
19	Suburban Atlanta	All Neighbor Newspapers	416,403

Reprinted with permission of Neighbor Newspapers, Inc.

tribution via mail to any areas desired. Ad rates are based on all 416,403 circulation or as little as 9,382 in selected neighborhoods. Advertisers get great marketing flexibility; Brumby gets ad revenue the Atlanta metros want.

The Neighbor papers return higher profit ratios than many paid-circulation papers (with their expense of broad news coverage) and are patently advertising vehicles, not quality newspapers. Yet, Brumby's editors claim a valid journalistic role. Executive Editor Bobby Nesbitt says, "We don't just throw a shopper at them. These papers give people a focus and a reason to feel good about where they live."[7]

---

[7] Ibid.

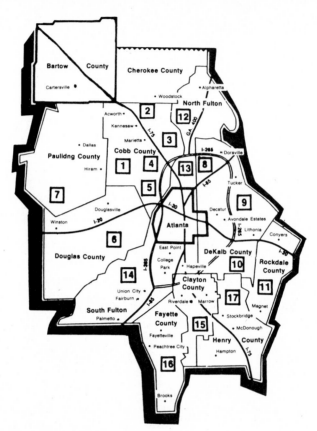

Figure 7.1 The Suburban Net of Neighbor Newspapers
Reprinted by permission of Neighbor Newspapers, Inc.

Completing the tight ring around Atlanta are other paid-circulation and free weeklies and dailies. One, the *Gwinnett Daily News*, exemplifies the rapid growth of small suburban papers. The *Daily News* went from weekly to six-day publication in 1965; by 1982, it was rated the fastest-growing U.S. daily by the Audit Bureau of Circulations. In 1983, it was publishing seven days weekly and had 25,800 paid circulation—over 30,000 in 1986. The *Daily News* also distributes a total market coverage (TMC) shopper to 37,000 nonsubscriber households; it claims its paid paper plus shopper reach 96 percent of its county's single-family homes each week.[8] Vigorous competition of that caliber

would trouble any metro. It was particularly difficult for *Journal* and *Constitution* strategists attempting to stabilize two papers that, though profitable, saw their long-range projections moving in the wrong direction—down. The afternoon *Journal's* circulation plummeted from 259,000 in 1962 to 182,000 in 1982—a 29.7 percent drop—before *Journal* executives stopped and then reversed the trend. The morning *Constitution* was down, though not so severely. (By 1986, it was at 228,000 and climbing; the combined Sunday paper had a healthy 570,000 circulation.)

Across the country, the pattern repeats: tight rings of suburban publications sprout in rich markets literally created anew in the 1960s and 1970s, as affluent residents fled from major

---

[8] Ibid.

cities. Suburban population nationwide grew 17.4 percent in the 1970s. By 1980, 44.5 percent of all Americans lived in suburbs—compared with 30.2 percent in central cities, 25.3 percent in rural areas.

It is that population shift which creates major news coverage problems for metros—and growth opportunities for suburban papers. Metros must cover not only their inner cities but also numerous small communities proliferating sometimes on a 360-degree perimeter around the city. In many of those communities, meanwhile, weeklies or small community dailies grow rapidly, boosted by new technology that simplifies and holds relatively low the cost of starting up a new paper. Suburban Newspapers of America (SNA), a trade organization of weeklies, free-circulation papers, and some dailies calculates that in the early 1980s, some 1,700 suburban publications were churning out a combined circulation of almost 22 million, up nearly 90 percent in ten years. And, in those ten years, SNA says, at least one-third of its weekly members moved up to daily or multiweekly schedules.[9]

Changing membership in ANPA illustrates the trend: In the 1970s, ANPA was a large-paper-oriented association of about 1,000 members. By 1986, membership was 1,393—and 78 percent had under 50,000 circulation; 22 were weeklies.

Small-paper growth is rapid especially in fertile Sun Belt suburban markets, around major cities that lost affluent residents 1960–80 due to inner-core deterioration and social upheaval. In 1960, for example, 18 suburban publishers ringed Miami with combined circulation of 152,000 paid and 5,000 free. By 1981, 37 publishers operated in those suburbs, with 173,000 paid circulation and 826,000 free. And those suburban markets now have highly attractive demographics formerly associated with Miami proper. In the same twenty years, the *Miami Herald*

and *Miami News*, based in the changing inner city and challenged by stern competition outside it, increased their combined circulation *just 14,000*, to 549,000 from 535,000.[10]

In St. Louis, two suburban groups of free-distribution papers played major roles in forcing Newhouse Newspapers to sell its profitless *St. Louis Globe-Democrat* (which later owners closed in 1986.) The *Globe-Democrat*, a morning paper, suffered many afflictions including union difficulties, but its biggest challenge was those suburbans—ten free papers published by St. Louis Suburban Newspapers, Inc., and twenty-three distributed by Donnelly Publications. (Both groups were sold to Ingersoll Publications Co., in 1984.) The thirty-three distributed 820,000 copies weekly and sold advertising in attractive combination packages permitting clients to take all or any of that 820,000.

New opportunities are opening, then, for the next generation of newspaper managers in expanding suburban areas. It is the growth area of American journalism.

How to Win in the Suburbs

Many suburban publications enjoy distinct advantages over their metro neighbors. If you enter suburban journalism, these are among steps you can take to win:

- Because each suburban audience tends to be socially and economically homogenous, you must ensure fine tuning of your editorial product and marketing strategy. It is counterproductive for a suburban paper to fashion, as many metros do, broad-based news products designed for audiences widely varying in educational background and interests. Suburbs tend to attract people of similar life-styles; you must be certain to meet their precise news needs.

- Make sure that your advertising rate struc-

[9] Suburban Newspapers of America, Chicago.

[10] Bruce E. Thorp, "Key to Success? Stay Local," *Advertising Age*, Sept. 29, 1982, p. 36.

tures are competitive, particularly with those offered by metros for zoned editions or part-run advertising. Lower operating costs permit many suburban papers to set rates substantially below the metros' and still enjoy profit ratios higher than the metros'. Lower costs are possible because relatively inexpensive, labor-saving technology is available for small papers, and lack of unions permits its widespread introduction without a costly "buyout" of displaced staff.

• As a suburban manager you must structure your operations to take full advantage of relatively simple distribution. Suburban

Home delivery is easier and cheaper for suburban newspapers than for larger, metropolitan papers. (Dan Chidester/The Image Works)

papers are already located in the rich areas that metros must reach via traffic-clogged highways. Short hauls cut gasoline costs, so home delivery is easier and cheaper for suburban papers. Use this competitive edge decisively to achieve the home delivery so highly attractive to advertisers. U. S. Suburban Press, Inc., representing more than 1,100 suburban dailies or weeklies, estimates that 90 percent are home-delivered.

• Your operation must be structured to exploit the enormous advantages that time/distance factors give suburban papers. Many suburban afternoon papers, for example, can hold for a press run of, say, 1 P.M. and deliver fresh, same-day news to front porches by 4 P.M. Distant afternoon metros are forced into early press runs, sometimes 8 A.M. to 9 A.M., to enable trucks to get papers to the suburbs for 4 P.M. delivery. That means suburban readers of an afternoon metro often see, at 4 P. M., a warmed-over rehash of last night's news. The advantage this gives suburban papers must be highlighted in both your news operations and sales promotion. Suburban morning papers have similar time/distance advantages over metros. They can hold press runs to well past midnight, then deliver night sports scores and other late-breaking news to breakfast tables. Distant morning metros must go to press early, often at midevening, and they, like afternoon metros, often arrive with outdated news content.

• As a suburban manager you must, above all, focus sharply on local news, for neither the neighboring metro nor evening TV can match you in quantity and quality. Many successful suburban papers treat news from world, nation, and state lightly, concentrating instead on local schools, the village council, Little League baseball. For householders concerned with their immediate surroundings, your suburban paper must be a necessity, not simply nice to have.

However, metros have strengths, too, and if you enter management of a large city daily, there are steps you can take to fight suburban papers.

How Metros Can Counterattack

Metros, if managed wisely, can meet suburban competition with confidence. As a metro manager, you should:

- Deploy your paper's relatively massive resources in all sectors—news, advertising, promotion, circulation—to put suburban papers under heavy pressure. Through zoned editions, metros can focus on narrow geographic or demographic market slices and offer detailed local news plus somewhat lower ad rates.

- Offer broad news coverage with world, national, regional, and state dimensions, appealing to well-educated, cosmopolitan suburban readers for whom the local paper's offerings of Little League baseball and church socials are not enough.

- Feature high-quality reporting and writing that can make suburban papers look amateurish by comparison. Special-interest sections—science, art, business—are particularly strong showcases in which a metro can display reporting depth.

- Strike into suburban markets with Sunday papers, those bulky, colorful and often highly profitable papers that give many metros strong competitive advantages. Few suburban papers, with their small staffs and limited budgets, can publish matching Sunday papers, with panoramic news coverage, entertainment sections, and advertising.

- Fully use the increasingly effective mechanical and distribution flexibility that is now available to metros for the purpose of zoning news and ad content. Satellite production plants in suburbs and morning publication (permitting predawn distribution over empty streets) give metros opportunities to compete in suburbs. The *Oklahoma City Oklahoman and Times* leapfrogs outside its core city to a $50 million production facility 8 miles from the downtown news, advertising, and circulation offices. This puts small papers throughout the state under heavy pressure as the morning *Oklahoman* prints a much later—and thus more journalistically valid—edition for distant regions of Oklahoma. Following affluent readers to small towns around Dallas is the *Dallas Morning News* strategy with its $57 million satellite plant in Plano, a rapidly growing suburban town.

Many metros possess managerial expertise in news, advertising, and circulation that small papers cannot match. It was managerial genius that devised the *New York Times's* strategy: skim off the most attractive readers demographically, in the prime city market, but then leapfrog over a constricting ring of small suburban papers (nineteen dailies are published within 40 miles of New York City) and achieve national newspaper status with satellite printing plants coast to coast. Although it publishes *some* suburban coverage, the *New York Times* chooses not to compete head-on against vigorous dailies and weeklies in Long Island, Connecticut, and New Jersey. Rather, the *Times* maintains perhaps the finest news-gathering staff in American journalism, turns it loose on substantive matters important to an intellectual (and economic) elite, and uses new technology to reach across the nation. Brilliant newsroom management led the *Philadelphia Inquirer* attack against the then-dominant *Philadelphia Bulletin* and a near army of local dailies and weeklies in Greater Philadelphia (by some counts, two hundred print competitors were out there). Eugene L. Roberts, *Inquirer* executive editor, first strengthened his paper as a metro daily, then as the region's best package of international, national, and state news. Finally, he added *suburban* news. "The *Inquirer* can't do everything the local papers do but distinguishes itself by running stories on trends relating to all the suburbs," he says.[11] That includes stories on taxation, education, street crime—news of pertinence in all Philadelphia suburbs. Roberts says the *Inquirer* approaches readers on many levels, claiming it has the best general news, best TV and movie listings, "and on top of that you don't neglect their high school basketball team."[12]

The *Atlanta Journal* and *Constitution* fight suburban competitors with detailed local news plus Total Market Coverage. *Journal* and *Constitution* vehicles:

- *The "extras,"* four tabloid weekly papers heavy with local news and zoned eight ways for ads. Extras are inserted in Thursday's *Journal* and *Constitution* for the inner city and for three county areas where suburban papers are most vigorous.

- *ZAP* (zone-area preprints), permitting advertisers to target any or all of twenty-nine zones for inserts on Sundays or in Wednesday's *Journal* and Thursday's *Constitution*.

- *REACH*, which delivers preprinted newspaper supplements to nonsubscribers via shared mail in zip code areas with as few as 5,000 or as many as 400,000 households.

Second-Layer Growth in the Suburbs

Some suburban markets mature so richly that their local papers grow into highly profitable, metro-like giants. Long Island's *Newsday*, once the epitome of the small suburban daily, has over 603,000 circulation (666,000 on Sundays) and is a world-class paper journalistically. In 1984, *Newsday*, owned by Times Mirror of Los Angeles, opened a bureau with forty-five reporters in midtown Manhattan and launched a

"New York *Newsday*" to gain subscribers in New York itself. This reversed the usual strategy of a metro attacking into the suburbs.

On the other side of Manhattan, in New Jersey's rich, suburban Bergen County ($39,664 average household income in 1986), the Hackensack *Record*, also once a small suburban paper, has 150,000 daily and 219,000 Sunday circulation. Like *Newsday*, it is a newspaper complete in all dimensions: international, national, and state news as well as local. In journalistic quality and sheer bulk, these "suburbans" match most metros and surpass many.

As suburban dailies mature to *Record* or *Newsday* levels, *they* come under attack by yet another layer of suburban publications tucked tightly beneath their shadow. As the *Records* and *Newsdays* broaden their news horizons to include Kabul and Katmandu, small local weeklies—of free or paid circulation—spring up to serve the narrow local news demands of small communities. For example, nine separate weekly organizations with about 200,000 total circulation publish in Bergen County, all around the *Record*.

A Fight Develops over Syndicates

One bitter struggle between metro and small suburban papers is over syndicated features and news services. No matter which side you are on as a manager, metro or suburban, you will probably be involved in it.

For generations, syndicates and, more recently, supplemental news agencies granted metro papers exclusivity over vast territories for desirable comics, features, columns, and services. Because they paid high rates, metro editors could tie up many leading features even if they did not publish them. A landmark breakthrough came with a 1976 antitrust case involving the *Boston Globe* in which the U.S. Justice Department pressed for restricting exclusivity to the city of publication. Three major syndicates—Chicago Tribune-New York News Syndicate, Field Enterprises, and King Features—

[11] C. David Rambo, "Suburban vs. Metros: Newspaper Civil War," *presstime*, August 1982, p. 38.
[12] Ibid.

agreed not to grant exclusivity to a central-city paper in any county where its household penetration was less than 20 percent.

The fight erupted again when the *Oakland (Calif.) Tribune* sued the *San Francisco Chronicle* and *San Francisco Examiner* on charges that they had violated the Sherman Anti-Trust Act by illegally holding exclusive rights to 115 syndicated features in the San Francisco Bay area. The suit charged that the metros had "obtained a stranglehold on syndicated features" by insisting on exclusive contracts for columnists such as George Will, William F. Buckley, James J. Kilpatrick, and Joseph Kraft plus comics such as "Peanuts," "Doonesbury," and "Blondie." *Tribune* publisher Robert Maynard says he did not sue syndicates because they demonstrated support for his position that the *Chronicle* and *Examiner* prevented his paper from giving its readers fully balanced editorial views and from publishing nationally recognized features.[13]

Syndicates and supplemental news agencies themselves see greater profit if they can serve small suburban papers and unhook from the exclusive agreements they granted in the heyday of metro journalism. Supplementals that once granted even statewide rights to single newspapers now try to limit exclusivity to a 25-mile radius from city of publication.

Let's turn now to another major change under way that has dramatic impact on newsroom strategy.

The Darkening Future of Afternoon Papers

It was in the columns of his own newspaper that Editor Steven Isaacs of Cowles Media's afternoon *Minneapolis Star* went public to complain that there had been a "change of society's timing" and that Americans no longer want an afternoon newspaper. At least, they did not want his.

---

[13] William Brand, "S. F. Dailies Sued Over Syndicated Feature Exclusivity," *Editor & Publisher*, Dec. 31, 1983, p. 25.

Isaacs, writing on March 25, 1982, explained why the *Star* would disappear a few days later as an independent newspaper and be merged with its morning sister, the 235,000-circulation *Tribune*. At the time, 170,000 Minnesotans were paying to receive the afternoon paper. Conservatively figuring two readers per copy sold (it's as high as 2.7 in some cities), perhaps 340,000 people were reading the *Star*, and yet, here was Isaacs publicly acknowledging that it could not market itself profitably. It is a revealing case study of afternoon newspapers and their role in American journalism.

Had "society's timing" changed to doom the *Star?* Or, was management error to blame? Both arguments are made in and outside Cowles Media's management suite. Some newspaper managers, stunned by deaths of once-great afternoon papers, accept Isaacs's catchy phrase as conventional wisdom, agreeing that whatever their market strength or competitive positions, however skilled their managers, afternoon papers are a dying breed. Others are not so certain about how to interpret what is happening. For example, morning newspaper circulation in 1985 led afternoon circulation 36.3 million to 26.4 million. But does that mean the momentum is shifting universally to morning papers because of some inherent weakness in afternoon publishing? Or, is it explained in part by the deaths of a few large-circulation PM papers that may have died for reasons not all related to the hour at which they arrived on doorsteps? Clearly, figures are distorted by the concurrent and atypical growth of a few morning papers such as *USA Today* and the *Wall Street Journal*. Those two alone add over 3 million circulation to morning figures. Unclear also is the meaning of changes in the numbers of afternoon and morning dailies. Morning dailies increased by 160 or 49.6 percent 1950–85; afternoon papers decreased by 230 or 15.8 percent. Still, afternoon papers outnumber morning papers by a wide margin—1,220 to 482. (In 1985; there were twenty-six all-day papers publishing both morning and afternoon editions.) Cast against traumatic change in other U.S. industries after 1950—the steel industry, for example—the decrease in PM papers looks small. Certainly, it seems relatively minor considering that afternoon papers take the brunt of competition from TV, which grew from birth to maturity as a commercial medium during that period.

Other factors:

- Most afternoon metros that fail are locked in deteriorating inner cores of older, mature cities and face vigorous crosstown rivals that are clearly market leaders. Those that fail suffer perhaps not so much from being afternoon papers as from being number two in a competitive market. Losers fail to maintain journalistic momentum, marketing focus, sales drive—and this seems more pertinent to newspaper success than does cycle of publication.

- Morning publication is not a ticket to automatic success. Morning papers in New York City, Detroit, Seattle, and St. Louis entered the mid-1980s deeply in trouble; some stood second to afternoon papers.

- Despite failure of weak big-city afternoon papers, PM papers in suburban and small town America generally are more successful than ever.

- Managers who presided over dying metros in the 1970s and 1980s never had a real chance for success, even though some showed alert sensitivity to special problems of PM publishing. Many were appointed only when conditions had become terminal. Once on the job, they found costs too high, revenue too low, time too short. Managers who might have saved the crippled metros were those of the 1960s, but they were often not alert to the socioeconomic changes then under way in big cities nor, when they finally did catch on, did they react in time.

- Afternoon papers that fail do not always fail in every operational respect. Some, for example, have hundreds of thousands in circulation and strong *reader* loyalty to the very end. Where they fail is in translating circulation strength into advertising support.

Not inconsequential in the public perception that afternoon papers are dying is the sheer drama of once-great metros closing their doors. TV is there, filming reporters sorrowing in the corridors. Catchy epitaphs by soon-to-be-unemployed wordsmiths gain currency (. . . "dinosaurs don't live here anymore," intoned widely quoted Publisher N. S. Hayden, as he padlocked the afternoon *Philadelphia Bulletin*.) It's enough to convince anyone that the breed is dying.

Yet the afternoon paper is better suited for some markets:

- Industrial cities whose blue collar workers have no time for a paper before work early in the morning and who prefer to read after leaving work at 3 P.M. or so. Detroit, Milwaukee, St. Louis, Pittsburgh and similar cities have large blue-collar populations.

- Towns with special life-style characteristics, such as those with many retirees with afternoon leisure time.

- Markets with special competitive characteristics. Small suburban papers overshadowed by strong morning metros, for example, are often better off publishing in the afternoon rather than competing head-on.

Well, then, exactly what *is* happening to afternoon papers? Let's seek further clues by examining the Minneapolis example more closely.

Changes Occur in the Afternoon

Writing the *Minneapolis Star's* obituary, Editor Isaacs filled almost two pages explaining why, in his stewardship of three years, a troubled newspaper (it was losing 6 percent circulation annually when he took it over in 1979) became terminal. Highlights:

- Most Americans (Isaacs says surveys show 82 percent) regularly or occasionally get national and international news from the evening TV; only 24 percent do so in the morning. Clearly, PM papers face the fiercest TV competition.

- Isaacs says morning readers want reorientation after a night's sleep and consider a hard-news, information-filled newspaper indispensable. However, readers regard the PM paper as a soft, featurish, warmed-over version of the morning paper and thus dispensable. He theorizes that afternoon readers, tired from work, want "reward," not a dose of hard news.

- In 1950–1980, 30 percent of Minneapolis's population moved out of the city center. A morning paper, trucked in predawn hours, can follow them to the suburbs. An afternoon paper must have earlier press time to gain truck time. The *Star's* was 9:30 A.M. Few newsworthy events break between midnight (press time for many morning papers) and 9:30 A.M., so afternoon papers reach readers with little hard news.

- Most news, Isaacs says, breaks during the morning newspaper cycle. His analysis of all breaking news printed by the *Star* and *Tribune* during a two-week period in 1980 shows that 90.5 percent broke for morning papers. The problem is accentuated because newsmakers (and not just in Minneapolis) want to appear on TV, and so schedule events at midday. This is right for the 6 P.M. TV news and the morning paper's cycle, but too late for afternoon papers.

- Isaacs finds that women working outside the home spend 27 percent less time reading newspapers than women who don't. More than 58 percent of Minnesota women

between twenty and thirty-five work. And, he says, in the Minneapolis area, 90 percent of childless women in that age bracket hold outside jobs. An extremely important segment of the newspaper audience has things to do in the afternoon other than read newspapers. From all this, Isaacs says, comes a "change of society's timing," dooming afternoon papers.

There is another view. Some observers see Isaacs's theory as not having industrywide application for afternoon managers. They say the problem was the way Cowles Media managed, or mismanaged, the *Star*. They also question the skill of Isaacs himself.

Two *Star* reporters—in a story the *Star* published shortly before its demise—described Isaacs as a "big, indiscreet, intimidating Easterner in a town known for its Scandinavian reserve" who ripped apart the paper's traditional content and layout too quickly.

> Suddenly, or so it seemed, the newspaper's most basic ingredients—city council meetings, news conferences, speeches—were gone. In their place was an unpredictable front-page mixture of blazing illustrations, Hollywood features and all sorts of things that had once been tucked away inside the paper.

Christopher Burns, associate publisher of the *Star and Tribune* (who, like Isaacs, fell victim to bloodletting following the *Star's* death) is critical:

> We fell into the trap; we wrote stories that were not essential. We made our hallmark out of the fact that we were background. . . . We were nice to know, we were fascinating, but not necessary. And whenever the crunch came, people would cancel us. Somebody came home and realized they hadn't read the *Star* for a week, and they'd say, "What the hell." . . . We walked away from the audience. The audience didn't walk away from us—from the *Star*. We just turned away and said, we don't want to write (local news) . . . this new *Star* is going to be much more fun for us. We're

going to glow in the dark. Incandescent newspaper. Young. Hip. With it. Innovative. Emphasis on television. Emphasis on style. . . . the *Minneapolis Star* just got up and walked out of the room as far as some of this city was concerned. . . .

There were inexplicable management moves. For example, the *Star* had 38 percent less circulation than the *Tribune* but some ad rates 21 percent higher—a disparity that must have puzzled even the most understanding advertiser.

In neighboring St. Paul, a different management style dealt effectively with problems similar to the *Star*'s. Knight-Ridder's *Dispatch* moved *with* change, restructuring carefully and quietly. In 1984, it merged news staffs with its morning sister, the *Pioneer Press*, but maintained strong presence in the afternoon field. Managing Editor William F. Centro of the *Dispatch* has this to say on handling change:

- Be alert to shifting reader and advertiser desire, but evolve slowly. The St. Paul papers radically changed content, format, layout—but over nearly ten years, not a few months.

- Listen to readers through research and conform to what they say they need, but do not abdicate a newspaper's traditional obligation to print the news as defined by trained editors.

- Do not desert hard news, or swing heavily to features. Remain a *news*paper.

- Design the paper for a busy reader and publish plentiful news digests, lots of stories ("high story count"), write and edit tightly, yet do frequent in-depth, investigative pieces on stories of substance.

- Plan coverage carefully; organize and package the paper with attractive display boxes, teasers, and other devices aimed at luring readers inside. Help readers read. [14]

Some PMs Convert to AMs

Many managers convert from PM to AM—105 in 1976–86 alone, ANPA says. It is a trend that is certain to continue.

Prior to converting its own 18,500-circulation *Bryan-College Station (Tex.) Eagle* to AM in 1981, Harte-Hanks studied 14 PMs that converted and found many sound reasons for switching:

- To increase circulation. *The Little Rock (Ark.) Democrat* reports a 16.2 percent increase in its 62,000 circulation the first year following conversion; the *Gainesville (Fla.) Sun*, which was projecting 2 percent annual growth in its 37,000 circulation, reports 7 percent growth its first year as an AM.

- To obtain rural circulation. Many PM papers have too little time to truck papers to distant delivery points; conversely, trucking in the predawn hours enables morning papers to escape afternoon traffic and gives them much greater "reach." When the *Pittsfield (Mass.) Berkshire Eagle*, a 31,000-circulation afternoon paper, converted, it quickly picked up 1,400 subscribers—1,000 beyond Pittsfield's traditional home market. The 40,000-circulation *Tallahassee (Fla.) Democrat* pushed out 90 miles to new population centers when it converted.

- To use mail distribution. Many smaller papers convert to reduce circulation expense and broaden their distribution ter-

---

[14] Joe Fenley, "Life and Death Among the PMs," Associated Press Managing Editors' Association, 1981–1982 report, p. 12. Also see Larry Fuller, "The *Star* Tried Harder, But Lost," Associated Press Managing Editors' Association, 1981–1982 report, p. 4, and "Demise of *Minn. Star* Blamed on Life Itself," *Editor & Publisher*, April 17, 1982, p. 12.

ritory by delivering by mail. Only AM papers can easily achieve same-day mail delivery. The *Festus (Mo.) Democrat-Pilot*, faced with increased motor delivery costs, converted to morning mail delivery and in 18 months increased circulation to 8,000 from 6,000.

- To present a stronger news package. Most prime news breaks for AM papers. Late-breaking nighttime sports coverage and fuller business coverage, particularly stock tables, are two particularly attractive offerings morning papers can carry.

- Advertisers like morning paper's "shelf-life"—having their messages accessible in a household all day.

Many small papers convert in one overnight step. AM-PM combinations owned by the same company often move first to all-day status, publishing in both cycles but gradually putting most emphasis on the AM edition. This invariably involves merging newsroom staffs and effecting other economies. Some papers merge newsroom staffs but continue separate AM and PM editions. The *Atlanta Journal and Constitution* did that to reduce costs.

Conversion to AM is often far from smooth. Increased costs follow some conversions. More employees are needed to continue staffing daytime news beats into evening. Some union contracts require nighttime wage differentials. Added features such as full stock tables and improved sports coverage for AM papers are costly. Circulation departments feel the heaviest burdens in conversion. Some report a 100 percent turnover among carriers, who do not want to deliver during the predawn hours. That can force a costly shift to adult carriers. Turnover is also high among district managers and other circulation supervisors.

Executives who have been through it offer this advice:

1. Carefully research reader and advertiser opinion on whether conversion should take place at all. Repeatedly, conversion veterans warn against tinkering with successful PM papers or simply rushing to convert because it seems fashionable.

2. If there is a go-ahead, conversion should be done while the paper is relatively strong and before it is backed into a corner by market changes. Planning at least one year ahead is recommended.

3. Detailed promotion is recommended to inform readers and advertisers precisely what is planned and why. Readers develop firm habits and should be told why they must change. Offer readers demonstrable improvement in the paper as it converts. Dow Jones' 40,000-circulation *Danbury (Conn.) News-Times* enlarged its news hole (total space available for news and information) and redesigned its format and typeface when it converted.

4. Detailed advisories to employees plus staff involvement in planning are necessary. Papers that keep employees informed report no significant morale problems following conversion (although converting to nighttime work causes marital and other personal problems for some staffers.)

5. Carefully time the move to AM—after, say, the first month, so that paid-in-advance subscribers will have nearly a full month to become accustomed to the change before they can cancel. Automatic or forced conversion of all subscribers is recommended.[15]

How about the reader in all this? Robert H. Wills, editor of the 183,000-circulation *Mil-*

---

[15] John H. Vivian, "PM Papers Wake to AM Trend," Associated Press Managing Editors' Association, 1981–1982 report; "Afternoon Newspapers: Is Future in Morning?" Toronto, Oct. 20–23, 1981, p. 8.

waukee Sentinel, a morning paper owned by the same company that owns the afternoon *Journal*, says that where competition exists, "editors are more alert and reporters work harder." When papers merge, "It's the readers who lose out," Wills says.[16]

In sum, readers, advertisers, and the career of every newspaper manager will be affected by changes under way in how newspapers must operate. Let's discuss how to design a news organization to handle such complex changes.

DESIGNING THE NEWS ORGANIZATION

In designing the newsroom's organizational structure and philosophy, you create an apparatus that must fashion the newspaper's relevancy to present and future readers—and that will account for 10 to 15 percent of the newspaper's total costs in the process. There are three important considerations:

First, insure the news organization's structure, personnel and attitudes effectively mirror your marketplace. Newsroom employees, their duties and titles, type of news covered, style of writing—all must meet your readers' needs. A southern small-town daily with mainly farm readers should not staff its newsroom entirely with reporters raised in northern big cities whose primary news interest is opera and modern dance. *Some* must be interested in agricultural news and high school football.

Second, integrate the newsroom into the overall marketing operation. Seat the chief news executive at top-management planning sessions and protect every editor's managerial prerogatives. A publisher who "end runs" the sports editor by telephoning compliments directly to a football writer for a story well done or who accosts a city hall reporter in the elevator for a story poorly done is a publisher who has de-

stroyed an editor's credibility. Design a clear-cut hierarchy and make sure it is followed.

Third, design for efficient management of resources—people, time, and money. Business-like methods must be accepted routine in the newsroom as in advertising, circulation, or other departments.

Let's look at how two completely different newspapers design quite different news organizations.

Metro vs. Small-Town Design

Newsday's primary market—affluent Nassau and Suffolk counties—compromises scores of "bedroom" communities for thousands of New York City commuters. The audience is upscale in income and education, demanding sophisticated coverage of art, music, entertainment, books, and other subjects in addition to hard news.

To meet that challenge, *Newsday* established a multifaceted newsroom organization tuned to the unique needs of its rapidly changing market. At the top, the management hierarchy is heavier than at many newspapers, and *Newsday* editors have strong voices in corporate affairs. The editor, for example, is one of four corporate vice presidents and one of eight executives on the top-management team.

From top down, lines of authority lead to first-level supervisors along both subject and geographic lines. For example, the managing editor, in day-to-day charge of newsroom operations, has two associate editors and three assistant managing editors—one each for Long Island, state news, and national/international news—plus a features editor.

Forty editors handle special-subject coverage—arts and leisure, sports, books, business, education, food, music, and so on. Geographic areas are also assigned to individual editors—one each, for example, to Nassau, Queens, and Suffolk counties in addition to bureau chiefs for New York City, Washington, D.C., and the state capital, Albany. One executive is designated "Senior Editor, Technology" and oversees computerized electronic editing systems.

---

[16] Clark Newsome, "Publishers Say Mergers Result in Better Product," *presstime*, January 1983, p. 49.

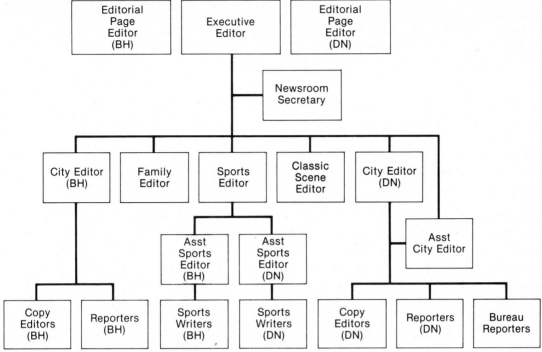

Figure 7.2 Athens (Ga.) Daily News & Banner-Herald

For a small-town daily, newsroom design is much less complicated. Figure 7.2 shows the table of organization for the 9,900-circulation *Athens (Ga.) Daily News* and the 12,700-circulation *Banner-Herald*, both owned by Morris Communications, Inc., and jointly produced in the same plant. Editorial page editors report directly to the publisher, and the executive editor is responsible for every other function in the newsroom.

Contrasted with *Newsday*'s scores of specialist editors and newsroom administrators, the *Daily News* and *Banner-Herald* make do with a city editor for the morning paper and one for the afternoon paper, a single sports editor (with one assistant for each paper), a "family editor" and a "Classic Scene editor" who prepares an entertainment tabloid section inserted in combined weekend editions. A single assistant city editor serves both papers as relief editor.

Though facing local weekly and radio competitors, the *Daily News* and *Banner-Herald* are 45 miles from Atlanta, the nearest large city. Athens is a small town surrounded by farmland. Its largest "industry" is the University of Georgia. So these small papers enjoy a lean managerial hierarchy organized in a straight-line pattern quite adequate for their relatively uncomplicated market and their readers' more traditional small-town news needs.

Designing the Newsroom into the Marketing Effort

Large or small, a newspaper's organizational design must truly integrate the news effort into the overall marketing thrust and facilitate two-way communication between news and other departments. One survey of 144 editors shows nearly 50 percent without access to figures on revenue, expense, profit.[17] How can they feel

---

[17] *Newsroom Management Committee Report, 1979, Continuing Studies,* Associated Press Managing Editors' Association.

equal partners in a team effort? Frequent meetings between publisher and editor help, as does automatic inclusion of the editor in cross-departmental strategy sessions. The alternative to such integration is an isolated newsroom "doing its own thing" and not efficiently supporting the marketing concept.

Effective organizational design should provide the chief news executive with an expanded management role. While directing news coverage and getting the next edition on the streets, the editor—as a member of management's strategy planning team—simultaneously must look ten years ahead to the future shape of the newspaper. Add the need for wise expenditure of, sometimes, tens of millions of dollars annually in a newsroom budget, and the chief news executive's responsibility assume awesome proportions. It's not an easy job. (See boxes for insights into just how complex it gets.)

Just as news executives must be involved in operational areas outside news, so must other managers—particularly in circulation and advertising—be kept current on what news is doing. Caution: Involvement in news by managers from outside the newsroom is a sensitive subject for many editors, who say that news must be covered almost instinctively in accord with standards developed through experience by professional reporters and editors and that intrusion by the "business side"—with its marketing, advertising, and circulation considerations—is disruptive at best, prejudicial at worst. This is a historic and very strong feeling, deeply rooted in some newsrooms, that stems in part from examples—every newspaper person knows

STRESS GOES WITH THE TURF

Editors say they enjoy their work, finding it challenging and well paid; but they warn that stress-related health problems go with the job.

Of 902 editors responding to an Associated Press Managing Editors Association survey, 39 percent report health problems they believe linked to job-related stress: 33 percent specify ulcers, asthma, hypertension, cancer, heart disease, arthritis, stroke, alcoholism, or drug abuse.

Most editors report being stimulated by the need to meet deadlines, manage newsroom competition between highly talented newspaper people, and produce quality newspapers. Their biggest frustrations come from bosses who ignore their advice and weaken their power or who decline to allocate sufficient resources to do the required journalistic job. Major stress follows any conflict with a boss who compromises newsroom integrity with decisions aimed only at producing higher profit.

Stress also comes from a fundamental change in their job function. Robert H. Giles, editor of Gannett's *Detroit News*, who supervised the survey, explains:

Fifteen years ago, editors were editors. Today, they are editor-managers. They direct the editing of the newspaper with one hand and, with the other, they are deeply involved in business management.

The editor is expected to carry on in the best traditions of journalistic excellence, but also is expected to share the responsibility for the newspaper as a "profit center." Many editors discovered that this dual obligation created unfamiliar stresses, stresses born of a conflict between the need to be good and the need to be lean.

Most editors report working more than 40 hours weekly: 22 percent say they put in 40 to 45 hours; 34 percent, 46 to 50 hours; 25 percent, 51 to 55 hours; 18 percent, more than 55 hours; and 53 percent say they work more than five days weekly, often at home.

A majority reported annual salaries under $34,999; 19 percent, $35,000 to $44,999; 13 percent, $45,000 to $54,999; 5 percent, $55,000 to $64,999; 7 percent, more than $85,000.

Stress or no, jobs as editors of America's leading newspapers are highly coveted, and for each there are hundreds of eager aspirants.

THE INSTINCTIVE, CURIOUS, DISPASSIONATE EDITOR

The people who run newspapers must have a flair for what is news, how to arrange it attractively, and what to include and what to leave out. There is just no formula for this. The instinct of a great city editor to look at an insignificant piece of information and to suspect it could lead to an important story is something born into some people and not others. The leading managers of newspapers must be forever curious about everyone and everything and eager to participate in all the events of the era they are living in. They should belong to no specific political party or ideology. Different problems require different solutions and people with set philosophies and institutional loyalties should never be in journalism.

Thomas Vail, editor and publisher, *Cleveland Plain Dealer,* letter to author.

---

several—of coverage being distorted for business reasons. As an aspiring manager, you must understand that this feeling pervades the very psyche of many experienced editors. It must be dealt with sensitively and carefully. But it cannot prevent dovetailing the newsroom, its executives, and its goals into the newspaper's overall mission.

Now we've discussed introducing marketing to the newsroom and designing a news organization. Let's turn to areas of particular interest to first-level managers in news who must carry the concept ahead.

RESEARCH IN THE NEWSROOM

The marketing concept requires a tight focus on meeting reader needs, hence newsroom managers at all levels must research precisely what those needs are and then plan carefully to fulfill them.

As discussed in Chapter 3, you must know the geography of your market and who lives there. You must now go beyond that, into a detailed audit of reader and nonreader thinking, interests, and attitudes—plus systematic research into how the newspaper as a product relates to them. It is important to research how readers are likely to receive change—a new section, a new feature, redesign of content.

In Dallas, Burl Osborne recalls once trying to save space in the *Morning News* by not running in all editions high school sports results from throughout the sports-crazy city. For one day, results were "zoned"—included only in editions sent to areas near the school mentioned. "The readers damn near stormed the gates," Osborne says, "and we repented the very next day."[18]

Aside from subjecting the newspaper to such wearing trial-and-error methods, you have other means of sampling readers and nonreaders.

Buy Research or Do It Yourself

Research aids range from complex and expensive to simple and cheap:

Professional readership studies, for those papers able to afford them, provide valuable guidance through personal in-depth interviews with scientifically selected probability samples of the public. Such studies can be expensive and take months to conduct and analyze. The *Los Angeles Times* spent more than $1 million in two years, researching reader and advertiser attitudes toward its new Sunday magazine.[19] If outside research firms are used, *always* help design the survey to make sure that questions are precisely tailored to your newspaper's specific needs. This type research is so important that many companies, Dow Jones and Harte-Hanks among them, have acquired their own research firms.

---

[18] Osborne, op. cit.
[19] Karl Fleming, "The New Los Angeles Times Magazine," *Washington Journalism Review,* April 1985, p. 48.

Subscriber questionaires can be published in smaller newspapers or mailed to readers and non-readers, if your corporate purse requires do-it-yourself surveys. Research expertise is as close as the nearest business or journalism school. At mid-1980s expense levels, a survey of 1,000 persons could be completed for substantially under $1,000.

Circulation-department feedback is invaluable. This department contacts readers and nonreaders daily, yet many newspapers have no systematic feedback to the newsroom. Every subscriber who halts delivery should be asked why; every nonsubscriber who declined the paper should be asked why; and the news department should hear why. The *Athens Banner-Herald and Daily News* ask every subscriber who drops the paper to complete a questionaire on why; this then goes to both the publisher and the newsroom.

Reader complaints or praise should be analyzed carefully. Letters plus memos on telephone calls should be circulated to editors as indicators (not, of course, totally reliable proof) of public mood.

Encounter groups provide excellent feedback if true cross-sections of readers are selected. Some papers hold coffee-and-doughnut meetings so editors and readers can discuss the newspaper in depth. Knight-Ridder's *Detroit Free Press* had its group study a competing paper, *USA Today*. (The seventy-eight person study group liked *USA Today's* color reproduction, shorter stories, and TV listings but not its lack of local news and local advertising, reports David Lawrence, Jr. then *Free Press* executive editor and now publisher.)[20]

Personal contacts number in the hundreds each week for managers of even a small paper—and each manager should listen to what is said about the newspaper.

Newsroom managers should be involved in such research from start. The goal is information needed to operate effectively, and news managers should help decide what that is. But also, news managers tend to deprecate as inaccurate—or reject as interference—readership research in which they have no part.

Editors and publishers clearly need scientific research. Surveys repeatedly show that instinctive interpretation by both of reader views on news can often be very wrong. A Lou Harris poll, for example, shows that fifty-two of the publishers surveyed hold news values quite different from those of their readers: 19 percent of publishers said that readers are very interested in international news while 49 percent of readers said they were; 98 percent of the publishers said that readers are very interested in local news, but only 72 percent of readers said they were.[21]

Editors don't score much better in a survey by United Media Enterprises, a Scripps-Howard company: 92 percent of the 101 senior editors polled said it is very important for a newspaper to provide community information, but of 1,000 members of the general public polled, only 76 percent agreed; 81 percent of the editors rated national/international developments a close second, but only 69 percent of the public agreed; 73 percent of editors said analyzing complex issues is a very important newspaper function, while only 42 percent of the public agreed.[22]

Unless they are careful, then, publishers and editors can produce newspapers that appeal to them or other publishers and editors yet miss the public's news needs and desires by a wide margin.

Working journalists, editors and reporters on the beat, often err, too. For example, seminal work on the public's views of newspapers was done by sixteen newspaper organizations in the

[20] "Free Press Awaits Today," *Advertising Age*, Feb. 21, 1983, p. 49.

[21] "Readers Give Newspapers Higher Marks Than They Did Eight Years Ago," *Southern Newspaper Publishers' Association Bulletin*, May 12, 1983, p. 2.
[22] "Reading The Newspaper Ranks Second Among Favorite Leisure Activities," *Southern Newspaper Publishers' Association Bulletin*, June 16, 1983, p. 3.

Newspaper Readership Project. Yet after years of committee work, Michigan State University researchers found that only one-third of 576 newsroom men and women ever heard of the project and only 8 percent ever saw any of its many reports.[23] Journalists were found to be so fundamentally misjudging the public's reading and life-style habits as to raise questions whether they could produce newspapers precisely tuned to their audiences: news staffers estimate that 51 percent of adults read a newspaper on an average day, while research places the national average at 67 percent; news staffers estimate front-page readership at 89 percent, while research places readership of an average hard news item at less than 50 percent. Journalists generally overestimate by far reader interest in sports, nongovernmental local news, fashion, food, society, homemaker topics, celebrities and personalities, the survey reports, and they substantially underestimate interest in national government, environment, and energy news.

In practice, many news executives combine careful research with a news instinct born of years in the business. Recommendations for using both, and a warning against sole reliance on surveys, come from Harold W. Andersen, president of the *Omaha (Neb.) World-Herald*, an AM-PM paper with 235,000 total circulation:

> Surveys often give conflicting signals—quite different answers when the same basic question is phrased differently and sometimes very vague or generalized answers from those being surveyed.
>
> Personally, I rely less on surveys (although we do survey) than on keeping my eyes and ears—and mind—open to all signs of what interests the people of Omaha and our region. . . . This "feel" for the needs and interests of our readers can be developed in a variety of ways, including surveys and occasional luncheon meetings with various

groups of readers. Another useful source: A careful reading of the newspaper itself, observing what writers are telling us in letters to the editor, what people are asking from their school board and city council and the state legislature, what various neighborhood groups are discussing at their meetings and what goods and services are being offered by advertisers in response to, or in development of, various consumer needs and tastes.[24]

In sum, techniques for sampling reader opinion are available to any newspaper, large or small, regardless of its resources. A manager must make sure that editors factor the results into their selection of stories and how they are reported and written. Only with research in hand can the manager turn to the next important step, planning.

PLANNING IN THE NEWSROOM

Newsroom planning is a multidimensional responsibility for the manager. Two broad areas are most important:

- Planning effective use of human resources. *No* newsroom can rise above the quality of its staff, and every newsroom manager's first responsibility is planning recruitment, hiring, training, motivation, and effective use of top-caliber people.

- Planning overall journalistic tone and the drive for quality.

A Planning Checklist for Quality

Let's look at a manager's checklist for planning journalistic superiority. We'll relate it to what Burl Osborne does at the *Morning News* in Dallas.

Make financial commitment.   There is no cheap route to journalistic superiority. In the first two

---

[23] Michael and Judee Burgoon and Charles K. Atkin of Michigan State University, quoted in "Declining Circulation—Who's to Blame?" report by Readership & Research Committee to Associated Press Managing Editors' Convention, San Diego, Calif., Nov. 9–12, 1982.

[24] Harold Andersen, letter to author, May 9, 1983.

years of Osborne's editorship, Belo Corp. doubled the *Morning News*'s newsroom budget. To correct journalistic weakness, newsroom executives must have sufficient financial resources.

Strengthen newsroom management. Stealing Osborne from AP is only one example of Belo's aggressive search for management talent. The *Baltimore Sun* was raided for Carl Leubsdorf, a skilled political writer who became the *Morning News*'s Washington bureau chief. Dave Smith, superbly talented editor of the *Boston Globe*'s prizewinning sports section, was recruited as sports editor. Other talented managers were found in newsrooms across the country.

Strengthen newsroom staff. This often, but not always, requires additional personnel. It *always* requires upgrading the staff's experience and ability—its general talent. In three years, the *Morning News* expanded its news staff to nearly 300 from 185. Says Osborne: "It is a matter of stated practice that any replacement must raise the level of the given position. . . ."[25]

Cover the ground. The best way to cover news is to have people there when it breaks. In 1980, the *Morning News* had bureaus in Fort Worth, Austin, Houston, Mexico City, and Washington. In three years, it opened new bureaus in San Antonio, El Paso (to cover West Texas), Tyler (East Texas), Mid-Cities (between Dallas and Fort Worth), Plano (a demographically attractive growth area north of Dallas), North Dallas, Toronto, New York City, Tel Aviv, and Oklahoma City. The Washington bureau's new chief expanded his staff to seven from three, and the state capitol bureau in Austin was strengthened. Few newspapers are able—fewer are willing—to spend the enormous sums necessary for such sudden bureau expansion or provide room in the paper for additional coverage. But managers must identify the newspaper's area of *opportu-*

nity, where investment in staff will bring appropriate return, and its area of news *responsibility*, which must be covered if the newspaper is to claim journalistic validity. Then they must plan for sufficient reporters on the ground.

Reexamine coverage strategy. Frequent and fundamental reexaminations of which areas are covered and why are mandatory, because a market's demographic character can shift rapidly. For reader and advertiser alike, management must move quickly into areas of new opportunity. The *Morning News* made a major staff expansion into rapidly growing and relatively high-income suburbs north and west of Dallas.

Reexamine newspaper structure/content. Just as demographics shift rapidly, so do readers' needs. Managers must frequently sample readers plus nonreaders and produce newspapers for them, not for other editors and not just because that's the way they always were produced. The *Morning News* overhauled its content and structure in what Osborne calls *internal zoning*. It blossomed with new sections, new features, new approaches to coverage—from local high school sports to international oil news.

Improve packaging/layout. Internationally renowned for journalistic quality and businesslike precision, the *Wall Street Journal* sells extremely well to its special audience (nearly 2 million copies daily in 1986) despite layout and design that are yet to emerge from the eighteenth century. Few newspapers, in this era of TV and color, could do so. The *Morning News* was redesigned to use color and catch readers with a wider, more open appearance. Attractive packaging as well as well-edited photos and graphics are musts.

　　This checklist deals with subjective judgments. There is no universal standard of excellence in layout, content, or coverage. Each must be examined for whether the chosen approach is correct for *this* newspaper in *this* market at *this* time.

---

[25] Osborne, op. cit.

Plan to Follow Reader Shifts

Many publishers and editors who are trying to establish news philosophies for the 1990s are heavily influenced by the research of Ruth Clark, who has studied shifting reader needs and desires.

In 1978, Clark reported that readers most wanted "local" news and felt alienated from newspapers. Readers wanted useful news to help them cope with a complicated world, delivered in newspapers that were better organized, easier to read, more relevant and personal, and less time-demanding, Clark said.

In 1984, a second Clark survey found reader desires shifting to "hard" news—daily, fact-filled coverage of such things as health, science, technology, diet and nutrition, and child-rearing— as contrasted with *soft*, featurish coverage of less essential subjects. Clark also found a desire for a broadened mix of local, national, state, and regional news. Clark found most readers regarding newspapers as indispensable, here to stay despite TV. But some still questioned whether newspapers are fair and unbiased. (See Chapter 10, "Newspaper Image and Promotion.")

Clark attributes the reader shift to the many traumatic events that occurred between surveys: U. S. inflation and recession, unemployment, international crises, and growing anxiety about nuclear war.

The studies, both sponsored by the American Society of Newspaper Editors, underline the speed with which reader views can change and how editors, and the entire marketing effort, must move quickly with them.

One controversy is whether readers, distrustful since Vietnam of distant conflicts and large institutions, are turning inward, restricting their news interests to local life; indeed, some say the reader wants only local news—Main Street, not Afghanistan; school boards, not the United Nations. All this inspires a paroxysm of seminars and studies dedicated to the proposition that if it is not "local," it is not relevant

news. Too often, "local" is given a parochial geographic definition: if it does not happen within the city limits, its news value is suspect at best. Calmer heads should prevail. "Local" should include any news development anywhere that affects "local" life. A manager's challenge is building a staff capable of sifting the world of news and extracting those items, regardless of dateline or subject, with bearing on the lives of the newspaper's readers, then reporting and writing those stories to properly highlight their relevance and meaning. A guerrilla war in Afghanistan is of "local" importance if it might someday involve U.S. tax dollars and young men; a school bond fracas in California has meaning in Newark if it parallels school controversies in New Jersey.

The Planned Shift Back to Hard News

There is a developing consensus that hard news is what newspapers should be all about in the 1990s and that the earlier preoccupation with soft, featurish approaches was perhaps overdone.

The featurish approach was, in part, an overreaction to the perceived threat of TV. Electronic journalism, some thought, would take the edge off hard news, leaving newspapers to featurish in-depth, "explanatory" journalism. That proved wrong. TV, despite rapidly improving professionalism, has not become a dominant or even satisfactory news medium—although, of course, a great many viewers *perceive* it as satisfactory. Many newspapers that virtually became magazinelike are swinging back to hard news.

It is a planned return to what football coach Vince Lombardi might have called the fundamentals, the journalistic version of blocking and tackling—precision identification of important issues plus in-depth reporting and clear writing that explains the news in terms meaningful to readers who are overwhelmed by daily developments. Surveys repeatedly show readers seeking information to help them cope, to handle complex social and economic problems.

Ruth Clark says the biggest switch in reader desires is "the new emphasis that readers are demanding from all newspapers for relevant, understandable hard news—be it international, national, regional, state, economic, local—and, yes, even community news." She adds:

It's not that sports fans will sacrifice good sports coverage, or that young people no longer want entertainment listings, or that special sections will disappear—though I'm willing to gamble on some fading away—but the big change in the markets we've surveyed is that today the main reason for buying and reading newspapers is hard news, properly and appropriately defined, compiled, digested, edited, explained and made relevant.[26]

A Small Paper's Redesign Plan

Here are ways a small paper can use Ruth Clark's guidelines in redesigning content and fashioning new links with readers:

- Personalize content by assigning staff writers to regular columns that are "anchored"—always published in the same spot so readers can find them easily. Invite guest columns from people in the community. Encourage letters to the editor. Give a banquet for writers of unusually good letters. Introduce staff members to readers through promotional ads in your own pages featuring photos and brief biographical sketches.

- Help readers cope with the information explosion by designing columns of news briefs, each of perhaps fifteen or twenty short items. Organize the paper along predictable lines: one section for local news, another for national and world news. Research by Clark and others finds readers overwhelmed by news and desiring a more predictable organization of the paper.

- Make the paper more readable and enjoyable. Study reader criticisms and surveys for hints on what is wrong. Type too small? Too many stories "jumped"—continued on another page? Stories too long? Use a color photograph above the front-page fold when possible; color attracts readers.

- Meet a continuing criticism that newspapers don't publish "good" news. Set aside a page for "Dear Abby," crossword and horoscope features, humorous pictures, a "people" column—all things readers find entertaining. Report the good things that happen to people—graduations, promotions, scholarships, elections.

Plan "Showcase" Improvement

Plan for news superiority in these showcases:

Front page. The explosive growth of "inside" sections rivals the front page for reader attention. But the front page still is where the day's best stories and photos are displayed and is extremely important in establishing public perception of the newspaper. It sets the tone for the entire paper and is a reader lure that the newspaper's best layout designers should construct carefully. One commendable change at many newspapers is to open the front page to all types of news, not just stories from Washington, London, or state capitals. Smart editors "front" outstanding stories—business, sports, real estate—that a decade ago would have been consigned to deep inside play regardless of news merits.

Business section. Probably the greatest single improvement in recent years is in business, financial, and economic news. This responds to the way in which everyday life is influenced for millions of Americans by the money supply, interest rates, the Federal Reserve Board, and other business esoterica once thought meaningful only to stockbrokers and bond traders. But also, smart managers know that outstanding business coverage can deliver readers who are

---

[26] "A Shift Back to Hard News," *Editor & Publisher*, July 16, 1983, p. 44.

demographically attractive to advertisers. Business coverage is not only necessary if a newspaper is to discharge its obligations to readers—it is also good business. Managers must make sure that business reporters are skilled "interpreters," capable of reducing highly complex stories to understandable terms that are meaningful to readers.

Editorial page. As the front page showcases a newspaper's best reporting, the editorial page displays its conscience. Unfortunately, some newspapers attempt to serve all factions with dispassionate editorials exploring all sides of an issue, never venturing to express an opinion. Result: deadly dull editorial pages and a withering of the leadership spirit many newspapers once displayed to the good of their communities. To assert leadership, a newspaper should thoughtfully explore all dimensions of a subject but then take a hard-hitting stand that makes a choice. Op-ed pages are expanding as reader soapboxes featuring guest writers, letters to the editors, and columnists.

Sports sections. Sports fans are insatiable. They want to know who batted first in the fourth inning of a local Little League game, as well as the sports editor's opinion on the Super Bowl. And, these sports fans, though difficult to satisfy, are a hard core of readers cherished by newspaper editors the country over. To meet the fans' needs, expanded sports sections carry, it seems, yards of statistical material plus in-depth, analytical behind-the-scenes coverage. With TV showing the game in living color, newspapers must not rush out with who won—but *how* they won.

"News of record." The newspaper is the best easily accessible source of life's statistical detail in any community. It alone records births, school graduations, marriages, deaths. Regardless of your newspaper's journalistic character or overall mission, you must devote significant resources to providing news of record. Says Tom Jobson, managing editor who guided growth of the *Asbury Park (N. J.) Press* from just over 40,000 circulation in 1961 to 116,000 daily and 168,000 Sunday: "We have a total 'local' coverage concept—I feel there's just about enough room for any level of news, promotions, dean's lists, births, in our paper along with news generating from outside our territory."[27]

Also Plan Special Sections

It is a formidable task to sift the entire range of newsmaking events, collating and packaging the most important in orderly fashion for readers with many news interests, needs, and desires. Planning the hard-news element is comparatively simple. The day's top story often is obvious and gets page one's top spot; the number-two story gets subordinated, and so forth. But how to handle thousands of other important stories that pour in daily? In many newsrooms the answer is an explosive but carefully planned proliferation of special sections. A prime example is in Denver, where Scripps-Howard and Times Mirror use special sections to create new sources of revenue to finance their newspaper war.

Scripps-Howard brought in Ralph Looney as editor of its *Rocky Mountain News.* (He had been editor of the group's *Albuquerque [N.M.] Tribune.*) Looney quickly introduced new special sections:

Mondays—"SportsPlus," beefed-up coverage of weekend sports.

Tuesdays—"Business," with ample space for in-depth coverage of this important news.

Wednesdays—"Mid-Week," a special section for women.

Thursdays—"Style," a fashions section.

Those sections were added to others already run: "Food Fare" on Wednesdays (the day many

---

[27] Tom Jobson, letter to author, March 19, 1983.

newspapers run the bulk of their food advertising); "Center Section" (an entertainment guide) on Fridays; "Home and Car" on Saturdays; and "Now," an in-depth Sunday feature section. (Looney's changes included an expanded index of leading stories and a "people" column for page two; improved weather coverage; new columns for the "Commentary" section; appointment of a religion editor and increased coverage of religious affairs; and a redesigned comic section.)[28]

The *Denver Post* added five new weekly sections:

"Fashion West"—fashion, fitness, life-style for Colorado.

"Travel"—a section claiming the "nation's top travel writers."

"TV Week"—listings and entertainment columns in magazine-size format inserted in the paper.

"Entertainment"—arts, books, music, film, theater on Sundays.

"Wheels"—a full size auto section "including car care advice, test drive reports and news from Detroit."[29]

For many newspapers, annual or occasional special sections are favorite devices for news roundups and special ad sales campaigns.

The *Muskegon (Mich.) Chronicle*, a 45,000-circulation afternoon paper owned by Newhouse, publishes these: "Progress" (city history and development, in January); "Brides" (February); "Home Improvement" (March); "Yard & Garden" (April); "Real Estate" (April); "Wheel & Keel" (May); "Summer Along Lake" (May); "Brides" (June); "Sportsfishing" (July); "Back-to-School" (August); "Football" (September);

"Homemaking" (September); "Real Estate" (September); "Car Care" (October); "New Cars" (October); and "Winter Sports" (November).

Another Michigan paper, the *Owosso Argus-Press*, a 14,700-circulation evening paper, publishes fewer annual special sections: "Year's End," "Back-to-School," and "Christmas."[30]

The Importance of Sunday Planning

Sunday newspapers—attractive, bulky and profitable—are the single most important edition for many managers and are sure to become even more important.

Sunday papers grew explosively in numbers after World War II, while their Monday-through-Saturday brethren were shrinking. (See Table 7.2.)

Sunday growth results in large measure from advertiser awareness that readers have more time to leaf through their papers on Sundays and can thus be exposed to more ads for longer times. And the Sunday paper can be designed to "pull" all occupants of a household—children (in for comics today but serious readers tomorrow); teenagers, prime targets for advertisers because they are big spenders (teenagers spent an estimated $30 billion in 1986); housewives, who—with their food and other expenditures—virtually control the budget in most households; and head-of-household men who make "big ticket" purchases—cars, boats, houses.[31]

The Sunday paper is so popular with advertisers that its ad content outruns ads in Monday–Saturday papers. Total ad content was 68.8 percent on Sunday in 1984, 60.7 percent in daily morning papers, and 61.2 percent in evening papers (it was 63 percent for all papers—morning, evening, and Sunday).[32] Sunday ad

---

[28] "Weekday Circulation Lead Widens," *Editor & Publisher*, Dec. 12, 1981, p. 17.
[29] Advertisement, "A New Excitement Unfolds in Denver" *Denver Post*, July 31, 1982, p. 18.
[30] "Special Editions," *Editor & Publisher International Year Book*, 1980, p. I-145.
[31] "Putting On The Best Of Faces," *Advertising Age*, Aug. 1, 1983, p. M-10.
[32] *Facts About Newspapers '86*, American Newspaper Publishers' Association, p. 9.

Table 7.2 Growth of Sunday vs. Weekly Papers

	1946	1985	Change
Daily newspapers	1,763	1,676	−87 (−4.9%)
Sunday newspapers	497	798	+301 (+60.5%)
Daily circulation	50,927,505	62,723,438	+11,795,933 (+23.1%)
Sunday circulation	43,665,364	58,816,734	+15,151,370 (+34.6%)

Facts About Newspapers '86, American Newspaper Publishers' Association, 1986.

lineage is 22 to 35 percent or more of some metros' total for some weeks. Circulation often runs substantially ahead. For the *Dallas Morning News*, it is 22.3 percent higher; for the *Philadelphia Inquirer*, it is double that of weekday circulation.

The Sunday paper's contribution to total revenue is a tightly held secret in most management suites, but for some it's 30 to 40 percent. Costs for a bulky Sunday paper can run 30 percent or more higher than for a weekly edition, but the Sunday paper often delivers a higher percentage of profit. The *New York Times's* Sunday magazine, just one of that newspaper's impressive (and unique) Sunday components, drew $95.8 million ad revenue in 1984, according to the *Times* (the Publishers' Information Bureau put the figure at $108 million.)[33]

The title "Sunday Editor" is escalating in pecking-order importance in hundreds of newsrooms. The Sunday editor's challenge is quite different from that of daily newspaper colleagues. The Sunday editor must plan to cover spot news breaking Saturday for Sunday and sum up, with in-depth analysis, the past week's top news for thousands of readers not taking the daily paper. The Sunday editor must project ahead into what the coming week's news might be and delve into areas that are outside the news mainstream but of compelling interest to demographically upscale readers: the arts, food,

wine, books, "inside" business and sports, travel—all the informative esoterica that draws leisurely Sunday readers. This requires an acute sense of timing. To spread out printing demands and not strain press facilities, the Sunday editor plans to put many relatively timeless sections "to bed" early in the week.

The hard-news content of many Sunday papers shrinks as their sheer bulk forces earlier press times for even the front page ("Sunday" editions become available early Saturday evening in many cities.) But to be valid as a *news*paper, the Sunday edition must have substantial hard-news content, and that demands vigilant last-minute monitoring of news-agency wires and local spot-news beats before the presses roll on Saturday.

Because of this timing problem and the Sunday reader's leisurely reading habits, the Sunday paper is evolving strongly toward background and entertainment copy. That gives rise to special Sunday feature writers, columnists, book and arts reviewers, gardening and home maintenance specialists—and the Sunday magazine.

By 1987, 57 newspapers were producing their own Sunday magazines. For a few, it is a journalistically valid, profitable venture; for others, the Sunday magazine simply bleeds advertising from other sections or degenerates into a second-rate journalistic effort. After a fifteen-year fight, the *St. Petersburg (Fla.) Times,* an otherwise extremely successful newspaper, shut down its magazine, the Floridian, because, though journalistically sound, it was losing about $300,000

[33] Craig Endicott, "New York Times Magazine Not Resting On Laurels," *Advertising Age,* Jan. 24, 1985, p. 34.

annually. James Davy, president of MAG/NET, an association of fifty-six newspaper supplements, estimates that a third of his members made money that year on Sunday magazines, a third lost money, and a third broke even.[34]

Many Sunday editors contract to carry *Parade* or *USA Weekend* (formerly *Family Weekly*) magazines, both highly profitable national advertising vehicles. *Parade* in 1986 had 292 clients, with 31.6 million total circulation. Some *Parade* clients, including the *Dallas Morning News* and *Washington Post*, have their own magazine but still pay high tribute to *Parade*'s reader draw. The *Dallas Morning News* grabbed rights to *Parade* when the competing *Times Herald,* in a major tactical goof, dropped the popular magazine. At the *Washington Post,* President Thomas Ferguson, a former *Parade* executive, says *Parade* is more widely read than anything in his paper except the front page.[35] *USA Weekend* (acquired in 1985 by Gannett) served 263 papers with 13 million total circulation. Most are too small to create their own magazines. Some newspapers, particularly smaller ones, are unable to obtain *Parade* because that magazine has granted exclusive franchises to other newspapers.

In sum, in any newsroom's plan for quality the Sunday magazine is important. But as in all things journalistic, magazines that are poorly executed detract from editorial quality throughout the paper and are expensive. It will be safer for you, an aspiring manager, to learn it here, in this book, rather than in the real world of newspapering: Your newsroom planning must safeguard against wasteful spending. Failure to learn that early can cost you heavily when you launch your career. Wanton spending isn't permitted.

---

[34] "Future Cloudy For Sunday Supplements," *Advertising Age,* March 13, 1983, p. 3.
[35] "More Papers Publish Sunday Magazines, Gaining Prestige and Challenging *Parade,*" *Wall Street Journal,* June 1, 1982, p. 31.

HOW TO MANAGE THE NEWSROOM'S RESOURCES

A newsroom manager commands four basic resources, each of which must be employed with telling precision:

- First, *human resources,* Any newsroom manager responsible for more than two staffers is a manager of people—and their time—as much as an editor or journalist. If you don't like managing people, solving their problems, and motivating them to produce, you don't belong in management. Most of *your* time will be spent making sure that *their* time is used efficiently and effectively.

- Second, *money* for salaries, bonuses, travel— money to get the right people in the right place at the right time.

- Third, *external resources,* such as news services and syndicates, all major contributions to any newspaper's content (and costs).

- Fourth, the *newshole,* precious space accorded the newsroom for each day's coverage, from Afghanistan to Main Street, from politics to "Dear Abby."

From an editor's view, there is never enough of the four; however, the business office often feels that there *is* enough. That difference of opinion can preoccupy both news and business managers.

Managing Internal Resources

In the newsroom as elsewhere in the newspaper, a manager's basic task is to recruit the staffers required (or permitted by the budget), train and motivate them to perform in accord with plan, then control and adjust their performance. Chapter 5 covers principles of the basic human resources task. We will zero in here on specific newsroom issues.

It often is said that you need one staffer per 1,000 circulation. It's a rule of thumb that won't stand examination: surveys show that newspapers employ anywhere from 0.7 staffers per 1,000 circulation to 1.4 or more. The difference ties back to two issues:

- The overall strategic goals of the newspaper, its competitive strength, and the financial strength it enjoys and is willing to commit. In a competitive fight, with a goal of winning through superior news coverage, more staff obviously will be employed if the corporate pocketbook permits.

- The state of the newspaper's technology. When first introduced, new technology tended to reduce the newsroom staff through automation. However, subsequent automation in production and other departments has shifted to the newsroom new functions in *manufacturing* the newspaper as well as producing journalistic content. That tends to force increases in newsroom staff (and, because technology varies, it throws into a cocked hat any traditional staff-to-circulation ratios).

In its drive for market supremacy, the *Dallas Morning News* added staffers so quickly that the ratio dropped from nearly one staffer per 1,000 circulation to about one per 950 in just months. One large regional paper, the *Des Moines Register & Tribune*, had a ratio of one to 1,458; a smaller Iowa paper, the 21,500-circulation *Burlington Hawk Eye*, at the same time employed 1 to 1,264. A survey of 153 papers of 20,000 to 100,000 circulation showed that they averaged 1.1 staffers per 1,000 circulation.[36]

Training for Quality Results

The newsroom manager aggressively recruits the most talented staff available, of course. But then what? Proper training can have great impact on quality performance. In-house training by senior reporters or editors is fine, but in reality deadline pressure often limits the number of experienced trainers available. Key staffers should be given outside training. Some of the best programs available are at the following:

- *American Newspaper Publishers' Association*, Training Services Department, The Newspaper Center, 11600 Sunrise Valley Drive, Reston, VA 22091.

- *American Press Institute*, 11690 Sunrise Valley Drive, Reston, VA 22091. (Strong on training for small-paper community journalism.)

- *National Newspaper Association*, 1627 K St., NW, Suite 400, Washington, DC 20006. (Its members are weekly and small daily newspapers and it often conducts training programs with state press associations.)

- *Inland Daily Press Association*, Suite 802 West, 840 N. Lake Shore Drive, Chicago, IL 60611.

- *Southern Newspaper Publishers' Association*, 6065 Barfield Road, Suite 222, Atlanta, GA 30328. To assist community newspapers, SNPA maintains a "Smaller Newspaper Committee."

- *Suburban Newspapers of America*, 111 E. Wacker Drive, Chicago, IL 60601.

The Associated Press Managing Editor's Association found that two-thirds of 150 newspapers in one survey had *no* budget for training meetings, seminars, or staff education programs. Funds switched to training from other budget areas, such as travel, ranged from $2,900 average for papers under 20,000 circulation to $12,000 for those over 100,000 circulation.[37] Such an unstructured, underfunded approach cannot produce quality training.

---

[36] *Newsroom Management Committee Report*, op. cit.

[37] *Newsroom Management Committee Report*, op. cit.

Trained news specialists can yield great dividends in readership. The general-assignment reporter, the journalistic switch-hitter who (some say with varying degrees of accuracy) quickly can get atop just about any type story, is still welcome in the newsroom. But in covering and "translating" enormously complex stories in law, medicine, science, and other highly technical areas, a reporter must have a solid academic background or proven expertise, developed on the beat, in reading or patient, time-consuming digging. Stories are too important and readers are too sophisticated, well educated, and skeptical to accept slapdash reporting and writing. Indeed, with newspapers dispensing advice on everything from the health of the heart to health of the mind, stories are too crucial to life itself to be left to amateurs.

Planning Staff Time Carefully

With salaries rising steadily and the work week getting shorter, the newsroom manager must budget staff time for effective use of every minute.

A reporter hanging around the coffee machine waiting for the next assignment is a valuable resource that is not being used effectively. A copy desk without time management will be overstaffed at some times and understaffed at others.

Union contracts or company policy establish work regulations—how many hours, how many days, whether the night-side staff works fewer hours than the day side, how much vacation time to grant, and so on. But within the confines of such policy, each newsroom manager must establish detailed time management. A few essentials:

- Time is money, and you never have enough of either. Look upon time, yours and the staff's, as one of your most valuable resources. Don't waste it.

- Lay down a written plan for how your staff will be employed. Schedule workdays and

hours in advance, two weeks or more, if possible, so employees can organize their personal lives and lay down *their* time management plans.

- Write a daily budget assigning each on-duty staffer. Be specific: story (or other task), time, location, approximate time to be spent, results expected.

- Be demanding. One of your important managerial responsibilities is to obtain optimum payback from every resource utilized. Demand effective payback for time spent.

Caution:

- Newspapers don't manufacture widgets and newsroom staffers are not unthinking robots who are paid for piecework. Creativity is the newsroom's business, and it doesn't come in planned, predictable bursts Monday through Friday, 8 A.M. to 5 P.M. Be flexible in time management, and when you smell a good story let them run after it without punching a time clock. And be prepared for them to come back dry occasionally, without the story; that's the news business.

- Reporters, writers, and editors are highly individualistic in talent and abilities. Consider each staffer's very own strengths and weaknesses and budget time accordingly. Staffer A will whip through a complicated financial story in no time flat; Staffer B will sweat for hours over it. In news, unlike a factory production line, a body is not just a body. (See box for the profile of the American journalist.)

Plan Your Money Management Carefully

Even on smaller papers, editors today spend a great deal of money; unless you can handle it

PORTRAIT OF THE JOURNALIST

Who is the American journalist? A survey of 1,000 newspaper journalists financed by Gannet Foundation in 1982–83 drew this portrait:

Male, 66%

White, 95%

Brought up in a church, 93% (Protestant, 60%)

Has B.A. degree, 55% (took at least some courses in journalism, 60%)

Married, 56%; has children, 73%; is age 32

Reads *Editor & Publisher Magazine*, 63%; *Columbia Journalism Review*, 60%; *Time*, 49%; *Newsweek*, 43%; *New York Times*, 33%; *Wall Street Journal*, 25%

Watches local TV news five times weekly, network news three times weekly

Is middle-of-road politically, 59%

"Helping people" is major job satisfaction, 61%; is fairly satisfied with job, 44%; very satisfied, 40%

Financial matters may cause him or her to seek new job, 50%

Sees investigating government claims and informing public quickly as key journalistic roles, 90%

Richard G. Gray and G. Cleveland Wilhoit, paper presented to American Society of Newspaper Editors, Denver, Colo., May 9, 1983.

---

effectively, you don't qualify for newsroom management.

A basic accounting course gets you over "math fright" and enables you to construct a budget as an evaluation and control tool. But to employ newsroom funds effectively, you must learn through experience where to use your money resources and when.

How much money is enough? That depends on the newspaper's overall financial condition and its goal in journalistic quality and profit. The editors of the largest papers spend $50 million or more annually; editors of smaller dailies and weeklies obviously make do with considerably less. In one survey, 144 editors revealed their newsroom costs on average are 15.16 percent of the newspaper's total "operating expense" and 11.75 percent of "total revenue." News expense is about 18 percent of "operating revenues" for papers under 20,000 circulation; over 100,000, about 12.5 percent. Measured against "total expense," newsroom budgets range from 7 percent to 20 percent (higher the circulation, the lower the percentage, because of

the economies of scale achieved by larger-circulation papers.)[38]

Fourteen papers of 38,000 circulation or less studied by ANPA's *presstime* magazine averaged slightly more than 15 percent of total operating expense with a high of 20 percent.[39] The weakness in such figures is apparent: None reflects such variables as competitive posture, market share, sense of journalistic mission, desire for quality.

Newsroom money management, in effect, is people management. Before it was sold in 1985 to Gannett, the 315,000-circulation *Des Moines Register & Tribune* spent 79 percent of its newsroom and editorial department budget on payroll. And that did not include fringe benefits and payroll taxes or the top two editors, whose salaries were on a separate payroll. The

---

[38] "Editors Need Larger Role In Budgeting Process, INCFO Told," *Southern Newspaper Publishers' Association Bulletin*, July 7, 1983, p. 3.
[39] C. David Rambo, "Excellence," *presstime*, November 1984, p. 15.

21,000-circulation *Burlington (Iowa) Hawk Eye* spent 68 percent of its newsroom budget on payroll. (The *Hawk Eye* spent $293,322 on news editorial costs but $330,083 for newsprint; the circulation department spent $260,042 delivering the paper, including $62,145 for postage.)

So, if you want dollar effectiveness, look to people costs. Three expense problems relate to how people are managed:

1. The number of employees inevitably expands without plan. Part-time employees show up on a full-time basis; temporary hires for a single project suddenly become indispensable. *No* addition in either category should be made without careful study of need and formal approval by the newsroom manager.

2. Overtime. Paying 1½ to 2 times regular salaries for overtime can raise costs quickly. Often, managers try to avoid adding a regular staffer, who can be paid at regular rates, by filling schedule gaps with overtime assignments—at a cost much above an additional salary. Calculate which costs less.

3. Variable costs—telephone, travel, expense accounts—can get out of hand quickly. In one year, the *Des Moines Register & Tribune* spent $116,000 on plane tickets for reporters and photographers; $96,000 on taxis, rental cars, and gasoline for their own cars. The newsroom's telephone bill was $112,000. The *Burlington Hawk Eye*, with seventeen reporters and editors, spent $10,687 on travel, $16,720 on long-distance telephone.

The newsroom manager—whether the title is executive editor, editor, or managing editor—carries final responsibility for constructing the department's budget and making sure that it is followed. However, many newspapers delegate day-to-day monitoring of budget performance to an administrative assistant—a person with news background plus a bent for financial detail. This person helps draw up the budget, approves all expenses, tracks down and corrects any unfavorable variances from budget, and has authority to cut back in one expense area to compensate for unfavorable variances in another. In sum, the challenge is to use every dollar effectively in the drive for improved journalistic quality.

Managing External Resources

We have seen that a table of organization sketches control of *internal* news-gathering resources. For the *Athens Daily News* and *Banner-Herald*, it leads from publisher to managing editor and, eventually, to a stringer paid by the published story for community news.

A newspaper also marshals major *external* news-gathering resources for readers. These resources can be formidable in size and quality, costly, and pivotal in news operations. Each manager must understand clearly how they operate. They are *news agencies*, primarily the Associated Press and United Press International; *supplemental news services*, such as the New York Times News Service and the Los Angeles Times-Washington Post News Service; and the *syndicates*, United Features Syndicate, King Features, and scores of others.

Managing News Service Relationships

The Associated Press—the name dates to the 1840s—was reorganized in 1894 as a nonprofit cooperative, and now approaches the 1990s as the world's dominant general news agency. It serves newspapers with 91 percent of the U.S. daily circulation.

AP's worldwide revenue in 1985 was $206 million. Its competitive strength stems from its cooperative nature, which gives even the smallest newspaper member representation on a twenty-two-person board of directors and a direct vote at the annual meeting in AP affairs.

Member newspapers are obligated contractually to contribute their news to the cooperative. That means AP's news-gathering resources include 1,500 U.S. newspapers and 5,700 radio and TV stations. News-exchange agreements with thousands of overseas newspapers and broadcast stations, directly or through national news agencies, give AP unrivaled news-gathering resources.

The newspaper desiring AP news or photo service must be voted into membership by the cooperative and must agree to pay weekly assessments levied as the newspaper's proportionate share of AP's costs.

Broadcast members and overseas subscribers cover much of AP's costs. Newspaper members in the United States contribute about 48.5 percent. AP service costs substantially more than that of other agencies. Some newspapers, the *New York Times* and *Los Angeles Times* among them, pay $1 million annually for AP services, although assessments of $200 weekly or so are common for small dailies.

Two factors are particularly operative for you as a manager:

1. AP member newspapers large or small are entitled to call on AP for special coverage—a story on a local man injured skiing in Switzerland, for example, or national and state divorce rates as background on a local story about divorce. Make sure all editors are aware of this.

2. AP's membership contract requires two years' notice of intent to cancel, and the contract is an open-ended commitment to pay whatever assessments the board levies. That means there is no negotiating AP's basic membership fee.

United Press International, financially weak and scrambling in the 1980s to stay in business, is easier to deal with on rates (UPI's 1985 revenue was $90 million; it had an operating loss of $1.3 million). UPI attempts to model its business practices after AP's but has a reputation for chopping rates to get business. In 1985, for example, the *Los Angeles Times* paid AP at the annual rate of $1,066,988, UPI $682,916. Price chopping inevitably feeds a downward spiral of reduced revenue, forcing service cutbacks that weaken the news report and, in turn, putting more downward pressure on rates.

An unending economic squeeze (UPI lost money *each* year from 1964 to 1984) brought despair to E. W. Scripps Co., 90 percent owner of UPI (Hearst Corp. owned 10 percent). Scripps put seventy-six-year-old UPI up for sale, but for two years there were no takers. Then, in 1982, little-known Media News Corp. acquired UPI. The company has been reorganized since then under a wealthy Mexican publisher, Mario Vazquez-Rana, but UPI is still without AP's cooperative, nonprofit structure and financial strength.

Both AP and UPI provide many services: computerized high-speed general news wires, full-time sports and photo services, state news circuits, mail packets of columns and features for smaller papers. Selectively acquiring AP or UPI services will give a newspaper powerful news resources at costs low compared to cost of internal resources. This sometimes leads papers to fill columns with wire copy simply to reduce expenses.

AP surveyed 2,336 publishers and editors in 1986, and the 40 percent who responded reported that on average, 37 percent of their newshole was filled by AP copy for 17 percent of their newsroom budget. Large papers spend an even lower percentage on AP. Reg Murphy, publisher of the *Baltimore Sun*, calculates that in 1983 AP costs were 4 percent of his *news* budget (not total newspaper budget) and that AP provided 24 percent of news the *Sun* published. The *Phoenix Gazette and Arizona Republic* spends 4 percent of its editorial budget for AP service in return for 37 percent of its news content. Smaller papers can get a combined service of international, national, and state news for the cost of a full-time reporter or two. Compare your news service costs and usage with those figures.

A third international agency, Reuters, historically owned primarily by British and Commonwealth papers but since 1984 publicly owned, occasionally tries to penetrate the U.S. newspaper market. But Reuters concentrates worldwide on delivering economic, financial, and commodity news to private subscribers. It is well managed and profitable (profits of $79.6 million in 1985 on revenues of $629.5 million), providing strong coverage from some parts of the world, primarily the Commonwealth and former British Empire. But it lacks U.S. domestic news in depth and is only a secondary agency for its handful of U.S. newspaper subscribers (it has just a few U.S. bureaus; AP has 135 in the United States and 83 overseas). Reuters entered the photo business by purchasing UPI's overseas photo operations.

Dealing with Supplementals and Syndicates

Strong supplemental news services are operated by a number of U.S. newspapers. They started as salvage services, selling news and feature copy prepared for their mother papers, but they gradually moved into true agency operation by originating copy exclusively for their wires and tailoring news reports for both morning and afternoon papers. One effect is that many editors drop UPI and retain AP as a basic service backed by a supplemental. The most important supplementals are operated by the *New York Times* and jointly by the *Washington Post* and *Los Angeles Times.*

Dow Jones and Knight-Ridder have services, too. Their attractiveness is twofold: (1) they carry excellent copy from some of the world's most prestigious papers and (2) clients can get exclusivity in a market (AP and UPI must by law serve all qualified applicants). Most supplementals will negotiate rates and contract terms.

In a highly competitive environment, syndicates negotiate their prices wildly for thousands of offerings—comic strips, crossword puz-

zles, horoscope features, you name it. Small papers pay as little as $4 to $5 weekly for even nationally syndicated columns, large papers pay $300 or more.

Popular comic strips ("must" Sunday reading for more than two-thirds of child readers, polls show, and more than half the adults) draw substantial prices. Large papers pay $1,000 or more weekly for a popular strip like "Peanuts" (which in 1984 became the first comic to run in more than 2,000 papers in the United States and abroad). Other comics are often cheap.

Syndicate rates are ostensibly based on circulation, but they really are what you can negotiate. (At a time when the *Des Moines Register & Tribune* paid $37.50 weekly for the Ann Landers' column, the *Burlington Hawk Eye* paid $7.65 weekly for "Dear Abby.")

From many internal and external resources, then, news flows into the newsroom in great volume. AP alone can deliver millions of words daily without strain. So the newsroom manager must carefully use this precious resource, space. The news hole can range from, say, 25 percent of a large metropolitan daily on heavy advertising days to 60 percent or more of the small daily. An Inland Daily Press Association study shows that papers up to 50,000 circulation on average devote 52 percent of total space to news and information. (Paid advertising gets 46 percent, unpaid advertising, such as house ads, gets 2 percent.)

An increase in number of pages printed has increased the news hole substantially. A Newspaper Advertising Bureau study shows that the average weekday edition grew from 20.5 pages of news and editorial matter in 1977 to 27.5 in 1983, an increase of more than 34 percent. The average Sunday edition grew from 45.5 news and editorial pages to 79.2, a 40 percent increase.

Newshole size varies widely, but *not* in direct response to news availability; it is determined by the advertising department. On the basis of advertising sold, the ad department calculates number of pages needed. Ad layouts are made on page forms and given to the

SETTING *USA Today's* "TONE"

USA Today, Gannett's national daily launched in 1982, boasts a colorful "with it" tone that created the fastest circulation success of any American newspaper: In seven months, it grew to more than 1.3 million circulation. The paper's start-up editor, John Curley (now president of Gannett), says the experience gives him a few clues to editing a national newspaper:

- Keep stories short. Upscale readers have many demands on their time and desire brevity.
- Edit for clarity, particularly in sports.
- Hire more editors even at the expense of reporters.
- Stories should inform and be interesting, not boring.

- Emphasize graphics that help tell a story. Crop photos effectively and make sure cut lines make sense.
- Do more stories on personal finance, new technology, and gimmicks that people can use in daily life.
- Don't always run negative stories.
- Weather news is important.
- Readers want portions of newspapers at different times for different things—in the morning for sports and hard news, later for leisure reading of feature copy.

Curley tells fellow editors faced with the daily challenge of producing a paper amid chaos and disorganization: "Regain control of the asylum from the inmates."

---

newsroom, which only then learns how many columns it has to fill with news and which pages are "open" for news and photo copy. Note that it is not the newsroom that decides on the news hole or what the ad/news ratio will be on a given page. For many papers, the size of the day's paper often is set in response to food advertising, the largest single ad revenue source for many dailies and weeklies and estimated at well over $1 billion nationwide.[40] An Advertising Bureau survey of 130 food retailers shows that 73 percent advertise on Wednesdays (when housewives plan food shopping for weekends), 38 percent on Sundays, 31 percent on Thursdays, 29 percent on Mondays, 20 percent on Tuesdays, 7 percent on Fridays, and 6 percent on Saturdays. News-coverage planning often revolves around such considerations. Wednesday papers are "big," Saturday papers "thin."

The key to efficient use of both news resources and newshole lies in selecting which

stories and photos to print and basing their length and display on news merits. It is a delicate process.

Initial winnowing and sifting of copy is extremely important. The immediate task is to quickly discard the irrelevant and unimportant and begin "working" copy that might qualify for publication. A manager must direct sharp attention to this point in the copy-handling chain, examining both the efficiency of the systems for selecting copy and the professionalism of the men and women doing it. Call them "copy testers," "gatekeepers," or "editors," the desk people who handle those thousands of words minute by minute greatly influence a newspaper's content and its journalistic stance (See box for the views of President John Curley of Gannett.)

There are many "copy flow" charts and systems. (There is even the "furniture mover" school of newsroom management, which experiments continually with flow of copy over square desks, around round desks, or through L-shaped desks, searching for ever-elusive optimum efficiency. The author once labored under an editor

---

[40] David Astor, "Food Shopper Shifts Help Newspapers, Says Survey," *Editor & Publisher,* April 2, 1983, p. 14.

who tried them all until, it seemed, every conceivable configuration had been exhausted. The editor then sawed 6 inches off all desk legs, explaining that lower desks are easier to work at. Speechless, the staff squatted down and got to it.) Each manager should develop the system that is best for the newspaper's individual needs and, importantly, for the staff talent available. It would be futile for the editor of the 14,700-circulation *Owosso (Mich.) Argus-Press* to model a system for handling a small staff and comparative trickle of copy on the system developed at the *New York Times*.

Whatever the system, it must provide for copytasting simultaneously on various desks—city, business, state, national, sports. And as deadline approaches, so does another crucial point in the copy-handling chain where a newsroom manager must assert firm control. This is the story conference. It is a daily brawl at some newspapers; a quiet, scholarly discussion at others. Whatever the level of emotion, it is the time when editors from various desks begin competing seriously to get their copy into that day's paper. The newsroom manager must intervene decisively to avoid deadlock if, say, the foreign editor demands the front-page lead position for the latest guerrilla attack in Afghanistan while the city editor argues that last night's city council meeting is the lead.

Managing the Newspaper's Tone

The newspaper's journalistic tone is set in the process of selecting which stories to publish, how they will be written, which headlines to run, and how pages will be laid out. Choices are infinite—anything between rape, pillage, and burn in bold colors beneath shouting headlines on the one hand and, on the other, routine stories written by uninspired writers under sleepy headlines for a gray front page.

There is no universal standard of what is correct and what is not. The *New York Post*, its red-daubed front page screaming about the day's icepick stabbing in Central Park, would wither corn and dry up cows if it were sold on street

corners in Athens, Ga. The *Athens Daily News* and *Banner-Herald*, their quiet and conservative front pages attuned to their small-town and rural audience, could only murmur ineffectually at thousands of harried New Yorkers streaming past subway newsstands. Don't copy another paper's approach. Design *your* paper's tone to meet *its* market's needs. Matching tone to market determines your paper's success in circulation, advertising, profitability. (See box for a list of papers considered successful in accomplishing that in their markets.)

If the newspaper is designed as a more attractive news and information tool that readers can use effectively, the logical packaging of both news and ads will pull readers more deeply into the newspaper and hold them there longer. And the more time readers spend going through pages, the happier your advertisers will be.

Increasingly, newspapers use design specialists called art directors, creative directors, or design editors. Their tools are photos, graphics of all kinds, color, and creative thinking about layout and design. The pressure to achieve better design stems primarily from three sources: (1) improved production techniques, permitting more and better color throughout a newspaper; (2) *USA Today's* example of successful graphics and color; and (3) market research showing that readers want newspapers that are better looking and easier to use.

Helpful hints on better layout and design came from a Southern Newspaper Publishers' Association Conference in 1985. The following list is adapted from a discussion led by Nanette Bisher, assistant managing editor for graphics of the *Santa Ana (Calif.) Orange County Register*:

1. Design pages for simple reading; lead readers to stories and steer them through.

2. Strive for horizontal design; don't revert to the traditional up-and-down design.

3. Fit design to reader habits. Modular makeup, constructed block by block, helps readers concentrate on one element at a time.

Time's TOP TEN

Few subjects create more controversy among journalists than which daily newspapers are best. Some journalists (and the author) maintain that there is no universal standard of excellence—that a newspaper should be judged only on whether it properly serves its own readers, advertisers, and community, not on any national or industrywide scale.

Nevertheless, periodic attempts are made to draw up "ten best" list. In 1984, *Time* magazine published a list based on its staff's study of "imaginative staff coverage of regional, national and foreign issues; liveliness in writing, layout and graphics; national impact achieved through general enterprise, command of some particular field of coverage on a track record of training top-rank younger journalists."

In alphabetical order:

	DAILY CIRCULATION	SUNDAY CIRCULATION
Boston Globe	515,000	782,000
Chicago Tribune	751,000	1,116,000
Des Moines Register	239,000	381,000
Los Angeles Times	1,038,000	1,294,000
Miami Herald	407,000	495,000
New York Times	911,000	1,523,000
Philadelphia Inquirer	533,000	995,000
St. Petersburg Times	243,000	310,000
Wall Street Journal	2,020,000	—
Washington Post	719,000	997,000

Source: "The Ten Best U.S. Dailies," *Time* magazine, April 30, 1984.

4. Avoid continuing stories to another page; if jumping stories is unavoidable, jump as many as possible to the same page.

5. Build each page around a dominant story, signaling readers which story editors regard as most important.

6. Use dominant art—one strong story or a story/photo/graphic package.

7. Balance the page and design the entire page, not just the top half ("above the fold") or the dominant element.

8. Organize material with boxes, but don't overuse this device; two per page is probably the limit.

9. Typeface helps determine a newspaper's personality, so don't confuse readers by varying it too much. Use type creatively and consistently; it's effective in breaking up gray areas.

10. Have fun.

Caution: The most creative design director cannot overcome fundamental weaknesses in news coverage and content. Emphasize news substance first. Beware of what Richard Smyser, editor of the *Oak Ridge (Tenn.) Oak Ridger*, calls the "pretty newspaper syndrome." Don't go too far and use pictures for the sake of pictures, color for the sake of color. *News* is still a newspaper's primary attraction.

Now, is it all working? Is your paper improved? Are you meeting reader needs? Let's turn to some ways of measuring.

EVALUATING AND CONTROLLING IN THE NEWSROOM

As newsroom manager, you design what you hope is an effective organization, you motivate people, and you plan the efficient use of money, time, news hole. Are you succeeding? Perhaps nowhere else in the newspaper is answering that so difficult.

Evaluating newsroom performance and controlling the effort to reach planned goals involves subjective judgments. Oh, you can evaluate your work schedules and employee motivation by whether people show up for work on time. And comparing costs to budget will determine whether the staff is spending beyond your means for telephone calls or travel. But what you must *really* evaluate at the end of each day, week, and month is whether your newspaper's overall impact in news—its professionalism, its tone—meets your audience's needs and meshes with the overall marketing effort. To judge, run down the following checklist.

The Busy Manager's News Checklist

Ask these questions:

- Is the paper accurate in minor as well as important detail and does it enjoy reader trust? Does it have credibility?

- Is it balanced and fair, reporting all sides of an issue in an objective, dispassionate manner?

- Does it cover the local scene? Can your readers learn from it what is happening in their hometown?

- Is it geographically complete, covering area, state, national, and world news? Is it well rounded, with full subject diversity, covering all types of news?

- Does the newspaper demonstrate enterprise, going beyond the routine to seek out and explain meaningful developments?

- Does it capture the drama of life or is it dull, unexciting? And does it have that occasional humorous story that brings a smile to reader lips?

- Acknowledging that news values vary, does the paper display judgment in emphasizing meaningful news and ignoring trivia?

- Is its writing professional and grammatically correct? Is copy clear, concise, readable?

- Is it a newspaper of good taste and can it be taken into the homes of your town?

- People are news. Are people in the newspaper?

- Do photographs and cut lines help tell the story? Does the paper have professional, understandable graphics?

- Is the layout open and airy, and does it make efficient use of news hole? Are headlines clear and well written?

- Is the paper competitive? To win in this business, a newspaper must beat somebody. Did you beat somebody today?

SUMMARY

A newspaper's survival ultimately depends on whether its news content meets the needs of its readers, and this news effort must be dovetailed into the overall marketing concept. Whether the competition is another paper of like size and characteristics or an entirely different medium, news is at the tip of the marketing spear.

The design of the news organization takes shape against the backdrop of important changes in the newspaper industry. Suburban journalism is growing rapidly and many afternoon papers, particularly those in large cities, are in trouble. Managers must adapt to their marketplace and plan the coverage it requires. For a metro daily or rural weekly, the table of organization must bring the newsroom and editors into the mainstream of planning.

Planning for quality must include a willingness to spend for newsroom resources; the hiring of strong news managers, reporters and editors; identification and coverage of the newspaper's area of opportunity; researching of reader needs and desires; and then designing the paper for its own particular market.

From all this, plus the responsibility of spending sometimes millions of dollars annually, comes an expanded definition of the newsroom manager's job. Top editors today are deeply involved in "business" affairs and the efficient use of newsroom resources—people, money, time, and the news hole.

Publishers and editors often misjudge reader needs and desires. Detailed readership research is a must, whether through expensive surveys by outside firms or inexpensive, do-it-yourself techniques such as encounter groups.

Plan to personalize the paper, organize its content, make it more readable, particularly the showcases: front page, business section, editorial page, sports section, and those pages of statistics on birth, death and life in your town. Plan for efficient use of internal news resources, such as staff and stringers, plus external resources such as news agencies and syndicates.

Then, decide whether your newspaper's news and information content—its journalistic "tone"—matches needs of its market and its time.

RECOMMENDED READING

On a continuing basis, outstanding work in newsroom management is reported in ANPA's *presstime*, ASNE's *Bulletin*, and APME's *Continuing Studies* and *APME Red Book*.

Also note, *Relating to Readers in the 80s*, readership research commissioned by ASNE, funded by United Press International and conducted by Clark, Martire & Bartolomeo, Inc. *Journalism Quarterly* presents scholarly analysis of newsroom issues; *Washington Journalism Review* and *Columbia Journalism Review* are excellent monthlies.

Note David Halberstam, *The Powers That Be*, New York, Knopf, 1979; Ben Bagdikian, *The Information Machines*, New York, Harper & Row, 1971.

Two excellent sources are Philip Meyer, *The Newspaper Survival Book: An Editor's Guide to Marketing Research*, Bloomington, Ind., Indiana University Press, 1985; and G. Cleveland Wilhoit and David H. Weaver, *Newsroom Guide to Polls & Surveys*, Reston, Va., ANPA, 1980.

CHAPTER EIGHT | Circulation

In Chapter 7 we discussed your role as a manager in creating the right news product. We now turn to getting that product to the right consumers at the right time. If you think this involves only a simple sales and distribution project, think again. Newspaper circulation work is highly complex.

In large measure, the complexity ties to a change in advertiser thinking. No longer is the sophisticated advertiser interested merely in how many papers you sell. Today, that advertiser wants, first, assurance you are selling a newspaper which will satisfy reader needs and thus be closely read and, second, that you are delivering it in timely, reliable fashion to the right people—those ready, willing, and able to purchase the advertiser's goods or services.

For you as a manager, the challenge is to thoroughly integrate your circulation effort into the newspaper's overall marketing strategy and then, at acceptable cost, get the paper to sufficient numbers of consumers that strategy identifies as primary targets. It is worth emphasizing that the marketing concept requires tightly coordinated, interdependent effort by all principal departments: news, advertising, production, promotion, and circulation. We treat them sequentially not to suggest priority but because, unfortunately, in a book one chapter must follow another.

So, we turn to circulation, an immensely complicated, important part of the newspaper's integrated marketing thrust.

THE SITUATION TODAY

Slippery variables make it difficult to fashion circulation strategy for the 1990s. Traditional methods are inadequate. Fresh thinking is needed. In brief, this is what is happening:

- Advertisers are redefining what is attractive circulation and what isn't. They want to pay for delivering their message only to prospective customers living close to retail outlets and ready and willing to buy. For many newspapers, distant circulation built over decades at enormous cost is suddenly "inefficient" and must be terminated.

- Readers pay huge amounts of money for daily and Sunday newspapers (well over $6 billion nationwide), but this sum provides only about 20 percent of most papers' total revenue and often does not cover newsprint costs, let alone the costs of news collection, printing, and distribution. Reader contribution to revenue must be increased.

- Soaring distribution costs, particularly for labor and gasoline, raise to 30 percent or more the circulation department's share of most newspapers' total costs, thus sharply threatening profits.

- Changing American life-styles, particularly the expansion of single-parent households, could invalidate newspaper content and distribution techniques tailored for traditional households of mother, father, and children.

Broadcast media, shoppers, and direct mail challenge newspapers by offering both total market coverage (TMC) to reach all households in a market and selective market coverage (SMC) to reach narrow market segments or just the affluent readers so desired by advertisers.

Anyone aspiring to a manager's role in the 1990s must understand the impact of these changes on operations. Let's look at what hap-pened to newspapers in the Twin Cities of Minneapolis and St. Paul, Minn., as such changes swept those markets.

In the 1930s, John Cowles, Sr., thought big in planning a circulation market for his *Minneapolis Star* and *Tribune*. The entire Upper Midwest would be his turf; his newspapers would span Minnesota's forests and the Dakota prairies, perhaps reaching even beyond. Cowles succeeded, establishing by the 1960s a complex system of more than 14,000 carriers covering thousands of square miles and offering doorstep delivery in far-flung outposts, including Igloo, S.D., 700 miles from Minneapolis. By 1973, combined circulation for Cowles's morning and afternoon papers topped 485,000; their editorial voices were powerful throughout the region.

But beneath the rosy surface, all was not well. Newsprint, $179 a ton in 1970, skyrocketed to over $500 in the early 1980s. Gasoline and other distribution costs rose rapidly. Wages, crucial in labor-intensive circulation work, jumped ahead. Subscription prices, however, lagged. Local retail advertisers, the single most important source of newspaper revenue, lost interest in paying for circulation in Igloo or anywhere else far away. Suddenly, yesteryear's circulation triumph was *today's expensive liability*.

The company had not adjusted gradually to change—had not shifted circulation priorities to meet new marketplace realities—and now it was forced into draconian measures. John Cowles, Jr., who succeeded his father as president in 1968, began a full retreat toward home base, vacating the vast marketplace the elder Cowles had so painstakingly built. Like many regional papers, the *Star* and *Tribune* found the circulation empire's outer reaches no longer tenable. In 1982, Cowles merged them into a single paper, The *Star & Tribune*, with 360,000 initial circulation, down a whopping 25 percent from 1973.

Even in its shrunken form, however, the *Star & Tribune* tried to handle a huge circulation territory—a seven-county metro area around

Minneapolis and St. Paul. It was still too big.

In neighboring St. Paul, meanwhile, Knight-Ridder's *Pioneer Press and Dispatch* were anticipating change and adjusting, not reacting, to it. Key to *Pioneer Press and Dispatch* strategy was intensive cultivation of a tight three-county area around St. Paul. In light of cost/revenue realities in the 1980s, that was wise. Donald Dwight, then presiding as Cowles' publisher in Minneapolis over an extremely high-cost operation, was envious: "St. Paul's distribution costs are just so appreciably lower than ours because they distribute in a much smaller area—wisely, because the profitability has got to be much better."[1]

In sum, circulation success traditionally meant selling more and more newspapers, regardless of who bought them or where they lived. No more. Circulation today must be established among consumers in areas carefully selected for advertiser needs. For, without advertising support, circulation is a cost factor, not a profit generator. Cowles didn't recognize that early enough; Knight-Ridder did. In attitudes and structure, the circulation organization must be designed to look anew at how newspapers are sold and distributed.

DESIGNING THE CIRCULATION ORGANIZATION

The circulation department's primary objective is planning, then achieving circulation expansion in accord with the newspaper's overall strategy. It is a formidable challenge requiring that the department be organized properly.

First, organizational design must ensure that circulation pulls effectively with news, advertising, production, and promotion departments.

Second, circulation must receive sufficient

---

[1] Don Clark, "Economic Stress Changes Shape of Newspaper," *St. Paul Pioneer Press/Dispatch*, March 27, 1982, p. 1.

resources, including truly outstanding managerial talent. The department is key to marketing success and cannot be starved for resources.

The Table of Organization

Changes under way externally in the newspaper's marketplace, plus internal adoption of the marketing concept, require transforming the circulation department from a semiautonomous unit reporting directly to the publisher into one that reports to the chief marketing executive. Top management must grant circulation managers major voice at the policymaking level. For many newspapers, this means circulators for the first time will help plan strategy. Top managers themselves must get involved in circulation—its planning, strategy, and execution. Many managers never have done this. Barriers between departments must come down—something other departments, particularly news, often resist. Marketing managers must keep circulators aware of what advertisers want; news managers should receive feedback from circulation salespeople on how the public regards the product.

Within the circulation department, thinking must expand beyond simply selling and distributing newspapers into entirely new dimensions of marketing strategy. For example, sales pushes cannot be made into new neighborhoods merely because, like mountains, they are there to be conquered; rather, sales efforts must be made in areas that are attractive to advertisers and covered by the newsroom.

Departmental design must also establish a hierarchy along unequivocally clear lines. The organization itself need not be complex, though the task is. See Figure 8.1 for a simple but effective table of organization for the *Athens (Ga.) Daily News* and *Banner-Herald*, which has a 9,900 morning and a 12,700 afternoon circulation.

Six subordinates report directly to the circulation director who, in turn, reports directly to the publisher. At these papers, the publisher serves as chief marketing executive.

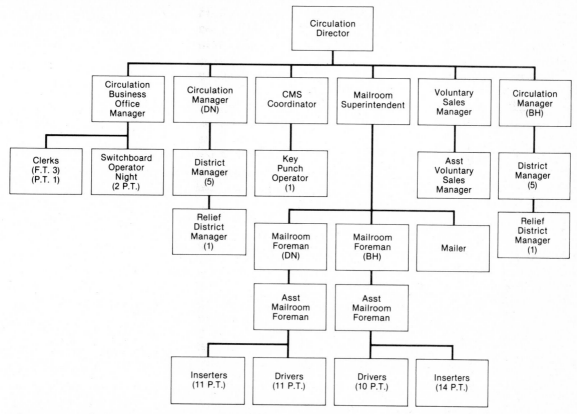

Figure 8.1 *Athens (Ga.) Daily News* **and** *Banner-Herald*

1. A *business office manager* supervises clerks and telephone operators who take "start" orders for new subscriptions and "stop" orders for cancellations. Note that part-time operators are available at night to customers who have delivery complaints.

2. *Circulation managers* (one for the *Daily News*, another for the *Banner-Herald*) supervise district managers (DMs), who in turn recruit, train, and supervise carriers.

3. A *circulation management systems (CMS) coordinator* is responsible primarily for computerized lists of subscribers and non-subscribers essential in methodical sales.

4. A *mailroom superintendent* handles mail circulation, of course—but also much more.

All functions between the press and delivery to carriers and single-copy sales points are supervised by this manager.

5. A *voluntary sales manager*—known as the "single-copy sales manager" at some newspapers—is responsible for sales at newsstands, drugstores, and vendor boxes.

Other important functions are part of circulation work at larger papers. The 110,000-circulation *Lexington (Ky.) Herald-Leader* has these:

State managers, who supervise circulation outside the city, a challenging job of efficiently planning motor routes and other distribution schemes to reach far-flung subscribers.

City managers, who supervise home delivery, a formidable task of recruiting, training, and motivating carrier youths. (Long Island's *Newsday* has 10,000; the *Detroit News*, 12,000!)

Marketing managers in circulation, who coordinate promotion through house ads, sales literature for carriers, and other media.

Transportation managers, who supervise truck and car fleets. Big job? Remember, nearly 63 *million* copies of U.S. newspapers must be transported each weekday. The *Des Moines (Iowa) Register & Tribune*'s circulation vehicles used in delivery, sale, and supervision drive 1.2 million miles annually.

Phone-room supervisors, who manage a sales force that works exclusively by telephone. It's an important source of "starts" plus cross-checks on delivery service and "stops."

For the circulation director, a tough challenge is opening effective relations with the newsroom, where editorial prerogatives are zealously protected and outside influences sometimes rejected out of hand as unwholesome efforts to distort the news process. But the sales force's view of the product must be considered in news planning; those who sell newspapers develop, from their contacts with the public, keen insights that are often valuable to the newsroom's decision-making process. But circulation managers should be aware that they tread here on sensitive ground. The news process must consider circulation's needs. If the marketing concept calls for a sales push in, say, a suburb north of town, reporters obviously must make sure that suburb is covered. But the daily judgment calls on what is news and what isn't must be made in the newsroom by seasoned editors, not in circulation or any other department.

Some newspapers design formal procedures to get circulation feedback into news planning. The *Louisville (Ky.) Courier-Journal*, widely applauded for journalistic excellence and independence, makes sure that circulation is consulted on where deployment of new reporters likely will yield greatest benefit.

Russell Barcroft, circulation manager for the *Santa Barbara (Calif.) News Press*, a 46,000-circulation evening paper, suggests that circulators can be helpful particularly to the newsroom in judging whether the "personality of the newspaper meets the personality of the community. . . ."

Barcroft urges close coordination with the research, advertising, and promotion departments in mapping sales drives. Research should spot areas that are likely to be receptive to new sales efforts and sales themes; advertising must make sure that advertisers' needs are factored into sales strategy; promotion must use television, radio, direct mail, and other media to prepare the way for high-intensity sales drives in narrowly focused geographic areas. Says Barcroft: "The circulation and promotion departments that use the shotgun approach are apt to be doomed for failure . . . with a rifleman's technique, the chance for success is great."[2]

The circulation department is heavily dependent on the production department: late press runs mean missed schedules all along the distribution chain and angry subscribers at the end of it. Circulation veterans say that no publisher would permit late press runs if he or she were ever held personally responsible for delivering bundles to trains, buses, airplanes, or teenagers on bicycles, none of which wait for newspapers that arrive late.

Integrated thrust by all departments toward marketing objectives may create personality clashes or turf battles between strong-willed and previously autonomous departments. If so, management must step in forcefully. Waiting for consensus to develop—waiting for them to sort things out—can waste valuable time. Strong managers set things right when they spot trouble.

[2] "The Circulation Perspective," Russell A. Barcroft, speech, International Newspaper Promotion Association, Chicago, May 15, 1983.

Design Manager Involvement in Key Areas

Many managers pay great attention to their newspapers' news and advertising operations but, amazingly, ignore efforts to get the papers to paying customers. Many feel ill at ease in circulation work because they lack hands-on experience.

Virgil Fassio, publisher of the *Seattle Post-Intelligencer* and one with that experience, says "Circulation is probably the area of least practical working experience (for) most publishers. As a result, circulation executives get less input on how to run their operations, but more second guessing from publishers. . . ."[3]

Not many managers have Fassio's background, which includes being circulation director for several major newspapers. But departmental design—in both structure and attitudes—must be such that managers supportively put their hands on key links in the circulation chain. Here are five of these links:

1. Sales strategy.   Too many circulation departments, under strong deadline pressure, are driven by a frenetic spirit of grabbing bundles of papers from the pressroom and trucking them wildly to distant sales points. A manager must make sure that there is a *strategy* designed to reach the right readers at the right time. Any circulation manager who cannot present, on paper, a strategy for the next three to five years—in addition to specific sales goals for the next twelve months—is failing.

2. Sales techniques.   Things can go badly wrong in sales. One survey shows that 64 percent of nonsubscribers in metro areas were never asked to subscribe to a newspaper.[4] There must be

precise techniques for canvassing target areas on a block-by-block basis, methodically and regularly. A circulation manager must plan in detail how available sales resources—people, time, money—will be used for optimum results.

3. Salesperson training and motivation.   Ill-equipped salespeople who are not personally motivated to sell effectively will do worse than not sell the paper; they will create a negative image that can be extremely difficult to overcome. Sales trainers should be selected internally, from the ranks of experienced circulators, or imported from outside. There is a science to selling, and good trainers can teach it. Check your existing incentive plans carefully. They can vary in detail but must link reward to sales performance and be attractive enough to inspire hard selling. Be aware that it is costly to sell effectively.

4. Pricing and payment collection.   This is such a key link in the circulation chain that we'll discuss it later in detail; for now, suffice to say that if a newspaper is priced unprofitably low or if collections are inefficient, the entire circulation exercise is wasted.

5. Effective distribution.   This, too, warrants detailed discussion later, but of course any newspaper—even if it is beautifully crafted by the newsroom, jammed with attractive advertising, and then printed with loving care—is worthless if it is not delivered to the right people at the right time. Ensuring that the trucks, rural route drivers, and thirteen-year-olds on bicycles do their duty is the responsibility of every manager.

The most important single resource of any circulation department is a highly professional circulation director backed by trained, capable middle-level managers and first-level supervisors. The director must be a master of marketing strategy at the highest levels and be able to plan and manage circulation operations on a daily basis. This requires the ability to use modern

---

[3] Celeste Huenergard, "Publisher Tells Circulators: 'Don't Be So Defensive,'" *Editor & Publisher*, June 25, 1983, p. 8b.

[4] "Newspapers Must Hustle For More Readers: Bogart," report on Newspaper Advertising Bureau survey, *Editor & Publisher*, June 25, 1983, p. 8a.

research, fight competitors head on, motivate people, and deliver profitable results. The job is a pressure cooker of responsibilities. In keeping with the newspaper industry's early production (rather than marketing) orientation, circulation managers were traditionally expected to be primarily distribution experts. No more. Today, *general* management skills are needed at all levels in circulation. Many newspapers recruit college graduates for first-level and middle-level management positions, although older circulators, reared in another era, are mostly a different breed. For example, the International Circulation Managers' Association surveyed 283 newspapers and found that only 34 percent of the circulation directors had college degrees. Behind them, however, 69 percent of the younger middle managers had degrees. (See box for one expert's view of the skills needed in circulation management.)

Many newspapers retire the old title "circulation manager" for "circulation director" or "vice president/circulation" in order to recognize the increased responsibilities that go with the job today. For some, these include operating a "profit center."

Design for Diversification

A basic consideration in designing the circulation department is whether it should be simply a service arm of the newspaper or a "profit center" as well.

Should the department be permitted to operate at a financial loss—accounting for 30 percent of the newspaper's total costs but only 20 percent of the revenue—if it sells and distributes the newspaper properly? Or should it also be required to generate a departmental profit? Increasingly, newspapers decide that both must be the goal—that circulation must view itself as an operating entity with profit-generating responsibilities beyond just keeping thirteen-year-olds happily mounted on bicycles and delivering newspapers. That requires circulators to initiate and operate TMC or find

---

TONY J. DELMONICO

For twenty-six years, Tony Delmonico fought the *Rocky Mountain News's* circulation wars in Denver, first part-time while obtaining a master's degree in secondary school administration from the University of Denver, then full-time. By 1983, Delmonico was circulation director for the *News's* parent, Scripps-Howard Newspapers, a Cincinnati-based group of sixteen dailies with 1.16 million daily circulation.

Through it all, Delmonico sharpened his view of the type of person who could succeed in Scripps-Howard circulation work. Needed, he writes, is one who is "very outgoing, talkative, and interested in being with people" who has "a forcefully persuasive, empathetic style of communication." A winner in circulation is "an opportunist with self-starting, hard-driving characteristics" capable of "building teams and attracting strong people to support him. He delegates authority, responsibility, and detail, and has a strong sense of urgency. A very high-energy individual."

A circulator's greatest challenge in the years ahead? "The challenge is competition. Competition from printed matter and other media for service (to reader and advertiser), for time, for value received, and for money spent."

And what must newspapers do to prosper?

> We must creatively design and aggressively market our products so that we can capture and maintain new readership. We also need to fully utilize the new technology and equipment that is available to upgrade the quality and re-design our products. Then recruit, select, train, and develop our people so that they can formulate new strategies that will enable them to be more productive and efficient in providing the service required to keep our readership growing.*

* Tony J. Delmonico, letter to author, Sept. 23, 1983.

other profitable uses for departmental resources that are normally only partially used in delivering the paid-circulation newspaper.

One idea is that circulation departments could use existing delivery systems to place products other than newspapers before the householder. That's called "alternate delivery." Consider: Delivery to the American front door is talked about by many people—magazine publishers, advertisers, producers of goods and services of all kinds. But now that the iceman, grocer, and milkman have dropped out, only the U.S. Postal Service and the daily newspaper deliver door-to-door on a regular nationwide basis. Only the newspaper does it on a seven-day basis. But the newspaper's elaborate, expensive, and unrivaled delivery capability is used just once daily in limited fashion. Carriers and drivers fan out across a market with newspapers for, say, 30 or 40 percent of households. They walk, ride, or drive past nonsubscriber homes—homes thousands of firms want to reach. Because not enough newspapers exploit the opportunity in that, vigorous direct mail and independent alternative-delivery competitors spring up. For competitive purposes and profit, circulation strategists must carefully investigate the possibilities of offering alternate delivery themselves.

Early experimenters delivered magazines inserted in their papers. *Time, Newsweek,* and others find, however, that such delivery is only minimally cheaper—or sometimes more expensive—than mail and it is also inaccurate. Magazine delivery appears to offer low profit potential. There often *is* profit and protection against competitors, however, in the delivery of preprints and other advertising. Some newspapers deliver material from a number of advertisers in a single plastic bag or wrapped in grocerystore preprints.

The competitive threat from independent alternate-delivery companies is illustrated in Columbus, Ohio, where a firm started operations during a newspaper strike. The company quickly grew to $3 million annual revenue and held important food advertisers even after the strike ended. The *Columbus Dispatch* eventually bought the company for about $5 million.

A survey by the International Circulation Managers' Association shows that 53.5 percent of 449 daily papers polled in 1980 deliver only their daily papers. Many circulators fear carrier rebellion if new distribution burdens are added. But 46.5 percent conduct some form of alternative delivery, and 31.3 percent claim to reach all households in their markets.

RESEARCHING THE CIRCULATION EFFORT

There is an ongoing social revolution in America that forces circulation managers to research their strategy for the 1990s carefully. Metropolitan daily newspaper circulators must use research to predict the newspaper's socioeconomic environment a decade ahead. Will inner-city deterioration spark further flight of affluent residents to suburbs? If so, should the newspaper follow? Who will remain behind as prospective readers? How can the newspaper—its marketing strategy, its sale techniques—meet inner-city life-style needs *and* appeal to suburbanites?

Small dailies and weeklies must research equally important unknowns. What will suburban and small-town life be like a decade ahead? Will the traditional family household unit exist widely? How will it spend its time and money? How will the newspaper penetrate the household and meet its need?

These are enormously important questions because, like army generals preparing to fight the last war, many newspapers are suited for a socioeconomic environment that was, to some extent still is, but in the future might not be.

Focus Research on Household Strategy

Basic circulation strategy for American newspapers is to penetrate the household with home delivery. The household is where buying power is and that's where advertisers want sales messages delivered. It is when they form traditional households that most readers take up the newspaper habit, particularly at age thirty-five or so, when they must know about schools, taxes, street crime, and the cost of groceries. The problem: fewer Americans today form traditional households. Those who do wait much longer to start. And when they do, they don't *act* the way they used to.

Particularly significant is the rapid growth of alternative living units, such as single-parent households. During the 1970s, married-couple families headed by householders age thirty-five or younger *grew* by about 147,000 annually. In the 1980s, the number has been *declining* by about 220,000 each year. There were 13,867,000 such households in 1983, down 343,000 from 1982. The proportion of one-parent families nearly doubled in the 1970s and by 1984 constituted 25 percent of all families. Mothers headed 89 percent of one-parent families. In 1985, the Census Bureau reported that nearly half the households added in the United States since 1980 consisted of people living alone or with nonrelatives. Now, how can such research be applied to circulation strategy? Well, consider the American newspaper:

Except for a few big-city papers that depend primarily on single-copy or street sales, most newspapers aim at traditional households of father plus mother and children. For delivery, this package of news and advertising directed at householders is printed attractively and dropped on front porches before 6 A.M. or, for afternoon papers, around 4 P.M. Circulation success is measured largely in number of households thus "penetrated." Advertisers are assured that once in the living room, the paper is easily disassembled and parceled out—sports to father, comics to children, and a favorite section for mother, too. It's all perfect for leisurely reading.

But will that content meet the needs of an unmarried thirty-year-old mother who hurries to put her children in a day-care center while she works? How about the thirty-year-old single male who has no head-of-household responsibilities and whose leisure time is spent in fishing, golf, or tennis? What content will attract him? And is throwing the paper on the front porch the way to reach either of them? They might, in fact, not have a front porch. Nearly one-third of U.S. housing units are multifamily structures, high-rise buildings, or condominiums. Penetrating them with newspaper delivery is like attacking a fort. That's because many are built like forts to protect residents from crime, inconvenience, and interruption. They offer no opportunity for a smiling thirteen-year-old carrier to walk onto the front porch and clinch a sale. Collections suffer too. Carleton Rosenburgh, when circulation director of Knight-Ridder's *Philadelphia Inquirer* and *Daily News*, said his company's bad-debt write-offs ran about 8 percent in multifamily dwellings as against 3 percent elsewhere.

Research should be sensitive to such lifestyle changes. Papers such as the *Inquirer* and *Daily News*, whose research spotted Philadelphia's trend to multifamily buildings, can adjust news strategy and circulation techniques accordingly. For example, high-rise "forts" can be penetrated by enlisting building personnel to sell subscriptions for hefty commissions. A building superintendent can be paid for making door-to-door deliveries or distributing newspapers through boxes in the lobby. Particularly in retirement communities, some circulators develop social get-togethers to introduce residents to the paper and entice them into pressuring building managers to permit effective delivery.

Continuing research also is needed on the following:

• The impact of education and income on reading habits. They are, in that order, the most accurate predictors of newspaper readership, more so than race or other factors. The higher the education and income, the greater the readership.

• Age as a factor in readership. In 1985, the Newspaper Research Council reported that

72 percent of all adults surveyed read a newspaper on an average day, 91 percent over a typical week (when casual readers were included). Among those surveyed, 65 percent aged eighteen to twenty-four were regular readers; in the age bracket of fifty-five to sixty-four, 80 percent were.

- Readers in demographically attractive suburbs who are highly desirable circulation targets for both small suburban and larger metro papers. Research by ANPA and the Suburban Newspapers of America shows suburbanites enjoying incomes and educational levels higher than those of most Americans. If suburbanites commute into a nearby city, the metro daily can often attract them with city coverage. But fewer use trains or buses and more drive—and one person to a car, at that—so they are difficult to reach. If a suburb becomes a self-sufficient community, offering jobs as well as bedrooms, suburbanites tend to shift preference to a local daily. That happened for *Newsday* when its market, Long Island, developed into a self-contained commercial and industrial center. It also happened for the *Bergen Record* in northern New Jersey suburbs of New York City. When their markets thus "mature," many suburban readers favor a local paper, particularly if it broadens its content beyond strictly local news to include national and international coverage, plus television news. Both suburban and metro papers need more research on the precise balance of content that will attract suburban readers.

- Growing leisure time and money to enjoy it change reading habits. The householder who once settled into an easy chair with the paper after work now can ski, hunt, fish—intrusions into reading time are countless. (Saturday afternoon papers are casualties; only a handful made it into the mid-1980s.) Newspapers, once primary sources of *entertainment* as well as news

and information, now compete against many affordable entertainment options such as home movies and cable TV. What content mix, promotional themes, sales approaches are needed? Conduct research to find out.

- Disappearance of the two-newspaper habit from most households narrows the circulation potential. It's not just life-style that's causing this; newspapers are bulkier and more comprehensive in content, eliminating need to buy more than one for ample news and advertising.

In sum, it may seem that an entire life-style is the circulator's principal competitor. That's not totally true, of course; there are other, vigorous competitors. But life-style changes *do* pose enormous problems for circulation directors because of rapid shifts in where and how Americans live. Alert researchers must track each shift carefully, for news content and circulation strategy must shift equally fast.

The Research Scenario Ahead

Consider this scenario: Circulation and advertising managers jointly visit the city's leading department store to solicit advertising; they learn that the store is launching special efforts to bring in residents with, say, $50,000 or more annual income—people who drive Cadillacs, ski in Switzerland, and buy fur coats and expensive perfume. Direct-mail firms can locate and reach people of that demographic profile, store executives say; so can specialty magazines. Can the newspaper?

The circulation manager must be able to say yes, along these lines:

There are 48,932 such households in our retail trading zone, almost all in three zip-code areas on the northwest side. Our computer has matched our demographic targets with our subscriber list, and your ad in our paid newspaper will reach 78 percent of them. The addresses of the others are also in our computer and we will reach them for you in our own direct-mail program.

Now, that is far from handing the paper to a thirteen-year-old carrier headed in the general direction of the wealthy northwest suburbs. But circulation departments must develop such precision-target marketing to remain competitive in the 1990s. Some already can.

Beverly Barnum, Harte-Hanks corporate director of market research, reports considerable success with the computer analysis of census materials to identify household characteristics that correlate tightly with newspaper circulation. Thus, Harte-Hanks can identify target areas where circulation sales drives are likely to succeed or, conversely, where results will not justify the time and expense involved. The *Los Angeles (Calif.) Daily News* retains outside research firms every two years for probing studies of population trends in its market.

Computers are used widely in circulation work. The International Circulation Managers' Association reports that 239 of 285 dailies surveyed computerize subscriber and nonsubscriber lists, circulation accounting, and billing.[5] Managers of even small papers must plan the capital investment required to computerize circulation record keeping. Knowing precisely who lives where in the market, how much they earn and how they spend their money, what they like and dislike about the newspaper—it's a fund of information the circulation department needs.

The circulation department, then, needs research tools to operate as a *problem solver* for advertisers. It must meet the advertiser's needs, perhaps with its own shopper or direct-mail effort, and not simply offer a single vehicle, the paid daily paper, on a take-it-or-leave-it basis.

PLANNING CIRCULATION STRATEGY

Circulation strategy essentially involves a plan for effective performance in three broad areas:

1. Plan to protect—enlarge—your newspaper's franchise as principal source of printed news, combating other newspapers, specialty publications, city magazines.

2. Protect your newspaper's dominance as an advertising vehicle by fighting off radio, TV, shoppers, and direct mail.

3. Guard your newspaper's role as an effective door-to-door delivery vehicle against competition from the U.S. Postal Service and independent alternate delivery systems.

This must be accomplished while selling subscriptions, delivering the paper efficiently and on time to keep subscribers happy, and collecting and pushing single-copy sales. It takes a great deal of planning.

Key Elements of Strategy

With adjustments for local conditions, strategy for any newspaper, large or small, must include key elements:

- Improve household penetration. This requires continuing research to determine the news needs in households, traditional or nontraditional, then constructing a news product to meet them. Sales resources—people, time, money—should be concentrated on selling home-delivery subscriptions. Convert casual, several-times-weekly buyers to the seven-day habit with, again, research determining their news needs and helping the newsroom to construct a product to fulfill them.

- Increase prices to elicit from readers greater revenue and thus relieve the burden on advertisers, who contribute 80 percent of a newspaper's total revenue. The basic necessity, of course, is a news product that readers perceive as essential, so that higher prices will become a secondary consideration or will at least seem palatable.

---

[5] Elise Burroughs, "Computerized Circulation Comes of Age," *presstime*, December 1982, p. 28.

- Control costs. Circulation's share of the newspaper's total costs will probably climb substantially beyond the current 30 percent or so, and most newspaper bottom lines will be hard hit by delivery expense.

- Improve management. This includes ensuring better marketing expertise, more professional human resources supervision, and effective training programs that include even first-level managers.

- Improve selling techniques. The primary sales force for this multibillion dollar industry is the teenage carrier. New ways must be devised for reaching prospective subscribers effectively while also retaining the carrier sales force and motivating it to perform better.

- Improve customer service, particularly delivery and billing.

Penetration—the Number-One Goal

The statistics are dismally clear: paid newspaper penetration of U.S. households is falling far behind household growth and, certainly, behind advertiser demands. It is the "silent crisis" of U.S. newspapering, a circulation weakness in the industry's ability to fulfill its basic mission for advertisers. The problem will not be disguised by ever-increasing newspaper profits, innovative news coverage, or improved production technology. The plain facts are that an industry which sold 124 papers per 100 households in 1950 sold just 77 per 100 in 1980, and that while the number of households grew by 2.4 percent 1970–80, daily circulation grew only 0.1 percent.

Katharine Graham, Washington Post Co. chairman, (see box for background), sounded the warning after serving as chairman and president of the American Newspaper Publishers Association: decline in household penetration leaves newspapers vulnerable to competitors "ranging from shoppers and marriage mailers to

any variety of target marketing and total market coverage schemes," she said. Newspapers must rebuild penetration or face "encroachments by the electronic media as well."[6]

Many metros have very shallow penetration. In its home county, the *Los Angeles Times* has 24.5 percent household penetration; the *Miami Herald*, 39.8 percent; *Atlanta Journal* and *Constitution*, 31.8 percent in the morning, 25.4 percent in the afternoon; *Chicago Tribune*, 26.3 percent; *Baltimore Sun*, 25.8 percent in the morning, 24.4 percent in the afternoon; *Philadelphia Inquirer*, 26.4 percent. Some smaller papers, however, claim impressive penetration—250 say they had 75 percent or more in their ABC city zones. Harry W. Edwards, when ANPA's membership director, found that the key ingredients to their success were those that take years to build: "A quality local news product, high credibility, community involvement, and dedication."[7] See Table 8.1 for the extraordinarily high penetration achieved by some small dailies.

Retail chains with multiple outlets now demand penetration of 80 percent or more, even outside the city zone. James F. Boynton, J. C. Penney manager of media services and guardian of a $270 million annual advertising budget, puts it this way: although most of his spending is with daily and weekly newspapers, he considers using "direct mail or some other media option when paid circulation drops below 50 percent penetration, and where we are getting less than 55 to 60 percent from the newspaper, we will add broadcast."[8]

Faced with such advertiser demands, your circulation strategy must include invigorated efforts over the long term to expand paid circulation *plus* immediate TMC programs.

---

[6] "Household Sales Slide Plagues Daily Papers," *Editor & Publisher*, May 1, 1982, p. 12.
[7] "Leaders in Penetration Rates Share Key to Their Success," *presstime*, May 1983, p. 60.
[8] "How J. C. Penney Uses Newspaper Audit Reports," *Audit Bureau of Circulations Case Book*, 1983, p. 5.

KATHARINE GRAHAM

Katharine Graham catches wide attention with comments on the American newspaper industry. This remarkable woman has been a leading player in big-league journalism for more than two decades.

Born June 17, 1917, to Eugene Meyer, a wealthy financier, and married in 1940 to handsome, brilliant, and erratic Phillips Graham, Mrs. Graham seemed destined for a completely *unre-markable* life. Two things changed that. Her father bought the *Washington Post* at a Depression auction in 1933 for $825,000, and in 1963, her husband, then *Post* publisher, killed himself.

Mrs. Graham, shaken and unskilled, took leadership of the Washington Post Co., which by then included *Newsweek* magazine. The company rose to new heights in both journalistic achievement and profitability. With great managerial courage, Mrs. Graham withstood heavy pressure from the Nixon administration to call off Executive Editor Ben Bradlee and his investigative reporters, who broke the Watergate scandal. Much more was at stake than her social reputation in capital inner circles. The *Post's* credibility and even a TV license held by the company were threatened. But she stood firm. Soon, the *Post* was setting national standards in political reporting and dominating the Washington newspaper market. The company grew rapidly, to $1 billion total revenue in 1985.

Mrs. Graham crossed many frontiers, becoming the first woman to head the American Newspaper Publishers' Association and first to serve on the Associated Press board of directors, where, it is said, she was sometimes the "toughest guy in the boardroom." For years, the *Post, Newsweek,* and her company's other communications properties—plus her aggressive leadership—made Katharine Graham the most powerful woman in the United States.

Your problems will be many. To deliver deep penetration, the circulation of free papers must be double or triple that of the paid ones—and that creates huge operational difficulties. Costs leap upward, and achieving accurate, on-time delivery to all households becomes complicated.

But no problem is larger than staff attitudes. Generations of newspaper people grew up thinking of shoppers as rather shabby devices. Some newsrooms disdain any publication devoid of news and thrown free on doorsteps; ad departments long preached that advertising adjacency to quality news in a paid paper is the way to sell products. Even in upper management, where the view of the penetration crisis should be clearest, there is often reluctance to publish shoppers.

If your newspaper has such attitudes, it lags behind its public in comprehending that shoppers have arrived. An NAB study shows that 57 percent of all U.S. adults live in communities with free papers; 46 percent report that free papers are delivered regularly to their homes—59 percent of adults are aware of free papers, have read, or have looked at one in the seven days preceding the survey; 34 percent of *all* U.S. adults read one or more over seven days (the same percentage, incidentally, read a paid-circulation weekly).[9]

A startling reality: for many consumers it obviously matters little whether you deliver a "traditional" newspaper or a free-circulation shopper. What counts to them is whether their needs are fulfilled by a publication's cost, content, and usefulness. Increasingly, the readers' verdict gives the shopper a place in the American home despite its lack of news content.

---

[9] C. David Rambo, "Special Report," *presstime,* October 1980, p. 5.

Table 8.1   Metro Area Penetration Leaders*

Morning and All-Day Papers	Households (in thousands)	Circulation	Percent Penetration
1. Owensboro (Ky.) Messenger Inquirer	31.5	23,383	74.2
2. Bloomington (Ill.) Daily Pantagraph	43.6	31,839	73.0
3. Sioux City (Iowa) Journal	43.4	31,677	73.0
4. Burlington (Iowa) Free Press	40.5	29,544	72.9
5. Bangor (Maine) Daily News	47.7	34,429	72.2
6. Elmira (N.Y.) Star-Gazette	35.0	24,882	71.1
7. Billings (Mont.) Gazette	42.7	30,290	70.9
8. St. Joseph (Mo.) News-Press, Gazette	38.6	25,937	67.2
9. Casper (Wyo.) Star-Tribune	27.9	18,589	66.6
10. Great Falls (Mont.) Tribune	30.0	19,927	66.4
Afternoon Papers			
1. Dubuque (Iowa) Telegraph-Herald	31.1	24,552	78.9
2. San Angelo (Tex.) Standard, Times	32.1	24,511	76.4
3. Owensboro (Ky.) Messenger Inquirer	31.5	23,771	75.5
4. Erie (Pa.) Times, News	100.2	75,296	75.1
5. Great Falls (Mont.) Tribune	30.0	22,529	75.1
6. St. Joseph (Mo.) News-Press, Gazette	38.6	28,971	75.1
7. Cedar Rapids (Iowa) Gazette	63.9	47,908	75.0
8. Green Bay (Wis.) Press-Gazette	63.0	47,072	74.7
9. Bloomington (Ill.) Daily Pantagraph	43.6	32,522	74.6
10. Cumberland (Md.) News, Times	39.5	29,369	74.4

* The unrivaled winner in metro area penetration is the *St. Joseph (Mo.) News-Press and Gazette.* Its combined AM–PM penetration is 118 percent!

Source: *Circulation.* '83/'84. Reprinted by permission.

Many paid-circulation papers were late in recognizing the necessity of TMC as a competitive tool, but now 73 percent of all U.S. dailies offer some type of TMC. One survey indicates 94 percent will do so by 1990.[10] Converts to TMC include some of the best and brightest names in American publishing: Harte-Hanks, Times Mirror, Tribune Company, Knight-Ridder, and the New York Times Co.

When they finally enter the field, paid papers often find they have many strengths in TMC operations: they know their markets, have advertiser contacts, and their sales force are ready to sell the new medium. They have printing presses, newsprint sources, trucks— the necessary production and circulation structure exists. TMC operations often prove highly profitable. Converting 35 to 40 percent of revenue to operating profit (double the performance of many paid dailies) is not unusual. TMC vehicles also protect a newspaper's franchise against outside attack and serve as promotional vehicles for selling paid newspaper subscriptions.

[10] "Survey Finds Surge in TMC Programs," *presstime*, April 1983, p. 19.

Hints on Launching Shoppers

If you launch a TMC operation, carefully select the format and marketing plan to suit your own market's needs. The style and quality of free-circulation papers and shoppers vary widely. Some are full-size broadsheet papers, others are tabloids or 8½ by 11 inches (the *Pennysaver* format). There seems to be no "typical" shopper operation, but Belden Associates researchers find certain common approaches:

- 67 percent of newspapers publish TMC products once weekly, on Wednesday, 19 percent more frequently; 26 percent prefer Thursdays, 10 percent Sundays.

- 57 percent deliver by carrier, 36 percent by mail.

- 57 percent report shared-mail competitors operating in their markets; 56 percent report that the biggest users are Sears; K-mart, 31 percent; Montgomery Ward, 15 percent; Kroger, 10 percent; lumber companies, 20 percent; other department stores, 18 percent; other food stores, 15 percent.

- 62 percent term their TMC operations "excellent" or "good" in advertising revenue; 65 percent, successful overall.

- 20 percent terminated TMC operations—28 percent because advertiser support dwindled, 21 percent over delivery problems, 14 percent because they were not profitable, 7 percent because of lawsuits by competitors.[11]

The *Denver Rocky Mountain News* offers TMC by delivering preprints to any or all forty-five metropolitan zip codes, inserting them on Wednesdays in the paid paper. Nonsubscribers get theirs in plastic bags hung on doorknobs by Wednesday evening. Advertisers can have pre-prints delivered to all homes, just single-family units or apartments, multifamily units, or combinations. The *Santa Ana (Calif.) Orange County Register* delivers preprints to any or all of sixty-nine zip-code areas through a combination of the paid paper and a four-color tabloid mailed second class to more than 400,000 nonsubscribers. The *Los Angeles Daily News* offers delivery to 461,000 homes in sixty zip code areas. The *Baltimore Sun* offers "Sun Plus," claiming nearly 93 percent household penetration in five counties—371,000 subscribers of the morning and afternoon *Suns* and 320,000 nonsubscribers reached via mail.[12]

Using Direct Mail for TMC

Operating a direct-mail effort could be part of your circulation department strategy for the 1990s. It builds household penetration, constructs yet another defense of a paid newspaper's franchise, provides valued advertisers with one more service, and, if operated properly, can be profitable.

Direct mail, long a selling technique, blossomed in the 1970s when lower third-class postage rates made it a viable alternative to newspapers for distributing preprints. More than $15 billion annually, more than 16 percent of total U.S. advertising dollars, are spent on direct mail.[13] So the potential for newspapers is huge. But why the *sudden* entry by newspapers into direct mail? The computer. Computers permit circulation departments for the first time to provide cost-effective service with high accuracy and reliability. About 150,000 address lists covering most U.S. households are available commercially. Computers can cull them for the demographic and geographic markets demanded by advertisers. For example, Lifestyle Selector

---

11 "Belden Reports Results of TMC Product Survey," *Editor & Publisher*, July 24, 1982, p. 15.

12 Celeste Huenergard, "Upscale Shopper Eyes National Distribution," *Editor & Publisher*, Nov. 20, 1982, p. 20.
13 *Facts About Newspapers '86*, op. cit.; also see Kirk Johnson, "New Mail-Order Techniques," *New York Times*, July 30, 1983, p. 33.

of Denver says its computers hold more than 10 million names and addresses and can cross-check them for eight characteristics such as age, sex, and occupation plus fifty-two life-style interests such as outdoor sports, foreign travel, gourmet foods, wine, and so on.[14]

Retailers like direct mail because it reaches primarily only those audiences of real value to them and thus reduces advertising costs. Says James Hollis, NAB expert on direct mail: ". . . the average discount store in this country does about $7 million in volume . . . 25,000 circulation is all that is needed to generate sales far above this average . . . generally, a store will not draw from an area larger than the area its employees come from. . . ."[15]

William McConnell, executive vice president/sales for Advo-Systems, Inc., the nation's largest direct mail firm says, "If I'm K-mart and want to buy all households within a mile and a half, I should get marriage mail . . . most newspapers would force me to buy a larger area."[16]

Direct mail's competitive threat is real, then, particularly for newspapers with high advertising rates and low household penetration. Retailers often view direct mail as offering immediate sales assistance at reasonable cost.

Direct mail's low cost is underlined by an NAB survey showing that shared-mail firms charged about $35, compared with $45 to $50 for many newspapers, to deliver 1,000 eight- to twelve-page advertising tabloids weighing up to 1.25 ounces.[17]

Your major operational problem in starting a direct-mail effort would probably be establishing address lists. Many papers begin by purchasing lists from commercial mail firms ($40 per 1,000 addresses with 75 percent guaranteed

accuracy was standard in the mid-1980s). Newspaper carriers or special teams make house-by-house checks; once they have 90 percent accuracy in street names and addresses collated by zip codes, the post office (under Section 945 of the *Domestic Mail Manual*) is obligated to make corrections, additions, and deletions for 10 cents per address.

The *Los Angeles Times*, in one of the country's most sophisticated direct-mail operations, uses a system of 109 grids covering 2.7 million households in southern California. Zoned groups are as small as 6,126 homes but average 40,000 addresses. On average, about 10,000 are *Times* subscribers; 30,000, direct-mail candidates. In 1983, *650 advertisers* used the program to distribute 400 million pieces. Small newspapers that publish a shopper for free distribution can broaden ad client support with mail delivery in rural areas. Shoppers often draw business from many small-town retailers who otherwise would not advertise.[18]

Direct-mail services should be promoted heavily. A competitor's direct mail may be "junk mail,'" but *yours* is exciting, effective advertising. Note the picture emerging from promotional efforts by the *Atlanta Journal* and *Constitution* to counter doubts about its direct mail:

- *Doubt:* Direct mail is junk mail, with no image, no firm readership. *Answer:* Our direct mail isn't just any mail advertising. It is produced by the *Journal* and *Constitution* and carries its reputation.

- *Doubt:* Direct mail is too costly. *Answer:* Our program affords efficient, selective market targeting by using mail in tandem with the newspapers, and cost compares to regular direct-mail postage rates.

- *Doubt:* Direct mail via third class cannot be guaranteed for timely delivery. *Answer:*

[14] Ibid.
[15] "Newspapers Urged to Embrace Shared Mail TMC Programs," *Editor & Publisher*, July 31, 1982, p. 18.
[16] "Marriage Mail: A Letter-Perfect Match," *Advertising Age*, May 30, 1983, p. M-15.
[17] "Newspapers Urged to Embrace Shared Mail TMC Programs," op. cit.

[18] Terry E. Brennan, "The Hows and Whys of Marriage Mail," *Editor & Publisher*, Oct. 16, 1982, p. 16.

Our program was developed in consultation with the U.S. Postal Service and at least 75 percent of each mailing will be delivered on the target date, the balance the following day.[19]

*Un*answered, however, in Atlanta and elsewhere, are several fundamental questions: Is the current attraction of direct mail due to basic strength as an advertising medium or to perceived weakness in newspaper penetration? Is direct mail simply attractive as stop-gap TMC, and will direct mail fade if newspapers gear up both their combined paid-circulation efforts and free-distribution papers to offer much demanded TMC?

In sum, whether you choose direct mail, shoppers, or other means, your circulation strategy must combat the "silent crisis" of shallow household penetration. TMC must ensure five basic strengths: ability to reach large numbers of households, concurrent zoning capability to focus on small segments of the market, highly accurate delivery, a competitive rate structure, and credibility among discerning advertisers as a cost-effective vehicle.

The best long-term strategy is improving journalistic content and marketing practices to open sufficient doors for the paid newspaper, for paid newspapers *are* better read than free-circulation papers or direct-mail circulars and *do* offer the best possible advertising environment. But increasing paid circulation is a long-haul proposition requiring major investment in content, promotion, sales—and time. So short-term TMC remedies must be planned.

A Basic Strategy Question: Elitism?

Basic strategy for the 1990s must determine how narrowly newspapers will focus their paid circulation. More readers are wanted, all right, and advertisers do demand TMC. But there is simultaneous pressure, often from those same

advertisers, for selective market coverage (SMC), delivering readers who are particularly attractive in income and buying habits or who live in precisely delineated areas targeted by retail advertisers.

Many advertisers put it simply: better to reach families with, say, $50,000 annual income living close to my store than those with $15,000 living far away. Other media—direct mail, specialty magazines—can deliver to attractive households and eliminate the cost of reaching those less attractive. Can newspapers? A concurrent question for circulation strategists is whether, with newsprint and other distribution costs rising, newspapers can afford to serve readers who are unattractive to advertisers.

Such questions are enormously important for newspapers in philosophical as well as strategic terms. Should a traditionally mass-medium industry now go elitist? Should it label some readers unwanted? What would *that* do to the newspaper's historic role in raising the public's educational and social consciousness?

Some newspapers frankly create "elitist" (and highly profitable) strategies to skim demographically attractive readers off the market. Metropolitan dailies such as the *New York Times* and *Los Angeles Times* offer advertisers a class of readers with very high incomes and education and make no pretense of deeply penetrating the mass market. The *Los Angeles Times*, for example, though it penetrates only 24.5 percent of Los Angeles County households, claims that its Sunday issue reaches 73 percent of those with annual incomes of $50,000 or more and 80 percent of the county's college graduates.

The *Wall Street Journal*'s circulation strategists are unrivaled in gathering readers of high demographic appeal. They engineered a circulation of nearly 2 million—largest among dailies—yet built such demographic "purity" that advertising is occasionally turned away for lack of space. Says Chairman Warren Phillips:

We have been careful as our circulation has grown to monitor very carefully whether the

---

[19] *Product Profile*, a brochure issued by the *Atlanta Journal and Constitution* in 1983.

quality of our demographics is being diluted—whether . . . we will retain [our] hardrock businessman subscriber. We have found that our demographics have actually been growing stronger in recent years, rather than the reverse, and we can provide the research to document this. As we enlarge the content of the *Journal,* we take care not to turn it into a general newspaper but rather to try to strengthen its appeal to our basic business audience by improving the paper's coverage of business matters (as occurred with the second section and the economic news on the new international pages) and at the same time supplementing this core coverage with news of foreign politics, leisuretime activities, health, education and other matters that have strong impact on the lives of our business subscribers. We believe the *Journal* is a long way from reaching any saturation level in its circulation.[20]

The *Journal* isn't slapped together haphazardly by editors who are isolated from reader desires or advertiser thinking. Rather, it is painstakingly constructed five days weekly for a hand-picked audience whose news needs are identified through precision research. The *Journal* is shrewdly promoted as *the* quality newspaper of its class, and the circulation department seeks out, one by one, those demographically attractive buyers, To ensure prompt, efficient delivery, seventeen satellite printing plants are located strategically around the country, and the paper is typically available at breakfast almost everywhere on the business circuit, coast to coast. Having accomplished that stunningly difficult journalistic, production, sales, and distribution task, *Journal* strategists focus on big-league advertisers willing to pay high ad rates that make the newspaper as successful financially as it is journalistically. In 1985, for a single page in its national edition, the *Journal* charged $75,356. That works out to $38.75 per agate line to reach high-income, decision-making executives through the *Journal's* pages. *That* is success in elitist circulation strategy.

The Market Segmentation Strategy

Few newspapers can focus strategy as narrowly as does the *Journal.* Not many smaller papers want to. Their markets are often homogeneous and can be served with a single editorial product, a single advertising strategy. Nevertheless, circulators who look into the future see that obtaining widespread general circulation will probably be (1) extremely expensive and (2) not all that attractive to advertisers anyway. Many see a strategy of market segmentation—*geographic zoning* and, perhaps eventually *interest zoning*—as a solution.

Geographic zoning attracts many advertisers, small and large, by reaching market segments with editions tailored in news and ads for those areas. For large papers, this can be enormously complicated, as Richard Capen, publisher of the *Miami Herald,* explains:

> The *Miami Herald* publishes 11 editions circulated throughout the state of Florida, plus an International Edition air-shipped each day to some 40 cities in the Caribbean and Latin America. We have developed a weekly Business/Monday tabloid section. To serve the needs of our local communities, the *Herald* publishes, twice a week, 11 Neighbor editions circulated in 20,000–40,000 subscriber increments.
>
> As we look at the future, our success will be based on our willingness to adjust to change while giving high priority to the expanding needs of our readers and advertisers.[21]

The *Chicago Tribune* offers six advertising zones daily for both display and classified plus four-way zoning of local news for Chicago and suburbs. Zoning is a strategy primarily for papers in large markets, such as Chicago, with great cultural or economic diversity and sprawling geographic areas to cover. A sense of neighborhood uniqueness in, say, the wealthy suburbs north of Chicago makes that area a prime target for a zoned edition. Zoning is less attractive in

---

[20] Warren Phillips, letter to author, March 18, 1983.

[21] Richard Capen, letter to author, May 27, 1983.

smaller, more homogeneous markets. Residents in a small town, for example, have common news interests and merchants feel no need to zero in on a special market segment; they draw shoppers from throughout the town. Also, many small papers lack the production and distribution flexibility necessary to split a press run of, say, 15,000 copies into three runs of 5,000 each—and to deliver different, tailored news packages to narrow slices of their market.

For newspapers large or small, getting the right papers to the right zone at the right time is a difficult logistical task in geographic zoning. Papers must be bundled by zones and trucks must take the right bundles to the right drop-off points. An edition zoned for the northwest suburbs is of no value delivered on the southeast side.

Interest zoning is an increasingly attractive idea—if not yet an operational reality—as new production and distribution techniques promise at least the technical capability for publishing daily editions zoned for special reader interests. It is possible, for example, to split press runs into segments aimed at, say, business-oriented readers, sports fans, or arts-and-leisure audiences. Computerized subscriber lists segmented by reader interest are feasible; on the drawing boards are ink-jet, plateless presses that could switch easily and cheaply from running papers heavy with, say, business news to some designed for sports fans or science buffs. Does it all point toward computer-sorted bundles being dispatched so carriers can throw, say, the sports-heavy paper to the first house on the block, the business-oriented paper to the second, and so forth? Technically, it will be feasible. But in addition to fearing that this could create a distribution nightmare, many circulation strategists argue that the newspaper is a mass-distribution product of wide-ranging news and advertising content for general, not specialized, audiences, and that tinkering with that could undermine its strongest quality.

In sum, *geographic zoning* will probably be an essential strategy for dailies whose adver-

tisers demand the servicing of narrowly focused market segments. However, *interest zoning* will probably be restricted to direct mail or other ancillary services. For certain, strategy in the 1990s will involve eliminating circulation unwanted by advertisers.

Plan to Cut "Inefficient" Circulation

Circulation strategy must eliminate "inefficient" circulation—circulation that is too costly or unwanted by advertisers who need to reach potential customers near their stores and not disinterested readers far away.

The *Washington Post*, for example, avoids reaching out too far despite the temptations of going national, like the *New York Times*. The *Post*'s cost/benefit studies in the early 1980s were negative, showing, among other things, that an average daily issue priced at 25 cents contained 26 to 27 cents worth of newsprint alone. Potential *subscribers* to a national edition wouldn't begin to cover costs, and the *New York Times* and *Wall Street Journal* are established solidly with *advertisers* as major national newspapers. So the *Post* stays profitably home (although it does distribute nationwide a weekly publication covering mainly national politics).

Some newspapers historically burdened with inefficient circulation now charge more for copies distributed, say, 50 miles from home base; others simply eliminate such circulation. The *Miami Herald* is among major regional papers trimming distant circulation. "We're concerned about the readers that matter to advertisers," says James Batten, president of the *Herald*'s parent, Knight-Ridder.[22]

The *St. Louis (Mo.) Post-Dispatch* once trucked 400 papers daily across Illinois to distant Indianapolis, Ind., at a $5,000 annual loss. Not anymore. Nicholas Penniman IV, general manager, says out-of-state circulation was built by publishers with big egos and is now unaffordable.

---

[22] Daniel Machalaba, "Some Papers Again Extending Their Turf," *Wall Street Journal*, Jan. 16, 1983, p. 21.

He says it's showy and costly—"Buffalo Bill circulation."[23]

The *Boston Globe*, which once considered most of New England its turf, changed strategy under Thomas Winship, its former editor, who said: "We do strive to continue our presence in the distant areas of New England but on rather a limited basis. We have found that from a realistic advertising point of view, that we should concentrate within a radius of 50 miles of Boston. . . ."[24]

Some managers let inefficient distribution wither, not replacing losses, or they gradually redeploy news and circulation resources in more attractive areas. The *Tulsa (Okla.) World*'s Executive Editor Bob Haring says:

> The *World* is not pulling out of any circulation areas, but we are concentrating in the newsroom on expanding our efforts where they make most economic sense . . . for example, changing the focus of our mail edition to appeal more heavily to those prospects who live near Tulsa but who, for reasons of distance, etc., cannot be efficiently served by carrier and thus must get the paper by mail. We will spend more money to cover Bartlesville, where we sell 7,500 papers a day, than we will Muskogee, where we sell 1,500.[25]

For a few newspapers, some widespread circulation is attractive for strategic reasons. The *Dallas Morning News* seeks enhanced regional stature, but only with distant readers who are special. Says President Osborne:

> We sell some papers in Texas and other areas of the Southwest outside of Dallas but . . . to very high-demographic groups. We sell very well in Midland, Texas, an oil center [290 miles southwest of Dallas]. The readers are people who get on their private jets and come to Dallas to shop at Neiman-Marcus and Saks. The advertisers don't complain.[26]

However, Osborne pointedly notes that under 10 percent of his circulation is outside the immediate Dallas market.

One classic regional paper that still circulates widely—and claims advertiser support for it—is the *Omaha (Neb.) World-Herald*. Says President Harold Andersen:

> We still are a regional newspaper, delivering every morning along a regional "main street" which stretches some 500 miles, from northwest Missouri and southwestern Iowa through Nebraska to South Dakota and Colorado.
>
> Since we have kept our retail advertising rates reasonably low, retailers do not seem to object to buying space in a regional newspaper—especially since the Omaha retail market stretches a good distance from the city of Omaha.
>
> Additionally, a number of our major retailers have branch stores in our circulation area outside of Omaha. And retailers who use preprints can choose to buy only a portion—the metropolitan area, for example—of our total circulation.[27]

Circulation's changing economics can mean a dramatic *negative* impact on newspaper profits due to sudden growth. When the *Washington Star* folded, the surviving *Washington Post* quickly increased circulation by 25 percent. There was a day when that would have been a bonanza. For the *Washington Post* of 1981, it had short-term contrary meaning: serving the larger number of subscribers—buying extra newsprint, driving delivery trucks extra miles—raised the *Post*'s operating costs so much that its third-quarter pretax operating earnings dropped about $2.5 million. Newly gained circulation revenue did not cover the cost of the new circulation and the *Post* could not raise ad rates quickly enough to make up the difference.[28] The *Philadelphia Inquirer* suffered similar temporary dilution of earnings when circulation soared following death of the competing *Philadelphia*

[23] Ibid.
[24] Thomas Winship, letter to author, March 11, 1983.
[25] Bob Haring, letter to author, March 2, 1983.
[26] Burl Osborne, letter to author, April 11, 1983.

[27] Harold Andersen, letter to author, May 9, 1983.
[28] "Washington Post Co. Says 1981 Net To Drop, Sees Good Year in 1983," *Wall Street Journal*, Dec. 1983, p. 17.

Bulletin. Of course, both the *Post* and the *Inquirer* now profit from increased circulation and have emerged as the only major dailies in their markets.

In sum, retailers are redefining where, how, and at what expense they want their message circulated. This, plus rising production and distribution costs, forces change in circulation strategy. Strategic planning in circulation must also consider other factors.

Target Blacks and Young Adults

Circulation managers must work closely with editors to expand readership among blacks and young adults. Newspapers have societal responsibilities to fashion news and advertising relevant to both groups. And, in self-interest, both are important in numbers and future demographic attractiveness.

In a 1979 survey, Leo Bogart, executive vice president of the Newspaper Advertising Bureau and one of the industry's premier researchers, found that 72 percent of whites read a daily paper "yesterday"; 70 percent read the previous Sunday's. For blacks, the figures were 59 and 61 percent, respectively.[29] In 1985, the Newspaper Research Council put average daily white readership at 74 percent and black readership at 67 percent. The Council attributes the difference to disparity in education and income, suggesting that black readership will lag until blacks catch up with whites in both areas. Bogart suggests that some blacks may perceive newspapers as part of the "system" that makes them feel indifferent or even alienated. However, newspapers themselves may contribute to the lag.

First, with affluent suburbs offering greater and more immediate potential reward, news and circulation strategies are often oriented away from city inner cores, where many blacks live. Content fashioned for middle-class suburbanites

will lack relevance to blue-collar inner-city residents. Also, street crime and traffic congestion in core cities complicate the delivery and sale of newspapers.

Second, newsrooms and management ranks are predominantly white, making it difficult to execute news, promotion, and circulation strategies that will capture black readers. Until more reporters, editors, and managers are drawn from black communities, the weakness will continue.

Attracting young adults to reader ranks may seem less complex because there is evidence that the newspaper habit comes with maturity and the assumption of adult or head-of-household responsibilities. Circulation managers have traditionally banked on it: A nineteen-year-old doesn't read newspapers because the newspaper isn't *needed* at that age. But, the argument continues, once married and concerned about taxes, children's education and shopping bargains, the former teenager *will* need it.

That traditional argument may be unrealistic in this era of changing life-styles. As discussed earlier, head-of-household responsibility is not accepted by some young people today; others delay it into their late twenties or early thirties. And the longer the delay, the greater the chance that alternate sources of information will be developed, with the newspaper *never* becoming integral to the individual's daily life. Each newspaper must provide content that is immediately attractive to young people, starting with comics and school news pages for children and then for all age groups leading to adulthood. For example: music is an obsession with millions of American teenagers; billions of dollars are spent annually for records, tapes, and music festivals. Yet few newspapers boast even adequate coverage of that music world in a way that is appropriate in language and style to a teenage audience.

Given appropriate content, circulation departments must get the paper before young people with promotion underlining its usefulness in terms that young people understand. One excellent avenue is the Newspaper in

---

[29] Leo Bogart, *Press and Public*, Hillsdale, N.J., Erlbaum, 1981, p. 75.

Education program, under which papers are provided free or at low cost to schools as teaching aids. Teacher usage of newapapers is strong. An *Atlanta Journal and Constitution* survey of teachers using its papers finds that 99 percent regard them as viable teaching tools; 63 percent use papers in teaching English or language arts; 61 percent, reading and writing; 53 percent, current events; 47 percent, social studies; and 26 percent, math.

Most papers in the NIE program also use other means of attracting student readers, including publication of school news written by students or examples of student art. Details are available from Manager/Educational Services, ANPA Foundation, The Newspaper Center, Box 17407, Dulles International Airport, Washington, DC 20041.

HOW TO MANAGE THE CIRCULATION EFFORT

Circulation management is a never-ending process of planning, making decisions, setting goals, organizing resources, motivating of people, and monitoring and controlling performance. Let's discuss applying that process in three areas particularly crucial to any newspaper, large or small, and to your success as a manager in circulation:

- Selling the newspaper

- Pricing the newspaper to achieve market dominance and profit

- Distribution and collecting

Unless you are aggressively successful in those three areas, you will fail in the short term, and so will your newspaper in long-term strategy. A fourth area, circulation promotion, is so important that we will cover it in greater detail in Chapter 10, within the context of the newspaper's overall promotion effort.

The core of the circulation effort is obtaining readers, both through home delivery and single-copy sales; retaining them with proper service that holds their loyalty; pricing the paper at attractive yet competitive levels that are profitable for your newspaper; collecting from subscribers; and replacing subscribers who move away or drop the paper for other reasons.

Selling the Newspaper

In planning circulation strategy, the manager defines the geographic areas and demographic characteristics that advertisers want brought into the fold. Selling starts with devising a marketing mix of type and quality of product needed by the market targets as well as price, promotion, type of sales effort, distribution network—all the devices for achieving either household-delivery subscriptions or single-copy sales. Two factors should dominate the manager's thinking in establishing selling "tone" and managing the sales structure:

First, sell not merely the newspaper but rather solutions to readers' needs. Newspapers will not sell over the long haul if they are merely nice to have; newspapers must become crucial to readers in daily life.

Second, in most complex, heterogeneous markets, successful selling cannot be based on a single "product." For advertisers, offer a variety of products, perhaps a shopper or direct-mail service in addition to the paid paper. For readers, the sales force must be able to differentiate the newspaper's wide variety of offerings as a solution to a variety of their needs—business section for the businessman, for example, sports for one group, arts-and-leisure section for another.

Selling must entice householders to subscribe but, equally, persuade them to continue subscribing. Too many sales programs are aimed solely at gaining new subscriptions, and the turnover rate ("churn") of existing subscribers is extremely high. It's a closely guarded secret at many newspapers, but churn exceeds 50 percent annually at some metropolitan dailies.[30] Churn presents a significant problem: advertisers seek continuity of readership and distrust newspapers with high churn. It has been fashionable among circulators to say that circulation departments can only sell new subscribers; the newsroom must hold them. That copout is no longer acceptable. We'll discuss details later, but the circulation department must keep subscribers happy with on-time delivery and correct billing procedures, using continuing promotion to "resell" subscribers on the merits of continuing to take the paper.

Focus sales campaigns on narrow market segments. Maximum impact is gained with alert promotion and hard selling in, for example, a single zip-code area or similarly narrow target selected in consultation with news and advertising. Trying to sell in an area that is ignored by the news department is futile; people want to buy a paper with news from their area. And selling in an area that is of no interest to advertisers is counterproductive. They won't pay for your achievements there. Zip code areas commonly are targeted for sales efforts because they are increasingly used by advertisers in their sales campaigns.

Many newspapers concentrate sales efforts in affluent areas, not only because residents there are favored by advertisers but also because high-income families, once sold, tend to continue subscribing. Often, higher incentives are paid to salespersons for subscriptions signed in those areas.

For most papers, carriers are the basic sales force. At the *Milwaukee Journal*, for example, three-fourths of "starts" are sold by carriers. Young carriers require basic instruction on how to make a sales pitch. The circulation department must provide promotion material that even a tongue-tied thirteen-year-old can use effectively.

Sales crews of youths other than carriers can effectively flood an area under adult supervision and knock on doors. Intensive training by newspaper employees is key. Adult salespeople are also used, particularly in high-rise or other multiple dwelling units where negotiations with building managers are necessary. Adults must be better compensated and thus are expensive, particularly in rural or low-density areas where they must spend a great deal of time to obtain a few subscriptions.

Telephone crews—"phone rooms" in industry parlance—are kept in continual operation by many newspapers. Adult solicitors are used. Smaller papers often achieve good results with occasional telephone efforts, either using employees or outside solicitors paid on a percentage basis.

Direct mail is useful with scattered prospects or those difficult to reach otherwise, in apartment buildings, for example. Magazines successfully sell subscriptions and renewals by mail. But it is a technique considered coldly informal by some newspaper circulators and likely to get lost in the river of direct mail flooding many households.

Whatever techniques are used—and most papers use several simultaneously—there must be intensive, concurrent promotion in the target area. Radio, TV, and outdoor advertising can create a sales environment that is helpful to the carrier who knocks on a door, order blank in hand. "Sampling," delivering free copies to nonsubscribers for a week or so, is often successful. (See box for the story of a particularly adroit promotion used to sell *USA Today*.)

A small paper, the *Corinth (Miss.) Daily Corinthian*, increased circulation by 25 percent—to 9,100—in a twenty-two-month sales campaign featuring a variety of methods. "We have done everything you can do to seek new business," says Publisher John Fitzwater. "Four night a week we telephone area residents. We ask first if they have home delivery of the *Daily Corinthian*. If 'yes,' we ask about service. If 'no,' we go into a sales pitch." In an effort to

---

[30] Patrick O'Donnell, "The Business of Newspapers: An Essay For Investors," New York, E. F. Hutton, Feb. 12, 1982.

THE EXAMPLE OF *USA Today*

Though the paper struggled toward profitability, adroit promotion helped USA Today *achieve the most rapid circulation success of any American newspaper.*

After spending more than $2 million in market research, Gannett Co. launched the national newspaper on September 15, 1982. It jumped to over a million circulation in one year, behind only the Wall Street Journal *(about 2 million) and the* New York Daily News *(1.3 million). Expensive, tightly coordinated promotion and sales boosted* USA Today. *Highlights:*

Advertising through newspapers, radio-TV, and billboards introduced *USA Today* two or three weeks before it was "rolled out" in each market. Promotion stressed its delivery via satellite to nearby production plants; the paper's use of color; its lively, exciting, fresh approach to the news.

Special displays in shopping malls before launch showed TV commercials and promotion tapes on TV monitors and videocassettes. Gannett reports signing substantial numbers of subscriptions in malls.

Free samples were distributed at strategic locations throughout the market. Newspaper ads described where they were available and touted mall displays.

Launch events—dinners, breakfasts, cocktail parties—were held (at great expense) to create excitement and get people talking about the new paper.

Gannett's other papers (then numbering eighty-five) were enlisted in focusing total resources on market-by-market launch. Some papers held subscription contests, giving employees prizes for signing customers. Promotion brochures that included order blanks were delivered to homes. Gannett Tel-Sell, a subsidiary, sold subscriptions nationwide by telephone.

Extensive door-to-door sampling and selling followed. Customers received thank you notes and money-back guarantees.

Colorful, modernistic *coin boxes* were set out by the thousands, appearing quickly throughout selected markets and providing opportunities for purchase. The per-copy price was kept low, at 25 cents, in the first two years, after which it was raised 40 percent to 35 cents and then to 50 cents in 1985.

---

convert casual readers into regular subscribers, the circulation department inserts mail-back subscription cards in each copy sold in racks. Cards are inserted in the paper's shopper, mailed to 13,000 households in five counties. Door-to-door sales are made by carriers. The newspaper also provides free delivery tubes to subscribers.[31]

Develop Single-Copy Sales

Even for newspapers whose basic circulation strength must be home subscriptions, single-copy sales can add circulation numbers, increase revenue, make the paper visible throughout the market and, importantly, give sales access to the casual reader who should be converted to the seven-day habit. And sales costs are lower in single-copy sales. Each home-delivery subscription can cost $5 to $20 in promotion, commission, and other selling expenses.

The biggest challenge in single-copy sales is that those who purchase the paper today must be convinced to buy again tomorrow. Bringing single-copy buyers back day after day challenges the entire staff: editors and reporters must fill the front page with substantive, attractive news; advertising salespeople must provide high-interest ad copy; production managers must get the paper off the presses on schedule; and circulation managers must get it to sales points on time. Missed objectives in any department—

---

[31] Southern Newspaper Publishers' Association, Circulation Bulletin, Oct. 3, 1984, p. 2.

a dull front page or late delivery—can mean thousands of sales missed. A big-city paper aimed at single-copy sales among commuters has a disastrous day if papers reach train and bus stations after the commuter rush. Yet expertly run single-copy sales campaigns often yield faster results than subscription sales efforts. Attractive newspapers made easily accessible sell quickly on heavily traveled streetcorners, in train and bus stations, hotels, shopping malls.

About 23 percent of all daily papers are sold one copy at a time.[32] Of *USA Today*'s 1.3 million circulation in 1986, 76 percent was single-copy sales. About 80 percent of the *Boston Herald*'s circulation represent single-copy sales; the *New York Post* and *Daily News* are sold mostly one copy at a time. There is a strong tradition for street sales in some large cities because many potential buyers can be reached quickly.

However, NAB says its research shows that small newspapers also have great opportunity for expanding single-copy sales after decades of emphasizing home subscriptions at the behest of advertisers. In some markets, particular lifestyles improve single-copy sales. Florida cities with seasonal influxes of vacationers, for example, are prime areas for single-copy sales. Newspapers there report dramatic recent sales improvement. David Fluker, St. Petersburg's circulation director, says it is "reasonable to expect" single-copy sales for his paper will constitute 30 to 35 percent of total sales by 1995.[33]

Important buyer psychology is involved in single-copy sales. Some readers prefer paying 25 or 30 cents for a single copy rather than a dollar or so for a weekly subscription—even though the latter is significantly cheaper. Interestingly NAB finds that 7 of 10 single-copy

Table 8.2   Single-Copy Sales as a Percentage of Total Sales

	1965	1984
St. Petersburg Times/Independent	7.5%	13.4%
Miami Herald	5.8	24.6
Sarasota Herald-Tribune	4.4	20.0
Tampa Tribune & Times	4.0	23.8
Orlando Sentinel	2.8	24.7
Ocala Star-Banner	2.2	21.7

buyers read a paper every day. They are "habitual" single-copy buyers. However, single-copy sales often catch occasional readers who say they don't have time to read a paper every day or those who buy only on certain days for special reasons—on Wednesdays for food ads, for example.

A developing problem is that street newsstands are disappearing and, as large supermarkets and chain stores prosper, the number of small retail stores drops, reducing over-the-counter sales outlets. This forces wider use of vending machines—"news racks"—to get newspapers before the public. Vending machines are expensive. Gannett paid over $200 for each of more than 10,000 futuristic boxes used to launch *USA Today* (and reports that more than 1,000 were destroyed or damaged by vandals in nine months in 1983 in the Philadelphia-New York City region). Loose change in boxes tempts vandals and dishonest employees. "Returns"—papers placed out for sale but returned unsold—are another expense. Accurately predicting the number needed for each box is an inexact science at best.

Successful single-copy sales require the following:

- Attractive front-page layout that makes the passerby dig down for coins. Many circu-

---

[32] *Circulation: Key to Successful Newspaper Marketing,* New York, Newspaper Advertising Bureau, Inc., September 1982 (research report).

[33] *Southern Newspaper Publishers' Association Bulletin,* April 10, 1985, p. 5.

A significant portion of many newspapers' circulation comes from single-copy sales. (Alan Carey/The Image Works)

lators feel that the news department must strive to make the front page particularly colorful above the fold—the portion that shows through the vending machine's window.

- Heavy promotion of that days' front-page news plus banners or other visuals that draw the buyer's eye to the vending machine or stack of papers.

- On-time delivery. Be there when readers are—or else. The late Dolly Schiff told the author, before she sold the *New York Post* to Rupert Murdoch, that she nearly created her own navy to get the paper out on time. *Post* trucks could not penetrate Manhattan traffic to catch the afternoon commuter rush, and she investigated using speedboats on the East and Hudson rivers. That didn't work; neither did her later study of using helicopters to fly papers over the traffic.

Another crucial factor in newspaper sales, for both home delivery and single-copy sales, is price. It merits careful study.

Aggressive Pricing a Top Priority

Newspaper pricing strategy should either maximize profit or achieve maximum sales volume and share of market. Of relatively minor concern in our discussion is pricing to achieve a certain quality image or to serve ethical or social considerations—sometimes factors in other industries.

Profit-oriented pricing aims at halting just short of that point where price increases cause disproportionate decreases in sales. Pricing strategy fails, obviously, if an increase designed to raise, say, $10,000 in new circulation revenue annually so angers readers that they cancel subscriptions worth $12,000. The strategy succeeds if it permits the newspaper both to raise prices *and* increase circulation. There is no industry formula for achieving that happy result; each manager must judge where price increases will meet reader resistance. NAB simply advises: "If we sell our paper for less than our readers think it is worth, we may be losing revenue. If we sell it for more than our readers think it is worth, we may be losing circulation. If we hit the bull's-eye, we may be maximizing both revenue and circulation." In the author's view, the newspaper industry generally is stricken with pricing timidity and unnecessarily shies away from aggressive, profit-oriented pricing.

Volume-oriented pricing aims for maximum sales or market share as more desirable long-term objectives than immediate profit. This approach is often used in competitive situations. Due largely to its competitive past—but also, the author contends, because of latent fears that newspapers aren't perceived by the public as worth more—the newspaper industry emphasizes volume-oriented pricing.

External influences on pricing include competition and custom. Unfortunately, the newspaper industry permits the ingrained custom of buying a newspaper for a stray coin or two. See Table 8.3 for a listing of newspaper prices. Note that newspapers sell their costly wrap-up of news from around the world—*plus* pages of interesting advertising—for pocket change.

Competition influences pricing not because newspapers generally battle other papers of like size and characteristics but because there are many other competitors for the reader's time and attention—and pocket change. In terms of pricing theory, many newspapers may appear to enjoy monopoly status because they are the only paid daily or weekly in their market. But many are engaged in pure competition—fighting large numbers of competitors, some of whom can enter the market easily and clamor for reader attention and all of whom influence a newspaper's pricing flexibility.

Many newspapers are trapped by decades of unimaginative efforts to meet all marketplace challenges simply by keeping prices low. Each manager must ask whether low pricing hasn't been the expedient answer to such things as quality lapses in the newsroom or lapses in distribution.

Whatever the cause, prices are deplorably low. Even in 1985, in the era of 80-cent soft drinks and 50-cent cups of restaurant coffee, the single-copy price of 5 U.S. daily newspapers was 10 cents. For 31, it was 15 cents; for 84, 20 cents. Even the 1,245 dailies boldly priced at 25 cents were cheaper than the cups of coffee drunk over them.[34]

The picture worsens when rate discounts are used to induce householders to subscribe, further reducing realized revenue. Discounting rates for 50 percent of total circulation is not unusual for some metro dailies.[35] For example, in 1985 Knight-Ridder sold its journalistically outstanding *Free Press* for the low rate of 20 cents daily or 75 cents on Sundays at newsstands; $1.90 for seven-day home delivery. Yet it acknowledged discounting prices on 132,942 daily copies (20.5 percent of the total) and 173,081 copies (21.5 percent) on Sundays. The *Detroit News*, also a journalistically outstanding paper, was priced at 15 cents daily (20 cents outside

---

Table 8.3   Single-Copy Prices, 1985

Daily Newspapers

10¢: 5	30¢: 130
15¢: 31	35¢: 169
20¢: 84	40¢: 3
25¢: 1,245	50¢: 4

Sunday Newspapers

20¢: 5	65¢: 1
25¢: 76	70¢: 0
30¢: 6	75¢: 229
35¢: 26	80¢: 2
40¢: 3	85¢: 5
45¢: 0	90¢: 2
50¢: 282	95¢: 1
55¢: 0	$1: 123
60¢: 15	$1.25: 1

Source: ANPA. Specialized newspapers and those selling for odd cents are omitted.

[34] *Facts About Newspapers '85*, Washington, D.C., American Newspaper Publishers Association, p. 5.
[35] Gregg Sutter, "Duel in Detroit: Who Will Go The Distance?", *Advertising Age*, Sept. 19, 1983, p. M-52.

the city), $1.40 for home delivery per week, and 75 cents on Sundays. Knight-Ridder claimed the *News* was discounting prices on 394,873 (or 60.6 percent) of its daily circulation, 431,823 (or 50.2 percent) of Sunday sales.[36] Obviously, the Detroit papers are special cases. Their fight was for survival. Each lost money and feared that if it fell too far behind it would be assigned permanent number-two position in a Detroit market that eventually might support just one paper. (In 1986, those fears drove the warring papers to petition the U.S. Justice Department for exemption from certain antitrust laws so they could combine their production and business operations under a single roof in a joint operating agreement, which will be discussed in a later chapter.)

Deep discounting of subscription rates is particularly damaging because it greatly dilutes the primary source of circulation revenue— home delivery. The typical U.S. daily delivers about 83 percent of its circulation to homes.

In setting prices, remember that you deliver comprehensive news, information, and entertainment plus colorful, detailed advertising to the door each day for pennies! The subscriber must be made to understand what a bargain that is. The daily newspaper's price must be edged up to and past the cost of that cup of coffee. After all, magazines commonly are priced at $2 or more and get more than 50 percent of their total revenue from the reader (compared to 20 percent or less for most newspapers). Cable TV fees are rising; book prices are up. This inevitably cheapens the newspaper's image in the public's eye, for it reveals deep concern among newspaper managers that their product has only a tenuous hold on its market position. Unless the entire industry moves quickly, ridiculously low prices will be so ingrained in the newspaper's relationship with readers that significantly higher prices will be impossible. Three

basic concerns militate for higher prices to readers:

First, escalating advertising rates throw an increasingly inequitable share of newspaper costs onto advertisers, and that soon may be unacceptable in this competitive world.

Second, even minor circulation price increases can yield significant new revenue. A 5 percent increase in Gannett's circulation revenue in 1985, for example, would have yielded more than $23.2 million additional.

Third, circulation costs are rising rapidly, particularly in labor (often 60 percent of the department's total) and energy (sometimes 20 percent of total). Unless circulation departments can bring in more direct revenue, they will fall even more deeply into deficit operations.

There is *some* evidence that the public generally feels rate increases would be justified. In her major readership survey (*Relating to Readers in the '80s*), Ruth Clark found that 85 percent of the public regard newspapers as "one of the biggest bargains there are these days." Clark quotes one housewife as follows: "Our paper costs only a nickel or dime more than it did ten years ago. Show me any product in the supermarket that can make the same claim." Belden Associates found in a study of metro markets that 60 percent of adult respondents considered newspapers "inexpensive"; only 29 percent termed them "expensive." The *Orlando (Fla.) Sentinel* determined that 72 percent of its readers found the paper "a good value for the money" (vs. "poor value").

Is the public already psychologically prepared for increases? Some managers think so. When the *Los Angeles (Calif.) Daily News* found that readers felt the paper to be worth more than its price, the paper raised prices eleven times in seven years. The *Wall Street Journal* was emboldened in 1984 to raise its annual subscription to $101; the per-copy price was raised 25 percent, to 50 cents. The *Journal* said the increase over $100 created a psychological barrier and caused a 2 percent circulation loss in the second quarter of 1984, but growth

---

[36] *1984 Annual Report*, Miami, Fla., Knight-Ridder Newspapers, Inc.

resumed quickly. *USA Today*, from its first day a hit with readers, dropped 9.5 percent in circulation in 1984, when it increased single-copy price from a quarter to 35 cents. But in 1985, the paper went to 50 cents. The *New York Times* in 1986 sold weekday plus Sunday mail subscriptions for $211 annually. The *Times* is deemed so important by readers across the country that it commands much higher prices in markets distant from New York City. Its Sunday readers, something akin to cult followers, pay $3 or more in some cities.

The *New York Times* and *Wall Street Journal* are aggressive pricing leaders in the industry. Implicit in that leadership is confidence in their competitive strength, confidence that their news and advertising are worth more and that readers perceive both newspapers as being so crucial to their daily lives that they will pay, within reason, the prices demanded.

Most rate increases cause at least temporary losses of circulation. Reader reaction to price hikes depends in large measure on how well newspapers serve their readers—and the availability of media alternatives. Certainly, no circulator can boldly increase prices without preparing the public carefully. Circulators must coordinate a fully integrated effort by all departments to improve the product so as to warrant increased prices; promote it effectively to ensure that the public will agree; and deliver it smoothly and on time. *Then*, prices can be hiked.

John Truitt, circulation director for the 48,000-circulation *Anderson (S.C.) Independent-Mail*:

- Never call it an "increase," always a "price change."

- Schedule change for early fall, when demand for the paper is highest (because of back-to-school news interest, shopping activity, etc.)

- Alert carriers two weeks in advance; give subscribers three days' notice, on the front page. The less advance notice to subscribers, the better.

- Don't stop the paper even when subscribers order it halted because of the price change; keep the paper arriving and give subscribers a cooling-off period to adjust to the new price.

- Any subscriber who insists on a halt in delivery should get a "preferred-customer kit" that includes a letter from the carrier, requesting reconsideration.

Some circulators say the reading public simply will not accept aggressive pricing and that newspapers cannot stand any drop in household penetration resulting from higher prices. Jack Butcher, circulation director for the *Tampa (Fla.) Tribune*, says, "Direct mail is now a major competitive price comparison [for advertisers]. Penetration declines can be reversed in the absence of circulation price increases. On the other hand, it would appear that every price increase causes a permanent penetration percentage decline." [37]

Some circulators say that the pricing leaders, the *Wall Street Journal* and the *New York Times*, are special cases and that the marketplace has room for few newspapers of their types. These circulators say that if most newspapers were priced appreciably higher, they would only be denied the mass-market acceptance that has traditionally been their basic appeal to advertisers. Low-price advocates note that TV and radio are "free" to viewer or listener and that their cost is borne by the advertiser. They cite proliferating free-circulation publications and direct mail, also free to recipients, as competitive reasons for keeping newspaper rates low. There is even talk of free daily newspapers being the wave of the future.

---

[37] Jack Butcher, speech to annual conference of Audit Bureau of Circulations, Nov. 10, 1983, Los Angeles.

DISTRIBUTING THE NEWSPAPER

Manufacturing more than 63 million copies of a product acceptable in quality and on time each day would challenge many industries. Most would be stunned at the idea of giving their expensive product to teenagers to distribute. But that's how the daily newspaper distributes most of its product. So an aspiring manager must become expert in the "little merchant" teenage carrier system and other ways of distributing newspapers to the right people in timely fashion and collecting for them.

Handle Little Merchants Carefully

Most teenage carriers are independent contractors, not employees, who buy newspapers at wholesale prices, deliver, and collect—thus they are known as "little merchants."

The newspaper's contractual and working relationship with carriers must be crafted carefully, with legal advice. Little merchants are exempt from minimum-wage laws. Their independent status exempts the newspaper from pension and benefits responsibilities and other legal burdens. Inappropriate contract language or job supervision can create an employer-employee relationship requiring the newspaper to shoulder enormous financial responsibility and exposing it to penalties under the law.

First make sure that the contract language for carriers explicitly states that they are independent contractors, not employees, and that the contract meets other current needs under state and federal law. The law changes, so stay alert. Essentially, the newspaper must protect the little merchants' independent status by compensating them for services rendered, but it may control only the result of their labor, not how it is accomplished. The newspaper cannot set prices, for example, or delineate sales territories or otherwise tightly supervise daily sales and distribution activities. It's a tricky area, hence legal counsel is required. Although the law doesn't require it, you should make sure

that carriers receive compensation close to the legal minimum wage. Compensation below that contributes to turnover in carrier ranks and draws trouble. (Other extremely important legal questions affecting circulation strategy are discussed in Chapter 12.)

Effective programs for recruiting, training, and motivating carriers are necessary to make sure that delivery keeps those valuable subscribers happy. Circulators perforce become expert in dealing with juvenile carriers and the problems of youth. Of approximately a million carriers in the United States, 85 percent are age eighteen or younger. Carriers are difficult to recruit, sometimes hard to motivate, and often fickle about staying on the job. Turnover is high: 90 percent annually nationwide, 200 percent or more at many newspapers.

A nationwide trend toward smaller families means fewer children for carrier jobs, an important factor for newspapers needing hundreds or thousands. The number of children between twelve and fourteen dropped 12 percent in the period 1970–1980; a further drop of 12 percent is predicted for 1980–1990.[38] Growing affluence means larger child allowances, so dollars earned as a carrier are less enticing.

Schools, churches, YMCAs, Scoutmasters —all are sources of serious, reliable youngsters. Motivational training, financial incentives, and adult supervision are crucial. Most newspapers conduct contests and award prizes—cash, stereos, baseball tickets, vacation trips—to carriers who sign the most new subscribers. *The Des Moines Register & Tribune*, with 8,000 carriers, 7,500 of them teenagers, offered personal computers to those who sold seventy-four subscriptions. But most carriers want a cash reward, so the *Register & Tribune* pays $3 for each eight-week subscription. *The Sacramento (Calif.) Bee* offers incentives (1985) averaging $3.12 per subscription sold.

For delivery, carrier compensation varies,

---

[38] Bogart, op. cit.

but the typical carrier (1984) delivers sixty papers daily and earns $20 weekly. Table 8.4 shows the 1984 compensation plan of Long Island's *Newsday*, with an army of 10,000 carriers ages eleven to eighteen.

Newsday carriers average forty to fifty papers delivered and $25 to $30 weekly compensation, including tips. Despite this compensation and unusually active motivational programs, *Newsday* carriers deliver on average for only sixteen months, then quit.

The key first-level supervisor in all this is the district manager (DM), who recruits, trains, motivates, and supervises carriers. DMs themselves should be recruited and trained very carefully. They can make or break circulation efforts.

The *Detroit News* employs 250 DMs for its 12,000 carriers, the largest such force in the country. They deliver 75 percent of total circulation to households, one of the highest home-delivered ratios among metropolitan dailies. On average, then, each DM supervises forty-eight carriers and routes. When a carrier is recruited, the *Detroit News* DM includes the family in a discussion of three important tasks—sales, service, and collection. Selling every day on the route is emphasized, but four times annually the *News* makes a special push with major promotion and sales campaigns of four to six weeks. DMs conduct motivational meetings, outlining prizes available and passing along sales hints: how to discuss the newspaper with prospects, how to describe its news and feature sections, and how to outline other incentives, such as food coupons available for clipping.

Milwaukee Journal DMs use slide shows featuring rock music and teenage humor. The idea is to put fun into selling.

Delivery problems are often complicated, in part caused by rapid turnover among DMs themselves. Tony Delmonico, circulation director for Scripps-Howard Newspapers (see box earlier in this chapter) reports that one of his group's papers, the *Denver Rocky Mountain News*, one year had an 89 percent turnover among its ninety-one DMs. He says it cost the company about $7,500 to recruit and train *each* replacement. Screening and better training of new DMs dropped turnover to 61.3 percent and, he says, saved $427,000. (The *News*'s circulation director, R. J. Myatt, says he knows the problem: A district manager must be a sales manager, teacher, psychiatrist, truck driver, public relations person, bill collector, and accountant—"we're looking for a Superman or Superwoman, and too often we hire a nerd.")[39]

A basic difficulty is the type work DMs must do. Often, that includes delivering a "down" route—one dropped without notice by a teenage carrier. As a manager, you can do little to change the nature of the DMs' work. But you *can* bring to bear leadership and motivational skills to keep them posted on the newspaper's strategy and circulation goals. Pay your DMs appropriately and make them feel that they are members of the management team.

The hassle of collecting is the reason carriers give most frequently for quitting. The collection process also irritates subscribers and leaves loose change rattling around, a temptation for the dishonest. Many papers switch to payment-in-advance (PIA) and bill by mail. This eliminates the administrative burdens teenagers feel in weekly door-to-door collecting and is attractive

---

Table 8.4   Carriers' Rates of Pay*

For delivering	Carrier was paid weekly
Seven-day subscription costing $2.50 weekly	48¢
Six-day subscription @ $1.50	30¢
Sunday-only @ $1	18¢

* Note the cost of delivery: the carrier received 19.2 percent of the seven-day subscription price, 20 percent of the six-day subscription, and 18 percent of the Sunday-only price.

---

[39] "Newspapers Told to Hire Better DMs," *Editor & Publisher*, June 25, 1983, p. 8a.

from your viewpoint because it actually gains interest-free loans from subscribers. A severe drawback is that it reduces personal contact between carrier and subscriber, in effect withdrawing the newspaper's front-line sales staff from frequent contact with customers. Some newspapers report that this has a negative effect on subscription renewals.

In sum, in managing the little-merchant system, you must pay close attention to three steps—recruitment and motivation of carriers, training and retention of district-manager supervisors, and collections.

Managing Other Distribution Systems

Newspapers sometimes contract with *independent agents* who handle all distribution, from press to subscriber household or point of single-copy sale. Often, independent agents handle many newspapers and magazines in the same area.

Over the short run, working through independent agents might look like the most profitable and certainly the easiest option for circulation departments. It avoids the need for large staffs, since recruiting and maintaining carriers are someone else's headaches. *Beware*. The independent-agency system can cause a newspaper to lose ultimate control of its product, pricing, distribution, and—importantly—customer relations.

Courts have ruled under antitrust legislation that once an independent agency buys newspapers for resale it may set its own prices and sell wherever and to whomever it pleases. Thus, a newspaper may find that its product is being handled by several agencies which are selling at various prices in competition with one another in the same general area. Also, newspapers can have no precise idea of who their subscribers are or where they live if distribution is handled by independent agencies (or loosely supervised nonemployee little merchants).

There are strong reasons, then, for every

manager to study closely a third option: *employee distribution*. Newspapers increasingly use only employees for moving papers from press to street sale points, stores, and vendors. Some also convert little merchants to employee status and pay them hourly wages. Under little-merchant or independent-agency systems, newspapers typically receive 70 to 75 percent of total single-copy and subscriber revenues. Carriers receive the rest. Calculate whether employee delivery would increase your newspaper's percentage. Another major consideration is that computers permit newspapers to maintain accurate subscriber lists. With employee delivery, this gives many newspapers unprecedentedly close adult contact with subscribers, and that is attractive. Robert Whalen of Whalen Computers, specialists in circulation systems, says, "A lot of newspapers have come to the conclusion that it is too dangerous to have their only contact with customers come through a 12-year-old boy."[40]

Computers aid payment-by-mail programs, eliminating another need for the little-merchant system. With the expansion of motor routes and the need to service multifamily and high-rise dwellings, adult delivery has become increasingly popular. Some circulators argue that the day of youthful carriers is passing—that legal, operational, and cost factors dictate a shift to adults. Others, however, feel that little merchants are the newspaper industry's greatest circulation strength and that, in selling newspapers, nothing beats the smiling teenager who lives down the street.

Mail delivery is used for 6 to 10 percent of all daily newspaper circulation, according to ANPA. This is attractive, particularly for morning papers with substantial rural or apartment-house circulation. Papers taken in presorted batches to post offices before dawn can be delivered the same day. Afternoon papers, of course, have little chance for same-day delivery by mail. Many weeklies distribute exclusively

---

[40] Burroughs, op. cit.

by mail because it is inefficient to maintain expensive carrier systems for once-weekly use.

Economical delivery by mail is generally possible only under second-class rates, based on the distance the newspaper is mailed and its weight. To ensure qualification for a second-class permit, management must attest to the post office that the paper, among other things, is published on a regular schedule at least four times annually, has a list of legitimate subscribers, and devotes not more than 75 percent of its space to advertising in more than half its issues over a twelve-month period.

Mail delivery is extremely important in TMC operations. The International Circulation Managers' Association says that 68 percent of all TMC publications are mailed.[41] But relatively high costs and postal delays (the postal system handled 131 *billion* pieces of mail in 1984, up from 106 billion in 1980) threaten timely delivery at acceptable cost.

Understanding and conforming to postal regulations is extremely important, and you should establish personal ties with the local postmaster, and stay informed on changes in regulations through publications of the Public and Employee Communications Division, U.S. Postal Service, P.O. Box 1600, La Plata, MD 20646.

SUMMARY

Under the marketing concept, the circulation department must be truly integrated with news, advertising, production, and promotion in a focused thrust toward the newspaper's overall goals.

Advertiser redefinition of what attractive circulation is plus rising distribution costs force many newspapers to eliminate circulation that is distant from their home markets. Advertisers want to pay only for circulation that reaches prospective customers living near retail outlets. Thus, distant circulation can be "inefficient," for circulation without advertising support is a cost factor, not profit generator.

Life-style changes force changes in circulation thinking. The newspaper is packaged and marketed under the basic strategy of penetrating the traditional mother-plus-father-plus-children household. The growth of other types of family units—single-parent families, for example—challenges long-held assumptions about the content and sale of the American newspaper.

With new competition springing up, circulation strategy must protect the newspaper's franchise as principal source of printed news, dominant advertising source, and door-to-door delivery vehicle.

Circulation accounts for about 30 percent of a newspaper's total expense but 20 percent or less of total revenue. Increasingly, circulation managers are expected to launch TMC or direct-mail operations and generate departmental profit as well as to perform more traditional distribution tasks.

An industrywide problem is fear that higher prices will lead to a loss of circulation. Improved content and aggressive promotion to make sure the public perceives the paper as being worth more are keys to raising prices.

"Selling" the newspaper involves obtaining readers, servicing them to retain their loyalty, collecting from them, and replacing those who cancel. The manager must intervene in the process at key points and times to ensure the staff quality and operational smoothness needed to accomplish those tasks.

RECOMMENDED READING

See particularly Leo Bogart's *Press and Public: Who Reads What, Where, When and Why in American Newspapers*, Hillsdale, N.J., Erlbaum, 1981. Association sources include Association of Paid Circulation Publications, P.O. Box 33641, Washington, DC 20033; Audit Bu-

---

[41] *Southern Newspaper Publishers' Association Bulletin,* June 5, 1985, p. 3.

reau of Circulations, 900 N. Meacham Road, Schaumburg, IL 60195; International Circulation Managers' Association, The Newspaper Center, Box 17420, Dulles International Airport, Washington, DC 20041; International Newspaper Promotion Association, The Newspaper Center (note INPA's *Census Applications in Newspaper Management and Marketing*, edited by Paul S. Hirt, 1981).

GLOSSARY

Many newspaper managers rise through news or advertising departments without hands-on circulation experience. Any manager who seeks credibility among circulators should learn their language, some of which is defined here.

Audit Bureau of Circulations (ABC). A nonprofit cooperative that audits and publishes member newspaper circulation figures for advertisers and others. Each member circulation department must keep daily and monthly records in accordance with ABC rules.

Blitz. Free delivery (also known as "sampling") to nonsubscriber homes for a week or so, followed by intensive sales effort.

Bootjacking. A term of yesteryear for selling single copies on the streets.

Bulk. Distribution of bundles trucked in large quantities for sale to, for example, hotels or airlines; there is disagreement as to whether bulk sales should be counted as paid circulation under ABC rules.

City Manager. Supervises the street sales manager, district managers, and others responsible for city circulation.

Contract haulers. Independent truck owners, not employees, who deliver bundles.

Country manager. Supervises district managers, motor route drivers, and others distributing outside the city.

District (or "branch") manager. Responsible for a specific territory; hires, trains, and supervises the carriers in it.

Door knockers. Sales crews, usually young people other than carriers, who sell subscriptions door to door on a commission basis.

Draw sheet. Count of copies ordered each day by each carrier, dealer, or others who distribute papers. Incorporates each new "start" or "stop" of subscriptions for that day.

Honor racks. Contrasted with coin-operated racks, these put buyers on their honor to leave money for the papers; a high theft rate is normal.

International Circulation Managers' Association (ICMA). A nonprofit research and service group at P.O. Box 17420, Dulles International Airport, Washington, DC 20041.

Little merchants. Boys and girls, not employees, who buy papers at discount, then deliver and collect. Check local/state laws for minimum ages, work hours, and other regulations.

Motor route drivers. These people drive distribution routes, normally in rural areas, throwing papers or placing them in roadside "tubes"; normally they are independent, not employees.

Ownership statement. Federal law requires the publisher of each general-circulation paper with a second-class postal permit to submit by October 1 of each year a sworn statement of paid circulation, ownership details, executives' names and addresses, and point of publication. This statement must be published in first or second issue of the paper following submission.

Payment in advance (PIA) or pay by mail (PMB). Payment through office, not carrier; is designed to sign subscribers to longer periods, usually a month or more, and relieve little merchants of collection hassles, the number-one cause of carrier turnover.

Phone room sellers. Employees or outside salespersons who canvas for subscriptions by telephone.

Promotion manager. Designs, supervises sales campaigns by carriers, phone rooms, outside sales crews, direct mail, other media.

Returns. Newspapers returned unsold to the

circulation department; an important indicator of a newspaper's circulation success in single-copy street sales. A high return rate can be enormously expensive.

Route list. A carrier's list of subscribers, usually requested annually by ABC.

Sampling. Free delivery to nonsubscribers for a week or so, followed by sales contact. This is expensive and must be tightly controlled.

SMC. Selective market coverage, circulation designed to reach a narrowly focused area of prime interest to advertisers.

Start. An order for delivery to a new subscriber.

Stop. An order to halt delivery.

Stuffing. Inserting preprinted material, often manually on smaller papers, prior to delivery.

Throwaway. A free- circulation paper or "shopper" with little news content; often thrown on front porches.

Total market coverage (TMC). An approach designed to reach all or nearly all households in a market; it often combines the newspaper's paid circulation with a free-circulation companion publication or direct mail.

CHAPTER NINE | Advertising

Frankly, you can be a successful newspaper manager even if you don't understand the inner workings of a press or how computers are programmed. But if you don't understand advertising, your manager's career will be short and unspectacular regardless of the department in which you work.

Advertising is the financial heart of the newspaper. Every manager at every level in every department must understand that, and help create a newspaper that is a successful advertising medium, because readers alone don't come close to fully supporting the newspaper. It is advertisers, contributing 80 percent or more of total revenue, who determine whether a newspaper will succeed financially.

In this chapter, we will discuss managerial principles you can use in designing and leading the advertising department of a new newspaper or shaping up the faltering ad department of an existing paper. Those principles include designing organizational structure, planning ad strategy, and then managing and controlling performance.

WHY ADVERTISING MATTERS

If simply selling more papers had been the only newspaper game in the early 1980s, the newspaper death list would have been considerably shorter. The *Washington Star*, after all, had a very substantial 340,000 circulation when it failed. The *Cleveland Press* claimed 316,000, nineteenth largest in the nation, just before it died. The *Philadelphia Bulletin* went down with close to 400,000, fourth largest for any afternoon paper in the country. Reader loyalty in those cities translated into millions of dollars in circulation revenue each year. In other cities, in different competitive and cost environments, circulation of that magnitude would mean immensely profitable operations. What went wrong? How could those newspapers fail financially when thousands and thousands of subscribers plunked down cash to buy them each day?

The equation of failure in newspaper publishing is extremely complex, and disaster wore many faces when it struck in Washington, Philadelphia, and Cleveland. Yet a common theme ran through those sad stories: *Each failed newspaper lost advertiser loyalty and share of advertising market.* For each, there came a time when revenue would not cover out-of-control costs, management error, journalistic weakness, onrushing competitors—all the ills that can afflict a newspaper—and those papers starved to death financially.

Loss of advertising market share is a manifestation of ills, not the cause; often, when share deterioration becomes glaringly visible, the newspaper's situation is already precarious. Large or small, published in village or metropolis, the newspaper is then vulnerable to internal disruption or error, such as a strike or management fumble, and to external forces, such as an economic downturn or competition from other papers or media. An example was the *Cleveland Press* in its final months.

The *Press*, demonstrating under the ownership of E. W. Scripps Co. how resilient a stricken newspaper can be, somehow survived years of internal and external affliction until rising costs and faltering revenue brought it to the breaking point. With its 45.1 percent share of Cleveland's metro daily *circulation* but at best only 35.5 percent of its daily *advertising*, the *Press* was caught in the classic "Catch-22" of a number-two newspaper: high costs of maintaining large circulation but low advertising revenue to support those costs.

Then came economic recession. Cleveland businesses shut down; unemployment skyrocketed. Retailers, still suffering from the city's 23.6 percent population loss between 1970 and 1980, were in agony. The *Press* was ravaged. Real estate advertising, for example, dropped one-third. Costs did not fall, however, and *Press* executives announced a 12 percent raise in local retail ad rates.[1] A 12 percent increase for hard-pressed retailers in a stricken city buffeted by recession? It couldn't fly—and didn't.

The *Press*, now owned by local entrepreneur Joseph E. Cole, announced rebates aimed at making rate increases more palatable. At the same time, it tried to improve news content and the paper's overall competitive posture. But time ran out and the newspaper shut down.

Says owner Cole:

> With better economic conditions, I believe we could have made it. But the economic environment, combined with . . . depressed real estate, automobile, housing and retail sales, contributed to our inability to secure sufficient advertising revenues. The times were simply against us.[2]

Strangely, Cole's eulogy did not mention competition, for in its extremity the *Press* battled formidable competitors for a share of Cleveland's shrinking ad revenue:

- The *Cleveland Plain Dealer*, 380,000 daily and 450,000 Sunday circulation, owned

---

[1] "*Cleveland Press* Offers Rebates For Plus Lineage," *Editor & Publisher*, Dec. 26, 1981, p. 17.
[2] "We Gave It Our Best—Joseph Cole," *Cleveland Press*, June 17, 1982, p. 1.

by well-financed, nationwide Newhouse Newspapers.

- Eleven suburban weeklies and shoppers, with 273,000 free and paid circulation, owned by Com Corp. Sun Newspapers, Inc., plus three independent weeklies with 45,000 combined circulation.

- *Cleveland Magazine* plus four TV stations and twenty radio stations (more in nearby suburbs and towns).

- Others included sixteen foreign-language newspapers aimed at the city's ethnic groups, forty-six business and trade periodicals published in Cleveland, seven college publications, vigorous direct-mail and outdoor-advertising companies, plus a tight ring of dailies and weeklies in smaller cities around Cleveland. [3]

The *Press* had to fight desperately for market share, because every ad dollar spent with a radio station, Hungarian neighborhood weekly, or suburban shopper was an ad dollar the newspaper did not get.

In sum, an aspiring manager who studies advertising's role in newspaper operations must consider several key points:

- Unless *reader loyalty* can be translated into *advertiser support* a newspaper is doomed.

- A circulation/advertising imbalance—high circulation costs, low ad revenue—creates a cost structure so high that the newspaper is vulnerable to disruptions in internal operations or external environment.

- Regardless of size, whether weekly or daily, a newspaper must have an advertising organization that—aided by all other departments—can compete against competitors of all types on all sides.

Let us now turn to designing an advertising organization capable of dealing effectively with those complex challenges.

DESIGNING THE ADVERTISING ORGANIZATION

The advertising department is in a "betwixt and between" position at any newspaper. It is the crucial link between the newspaper's need for revenue and the prime source of it, the competitive marketplace. But, it is totally dependent on other departments—news, circulation, production—for what it sells: solutions to advertisers' problems.

Take great care, therefore, in designing your advertising organization to operate efficiently in both its internal and external environments. Obviously, for most managers newly entering the field, the task will be to redesign an existing department. Try to create new attitudes throughout the newspaper to motivate each manager, in advertising or out, to nurture the advertising organization, giving it appropriate human and financial resources and supporting its efforts. And, importantly, design to accommodate internal changes in the way newspapers do things.

Design for Change Within

Newspapers in colonial days gained all their revenue through circulation alone. By 1887, when the American Newspaper Publishers' Association was formed and began keeping records, about half of newspaper revenue came from circulation. By 1909, it was down to one-third; by the early 1980s, it was 20 percent or less.

The change reflects slow circulation growth by newspapers and a reluctance to risk losses by charging readers more. Many newspaper managers feel that readers will not accept higher

---

[3] Cleveland competitors, from *'78 Ayer Directory of Publications*, Philadelphia, Ayer Press, 1978; and *Broadcasting Yearbook 1978*, Washington, D.C., Broadcasting Publications Inc., 1978.

costs and that the main burden, therefore, falls to the advertiser. The fact that the advertiser accepts repeated ad rate increases shows how essential the newspaper is to business, commerce, and industry.

Therefore advertising's contribution to total revenue has risen to 80 percent or more at most newspapers, while it is the least expensive department to operate—only 6 to 8 percent of total expense. To survive without advertising, newspapers would have to increase their circulation rates fivefold or more *and* maintain present circulation levels. Of course, newspapers priced that high and lacking full advertising—a reader draw, just like news—would lose circulation speedily.

The first reality in designing the advertising organization, then, is its relative position within the newspaper's structure; it is crucial in generating revenue and comparatively cheap to operate.

A second reality is that you must integrate advertising with other departments and see that they work together smoothly. The ad department must be involved in every step of the marketing effort, including creation of the news product, production, and distribution. That's still a revolutionary idea at some newspapers, particularly in newsrooms where *any* suggestion that advertising considerations enter the news process can create immediate tension. Start with a clear explanation to editors of advertising's financial importance, but stop well short of suggesting that the newsroom sell its journalistic soul to advertising. That won't work and it's wrong.

In the corporate hierarchy, the advertising department must report directly to the chief marketing executive: the marketing director in larger papers, general manager or publisher in smaller paper. Looking downward, the advertising director must plan and continually evaluate, control, and adjust as necessary performance of important subunits. Depending on newspaper size, these subunits vary in number and character.

Figure 9.1 shows the organizational structure of the ad department at the *Athens (Ga.) Daily News* and *Banner-Herald*. These subunits report directly to the ad director:

- The *national ad coordinator* seeks all available national or "general" revenue, but relative to other sources of revenue, it won't be significant on a newspaper this size. The coordinator works through a "national rep," a firm that sells space, on a commission basis, to national advertisers for many newspapers.

- The *retail manager* runs the single most important subunit. Retail or "local retail" ads from local merchants provide most revenue for all newspapers except those that are national in scope.

- The *chief artist* directs layout and design services for advertisers. Vital to the sales effort is the speculation or "spec" ad created by artists to entice advertisers into signing a contract. Advertising graphics that are esthetically pleasing—in addition to being persuasive—contribute greatly to a newspaper's readability and appeal. Increasingly, ads are being laid out, graphics and all, on computer screens. Eventually this process will be dovetailed into pagination—the computerized layout of pages.

- The *classified manager* directs a booming sector of newspaper advertising. We will discuss this and other forms of advertising in detail later.

Design for External Change

The advertising department must be designed to meet rapid change outside the newspaper. First, total advertising expenditures are growing faster than the U.S. gross national product (total goods and services produced) and have done so for more than forty years, through thick and thin in the national economy. (See box for a

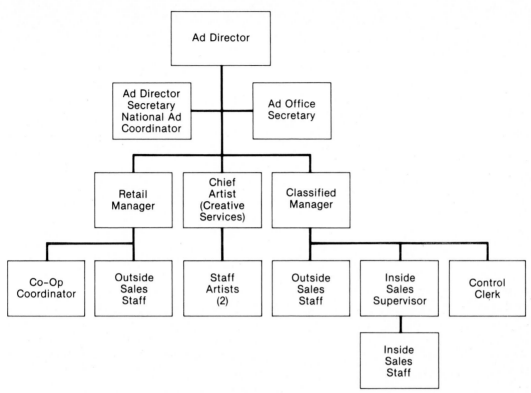

Figure 9.1 *Athens (Ga.) Daily News and Banner-Herald*

chart illustrating that.) Total newspaper ad dollars are growing rapidly too. (See Table 9.1.)

But, second, competitors also are growing rapidly, so the advertising organization must be designed to ensure that highly professional, competitive people are assigned to advertising. In just 1984-1985, for example, total advertising in all media rose 7.8 percent, to $94.7 billion from $87.8 billion. TV, not even a significant competitor when many 1980s publishers first entered newspapering, took 21.9 percent. Direct mail, relatively new as a serious competitor, took 16.3 percent. Radio, magazines, specialized business publications—all chipped at newspapers' share, which in 1985 was 26.5 percent, almost equaling TV and radio combined but still down from 28.4 percent in 1981.[4]

A third major external change to factor into organizational design is that retailing is changing as advertisers seek more than simple exposure

Table 9.1 Daily Newspaper Advertising Volume (millions)

	National	Local	Total
1950	$ 518	$ 1,552	$ 2,070
1960	778	2,903	3,681
1970	891	4,813	5,704
1980	1,963	12,831	14,794
1981	2,259	14,269	16,528
1982	2,452	15,242	17,694
1983	2,734	17,848	20,582
1984	3,005	20,830	23,835
1985	3,352	22,818	25,170

Source: American Newspaper Publisher's Association.

[4] *Facts About Newspapers '86*, Washington, D.C., American Newspaper Publishers' Association, p. 8.

ADVERTISING AND THE GNP

Total U.S. advertising expenditure is growing faster than the gross national product (total goods and services produced). Here are some representative figures (dollars in millions):*

YEAR	GNP	PERCENT CHANGE	DOLLARS AD	PERCENT CHANGE	PERCENTAGE AD OF GNP
1975	$1,549.2	8.0%	$27.9	4.8%	1.801%
1977	1,918.2	11.7	37.4	12.4	1.952
1979	2,417.8	11.7	48.8	12.6	2.018
1981	2,937.7	11.6	60.4	12.8	2.057
1982	3,059.3	4.1	66.6	10.2	2.176
1983	3,291.1	7.6	73.0	9.6	2.218
1984	3,609.0	9.7	81.5	11.6	2.258

For newspaper advertising, the picture 1946–1981 is one of upward movement along with the GNP, even though that period included television's birth as a commercial medium and strong competitor for ad dollars.†

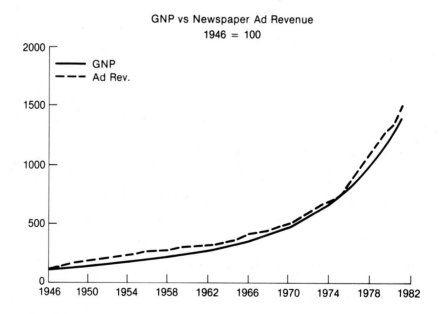

GNP vs Newspaper Ad Revenue
1946 = 100

* C. Patrick O'Donnell, Jr., *Industry Viewpoint*, New York, Donaldson, Lufkin & Jenrette, March 19, 1984, p. 4.

† Alan S. Donnahoe, "Will Newspapers Survive?" *Editor & Publisher*, July 17, 1982, p. 22.

of their message to large numbers of diverse readers via just any mass-circulation medium. Rather, they demand meaningful impact on potential customers through precision advertising vehicles with proven ability to create response.

Advertisers want a newspaper's news and feature copy to create believability and reliability, thus lending credibility to ads and motivating response. For example, the *New York Times* offers an environment of high-quality journalism that delivers upscale readers. This strategy captures 60 percent of the three-paper New York City ad market even though *The Times* is second in daily circulation to the *Daily News*.[5] (*The Times* gained that share even when it was third in circulation; it beat out the *New York Post* for second position in 1984.)

Advertisers are also carefully analyzing media costs, watching "cost per thousand" rates ("CPMs" in the trade), which newspapers and their competitors charge to deliver an advertising message to a thousand readers. CPM comparison is an important advertiser yardstick in judging the relative cost-effectiveness of various media; newspaper managers *must* design an organizational structure capable of meeting competitors on that battleground.

As newspaper CPMs escalate due to higher costs—plus shareholder profit demands—and as alternative media become more attractive, some advertisers withdraw from newspapers or seek a "mix" of, say, one newspaper supplemented by TV, radio, or others. Jewel Food Stores, for example, a major advertiser, advertises in a mix of about 52 percent newspapers, 23 percent TV, 13 percent radio, 12 percent direct mail, and other vehicles. Supermarkets nationwide generally use 57 percent newspapers, 7 percent TV, 7 percent radio, 29 percent direct mail, and others.[6]

In two-newspaper towns, some advertisers withdraw from the number-two paper on grounds they can reach desired audiences more economically through one newspaper, the market leader, plus such a mix of other media. For the advertiser, this eliminates the cost of "duplication"— advertising in two newspapers whose circulations overlap and to some extent deliver the same readers. It also helps kill number-two newspapers. It certainly did in Washington, Cleveland, and Philadelphia.

Increasingly, all this is no longer sorted out one to one between newspaper salesperson and corner grocer. More than half of all newspaper advertising is planned or bought outside the local market, at distant headquarters of store chains, where research-oriented specialists demand precise information on newspaper markets, audiences, and competitors. Traditionally, many newspapers sent backslapping sales people into the fray equipped with little more than pleasant personalities; these same papers now scramble to deliver computer-generated market studies to this new breed of advertising executive.

Designing Advertising Research

In Chapter 3 we discussed research of a newspaper's market, product, and competition in overall strategic planning. Those same three steps are necessary in planning ad sales strategy, and we must add a fourth—researching the *advertisers'* businesses to determine their needs and how we can meet them.

Research must be continuous, using "intelligence" generated internally and externally by government or research bodies. Larger papers must have research units with computer capability to digest vast amounts of raw information. Smaller papers can and must make sure that they also have research capability, no matter how primitive technologically.

Always, research must focus on marketing the newspaper better and more profitably, suggesting practical steps toward basic objectives: identifying marketing opportunities or prob-

[5] "New York's *Daily News* Girds For Next Round vs. Murdoch," *Adweek*, April, 1984, p. 10.
[6] "Ad Directors Urged To Set Up Co-op Departments," *Editor & Publisher*, July 23, 1983, p. 13.

lems, designing tentative solutions, and then helping the decision-making process move ahead. Research for external use should be designed to solve advertiser needs and assist you in what advertising sales is all about: getting signed contracts. Base your sales effort on solidly researched information and facts, not the personality or flair of salespeople.

The *Denver Rocky Mountain News* gives clients a fifty-four-page market analysis by Belden Associates, a Dallas research firm used by many newspapers. As an example of the report's detail, Belden found there are 71,000 widows in the Denver-Boulder market or 11 percent of all women, and that 54 percent of these read the *Rocky Mountain News*. The *Tampa (Fla.) Tribune* distributes a twenty-eight page Belden report revealing, for example, that 34 percent of Tampa homes have $20,000 or more annual income.

Market surveys by outside firms can be expensive. The *Atlanta Constitution* and *Journal* paid more than $200,000 to Scarborough Research Corp. of New York for a market study. Was it worth it? Ferguson Rood, vice president for marketing and advertising, has this to say:

> Research such as Scarborough is essential to the sale of advertising. It is necessary that we measure our markets in terms of readers rather than simply count circulation. Knowing who our readers are in terms of their demographics and lifestyles helps us and our advertisers target advertising messages for everyone's benefit.
>
> We have found through years of experience that when we relate our readership to shoppers at specific stores, we help advertisers buy more space more efficiently, thus making their advertising an investment rather than an expense.

If you cannot afford outside research, do-it-yourself kits are available. Suburban Newspapers of America distributes readership survey materials complete with sampling methodology and questionaires.[7]

However it is obtained, newspaper research must help advertisers find the geographic or demographic targets they want to reach, then assist in precision delivery of the client's message via target marketing. Says Donald R. Hatley, ad director for the *Montgomery (Ala.) Advertiser* (48,000 morning circulation) and *Alabama Journal* (23,000 evening): "I can see the day when we'll be able to hit all the left-handed cigar-smokers on the left side of the street whose names start with 'M.' Nobody else is better suited to do it."[8]

Research must determine how the newspaper is performing in its market. Without this, strategy can go astray. Sometimes, for example, huge chunks of newspaper circulation become unattractive to advertisers. Such a development must be picked up in research so managers can adjust accordingly. At the *Cleveland Press*, it wasn't, managers didn't—and that compounded the *Press*'s problems. To explain:

In January 1982, *Press* circulation penetrated 47.9 percent of households in its ABC City Zone. That ranked an impressive sixth among the twenty-five largest-circulation U.S. newspapers. However, Cleveland's inner core had been through a decade of wrenching socio-economic change, and many demographically attractive customers had fled to suburbs in the Retail Trading Zone (RTZ). Out there, the *Press* ran into Com Corp.'s eleven suburban weeklies and shoppers, each entrenched in its narrow local market, plus zoned editions launched earlier by its alert crosstown rival, the *Plain Dealer*. The *Press* was late in detecting the shift to the suburbs; when it finally reacted, the competitive situation had deteriorated beyond repair. The *Press* never penetrated more than 14.6 percent of those desirable RTZ households and was able to offer its advertisers mainly circulation in relatively unattractive inner Cleveland. Advertisers insist on lower ad rates for unattractive circulation—if they pay for it at all—so the *Press*

---

[7] *Market Research*, a kit from Suburban Newspapers of America, 111 E. Wacker Drive, Chicago, IL 60601.

[8] Elise Burroughs, "More Dailies Offer Advertisers Chance To Reach Target Markets," *presstime*, August 1983, p. 19.

was forced to lower rates and then provide rebates, which reduced revenue even more.

Lessons for all managers: research must pick up trends such as those that trapped the *Press* early enough so that adjustments can be made. *Press* ad salespeople were ill equipped to meet advertisers' objections that they were not interested merely in large circulation, that they wanted the *Press* to deliver the right kind of readers—the affluent, ready-to-spend readers who lived near retail outlets. *The Press*'s research should have found these readers so that the newsroom could develop a product for them and circulation, in turn, could deliver them for the advertising department to sell to clients.

A different but equally instructive research problem plagued Gannett's *USA Today* in its early years. The paper enjoyed astounding circulation success, but many advertisers complained that 70 percent of sales were single copies from newsstands and racks and that, therefore, there was no reliable research on precisely who the readers were. Advertisers want continuity among readers, and they asked for research on whether the same people were buying the paper each day. Some wanted to know whether readership was heavily sports-oriented—drawn by the paper's outstanding sports section—and whether as a daily *USA Today* had a "shelf life" of several days, as did *Time, Newsweek*, and other magazines.

Breaking through the image problem and selling advertisers on the value of *USA Today*'s very substantial circulation was frustratingly difficult for Gannett executives. Their inability to plan an advertising strategy that answered those questions satisfactorily contributed to *USA Today*'s start-up losses, which ran into the hundreds of millions of dollars.

PLANNING ADVERTISING SALES STRATEGY

Now comes one of a manager's most important responsibilities: Planning a dynamic sales strat-

egy to achieve the advertising department's assigned goals. This must be done for major advertising categories—local retail, national, and classified—and, as well, for preprint/insert advertising, co-op, legal or public notice, and coupon advertising. All are important revenue sources.

As you study each category in detail, you may easily lose sight of the overall strategic picture. So keep in mind that advertising sales strategy must be planned in complete consonance with the strategies of other departments, particularly news and circulation. Here is an example of what can happen when that underlying principle of the marketing concept is ignored.

When Australian publisher Rupert Murdoch bought the *New York Post*, he laid down a news strategy featuring highly sensational coverage—rape, murder, pillage, and arson are standard fare. His circulation strategy aims at New York City readers left behind by the *Daily News* in its climb to somewhat higher journalistic ground and, certainly, by the high-toned *New York Times* and *Wall Street Journal*.

Murdoch's advertising strategy? Well, a story (perhaps apocryphal) illustrating his dilemma made the rounds. It has Murdoch trying to convince an executive of an upscale New York City department store to switch advertising to his *Post* from the *Times*. Murdoch's flamboyant afternoon tabloid was, after all, then delivering more readers than the *Times*. "Mr. Murdoch," the executive is said to have replied, "The *Times*' readers are our shoppers. The *Post*'s readers are our shoplifters."[9]

True or not, the story damaged the *Post*. As the paper tried to carve out a share of an advertising market crowded by the *Daily News*, largest general-circulation daily in the country, and the *Times*, perhaps the most prestigious, the tale was circulated by, among others, *Advertising Age*, a trade publication widely read

---

[9] "*Post* Has The Numbers, But Lineage Trails," *Advertising Age*, Nov. 29, 1982, p. 26.

by advertising executives and retailers nationwide. The magazine quoted "one New York
media buyer" as follows:

> I look at their numbers [the *Post's* readership
> research] and I see that they reach more college-
> educated readers than the *Daily News* and that
> they have a younger audience than the *Times*, but
> just when I think that—maybe—I should recom-
> mend the *Post* to a client, I look at those screaming
> red headlines, and I think, God, no, I just can't
> go in there.[10]

The failure of the *Post's* advertising strategy
seriously detracted from one of the industry's
great circulation success stories: from 400,000
to 960,000 in just six years. Circulation plummeted to 732,000 in 1987. It was self-defeating
for one *Post* department, news, to create a
sensational newspaper and for another, advertising, to try to sell to advertisers on fashionable
Fifth Avenue the type reader that content at-
tracted. For years, this inconsistency in policy
reportedly cost Murdoch some $1 million or
more *monthly* in operating losses.

Now let's look at where advertising dollars
come from, how the competitive battle for
market share is heating up, and where newspaper strengths and weaknesses lie.

Local Retail Display Advertising

Local retail merchants, who sell directly to
consumers, are mainstays of newspaper advertising. They spent $41.3 billion in 1985, or 43.6
percent of the total $94.7 billion advertising
outlay in the United States. Of that local retail
total, newspapers received 52.7 percent, or
$22.8 billion.

TV, with $5.7 billion or 13.8 percent, was
the newspaper industry's closest single competitor in local retail, but a distant one. Radio's
share was about 11 percent.[11]

For all but national newspapers, local retail
dominates revenue. Often, 50 percent of the
total—70 to 80 percent or more on smaller
papers—comes from local retail. So the local
retail fight into the 1990s promises to be one in
which newspapers battle rising numbers of vigorous competitors lusting for their very life-
blood.

Direct-mail companies, using computerized address lists to seek out tightly stratified,
demographically attractive advertising targets,
took in $15.5 billion total revenue in 1985, and
they certainly will be in the forefront of competitors. So will free-circulation papers. They
offer, of course, highly sophisticated SMC plus
the ability to blanket geographic areas with
nearly 100 percent TMC penetration.

Because newspapers have traditionally
dominated local advertising, some managers
even today project their local revenue as a
guaranteed fixed percentage of advertisers' store
sales. This will change now that local merchants
increasingly seek media alternatives. Also sure
to change is the attitude, among some managers
of small- and medium-size papers, that they can
raise rates nearly at will. Advertisers started
rebelling over automatic increases designed to
cover rising newspaper costs in the late 1970s,
when some papers passed along double-digit,
twice-annual increases that totaled substantially
more than inflationary cost increases.

Your sales strategy, then, must recognize
that newspapers face an unprecedented challenge in local retail due to strengthening competitors, advertisers' increasing sophistication in
media affairs, and the inability of some editors
and circulation managers, as at the *Cleveland
Press*, to shift journalistic and marketing strategies so as to meet socioeconomic changes in
their markets. Don't overlook, either, pressure
created by advertisers who got quite an education when a number of newspaper companies
went public and were required to publish financial results. Advertisers learned that the ad rates
they were paying supported newspaper profit
ratios higher than those enjoyed by many in-

---

[10] Ibid.
[11] *"Facts About Newspapers '86,"* op. cit.

dustries and, indeed, often by the advertisers themselves.

Let's look now at some of the strengths newspapers have in the fight for local retail advertising and how you can bring them to bear:

- As the primary, often unrivaled source of substantive local news, community newspapers can generally demonstrate reader acceptance that promises widespread and credible exposure of advertisers' messages to their primary consumer target—local residents. Indeed, many readers buy newspapers for advertising as well as news. Sell the newspaper as a family tool that is actively used in the search for shopping guidance by serious, habitual readers.

- Point out to advertisers that the very nature of a newspaper, as contrasted with TV or radio, permits graphic display of detailed local retail shopping information—full-page ads of grocery prices, for example, or dozens of hardware items.

- Newspaper readers are generally upscale in education, income, and buying habits. Your research of your own market should reveal this; then, demonstrate how your integrated marketing effort creates and distributes a product that reaches attractive consumers.

- Merchants selling consumables (foods or drugs, for example, not autos or refrigerators) tend to advertise at predictable levels in good times; yet they also advertise even in bad times just to maintain their institutional image and market share. Newspapers have "shelf life" or availability and usefulness in the home—all day for a daily, five or six days for a weekly—that is well suited for that type of advertising. Make it a selling point.

- Alert newspapers can meet, better than any competitor, the pressing need of core-city advertisers by "chasing" affluent customers who move to the suburbs and beyond. The *New York Times* does this for Fifth Avenue merchants by delivering demographically attractive readers via its circulation in the rich suburbs of New Jersey, Connecticut, and elsewhere. Smaller dailies and even weeklies can offer target marketing, particularly if they provide TMC with a combination of their paid-circulation plus a free-circulation paper to nonsubscribers. TV, a mass-appeal medium, cannot focus its effort that way. It casts a net for scattered millions. Radio can "zone" with programming—rock music to draw young listeners, "golden oldies" for older listeners—but it still cannot match newspaper zoning.

- Newspapers require less "lead time" than TV for ad copy, so advertisers can quickly exploit an event (a swimsuit sale, for example, soon after unexpectedly good spring weather). TV requires lengthy lead times for commercials, and commercials are far more expensive to produce than are newspaper ads.

However, newspapers battle for local retail ads with a number of weaknesses:

- Paid circulation generally penetrates too few households. Your strategy must be to improve news content to eventually attract more paid readers while also providing TMC.

- Because it is essentially a news medium, the newspaper cannot attract the huge audiences lured by TV's entertainment. Your strategy must be to show advertisers (through research) that you, however, deliver demographically attractive albeit smaller audiences.

- Newspapers, unlike TV or radio, use a very expensive commodity—newsprint—and, also unlike broadcast, are labor-intensive. This drives up costs, which, in turn, forces newspaper ad rates higher until competitors can sometimes undersell. Free-circulation papers have costs substantially lower than those of a paid circulation newspaper: shoppers have no expensive news staffs. To counter both low-cost competitors, you must sell advertisers on the fact that paid circulation papers (1) attract more affluent readers and (2) are read with greater care and thus are a better advertising medium.

- Newspapers suffer competitively due to their cumbersome, expensive distribution process—kids on bicycles, adults on motor routes. Contrast flicking a dial to tune in an anchorperson to retrieving a newspaper thrown in the bushes by an errant teenager (and newspaper ink smudges readers' hands—serious reason, incidentally, why some people avoid reading newspapers). As discussed in Chapter 8 your best response is to create a capable circulation organization that works closely with the advertising department to ensure timely delivery and efficient subscriber service.

- And, to be blunt, some newspapers lose local retail simply because they are archaic in marketing strategy, sales techniques, and research. Often, TV just outsells them. We'll discuss later how to avoid this.

In counterattacking, particularly against TV, many newspapers find great opportunity in part-run local retail advertising—ads that run in just some editions. In Dallas, the *Morning News* and *Times Herald* offer part-run advertising techniques that are models for all managers. Witness:

1. Dallas is a sprawling "metroplex," and huge portions of the *Dallas Morning News* and *Dallas Times Herald* circulation are of no interest to many small advertisers. A store owner in, say, southwest Dallas, whose customers come from the immediate neighborhood, does not need to advertise in distant northwest Dallas.

2. Rising costs, particularly of newsprint, push ad rates based on total circulation up beyond the reach of small advertisers.

3. Competing media, particularly shoppers or neighborhood weeklies and small dailies, can deliver narrowly focused circulation zones suited to small advertisers, *and* at lower rates.

What to do? The *Dallas Morning News* and *Times Herald* both offer lower-cost space in just a portion of total circulation, rather than only "run of paper" (ROP) advertising in all editions. The *Times Herald*, for example, covers Dallas with five weekly editions called "Community Closeup," with local news produced by special staff. Using those editions, advertisers can:

- Reach any of five regions through one "Community Closeup" or in any combination of all five plus the main paper.

- Use a *Times Herald* direct-mail operation reaching 320,000 households that don't purchase the paper. The *Times Herald* promises to deliver 750,000 households with its paid circulation to subscribers plus direct mail to nonsubscribers.

- Insert preprints in the *Times Herald* (minimum 40,000 copies) for readers in seventeen preprint zones that slice the city into small geographic blocs (importantly, this can produce neighborhood economic or social homogeneity and permit narrow target marketing).

To similarly serve advertisers, many papers are turning to part-run advertising. In one month, the *Chicago Tribune* ran 275,000 column-inches of ROP advertising in all editions and 410,000 part-run; the *Detroit News*, 289,000 full-run and 105,000 part-run; the *Memphis Commercial Appeal*, 149,000 full-run and 85,000 part-run.[12]

---

[12] "1986 April Lineage," *Editor & Publisher*, June 7, 1986, quoting Media Records, Inc., p. 42.

For many papers, part-run reverses a dangerous situation: as full-run rates get higher, they appeal only to larger advertisers, and papers thus must depend on a shrinking handful of clients. Part-run broadens the revenue base to include smaller advertisers and makes newspapers less vulnerable to economic dislocation or the whims of a few large ones.

Part-run advertising, in sum, is just good business. Wall Street analyst C. Patrick O'Donnell, Jr., examining for his investor clients the finances of a 75,000-circulation "model" newspaper, points out that incremental cost increases for part-run "are not burdensome . . . and such advertising revenue adds to the overall operating margins of any newspapers." O'Donnell's model paper would charge $2,000 for one-time insertion of a full-page ad that goes to all 75,000 subscribers, $800 to deliver the same ad via part-run to 15,000 subscribers.[13]

National (General) Advertising

In this category, your strategy must be to expand by attacking the dominance of TV. Stakes nationwide are huge. National advertising, mostly by firms offering mass-produced goods and services for multioutlet sale, reached an astounding $53.3 billion in 1985, up 7.2 percent from 1984. Of that, newspapers got just 6.2 percent—or $3.3 billion. Network TV got $8.3 billion. National ads placed directly with local TV stations ("spot" national) hit $6 billion. That gave TV, then, $14.3 billion. Newspaper national in 1985 increased 7.1 percent over 1984, signaling strong efforts by many managers to elbow into the national arena. It will be a tough fight.

TV has great strength in advertising products such as, say, razor blades or beer, mass-produced and sold coast to coast to demographically diverse audiences. The Newspaper Advertising Bureau (NAB) notes, for example, that

98 percent of U.S. households have TV sets and three out of five have at least one turned on during prime viewing hours. But NAB also provides you with hints on how to sell advertising against network TV competition:

- Point out that national TV might deliver huge audiences for a given *program*, but there is argument whether it delivers them for *commercials*. Viewers often regard commercials as intrusive, to be avoided by leaving the room, talking, reading, or switching channels. NAB says that only 60 percent of a program's audience is even in the room and paying attention when a typical commercial runs. (Conversely, NAB says, 84 percent of a newspaper's pages are opened by the average reader; thus the ads are delivered to four of five readers per paper.) Flipping channels to avoid commercials reaches such dimensions that advertisers have called it "zapping." It's particularly easy with a remote-control device operated from a favorite armchair. General Foods, the nation's twelfth largest advertiser ($450 million in 1985), calculates that it loses as much as $1 million annually to zapping. General Foods counterattacked with "roadblocking"—running the same commercial on three networks *and* cable TV—so that channel jumpers would have a good chance of seeing it wherever they switched. However, that doesn't catch viewers using VCRs to record programming and eliminate commercials by "zipping" past them.

- TV viewers cannot easily recall commercials. One NAB study shows that only 5 percent of viewers could recall brand names that had been mentioned in commercials four to eight minutes earlier; none recalled names mentioned *more* than eight minutes earlier.

- Network TV viewing drops as cable TV proliferates. Research in Tulsa, Oklahoma,

---

[13] "The Business of Newspapers: An Essay For Investors," industry review by Patrick O'Donnell, Jr., senior publishing analyst, E. F. Hutton, Feb. 12, 1982.

shows that prime-time network viewing averaged 90 percent in homes without cable TV but that it dropped to 74 percent in 12-channel-cable homes and 56 percent in 36-channel homes.[14] In 1987, some 44 percent of U.S. TV homes had cable; some estimates are that 50 percent or more will have it by 1990 and that network viewing could fall to 60 or 65 percent. Network TV won't fade away as a national advertising competitor, but point out that there *is* a question mark over its future.

- Point out also that 20 percent of the population does 43 percent of the total TV viewing, so sole reliance on TV means reaching only one-fifth of the population.

- NAB says that TV "has difficulty reaching upscale socioeconomic segments of the population." Households of $40,000 or more annual income watch TV 19.9 hours weekly; under-$10,000 households, 27.5 hours. With improved zoning and sophisticated marketing, newspapers can offer national advertisers a precision vehicle for reaching demographically attractive consumers—and at CPMs lower than TV's. Thirty seconds of commercial time can cost (1986) $300,000; the highest price ever paid for TV time (sixty seconds on the 1986 Super Bowl telecast) was over $1 million. For just *thirty* seconds on the 1987 Super Bowl telecast, the cost was $600,000.

Newspaper enthusiasts spot consumer and corporate attitudes that could increase national newspaper advertising. According to Craig C. Standen, NAB president, consumers are better educated, more demanding, and no longer buy automatically. They require more information on, say, a car, and newspaper advertising is best suited to provide detail. Also, Standen says, business leaders and corporations are taking to advocacy and institutional advertising, discussing not only their products but also public issues. This kind of thoughtful, detailed advertising is best delivered in newspapers.[15]

However, your national ad sales strategy must also recognize that newspapers have weaknesses:

- The big dollars available draw many competitors, and the newspaper industry's share is slipping. With a generation of TV-oriented advertising executives, it will not be easy to reverse that trend.

- Newspapers spend heavily to modernize plant and equipment, but many still cannot provide the reproduction quality—particularly in color—demanded by national advertisers in this era of crystal-clear TV transmission (456 papers surveyed by ANPA spent over $1 billion in 1986 on plant and equipment).[16]

- There lingers an old newspaper habit of charging more for national advertising than for local. Avarice aside, newspapers have higher costs than TV and must compensate their national sales reps. This requires higher ad rates.

- Newspapers also argue that national advertisers benefit from all circulation—even, say, out-of-state circulation that is of no interest to local advertisers. National rates in 1984 averaged 64.6 percent higher than local rates, according to ANPA. The American Association of Advertising Agencies said that the disparity in the mid-1980s was greater than any time since 1933, when the

---

[14] "The People On The Left Are Still Charging You As If The People On The Right Didn't Exist," advertisement in the *New York Times*, April 7, 1983, p. 48.

[15] Craig C. Standen, "Why And How Papers Can Get Bigger Share of National Ads," *presstime*, January 1983, p. 32.

[16] "Survey Shows Record Expenditures," *presstime*, June 1986, p. 86.

association began keeping records. (In 1933, the differential averaged 37.9 percent).[17] Prestigious *Advertising Age* magazine warns newspapers that their "pricing arrogance" is the greatest barrier to increased national advertising.

We'll now discuss how your strategy must close that rate gap and increase national ad revenue.

Join Industry's Campaign for National Advertising

As never before, the newspaper industry is campaigning for national advertising. Dovetail your sales strategy into the effort by NAB and ANPA to make it easier and cheaper for national advertisers to use newspapers. A key element in accomplishing this is the standard advertising unit (SAU) system.

ANPA is convinced that newspapers will gain national advertising as network TV, long dominant, loses significant market penetration to cable TV and other forms of electronic home-delivered entertainment—*if*, that is, newspapers become easier to deal with. In 1980, while she was chairman of ANPA, Katharine Graham, also chairman of the Washington Post Co., ordered a special committee to develop the first SAU system. Walter Mattson, president of the New York Times Co., headed the committee.

By July 1, 1984, when the system went into effect, dailies representing 96 percent of total U.S. circulation accepted all or most of the new system. To fully conform, full-size ("broadsheet") newspapers accept a format of six columns, each $2\frac{1}{16}$ inches wide with $\frac{1}{8}$-inch between columns. Columns are 21 to $22\frac{1}{2}$ inches deep. Printed pages are 13 inches wide. Ad rates are based on the column inch (not agate line, used generally by newspapers since the

early 1800s). Tabloid pages are $10^{13}/_{16}$ inches wide and 14 inches deep, with five columns, each $2\frac{1}{16}$ inches wide and $\frac{1}{8}$ inch apart. There are minor variations for some tabloids, particularly New York's *Daily News* and *Newsday*, which face multimillion dollar press modifications if they conform completely. (See Figure 9.2 for an illustration of "specs.")

The SAU system involves 57 standard ad sizes, 56 of which fit full-size newspapers; 16 fit tabloids. This permits advertisers to create a single ad for all SAU newspapers throughout the country. Newspapers are free to accept other sizes, too. Even smaller newspapers normally attracting little national advertising should adopt SAU standards, because major regional and even local advertisers seek standardization among newspapers. Regional advertising headquarters for food or discount stores, for example, exert pressure for conformity. Classified advertising is exempt from SAU standards.

A second industrywide bid for national ads backed by the NAB and ANPA is Newsplan, under which more than a thousand newspapers offer 3 to 30 percent rate discounts to national advertisers who contract to buy 6 to 104 pages annually.

The NAB also operates computer-analyzed newspaper data on-line (CAN DO) to provide national advertizers with demographic data and market research from hundreds of newspapers.

Other industry groups woo national advertisers too:

- The International Newspaper Financial Executives' Association recommends a standard invoicing form containing basic information elements to reduce paperwork headaches for national advertisers. (See Figure 9.3 for information on the form.)

- International Newspaper Advertising and Marketing Executives, another industry association, proposes a standardized rate card based on data published by the widely-used Standard Rate & Data Service, Inc.,

---

[17] Phillip H. Dougherty, "Newspapers Seek More National Advertisements," *New York Times*, April 25, 1983, p. B4.

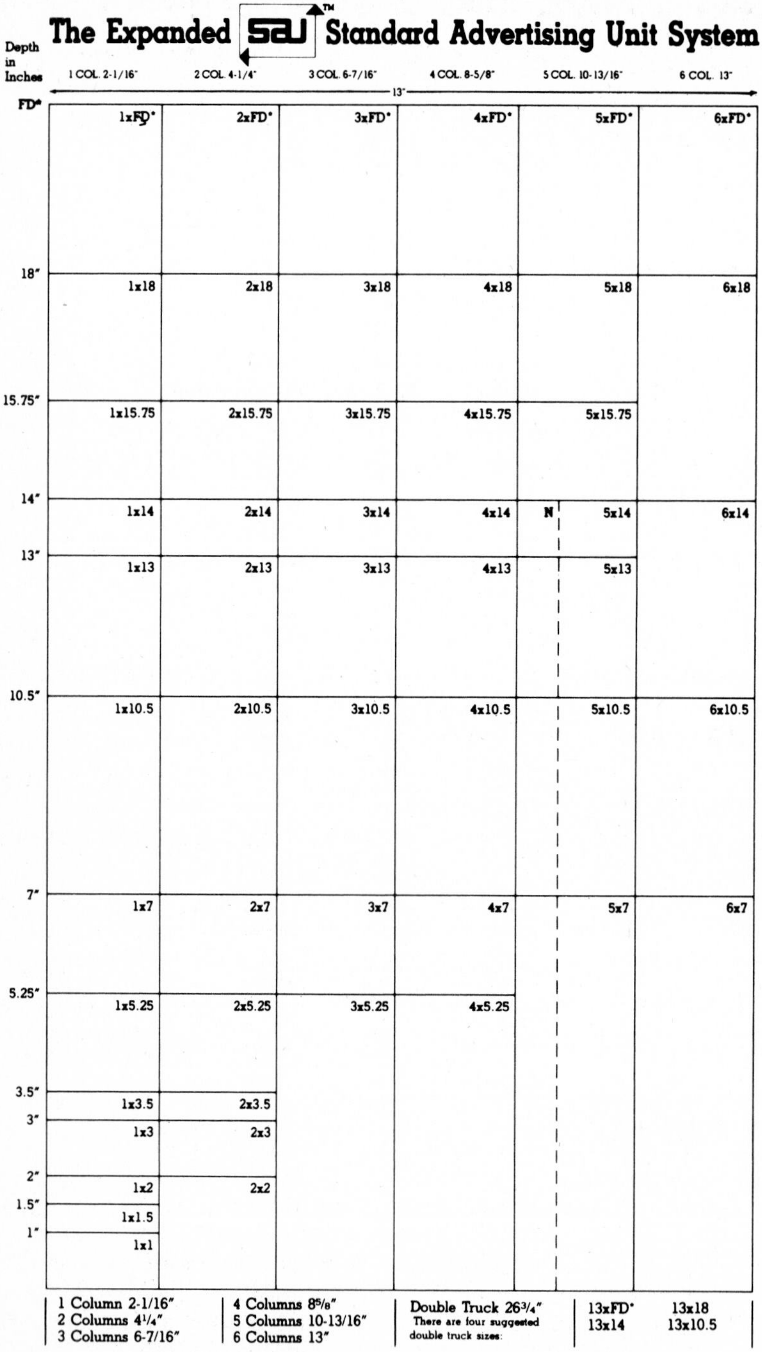

The Expanded SAU™ Standard Advertising Unit System

Depth in Inches

Depth	1 COL. 2-1/16"	2 COL. 4-1/4"	3 COL. 6-7/16"	4 COL. 8-5/8"	5 COL. 10-13/16"	6 COL. 13"
FD*	1xFD*	2xFD*	3xFD*	4xFD*	5xFD*	6xFD*
18"	1x18	2x18	3x18	4x18	5x18	6x18
15.75"	1x15.75	2x15.75	3x15.75	4x15.75	5x15.75	
14"	1x14	2x14	3x14	4x14 N	5x14	6x14
13"	1x13	2x13	3x13	4x13	5x13	
10.5"	1x10.5	2x10.5	3x10.5	4x10.5	5x10.5	6x10.5
7"	1x7	2x7	3x7	4x7	5x7	6x7
5.25"	1x5.25	2x5.25	3x5.25	4x5.25		
3.5"	1x3.5	2x3.5				
3"	1x3	2x3				
2"	1x2	2x2				
1.5"	1x1.5					
1"	1x1					

1 Column 2-1/16"	4 Columns 8⅝"
2 Columns 4¼"	5 Columns 10-13/16"
3 Columns 6-7/16"	6 Columns 13"

Double Truck 26¾"
There are four suggested double truck sizes:

13xFD*	13x18
13x14	13x10.5

Figure 9.2 SAU Format Chart

This illustrates 53 of the 57 advertising sizes developed under the standard advertising unit (SAU) system implemented on July 1, 1984. Special sizes were adopted by two tabloids. New York's *Daily News* and *Newsday*.

Reprinted by permission of Newspaper Advertising Bureau, Inc.

The 29 elements of the Standard Advertising Invoice (SAI)*

1. Name of Particular Newspaper, Address and Phone No.: The name of your newspaper and contact person with mailing address, including provision for nine digit ZIP codes and phone number, including area code.

2. Billed Account Name and Address: Name of the advertiser or advertising agency that placed the advertising, and the complete billing address.

3. Invoice/Document Number: A numerical control procedure that will provide a unique number for each individual invoice, invoice/statement or document.

4. Billing Date: Last day of current billing period or cycle.

5. Billing Period: Period of time covered by the invoice (week(s), month, etc.)

6. Terms of Payment: A statement of when the invoice becomes due and payable.

7. Billed Account Number: The unique number or letter/number sequence assigned to each advertiser or advertising agency by the newspaper. This number would generally be part of the newspaper's accounts receivable control system.

8. Advertiser/Client Number: If different from account being billed.

9. Advertiser/Client Name: If different from account being billed.

10. Date of Insertion or Transaction: The date(s) of publication of the advertisement (month and day(s)), or a transaction date for other items (payments, adjustments, etc.).

11. Newspaper's Reference Number: A newspaper's internal reference number for document retrieval, cash application, or for other purposes.

12. Other Charges or Credits: Identification of transaction such as color charges, position charges, production charges, art charges, zone area, penalty carrying charges, etc. (A legend identifying any codes used should be shown on the invoice.) If code legend is not used, explanation of transaction should be provided as part of description.

13. Description of Ad: Identification of the ad for the advertiser. Description may include the advertiser's insertion order number, advertiser's name, key words in the ad, products advertised, a number furnished by the advertiser or advertising agency used to identify the advertising order, etc.

14. Product/Service Code: A number identifying both manufacturer and product, or service.

15. SAU/Dimensions: For display ads, the self-descriptive nomenclature of the columns by inches (e.g., 3 x 14 inches would be the SAU number for a three-column-by-14 inch display ad). For other ads, appropriate dimensions (e.g., 1 x 6 lines for a classified ad).

16. Number of Times Published: The total number of appearances of an ad.

17. Billed Units: The size of the ad in column inches, lines, number of preprints or other billed units.

18. Applicable Rate: The rate per inch, line, number of preprints, or other billable unit charged based on the rate card and contract in effect.

19. Gross Amount: The extension of total billed units at the applicable rate before agency commission and cash discounts.

20. Net Amount: Gross charge less agency commission.

21. Current Gross Amount: Total of gross charges for advertising, color, production charges, art charges, position charges, etc., appearing on the invoice for the current billing period.

22. Current Net Amount Due: The total of net charges for advertising, color, production charges, art charges, position charges, etc., appearing on the invoice for the current billing period.

23. Cash Discounts: A discount allowed for the early payment of amounts due. This may be included in the terms of payment or shown separately, if applicable.

24. Aging of Past Due Amounts: An aging of overdue charges according to billing terms, based on the number of days outstanding from the billing dates, usually stated in 30-day increments (e.g. 30-60-90). This is a statement item and is optional for those newspapers that prefer to send separate statements of account.

25. Total Net Amount Due: The total of all current net charges plus those charges still outstanding from previous billing periods. This is a statement item and is optional for those newspapers that prefer to send separate statements of account.

26. Billed Account Number: Optional repetition of item 7 if remittance stub is used.

27. Billed Account Name: Optional repetition of name part of item 2 if remittance stub is used.

28. Name and Address for Remittance: The name and address to which payment is to be sent. A return payment document may be included with the invoice.

29. Contract Performance: Information regarding contract period and requirement as well as current billing period and cumulative performance. This information can also be supplied in the description portion of the invoices or on a separate statement.

*These invoice elements represent minimum data requirements. Individual newspapers may, at their option, include or incorporate additional data relevant to their publications and customers.

Figure 9.3 Standard invoice recommended by International Newspaper Financial Executives' Association

Reprinted with permission of the International Newspaper Financial Executives. SAI™is a trademark of INFE.

YOUR NEWSPAPER (Logo, etc.)

ATTENTION
ADDRESS
CITY/STATE/ZIP • 4
PHONE NO

ADVERTISING INVOICE/STATEMENT

3 DOCUMENT NO.	4 BILLING DATE	5 BILLING PERIOD	6 TERMS OF PAYMENT

2 BILLED ACCOUNT
CUSTOMER NAME
ATTENTION
ADDRESS
CITY/STATE/ZIP • 4

7 BILLED/ACCOUNT NO.	8 ADVERTISER/CLIENT NO.
9 NAME OF ADVERTISER/CLIENT	

10 DATE	11 REFERENCE NUMBER	12 13 14	CHARGE OR CREDIT DESCRIPTION/PRODUCT CODE	15 SAU/ DIMENSIONS	16 TIMES	17 BILLED UNITS	18 RATE	19 GROSS AMOUNT	20 NET AMOUNT

OTHER CHARGES/CREDIT LEGEND

A – COLOR
B – POSITION
C – PRODUCTION
D – ART
E –
F –
G –
H –

23 CASH DISCOUNT
DEDUCT $ _____ IF PAID WITHIN _____ DAYS

21 CURRENT GROSS AMOUNT	22 CURRENT NET AMMOUNT

24 AGING			25 TOTAL NET AMOUNT DUE
30 DAYS	60 DAYS	90 DAYS	

29 CONTRACT PERFORMANCE
EXPIRATION DATE
REQUIREMENT
CURRENT MONTH
CUMULATIVE

26 BILLED/ACCOUNT NO.

28 REMIT TO

27 BILLED ACCOUNT NAME

AMOUNT ENCLOSED

REMITTANCE ADVICE

Figure 9.3 Standard invoice recommended by International Newspaper Financial Executives' Association (*Continued*)

Reprinted with permission of the International Newspaper Financial Executives. SAI™ is a trademark of INFE.

226

THE RATE CARD

A rate card must state advertising policies and rates with clarity and precision in a format that promotes the newspaper's value to advertisers. In an industrywide effort to make it easier for advertisers to use newspapers, the International Newspaper Advertising and Marketing Executives, with concurrence from the American Newspaper Publishers' Association and the Newspaper Advertising Bureau, recommends a standardized 8½ × 11 inch rate card. It presents data in the sequence used by the Standard Rate and Data Service, which publishes monthly rate information from newspapers nationwide. The recommended order:

1. *Personnel*
   Publisher, marketing director, ad manager, etc.
2. *Representative*
   Name, address of "rep" firm selling space to national advertisers.
3. *Commission and Payment Terms*
   Whether cash discount is offered; agency commission.
4. *General Policy*
   Policy on forbidden ad copy, days of publication, contract rates, rebates.
5. *ROP/Reprint Rates*
   Black-and-white rates for Standard Advertising Units, insert rates, discount policy, delivery specifications.
6. *Group Combination Rates*
   Rates for ad in more than one jointly-owned newspaper; also co-op rates.
7. *Color Rates*
   Available days, rates for color.

8. *Special ROP Units*
   SAUs; see No. 5.
9. *Split-Run Ads*
   Rates for ads in less than full circulation.
10. *Special Services*
    Creative services, market research newspaper provides advertisers.
11. *Special Days/Pages/Features*
    Guide for advertisers who want copy to run on days when certain news copy is featured.
12. *ROP Depth Requirements*
    Minimum sizes for ads.
13. *Contract and Copy Regulations*
    See No. 4.
14. *Closing Times*
    Deadlines for receipt of copy.
15. *Mechanical Requirements*
    Column depth in lines; number of columns to page, other mechanical information.
16. *Special Classification Rates*
    Rates for guaranteed position; rates for special advertiser groups.
17. *Classified Rates*
    Sometimes presented in separate rate card.
18. *Comics*
    Rates, policy covering ads for comic pages.
19. *Magazines*
    Rates, policies for ads in TV or other magazine published by newspaper.
20. *Miscellaneous*
    Circulation, market information, audience demographics, etc.

so national advertisers need not wrestle with many different forms of rate cards. (See box for an example.)

Many large papers and groups maintain their own national sales staffs. In 1984, Knight-Ridder had offices in eight cities; Tribune Company sold space in the *Chicago Tribune* and other group papers from offices in eight U.S. cities and Mexico City. Most papers, however, rely on agencies representing scores of newspapers. One of the largest, Landon Associates, Inc., bases sales forces in New York City and 22 other cities to sell for newspaper clients in more than 40 states. Branham Newspaper Sales has salespersons in 17 cities to represent papers in all 50 states.

Standard commissions paid to agencies range

from 10 to 15 percent under contracts continuing automatically from year to year unless they are canceled by either party. Groups with many papers negotiate more favorable terms. Managers of small papers, individually representing a tiny fraction of any agency's total revenue, must be certain they don't get overlooked by sales reps obsessed with the "big view" from New York City or Los Angeles. Although national revenue often is only 5 or 6 percent of total revenue for small papers, it can, given due attention, be expanded considerably. Small-paper managers must open personal contact with their reps to make sure that the reps receive a steady flow of information about the paper. A significant increase in circulation, a competitive improvement, news content restructuring—all should be passed to the rep. Send along a fact book; it need not be expensive. The best such books state, simply and clearly, the market's strengths and the paper's ability to exploit it for the national advertiser. "Any rep is as good as your push," the ad director of one small paper told the author.

Whenever possible, small papers should join statewide or regional groupings of papers that offer national advertisers a single buy covering many markets. National advertisers don't often reach down to make a single buy in, say, a daily of 25,000 circulation. But that daily is attractive if, with ten others, it offers 250,000 or more circulation. Many state press associations offer such "ad networking" of weekly or small daily papers.

In sum, the fractionalization of network TV opens great opportunities for newspapers in national advertising. Each manager should join industrywide efforts to court national advertisers with uniform mechanical specifications, standardized rate cards and invoices, and volume discounts. But national ad rates are substantially higher than local rates. Unless that changes, luring more TV-oriented advertising executives into newspapers will be difficult. (See box for one major advertiser's views on how newspapers can make progress.)

Classified Advertising

Your ad strategy should assign some of the newspaper's brightest talent to classified advertising. Here is why:

1. Classified revenue *tripled* in the 10 years ended 1984, when it hit $7.4 billion.[18]

2. Industrywide, classified is 31 to 33 percent of total newspaper ad revenue, closer to 50 percent for some metros.[19]

3. Classified yields the highest per-page profit for most newspapers with, one analyst estimates, more than 50 percent of incremental revenue sometimes going directly to operating profit.[20]

4. Although electronic systems could provide future competition, classified is one ad sector where newspaper strategists can plan on near monopolization of their markets' potential.

5. Readership research, including highly regarded Ruth Clark studies, indicates that classified ranks strongly with readers as favorite *news* coverage. It's a sort of guide to what is happening in town, who is having a garage sale, and so forth.[21] On average, 53 percent of all readers (58 million adults) see some classified on a weekday, according to one survey. It's 54 percent for Sunday or weekend papers.[22]

Other attractions of classified are its low cost to the advertiser and its proven ability to

[18] Southern Newspaper Publishers' Association, *Bulletin*, May 22, 1985, p. 1.
[19] "Managers View Behind-The-Pages Scene," *International Newspaper Advertising and Marketing Executives' News*, December 1982, p. 4.
[20] "The Business of Newspapers," op. cit.
[21] *Changing Needs of Changing Readers*, a study commissioned by American Society of Newspapers Editors and conducted by Ruth Clark, then vice president of Yankelovich, Skelly and White, Inc., May 1979.
[22] "Classified Receives High Performance Rating," *International Newspaper Advertising and Marketing Executives News*, December 1982, p. 11.

AN ADVERTISER'S OPINION

Here is what Walter M. Haimann, president of Jos. E. Seagram & Sons, a major advertiser, has to say on ways newspapers can increase national advertising:

- Improve reproduction, change formats to reduce page "clutter" and "fill-in, small-space" advertising that surrounds ads and "cheapens the image of my product"; reduce the "incredible" 60/40 ad-to-news ratio.
- Provide an "editorial environment that stimulates interest in a product" and do not place an ad next to "blatantly unacceptable" editorial matter (i.e., a Seagram liquor ad next to a story on drunk driving).
- Create a newspaper that "stimulates an immediate sales reaction," one consumers "shop" for information on product availability and price; newspapers "shine" in this area.

- Produce a newspaper giving a national advertiser "impact against his target . . . and color is impact; newspapers with good color will be read all over, even the ads."
- Guarantee "competitive product protection"—separation between his ad and a competitor's; Seagram insists on at least six pages separation in magazine advertising, which newspapers try not to promise because it creates page layout and production problems.
- "Research is the name of the game," and newspapers must provide better target-audience data for comparison against other media, so advertisers can determine optimum ad sizes, how many times to run an ad, and so on.
- Stop charging national advertisers "rates that are sometimes 50% over the local rates." National advertisers insist on advantageous or at least competitive pricing.

sell. A major problem, however, is classified's vulnerability to economic downturn. If the local economy sneezes, classified gets pneumonia. When recession hit Los Angeles in 1982, the *Los Angeles Times* reported help-wanted classified in one month (August) fell 40 percent, real estate, 35 percent.[23] The *Times* noted that classified is "so reflective of the nation's economy that the 'help wanted' category is used as a leading indicator of economic activity" nationwide.[24]

Any manager depending on classified for major share-of-profit performance must be ready with contingency plans, so that, if an economic downturn should dislocate classified volume, immediate cost reductions can be put into effect to protect margins.

Classified has a high profit ratio because no expensive news coverage is necessary for its pages (although some papers position news in classified—an auto maintenance column in the used car section, home building hints in real estate, etc.). You can use two other tactics to boost the profit ratio in classified:

- Economical layout can cram maximum ads into minimum space. Many papers with standard six- or eight-column formats for other pages go to nine or ten narrow columns per page for classified. This greatly increases revenue per page when classified is sold on a per-column-inch or per-line basis.

- Sophisticated computerized systems permit efficient, low-cost order taking via telephone. Typesetting and billing can be automatic. The elimination of manpower adds to classified's profit.

[23] Jonathan Friendly, "Coast Paper Feeling Pinch of Recession," *New York Times*, Aug. 15, 1982, p. 28.
[24] Annual Report, Times Mirror Corp., Times Mirror Square, Los Angeles, CA 90053.

Three categories of advertisers provide most classified: auto sales, real estate, employment. But new categories, arranged by classification (thus, "classified"), develop all the time. "Garage Sale" arrived relatively recently, for example, but it is significant business for many newspapers.

Some advertisers prefer to use photographs or illustrations with word copy. This creates "classified display," particularly in auto and real estate. It is welcome revenue *if* it is new business; unfortunately, much is merely shifted from local retail and does not represent any net increase in business.

In addition to local retail, national, and classified, four other types of advertising are important to your strategy—preprints, legal or public notice advertising, co-op advertising, and coupons.

Preprint (Insert) Advertising

The distribution of nearly 30 billion preprints as inserts in daily and Sunday papers in 1983 brought in an estimated $2.5 billion revenue— 10.5 percent of total local retail.[25] Two or three of the colorful, different-size preprints shake out of many weekday papers; on Sundays, a fallout of ten or twelve is not unusual. Preprints are big business.

Preprints arrived on the newspaper scene after World War II, when discount houses began demanding well-printed, colorful advertising— almost minicatalogs—delivered to households in their markets. Many newspapers cannot offer precision color printing but are efficient distribution vehicles. So retailers ship preprints in bulk to newspapers for insertion and delivery. Newspapers get about 45 percent of total preprint revenue; 55 percent goes to commercial printers. But preprints are nevertheless highly profitable for newspapers: some collect $50 or more per thousand delivered, and almost no

Colorful, preprinted advertising is common in many daily and Sunday newspapers.

incremental new cost is involved—carriers deliver somewhat bulkier papers for the same fees.

The primary competitor is direct mail. That became clear when K mart, the nation's ninth largest spender for advertising ($554 million in 1985), sent tremors through the newspaper industry by switching its preprints from newspaper distribution to direct mail in four states. Advo-Systems, Inc., the nation's largest direct-mail firm, took over K mart's 10 million *weekly* preprints in Kentucky, Ohio, Indiana, and Michigan because 200 daily and weekly newspapers that were formerly used could not penetrate enough households and, K mart executives said, "We can get 100 percent coverage with Advo."[26]

---

[25] Margaret Genovese, "Preprints," *presstime*, August 1983, p. 4.

[26] "K mart To Switch Inserts From Newspapers To Advo In Four States," Southern Newspaper Publishers' Association, *Bulletin*, Aug. 5, 1983, p. 1.

The threat was not unexpected. For years, publishers watched U.S. postal rates lowered to accommodate direct-mail firms. NAB President Standen reacted angrily: "It costs me 20 cents [now more, of course] to get a letter from my daughter at camp, to send a Christmas card . . . a three-ounce package of advertising costs a mailing house 7.4 cents. I think that's wrong. . . ."[27]

Advo originates more than half the nation's third-class mail, according to ANPA, and maintains computer banks of 83 million individual addresses constituting more than 97 percent of all U.S. households.[28] The company expanded rapidly in the mid-1970s by courting leading preprint users that were crucial to newspapers—J. C. Penney, Montgomery Ward, department stores, discount houses.[29] In 1986, however, rising costs and newspaper counterattacks led Advo to concentrate on more limited operations in the most lucrative markets.

Nationwide, direct mail is booming. One potent attraction is "marriage mail," stuffing two or more noncompeting preprints into the same envelope and thus reducing each user's postal costs. It all helped push direct mail to well over $15 billion annual revenue in 1986.

Newspaper managers have long argued whether to curse preprints or be thankful for them. Profits are high. But haven't newspapers for generations educated advertisers to believe that tight adjacency of ad and news copy best assures high readership? Isn't the basic appeal to advertisers that news copy pulls readers into reading ads? And don't preprints destroy adjacency, turning newspapers into simple delivery vehicles?

Editors are concerned because a switch of advertising from the newspaper itself into preprints will shrink newshole, the total space available for news. Newshole is established by the amount of ROP advertising scattered throughout the pages. Some editors demand a guaranteed number of news columns to maintain the newspaper's journalistic integrity even without ROP advertising to support them. But that is expensive—a direct drain on profits, and the issue is unresolved at many newspapers.

Lee Enterprises, Inc., a company that owns eighteen newspapers ($207 million revenue in 1985), complained in its annual report that "Large-volume customers continue to increase advertising, although their use of preprints and supplements is sometimes at the expense of the local display lineage."[30] A shift in ad strategy by Sears, Roebuck and Co., underlines the problem: In 1973, 73 percent of Sears' local print advertising was ROP. By 1978, 54 percent was ROP; it was an estimated 19 percent in 1983. Sears, using ever more preprints, said newspaper ROP rates were too high and that newspapers could not penetrate sufficient households or improve color reproduction.

Retailers, then, are finding cheaper ways to deliver preprints via mail, shoppers, or door to door with independent delivery systems, and they cut out the newspaper middleman. To hold your newspaper's preprint business, take these steps:

- Maintain sufficient total circulation, perhaps combining paid circulation with TMC to eliminate the argument that only direct mail can blanket a market with preprints.

- Simultaneously provide target marketing to deliver preprints to attractive households in tightly segmented blocs.

- Constantly promote the value of news-ad adjacency and sell the theme that the inclusion of ads in a news-and-feature package lends credibility that direct mail or shoppers lack.

---

[27] Craig C. Standen, "Marketing Against Other Print," speech to Operations Management Conference, Las Vegas, Nev., June 11, 1983.
[28] Genovese, op cit.
[29] Genovese, op. cit.

---

[30] Report to shareholders for third quarter ending June 30, 1983, Davenport, Iowa, Lee Enterprises, 1983.

- Bring to advertisers' attention the relatively poor readership of preprints and shoppers that arrive on the tide of hundreds, if not thousands, of pieces of direct mail delivered to a household annually. For example, the *Phoenix Gazette* and *Arizona Republic* cite a study they commissioned showing that 25 percent of all direct mail preprints are thrown away unread.

Co-op Advertising

A rapidly expanding revenue sector is co-op, whereby national manufacturers reimburse local retailers for much—sometimes all—of the cost of advertising their products. Using co-op, retailers double or triple their ad budgets but increase their own direct costs only 10 to 20 percent.

Available co-op dollars hit an estimated $10.2 billion in 1985, up from $900 million in 1970.[31] Much co-op revenue comes from makers of cameras, jewelry, home maintenance products, and furnishings and apparel who want to advertise their specific products and simultaneously identify local retail stores where they are available. Many newspapers overlook this revenue source, and local retailers often do not understand it either. NAB estimates that only two-thirds of available co-op support is spent each year. Competitors are not slow in lunging for co-op dollars. Newspapers' share dropped to an estimated 68 percent in 1984 from 82 percent in 1975. Much of the loss goes to direct mail.[32]

You should establish a special co-op department; the results can be spectacular. The *Pittsburgh Press and Post-Gazette* invested $130,000 in a two-person co-op department and the first year received $787,464 co-op revenue.[33]

Newspapers often print special forms that retail clients can use for claiming co-op reimbursement from suppliers. Anything that helps merchants in your town extract co-op support from manufacturers is money in your newspaper's bank.

Frank Hennessey, NAB vice president for co-op, estimates available revenue by dividing in half the retail sales in a newspaper's retail trading zone, then multiplying by 3 percent. That worked out, for example, to a "$17 million opportunity" for the *Roanoke (Va.) Times & World News*, he says.[34] NAB has two programs to help newspapers exploit co-op:

> *Retail Co-op Recovery* has details on thousands of co-op plans, how much money is available, and how newspaper clients can collect it.
>
> *Newspaper Co-op Network* permits manufacturers to sign a single contract and receive a single bill for ads placed in up to 1,500 newspapers by markets or regions.

Coupon Advertising

Every shopper, it seems, heads for the supermarket clutching coupons snipped from the local paper. It's big business for newspapers—163 billion coupons were distributed in 1984, 82.1 percent in newspapers.

Coupon values range from a cent off a bar of soap to $2,500 to $10,000 off prices of foreign cars imported by a car dealer in Richmond, Virginia (twenty-one of his car coupons were redeemed, one for a $10,000 reduction in the $48,174 price of a Porsche 928).[35] The total value of coupons in any day's paper can range into hundreds of dollars in major metro markets. The *Athens Daily News* and *Banner-Herald* often carry $100 worth or more each week.

Four of five coupons are placed by the grocery industry. For all newspapers, large or

---

[31] "As Co-Op Dollars Rise, Dailies' Share Drops," *presstime*, April 1983, p. 34; also see Dorothy G. David, "Newspapers Packaging Successful Co-op Packages," *INAME News*, July/August 1985, p. 12.
[32] Ibid.
[33] "Ad Directors Urged To Set Up Co-Op Departments," op. cit.

[34] Ibid.
[35] "Competitors Eye Newspaper Bonanza As Advertisers Expand Use of Coupons," *presstime*, April 1983, p. 35.

small, they are significant readership attractions. Second to daily newspapers as coupon carriers are magazines, with 11.4 percent; containers (such as cereal boxes), with 6.9 percent, and direct mail, with 3.8 percent. Direct mail will pose severe competition in the future.

Selling advertisers on your newspaper as a coupon vehicle is part of the overall challenge of positioning the newspaper effectively in its marketplace. Start by offering advertisers free trial with a coupon—buyers coming through the front door clutching the coupon will convince many retailers.

Legal (Public Notice) Advertising

This advertising is important, particularly for small dailies and weeklies. For papers with a daily circulation papers of 10,000 to 15,000, legals often are 1 to 2 percent of total revenue. The $10,000 or so sometimes available annually in small towns can make the difference between profit or loss for weeklies.

Legals may cover many subjects—bidding for city contracts, executors of wills seeking survivors, new laws, divorce notices. They are sometimes awarded by government jurisdictions on a bid basis, sometimes on a rotating basis between two or more qualified newspapers. Qualifications vary between states, but normally legals are awarded only to newspapers of general news content with paid circulation and second-class postal permits that publish on a continuous basis, at least in part in the city where the newspaper office is located. In some states, including California, publications must be adjudicated as bona fide newspapers for legal advertising purposes. Rates for this type advertising are set by the awarding governmental body.

HOW TO MANAGE THE SALES EFFORT

Picture your favorite football team with the ball on the opponent's 1-yard line in the year's most important game. Your team worked hard to get there, organizing, planning and scouting the opponent's strengths and weaknesses. If your team gains that last yard and scores, it succeeds. If it doesn't, all the hard work fails. And so it is in managing newspaper advertising. You can organize, research, and plan, but if your department doesn't *sell*, you fail. And you don't get applause for merely playing the game well, either. It's what's profitably on the scoreboard— the advertiser's signature on a sales contract— that counts.

There are many routes to the 1-yard line— many approaches to organizational design, research, planning. But one thing is clear: To score, there must be professional, hard-hitting sales work. Without hard selling, a paper can make all the right moves in circulation, news, and other areas and still not reap full benefit in advertising. But, let Tom Vail, publisher and editor of the *Cleveland Plain Dealer*, describe what happened when he launched his paper on a campaign to overtake the *Press*:

> ". . . at that time we were 80,000 a day behind the *Cleveland Press* [in circulation], although we were the only Sunday paper in Cleveland, and we trailed on a daily basis our competitor in both retail and national advertising. . . . When we passed the *Press* in daily circulation in 1968, I thought the advertising leadership would shift to us automatically. How wrong I was! Not only did it take us eight more years to get the advertising leadership, but of course we had to show circulation leadership not only in the total area but also in our home county, city zone, the Standard Metropolitan Statistical Area, and other categories of circulation leadership interesting to advertisers.[36]

American advertisers, economic underpinning of the world's largest, most active free press, have become a demanding, discerning force. They know what they want and must be

---

[36] Thomas Vail, letters to author, April 8, 1983.

served, or they will go elsewhere. Those advertisers *have to be sold.*

Your sales campaign must be multidimensional, ranging from institutional promotion of print as an effective medium to tailoring an ad schedule to a local retailer's needs and budget. You must be not a seller of space but a solver of problems. Successful selling requires having an imaginative variety of products and services rather than, say, simply trying to push a full-page ad in Wednesday's food section. That requires thorough research of the market, the newspaper's position in it, and competitors. It requires understanding the advertiser's needs and business so solutions to those needs can be put forward.

Harte-Hanks employs this concept as a fine art, operating a consumer distribution marketing (CDM) division, in addition to its newspapers. Harte-Hanks bills CDM as a "complete publishing/distribution support system that helps advertisers target their messages to their prime prospects in the most cost effective way."[37] CDM offers commercial printing and distribution of printed advertising via private carriers and mail, which it claims can reach 90 percent of all American homes via computerized address lists. CDM also offers research services and, importantly, publishes shoppers zoned for 300 separate editions reaching 3.2 million households weekly.

"We have the ability," says President Marbut, "for newspapers and CDM salespeople to jointly call on major advertisers such as Sears and K mart, and the like."[38] Thus, a Harte-Hanks sales team can offer full-run advertising ROP in one of the group's paid-circulation papers, space in its shoppers, plus inserts which Harte-Hanks will print and distribute in its own publications, via direct mail handled by the company or, if the client wishes, in a plastic bag hung on doorknobs by one of the company's

direct-distribution units. Harte-Hanke's own research companies can survey the client's market and suggest efficient ways to advertise. Not many sales managers, particularly in early career years, run operations that complex. But the principles of sales management are the same if you are supervising a $500 million corporation or a two-person sales staff on a small weekly. You can follow the same checklist.

The Sales Manager's Checklist

Let's look at organizing—and energizing—an effective sales force to accomplish your top-priority responsibility in sales management: getting through the prospect's front door and coming out with a signed advertising contract. Key steps:

- Analyze market, types of advertisers, competitive situation, your own newspaper's strengths and weaknesses, and formulate attack plan.
- Recruit and train sales force.
- Organize individual salesperson tasks and assign client lists.
- Lead, motivate, compensate.
- Evalute, control, and adjust individual sales efforts.

Plan Your Sales Attack

Painstaking audit of significant advertising prospects in the market comes first. Who is out there? Where do they now advertise? What potential revenue do they represent?

Now, lay that intelligence against your sales goals developed in corporate and departmental strategy sessions. Where can you get business needed to improve revenue, increase number of advertising clients, and boost your market share?

List your competitors' accounts and those they share with your newspaper. Target theirs

[37] 1981 Annual Report, San Antonio, Tex., Harte-Hanks Communications, 1981.
[38] Robert Marbut, letter to author, March 3, 1983.

for special attention by your sales force. Analyze sales themes and techniques competitors use against your paper, and equip each salesperson with telling counterarguments (listed in our earlier discussion of different advertising categories).

Compare rates, CPMs, and rate-increase histories. Are yours dangerously high—or low enough that an increase will be palatable to advertisers?

Establish programs of penetrating new areas of business, not simply reworking old ones. For example, newspapers have, in recent years, opened new major revenue sources with banks and other financial institutions.

Your attack plan must cover the relevant geographic market and focus on prospects with true potential for significant revenue. Select prospects who *need* to advertise (whether they recognize it or not) and who have the business volume to support cost of advertising.

Recruiting, Selecting, Training

Libraries full of books have been written on the selling process. But what makes one person effective at it and another ineffective is still a bit of a mystery.

Some successful sales people rely on personality—the ability to approach an advertising prospect with poise, tact, and good cheer. Others rely primarily on the ability to manipulate and persuade, to identify the prospect's needs and demonstrate persuasively how the newspaper can fulfill them. Still others can *adapt* to any situation, zeroing in on the prospect's wants and demonstrating our understanding of them.

Whatever the technique, successful selling requires the salesperson to listen carefully to the prospect—to understand and sense the prospect's thinking and react accordingly. Importantly, the salesperson must need to succeed in selling—must be ego-driven and goal-oriented. Look for those characteristics in recruiting a sales force.

Talent is all around: at smaller newspapers

nearby (don't overlook competing papers), in other sales businesses, in junior ranks of your own newspapers, among recent college graduates. Beware of job-hoppers, whose records show personal instability or have unexplained gaps. Don't be diverted by the old argument over whether it's the product's quality that sells or the salesperson's ability. You need both.

Training is a continual process, regardless of the experience or success of your sales force. Start by ensuring a smooth flow of information to the staff on overall corporate goals and departmental objectives; any improvements in the newspaper—new sections, new columnists—and circulation and penetration successes; and what your competitors are doing. Training aids include lectures, role playing, one-on-one assistance, training films, guest speakers. Experienced salespersons may balk at training on the grounds they know it all. They don't. Bring them into refresher courses.

Organizing the Salesperson

This is a particularly crucial function for every sales manager. First, you must organize each salesperson's efforts in a fail safe system that ensures regular sales calls on *all* prospects. If you don't, some prospects and clients will be neglected. Salespeople become "account executives" and are assigned to "accounts" or customers.

Second, salespeople need direction and standards against which to judge their own performance. As sales manager, you can nudge—prod, if necessary—each individual to reach personal sales goals.

Third, good salespeople are thoroughbreds and ego-driven self-starters. But they need lots of attention. Don't forget to stroke their psyches a bit.

Fourth, in organizing sales territories and prospect lists, you will, to a great extent, be determining the salesperson's earnings potential and whether he or she qualifies for advancement. You will ruin a salesperson's morale if you consistently provide only low-quality prospect lists.

You must make sure that each salesperson organizes time, planning each day's effort efficiently. It wastes time to make a few calls that are widely scattered throughout a large territory; it's better to bunch them. Even telephone calls should be organized methodically. Each salesperson must be organized each day to represent the newspaper properly. An ill-prepared sales call waste the prospect's time and can damage the newspaper's image.

Make sure that each salesperson has a clear understanding of precisely what performance is required. That includes not only signing new prospects but also increasing revenue from existing clients. It includes the administrative duties involved in selling—writing regular summaries of activity and submitting expense accounts on time. Don't overdo it, however. Don't keep those thoroughbreds off the sales track just to shuffle irrelevant paper.

Lead, Motivate, Compensate

The Marine Corps motivates people with flag, country, patriotism. Coaches lead football teams by invoking the alma mater's name. With a sales force, leadership based on such appeals inspires team spirit and drive; momentum is built by the challenge of competition; appeals to pride motivate individuals to improve their personal sales records. Those techniques—and others discussed in Chapter 5, "The Human Element"— will help you assemble aggressive, professional salespeople and train and lead them well. It is important that, as sales manager, you determine each individual's needs and help fulfill them. Be supportive in both a personal and an organizational sense.

But whatever factors enter your motivational strategy, *the central ingredient must be worthwhile compensation.* Best is a commission plan tied directly to performance plus careful assignment of client lists from which commissions are earned. The advantages of commission-based compensation are many: It is a strong incentive for salespersons because it relates pay directly to results. Each salesperson easily understands a compensation system based on performance. The newspaper's costs in base salary are reduced and sales costs rise only proportionately to revenue gained. Some disadvantages are these: Heavy reliance on commission payment feeds the sales force's already strong money orientation and doesn't build company loyalty. Salespeople tend to "work" only active accounts that are likely to yield quick sales, and neglect the service of existing customers or the spadework to open new accounts. They tend to neglect administrative duties. And a few highly talented salespeople—or those with the best account lists—will earn more than their colleagues, creating tension in the department.

Strive for balance to maintain the motivational value of commissions, yet build loyalty to the newspaper with salary. A survey of 294 newspapers by the Association of Newspaper Classified Advertising Managers found that salary-plus-commission was the payment scheme for 69 percent of outside salespersons and 71 percent of telephone salespersons. How much base salary to pay depends on local conditions. Newspapers with long-established clients should pay higher salaries so as to maintain experienced professionals to service valuable existing accounts. In 1985, the *Dayton (Ohio) Journal-Herald* paid outside salespeople 75 percent salary, 25 percent commissions; inside telephone salespersons, 60 percent salary, 40 percent commission.

Evaluating and Controlling

The evaluation and control of performance must occur on two levels—with individual salespersons and for the entire department. First, evaluate the individual. Judge an advertising salesperson primarily on whether sales goals are met—that is, on dollar volume of sales brought in. There are few valid excuses for a salesperson who consistently fails to meet goals. Conversely, high sales volume can make other shortcoming irrelevant.

Dollar results aside, evaluate individuals for:

- Time spent in office. Sales are made in clients' offices, not at the newspaper.

- Personal neatness, including hair and clothes.

- Number of calls on existing accounts. No efficient salesperson permits accounts to languish.

- Number of new accounts opened. Each salesperson must constantly open new sales prospects.

- Promptness and accuracy; completeness of sales orders, call reports, and other administrative procedures.

- Cost of sales, including entertainment, travel.

- Salesperson's knowledge of newspaper industry, your newspaper and its circulation, readership and demographic strengths. Important: does the salesperson know the competition and sell effectively against it?

- Efficiency in planning the work day, including routing and frequency of calls.

- Persistence in pursuing the sale, asking for the order and then the reorder.[39]

Continuing evaluations spot those who need help and perhaps retraining and those who consistently fail to perform. Terminate the chronically unproductive, reward your producers. Shift inactive accounts to new salespeople.

Evaluation of departmental performance rests on whether goals are met. But that doesn't mean relying solely on revenue measurements. Quite the contrary. *To be an effective sales*

---

[39] For additional helpful details see *Measuring Salesforce Performance*, Management Aid No. 4,003, Fort Worth, Texas, U.S. Small Business Administration, 1981.

Table 9.2 Sales Cost as a Percentage of Advertising Revenue

	High	Low	Mean
Retail	11.3%	2.9%	6.2%
National	21.2	0.3	7.9
Classified	26.2	1.2	10.3
Miscellaneous	1.0	0.1	0.63
Total	12.7	6.9	9.8

"Company Average Sales Costs To Revenue For Advertising," *Newspaper Controller,* Washington, D.C., Institute of Newspaper Controllers and Finance Officers, December 1982, p. 3. Reprinted by permission.

manager, you must hold cost of advertising sales to efficient levels. What is "efficient" varies with market, competition, and operational factors. However, the Technical Advisory Board of the International Newspaper Financial Executives surveyed its newspaper members and drew up some guidelines based on the composite of sales cost as a percentage of advertising revenue (see Table 9.2).

Let's take that approach to a "typical" 75,000-circulation daily with annual advertising revenues of $14,750,000 and advertising department costs of $1,150,000.

$$\text{Cost/sales ratio} = \frac{\$1,150,000}{\$14,750,000} = 7.7\%$$

That 7.7 percent compares favorably with the mean of 9.8 percent. But what ratio is satisfactory to *your* newspaper depends on the competition you face and other local conditions. For one measure, compare your ratio against those of previous years, then factor in such subjective considerations as whether new competition entered the market or whether other external factors have raised costs, for example, or lowered revenue.

Note that the cost/sales ratio will signal difficulties or successes in the department. But it doesn't reveal causes. For that, you must compare each salesperson's performance against standards for sales and expenses.

Check These Off, Too

Your sales manager's checklist is incomplete if you don't check off a few final points:

- Do you walk through the ad department frequently ("management by moving about") and insist on an alert, well-dressed cheerful staff that spends most of its time outside the office? Unkempt, downbeat salespersons gathered around the coffee machine are not representing your newspaper properly.

- Do you personally make sure that your national ad rep is being fed new and frequent descriptive material on the newspaper's market and competitive position? Is the rep getting selling hints on properly representing your newspaper?

- Do you monitor the NAB, ANPA, International Association of Newspaper Advertising and Marketing Executives, and other trade groups for selling hints?

- Importantly, are *you* doing your share by calling on major advertisers and nonadvertisers, offering them information about your newspaper and obtaining guidance for your own staff? Are you involved in your department's main role?

- Have you organized—and energized—an effective sales force to get through a client's front door and come out with a signed order? That, after all, is your top priority responsibility.

Listen to Walter M. Haimann, president of Jos. E. Seagram & Sons, a major national advertiser:

> Quite frankly, a lot of us are beginning to wonder if newspapers don't *want* national business. You certainly don't give any indication of it by your actions. And I can't tell you how long it's been since my people or I have even had a newspaper rep knocking on our doors. I see magazine people in our offices constantly.[40]

SETTING ADVERTISING RATES

In establishing ad rates, you must perform with high professionalism, mustering judgment plus keen insight into your marketplace, the competition, and the newspaper's marketing objectives. As discussed in Chapter 8, pricing can have several objectives: profit, market share, or high sales volume for competitive purposes, and it can be influenced by social or ethical considerations. Rates can also be influenced by legal factors, and this will be discussed in Chapter 12.

Rates pegged too high kill the most imaginative, energetic sales efforts if they provide openings for competitors or are rejected by advertisers. Pegging rates too low makes mockery of your entire sales effort. If costs are not covered, if no profit is forthcoming, why go through the exercise? The manager shoots for a spot somewhere between those extremes. Precisely where that point is and how to find it is much discussed among advertising managers.

Some maximize profit by edging rates upward until there is a disproportionate drop in volume of ad dollars. Others sacrifice immediate profits to maximize sales and achieve long-range improvement in market share.

Another approach is cost-plus: adding relevant costs plus a percentage for profit. But calculating relevant costs, particularly a percentage of fixed overhead costs such as rent or utilities, is difficult. And cost-plus doesn't consider competitive rates or other realities of the marketplace.

So managers speak of establishing "feel"

---

[40] Walter M. Haimann, speech to International Newspaper Advertising and Marketing Executives' sales conference, Las Vegas, Nev., Jan. 23, 1983.

rather than "formula" for setting ad rates. In gaining your "feel," consider a checklist of factors.

Use a Rate-Setting Checklist

- Costs. Key here is understanding precisely what and where costs are in your newspaper's operations. Managers who don't know what costs must be covered are crippled. You must also judge where costs are likely to move in the period ahead for which rates are being established.

- Profit level required by the ownership, whether a single individual, family or thousands of shareholders represented by a board of directors. The operating statement (see Chapter 4) approved by the ownership should state the newspaper's specific profit goals for the forthcoming year. Your departmental goals will state revenue and cost objectives. Absent such precise direction, performance appreciably "better than last year's" is a good rule of thumb if you like your job. Set rates accordingly.

- Quality of service. Rates should reflect whether the paper is performing as advertisers demand. Set high rates with confidence if the paper penetrates sufficient homes in the relevant market, reaches the right, demographically attractive readers, and stimulates sales. Managers who cannot claim such performance must be more tentative in setting rates. Note there sometimes is image *advantage* in high rates; the higher the rates, the higher the perceived value of the advertising service.

- Competitive rates. You cannot raise rates far above a serious competitor's—be the competitor another paper, a radio or TV station, direct mail, or whatever. Only with clear competitive superiority can your newspaper greatly outstrip competitors' rates. Advertisers are mobile, capable of shifting quickly to any medium promising better results at lower costs. Try to determine your competitors' *costs* and rate histories; if things get tough, how far can they lower rates?

- Inflation indices. Many advertisers compare your rate increases with inflation, the Consumer Price Index, or other cost indices. Rate increases that consistently outstrip the inflation rate will draw advertiser ire.

- Rate-increase history. Regardless of other factors, too many increases too frequently will draw trouble. Pacing and a sense of timing are crucial. If possible, peg increases to improved service, better journalistic content, expanded circulation.

- Sell your rates. Pure salesmanship plays a huge role in demonstrating the value of newspaper advertising, its strengths over competitors, its ability to get results. It is not enough for rates to be competitive, fully justified, and logical from your newspaper's cost point of view. Each advertiser must be sold on the idea that all this is true.

- Whatever the market will bear. It all comes down to what the advertiser will pay. Stay in close touch with advertisers and react quickly to any shift in sentiment. Know what they think about your rates.

"Flexible" Pricing Is In

Facing competition plus advertiser resistance to rates, newspapers increasingly use "flexible" pricing tactics. It amounts to solving the advertiser's problems with imaginative sales assistance—through rates and other devices—rather than a take-it-or-leave-it sales posture and rigid price structure.

A manager's aim in this is to attract more advertising but also to address specific problems that crop up for newspapers. For example, some businesses concentrate advertising on certain days—Wednesdays for food stores, Sundays for department stores, and so forth. This leaves some issues, particularly on Mondays and Tuesdays, short of advertising. Perhaps your newspaper should offer discounts for advertising on weak days.

Substantial discounting is aimed at attracting advertisers to ROP use of the newspaper's pages themselves rather than preprinted inserts. This creates a larger news hole and, for many papers, solves a difficult problem of physically inserting preprints. Inserting equipment is expensive and often cranky mechanically.

Newspapers have traditionally offered volume discounts: the more you advertise, the lower the rate. Under flexible pricing, that practice is extended. For example, newspapers with zoned editions or TMC programs offer discounts for placing ads in those special products as well as ROP. Or special positioning of ads in the newspaper is offered in "flexibility" pricing. A special section on real estate is the place for a realtor's ad; restaurant ads belong in "Arts and Leisure," auto ads in sports or business.

Design Effective Rate Cards

You must pay special attention to how your newspaper, rates, and policies are presented to the marketplace. Of particular concern is "drop material" provided for salespeople to use and leave behind during sales efforts. Without detailed, hard-hitting, and colorful promotion material, few salespeople can be fully effective.

Key pieces are rate cards. They range in size and complexity from a simple four-page, 3 by 8 inch black-and-white pamphlet of the sort issued by the *Iron Mountain (Mich.) Daily News* (10,000 afternoon circulation) to the three slick, highly detailed brochures of twelve to sixteen pages printed in color by the *Dallas Times Herald*. They cover local retail, classified, and national advertising plus specialty business such as preprints and job printing.

The essential element in any rate card is clear, understandable statement of rates, production schedules, and advertising policies. Make sure that the advertiser does not need a lawyer and pocket calculator to understand the rate card. Rate cards should include any conditions— such as prohibited advertising (some papers refuse ads from fortune tellers, liquor companies, or others)—and a clear statement that rates may be changed with notice (usually thirty days) for advertisers with volume contracts and without notice for noncontract advertisers. (Review earlier box entitled "The Rate Card" for recommended content.)

Circulation figures and other facts about the paper must be completely accurate. The *Sacramento (Calif.) Union* agreed to reimburse advertisers up to $2 million after it was charged that a former circulation manager had inflated the circulation figures on which ad rates were based.[41]

PERSONAL SELLING IN THE MARKETPLACE

You will probably be introduced to advertising by selling it, not managing the department. So you need personal selling skills for use in the marketplace. Anyway, you cannot manage other people who spend each day pounding the bricks unless you understand what it is like. If you have management aspirations in advertising, seek on-the-job selling experience. What follows can be the basis of a training program for salespeople you manage or for selling a client yourself.

Let's set forth on a typical selling mission: Psyche yourself up. Ready for a hard day's work? Do you want to succeed, to win? Check your time-management plan. Telephone ahead for appointments and arrange your visits with the

---

[41] "Sacramento Union's Advertisers Will Get $2 Million Settlement," *Wall Street Journal*, Aug. 16, 1983, p. 16.

most efficient routing. Organize your presentation. Who precisely is your target? What is their business? How can your newspaper solve their sales problems? What sales resistance will you encounter? Where do they now advertise? How can you counter that? What can your newspaper do that competing media cannot? Make certain your presentation will be delivered to the prospect's decision maker.

Check your briefcase. Rate cards and *contracts*? "Drop" material on your newspaper's strengths, circulation, advertising volume? Tear sheets illustrating how your target's competitors advertise? "Spec" layouts of ads you think your target should buy? A copy of the newspaper?

Now, you are ready for the prospect. Let's follow a five-step procedure recommended by the Newspaper Advertising Bureau (NAB) and used by many newspapers.[42]

Selling Retail Clients—I

As either a salesperson or ad manager, you must understand retailing and your target's business. The NAB averages in Table 9.3 show you and your target how much other store owners spend on advertising.

Selling Retail Clients—II

Gauging household spending flow is crucial in any advertiser's decision on when—and how much—newspaper advertising should be bought. Table 9.4 shows the monthly patterns of spending by the average U.S. household in representative stores. You can show them to your target. These figures, supplied by the U.S. Department of Commerce, can be multiplied by the number of households in your market to yield the market's sales potential.

---

[42] Newspaper Advertising Bureau, 1180 Avenue of the Americas, New York, N.Y. 10017.

Table 9.3 Selling Retail Clients—I

Type of Business	Average Percent of Sales Spent on Advertising
Appliance, radio, TV dealers	2.3%
Auto dealers (new car/franchised)	0.8
Banks (commercial)	1.3
Beauty shops	2.0
Credit agencies (personal)	2.4
Department stores	2.8
Discount stores	2.4
Drug stores (chain)	1.7
Drug stores (independent)	1.3
Food chains	1.1
Furniture stores	5.0
Gas stations	0.8
Hardware stores	1.6
Jewelry stores	4.4
Motion picture theaters	5.5
Music stores	1.8
Real estate offices (and combinations with insurance, loan, law offices)	4.0
Savings and loan associations	1.5
Sporting goods stores	3.5
Tire dealers	2.2
Travel agents	5.0

NAB recommends convincing your retailer target to spend for advertising when customers are in a buying mood ("shoot when the ducks are flying"). Establish monthly buying patterns using the national figures in Table 9.4 and each stores' *own* pattern, then suggest your target spend for advertising in the relationship depicted in Figure 9.4.

The relationship of sales to advertising should *not* look as it does in Figure 9.5.

NAB suggests alerting the target that a store department that is efficiently delivering maximum buyer traffic at the lowest possible

Table 9.4 Selling Retail Clients—II

	Household Appliances, Radio/TV	Department Stores	Furniture Stores	Grocery Stores	Women's Clothing, Furrier
January	$12.36	$73.71	$14.45	$221.46	$15.04
February	11.91	73.54	14.09	204.58	14.65
March	13.24	94.30	16.14	221.68	17.32
April	12.64	100.89	16.07	227.33	18.80
May	12.66	106.72	16.40	234.00	18.36
June	13.73	100.53	16.78	229.04	16.55
July	14.77	100.02	16.64	248.25	17.85
August	13.60	104.23	16.39	227.71	18.56
September	13.16	100.33	15.84	229.82	18.09
October	13.65	109.74	16.58	237.20	19.78
November	15.26	130.28	17.79	226.70	20.77
December	22.34	207.71	19.34	256.77	31.25
Total	$169.32	$1,302.00	$196.51	$2,764.54	$227.02

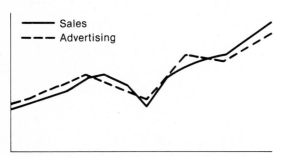

Figure 9.4 A Good Relationship of Sales to Advertising

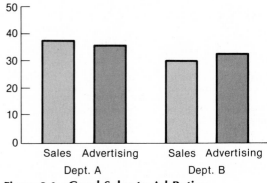

Figure 9.6 Good Sales-to-Ad Ratios

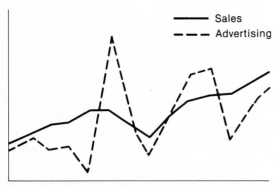

Figure 9.5 A Poor Relationship of Sales to Advertising

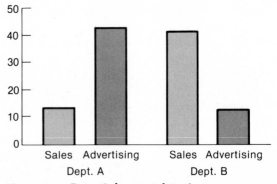

Figure 9.7 Poor Sales-to-Ad Ratios

	1 Sales last year	2 % of year's sales	3 Advertising last year	4 % of year's advertising		5
Jan.						
Feb.						
Mar.						
Apr.						
May						
June						
July						
Aug.						
Sept.						
Oct.						
Nov.						
Dec.						
Total		100%		100%		

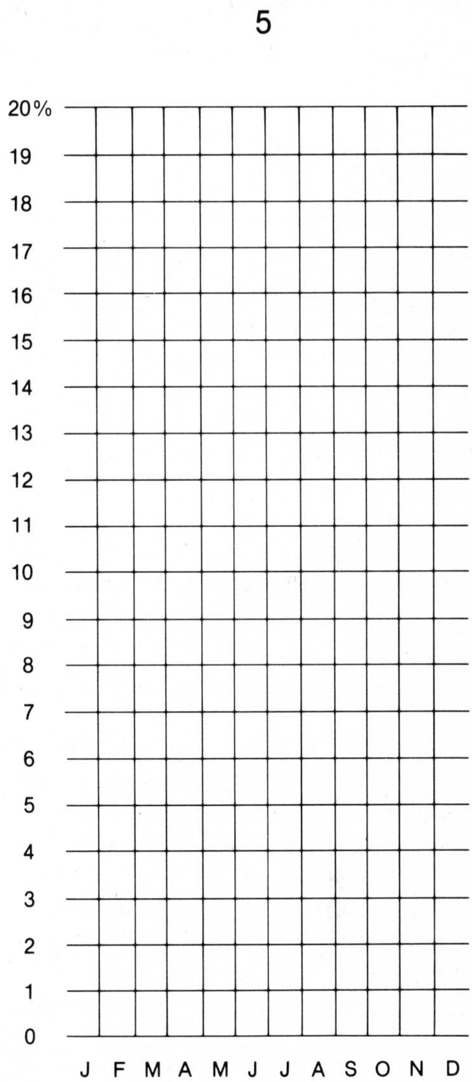

The grid in column 5 has a vertical scale from 0 to 20% and a horizontal axis labeled J F M A M J J A S O N D.

Figure 9.8   Selling Retail Clients—III

advertising cost will have a sales-to-ad ratios such as those in Figure 9.6.

The sales-to-ad ratios should *not* look as they do in Figure 9.7.

Selling Retail Clients—III

You must help your target understand the store's sales-to-ad ratios. NAB suggests using the grids shown in Figure 9.8. The procedure is this: Write in column 1 the retailer's monthly sales last year. Divide last year's total sales into each month's sales, entering the resulting percentage in column 2. In column 3, enter each month's advertising last year (in dollars or column inches). Divide last year's total into each month's figure, entering the percentage in column 4.

Plot monthly sales and advertising percentages on the graph (column 5). If sales and advertising lines don't run close to each other, advertising is too late or too early—and sales are being missed.

Selling Retail Clients—IV

Help your target judge proper allocation of ad dollars to different departments or merchandise lines. Using Figure 9.9, write in column 1 a randomly selected month, in column 2 the store department or line. In column 3, write each department's (or line's) sales last year, then total. Divide the month's total sales into each department's (or line's) sales, writing the percentage in column 4.

In column 5, enter each department's (line's) advertising expenditures during the month. Divide month's total advertising (figured in step three) into each department's (line's) advertising, and enter in column 6 the percentage of advertising run.

Examine two departments, and (in column 7) shade in bar graphs representing sales percentages, along with advertising percentages. Has proper advertising emphasis been given each department (or line)? Are some departments underadvertised?

Selling Retail Clients—V

Counseling your retailer to use methodically planned advertising campaigns of lengthy duration should be your strategy. NAB recommends that, having helped the retailer understand the store's past performance, you try to become the retailer's partner in planning the store's sales strategy and advertising spending. NAB suggests a four-step plan.

Step 1: Set Sales Goals. Starting with last year's sales for one month, consider market changes in population, income, and employment since last year. Figure in special sales or merchandising events planned for the forthcoming month (special holiday sales and so on). Judge as best you can what competing stores are doing and estimate their relative success. Consider any expanded or new departments in the retailer's own store and instill determination to advertise and sell more aggressively. Enter in Figure 9.10, for the relevant month, last year's sales in dollars (or column inches) plus percentage. Consider last year's performance and market plus competitive conditions, then rough in sales goals for the same forthcoming month.

Step 2: Set Advertising Budget. Determine next month's advertising expenditures, first checking co-op dollars available from suppliers. New or expanding stores should advertise more, as should any in less favorable locations. Larger budgets are required for stores with strong competition or whose primary appeal is low prices. Special dates or events offer additional sales opportunities and, NAB points out, should be budgeted for.

Using Figure 9.11, enter (1) percent of sales invested in advertising for same month last year. Write in (2) dollars, including co-op, invested last year. Enter (3) inches (or lineage) bought last year.

Enter (4) month's sales goal, and (5) multiply it by percent planned for advertising. That yields (6) the month's ad budget. Dividing the budget by the newspaper's space rate will give (7) the inches (or lineage) available to promote the store for the month.

Step 3: Decide What to Promote. In helping the retailer determine which departments or products to advertise, consider the sales goal for each. "For instance," says NAB, "if the sales goal of Department A is 9 percent of the total store sales objective this month, then earmark for it something like 9 percent of the month's planned advertising space."

1 Month						1 Month				
2	**3**	**4**	**5**	**6**		**2**	**3**	**4**	**5**	**6**
Department	Sales	%	Advertising	%		Department	Sales	%	Advertising	%
	$		$				$		$	
Totals	$	100%	$	100%		Totals	$	100%	$	100%

7		**7**		**7**		**7**	
Department _____		Department _____		Department _____		Department _____	
Sales	Adv.	Sales	Adv.	Sales	Adv.	Sales	Adv.
50%		50%		50%		50%	
40%		40%		40%		40%	
30%		30%		30%		30%	
20%		20%		20%		20%	
10%		10%		10%		10%	

Figure 9.9 Selling Retail Clients—IV

Next month is _____

Department or merchandise group	Month's sales last year	%	Month's sales goal this year	%
	$		$	
	$		$	
	$		$	
	$		$	
	$		$	
	$		$	
	$		$	
	$		$	
	$		$	
	$		$	
	$		$	
	$		$	
	$		$	
Totals	$	(100%)	$	(100%)

Figure 9.10 Selling Retail Clients—V

Month's planned advertising THIS year

Next month is _____

4 Sales Goal __ __ __ __ $ _____

1 % of sales invested over all _____

5 % for advertising __ __ X _____%

Month's advertising LAST year

6 Advertising Budget __ $ _____

2 Dollars _____ (Co-op _____%)

7 Lineage _____

3 Lineage _____

_____ _____
Earned rate per column $ Budgeted
inch or agate line

Figure 9.11 Monthly Ad Budgeting Chart

Using Figure 9.12, draw up a flexible outline factoring in items likely to attract shoppers in the month ahead (no snow tires in July). Consider "sleepers" or products that are currently hot but which didn't show up in last year's figures. Again, determine which goods have co-op support. Plan to promote new or expanding departments plus products that are seasonal and likely to face decreased sales next month.

Step 4: Complete a Day-to-Day Schedule. Using a large calendar (the NAB's *Newspaper Advertising Planbook* is excellent), calculate ad expenditures for each day in coming month. Consider such things as when large local firms pay employees and thus make money available for shopping; days when traffic is heaviest; nights when the store is open; merchandising events, local or national, when shopping traditionally is done; departments to be opened or expanded; current prices and stock on hand. Enter items, prices, and ad sizes for each day. You should urge a trial period of at least four months for this four-step program of increasing a retailer's

advertising. Anything less is unlikely to prove the value of consistent advertising.

Ask for the Order

A sales presentation should focus on the *prospect's* needs (never, "*I* sure need a good order today") and how your newspaper can fulfill them. Concentrate on a central theme, avoiding too many sales points. Don't confuse the issue. Keep your presentation simple. Always be honest with every claim. State your case briefly; if you waste the prospect's time, you will not be welcomed again.

Stay flexible, ready to depart from your planned presentation if it isn't going well (watch your prospect for signs of impatience) or if your prospect presents you with an unexpected opening. For example, if you go in with a presentation on advertising shoe sales and the prospect starts talking about boots, *you* switch signals too.

Opinions vary on how hard to sell against competition. Some sales managers say that competition should never be mentioned; others say a presentation that doesn't bounce off compe-

Department or merchandise group	Percentage of month's sales	Percentage of month's advertising	Lineage
	%	%	
	%	%	
	%	%	
	%	%	
	%	%	
	%	%	
	%	%	
	%	%	
	%	%	
	%	%	
	%	%	
	%	%	
	%	%	
Totals	100%	100%	

Figure 9.12 Monthly Ad Sales Record

tition is inadequate. On balance, talk positively about your newspaper and its strengths and not too much about competitors' weaknesses.

Be sure you state cost of the advertising program you propose and quickly translate that into likely effectiveness. That includes CPMs and how they compare to other media. Always describe advertising as a necessary *investment* by the retailer in improved business, *never* as a *discretionary expense*.

Ask for the order, *always*. You know that's why you're there. So does the prospect. Get a signature on that contract!

Follow Through with Effective Ads

Only if advertising is effective will the client return to the newspaper. So your job includes making certain that ads are well done. Here are some NAB guidelines for effective ads:

1. Create an identity with distinctive artwork, layout, and copy. This attracts more readers. Don't look like the competition.

2. Use simple layout. Be clever but not cryptic. Move the reader's eyes logically from headline to illustration to explanatory copy to price to store name and logo.

3. Have a definite focus. Newspapers are a visual medium and readers' eyes are drawn to well-chosen photographs or interesting artwork that, in turn, leads them to read about what you are selling.

4. Feature consumer benefits. Answer the customer's question "What's in it for me?" If it's lower price, feature that.

5. Avoid congestion. Use white space to separate your ad from the print surrounding it.

6. Tell the whole story. Cite color, size, and price in appealing, enthusiastic, complete sentences and with illustrations.

7. Name the price. List the item's outstanding features to justify higher price. With lower prices, mention "closeout" or "clearance sale" to dispel any notion of low quality. Explain credit and layaway options.

8. Specify branded merchandise. Capitalize on the manufacturer's previous advertising to establish a brand name. Enhance the store's reputation by featuring known brands.

9. Include related items. Strive for two sales instead of one by, for example, showing a clothes dryer in an ad featuring a washer.

10. Urge readers to buy now. Stimulate prompt action with "limited supply" or "this week only."

Warning:

- Don't forget store name, address, telephone number, and hours. One out of ten American families moves annually and may not know the store. Even if the store is long established, mention its name several times in the ad.

- Don't be too clever. Some consumers distrust cleverness in advertising, as they distrust glib salespeople. Straightforward copy is most effective.

- Don't use unusual or difficult words. Many consumers won't understand "couturier" or "gourmet" or technical terms. Use simple language; everybody understands it.

- Don't generalize. Shoppers want facts; facts sell.

- Don't make excessive claims. The surest way to lose customers is to make claims the store cannot back up.[43]

---

[43] "1984 Newspaper Advertising Planbook," NAB.

THE FUTURE

One unchanging law of newspaper management is that many things are changing.

If you are not yet in management, things will be changed by the time you get there. Let's look at a few changes that are likely to affect newspaper advertising.

Looking ahead to the year 2000, some futurists predict an enormous increase in advertising volume. An NAB survey of advertiser and agency executives in 1984 yielded predictions the number of print and broadcast ad messages would *double* in twenty-five years.

Other predictions:

- Broadcast may be disadvantaged because it will be forced to use fifteen-second commercials to handle its extra ad load. That will cause "clutter," an airways crowding advertisers dislike because their messages are lost. Newspapers will add extra pages to escape clutter.

- Cable or satellite systems will reach 90 percent of U.S. homes by 1990; 75 percent will subscribe to pay TV. Network TV's prime-time viewing share will drop to half of today's 78 percent. Newspapers will become proportionately more important to advertisers.

- Specialized media aiming at narrowly defined target marketing will double in number by the year 2000, forcing newspapers to improve their zoning and target-marketing capabilities to meet advertisers' needs.

- The one hundred top national advertisers will account for 70 percent of total ad volume, up from the present 56 percent.

- The big-spending American will be the target; 80 percent of all ads will aim at the population segment responsible for 50 percent of all consumer spending.

- Important demographic changes will include an increase to 75 percent from today's 62 percent of working-age women in the work force; the number of Americans in their late twenties who are college graduates, now 21 percent, will double by the year 2000. Ad strategies will have to adjust to such marketplace changes.[44]

SUMMARY

Advertising market share, more than circulation share, tells the tale in newspapering today. Dailies in Washington, Cleveland, and Philadelphia died even though they had substantial reader loyalty.

For smaller dailies and weeklies as well as metros, financial success depends on achieving sufficient ad share against many competitors—TV, radio, shoppers, direct mail—and not simply fighting off competing newspapers of like size and characteristics. Advertising departments must compete for ad dollars and reader time against all media.

Newspapers continue strongest in *local retail* and *classified* advertising. Opportunities are opening for expansion of *national* advertising as cable TV and other electronic systems fractionalize the network TV market. But TV's entertainment value delivers huge audiences that are attractive to many national advertisers, so the battle will be tough.

Research is fundamental to effective advertising strategy. Advertisers want newspapers to deliver selected affluent, ready-to-buy prospects living near retail outlets. Research must find those prospects.

Newspaper advertising strategy must include target marketing. More so than broadcast, newspapers are superbly equipped for zoning

---

[44] Leo Bogart, NAB executive vice president, speech to ANPA, Montreal, May 1, 1984.

editorial and advertising content to deliver pin-point marketing.

Newspapers' biggest single problem is the relatively shallow household penetration that many deliver in their primary markets. Managers must offer total market coverage (TMC) to quickly deliver all or nearly all households for demanding advertisers while simultaneously improving news content to improve paid circulation.

Each manager must develop modern marketing leadership, integrating sales-related functions and launching highly motivated, well-trained sales forces into the marketplace.

RECOMMENDED READING

Continuing research is issued by a number of advertising-oriented industry groups: the Newspaper Advertising Bureau, 1180 Avenue of the Americas, New York, NY 10036; Advertising Media Credit Executives' Association International, Inc., 3803 S. Beverly Hills Drive, Toledo, OH 43614; Association of Newspaper Classified Advertising Managers, P.O. Box 223, Danville, IL 61834; International Newspaper Advertising and Marketing Executives' Association, The Newspaper Center, P.O. Box 17210 Dulles International Airport, Washington, DC 20041; National Association of Advertising Publishers, a group of free-circulation papers, 111 E. Wacker Drive, Suite 600, Chicago, IL 60601; Newspaper Advertising Co-op Network, 501 W. Algonquin Road, Arlington Heights, IL 60005.

GLOSSARY

Advertorial. An ad advocating a political or philosophical concept—often controversial because it may be interpreted by readers as regular news content.

Agate line. A space measurement, one column wide and 1/14 inch deep.

Agency commission. Usually 15 percent, paid to recognized ad sales agencies for selling space to national advertisers.

Better Business Bureau. A local watchdog group supported by businesses to guard against business fraud and deceptive advertising.

Broadsheet. A "standard" newspaper page, normally 13 inches wide and 21 inches deep (measurements vary.)

Center (or double-page) spread. Ad space on two facing pages.

Checking copy. Ad copy sent advertiser to prove publication.

Circular. An ad printed on a stand-alone single sheet or folder.

Classified. Ads arranged by "classification" such as help wanted, autos for sale, etc.

Column inch. A space measurement one column wide and an inch deep.

Combination (or combo) rate. A reduced rate offered advertisers for also using another publication, usually one owned by same publisher.

Cooperative (or co-op) advertising. Ads for which national advertiser, usually a manufacturer, pays some or all of the local costs to promote a product jointly with a local retail outlet.

CPM (cost per thousand). Advertiser's cost for ad reaching a thousand readers (or, in TV and radio, viewers or listeners).

Cumes (cumulative audience). The total of unduplicated persons or homes reached in given time by an advertising schedule; used mostly in TV.

Demographics. Vital statistics of a population, such as age, income, occupations.

Direct mail. Mail-delivered direct-response advertising.

Display advertising. Ads other than classified often set in type larger than body type and "displayed" in larger spaces to attract attention.

Double billing. A billing method whereby an advertising medium gives a retailer two invoices for the same ad. The retailer pays the lower one and submits the other to the manufacturer for co-op funds (which are actually unjustified). Highly unethical.

Double truck. A single unbroken ad on two facing pages.

Drive time. The time during which commuters drive to and from work and for which radio charges the highest rates; normally 6 A.M. to 10 A.M. and 3 P.M. to 7 P.M.

Due bill. The exchange of ad space for services or goods from restaurants, theaters, etc.

Ears. The upper corners of front pages, often boxed and sold for ads.

Federal Trade Commission (FTC). Monitors interstate commerce to, among other things, prevent unfair competition and fradulent or deceptive advertising.

Flat rate. Space charge without quantity or frequency discounts.

Following (or full) position. Ad space next to specified editorial matter, for which the newspaper charges a premium rate.

Food and Drug Administration (FDA). The federal agency with, among other things, authority over the labeling of products.

Forced combination. The selling of ad space only if space in another publication is purchased. May be illegal.

Frequency. The number of times readers or household is exposed to an ad within a specified period.

Full (or following) position. Ad space in preferred space, next to certain reading matter or at the top of a page.

General (or national) rate. Rates for nonlocal advertisers.

Gross rating points (GRP). A measure of overall effectiveness of an advertising medium—percentage of audience reached and how frequently. Each point equals one per cent of households or persons being measured; usually used in radio, TV or outdoor advertising.

Gutter. Blank inside margins of printed page.

Inserts. Preprinted ad matter delivered in newspapers, normally for a fee per thousand.

Island position. Ad space completely surrounded by editorial matter.

Layout. Finished design or rough sketch showing how an ad will look.

Legal (or public notice) advertising. Ads fulfilling legal requirements that certain governmental reports and statements, such as new laws or election notices, be published; also, ads by individuals or institutions on divorce, financial statements, bankruptcy proceedings, etc.

Lineage. Total ad lines printed or lines in an individual ad (14 lines to a column inch).

Local advertising. Ads from local merchants, as distinct from national (or general) advertisers.

Makegood. Free ad to correct error or other problem in previous paid ad.

Marriage (or, piggyback) mail. Mail in which two or more advertisers use the same cover and share costs in a direct-mail campaign.

Milline rate. Cost for one line in ad appearing before one million readers; used to express ad rates in relation to circulation.

National advertising. For products or services sold through many outlets, as contrasted with single-outlet local advertising.

Newspaper Advertising Bureau (NAB). Membership organization promoting advertiser use of newspapers. Address: 1180 Avenue of Americas, New York, N.Y., 10017.

Newsplan. Industrywide effort launched by NAB in 1979 under which individual newspapers offer quantity/frequency discounts to national advertisers.

Open rate. Highest ad rate, paid by users who don't qualify for discounts; also called basic, transient or one-time rate.

Preferred-position. Special position for which advertiser pays premium rate.

Prime time. Peak TV viewing hours, usually 7 p.m.–11 p.m., for which higher rates are charged.

Psychographics. Market description in terms of lifestyles, attitudes, opinions, etc.

Publisher's statement. Usually sworn statement by publisher of circulation, on which ad rates are based.

Rate card. Listings of rates, mechanical specifications, advertising policies and other matters affecting advertisers.

Rate holder. Used normally in local advertising to indicate ad published to maintain time or quantity discount guaranteed under contract.

Reach. A newspaper's total audience.

Reading notices. Ads set to look like editorial matter. Many newspapers refuse them or require clear labelling as advertising.

Rebate. A payment to an advertiser whose increased activity qualified for a larger discount; or payment by a newspaper when circulation falls below guaranteed levels.

Retail advertising. Ads placed by local merchants who sell directly to users.

Robinson-Patman Act. An FTC-enforced federal law to protect smaller merchants by ensuring that they receive same ad discounts given to larger advertisers in same market.

Run of paper or run of press (ROP). An ad position anywhere in paper at the discretion of the publisher.

Scotch double truck. One ad taking up two facing pages, bordered on each side and at the top with editorial matter.

Short rate. A rate applying to the payment of an advertiser who enjoyed space discounts but failed over the contract period to buy the minimum space required under contract.

Space buyer. Ad agency employee who selects print media for advertising clients.

Space discount. A discount given for a contractual agreement to buy certain amount of space.

Standard Advertising Unit (SAU) system. A system developed by the American Newspaper Publishers' Association in an effort to standardize newspaper advertising sizes and dimensions and increase national advertising by making it easier to plan, order, create, and pay for newspaper ad space.

Supplements. Preprinted inserts distributed in newspapers.

Till forbid (or, run TF). Normally used in local advertising to order continuous publication until the advertiser withdraws the order.

Transient rate. See "open rate."

CHAPTER
TEN

Newspaper Image and Promotion

The issue of newspaper image and promotion was, for a very long time, taken lightly among publishers and editors; a fashionable wisecrack along these lines was that "For people in advertising, we sure do a lousy job of advertising our business." Not many managers got excited about image, and promotion was sorely neglected by the industry and individual newspapers alike. But times have changed.

Promotion today is an extremely important managerial responsibility and must be integrated into every newspaper's marketing effort. Image in the marketplace must be built carefully and protected devotedly. Because of their importance, we are treating promotion and image in this separate chapter. But if you're headed for a career in general management, circulation, advertising, or news management, don't separate promotion or image in your mind from your most fundamental priorities.

We will look first at the wider newspaper industry image and then at how you can organize and manage a promotion effort to improve your newspaper's general image, increase circulation, and augment advertising sales.

NEWSPAPER IMAGE AND CREDIBILITY

On February 27, 1984, the *Wall Street Journal* published an item favorable to Chicago Milwaukee Corp. Next day, the company's stock value jumped more than $7 per share. It was another example of investors' extraordinary faith in the *Journal*'s accuracy; it was commonplace, this investor willingness to bet large sums of money on the *Journal*'s insightful reporting. Generations of dedicated reporters and skilled editors, schooled in the *Journal*'s ethics of handling sensitive news, labored to build that trust. So Chicago Milwaukee's $7 jump raised no suspicions at the *Journal*. But it did at the Securities and Exchange Commission.

Unknown to the paper's management, the SEC was tracking the market impact of stories written for the paper's "Heard on the Street" column by thirty-five-year-old R. Foster Winans, author of the Chicago Milwaukee story. The SEC had been informed by the American Stock Exchange that suspicious trading patterns surrounded mentions of companies in "Heard." In sum, the SEC later reported, Winans on many occasions leaked to associates advance word of what "Heard" would say. They traded before the paper was published and well before the general investing public could react. Large profits were made and Winans shared them, the SEC said.

The story was big news, the talk of Wall Street. Radio, TV, and other papers ran detailed accounts. The *Journal*, writhing in anger and embarrassment over what it called this "betrayal," published thousands of words on the affair, even describing Winans's sex life, obviously determined that whatever surfaced would see first light in the *Journal*, not a rival paper. It was a dagger in the heart of the *Journal*'s only strength in the advertising and circulation marketplace—its credibility—and a blotch on its image as *the* source of accurate and reliable financial, business, and economic news. (Winans was later sentenced to eighteen months in prison.)

The *Journal* is not the only paper that has been hurt in this way. The *Washington Post* was hoaxed by a staffer who tugged at readers' heartstrings with the piteous story of a child heroin addict who, it eventually was revealed, did not exist. The *New York Times* ran a beautifully written, first-person account of a guerrilla war in Cambodia by a reporter who got no closer to the jungles of Southeast Asia than a comfortable seaside resort in Spain. Many other papers must acknowledge that momentary breakdowns in editing safeguards let raging errors—or outright hoaxes—slip through. So in a very real sense, the first line of defense in newspaper promotion must be awareness that the *entire staff* must guard against journalistic lapses that will cause the newspaper great embarrassment. Every member of the staff must make sure that:

- Reporting is perceived by the public as presenting all sides of an issue and giving all principals in a story, particularly those accused of wrongdoing, an opportunity to respond.

- Writing is as objective and dispassionate as possible and clean of bias. Make certain Republicans don't "smile" in your columns while Democrats "smirk," or vice versa.

- "Informed sources" and "observers" aren't quoted too often. Even casual readers understand that those terms often cover only the writer's own opinions.

Simply put, the entire staff must ask, "Is that story just too good to be true? Are those quotes just a little too slick?" Had those questions been asked at the *Washington Post, New York Times, Wall Street Journal*, and other newspapers, some major blemishes on newspaper credibility would have been avoided. However, even the most alert newsroom has difficulty preventing betrayal by an individual.

In the cases cited, the *Journal*, *Times*, and *Post* had formal codes of ethics or standards of professional conduct that were betrayed by individuals. What counts when that happens is how the newspaper in the short term handles the explanation to readers and advertisers and how, over the long term, it rebuilds its image. There can be no haphazard approach to image and promotion. It must be a professional, ongoing effort. And as with any of your managerial responsibilities, you must first turn to planning and organizing the effort.

PLANNING AND ORGANIZING THE PROMOTION EFFORT

As a key player on the integrated marketing team, the promotion department pursues planned goals. Two are most important:

First, the department conducts *institutional promotion* of the overall character of the newspaper—its business and editorial philosophies. This establishes the paper's "tone" in its market.

Second, the department conducts *marketing promotion* to increase sales by informing readers and advertisers of the newspaper's availability, stimulating their needs and convincing them the newspaper's advertising and news fulfills those needs.

Promotion also is a *competitive weapon* to compare the newspaper with competing media, drawing distinctions and differentiating the media. Guidance for promotion activity comes from two sources and can cover both short-range and long-range activity.

First, overall strategic guidance comes from the newspaper's long-range planning process. This should include, for example, general guidelines on how to "position" the newspaper in "image" or public and consumer perception five or ten years in the future.

Second, the newspaper's short-term plan must assign specific immediate activities that are tightly coordinated with the circulation and advertising departments to increase sales or achieve other objectives within the one year ahead.

Promotion takes various forms: *advertising* in the newspaper itself (house ads) or other media; *publicity*, such as news releases for other media; *sales activities*, such as trade show booths and displays. There also must be for salespeople effective "drop" or *promotion material* focused on the selling function.

In organizational structure, promotion should report to the marketing director and have easy access to the directors of advertising and circulation. Close coordination with other departments, particularly news, is important. Top management must assign appropriate human and financial resources to promotion. Avoid the common error of running a low-budget promotion department headed by a powerless third-rank executive who gets the job only because he or she doesn't quite fit in elsewhere. Such a promotion director is never admitted to decision-making circles, of course, and promotional considerations never enter the overall newspaper strategy. This type of promotion executive is never asked to help fashion the news and advertising strategies that create a newspaper's image but is asked, occasionally, to clean up a public relations mess—explain away major error or hoax. And the publisher will wonder why the paper has low credibility in its market.

Some papers spend 1 to 2 percent of gross annual revenue on promotion, but deciding how much to spend is difficult. Should the figure be a percentage of sales, a little bit more (or less) than last year, or pegged to what competing media spend? In practice, many newspapers give promotion a bit of what is left over after other departments share next year's budget pie. But if you are a promotion-smart manager, you will assign precise goals to the promotion department and then provide the financial resources needed to meet them. If you manage a small paper, you cannot afford a large promotion organization. But you must *think* promotion and maintain effective efforts even if that means you can assign promotion only as a part-time responsibility for a manager.

Increasingly, research into reader and advertiser attitudes is used to identify what is liked or disliked about the newspaper, so that the promotion director can define departmental objectives and plan means of accomplishing them. Two thoughts to keep in mind:

- All the promotion in the world cannot explain away basic flaws in a newspaper's journalistic content, advertising practices, or production and delivery systems. The best way to create a quality image is to produce a top-flight journalistic product and business operation.

- Absolute honesty in promotion is essential. Promotion should *never* step beyond facts into unfounded claims. The newspaper industry has a serious credibility problem and promotion must be part of the solution, not part of the problem.

FIRST UNDERSTAND THE INDUSTRY'S IMAGE

To effectively manage a *newspaper's* image, you must understand the *industry's* image. For although polls show readers hold their own paper in higher esteem than the "media," no individual newspaper is free from the rise or fall of public esteem for newspapers as a whole.

Your basic challenge in this image business is that your newspaper sells readers and advertisers something difficult even to define, let alone achieve and maintain: credibility. But it's all that you have to attract readers and advertisers. It takes generations to build and unceasing vigilance to protect. But in a flash, despite constant watchfulness, grievous damage can be done to it. A single hoax or error might not destroy credibility, but it can draw down the

reservoir of public confidence to dangerous levels. Probably more serious over the long haul is gradual erosion of public confidence due to errors in fact or to perceived bias in handling news, lack of good taste, or insensitive and unfair invasions of privacy. All find their way into daily and weekly papers large and small, and though each may seem insignificant, their cumulative impact can be devastating and long-lasting.

Polls reveal many negatives in public perception of the press. And, contrary to long-held industry belief, polls show that the criticism is not simply of the press as a messenger of bad tidings but rather as an impersonal, arrogant, and manipulative element that intrudes into political, social, and economic life. The press is often seen as a self-appointed participant in—not merely an observer of—the decision-making process. And some critics ask: Who elected the press to run my life?

Studies Reveal Serious Public Doubts

You must design promotion strategy against a backdrop of nearly unanimous findings by reputable research organizations that the public has severe doubts about the press and its motives. A major study by the American Society of Newspaper Editors (ASNE), *Relating to Readers in the '80s*, revealed in 1985 that:

- Three-fourths of the adults surveyed have problems with the news media credibility; one-fifth deeply distrust the media.

- Three-fourths say that reporters only want a good story and don't worry about hurting people.

- One-sixth say that the media are biased—that they sensationalize, invade people's privacy, and emphasize bad news too much.

- Half say they would turn to television if forced to choose a single source of local news; only one-third chose newspapers.

Belden Associates, a leading newspaper research company, finds these criticisms of newspapers:

- They are biased in handling news, carrying "slanted" news and too much "bad" news.

- They are guilty of inaccurate reporting (both typographical and factual errors).

- Content is "irrelevant."

- Not enough news is local.

- Then, mechanical problems: stories are too long, there are too many jumps, there is poor organization within the paper.[1]

In her study for ASNE, researcher Ruth Clark finds that public perception of newspapers has improved since her 1978 study *Changing Needs of Changing Readers*. Readers, she says, like newspapers and their editors; a majority think that newspapers are indispensable (though younger readers are less sure). A Times Mirror Corp. survey released in 1986 found a wider base of public support for newspapers than was generally expected and that vociferous critics were in a minority. But major reservations persist. Clark: "We [readers] still question, however, whether you are fair and unbiased when it comes to covering and allocating space to all your constituents. And we sometimes think you are trying to manipulate us."

Clark finds the industry in general judged more harshly than each reader's own newspaper:

- 57 percent expressing opinions do *not* feel that newspaper stories are usually fair; only 39 percent believe their own paper is biased.

- 53 percent do *not* believe newspapers are usually accurate; 84 percent describe their own paper as accurate.

Table 10.1 Confidence in Institutions

Church/organized religion	62%
Military	53
Banks and banking	51
U.S. Supreme Court	42
Public schools	39
Newspapers	38
Congress	28
Big business	28
Organized labor	26
TV	25

Gallup Report, August 1983.

"While the perception of bias among newspapers in general has immense implications," Clark says, "it is apparent that the problem is one for the industry as a whole rather than for individual newspapers. One reason, of course, is that people's ties to their own papers are far stronger and warmer; 88 percent believe that the paper they read most often really cares about the community."[2] However, 42 percent expressing opinions say even their own newspaper attempts to manipulate them.

Gallup asked 1,497 adults of age eighteen or above this question: "I am going to read you a list of institutions in American society. Would you tell me how much confidence you, yourself, have in each one—a great deal, quite a lot, some, or very little?" Table 10.1 shows the responses of those who replied, "a great deal" or "quite a lot."

Zeroing in on newspapers themselves, Gallup finds mixed reader confidence, as shown in Table 10.2.

A Harris poll finds severe slippage over an eighteen-year period in the percentage of U.S. adults expressing a great deal of confidence in the press. In 1966, it was 29 percent; 1973, 30 percent; 1977, 18 percent; 1982, 14 percent.[3]

---

[1] Deanne Termini, senior vice president, and Sheila Miller, research associate, Belden Associates, Dallas, in a paper delivered to the Southern Newspaper Publishers' Association editorial clinic, Dallas, April 3, 1984.

[2] Ruth Clark, president, Clark, Martire & Bartholomeo, Inc., Dallas, *Relating to Readers in the '80s*, research sponsored by American Society of Newspaper Editors.

[3] Termini, op. cit., p. 15.

Table 10.2 Confidence in Newspapers

A great deal	11%
Quite a lot	27
Some	41
Very little	18
None	1
No opinion	2

Gallup Report, August 1983.

The public's view is even more mixed on confidence in the men and women collectively called the "press." Harris asked, "As far as people in charge of running [the press] are concerned, would you say you have a great deal of confidence, only some confidence, or hardly any confidence at all in them?"

Note that, as an *institution*, newspapers gain a higher confidence rating than TV. But in confidence in the *men and women* behind the scenes, newspapers are rated substantially below TV news. Studies show that the public does not know much about the men and women who publish newspapers. Contrast that with viewer identification with a TV anchor who comes across as a real person, even a friend, invited into the home each evening to read the news. Consider the total anonymity of most publishers and

Table 10.3 Percent of U.S. Adults with a Great Deal of Confidence

Medicine	32%
Military	31
Education	30
U.S. Supreme Court	25
TV news	24
White House	20
Organized religion	20
Major companies	18
The press	14
Congress	13
Organized labor	8

Gallup Report, August 1983.

editors or, indeed, save a few bylines, most reporters. Contrast that with how CBS anchor Dan Rather drew solemn comment in the trade press and even in general-circulation papers when he first chose to read the news occasionally wearing a sweater under his jacket. Only the naive believe Rather wears a sweater because he gets cold under those bright (and very hot) studio lights. TV strategists select such sartorial touches to build personal linkage between anchor and viewers. Conversely, it's a newspaper tradition to scorn such trivialities, to glorify the copy desk's anonymity, to root out of a writer's reporting little touches of warmth and personality that could fashion personal links with readers. (Homer Bigart, whose reporting won two Pulitzer Prizes, once told the author that in Vietnam he had survived unscathed when bullets hit every other man he was riding with in a helicopter. Bigart could tell only another correspondent, not his *New York Times* readers. The *Times* copy desk, he said, edited from his account all personal references to his narrow escape. Picture how TV news would handle it: correspondent in tailored bush suit breathlessly describing the firefight while camera pans across bullet-riddled chopper. And guess which account would come alive for the public back home.)

By neglecting such personal touches, the newspaper industry demonstrates that it doesn't understand readers. Ruth Clark finds that 56 percent of her sample group *want* to know more about editors and reporters who publish the local paper; only 40 percent want to know more about production technology—a favorite promotional theme for scores of papers for a decade or more.

Believability a Major Goal

Without believability, the newspaper industry cannot function as the credible primary source of in-depth information so essential in a democratic society. An individual newspaper lacking

Table 10.4 Most Believable News Medium

Television	51%
Newspapers	22
Magazines	9
Radio	8
Undecided	10

Gallup Report, August 1983.

believability cannot succeed in circulation or advertising.

Achieving believability is a complex challenge. A Roper poll on *news* believability asks, "If you got conflicting or different reports of the same news story from radio, television, the magazines, and the newspapers, which of the four versions would you be most inclined to believe?" Table 10.4 shows the results.

However, polls consistently find newspaper *advertising* ranked as more believable than TV ads. The results of one poll—published by the industry's chief advertising promoter, the Newspaper Advertising Bureau—are shown in Table 10.5.

Differing believability scores for news and advertising stem in part from basic differences between newspapers and TV:

- Some TV viewers feel that they "see" news develop on TV. Could a camera lie? Would the anchor, "Mr. Sincere Himself," shade

Table 10.5 Most Believable Advertising Medium

Newspapers	42%
TV	26
Magazines	11
Radio	11
Direct mail	5
All about equal	2
No opinion	3

Key Facts About Newspapers and Advertising, 1984, New York, Newspaper Advertising Bureau, 1984, p. 23.

the truth? In contrast, 33 percent of those surveyed by *Newsweek* magazine said that newspaper reporters—unfamiliar, anonymous, impersonal—"often make things up."

- In advertising, TV commercials are intrusive and often avoided by viewers; recall of specifics is difficult after even a short time. Newspapers, conversely, are purchased by many *for* advertising. They carry detailed ads that can be clipped for future reference. They are not burdened by the strident hucksterism that plagues so much TV advertising.

Three Other Problem Areas

Polls reveal problems in three other areas:

First, the public, better educated and more sophisticated, makes an important distinction between what the press does and how it does it. For example, there is strong support for investigative reporting in concept but firm disapproval of undercover techniques in practice. Gallup asked, "As you probably know, the news media—TV, newspapers, and magazines—often do what is called investigative reporting: uncovering and reporting on corruption and fraud in business, government agencies, and other organizations. In general, do you approve or disapprove of investigative reporting by the news media?" The results are shown in Table 10.6; Table 10.7 shows views of reporting techniques.

Second, there is important evidence that the newspaper industry should speak not of *its*

Table 10.6 Views of Investigative Reporting

	Among U.S. Adults
Approve	79%
Disapprove	18
Undecided	3

Gallup Report, August 1983.

Table 10.7   Views of Reporting Techniques

	Disapprove
Having reporters *not* identify themselves as reporters	65%
Using hidden cameras and microphones	58
Paying informers	56
Quoting unnamed sources	52

Gallup Report, August 1983.

First Admendment rights but rather of the public's. Clark finds, for example, that 7.4 percent of her sample feel the press must be present when American military forces are sent to another country. "This high figure suggests," Clark says, "that newspapers might have obtained stronger public support against their exclusion from the Grenada invasion [in 1983] if the issue had been expressed differently: as the right of the public to know, rather than the right of the press to be there." Despite fears of many journalists that they alone defend the First Amendment, Clark finds 86 percent of her sample agreeing with the statement "If the government tried to close down a newspaper and stop it from publishing, I'd be upset enough to do something." Only 25 percent agree that the president has a right to stop a newspaper from printing a story he feels is biased or inaccurate.[4]

Third, much public criticism of the "media" really is directed at TV, not newspapers, and many in the newspaper industry feel promotion efforts should make this distinction. Creed Black, chairman and publisher of Knight-Ridder's *Lexington (Ky.) Herald-Leader*, in his final speech as president of ASNE, said:

> . . . I come to what I have become increasingly convinced is one of the major reasons our public standing seems to have declined while our

performance as an institution has improved. It is that the public lumps the printed press and television together in something called "the media" and makes little if any distinction between the two. The result is that we are blamed for the sins and shortcomings of what television—which remains basically an entertainment medium—calls news.[5]

Black criticizes what he terms TV's "show biz" approach to news, saying that much of its offering is not news at all. He urges newspapers not to include themselves in "the media"; newspapers are "the press." Says Executive Editor Ben Bradlee of the *Washington Post*: "Television has changed the public's vision of the reporter into someone who is petty and disagreeable, who has taken cynicism as an unnecessary extra step."[6] TV cameras, lights and recording devices are much more intrusive than a reporter with notebook and pencil. And, the process of getting a television news story can become part of the story itself in a dramatic, prying way.

In sum, your newspaper's promotional strategy must take into account public perceptions that newspapers are biased. Some readers fear newspapers attempt to manipulate them. Consequently, newspapers as an institution do not have the complete confidence of their readers. However, readers generally rank their own hometown papers much higher, and we now turn to your responsibility for your own paper's credibility.

HOW TO BUILD YOUR NEWSPAPER'S CREDIBILITY

Concerned that a "credibility gap" existed between their newspaper and its readers, managers of the *Orlando (Fla.) Sentinel* launched a major image-building campaign. Within two years,

---

[4] Ruth Clark, op. cit., p. 23.

[5] Creed C. Black, "Our Image Problem: A Paradox," speech to ASNE, Washington, D.C., May 9, 1984.
[6] "Journalism Under Fire," *Time* magazine, Dec. 12, 1983, p. 77.

Table 10.8   Results of Credibility Survey

The Sentinel is	Positive	Neutral	Negative
Believable	74%	21%	5%
Has integrity	70	23	7
Fair/objective in reporting	60	27	13
Accurate in reporting	65	26	9

H. R. Lifvendahl, president, *Orlando (Fla.) Sentinel*, in a letter of March 12, 1984, and a study entitled "Attitudes Toward The *Orlando Sentinel* in the Central Florida Market."

they claimed substantial success. Then Editor David Burgin said, "I can't say we've closed the gap, but certainly the results show we've narrowed it dramatically. . . ." Just talk? Note:

- Circulation expanded during the 1982-84 campaign faster at the *Sentinel* than at any other major paper in the Southeast, where Sun Belt papers outstrip others across the nation in growth. Daily circulation rose 6.1 percent; Sunday's, 8.6 percent.

- Belden Associates, retained for a continuing market study, discovered that *Sentinel* readers had noted and approved the paper's self-improvement campaign: 44.4 percent of respondents said the *Sentinel* overall was "better than it used to be." That was a 45 percent increase over those who said that in 1982. There was an equally impressive increase in number of respondents who judged the *Sentinel* improved in news coverage, appearance, design, and organization.

In improving credibility, Belden reports, the *Sentinel* achieved significant recognition, as shown in Tables 10.8 and 10.9.

An Image-Improvement Checklist

You can draw important lessons from the *Sentinel*'s campaign in structuring your promotion department and planning improved image:

Table 10.9   Results of Image Survey

	Agree	Disagree	Don't know
The *Sentinel* insists on the public's right to know	84%	10%	6%
The *Sentinel* is a positive force in community	85	9	6
The *Sentinel* has made some good changes in the paper in the past year or two	88	8	4

H. R. Lifvendahl, president, *Orlando (Fla.) Sentinel*, in a letter of March 12, 1984, and a study entitled "Attitudes Toward The *Orlando Sentinel* in the Central Florida Market."

- Ensure top management's full commitment. *Sentinel* President and Publisher H. R. (Tip) Lifvendahl was deeply involved in the campaign, along with Burgin and Arthur D. Farber, vice president and circulation director.

- Listen to readers. Research into readers' views must be the foundation for promotion strategy. The *Sentinel* listens through Belden's continuing market study. Less costly polls can be run by smaller papers, along with focus groups (see box for how they operate) or personal interviews that can reveal how readers and nonreaders perceive a newspaper.

- Improve image through substantive improvement in news and advertising. Effective image building is more than a new fifteen-second radio jingle boosting the paper, sponsoring a soapbox derby, or handing out T-shirts to joggers. It is enlarging the news hole, increasing story count, reorganizing and redesigning the paper to aid

THE FOCUS GROUP

Readership surveys sometimes return conflicting signals on public perceptions of newspapers. For example, respondents to one survey divided in three almost equal groups: One considered the press *unbiased* in business coverage; a second, *biased for* business; a third, *biased against* business. So, many editors and managers augment surveys with in-depth meetings with readers. Thus, the focus group.

If moderated expertly in a relaxed atmosphere, focus groups can provide valuable feedback. Focus groups are simple to conduct and provide inexpensive contact with readers. However, participants are often selected unscientifically and sessions can yield unrepresentative information. So beware drawing sweeping conclusions from them.

It's best to seek reader input on a specific subject, say women's pages or the sports section. Invite appropriate groups of fifteen or so readers to the newspaper office or to a neutral meeting room for a chat, perhaps over coffee and doughnuts. Participants tend to be reticent if newspaper personnel are present, so many sessions are conducted by an outside professional. Or, invite newspaper personnel in for a roundtable discussion during the second half of the meeting. Two hours is considered the effective maximum for such meetings.

The main benefit of such informal sessions is that, if skillfully run, they give small groups of readers a chance to speak their minds about the paper. But directing informal conversation into useful channels can be a challenge for even an experienced discussion leader. So again, results must be weighed cautiously.

readers, improving reporting and writing. The *Sentinel* did all those things during its campaign.

- Spend money. How much obviously depends on each newspaper's available resources. The *Sentinel*, a wealthy Tribune Co. paper, added thirty experienced writers and editors during its campaign, increasing its total news staff to 270 people with (in 1984) a budget "well over $10 million." The company's flagship, the *Chicago Tribune*, spends $3 to $4 million annually on promotion. The *Worcester (Mass.) Telegram/Gazette*, with 56,000 AMs, 86,000 PMs, and 117,000 Sunday circulation, has an eight-person promotion department that spends 2 percent of gross revenues on promotion (it declines to state that in dollars.)[7]

[7] Terilyn McGovern-Mazza, "An Interview With A Winning Promotion Manager," *Editor & Publisher*, July 19, 1982, p. 19.

- Exploit every positive development. the *Sentinel*'s campaign exploited a $40 million conversion to offset printing by promoting improved color and reproduction capability. The paper's name was changed from *Sentinel Star* to *Orlando Sentinel* to build stronger market identification. Opening a new bureau, adding a new feature or column or a major series of articles—all are positive developments you can exploit through promotion.

- Warm up the paper. The *Sentinel*'s index now says, "Good morning" every day. The paper doesn't order readers to turn the page if a story jumps; it says, "please see . . . ." And, Burgin directed the staff to "squeeze in as much wit and charm as we can. . . ." He assigned critics to cover movies, restaurants, classical music, art and architecture, all to make the paper a useful and readable friend of each reader.

- Talk about yourself. Many newspapers are reluctant to brag a bit in public. Such

The Orlando Sentinel's **promotional packet, which includes a newspaper and press kit, is part of the newspaper's credibility campaign with advertisers, journalism schools, and other newspapers.**
(Courtesy of *The Orlando Sentinel*)

reluctance is a bad habit. The *Sentinel* states in its masthead, "The Best Newspaper in Florida." It issues slick promotional packets on its credibility campaign. Publisher Lifvendahl signs cover letters sending packets to advertisers, journalism schools, and other newspapers across the country. Explaining to both reader and advertiser what you are doing to improve your newspaper is essential in any image-building effort.

Two dangerous extremes in newspaper promotion must be avoided. First, when major errors appear or hoaxes slip into print, many papers publish guarded "explanations" that cannot possibly be confused with an apology or even a correction. Other editors and publishers will understand, but readers are left confused about just what did happen. For many editors, it is most important that there be ritualistic (and, of course, symbolic) disembowelment by a responsible editor who courageously steps forward to accept blame at the annual convention of ASNE or another professional forum, appropriately out of view of readers and advertisers.

Resolutions should be passed, codes of ethics reexamined, and each editor, upon return home, must send to the editing desk a memo to "tighten up" and guard against hoax and error. For many editors, that fixes the matter. But, of course, for readers it doesn't. The guarded "explanation" at best treats only symptoms of an image problem, not the cause, and at worst adds to public doubt and suspicion. Too often, the entire exercise is internal, almost fraternal, conducted by editors for other editors. Clear, detailed explanations to readers of what went wrong are the only course. No reader could fail to understand what went wrong at the *Wall Street Journal* in the Winans case *or* doubt the *Journal's* determination to avoid another such lapse.

A second extreme to avoid is managing the newspaper with the "image factor" primarily in mind, sacrificing the journalistic fundamentals of printing the facts and exercising community leadership in an effort to be "liked." Never should a newspaper grovel for favor. Credibility comes not from being "liked" but rather from being respected for courageous, high-quality professionalism. Promotional considerations must enter strategic planning, but they cannot override the professional judgment of editors, advertising directors, or circulation managers.

Themes to Stress

Research into reader views clearly suggests promotional themes you can use to improve your newspaper's credibility. They include the following:

- The newspaper is the best possible source of complete, accurate, meaningful news and information. Stress "complete" to contrast with TV's shallow treatment of news, "meaningful" to contrast with its "show biz" tendencies and frothy stories used simply because they look fine in pictures. Stress "accurate" because factual errors in newspapers are a prime cause of loss of reader confidence. Donald Jones, experienced editor for the *Kansas City Star and Times*, says that factual errors "do more to undermine the trust and confidence of readers than any other sin we commit . . . the smallest error of fact (will) cast doubt on the whole story. . . ."[8]

- The paper must fairly and openly judge itself. Some newspapers appoint an "ombudsman" to handle reader complaints and judge, on the public's behalf, the newspaper's fairness and professionalism. Ombudsmen, drawn often from senior editor ranks but sometimes from outside the paper, achieve success directly proportionate to how seriously management views its credibility problem. If you are serious, your ombudsman will have credence and be helpful. If you don't care, neither will the public. A measure of your seriousness: Does your ombudsman have full rein to print sharp criticism of your paper? The

Washington Post's executive editor, Ben Bradlee, gave his space for thousands of prominently displayed words to berate the *Post* for mishandling the child heroin addict who did not exist. Only another editor can understand how each word, in his own paper, took a bite out of Bradlee. Not many newspapers take such self-inflicted punishment. Many play with the ombudsman concept, then quietly retire it. Less than 2 percent of U.S. dailies have ombudsmen.

- Make the newspaper accessible to its public and thereby attack a widely held view that editors and reporters hold themselves apart and are "arrogant." Promote letters to editors and invite guest columnists. Emphasize that no other medium can give readers such opportunities to have their say. If your paper has no ombudsman, switchboard and desk personnel should be schooled in handling telephone complaints or comments responsively. Use focus groups, kaffee-klatsches, and building tours to give readers access to newspaper personnel. Above all, correct errors promptly and fully. Reveal all. There can be no cover-up, no holding back. Take your lumps and then get on with rebuilding reader confidence. If a questioned story is correct, say so—and say why it is. Don't simply publish that lame old, "The *Daily Bugle* stands by its story."

- Promote "good" news content to counter persistent complaints that newspapers print only "bad" news. Ruth Clark finds that 66 percent of respondents feel newspapers pay too much attention to "bad" news, not enough to "good things" (64 percent made that complaint about TV). One reader told Clark: "If there is a drug bust in the high school, it is on the front page. If we raise money for the band to take a trip, it is not in the paper." If that is true for your paper, you have an internal problem with story selection that must be corrected. But most newspapers print plenty of "good" news—

---

[8] *Excerpts*, pamphlet from the Organization of Newspaper Ombudsmen, distributed by now defunct National News Council, March 8, 1983.

awards, scholarships, humor columns. Promote it.

- Explain the newspaper's responsibilities to cover the news, push for facts and, on occasion, seemingly pry into private lives. This is to counter complaints that reporters are insensitive and invade privacy just to "sell newspapers." Don't simply retreat behind what the First Amendment and the law permit reporters to do: explain *why* the newspaper must serve as community watchdog and professional adversary of government. Promote the paper's role as defender of the *public*'s right to know.

- Emphasize the fairness and balance of coverage. Present all sides of controversy. Cover all elements of the community, particularly minorities and the young. Be fair— and promote the fact that you are. Clark: "If there is a gap between newspapers and the public, it is on the fairness issue."

- Promote the newspaper's usefulness as a tool in everyday life. Want to know where to go for entertainment, how to get there, and how much it will cost? Health columns, recipes, TV listings, how to cope? It's all in the paper, so promote it.

- Underline the newspaper's independence from pressure groups, including advertisers. Ruth Clark says that 57 percent of her respondents say advertisers and other business interests often influence news coverage.

- Identify with the community. This does *not* mean unthinking "boosterism." It means promoting the paper as a constructive— and sometimes critical—force for community involvement. It means editorials on local issues, not always Afghanistan. It means translating world and national issues into local terms—and promoting the paper as complete, well-rounded, and watching the world of news for local readers. Group-

owned papers must avoid acting like local franchise outlets for some distant, impersonal corporate giant. Gannett for years promoted the theme, "Gannett, A World of Different Voices Where Freedom Speaks."

Promotional Vehicles to Use

Promotion managers tend to agree basic promotion strategies are applicable among all papers, large and small. Donald B. Towles, vice president and director of public affairs of the *Louisville (Ky.) Courier-Journal* and *Times* (299,000 daily, 322,000 Sunday), says that "newspaper promotion is basic. What will work for a 250,000 circulation daily will work just as well for a 25,000 circulation daily or 2,500 circulation weekly."[9]

That is, whether you are spending $1.7 million to promote the *Denver Post* or promoting a weekly on a low, low budget, you can use essentially the same approach. Some vehicles for spreading the message:

Your own pages. Large or small, a paper can use "house ads" to reach readers and advertisers. However, *non*readers and *non*advertisers, important targets, are not reached. So house ads cannot be the sole vehicle for successful promotion. But they are relatively cheap to fashion and can be run as space becomes available. House ads constitute 2.5 to 3.5 percent of total content in some newspapers. Use your shopper or TMC product to reach nonreaders.

Radio and TV. Some managers feel that using competing media might be endorsing them as advertising tools. However, radio and TV are widely used, and should be. William J. White, *Philadelphia Inquirer* promotion director, says, "Using other media is the only way to reach out

---

[9] Donald B. Towles, "Mailing Promotion Work," speech to National Newspaper Association, Louisville, Sept. 22, 1983.

beyond our own readers."[10] A Southern Newspaper Publishers' Association survey of 56 papers finds 41 advertising on radio, 13 on TV (2 used direct mail).[11] Radio is favored because of its relatively low cost and target marketing capability. Promotion Manager E. Russell Donnelly of the *Worcester (Mass.) Telegram and Evening Gazette* says that a 30-second TV commercial for a New England station costs (in 1983) $20,000 to produce, up to $3,000 to run once—and is viewed by thousands in four states too far away to subscribe to his papers. A 60-second radio commercial costs under $1,000 and can be aired for $15 to $18 each time. And local radio, with programming targeted at different age and income categories, reaches the people his papers want to reach.[12] Radio offers quick promotion of, say, a news exclusive in today's paper. Some papers telephone commercials to radio stations on just minutes notice.

Outdoor advertising.   It is often used for photos of individual columnists or reporters to "humanize" an otherwise anonymous news-gathering staff. But relatively few people see any single billboard, and copy must be limited to those few words motorists can catch while zipping by.

Direct mail.   SNPA found just 2 of 56 survey respondents promoting via direct mail. Large papers trying to reach huge audiences of nonreaders find direct mail prohibitively expensive. However, the *Bryan-College Station (Tex.) Eagle*, with 18,000 evening circulation and a total population of about 75,000 in its home county, spent just $10,000 to reach nonsubscribers by direct mail. The campaign brought in 1,100 new subscriptions and—at $9.09 per order—was termed cost-effective.[13]

Other vehicles.   These include magazines, cable TV, rack cards (printed promotion placed on coin boxes), or posters on circulation trucks. Many papers use other newspapers, particularly in New York City, to reach East Coast ad agencies and major advertisers. The *Wall Street Journal* is used by papers trying to reach advertisers likely to read the *Journal.*

In sum, building a newspaper's institutional credibility is extremely important. But the true goal of effective promotion is increasing readership and ad revenue. And that requires hard-hitting promotion aimed at specific circulation and advertising audiences.

PROMOTING CIRCULATION GROWTH

It was a promotion manager's dream—a photograph of smiling Al Neuharth, chairman of Gannett Co., Inc., holding up a copy of his new baby, *USA Today.* At his side, also smiling, were, no less, President Ronald Reagan, Senate Majority Leader Howard Baker; and House Speaker Tip O'Neill.

Neuharth, thus having boldly obtained virtual endorsement by the nation's then top three political leaders, was launching *USA Today* in its first "market rollout" in Washington on Sept. 15, 1982. Published prominently in leading newspapers and trade journals, the photograph set the tone for the costliest, most aggressive circulation promotion campaign ever conducted by a U.S. newspaper.

By May 1983, just eight months after Neuharth and friends were photographed, a survey for *Advertising Age* magazine found that 51 percent of the U.S. population had heard of *USA Today* and 46 percent had read it at least once. The paper at that time was available in just fifteen major markets.[14] By 1986, *USA Today*

---

[10] Elise Burroughs, "Airwaves, Billboards and TV Tout Newspapers," *presstime,* October 1983, p. 46.
[11] "Radio Is Most Popular Medium for Advertising Newspapers," *SNPA Bulletin,* April 7, 1983, p. 1.
[12] Burroughs, op. cit.
[13] Ibid.

[14] "*USA Today* Scores Well In AA Survey," *Advertising Age,* July 1983, p. 46. For details, contact SRI Research Center, 301 South 68th St., Lincoln, Neb., 68506.

had over 1.3 million circulation, was the nation's third-largest daily, and claimed 4,792,000 readers.

Gannett doesn't say how much it spends promoting *USA Today*, but Joe Welty, vice president for advertising, gave a clue: Gannett was spending in 1983 $1 million *per market* to introduce *USA Today*. Of course, Welty explained, spending would increase significantly when circulation was extended to Chicago and New York.[15] And that was just the first stage, when circulation was being emphasized. With advertising lagging (and *USA Today* losing a great deal of money), a second expensive promotional push was aimed at advertisers.

A Circulation Promotion Checklist

Whatever your circulation promotion budget, take lessons from *USA Today*'s campaign:

- A high degree of visibility must be achieved. *USA Today*'s name, its distinctively colored nameplate, and its futuristic coin boxes are everywhere. The nameplate is on coffee cups, cereal boxes, matchbooks, T-shirts, TV, radio, and other newspapers and magazines. It is difficult for literate, aware people in any primary market selected for circulation expansion not to know of *USA Today*.

- Great promotional intensity must be reached quickly and then maintained. The shock value of *USA Today*'s campaign is unmistakable. The message quickly inundates target audiences; it isn't dribbled out.

- The newspaper must be readily available for purchase. Intensive promotion of a newspaper that readers cannot find to buy is a waste of money. *USA Today* blossoms overnight at thousands of sales points when new markets are opened. Aside from coin

[15] "*USA Today* Hikes Ads," *Advertising Age*, Feb. 21, 1983, p. 16.

boxes, Gannett pushes single-copy sale at newsstands, hotels, airports and other places.

- Circulation promotion must relate directly to the paper's overall strategy. Gannett proposes *USA Today* as a unique national newspaper for traveling upper-income executives and other demographically appealing audiences. Promotion speaks directly of the paper's usefulness to that type person.

- Promotion must tie to the paper's distinctive appearance, characteristics, or features. Gannett's promotion touts *USA Today* as a different kind of paper, bright, fast-paced, with it. Gannett does *not* promote *USA Today* as a me-too version of the *Wall Street Journal*, the *New York Times*, or any other publication.

- Promotion must avoid exaggeration. *USA Today*'s circulation growth, fastest ever in the industry, is carefully documented each step along the way. An Audit Bureau of Circulations imprimatur certifies Gannett's claims. The new *Washington (D.C.) Times*, by contrast, claims that it is "a newspaper second to none," when in fact any knowledgeable observer can see that it is a distant tenth to the *Washington Post*. The *Times* claims "unquestionable excellence," a claim that is patently open to question. Ads boasting a "talented, award-winning staff of experienced journalists" carry photos of staffers who appear to be in their teens.

- Avoid the trite, the routine approach. Try for the unusual, catchy theme or idea.

Promote Fulfillment of Reader Needs

Successful circulation promotion stresses that readers can fulfill important needs by reading the paper. The best copy does so in direct, explicit terms. Examples:

- The *Wall Street Journal* sells itself as a tool for business success, a newspaper that will "save you from missing something that could help your career a lot."

- The *Milwaukee Journal* prides itself in its comprehensive international, national, state, and local news, advertising: "The *Milwaukee Journal.* Get the Whole Story." The less successful *Milwaukee Sentinel* makes a virtue of its smaller size by promoting itself as "tightly edited" and more manageable for the busy reader.

- *Newsday* promotes, among other things, its exclusive ability to reproduce photos and ads in four colors: "There's a More Colorful New York in New York *Newsday.*"

- The *Las Vegas (Nev.) Review-Journal*, 76,000 evening circulation, sells itself as offering "more"—"986 pages more than our nearest competitor during three weeks alone . . ."

- The *New York Times* even promotes the difficulty of its crossword puzzle: "If you thought today's crossword puzzle was challenging, see what the *Times* has in store for you tomorrow!"

There are hundreds of successful circulation promotion themes—convenience, low price, the prestige of being informed, the need to be informed . . . the list is endless. However, the core of circulation promotion must be the newspaper's news and information. A newspaper cannot match TV's sound-and-sight appeal, it cannot be more entertaining. But it *can* be more informative, more newsy by far, and that basic, unmatched strength must be emphasized in promotion.

Attack Problem Areas Directly

National polls or even a small paper's own low-budget research can uncover reader doubts, suspicions, and complaints. Your promotion should attack them directly.

The jointly owned *Dayton (Ohio) Journal Herald*, 102,000 morning circulation, and *Daily News*, 119,000 afternoon, attack feelings that they are distant from readers, perhaps arrogant or out of touch:

- Dayton residents are invited in for "Coffee with the Editor." Staff members speak to groups and answer questions.

- Telephone calls to a special number are taped and published in "Speak Up Dayton," a regular feature letting citizens speak their minds.

- To personalize the staff, full-page ads feature photos of staffers and list city area or suburb where they live—all under the headline, "Your Neighbors Cover the News." Says promotion Director Ken Walters: "The ad showed that the 'downtown paper' was really staffed with people who live throughout the Miami Valley—they are neighbors."[16]

Richard G. Capen, chairman and publisher of the *Miami Herald*, says newspapers "have problems with alienation from their readers and the public at large," so his paper takes steps to stay close to readers. The *Herald*:

- Holds monthly "Meet the Press" meetings of readers to help them "understand some of the things we do and create a substantially improved awareness on the part of our editors and reporters as to the sensitivities of our coverage and the problems we cause when errors are made."

- Holds regular breakfasts and lunches with community leaders and opinion makers, asking "top business people, cultural and civic leaders, top black, Hispanics, women and related segments of our community to

---

[16] "Editorial Staffers Introduced as Neighbors," *INPA Idea Newsletter*, Reston, Va., International Newspaper Promotion Association, April 1984.

discuss current problems and ways in which our newspaper can meet the needs of our readers."

- Carries an expanded "Reader's Forum" to publish reader letters.

- Offers space for guest editorials and feature articles on many issues.

- Runs a "Speakout" series in which readers challenge *Herald* editorials and op-ed articles.

Many papers—among them the *Pittsburgh Post-Gazette* and *Milwaukee Journal*—publish detailed stories about their newspaper operations, picturing staffers at work and identifying them by name, title, and function. The *Journal's* articles say, "This is another in a series of Sunday pages intended to help you become better acquainted with the *Milwaukee Journal*."

The *Clearwater (Fla.) Sun*, a 40,000-circulation morning paper, has a comprehensive "Outreach Program" that includes an ombudsman, monthly reader surveys on appearance and content, editor hotlines, focus groups, and appearances before local groups by senior editors.

When he was an editor, Publisher David Lawrence of the *Detroit Free Press* frequently wrote to his own letters-to-the-editor column in response to reader complaints. "People are scared of us," Lawrence says, "and think we have all the power and have to have the last word. Readers want to know we're human, imperfect and not very different from them."[17]

At times, circulation promotion must anticipate reader complaints. For example, like all newspapers, the *New York Times* expects complaints, even lost circulation, following a price increase. In anticipation of this, the *Times* published a news story in its own pages on why on March 1, 1982, its price would rise to 30 cents in the city:

Donald A. Nizen, the newspaper's senior vice president for consumer marketing, said the price increase was dictated by a "steady escalation of costs in all areas of producing the paper." As one example, he said, "the cost for just the newsprint and ink alone for a 96-page paper will be 26 cents a copy on March 1, when the price of newsprint will increase to $525 per metric ton."[18]

Deanne Termini, senior vice president of the research firm Belden Associates, lists reasons frequently given in polls for not reading newspapers.[19] The list as given below is adapted to suggest themes for countering complaints:

No time to read. Promotion could emphasize compartmentalization and indexing to aid the reader; the newspaper is presented as a menu from which reader quickly selects desired items.

Too expensive. Compare relatively low price— 35 cent paper with 50-cent restaurant cup of coffee; always mention in any story about a price increase how long it has been since the last increase; also mention rising costs and newsprint prices. Stress the paper's shopper coupons, sometimes worth hundreds of dollars in a single issue. The *Athens (Ga.) Banner-Herald* publishes house ads totaling coupon values in the previous week's issues, adding "it's like having money delivered to your door."

Poor delivery service. Aside from bearing down on the circulation department, establish a customer-service unit and promote use of trucks to get copies to complaining subscribers who missed theirs; always follow up with a telephone call the next day.

Prefer TV/radio news content. First, ensure that local news is covered, then promote its

[17] First Quarter Report, Miami, Fla., Knight-Ridder, Inc., 1984, p. 11.

[18] "Times' Weekday Price to Rise in City Region," *New York Times*, Feb. 22, 1984, p. B3.
[19] "Why Is The Press Disliked?" *SNPA Special Bulletin*, Atlanta, Southern Newspaper Publishers Association, April 1–3, 1984, p. 9.

exclusivity and depth. *No* other medium records births, marriages, deaths, and other local news as does the newspaper.

Dislike of content. Too much bad news, bias. Ensure that bias does not exist, then promote "good news" content, highlighting it in the paper itself and in promotional themes. Have a local humor columnist? Put his photo on billboards advertising his cheery message. Content for everyone is in the paper; promote it.

Dislike of editorial policy. Promote the difference between news columns and the editorial page; the author would never carry an editorial on news pages, particularly the first page, and only rarely a "news analysis" anywhere but on the editorial or op-ed page. Many readers do not distinguish between straight news and editorial pages. Promotion should highlight that an *editorial* point of view does not mean *news* stories are slanted.

In sum, promotional preemptive strikes should be launched against known reader doubts even if they have not yet manifested themselves in written complaints—or declining circulation. Find out what problems exist, fix them, then explain with frank, detailed promotion.

The Importance of Carrier Promotion

Much of your promotion must be directed toward recruiting and motivating carriers and acquainting the public with their importance.

House ads detailing potential earnings can help attract carriers. Gannett's *Wilmington (Del.) News*, 50,000 morning circulation, and *Evening Journal*, 85,000, publish photos of carriers along with job application forms. Many papers direct carrier recruitment promotion at parents, pointing out the value of instilling the work ethic in their teenagers.

The *Lynchburg (Va.) News*, 20,000 morning circulation, and *Daily Advance*, 21,000 evening, strike a community-service theme and promote carriers' efforts to raise money for United Way. "We do more than just deliver newspapers," the ads say.

Promotional material for use by carriers in door-to-door selling is extremely important. Not many thirteen-year-olds are accomplished salespeople. The *Bakersfield (Calif.) Californian*, 80,000 morning circulation, provides its carriers with selling hints written and illustrated like comic books. One shows how to explain a price increase to subscribers.

Many helpful hints in carrier promotion and other areas of newspaper image building are available through the International Newspaper Promotion Association, The Newspaper Center, 11600 Sunrise Valley Drive, Reston, VA 22091.

The Contest Controversy

One controversy in circulation promotion is over the value of sweepstakes, cash giveaways, and other contests variously called Bingo, Zingo, or other racy names.

Rupert Murdoch's papers, including the *Boston Herald* and *New York Post*, heavily promote cash contests and attribute much of their sometimes astounding circulation growth to giveaways. The Tribune Co.'s New York *Daily News* and *Chicago Tribune* also use cash contests to ignite reader interest. In New York City in 1983, the *Post* and *Daily News* took their bitter contest for circulation into the contest arena, offering a total of $225,000 in *weekly* prizes. Games involved lucky numbers printed daily by each newspaper. (The *Post* promptly tricked *News* Publisher James Hoge into being photographed holding a *Post* Wingo promotional card; the photos were duly published in the *Post*.)

Atlanta Journal and Constitution executives found to their surprise that 24 percent of Atlanta's adults participated in their Zingo contest. The players' demographics matched those of *Journal and Constitution* readers, although players were slightly older.[20]

---

[20] Minor J. Ward, then president, Atlanta Newspapers, conversation with author, Feb. 10, 1984.

Cash contests attract primarily nonreaders with only temporary interest in the paper and bring little permanent increase in circulation. However, contests at least entice nonreaders into trying the paper, and hard-hitting promotional follow-up can help hold some cash-oriented players.

Ask for the Order

The entire point of circulation promotion is to hold current readers and sell the paper to nonreaders. Surprisingly, many promotion efforts don't directly appeal to either group. Promotional ads should carry telephone numbers or addresses where subscriptions can be ordered. Include coupons that can be clipped and sent in. Don't avoid the point of it all: *ask for a subscription order.*

PROMOTING ADVERTISING GROWTH

Turning from circulation to advertising promotion, you must shift gears. A completely different audience must be wooed with different themes.

The targeted audiences are advertisers or their surrogates, the ad agencies. Both are sophisticated in advertising strategy and market research; they are, without question, discerning in where, when, and how to spend their advertising budgets. You must make sure that promotional messages aimed at these audiences are tightly researched, factual, and of high quality.

Advertising promotion revolves around the number of your readers, where and how they live—their demographic appeal—and your newspaper's ability to elicit from them shopper/buyer response to the advertisers' message. Thus, the fundamental theme of advertising promotion is that the newspaper is a useful, profitable tool for advertisers in improving their own business fortunes.

Sometimes, however, promotion must start with a much more basic theme—that a market indeed exists.

First Delineate the Market

Drive through Chicago's suburbs all you want. Ask at every gas station. You'll not find "Herald City." But it's there. The *Arlington Heights (Ill.) Daily Herald* says so.

The *Daily Herald* mapped out a market of sixteen communities in Chicago's northwest suburbs, called it Herald City, and tells advertisers that only the *Daily Herald* can "deliver" affluent suburbanites who live there. It's possible to argue that Herald City is in fact sixteen distinctly separate communities, that they lack commonality to constitute a single market, and that the *Daily Herald* isn't exclusive in delivering them. Other newspapers, including the Chicago metros, so argue. But despite vigorous attack from competitors, the *Daily Herald* has had enormous success in creating, through promotion, the concept that this market exists, that is it demographically attractive, and that the *Daily Herald* and its free-circulation sister, *This Week*, deliver it.

How successful? Between 1969 and 1986, the *Daily Herald* expanded from a twice-weekly with a limited marketing view to a seven-day morning paper with paid circulation over 62,000 daily and once-weekly TMC of 280,000 nonsubscriber households. The operation is the star performer of Paddock Publications, one of the nation's strongest suburban newspaper operations. *Daily Herald* Editor Dan Baumann says of the $200,000 Herald City promotion campaign: "The theme was to build the idea that this is a market that can be defined and separate from the amorphous [city plus suburban] mass.[21]

Times Mirror Corp., has similar promotion under way in Connecticut towns north of New York City, attempting to instill in advertisers' minds the idea of a suburban regional market served by the company's *Stamford (Conn.) Advocate* and *Greenwich (Conn.) Time*. This has been Times Mirror's strategy since acquiring

---

[21] Joanne Cleaver, "Making Herald City Come Alive," *Advertising Age*, Jan. 30, 1984, p. M-21.

both papers in 1978. Neither the *Advocate*, with 30,000 evening circulation, nor *Time*, with 16,000 evening circulation, fits the profile of a typical Times Mirror paper. The group is known for large-circulation metro operations—The *Los Angeles Times*, *New York Newsday*. But in those Connecticut suburbs there awaits rich opportunity for expansion. Stamford's home county, Fairfield, has well over $4.6 billion in retail sales. The *Advocate*'s news desk is now busily turning out regional stories that tend to knit together communities throughout the area; its promotion department is delineating the area as a single market that the *Advocate* alone serves well.

Sometimes smooth promotion won't create a market. For example, Gannett sees a rich *demographic* market available in affluent, much-traveled business executives, and heavily promotes the concept that *USA Today* can reach them anywhere in the United States. But advertisers are slow to accept the claim and their support of *USA Today* lags behind the readers' by a wide margin.

Promoting the Market's Attractiveness

With the market delineated geographically or demographically, your promotion must convince advertisers of its attractiveness. Because most newspaper ad revenue is local/retail, your first task is to promote effectively on Main Street.

Promote population size and attractiveness in the market, households, personal and household income, retail sales, and other indicators of wealth and willingness to spend it. For smaller papers, promotion materials can be a simple collation of vital statistics in a low-cost pamphlet; for larger papers, expensive advertising in a full range of media. (See box for an example of a market fact book.)

Promotion that you design to highlight a

THE MARKET BOOK

Call it a "market book" or "fact sheet," your newspaper should have a core packet of promotion highlighting for advertisers the market's strengths and how the paper exploits them.

Some papers publish slick, expensive market books for ad agencies, ad reps, and advertisers. Smaller papers can make do with inexpensive fact sheets. Whatever your budget, include key information:

- Market description, including retail sales, households, population, and an explanation of the geography. Maps showing zip code areas covered by TMC or zoned editions are helpful. Ages of the population, educational levels, incomes, buying habits—all are essential.
- Competitive situationer, including how your paper and principal competitors reach the market. This should be expressed in total and zip code area penetration plus circulation by demographic groups, such as women

between eighteen and thirty-five or $50,000-plus income categories.
- Readership profiles giving a clear picture of who reads the paper—expressed in age, education, income, occupation, whether they own their own home or rent, and so on.
- Newspaper growth records are helpful when they show expanding circulation and increasing ad lineage.
- Shopping mall and store studies showing who shops and where—all related, of course, to newspaper circulation and reading habits.
- Statement of source and methodology for any research or survey material. Undocumented claims are unacceptable to sophisticated advertisers.
- Background on newspaper and key personnel can personalize both the institution and its staff.
- And, of course, rate cards and contracts.

market's value must tie closely to your newspaper's overall strategy. For example, the *New York Times* doesn't pretend to be a mass-consumption newspaper—indeed, it studiously avoids being so considered. So, the *Times*'s promotion stresses the high incomes and educational levels of its carriage-trade audience. The *Times* promotes its national market as a relatively narrow but highly attractive *demographic* slice—just 1 percent of the U.S. population that is most affluent. More frequently, however, your newspaper promotion will stress the attractiveness of a *geographic* market and the quality of its readership. Your promotion must present truly important information in a form easily understood by busy, preoccupied advertisers and their agencies.

Promotion material must then be placed in the proper hand—preferably by a salesperson directly or via direct mail or, often, ads in the periodicals likely to be read by advertisers. Precision tailoring and delivery is a key link in the promotion chain.

Prove You Deliver the Market

The third step, after delineating the market and demonstrating its attractiveness, is to prove that your newspaper reaches the advertisers' potential buyers in the market.

Key elements are your newspaper's household penetration in a geographic market, such as city zone or retail trading zone, or its readership in demographic markets such as the *Wall Street Journal*'s nationwide business audience.

At this point, your promotion must *position* the newspaper competitively in its market. Some small-town publishers position their paper as "The only newspaper in the world that gives a damn about our town." That's not a bad statement of confidence, saying that any advertiser wanting to reach "our town" must do it through our pages. In one way or another, often at enormous cost, many papers position themselves through promotion as the number-one medium in delivering the market. One frankly positions

itself as number two—but it also claims that it's necessary for any advertiser who wants to reach its market. The *Los Angeles Herald Examiner*, casting about for some way to compete against the dominant *Los Angeles Times*, doesn't deny that it is number two. Its theme is that by *adding* the *Herald Examiner* to an ad schedule dominated by the *Times*, an advertiser can reach more households.

Opinions differ on whether promotional positioning should mention competitors by name. Some promotion managers argue naming competitors graces them with advertiser awareness they otherwise would not achieve. The *Herald Examiner* approaches that problem by somewhat disingenuously referring to the *Times* as the "Big Pickle":

> Making a newspaper (advertising) buy in Los Angeles County is about as much fun as bobbing for pickles, blindfolded. It's really easy to find the Big Pickle. But it only gives you one of every four households, so you have to tack on a bunch of baby dills to bring up your penetration. . . .[22]

USA Today doesn't mince around. It positions itself against *Time, Newsweek, Sports Illustrated*, and *U.S. News and World Report*—and names them in promotion designed to prove that *USA Today*'s audience is more attractive demographically than theirs.

Prove You Create Response

Demonstrating that your newspaper *reaches* an audience doesn't convince many advertisers today. This brings you to the fourth step in advertising promotion: proving that your newspaper can *pull response*, that an ad will draw customers into a store and move merchandise.

Nothing succeeds like a trial run of ads (always strive for more than one) to demonstrate response. But if the advertiser is unwilling to experiment, there are always testimonials and

---

[22] "I'll Get You Out of L.A.'s Penetration Pickle in A 2nd," advertisement in *Advertising Age*, March 28, 1983, p. 36.

the judgment of peers. A list of your advertisers, showing how long they have been customers and how much space they buy, can convince holdouts their peers see the newspaper as effective and that they must jump aboard. *USA Today* floods advertiser prospects with lists of companies, arranged alphabetically and by type of business, that use the newspaper. Testimonials from advertisers should describe the response from customers who see their ads in the paper. *USA Today* creates testimonials on number of customers as well as telephone calls or orders resulting from ads in the paper. ("*USA Today* is an action medium," promotion reads, "bold, inviting and uncluttered. If you send in the coupon, we'll send you actual case studies that'll knock your socks off!")

To prove reader interest, promote time spent by the average reader with each issue and the number of consecutive issues read. A newspaper skimmed for just a few minutes once every week or so by the occasional reader is not attractive to advertisers. *USA Today* uses one poll showing forty-one minutes average reading time by respondents and that they read, on average, 3.7 of the past five issues.

Don't Overlook National

You must create effective promotional material to boost national ad sales, providing it either directly to major advertisers and ad agencies or through your newspaper's own national ad rep. But be aware that promoting national is particularly difficult.

National advertisers and agencies generally have headquarters in distant cities. Their decision-making executives are often preoccupied with the quick, single buy of TV or magazine advertising. Most lack personal contact with your newspaper or awareness of what it is doing to capture your market.

To counter this, Lou Hagopian, chairman of the N. W. Ayer ad agency in New York City, says promotion aimed at national advertisers should:

- Stress circulation totals, particularly any saturation coverage available through TMC vehicles, but avoid total preoccupation with circulation numbers.

- Show demographic quality of your circulation, not just totals. Advertisers seek special-interest blocs of readers, so promotion must describe the diverse groups comprising your total circulation and how your newspaper reaches each. For example, demonstrate that your business section reaches highly affluent readers seeking personal investments information (of interest to bank or broker advertisers). Show you attract sports readers (of interest to liquor and tobacco advertisers).

- Simplify the national agency's job in buying newspaper ad space. Include standardized rate cards and promote the use of Standard Advertising Units and Newsplan. These devices to remove mechanical barriers to newspaper advertising are discussed in Chapter 9.

- Speak to your own strengths and don't attack competing newspapers. Some newspapers, he says, are "forever cutting down their competitors and, thus, themselves." A newspaper's strengths, he says, are couponing ("unbeatable"), TV support advertising, new-product introductions, local retail, and ads for tobacco, liquor, financial, and food products.

- Get copies of your newspaper into the hands of national advertisers and agencies, along with personal information on the men and women who produce it. Personalize the image.[23]

---

[23] Lou Hagopian, speech to International Newspaper Advertising and Marketing Executives, July 20, 1982. Also see "How to Make Newspapers Number 1 on Madison Avenue," *Editor & Publisher*, July 28, 1982, p. 14.

Promote Classified Advertising

Your first step in promoting classified advertising may be convincing key executives of your own newspaper that money should be spent for it. Inform unbelievers that classified, after all, is the second-largest source of ad revenue (after local retail) and is growing rapidly. All this is true. Yet, many newspapers, particularly smaller ones, neglect to promote classified effectively.

Here are some successful themes for the advertising public:

- It's simple to use classified. Just telephone us and we'll handle everything; we'll bill you, or you can drop off a check.

- It's cheap to use classified. A few dollars will sell your used car or get rid of those surplus kittens.

- Classified ads draw a fast, meaningful response. Testimonial promotion stressing number of responses to a single ad or quick sale of an item can be very effective.

Target two basic audiences for classified promotion:

- High-volume or "contract" advertisers, such as real estate firms, employers, and car dealers (largest three users of classified).

- Occasional or "transient" or "voluntary" user of classified.

Obviously, different approaches must be used to reach prospects who range from real estate firms that spend thousands of dollars annually in classified to the householder who wants to advertise, for $4.50, the once-in-a-lifetime garage sale. Streetwise, aggressive salespeople are the primary force for selling classified to high-volume advertisers, and they must have leave-behind or "drop" material, including rate cards and contract forms that are easy to understand and use. Promote classified's attractive rates for those prospects who find retail display rates prohibitively high but who, if convinced to use classified, can be attractive revenue contributors.

House ads in your own pages are the most widely used form of classified promotion. Your paper's existing readership, shown by research to frequently browse classified pages, is the largest, most attractive, and most easily reached audience available. Promotion campaigns built around house ads should have continuity and frequency—a front-page teaser, for example, alerting readers to an amusing or particularly interesting ad. Radio, outdoor advertising, direct mail—all are used, but generally less than for promoting local/retail or national advertising.

Persistent, imaginative promotion, in sum, can build classified success. "I got my job through the *New York Times*" is a promotional theme that made the *Times*'s classified employment section famous—and added millions of dollars to the *Times*'s coffers.

SUMMARY

Polls show that the newspaper industry is perceived by the public as guilty of bias in handling news or, by some readers, of intentional fabrication. When expressing confidence in American institutions, the public ranks the newspaper industry substantially below organized religion, the military, banks, the U.S. Supreme Court, and public schools (but ahead of Congress, big business, organized labor, and TV). The public has less confidence in the men and women who collectively make up "the press" than in the individual newspapers they read daily or weekly.

The industry obviously has an image problem as it strives for the credibility newspapers must have to discharge First Amendment responsibilities and achieve commercial success in advertising and circulation.

Each individual newspaper must bolster its own image through professional, imaginative promotional campaigns. Research—listening to readers and nonreaders—is the foundation of all promotion. Promotion cannot gloss over journalistic or product weakness; there must be substantive improvement in product quality, which promotion then highlights and exploits.

However large or small the promotion budget, one goal must be making the newspaper warmer, friendlier—personalizing it and its staff. These themes are important: the newspaper provides complete and reliable news and information; the paper is accessible to its public, responsive to its needs; "good news" is available along with the bad; the paper has a duty to probe and push for news and doesn't needlessly invade personal privacy; it is fair and balanced in coverage.

In promoting circulation growth, the paper should quickly achieve a high degree of visibility; it must be talked about. Promotion should stress benefits to readers that come with subscribing. It should avoid exaggeration. And without fail, promotion should ask for the order; it should urge purchase of the paper.

Advertising promotion is directed at a different audience, the advertiser or ad agency. Most are sophisticated in advertising, and promotion must be first-rate in terms of pertinence and quality. Promotion should delineate the market, describe its attractiveness, prove that the paper delivers it, and prove it pulls response from advertisers' prospective customers.

RECOMMENDED READING

International Newspaper Promotion Association, The Newspaper Center, Box 17422, Dulles International Airport, Washington, DC 20041, provides research and assistance in promotion and marketing programs for newspapers. Suburban Newspapers of America, 111 E. Wacker Drive, Chicago, IL 60601, issues do-it-yourself kits for reader surveys used in suburban newspaper markets. ANPA's *presstime* and *Editor & Publisher* regularly cover promotion subjects. Note also Charles Patti and John Murphy, "Cases in Advertising and Promotion Management," New York, Wiley, 1983; and William R. Shover, ed., "Promoting The Total Newspaper," INPA, 1973.

CHAPTER ELEVEN

Production and the New Technology

For three very good reasons, we turn now to "Production and the New Technology." First, the industry manufactures 63 million copies of daily newspapers each day; each week, 47.5 million copies of weeklies. Even if your career focuses on news, advertising, or another sector, you will inevitably be involved in production and technology. Second, production and new technology have turned newspapering into a capital-intensive business, and its sheer expense will be a pivotal consideration for you as a manager, whatever your department or level of responsibility. Third, fulfilling careers are available within production and managers who started there are moving into significant general-executive positions with top companies. Who knows? This might be where *your* march to the top starts.

Entire books could be written about production; indeed each technological breakthrough—electronic editing, offset printing, pagination—alone warrants highly detailed treatment that unfortunately is beyond the scope of this book. So we'll concentrate on current research and development in offset and other printing techniques, capturing keystrokes in electronic writing and editing, then pagination or electronic layout of pages. Production strategy for the 1990s involves exploiting cost reductions and product improvements promised by those developments. You should be familiar with them, regardless of your career interest. Note the glossary of production and technical terms at the end of this chapter. It will brief you on the special language spoken by production experts.

THE IMPLICATIONS OF NEW METHODS

New technology, the space-age way of doing things, is transforming newspaper production. Enormous technical genius and huge sums of money are being invested. Every sector of newspaper management, not just the "manufacturing" process, is being given better, more cost-efficient methods of meeting reader and advertiser needs. For example:

- In Chicago, a $185 million production center gives the once-gray *Tribune* state-of-art color printing and unprecedented distribution flexibility. This huge metro of panoramic sweep now produces sophisticated zoned editions and, in part, has become a group of community newspapers. The *Trib*'s newsroom edits news products for neighborhood readers; advertising offers zoned, lower-circulation editions to small accounts and, thus, lower rates that are competitive with those of even small suburban media; the circulation department gets better-looking papers produced earlier and onto trucks faster. The competing *Chicago Sun-Times* is severely outclassed.

- In Baltimore, the *Sun* churns out 75,000 copies per hour in a $50 million production facility built around four giant nine-unit Metroliner presses. New technology permits the *Sun* to jump a generation of production development and assume new competitive strength. It vanquished the *Baltimore News American*, folded in 1986, and now competes head-on with smaller dailies and weeklies throughout Maryland. New technology at this one newspaper has changed competitive patterns throughout an entire state.

- At the *Wall Street Journal*, *USA Today*, and the *New York Times*, satellite communications permit the development of true national newspapers for the first time in American journalism. The *Journal* uses seventeen plants throughout the country to print about 2 million copies before breakfast, Monday through Friday. For *USA Today*, a computer-driven system bounces signals off the WESTAR III satellite, 22,300 miles above earth, and down to sites that print the best newspaper color ever seen. The *New York Times* uses eight printing plants as it strides toward 1 million copies daily.

- Back on earth, at papers such as the 20,000-circulation *Concord (N.H.) Monitor*, new technology includes portable 4-pound personal computers that reporters use to write stories that are then filed by telephone into electronic copy-processing systems at the home office. It is fast and relatively cheap—no rushing back to the office to write, just a quick "dump" by telephone from motel or clubhouse.

For weeklies, a new world has opened. Robert Tribble, owner of Georgia's Manchester Tri-County Newspapers, Inc., is a publisher of small town weeklies who can recall the Linotypes, hot-metal composition, and sheet-fed flatbed presses of an earlier day. When he entered weekly newspaper work in 1960, he says:

> . . . the publisher, editor, ad salesman and many times bookkeeper had to spend long hours in the back shop around the hot metal. What you really had in those days was not a newspaper editor but a printer. His time had to be spent in production rather than newswriting and sales. I know of several old-time editors and publishers who never wrote a story or called on an advertiser. The stories and advertisements that ran in each edition of the weekly press "walked" in the front door. Editors and publishers were too busy in hot metal composition and job printing to bother with too many news stories or ads.[1]

---

[1] Robert Tribble, letter to author, Sept. 10, 1983.

Sophisticated manufacturing equipment such as these continuous-feed presses are one way in which newspapers use up-to-date technology.
(John Blaustein/Woodfin Camp & Associates)

WHERE THE MONEY GOES

Capital improvements by American newspapers feature heavy spending in pressrooms and for plant modernization.

The American Newspaper Publishers' Association estimates that the 456 dailies surveyed spent over $1 billion in 1986. Here (in millions) is where:

Pressroom	$272.8
Plant expansion/modernization	356.1
Computer/front-end systems (VDTs, etc.)	111.8
Computer/business and accounting	33.3
Mailroom	88.2

Proving that the industry is in the transportation business (as well as in journalism, advertising, manufacturing) is the fact that newspapers spent an estimated $33.5 million for autos and trucks.

Industrywide, capital expenditures in production technology exceed $1 billion annually—double 1977 levels, according to the U.S. Department of Commerce and ANPA. Most of this money goes for pressrooms, plant expansion, and computers. See box for a breakdown.[2]

All this is developing in an industry that is still celebrating itinerant printers who, legend has it, could move into town with a "shirttail of type" and go into the newspaper business! Today's senior managers, as young men and women, entered an industry chained to slow, clanking Linotypes; in just the span of their careers, it has become an electronically complex, capital-intensive industry. They install high-speed offset presses and cold-type processes that consign Linotypes to junkyards. They buy electronic editing systems and hire reporters who never worked on typewriters, only on video display terminals (VDTs) or personal computers (PCs.) The hum of computers hangs over the newspaper landscape.

Implications for aspiring managers are many: new technology raises the newspaper's fundamental cost base, yet it also promises better cost control. It shifts production work to departments, particularly news, that were never before involved in manufacturing, yet it also permits dramatic improvements in journalistic quality. For advertising and circulation, it opens entirely new marketing opportunities. Let's look at how all this can be organized.

DESIGNING THE PRODUCTION ORGANIZATION

If you were designing a production organization not too many years ago, you would walk quickly through the news and advertising departments to the "back shop," where it all happened. Not anymore. Today, you start by studying the entire newspaper for efficient, profitable ways to use new technology in a production chain running from the front door through all departments to loading docks out back, where trucks pick up bundles and speed off. The target is a unified system tying together the computer and data processing needs of all departments and thus achieving maximum efficiency and compatibility of equipment plus lower initial cost and economical operation.

Computerized writing and editing have transformed newsroom operations. VDTs and PCs "capture" reporter and editor keystrokes to drive high-speed electronic typesetters—eliminating the slow, costly Linotype operators once so crucial in production. Many production functions such as typesetting now fall to the newsroom. The wire desk, which once received news agency copy via land lines, at sixty-six words per minute, or by mail, now catches it with a satellite receiver on the newspaper's roof. Copy pours into newsroom computers at over a thousand words per minute. Newsroom "morgues," those dusty libraries filled with ragged envelopes of decaying clips, are computerized by a few papers for instantaneous recall on VDTs.

In advertising, classified clerks take copy customers dictate by telephone, write ads on VDTs, proofread, check credit references, submit copy to typesetting, and issue bills—all in minutes. Circulation uses mobile radios to maintain contact between home office and district managers; computers handle subscribers and nonsubscriber address lists. Business office inventory, accounts receivable, financial data of all kinds—the details on which enlightened managers move—are "massaged" by sophisticated electronic equipment and made available to decision makers when they need them.

In sum, efficient design of the production organization must integrate the missions, needs, and resources of many departments, not just the back shop. Maximize your exploitation of three major technological breakthroughs: computerized capturing of keystrokes, offset printing and cold-type processes, and pagination. Let's look at each in turn.

---

[2] "Newspapers' Capital Spending Exceeds $800 Million," *presstime*, July 1983, p. 57.

Design to Capture Keystrokes

Newspapers save millions of dollars because technology permits computer capture of keystrokes made by reporters, editors, and ad copywriters. This must be central to any organizational concept for your production department.

In precomputer days, a reporter typed up stories on a sheet of paper that the copy desk then pencil-edited and passed to Linotype operators, who produced the type used in page makeup. Similarly, all ad copy was "rekeystroked" in laborious and costly typing and retyping.

A cost-reduction breakthrough came in the 1960s with optical character readers—"scanners"—which can read copy prepared on special typewriters and convert it into electronic impulses that drive automatic typesetters. Although some scanners are still in use, they were short-lived as primary typesetting devices. VDT writing and editing became feasible in 1970 and spread rapidly thereafter.

VDTs virtually eliminate expensive rekeystroking. Reporters' keystrokes go into computer storage. The copy desk uses it own VDTs to edit reporters' stories and resubmits them to computer storage. Stories then go into phototypesetters. Using light flashed through negatives, or images formed on cathode ray tubes, phototypesetters spew out columns of type—"cold type"—to be pasted up in page layouts from which offset plates are readied for presses. Phototypesetters create the equivalent of a full-size newspaper page of type in about a minute (faster models are being developed).

"Capturing" the original keystrokes of reporters and editors is the basic, most important cost-reduction offering of the new technology.

Design for Offset's Advantages

A second major technological advance central to your organizational concept is offset printing.

Offset is based on cold-type processes that employ high-intensity light or laser beams to reproduce page layouts on light-sensitive plates. Once mounted on presses, the plates are treated with water and oil-based ink. Ink adheres to images on the plates, which transfer ink to "blankets" or cylinders which, in turn, transfer—"offset"—ink to newsprint running through the presses. In 1986, 82 percent of all U.S. daily papers were printed by offset.

The offset and cold-type process is a major advance from hot-metal printing. In hot metal, Linotypes create type for page layouts that are locked into a "chase" or metal frame. Papiermâché mats are made from the chase and, in turn, 40-pound hot metal stereo plates from the mats. When cool, the heavy plates are locked on presses, inked, and run against newsprint—the raised typeface creating inked images. Offset printing is cheaper, faster, and cleaner than hot metal. A fast Linotype operator can set five or six column lines of hot type per minute; computer-driven typesetting machines in cold type spew out over a thousand per minute.

Facing fewer union roadblocks to new technology and able to reequip at lower total cost, smaller papers switch to offset relatively easily. Metro dailies, however, face union restrictions and enormous replacement costs. The *New York Times* spent $14.1 million in a "buyout" of 147 union-covered composing-room employees displaced by new equipment. The *Chicago Tribune* spent $80 million in 1982 for ninety new Goss Metroliner presses. Most of the 133 displaced old Goss units were sold for scrap.

Relatively inexpensive equipment modifications permit some papers to use older presses for modern printing processes. Modified presses use special plates developed by DiLitho, Letterflex, NAPP, and other companies. Even as late as 1986, these modifications permitted 20.8 percent of U.S. dailies to use letterpress in production. Mostly larger papers, they accounted for 46.6 percent of total daily circulation. (Two percent of dailies use both letterpress and offset.[3])

Under test now by major press manufacturers is "flexographic" printing, around for years but used primarily by book printers. Flexography prints water-borne inks directly on newsprint, without offset's intermediate "blanket." Proponents claim that "flexo" promises higher-quality printing plus cheaper color. Flexographic units are less complicated mechanically than other press units and somewhat cheaper. They waste much less newsprint, are quieter, and cause less "show-through" of ink (thus reducing ink smudges on readers' hands).

Design for Pagination

It was the dream of newspaper managers for years: If only they could eliminate those time-consuming, expensive steps in the production chain between newsroom and press—if only editors and ad layout artists could handle the total appearance and production of the newspaper—it would revolutionize production economics, reducing manpower and lowering costs.

Great technical expertise and huge sums of money were thrown into pursuing the dream. First came cold type and offset, then VDT editing. Next came pagination—electronic makeup of pages. It could eliminate composing and platemaking departments and is a third major technological innovation around which your production organization must be designed.

Pagination works like this: News and ad copy created on VDTs by reporters and advertising personnel go directly into computer storage without additional rekeystroking. This copy then goes to a computer terminal operated by an editor or, if ads are being laid out, an advertising artist. Entire pages are laid out—stories, headlines, photos and artwork, ads, and all—on the VDT. Then, pages go directly to the platemaking process.

In some cases, composing rooms, which account for half of all production costs, will be eliminated. The *Long Beach (Calif.) Press-Telegram* installed pagination in 1985 for about $3 million, including equipment, building remodeling, and separation incentives paid to displaced workers. Composing room staff was reduced to 21 from 56 full-time employees; engraving department personnel fell from 8 to 6. Four positions were added in the newsroom, which took on tasks formerly handled in other departments. Editor Larry Allison says the newsroom got total control of content, design, and layout as well as better color and faster production. A disadvantage for the newsroom is that it must assume additional and very complex equipment and tasks. While this permits the design of smaller production departments, it requires adding staff in newsrooms, which must now take over many tasks that were formerly assigned to production.

Lester Wiltse, production manager of the *Pasadena (Calif.) Star-News*, a 52,000-circulation paper which went to 100 percent pagination of news and classified ads, says:

> In 1973, when we abandoned hot metal, we had 100 composing room employees. In late 1981, when we were still pasting pages, we had 22. Today, after 16 months of [using a pagination system bought in 1982 from Information International for $1.9 million], we have only 9, and the number will drop more . . . with hot metal, we required 7 composing man-hours per page. With [pagination], the figure is down to 0.6.

The *Niagara Falls (N.Y.) Gazette*, a 31,000-circulation Gannett afternoon paper, reduced

---

[3] ANPA's *Special Report* number 83-1, Jan. 31, 1983; letterpress figures from *Special Report* number 83-2, Feb. 7, 1983. Also see "Letterpress to Offset Conversion: A Supplier's Point of View," *Editor & Publisher*, Sept. 4, 1982, p. 34; and "Our Conversion Is Making Headlines," advertisement, *Editor & Publisher*, June 18, 1983, p. 25.

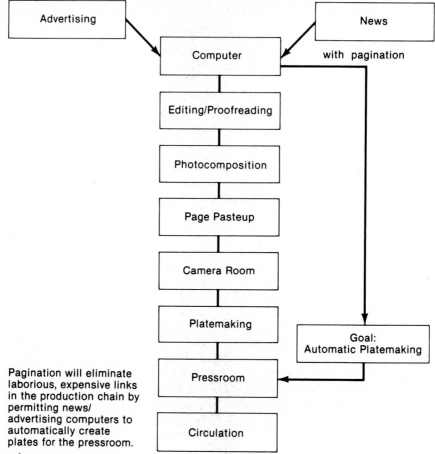

Pagination will eliminate laborious, expensive links in the production chain by permitting news/advertising computers to automatically create plates for the pressroom.

Figure 11.1   The Current System

its eighteen composing room employees to six in eleven months after installing pagination and cut to 1½ from nearly 3 the number of per-page man-hours needed in composition. The system saved 18,000 man-hours per year. Joseph M. Ungaro, president of Gannett's Westchester Rockland, N.Y., Newspapers, an early experimenter in pagination, says the process could save the newspaper industry more than $2 billion annually. Many medium-size newspapers can save $100,000 to $150,000 annually in materials, eliminate fifteen to seventeen jobs, and, he says, achieve sufficient cost reduction to pay off pa-

gination in three years.[4] Figure 11.1 shows how.

The design of the production department can take many forms, and its managers can take different approaches to achieving their objectives. Whatever your style, make sure that the department is structured to exploit the cost-

---

[4] Frank D. Simmons, "Dream System Pressed into Service," from *Telecommunications & Technology*, an Associated Press Managing Editors Continuing Studies Committee Report, San Diego, 1982, p. 3; and "Here's What The *Pasadena Star-News* and TRIPLE-I Learned About Pagination in the Past 16 Months," advertisement, *Editor & Publisher*, June 11, 1983, p. 81.

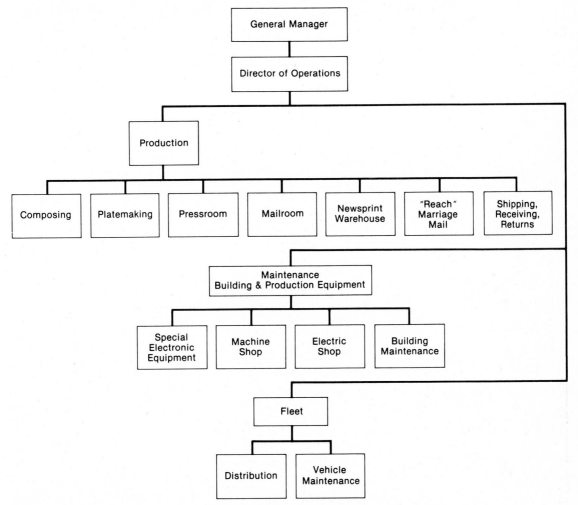

Figure 11.2 *Atlanta (Ga.) Journal* **and** *Constitution* **Operations Department**

Source: Hal Brown, *Atlanta Journal* and *Constitution* director of operations

reduction and product-improvement potentials of capturing keystrokes, offset, and cold-type printing, plus pagination.

Draw a Table of Organization

The *Atlanta Journal and Constitution* designed a production table of organization useful as an illustration (see Figure 11.2) of the complexity, today, of what was once a simple, straight-line hierarchial arrangement. Note how it assigns functions. They are as follows:

- General manager. Newspaper's chief business (as distinct from news) executive; reports directly to the publisher.

- Director of operations. Normally found only on larger papers. Atlanta's director is Hal Brown, an executive with an industrial engineering degree whose primary career

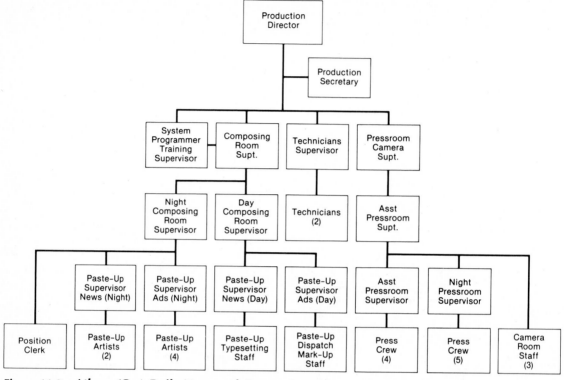

Figure 11.3 *Athens (Ga.) Daily News* and *Banner-Herald*

background before he joined the *Journal and Constitution* was Lockheed Aircraft and shoe manufacturing. He manages 900 employees.

- Production manager. Supervises traditional production subunits (composing, platemaking, pressroom, mailroom) and is responsible for newsprint, shipping/receiving, and returns (newspapers brought back unsold) plus the newspapers' marriage-mail program, "Reach."

- Maintenance manager. Has a new (and very important) function of supervising electronic equipment—computers and VDTs—plus machine shop, electric shop, building.

- Fleet manager. In addition to vehicle maintenance, supervises distribution of papers from loading dock to branch offices or other distribution points.

Small dailies feature much less complicated organizational designs. Note in Figure 11.3 that the *Athens (Ga.) Daily News* and *Banner-Herald* produce 23,000 copies daily in a comparatively simple production organization led by a "production director" who reports directly to the publisher and supervises four subunits. Design your production organization for your needs; don't duplicate somebody else's chart.

As these tables of organization illustrate, the production department requires massive resources—in money and managerial talent, particularly. At a typical 50,000-circulation daily, production accounts for 12 percent or more of *operating* costs and 21 percent or more in newsprint. For larger papers, operating costs and newsprint are 45 to 50 percent of total expense. In *capital* investment, production is the walkaway leader. Recall the cost of $185 million for the *Chicago Tribune's* production facility and the $50 million for presses at the *Baltimore Sun*. For smaller papers, computer systems to handle advertising, circulation, and in-house financial programs cost $100,000 to $1 million or more. Even systems based on low-cost personal computers for weeklies cost $25,000 and up.

Substantial managerial resources must be assigned to production. Special skills are required to manage the expensive equipment involved in such important, complex functions. What makes a good production manager? It varies. Consider the two award-winning production managers described below.

Norman P. Dusseault. Dusseault, operations manager of the *St. Petersburg (Fla.) Times and Independent*, frequently cited for technical excellence, graduated in social science from Holy Cross College, served in the U.S. Marines as a personnel and legal officer, and then joined the *Times and Independent* in 1957. He worked successively as personnel assistant, employment manager, assistant manager/classified advertising, and in 1974 became operations manager, responsible for all production activities. Says Dusseault:

> I am decidedly nontechnical, although I surround myself with top technicians and together we get the job done. I suppose a better technical orientation on my part would be a help, but the job is far too complex technically to be mastered by any one person anyway. I suppose some ability to draw together the diverse management and technical people toward common ends is important. So management training that emphasizes team building, the ability, and the willingness to delegate, etc., would be important preparation. I frequently find my own background in personnel management, promotion, written and verbal communications helpful.[5]

Ken Kniceley. Kniceley followed a different route in becoming production director of Charleston (W. Va.) Newspapers, which wins awards for printing the *Gazette* and *Daily Mail*. Kniceley worked for the *Daily Mail* in high school and became a composing-room apprentice after his graduation in 1950. Along the way, he crammed in two years in print management at West Virginia Institute of Technology and, after serving as manager of the advertising and composing-room departments, was made production director in 1977. Kniceley's techniques:

> Produce the very best paper possible on time, and at the most reasonable cost; place the right manager in the right job in each work area; properly train all managers; cross-train all employees, even between departments; stress neatness and cleanliness in all areas, which shows up in the final product; make sure all employees are made aware of all goals and give directions to achieve these goals. Each individual should have leeway to achieve these goals so that they can use their own abilities.[6]

Note Kniceley's emphasis on *goals*. Planning them and supervising their achievement is a major function for any production manager.

PLANNING IN PRODUCTION AND THE NEW TECHNOLOGY

Planning years ahead is difficult in all newspaper management but probably most difficult in production. First, production's basic mission shifts rapidly over the short term as the departments it supports—news, advertising, circulation—adjust operations to meet changes in the marketplace, competition, and reader and advertiser demands. Second, never before has there been such a rapid flow of technological change affect-

---

[5] Norman P. Dusseault, letter to author, Sept. 8, 1983; also see "Dusseault and Irwin Are St. Pete's Capt. Marvels," *presstime*, June 1983, p. 26.

[6] Ken Kniceley, letter to author, Aug. 18, 1983; also see "Production Award For Job Done 'Kniceley' At Charleston," *Production News Magazine*, Sept. 1982, p. 4.

COLOR IT BRIGHT

Production departments must create better newspaper color reproduction because color is a big hit with readers and advertisers.

Metro editors know that street sales rise when they front interesting, sharply reproduced color above the fold and catch the eyes of hurrying commuters. In small newspapers, color has strong appeal to home subscribers.

But not until the 1980s did technology permit widespread color usage. And, there now is a competitive spur: Gannett's *USA Today* blossoms five days weekly with brilliant color plus imaginative graphics editing and layout. *USA Today's* color is credited with an important role in its climb over 1.3 million circulation quickly after launch, and editors of other papers push their production departments for color weather maps, graphics, and photos of similar quality.

A Newspaper Advertising Bureau survey finds that readers perceive a newspaper as progressive if it prints quality color, but that poor color reproduction turns readers off. And color advertising sells more merchandise. Ad agencies told NAB that 70 percent of their ads run in color, many in magazines, which have generally better reproduction than newspapers. NAB and the American Newspaper Publishers' Association are moving to coordinate nationwide color reproduction standards, as they coordinated standardized mechanical specifications in advertising.

One problem in running color has been its cost. Direct cost to small papers can run $350 or more for a single color photo. State-of-the-art "scanners" that speed the processing of color art cost (in 1985) $100,000 to $400,000.

ing newspaper operations, and there is more radical change ahead. Third, it is imperative to long-range strategy that production planners pin down the expected cost of new technology, but this has proven almost impossible. Costs simply change too quickly.

A fourth difficulty is pinpointed by Peter P. Romano, director of ANPA's Research Institute: planning is particularly difficult because great lead time is required. In equipment development, laboratory breakthroughs normally take seven years to reach production trials, twelve years to widespread commercial application.[7] But plan we must.

Plan for 1990s Needs

A new production chain will have to be constructed for the 1990s. It could start with reporters "talking" stories into computers equipped

with voice recognition logic, and then proceed to editors sitting before VDTs and fulfilling all production functions short of the pressroom. There is a strong possibility of impactless printing by computer-controlled ink-jet systems using laser imaging. Technically, this could permit editors to produce as many different newspapers as there are subscribers. Production will have to automate mailrooms and customize newspapers by inserting special-interest sections for different subscribers. Efficient pagination systems plus relatively low-cost computerized systems and presses will be needed in satellite locations, even by medium-size papers. The mission will be to produce a multiplicity of zoned editions, TMC publications, and other tailored journalistic and advertising products at several sites other than the main plant.

Production will have to satisfy unrelenting demands from news and advertising for ever-improved color reproduction. *USA Today* proved that high-quality color is feasible and that it sells. There will be no turning back. (See box for details on why.)

---

[7] Peter P. Romano, American Newspaper Publishers' Association.

There could be joint use of production facilities by smaller papers. Many weeklies now share production facilities—central printing plants—which will become faster and more economical with the spread of electronic editing, pagination, and high-speed movement of copy by circuit from newsroom to remote printing plant.

On all papers, pressure will increase for the production department, through automation and other efficiencies, to save time and money. Competiton and more sophisticated readers will require more timely, better researched news content. Production will have to help provide it.

Even the smallest daily's production department will need a satellite receiver not only to pull in news copy from news agencies but also to obtain ad copy from national advertisers and agencies. National ads will be prepared just hours in advance and sent to newspapers by satellite.

Newspapers already sell information to customers other than subscribers. Some production departments maintain databases—"information centers"—capable of turning out newsletters, direct mail, and electronic transmissions to homes and offices.

There will be major changes in ink and, perhaps, newsprint. Researchers have already identified a possible less expensive substitute for the wood pulp that is now used in newsprint production. It's kenaf, and we'll turn to it in a moment. Ink that greatly reduces rub-off is being developed, although it is currently very expensive.

Keep Basic Goals in Mind

As you look ahead to production management and all those dazzling possibilities, it will be easy to forget basic goals and to buy new technology for the same reason some people climb a mountain—simply because it is there. Stick to these basic goals:

- Seek higher profits through automation and resultant manpower reduction. This is essential in production and maintenance, which account for 45 to 48 percent of total employees for many papers. New technology offers unprecedented cost reduction. Plan for it.

- Improve the news product with technology offering clearer printing, sharper photographs, vastly improved color. Construct systems, for example, to ensure that skilled journalists, not unskilled typists, are the last to touch news copy. That will improve accuracy and reduce typographical errors.

- Strengthen management's hand with unions by reducing back-shop work forces and installing equipment that is automated or can be operated by nonunion supervisors. Design production systems that unions cannot shut down.

- Improve research capability and give editors better information on reader likes and dislikes, marketplace demographics, competitors' strengths and weaknesses; give advertising managers retailing trends, lifestyle developments.

- Plan product diversification as new technology frees the news, advertising, and production departments to create zoned editions, free-circulation publications, and direct-mail services. Smaller papers particularly should plan to attract lucrative outside job printing. As never before, newspapers can establish themselves as "profit centers" offering new, profitable services to reader and advertiser. Some newspapers will sell access to their market research, for example, or permit users to dial into computerized morgues via telephone.

- Improve distribution flexibility with new technology permitting news, advertising, and circulation departments to target small segments of their markets, then deliver with great accuracy. Plan, for example, for presorting newspapers so motor-route drivers can insert a plastic identity card at the loading dock and automatically receive newspapers sequenced and bundled for fast delivery.

- Strive for overall improvement in management efficiency, probably the greatest payoff for decision makers from the computerization of record keeping. Financial officers must be able to offer, quickly, the meaningful, understandable data essential for any management team trying to calculate where a newspaper is financially and project where it likely will go. Computerized inventory records, for example, can give some managers their first-ever accurate picture of raw materials in storage, costs, and any impending shortages or expensive oversupply.

To exploit this great potential, a technology committee should be established to formulate long-range strategy. This committee should meet frequently with managers of all departments and seek for every dollar spent at least one dollar in cost reduction or product improvement. Proceed carefully, for although new technology opens opportunities undreamed of just a few years ago, it also opens traps.

Beware the Technology Trap

With just a misstep or two, you can take a wrong and very expensive fork in the technological road. The stakes are so huge that the manager who errs in this way will very likely suffer a career setback. Some dangers:

- The capital investment required for new technology can throw a paper deeply into long-term debt and add heavy interest payments that strap current operations. It's basic stuff, but never forget that interest of, say, 12 percent on a $50 million loan for new equipment will total $6 million the

first year. If you're managing a weekly grossing $150,000 annually, can you afford $3,000 annual interest to borrow $25,000 at 12 percent for new equipment?

- Unleashed, American technical genius develops complex systems, some offering—at unjustifiable cost—far more capability than needed. There is an inherent temptation to overbuy systems with bells, whistles, and flashing lights when just a buzzer or two would do. Beware consensus systems planned by interdepartmental committees, each clamoring for costly, tailored equipment that is no more functional than cheaper, off-the-shelf systems that have already been found successful at other papers. For most papers, standardized electronic editing systems—proven through years of experimentation elsewhere—are quite sufficient. Don't pay to reinvent the wheel. And beware the danger of planning a system for *what it will do*, not for what the newspaper *needs done*. Why pay limousine prices if an economy car will do?

- There is, conversely, danger in planning technology only for today's needs, without consulting all departments on what tomorrow's expanded needs are likely to be. Whether you're buying a building, a press, or a computer, allow for incremental additions that won't force you to rip out walls, replace entire lines of presses, or switch to new computer systems. In constructing a $16 million, 87,000-square-foot new plant, the *Bradenton (Fla.) Herald* provided for a 350 percent expansion in space through building additions, if needed, in future years. However modern, your new building or electronic system will not stay long at the tip of the technological spear; improvements are coming and your needs will change.

- Guard against newsroom and production department appetites for more and more new technology that can pressure you to invest without reward in systems that are ahead of their time. In the early 1970s, some papers wasted millions to research pagination, though they learned quickly that its time had not yet arrived.

- Never plan hurriedly. Analyze functions suggested for new equipment and obtain interdepartmental agreement on what they are. Invite at least three vendors to study those functions, design a solution, and submit cost estimates. Do not reverse the equation by buying a system, then attempting to adapt functions to it. Always haggle over prices. Tippen Davidson, general manager of the *Daytona (Fla.) News-Journal*, put out specifications for VDTs and computers to handle news and ad copy. Bids ranged from $350,000 to nearly $1 million. After settling on a $600,000 system, he advises: "Assume the initial proposal from any vendor is for his 'Cadillac' model and question him closely about less expensive alternatives . . . don't be bashful about dickering over prices . . ." Carefully select a single integrated "total system" to serve all departments. Incorrectly choosing even one piece of equipment can lead an entire newspaper toward a costly, soon-to-be-obsolete system.

In sum, the technological "Great Leap Forward" can do wonders for profitability, efficiency, and product quality *if* it is carefully researched and planned for proven application to your operating problems. But, the Great Leap also can take you over a cliff if you don't accurately calculate application, cost, and payback.

How long your newspaper can wait for payback—recovery of cost of new equipment—depends on many variables, including the newspaper's financial condition and tax situation. Seek expert counsel from your chief financial officer on this, but here is a rule of thumb: Calculate the average annual *net* savings the equipment will produce through staff reduc-

tions, increased efficiency and so forth. Divide that into the new equipment's cost to obtain the years to payback. You must then make a business judgment on whether the payback period is acceptable. In the early days of electronic editing and photocomposition, payback was sometimes extraordinarily fast—two years or less for entire new systems—because deep staff cuts were possible. Some composing room staffs were cut 50 percent or more; often, 75 percent of full-time proofreading staffs were cut. Today, such opportunities come less frequently. Ken Kniceley, at the *Charleston Gazette* and *Daily Mail*, seeks payback in five to seven years for most electronic equipment, twenty years for presses.[8] Norm Dusseault at the *St. Petersburg Times and Evening Independent* seeks payback in about two years for most equipment, but, he says,

> . . . this is not the only factor involved in deciding to buy new equipment. For example, we went into offset printing years ago, and are currently expanding again, not solely based on a proven cost justification formula, but rather because of our interest in producing quality. Ultimately, of course, this cost justifies in the general health of the newspaper.[9]

Gannett ranks its managers' capital investment requests from "must have" to "nice to have," then calculates the impact each will have on cash flow. If the investment promises an immediate return of 15 percent or so, approval is given. Dow Jones takes a longer view, seeking quick payback, of course, but also considering the long-range strategic value of the capital investment.

Obtain expert financial advice on tax implications: make *no* capital expenditure without exploring depreciation schedules under which the IRS permits tax deductions over a period of years for newly purchased equipment. Tax consequences are frequently pivotal in deciding

---

[8] Kniceley, op. cit.
[9] Dusseault, op. cit.

whether a capital investment should be made, and it will take years to sort out the real implications that the 1986 tax reform had for all this. Any purchase contract should be checked by the paper's attorney before it is signed.

Of course, in production planning, you must balance cost of equipment and payback against the support role your department plays for other departments. You don't manage production just for the sake of managing it; you manage production to assist news, circulation, advertising, and other departments.

HOW TO MANAGE THE PRODUCTION EFFORT

You may approach production and new technology with weak technical background and strong trepidation. You're not alone. Many aspiring managers fear its technical complexities and high costs. So, let's discuss how you can get along in performing the technical duties of a production manager and handling the human element.

Hints for Nontechnical Managers

How can the nonengineer manager get atop all this? In the words of Michael G. Gartner, now editor of Gannett's *Louisville (Ky.) Courier-Journal*: "That's a problem. 'It used to be,' a publisher told me not long ago, 'that the circulation department was the place the publishers avoided because they couldn't understand it. Now, it's the production department.'"

Gartner continues:

The good publisher has to do two things: First, educate himself about the new technology; second, hire a bright young engineer to run the production department. Between the two of them, then, they'll be able to stay abreast of developments and override the old-fashioned thinking that pervades the department. When the new technology came to the newsrooms, an editor I know went to night school to learn about computers.

He learned. "A wonderful thing just happened," he told me one day. "One of these young computer whizzes tried to get by with something, and I looked him in the eye and said, 'B.S.' I knew enough so I couldn't be walked over by those guys." The good publisher and the good editor and the good ad managers must now keep abreast of technology, too, so that the computer people don't take charge of the other departments. Business and editorial and advertising decisions should not be made on the basis of what machines can do.[10]

Advice, then, for the nontechnical manager in this technological age:

- Get involved. Don't avoid technology; it will not go away. Publisher Richard G. Capen of the *Miami Herald* says, "There must be willingness to learn about new technology, to not be afraid of it and to accept it willingly and enthusiastically."[11] Read trade publications, particularly the technology sections of *presstime* and *Editor & Publisher*. Attend ANPA's annual Research Institute Production Conference, *the* showplace for new equipment. Attend training programs offered by numerous trade associations; visit other papers, stay in touch with equipment vendors.

- Hire carefully, selecting employees who know the new technology and understand that production fulfills *service functions* for other departments (avoid those so enamored with new technology that they want the technical tail to wag the newspaper dog). Assign staffers with strong technical orientation to those departments, such as news, that might need assistance.

- Do not be awed by the new gadgets. Check what other papers are doing, listen to your vendors. But don't follow them blindly. As

---

[10] Michael G. Gartner, letter to author, March 1, 1983.
[11] Richard G. Capen, Jr., letter to author, May 27, 1983.

in all crucial management decisions, step back, take a deep breath, and ask: Is *this* system, at *this* cost, and *this* payback, best for *this* newspaper at *this* time?

- In daily operations, look for key indicators of high quality: on-time performance in all functions, particularly press runs; minimum downtime of equipment, a sign of good maintenance that reduces breakdowns; good printing, with sharp color reproduction, clean inking (no smudges), and minimum showthrough of ink from the other side of page.

Dusseault of St. Petersburg lists his priorities this way:

1. Quality—This is the religion around here and so I hear a lot about poor-quality products. Also it hurts my pride to turn out poor work. Quality is elusive, however. There are so many variables, and so many people involved. I would say that this is my major challenge, to keep quality standards high.

2. Maintaining good morale—This involves a host of activities, ranging from communications to good pay programs, to safety, etc. Mostly it is trying to get across that we care about our people working here, that they are important as individuals. We don't always succeed, but we try.

3. Planning equipment and processes and staffing to keep abreast of surging [market] growth in our area. We can get behind in a single season, and we have to look ahead intelligently or be drowned.

4. Cost control, staying within budget, holding down waste, and at the same time being flexible enough to change the budget when it makes sense.

5. Daily operations, meeting deadlines, spotting and correcting problems, etc."[12]

---

[12] Dusseault, op. cit.

Managing the Human Element

Managing people in any department is a challenge. It is even more so in production, because new technology brings with it traumatic change that deeply affects employees' lives.

A fundamental redistribution of work is under way. Employees are being assigned new, sometimes bewildering tasks. Some jobs are disappearing; many employees are worried, some are hurt. For example, a Rand Corporation study finds that by 1983 newspapers employed *52 percent fewer workers* in composing rooms than before cold type. That covered a ten-year period. And the survey finds the average composing room staff still 20 percent larger than necessary.

Many newspapers reduce production staffs through attrition, waiting for retirements and resignations over a period of time. But papers that must move quickly or are restricted by union agreements use the "buyout"—paying workers to leave. Among 400 papers surveyed by Rand, union papers averaged buyout costs of $500,000. About 11 percent of workers displaced by technology were simply laid off.

Job displacement will continue well into the 1990s, particularly with pagination. To be humane *and* achieve maximum benefit of the new technology, you must treat gently those whose lives feel the impact. This is necessary particularly with systems that transform job functions. Providing adequate information and training makes a huge difference. Newspaper employees, regardless of age or experience, can take smoothly to new technology. This was proven with VDT writing. Careful training equipped thousands of reporters and editors who used typewriters all their professional lives to take quickly to VDTs. To avoid fear of or resistance to new technology, you should:

- Explain overall strategy. Describe the newspaper's goal and how new equipment or systems fit into the larger operational picture.

- Immediately and frankly describe impact, if any, on jobs. If jobs will be eliminated, say so—and simultaneously announce how you will care for the displaced. Be candid about redistribution of workload. If, for example, the newsroom must accept tasks formerly performed in production, explain how they will be shared.

- Stress positive attributes of new technology. Many reporters and editors prefer VDTs over typewriters because they make jobs easier. Highlight such benefits.

- Whenever possible, let employees help design new systems. They often make sound technical contributions, learn what is happening, and, importantly, help quiet the fears of others.

- Always provide careful training to minimize shock of newness. Begin, for example, by changing only an editor's tool—a new VDT for an old typewriter. Don't also change job function. The editor who keeps the same job must then wrestle only with a new tool.

- Address authoritatively and in detail any fears that technology will affect health. Rumors have swept newsrooms that VDTs injure health, and ANPA has repeatedly produced expert medical testimony that they don't. Include such evidence in your *initial* announcement that new technology is coming.

- Create liaison teams for effective coordination in newly realigned departments. Quickly iron out any operational problems.

- Listen to your staff. If there are even seemingly minor complaints—that the positioning of VDTs creates glare, for example, or cricks in the neck—move rapidly with a remedy (in this case, mount VDTs on swivels so employees can adjust them comfortably). Don't let cricks in the neck

sour your staff on a multimillion-dollar system that will jump your technology ahead a generation.

Manage Newsprint Resources Carefully

High among any production manager's priorities is newsprint. Every effort must be made to lower newsprint costs and reduce waste. The figures in Table 11.1, from the Newsprint Information Committee, illustrate why.

Of all costs, only personnel expense is larger. And none is as subject as newsprint to marketplace pricing pressure. With exception of a temporary 6 percent reduction in 1982, newsprint prices in recent memory have increased steadily. Since 1974–1975, increases have exceeded rises in the Consumer Price Index. In 1987, prices for some newspapers hit $610 per metric ton, and no price plateau is in sight.

Ensure effective cost control, particularly in three areas:

- At purchase. Newspapers or groups that are large consumers must negotiate quantity discounts. Unfortunately, medium- and small-size newspapers must generally pay going rates.

- In handling and storage. A careless forklift operator who pokes a roll can destroy

Table 11.1 Newsprint as an Element of Total Publishing Cost

Typical Dailies (circulation)	Newsprint— Percent of Total Cost
750,000	32.9%
250,000	30.0
50,000	26.5
9,000	15.8

Newsprint Information Committee, New York, 1983.

many dollars worth of newsprint; rolls that become wet or too dry represent money wasted. (ANPA recommends storage at 60 to 70°F and 45 percent relative humidity.)

- In usage. Money is saved if presses are operated by trained (and cost-conscious) press crews.

The *Orlando Sentinel* calculated that at 1984 prices, each "web break"—a newsprint tear while presses are running—cost about $27 and took ten minutes to fix. A team of seven press employees won a cost-reduction contest by running 453 rolls of newsprint through the presses without a break, thus saving $73,305. One ingenious newsprint-conservation step is reducing "web width"—the width of each page. The *New York Times* reduced its width from 58 to 56 inches in 1981, then to 55 inches in 1983. The annual newsprint saving (at 1984 prices) *exceeds $8 million*. Some newspapers use lighter, less expensive newsprint. The standard basis weight is now 30 pounds. Newsprint is weighed in pounds per ream, or five hundred 24- by 36-inch sheets. In metric terms, weight is expressed in "grammage" (weight in grams of one sheet of newsprint measuring one square meter). A 30-pound basis weight is equivalent to a grammage of 48.8. Shifting to even lighter newsprint, with technology at hand, causes ink "bleed through" and severely impairs readability. But stay alert for new techniques that might make it possible.

Newsprint waste reports from hundreds of newspapers are analyzed by ANPA's Research Institute. Depending on printing process and other variables, waste ranges from about 2.2 percent of total newsprint used to 5.3 percent or more. Measure your waste against that range. The Institute monitors newsprint from Canadian and U.S. mills for variations in physical properties that influence printing quality. Published results identify each mill only through a confidential code. You can obtain details from ANPA, The Newspaper Center, Box 17406, Dulles International Airport, Washington, DC 10041.

To ensure newsprint availability and influence prices, many newspapers invest in mills. Canadian mills outproduce U.S. mills by far. In 1982, for example, Canadian capacity was 10 million metric tons; U.S. capacity, 5.2 million. U.S. newspapers and other users consume substantially more than double the U.S. production. About 57 percent of the newsprint used in the United States comes from Canada, 41.5 percent from U.S. mills, and less than 2 percent from other countries.

Your newsprint prices are sure to rise, for the newsprint industry's economics are stunning. One estimate is that it would cost (at 1984 prices) $300 million to build a plant capable of producing 500 tons daily. Costs are high for raw materials, labor (strongly unionized), and energy. As many as 22,800 gallons of water are used to produce one ton of newsprint, along with huge amounts of fuel oil. And because mills must be located close to wood supplies, the cost of transporting newsprint to U.S. papers is high. Abitibi-Price, Inc., North America's single largest producer, says its costs are as follows: wood, 25 percent; labor, 23 percent; energy, 15 percent; other mill costs, 21 percent; delivery, 16 percent.

All this inspires a search for new raw materials. Some experts, including William D. Rinehart, ANPA's vice president/technical, says the answer is kenaf, a nonwood fibrous plant that matures in four or five months—compared with twenty-five years for trees used in wood pulp—and provides a per-acre yield nine times that of forest land. It grows well in the South, southern California, Arizona. Importantly, it has proven cost-competitive with wood pulp and produces high-quality newsprint. Some futurists predict that new technology using kenaf will permit the construction of small mills, close to U.S. newspapers, producing 25 to 50 tons daily. Rinehart says that one day newspapers may invest as readily in newsprint mills as in presses and other equipment.

In sum, newsprint management must include stringent cost and waste controls plus, perhaps, capital expenditure in newsprint production facilities. Unless cost breakthroughs in newsprint use are achieved, many newspapers will suffer severe pressure on profits.

Managing Building and Site

Newspapers have traditionally been located in the city's center, close to business activity, government, and other news sources that must be covered. However, many city centers are deteriorating, readers and retailers are moving to the suburbs, news sources are dispersing—and many newspaper buildings are inadequate for new equipment or lack space for storing tons of newsprint.

It all raises nagging questions: Is there a social responsibility to remain in the city's center, to support the core of the paper's market? Or is there a business imperative to move to cheaper land (and lower taxes) outside town? Or should the operation be split, keeping editorial and business departments downtown and establishing production in a satellite location outside town? The *Atlanta Journal and Constitution* made what is becoming a standard move for many metro dailies: it constructed a $50 million satellite printing facility northeast of Atlanta but left other operations downtown. This locates some production capability in a growing population area and leapfrogs inner-city traffic.

If your paper contemplates moving all operations outside the city, consider whether the newspaper risks losing identity in its market core. Also consider the cost. ANPA's Rinehart suggests that a square foot of building is needed for each copy of the newspaper sold. Other experts suggest as much as 1.5 square feet per copy.[13] The *Harlan (Ky.) Daily Enterprise*, a New York Times Co. evening paper of 7,500 circulation, built a new 14,000-square-foot plant

and office complex. The building, press, and other equipment cost $2.3 million, or $164.28 per square foot. Gannett spent $300 per square foot—$15 million total—for a 50,000-square-foot satellite printing plant in Miramar, Florida, for *USA Today*. The *Asheville (N.C.) Citizen-Times* figured $275 per square foot for an $11-million 40,000-square-foot suburban printing plant.

In picking a new site, make sure that good transportation is available. Delivery trucks must have quick access to major highways leading throughout the market; easy commutes will mollify employees disgruntled over moving to a new plant. Considerations of taxes, topography (presses weigh tons and must have solid foundations), and availability of utilities all go into site selection and planning. If possible, arrange multiple service by utilities. Don't let a single power failure shut down a new multimillion-dollar plant.

In designing a plant, make sure that all department heads are consulted on projected long-term needs. Design today for tomorrow's needs. Use an architect experienced in the construction of newspaper plants. Obtain building and fire code requirements in advance. They vary, and you don't want a new building declared unsafe the day after it opens.

JOINT OPERATING AGREEMENTS

As Hearst Corp. pictures it, the group's *Seattle Post-Intelligencer* was not long for this world: It lost $14 million in 1970-81, and $8 million in 1982 alone. By mid-1983, Publisher Virgil Fassio says, the 191,000-circulation morning paper was hemorrhaging $175,000 in *weekly* losses.

Hearst's solution was a joint operating agreement (JOA) with the competing *Seattle Times*, combining all operations except editorial of both papers. The *Times* prints the *Post-Intelligencer*, sells its ads, distributes it, and performs business functions. In return, the *Times* takes the first 6 percent of profits as a manage-

---

[13] Paul Kruglinski, "Building A New Plant," *presstime*, June 1983, p. 4.

ment fee, then the two share the remainder—66 percent to the *Times*, 34 percent to Hearst.

Congress agreed as early as the 1930s and, most recently, in the Newspaper Preservation Act of 1970, to permit two newspapers in one city to combine all but their newsrooms free of antitrust considerations if one is provably failing financially and faced with closing down. Congress's intent is to maintain separate editorial voices in such cities. Predictably, JOAs are highly controversial. The U.S. attorney general must approve each and, as in Seattle, there are sometimes stiff court challenges. Opponents argue that JOAs give participants monopoly shares of a market and unfair advantage over competitors, particularly suburban papers but also radio and TV. A developing controversy is over whether JOAs should be permitted to jointly produce a shopper or other nonnewspaper product. Shoppers, opponents say, carry little or no news and should not be covered by legislation aimed at preserving independent editorial voices. Opponents also argue that JOAs keep ad rates artificially high and don't serve readers well, either. Supporters argue that many papers survive to serve reader and advertiser only because a JOA gives them a new lease on life.

Precise corporate outlines of a JOA—the

Table 11.2 *Herald* and *News* Comparative

	Herald	News
Circulation		
Daily	431,965	62,457
Sunday	523,847	(none)
Full-run ad lineage		
(000s, six-column inches)		
Retail	1,480.8	279.1
National	336.8	133.6
Classified	870.2	338.9
Total	2,687.8	751.6
ROP part-run	1,946.7	(none)
Preprints	1,102.5	24.2

Table 11.3 *Herald* Payments to *News*

	Editorial Expenses	Operating Profit
1984	$5,367,000	$8,751,000
1983	4,539,000	7,932,000
1982	4,445,000	6,523,000

division of duties, costs, and profits—are negotiated separately in each case, subject to Justice Department review. In most cases, dramatically improved financial results follow. In Seattle, Hearst says it reduced losses the first year under the JOA, then made a profit in the second, 1984. Publisher W. J. Pennington of the *Times* says his already profitable paper enjoys even higher profits. As in most JOAs, the key to this financial turnaround is staff reduction. Net staff reduction approached two hundred.

There is no doubt that a JOA signed in 1966 between Knight-Ridder's *Miami Herald* and Cox Enterprises' *Miami News* keeps Miami a two-newspaper city. Under the agreement, the afternoon *News* is autonomous journalistically, but the *Herald* prints and distributes the *News* and handles other business functions. Table 11.2 shows how the newspapers perform under the agreement.

On those figures, it is clear that the *News* could not survive if it were not in a JOA. Yet it flourishes financially in the JOA. The *Herald* pays an agreed sum for the *News*'s editorial expenses plus up to 15 percent of *combined* annual operating profits each year. Table 11.3 shows the *Herald*'s reimbursements to the *News*.

Those payments to the *News* came from combined revenue that hit $230.4 million for advertising and $40.7 million for circulation in 1984; $206.4 million and $38.9 million, respectively, in 1983; and $186.3 million and $27.9 million in 1982.[14]

---

[14] *1984 Annual Report*, Miami, Fla., Knight-Ridder Newspapers, p. 64.

Table 11.4   Existing Joint Operating Agreements

	Population	Began	Partners
Albuquerque, N.M.	321,000	1933	Scripps, independent
El Paso, Tex.	441,000	1936	Scripps, Gannett
Nashville, Tenn.	453,000	1937	Gannett, independent
Evansville, Ind.	131,000	1938	Scripps, independent
Tucson, Ariz.	350,000	1940	Pulitzer, Gannett
Tulsa, Okla.	370,000	1941	Two independents
Chattanooga, Tenn. (Dissolved in 1966, renewed in 1980)	181,000	1942	Two independents
Madison, Wis.	196,000	1948	Lee, independent
Fort Wayne, Ind.	183,000	1950	Knight-Ridder, independent
Birmingham, Ala.	270,000	1950	Scripps, Newhouse
Lincoln, Neb.	171,000	1950	Lee, independent
Salt Lake City, Utah	163,000	1952	Two independents
Shreveport, La.	192,000	1953	Gannett, independent
Knoxville, Tenn.	192,000	1957	Scripps, independent
Charleston, W. Va.	62,000	1958	Thomson, independent
Pittsburgh, Pa.	398,000	1961	Scripps, Block
Honolulu, Hawaii	360,000	1962	Gannett, independent
San Francisco, Calif.	632,000	1965	Hearst, independent
Miami, Fla.	354,000	1966	Knight-Ridder, Cox
Cincinnati, Ohio	370,000	1979	Scripps, Gannett
Seattle, Wash.	480,000	1983	Hearst, independent

In 1986, Knight-Ridder, owner of the *Detroit Free Press*, and Gannett, which had acquired the *Detroit News*, sought Justice Department approval of a 100-year JOA for the two papers. They announced that the *Free Press* had lost $35 million in the preceding five years; the *News*, $20 million. They agreed under a five-year sliding formula that Gannett would receive 55 percent of profits, decreasing to 50 percent after the fifth year. They agreed to split profits fifty-fifty for the next ninety-five years. Gannett published—and thus tacitly endorsed—an estimate by securities analyst John Morton that operating profits under the JOA would be $13.5 million the first year, $40 million the second, $57 million the third.

Financial success does not automatically follow JOA status, however. In 1983, Newhouse sold its *St. Louis Globe-Democrat*, a chronic loser despite its JOA with the *St. Louis Post-Dispatch*; the paper closed down in 1986. There are now 21 JOAs. (See Table 11.4.)

ELECTRONIC HOME DELIVERY

Much of the scare talk about newspapers becoming obsolete is ended. The industry is strong. Circulation approaches 63 million daily, advertising revenues leap forward. At every turn is promise of a bright, automated future . . . well, not quite.

At the end of the production chain, after the VDTs and high-speed presses finish, there still waits that thirteen-year-old newspaper deliverer. And every day, in this era of computers and space satellites, thousands of youthful carriers set off with bundles of expensive newsprint, tossing on front porches and lawns a product fashioned with journalistic skill from news collected at great cost and manufactured with enormous ingenuity—teenagers making deliveries the same old way, by bike or on foot, in an industry close to automating everything between reporter's mind and pressroom!

Concurrently, competing media are making striking technical breakthroughs, particularly in computer-based telecommunications. Constrasting with the rising cost of newsprint and its distribution, the cost of computer memory and electronic communication is falling.

From all that, communications futurists envisage new ways of transmitting news and advertising to the American consumer. Some predict the "wired city" of households linked by two-way interactive communications networks delivering massive amounts of data at high speed from central computers to desktop terminals on command from the household user. Is that the better way, the shape of communications to come? Or, is that vision far ahead of its time or, even, an hallucination?

Newspapers Keep Options Open

As a potential competitor in household delivery, the telecommunications industry has two things going for it: First, it is incredibly wealthy ($200 billion revenue in 1984, headed for double that in the early 1990s), and second, electronic home delivery systems are technically capable of speeding vast amounts of information into households with precision and efficiency.

It is all so impressive that many newspaper managers feel they must get involved in some form of home-delivery telecommunications just to keep their options open. Of 1,070 dailies large and small polled by ANPA in 1983, 48 percent were operating or planning new telecommunications ventures; almost 85 percent

with over 500,000 circulation were involved actively or expressed interest in electronic home delivery.

However, the nature of most experimentation shows that managers feel electronic home delivery may one day *supplement* newspapers but not *supplant* them. Many feel that the technical potential is enormous, but that costs are too high and householders reluctant to adopt a new communication form that has not yet proven to be easy or economical to use—or essential to daily life.

Times Mirror and Knight-Ridder both made expensive efforts to develop Videotext, the delivery of computer-generated material over two-way interactive circuits. Knight-Ridder invested over $50 million in a system that proved technically strong but unable to arouse sufficient consumer interest. Times Mirror invested $15 million. Both operations were shut down in 1986. What the two companies attempted—and why they failed—are issues of importance to newspaper managers, who will face in the 1990s renewed efforts to create viable electronic home-delivery information systems.

Knight-Ridder's system, Viewtron, linked user homes with computers to provide not only news, information, and advertising but also banking and shopping service, educational programs, games, community bulletin boards, and many other services. Hand-held keyboards summoned Viewtron services over telephone circuits and displayed them on home TV screens (a major disadvantage that put both telephone and TV temporarily out of action) or personal computers. The projected strategy was to build a nationwide network of allied papers and jointly make Viewtron available on a widespread basis. Each local participant was to own 75 percent of its joint venture and contribute local news and marketing expertise.

Linking the powerful news-gathering resources of twenty or thirty major newspapers through high-speed computerized networks was a mind-boggling idea, but consumers would not pay for it and the advertiser would not support it. The system aimed at high-income, demographically attractive users and, in raw numbers at least, the potential market was large. Studies indicated that by 1990, 30 percent or more of homes would have personal computers equipped to send or receive data over the telephone. Researcher Ruth Clark found that 68 percent of all regular newspaper readers were already participating in the "communications revolution" through cable TV or video games, personal computers, or video cassette recorders. However, users proved extremely cost-sensitive. Customers clearly will not pay substantial fees for general news that is also available, albeit somewhat later, in a 35-cent newspaper; few want to use a costly personal computer and telephone hookup for baseball or football scores they can get free on radio or TV, or in tomorrow's paper.

There is also doubt that the householder will adapt easily to a computer-based keyboard for such tasks as banking and shopping. Will shopping from the kitchen with an electronic version of the Sears catalog be considered essential? Or will it take some of the fun out of life? Will the buyer want to leave home to *feel* the fabric of a new dress, *sniff* the freshness of meat? And after all, how many need to use an electronic system for banking from home at midnight?

After a two-year experiement with ten newspapers and CompuServe, a computer time-sharing firm in Cleveland, the Associated Press sees "no clear and present danger to newspapers from electronic delivery of information to the home, but the dangers and opportunities are all out in the future."[15] AP says householders rapidly lose interest in interrogating distant computers for the latest news once the novelty wears off. In the experiment's final eight months, one-third of users looked at CompuServe's "elec-

tronic newspaper" only once. Average time spent with it dropped to five minutes.[16] Note that the target market was the "typical" household, and the services offered were general news and information.

Beyond doubt, a substantial *business* audience is eager for electronic delivery of news. Dow Jones & Co. proves that businesses that turn on news—brokers or commodities traders, for example—will pay handsomely for news that will help them make profitable deals. Dow Jones boasts (1985) more than 185,000 subscribers to its electronic news retrieval service—each paying $75 to join, $1.20 per minute in prime time to use it, and 20 cents per minute at other times. Reuters News Agency is also strongly positioned in the U.S. business market with electronic services. Knight-Ridder's New York-based *Journal of Commerce* sells shipping news services costing $250 or more monthly, plus a highly successful Commodities News Service. Note, however, that these successful services focus narrowly on news of profitable interest to a specific business audience. They avoid trying to appeal to typical householders with general news.

What Does It All Mean to You?

But what does it all mean to you? Well, if you enter newspaper management, you are likely one day to either (1) work for a company at least peripherally involved in electronically transmitting news or (2) compete against one that does. Read what one expert thinks you should be doing in the early 1990s. Lloyd G. Schermer, president of Lee Enterprises, owner of newspapers and broadcast stations, warns that newspapers have their research and development "radar" set only five years ahead—not far enough—and are looking in the wrong direction:

---

[15] "Electronic Newspaper Found Unprofitable," *Editor & Publisher*, Aug. 28, 1982, p. 7, quoting Lawrence Blasko, then Associated Press director of information technology.

[16] Jonathan Friendly, "Little Market Seen For Electronic Newspapers," *New York Times*, Oct. 2, 1982, p. 19.

I think we had better start developing a second radar system focused 10 years out . . . we must come to the realization that we are in the information business—not the newspaper business.

Our future competitors could be giants such as AT&T, Xerox, Exxon and IBM. Any one of these large companies is spending research and development funds far in excess of what our total industry spends and they are focusing on the information business . . . Of the two mass-media electronic delivery systems, cable and telephones, the telephone represents our greatest threat and our greatest opportunity. It will take . . . much longer, for cable to wire, and in most cases rewire, the nation with interactive systems.

On the other hand, Ma Bell's telephones and others are already in 98 percent of the homes; the paired wires coming into your phone can be souped up to deliver interactive audio visual services; the phone companies are nationwide in scope; they already have in place the computer and monopoly switching capability . . . to identify, record, invoice and collect . . . and finally, Baby Bell is big—big enough to do the job with people and dollars to maintain its dominant market position, as it transforms its traditional Yellow Page service into interactive electronic information systems.[17]

The specter of electronic delivery of advertising—Yellow Pages updated minute-by-minute and delivered to a home screen, for example—disturbs many newspaper strategists. Envisage a home user casting aside the newspaper and summoning from a telephone company's distant computer just those classified ads that are of interest.

Many newspaper strategists, however, find newspapers strongly positioned to meet new competitors. Lee's Schermer sees the newspaper possessing these qualities:

Print updated daily, a strong reputation, daily mass-market penetration, convenience, portability, local news generation, cheap [newsprint]

memory, an interactive distribution system [carrier with subscriber], reader habit, and an electronic information storage and transfer system that's up and running within the four walls of most newspapers today. It's only a matter of time before these systems break out of those walls and into the marketplace. Finally, our greatest long-term strength is our credibility to produce the content our customers expect of us and not from potential competitors.[18]

Content. It all comes back to quantity and quality of news and advertising that newspapers gather, produce in easily manageable form, and distribute quickly and cheaply. And, as Schermer points out, most newspapers already have internal news systems easily adaptable to electronic delivery, should that prove attractive. Many newspaper managers therefore talk *not* of using new systems to supplant the newspaper but, rather of employing its unique strengths in yet another, profitable, manner. Cannot that mountain of news, laboriously collected daily but only partially published, be used another way?

Cable TV—A Newspaper Option?

Many newspaper companies diversify into cable TV, profiting from the American public's voracious appetite for home entertainment. Huge cable systems serving hundreds of thousands of homes are owned by Times Mirror, Newhouse, Capital Cities, Landmark, Tribune Co., New York Times Co. (in that order, the largest newspaper owners of cable). Less clear, however, is how profitable *news* programming will be in cable.

ANPA counted 120 newspapers reaching over a million subscribers through cable TV in 1984, mostly by leasing a channel or collaborating with a local system owner. However, of 69

---

[17] Lloyd G. Schermer, president, Lee Enterprise.

[18] "Newspapers Believe Cable TV Ventures Will Be Profitable, Says NAB," *SNPA Bulletin*, Nov. 11, 1983, p. 2.

newspapers providing local news, only 11 claimed profitability. Newspapers programming for cable were of all sizes—26 percent had circulation over 100,000; 23 percent less than 10,000. Cost averaged $40,000 to $50,000 to start a service offering scrolled text news and classified ads (but few graphics). Programming most frequently was local news, sports, and weather. But 54 percent carried stock quotes; 38 percent, school lunch menus; 19 percent, horoscopes. Of 62 systems transmitting advertising, 73 percent carried classified and retail ads; 29 percent accepted national ads. One-way cable TV systems are not suited to classified advertising.[19] James L. Whyte, vice president and general manager of the combined 210,000-circulation *Jacksonville (Fla.) Times-Union and Journal*, says his paper folded a cable venture after four years because it had no revenue potential. Viewers will not sit before a screen waiting for classified ads to scroll by.[20]

Cable penetration of the nation's households is deepening. In 1987, 44 percent of all U.S. households were wired for cable. Penetration was much deeper in some cities: 66.2 percent of homes in Wilkes-Barre/Scranton, Pennsylvania, 60.8 percent in San Diego, California, and 57.3 percent in Pittsburgh.[21] But in the largest ten TV markets, 70 percent of households were *without* cable. Reasons included the high cost of installing systems, political problems with local governments, and adequate over-the-air television.

Only financially strong companies can become big players in cable. Wiring for cable is expensive—$12,000 to $15,000 per cable mile in suburban locations in 1986, $20,000 to $30,000 in cities such as New York and Boston. Cable companies fear that the monthly fee paid by cable subscribers ($16.80 average in 1984) will not permit profit in such expensive projects.

Some Seek to Offer Programming

Providing cable *programming* may open limited opportunities for profitable second use of a newspaper's main product—news. That's the bet of Gannett and others.

Gannett surprised many observers by not adding cable systems to newspapers, radio and television stations, outdoor advertising companies, and other businesses it rapidly acquired in the 1970s and 1980s. The high price of acquiring cable systems—$1,200 per subscriber was not unusual—dampened Gannett's interest. Instead, the company owns programming companies and many of its ninety newspapers lease channels on local cable systems or contract in joint ventures to provide news and advertising. But neither Gannett nor other newspapers report user acclaim or huge profits. In fact, of 69 papers surveyed by ANPA, 49 percent report they entered cable programming just to defend against competition; 60 percent term it mainly a good way to prepare for the telecommunications future—whatever that might be. Of 11 profitable efforts, 8 were operated by papers under 25,000 circulation offering local programming. All used existing newspaper staffs to prepare programming, thus incurring low start-up costs.[22] Many, however, find programming unprofitable.

There have been notable failures in interactive *two-way* services. The hapless *Minneapolis Star and Tribune* experimented but found it cost users 25 to 50 cents per story summoned for viewing—compared with 25 cents at that time for an entire newspaper with scores of

[19] "Jacksonville Newspapers End Four-Year-Old Cable Operation," *SNPA Bulletin*, Aug. 26, 1983, p. 3.

[20] "Cable Penetration," *Advertising Age*, Sept. 12, 1983, p. 60, and "Our TVs Are on 6 Hours, 55 Minutes Daily," *USA Today*, May 17, 1984, p. 1.

[21] Margaret Genovese, "More Papers Entered Cable TV For Competition Than Profits," *presstime*, Feb. 1984, p. 30.

[22] Don Clark, "Newspapers in Minneapolis Drop Electronic News Tests," *St. Paul Pioneer-Dispatch*, March 27, 1982, p. 10.

stories. The Minneapolis papers killed the experiment.[23]

Two major attempts were made to develop national cable services devoted exclusively to news. ABC Video Enterprises and Westinghouse Broadcasting and Cable jointly launched Satellite News Channel in 1982, failed, and one year later sold it (for $25 million) to Ted Turner. Turner, a colorful Atlanta entrepreneur, achieved critical acclaim with Cable News Network, a first-rate news service, but lost millions of dollars year after year.

There is not sufficient support for other 24-hour, all-news channels. Subscribers resist increased fees for news channels, and advertisers hang back for two reasons: First, the large number of cable channels available fractionalizes the audience; a network TV channel is a better advertising vehicle because it can deliver more viewers than can any single cable channel. Second, cable's household penetration, though most local systems average 55 percent, is uneven and in some cities low (25.8 percent in Chicago in 1985, for example).

Explore Other Ways

A newspaper manager must stay current on how technology is opening other ways of reaching the American home electronically. Examples:

- Fiber optics derived from glass can replace copper paired wires now used in telephone service. Fiber optics can penetrate the home with a single circuit of extremely high capacity, carrying not only telephone service but also a burglar/fire alarm system as well as home banking and shopping services—and many cable channels. Telephone companies may become primary carriers of home services and important providers of news and other programming as well. The day may come when newspapers collaborate with telephone companies to provide electronically delivered news and advertising *or* compete against them.

- Low-power television (LPTV), limited to 10 watts for very high frequency and 1,000 for ultra high frequency stations, opens opportunities for new TV stations to reach limited audiences in a radius of 10 to 20 miles. Because of relatively low start-up costs (substantially under $1 million in 1983), the Federal Communications Commission hopes to entice diverse "Mom and Pop" owners into TV broadcasting. More than 13,000 applications followed FCC announcement that 4,000 stations would be licensed. Between 30 and 40 percent of applicants were newspapers. But there were no early indications that LPTV would be a major competitor for local advertising and news.

- Direct broadcast satellite (DBS) in theory threatens cable TV because DBS programming is to be beamed up 22,300 miles to satellites, then back down to homes equipped with special rooftop antennas. It promises extremely high resolution pictures, even on large screens, by means of a technique called high-definition television. DBS, however, carries fewer channels than cable, is a one-way system, and is suited only for national, not local, programming. The cost of a DBS system, estimated in the mid-1980s at $400 million, is a barrier. CBS, Western Union, and Publisher Rupert Murdoch investigated DBS and then pulled out.

SUMMARY

Technology is transforming American newspapers into a capital-intensive, computerized industry, promising national dailies and country weeklies alike exciting new ways to improve content and reduce costs.

---

[23] Robert Garfield, "Fragmented Cable Can't Attract Ads," *USA Today*, Oct. 21, 1983, p. B1.

Three basic techniques are the core of a modern production chain: computerized writing and editing that captures newsroom keystrokes, offset printing and cold-type processes, and pagination or computerized layout of pages. Each offers staff reductions, higher profits, and improved journalistic quality.

There are dangers: the high cost of new technology can create heavy debt; it is easy to buy too much technology or, conversely, too little.

Even managers lacking technical background must get involved in the new technology. But buy carefully and never without haggling over prices or obtaining expert financial advice.

Newspapers must plan to sell news and information to customers other than subscribers. But most publishers feel that electronic systems will supplement—not supplant—newspapers.

The general public doesn't easily adapt to high-cost delivery of news via home terminals. However, delivery of news in a "bundle" of other services such as telephone, burglar/fire alarms, and so on might be a possibility. Certainly, the delivery of tightly focused "news to profit by" to the business community can be highly successful. In serving business, newspapers may find a way to use existing staff, facilities, and the huge databases they build each day.

RECOMMENDED READING

Technical bulletins issued by ANPA's research center are the best available sources of up-to-date information on newspaper production. Contact William D. Rinehart, vice president/technical, ANPA, 11600 Sunrise Valley Drive, Reston, VA 22091. ANPA standing committees report regularly on newsprint, telecommunications, and technical research. *Editor & Publisher* and *presstime* regularly report on technical developments. The Southern Newspaper Publishers' Association issues weekly technical bulletins. Also note Benjamin Compaine, *The Newspaper Industry in the Nineteen Eighties: An Assessment of Economics and Technology*, White Plains, N.Y., Knowledge Publishing, 1980; David Weaver, *Videotex Journalism: Teletext, Viewdata and the News*, Hillsdale, N.J., Erlbaum, 1983.

GLOSSARY

Access time. Delay between receipt of material and the instant the computer was ordered to deliver it.

Cable television (or community-antenna television, CATV). Delivery of TV signals via wired circuits.

Cathode ray tube (CRT). Vacuum tube that displays information on a screen, as in VDTs, or transmits images to photocomposition equipment.

Cellular radio. Telephone system that passes mobile user from one transmitter to another in a city; transmitters cover "cells."

Central processing unit (CPU). Computer element that fulfills instructions from programming.

Coding. Successive instructions assigned computer for processing.

Database. Information in computer storage.

Direct broadcast satellite (DBS). TV signals to statellites for relay to earth stations; permits long-range broadcast.

Direct lithography. Process of converting letterpress to offset with special plates, avoiding the cost of replacing the press.

Electronic data processing (EDP). Processing data electronically, especially with computers.

Electronic mail. Computer exchange of messages.

Federal Communications Commission (FCC). Licenses radio and TV stations, assigns wavelengths, and monitors public interest in broadcasting.

Fiber optics. A technology comprising circuits derived from glass with much larger transmission capabilities than copper wires; such circuits convert a signal into a light wave, which is reconverted to signal at receiving end.

Flexographic printing. Applies water-borne ink directly to paper without offset's intermediate "blanket"; presses are cheaper, less complicated, waste less newsprint.

Front-end system. VDTs and computers that handle news and advertising copy.

Gravure printing. Printing with images etched below the nonprinting surface to cup ink in hollows; noted for high-quality reproduction.

Halftone. Photo or other continuous-tone art specially screened with criss-crossing lines so reproduction appears as small dots.

Hardware. Computer components, including mechanical and electronic.

Interactive. System that both sends and receives.

Joint Operating Agreements. Agreements whereby the U.S. Justice Department exempts some newspapers from antitrust legislation and, if one paper is failing financially, permits them to combine production and other facilities.

Kenaf. Nonwood fibrous plant that some experts feel may replace wood as the primary raw material in newsprint.

Letterpress. Now nearly extinct newspaper printing process; uses hot metal typesetting and prints from raised surface of type.

Low-power television (LPTV). Limited to 10 watts for Very High Frequency stations and 1,000 watts for Ultra High Frequency stations; designed to diversify TV ownership and permit reaching audiences in a 10 to 20-mile radius.

Linotype. Keyboard machine for mechanical setting of type from hot metal; displaced for newspapers by photocomposition.

Management information system (MIS). Internal system for making pertinent data available to decision makers.

Microwave. High-frequency electromagnetic-wave transmission in straight line of sight.

Multipoint distribution service (MDS). Service whereby microwave transmitters send pay-TV programming to subscribers equipped with special antennas.

Optical character reader (OCR or "scanner"). "Reads" typewritten copy and translates it into electronic impulses that drive typesetters; has generally given way at newspapers to VDT editing.

Offset. Prints image transferred from plate cylinder to "blanket" or second cylinder which, in turn, transfers to paper; widely used in newspapers for clean reproduction at lower cost than letterpress.

Pagination. Computerized page layout on screen; promises eventual elimination of composing and platemaking departments.

"Payback" period. Time in which reduced costs and other efficiencies cover expense of new equipment; crucial in decision whether to buy.

Personal computers (PCs). Important in newspaper production because they cost less than most VDTs and are both lightweight and transportable; many are interactive with other systems.

Photocomposition. A method of typesetting involving a light-sensitive photo process.

Plateless printing. Goal of many newspapers that hope to eventually switch to lower-cost ink-jet printing; obviates the need for heavy presses and permits rapid changes in the material being printed.

Satellite earth station. Receiver for signals transmitted from communications satellites.

Satellite plant. Production facility distant from the news and advertising offices; typically, a suburban plant linked by microwave from downtown headquarters.

Software. Programmed instructions (tapes or disks) used in conjunction with a computer.

Subscription television (STV). TV programmed for subscriber sets equipped with special decorders enabling them to receive special pay programming delivered by standard signal.

Teletext. One-way transmission of characters and graphics, usually via TV frequencies.

Video display terminal (VDT). A terminal enabling one to type material on screen for transfer into a computer; newspapers use thousands in news, advertising, administration.

Videotex. Two-way teletext; user can interrogate distant computer.

Viewtron. Videotex service developed by Knight-Ridder Newspapers, Inc., and operated by its subsidiary, Viewdata Corp. of America. Though technically able to deliver huge volumes of data, the service got a lukewarm reception from the public in its initial years.

Web printing. Printing whereby continuous rolls of paper are fed to a cylinder press, as in newspaper production.

"Wired city". Term indicating high degree of household penetration by cable TV or other forms of electronically delivered programming.

The Law and You

CHAPTER TWELVE

We conclude Part II's survey of newspaper marketing and operations with a warning: It's a legal jungle out there for you aspiring managers. We've waited until now to deal with law in newspaper management because it needs the coherence and emphasis that only a separate chapter can give. But don't think the delay means that this is a subject of secondary importance; it isn't. Newspapers operate today in a litigious, legally belligerent environment. As never before, they are under legal attack in virtually every operating sector. Emboldened by a public mood that is often critical of the press, plaintiffs seek and sometimes receive huge judgments. Suing a newspaper, if not entirely fashionable, is at least an increasingly acceptable enterprise.

Losing a suit—or paying the often enormous costs of defending against one—can destabilize your paper financially and chill its reportorial ardor. It can blemish careers. Losing to a union or government regulatory agency can create third-party intervention in your newspaper's conduct of its own business.

Currently active areas of newspaper law include libel and invasion of privacy; open records and freedom of information; antitrust; advertising and circulation; and personnel and labor. Each merits a book by a lawyer (which this author is not). So for aspiring newspaper managers, some advice: As a first step, you must retain competent legal counsel (1) to construct preventive programs designed to avoid legal difficulties and (2) to defend you when litigation threatens. Not every manager can or should be a lawyer. But every manager must learn when to call one.

A CASE EXAMPLE

At the time, the *Alton (Ill.) Telegraph* was a prosperous 38,000-circulation evening paper known for vigorous, award-winning investigative reporting. Its crusading editors brought home awards and commendations. The paper's market value was $3 million or so.

Then, the shock: a local businessman filed a $10.5 million libel suit based on a memo, never published, that two *Telegraph* reporters sent to a federal agency while they were researching a story. After a legal battle for nearly seven years, the *Telegraph* lost in 1982. A jury awarded the businessman $9.2 million—$6.7 million for actual damages and $2.5 million in punitive damages. The *Telegraph* sought protection under bankruptcy laws. Then, with legal costs mounting ($100,000 simply to prepare a never-delivered appeal), the *Telegraph* settled out of court by paying the businessman $1.4 million, much of it borrowed. The paper's owners nearly lost everything, not just jobs but almost the paper itself. A chill descended over the *Telegraph*. Salaries were frozen. Newsroom vacancies went unfilled. Cautious editors banned the use of anonymous sources; reporters often destroyed notes after use lest they be subpoenaed in any future lawsuit.[1]

The case illustrates a worsening libel situation for papers large and small. Libel is big business for many plaintiffs and their skilled attorneys. Scores of suits are filed. Damages of tens of millions of dollars are sought. Hundreds of thousands of dollars, sometimes millions, are spent in attorneys' fees and court costs. And, once a libel case comes before a lower court jury, the outlook is dim. In 1979-1983, newspaper defendants lost 83 percent of jury trials; in 1984-1985, 62 percent (compared with 33 percent of defendants who lost medical malpractice suits and 38 percent who lost product liability cases). Awards in eighty libel cases averaged $2,174,633 (compared with $665,764 in malpractice and $785,651 in product liability). For newspapers, the picture improved only after expensive appeals were carried to higher courts. There, 70 percent of verdicts against newspapers were reversed; and when lower court verdicts against newspapers were upheld, damages were often trimmed by four-fifths or more.[2]

All of which is to say there is good reason to begin "The Law and You" with law in the newsroom.

IN THE NEWSROOM: LIBEL AND INVASION OF PRIVACY

With stakes so high, every manager must make sure that the entire staff—particularly in news, down to newest cub—understands the law of libel and privacy.

Libel is injury to reputation, a false statement communicated to a third person without consent or privilege that injures or tends to injure an individual's reputation by lowering community estimation and causing him or her to be shunned or avoided or exposed to hatred, contempt, or ridicule. Damages against newspapers often result when stories cause monetary loss to an individual or business. Provable truth is the only complete defense, but some state laws require truth with good motives or justifiable ends. Check with local counsel for a precise interpretation.

In some circumstances, newspapers have privilege. They are immune if they fairly and accurately cover certain sources—judicial, legislative, public, and official proceedings and most public records, even if those proceedings or records contain libelous statements. This is a tricky area; what constitutes "judicial proceed-

[1] John Curley, "How Libel Suit Sapped the Crusading Spirit of a Small Newspaper," *Wall Street Journal*, Sept. 29, 1983, p. 1.

[2] "Socking It to the Press," *Editor & Publisher*, April 7, 1984, p. 31; also see David Astor, "A Look At Libel," *Editor & Publisher*, Oct. 5, 1985, p. 14.

ings," for example, can vary. Again, consult a local attorney. The right of fair comment permits factually true, fair comment without malice on matters of public interest. (For background in how recent libel law was fashioned, see the box entitled "Landmark Cases.")

An increasingly active sector of law concerns invasion of privacy. Newspapers have been found liable for unreasonable intrusion into the seclusion or privacy of an individual because they publicly revealed embarrassing or objectionable private facts or held the individual in a false light. Stories held to shock or outrage the "reasonable person" are dangerous. Intrusion can include use of hidden cameras or microphones or theft of documents. Such tactics can be legally (and ethically) indefensible. In general, courts hold that individuals lose the right to privacy when they are involved in a news event or story of legitimate public interest, even against their will. But this is a gray area. Newspapers have been found liable for digging up distasteful, sordid details from the past of a person who currently lives a private life that is not newsworthy. That is, truth is sometimes no defense if there is no current newsworthiness or if the truth is sufficiently private and embarrassing. Another dangerous area is appropriation without consent of the name or photograph of an individual for commercial gain. This could include using a person's name or photograph in an advertisement endorsing a product, for example. It's all so complex that safeguards must be developed.

How to Avoid Libel: A Checklist

- Hire a lawyer expert in libel (not contract law, not real estate) who can explain current law in lay language. Let the lawyer construct your safeguards against libel. Whenever possible, retain the lawyer to read dangerous copy prior to publication or take telephone inquiries from your news desk—even at midnight.

- Hold regular staff seminars on libel, with both counsel and top executives participating to underline the subject's importance.

- Make sure that a libel manual is available in the newsroom and that each staff member signifies in writing that it has been read. A fine manual for the working journalist is in *The AP Stylebook* (The Associated Press, 50 Rockefeller Plaza, New York, NY 10020), but it should be amended by counsel for local applicability.

- Wage unrelenting war on careless, sloppy reporting and writing. This is the cause of most libel cases. Demand accurate handling of *every* story. Even the most routine, seemingly innocuous story can be libel dynamite. Insist that reporters assigned to highly technical stories—crime, law, medicine, business—have the expertise to write balanced, accurate stories.

- Weed out activist reporters who carry their causes into what should be dispassionate news columns. Beware of tendentious, argumentative, imprecise language. Some words—"Nazi," "communist," "liar," "drunkard," "fraud"—are libel per se in some circumstances.

- Discourage overuse of "informed source" or unnamed "official source" who gives your reporter a damaging story about someone. What are the motives behind this anonymous attack? Is the story of meaningful, substantive interest to readers or simply malicious? Is it probably worth the risk? Sometimes, you might insist that if anonymous sources must be used, they sign statements authenticating their information so there can be no reneging in court. *Always* make sure that a responsible editor knows the identity of the reporter's anonymous source.

- Carefully monitor investigative stories alleging criminality or malfeasance. Again,

LANDMARK CASES

Where libel law is going is unclear. Changes in the U.S. Supreme Court's makeup will probably have great impact on the law's evolution. But managers must make sure that newsroom staff at least knows how the law got where it is. The landmark cases are these:

New York Times v. Sullivan (1964)

The court ruled that public officials must prove actual malice to collect damages for a story on their official conduct. Malice was defined as publishing despite knowledge that the story was false or in reckless disregard of whether it was.

Associated Press v. Walker (1967)

This case extended Times v. Sullivan to include not just public "officials" but also public "figures" in whose "public conduct society and the press had a legitimate and substantial interest." In AP v. Walker and a consolidated case, Curtis Publishing Co. v. Butts, the court made a distinction between "hot news" stories and investigative reporting. Careful substantiation of all facts is doubly required in the latter.

Rosenbloom v. Metromedia (1971)

The court ruled that a private individual (as well as public official or public figure) must show malice to recover libel damages when coverage is on matters of public interest.

Gertz v. Welch (1974)

Here, the court signaled that it felt it went too far in Rosenbloom v. Metromedia. In cases not involving punitive damages, it said, private individuals did not have to prove malice, only fault by the newspaper. It left open to state courts the definition of what constitutes fault or negligence. The court also left it up to lower courts to decide who is a "public figure." In this case, it ruled that a well-known Chicago attorney was a private individual.

Time, Inc. v. Firestone (1976)

The court ruled that a prominent socialite who held press conferences and used a clipping service to collect stories about herself was a private individual in libel law. The decision seemed to limit the protection the press won in Times v. Sullivan, confining it to cases involving public officials and public figures who willingly step into the limelight.

Starting in 1979, a series of decisions created concern among newspaper executives that the Court was taking a conservative view of the press. Among other things, the court began to allow libel plaintiffs to probe the "state of mind" of reporters and their conversations with editors prior to publication of an alleged libel. However, two decisions in 1986 were interpreted as granting newspapers additional protection: In Philadelphia Newspapers, Inc. v. Hepps, the Court ruled that a person suing a news organization for libel must prove damaging statements to be false, at least on "matters of public concern." Until that ruling, the burden was on news organizations to prove that contested statements were true. In Anderson v. Liberty Lobby, the Court ruled that libel suits filed in federal courts by public officials and public figures must be dismissed before trial unless evidence suggests that libel can be proved with "convincing clarity." That was hailed as encouraging judges to dismiss weak cases and avoid expensive trials.

In an important case in 1987, a federal appeals court in Washington threw out a jury award of $2 million that had been won by William Tavoulareas, a former president of Mobil Corporation, in a libel suit against the Washington Post. The Post had reported Tavoulareas "set up his son" in a shipping firm doing business with Mobil. The appeals court ruled Tavoulareas was a "public figure" and thus must prove the Post defamed him with "actual malice." The court ruled the Post story was "substantially true" and said it agreed with the newspaper that "the First Amendment forbids penalizing the press for encouraging its reporters to expose wrongdoing by public corporations and public figures."

you may have to prove truth. Warn against unseemly haste. It can cause errors and errors may spell libel.

- Extend your libel watch to all pages— letters to the editor (your newspaper is legally responsible for *all* content), photographs, births, hospital notes, marriages, and that column called "Our Town 30 Years Ago Today" (you can be in big trouble if you resurrect the drunk driving arrest, thirty years ago, of a person who subsequently lived a blameless private life).

- Strive for sensitive handling of stories that are journalistically unfair—that hurt, embarrass, or cause monetary loss. Those stories are libel bait. Get balancing comment; be fair.

- And check the libel insurance. It's expensive, but you cannot be without it. Companies specializing in libel are Safeco of Seattle, Mutual Insurance Co., Ltd., of Hamilton, Bermuda, and Employers Reinsurance Corp. of Overland Park, Kansas. The Libel Defense Resource Center of New York City, a media-supported group, can provide additional background.

What to Do When Trouble Erupts

You must make sure that all employees understand how to handle a libel threat. Here are some pointers:

Assume that every threat of a lawsuit— even implied—is serious. Columnist William Safire of the *New York Times* terms libel lawsuits the "rich man's relief." Those who threaten to sue may be able to afford following through.

If an attorney telephones about a story, you, the layman, never do the talking. Instead, your attorney talks law with the complaining attorney. What is said or written following alleged libel can be crucial to a lawsuit's outcome. When danger flags go up, especially if the words "libel" or "lawsuit" are mentioned, give the matter to your attorney. Anxious young reporters trying to "straighten things out" themselves with an attorney or offended individual can dig your newspaper deeper into trouble. You must create a newsroom climate that encourages reporters to discuss libel threats with their superiors rather than acting independently.

In any discussion, *admit nothing.* Libel law is complex, and what appears libelous to the complainant or even to you might not be libel at all. Listen courteously to any complaint, take full notes, and promise to investigate. Then, call your attorney. Complaints often arise from momentary anger that people feel when they are hurt or embarassed in print. Sometimes, a fair hearing of their complaint will solve the problem. In delicate situations, consult your attorney in negotiating and writing corrections; *never* publish a retraction without counsel's advice. Retractions can later be held to be admissions of falsity or wrongdoing. Also, a retraction can repeat the defamation and thus increase the newspaper's liability. The best way to defend against a libel suit is not to let it get into court.

There is danger that you may so frighten the newsroom staff—or yourself—about libel that self-censorship settles over the newspaper. The rising number of suits filed by corporations may be aiming to do just that. Examples are lawsuits over stories critiquing new products or even reviewing restaurant food. Mobil Corp. in 1982 insured 100 top executives for up to $10 million in legal fees should any of them sue for libel. Achieving correct balance in alerting employees to libel but not alarming them is a delicate matter for any manager. You must come down on the side of aggressive but fair, courageous but careful journalism. Threats of multi-million-dollar libel judgments must be a business consideration but cannot be allowed to dampen your newspaper's reportorial efforts or the independence of its editorial pages.

Is Offense the Best Defense?

Weary of what they regard as unfounded libel suits, some newspapers are going on the offen-

sive. The *Charleston (W.Va.) Gazette* files coun-
tersuits against plaintiffs' lawyers when it feels
libel suits are without merit. The publisher who
established the paper's policy, the late W. E.
(Ned) Chilton III, said: "I decided this newspaper would not sit back and allow baseless suits
to remain unanswered. I wasn't going to file
against the plaintiff because he didn't know the
law. I went against the lawyer."[3] Chilton advises:
"If enough lawyers are forced to pay for their
unmeritorious lawsuits against newspapers, caution will grow among lawyers and fewer unnecessary libel suits will be filed."[4] Dow Jones &
Co. and Cowles Media also counterattack. Both
won back some legal costs from plaintiffs who
sued them and lost.

However, the largest recorded out-of-court
settlement was made by Dow Jones's *Wall Street
Journal*—$800,000 to two former federal pros-
ecutors named in a story. Some publishers fear
that such settlements encourage other libel suits.
The *Des Moines Register & Tribune* spread
word through the Iowa Bar Association that it
would settle no libel suit out of court even if
such a step would save money.

Let the Sunshine In

Who cared when the Knoxville, Tennessee,
school board elected officers secretly? The *Knoxville News-Sentinel* did. It sued under the state's
"Sunshine Law" to force the board to conduct
public affairs in full public light.

Not one network TV crew rushed to the
story in Knoxville; no national newspapers or
magazines covered it. It was left to the *News-
Sentinel* to make a fuss—one of uncounted legal
actions taken at considerable expense by newspapers throughout the country to protect the
public's right to know what its government is

up to and to guard the press's right to cover it.
The effort must extend up the government
ladder to highest federal levels. If the press
doesn't force light into those bureaucratic corridors, who will?

As a manager, you must participate aggressively in this effort if your reporters are to have
free access to news and if your newspaper is to
be a reputable community leader. Many government officials want to shield themselves and
their official activities from public view. But
federal and state laws give you strong weapons
to fight this. Here are some sources of help:

- Reporters' Committee for Freedom of the
Press. It has an FOI Service Center (800
18th Street, N.W., Washington, DC 10006)
that instructs reporters on how to use the
federal FOI Act. A telephone hotline (202-
466-6312) gives free aid in press law matters. The center provides sample letters
for requesting government information (see
box) and will even tell you how much
federal agencies charge for assistance ($6
per hour, for example, for clerical help at
the Central Intelligence Agency in 1984).

- State press associations usually retain legal
counsel and provide Sunshine Law assistance. The Georgia Press Association, for
example, publishes a tiny (2½″ × 3½″)
booklet on state public records and open
meeting laws. It fits easily into reporters'
wallets. (Georgia Press Association, 1075
Spring Street, N.W., Atlanta, GA 30309.)

- The Society of Professional Journalists, Sigma
Delta Chi, operates a legal defense fund
for First Amendment cases. (840 N. Lake
Shore Dr., Suite 803, Chicago, IL 60611.)

Other active press groups include ASNE,
ANPA, and Inland Daily Press Association.
Gannett Co. and the New York Times Co.
are among communications companies often
arguing for open access in FOI battles. Gannett
expects its reporters to object if a courtroom is

[3] Steve Weinberg, "Libel: The Press Fights Back," *Columbia Journalism Review*, November 1983, p. 65.
[4] "Charleston Gazette Continues Fight Against Unwarranted Suits," Southern Newspaper Publishers' Association *Bulletin*, June 1, 1984, p. 2.

FOI SAMPLE REQUEST

This letter is recommended by the Reporters' Committee for Freedom of the Press for requesting information under the Federal Freedom of Information Act. The committee's FOI Service Center *in Washington, D.C., provides guidance also for journalists in appealing FOI decisions or taking legal action.*

Telephone No. (business hours)
Return Address
Date

Name of Public Body
Address

To the FOI Officer
 This request is made under the federal Freedom of Information Act, 5 U.S.C. 552.
 Please send me copies of *(Here, clearly describe what you want. Include identifying material, such as names, places, and the period of time about which you are inquiring. If you wish, attach news clips, reports, and other documents describing the subject of your research.)*
 As you know, the FOI Act provides that if portions of a document are exempt from release, the remainder must be segregated and disclosed. Therefore, I will expect you to send me all nonexempt portions of the records which I have requested, and ask that you justify any deletions by reference to specific exemptions of the FOI Act. I reserve the right to appeal your decision to withhold any materials.
 I promise to pay reasonable search and duplication fees in connection with this request. However, if you estimate that the total fees will exceed $_____, please notify me so that I may authorize expenditure of a greater amount.
 (Optional) I am prepared to pay reasonable search and duplication fees in connection with this request. However, the FOI Act provides for waiver or reduction of fees if disclosure could be considered as "primarily benefiting the general public." I am a journalist *(researcher, or scholar)* employed by *(name of news organization, book publishers, etc.)*, and intend to use the information I am requesting as the basis for a planned article *(broadcast, or book)*. *(Add arguments here in support of fee waiver)*. Therefore, I ask that you waive all search and duplication fees. If you deny this request, however, and the fees will exceed $_____, please notify me of the charges before you fill my request so that I may decide whether to pay the fees or appeal your denial of my request for a waiver.
 As I am making this request in the capacity of a journalist *(author, or scholar)* and this information is of timely value, I will appreciate your communicating with me by telephone, rather than by mail, if you have any questions regarding this request. Thank you for your assistance, and I will look forward to receiving your reply within 10 business days, as required by law.

Very truly yours,

Reprinted with permission.

(Signature)

"YOUR HONOR . . ."

Gannett Co. equips reporters with wallet-size cards carrying guidelines on how to object if a judge closes a courtroom and expels the press. The message is short, respectful of the court, and to the point:

Your honor, I am _____, a reporter for _____, and I would like to object on behalf of my employer and the public to this proposed closing. Our attorney is prepared to make a number of arguments against closings such as this one, and we respectfully ask the Court for a hearing on these issues. I believe our attorney can be here relatively quickly for the Court's convenience and he (she) will be able to demonstrate that closure in this case will violate the First Amendment, and possible state statutory and constitutional provisions as well. I cannot make the arguments myself, but our attorney can point out several issues for your consideration. If it please the Court, we request the opportunity to be heard through Counsel.

---

closed to them. They carry small cards they can read to the judge (see box). The Gannett statement objects to courtroom closure on behalf of "my employer *and* the public. . . ." It is a *public* right the press defends. The issues, of course, are free press and fair trial, a clash inevitable at times between the First Amendment and the Sixth Amendment guarantee to criminal defendants of speedy and public trial by an impartial jury or the Fourteenth Amendment guarantee of due process under the law. Judges sometimes rule that news coverage prejudices juries, making fair trial impossible; they therefore close courtrooms or issue "gag orders" restricting coverage. Most such restraints are eventually struck down by the U.S. Supreme Court. But unclear is whether *pre*trial hearings are subject to closing. In this era of plea bargaining, pretrial hearings are often the only forum for criminal proceedings. If your newspaper is to operate with a sense of social responsibility, reporters should use the Gannett approach and lodge a protest at any judicial closing.

Shield Laws, Searches, the SEC

Shield laws, adopted by about half the states, give reporters some protection against being forced to divulge confidential information or testify in court or before legislative and administrative groups. However, laws vary widely and are open to judicial interpretation. Sometimes, they are not much help. New Jersey has a shield law, but *New York Times* reporter Myron Farber spent forty days in a New Jersey jail for refusing to turn over notes subpoenaed in a murder trial. It cost the *Times* $286,000 in fines. The *Times* recovered $101,000 when it was pardoned, with Farber, by the governor in 1982—but the courageous stand on principle by Farber and his paper was expensive.

Newsroom searches by police were held by the U.S. Supreme Court in 1978 (*Zurcher* v. *Stanford Daily*) to be constitutional if performed under a valid search warrant issued to obtain evidence that was reasonably thought to be at the newspaper office. This arose from a search in 1971 of the Stanford University *Daily*. The Privacy Protection Act of 1980 says that newsrooms can be searched only in rare circumstances, as when officials have reason to believe a search is necessary to save a life or prevent destruction of materials or when a subpoena would be ineffective. Remember: a search warrant authorizes police to use force if necessary. You may refuse to cooperate, stall, ask questions, call your attorney—but don't resist physically.

Securities and Exchange Commission regulations and how they affect the press are controversial and evolving. The subject became heated with SEC charges in 1984 that *Wall*

New York Times reporter Myron Farber (right), with his attorney. Farber spent 40 days in jail for refusing to turn over notes he took in investigating a murder, but was later pardoned by the New Jersey governor.
(UPI/Bettmann Newsphotos)

Street Journal reporter R. Foster Winans and four others had profited illegally from his advance knowledge of stories the *Journal* would publish. It was charged that they traded stocks, later benefiting when the stories caused prices to rise or fall. There was some sentiment in Congress and elsewhere for classifying reporters as "insiders"—people the SEC judges to have advance information that could move market prices. An insider is supposed to reveal inside information publicly or refrain from trading. The *Wall Street Journal*, like many newspapers, prohibits employees from buying or selling securities or sharing inside information until two days after an article about a stock is published. *Journal* reporters are not supposed to trade at all in the securities of companies they cover.

IN THE MARKETPLACE: ANTITRUST

Few problems are potentially more dangerous for newspapers than today's heated antitrust climate. As a manager, you must make *no* significant move in the marketplace without expert counsel on what, if any, are its antitrust implications. It's that bad.

Antitrust suits are proliferating and defense costs escalating; attorneys' fees in the hundreds of thousands of dollars are not unusual. You easily, unwittingly can make mistakes that leave your newspaper vulnerable in lawsuits. Losers in civil antitrust cases can face *treble damages* along with enormous legal costs—plus enforced change of the newspaper's competitive posture or severe restrictions on future operations. Criminal antitrust conviction can mean heavy fines and jail terms. Here are some examples:

The 5,600-circulation *Manteca (Calif.) Bulletin* was awarded $6.3 million damages from a competitor, the *Manteca News*, in an antitrust suit charging that advertising was sold illegally below cost and that secret, discriminatory discounts were offered to some advertisers. Gannett Co. opted for an expensive out-of-court settlement when its *Salem (Ore.) Statesman and*

Capital Journal was charged in a multimillion dollar suit with using illegal, predatory means to drive a shopper out of business; some Salem advertisers sued on grounds the newspaper (now consolidated into the *Statesman-Journal*) thus deprived them of an alternative outlet for print advertising. The Chicago Tribune Co. agreed to sell two shoppers and three weekly paid papers in Osceola County, Florida, when the Justice Department charged that their purchase by the Tribune Co.'s neighboring *Orlando Sentinel* would have the "probable effect" of substantially lessening advertising competition in the county. The Tribune Co. bought the publications in 1980 for $4.1 million, and Justice started an investigation within three months, saying the *Sentinel* had 40 percent of the county's print advertising and the five smaller publications, 20 percent.

Antitrust cases often arise from shifting competitive patterns that throw established dailies and weeklies into direct competition with shoppers, direct mail, and other newcomers. Along with radio, TV, and other media, all are fighting for essentially the same advertiser dollar. And some losers extend the war into the courtroom with antitrust charges.

The Legal Background

Federal and state antitrust laws are many and complex, covering wide areas of newspaper operations. Federal laws spring from these acts:

- The Sherman Antitrust Act (1890) is designed to protect free competition in business. It prohibits unreasonable restraint of trade involving a conspiracy of two or more persons. This includes competitors as well as buyers and sellers who conspire in such matters as price fixing, dividing markets, or boycotting or illegally damaging a third party. It prohibits monopolizing a market or conspiring or attempting to do so for illegal purposes. Generally, a newspaper with 70 percent of the "relevant" advertising market is presumed to possess monopoly power, although even 50 percent can trigger suits. These days, an ill-defined "substantial" share of the market—if unfairly gained—can run risk of suit.

- The Clayton Act (1914) broadens Sherman by prohibiting activities that could illegally stifle competition. Clayton prohibits discriminatory pricing that injures other media. It prohibits "tying arrangements" that force a buyer to purchase a product just to get another—ads in a shopper to get space in a newspaper, for example.

- The Federal Trade Commission Act (1914) created the FTC to enforce federal antitrust laws. Its scope includes business practices violating consumer interests regardless of competitive factors involved. The FTC watches for deceptive advertising.

- The Robinson-Patman Act (1936) prohibits price discrimination in interstate commerce (in which newspapers are generally found to be engaged).

A key word throughout all this is "conspiracy." You or other employees must avoid any contact with competitors that could be construed as aiming at an agreement to fix prices, divide markets, or otherwise contravene antitrust laws. This includes meetings at trade association conventions or other seemingly innocuous affairs.

Take Care with Shoppers

Much antitrust litigation revolves around shopper publications, often when an established daily or weekly launches one or otherwise responds to the arrival in the market of an independent shopper. No established paper should field a shopper without expert legal advice. Factors to consider:

The law does not frown on any newspaper launching a "fighting ship," a new publication designed to improve or regain competitive position. The law, indeed, is structured to promote vigorous, fair competition. However, from day one in the planning process you must demonstrate you desire only to improve your newspaper's own economic interests—that your motivation in launching a shopper is to respond to advertiser demands for a new publication. Detailed memos must be kept showing clearly that the shopper, its marketing strategy, and its ad rates are not structured to harm any present or future competitor. Launching a shopper with the intent of driving a competitor from the marketplace is reckless, dangerous, and—in most cases—illegal.

Understand that however pure your intent, you can still be sued. In some particularly competitive markets, established papers *assume* they will be sued if they launch a shopper. Juries sometimes vote their emotions in antitrust cases, which can be so complex that even skilled lawyers have difficulties understanding the law. And sometimes, juries indentify established papers as the "big guy," the wealthy, powerful villain; the shopper publisher sometimes comes off as the favored "little guy," the underdog. So, even though you may intend to compete fairly and legally, you need legal counsel from the start in establishing the structure and operating patterns of any TMC product. The thrust of many antitrust suits is that a newspaper uses illegal, predatory tactics to achieve or maintain a market monopoly. Ensuring fair intent plus legal operation of a shopper might not keep you out of court, but it could improve your chances of eventually winning if you do get sued.

Monopoly position is not illegal as such. Recent newspaper history demonstrates that papers die for many reasons, leaving a single paper the natural victor (still facing other types of media competitors, to be sure). But illegal use of monopoly power thus gained has a high probability of drawing fire.

So, first, you must be doubly cautious if you manage the only paid-circulation daily or weekly in your market. Newspaper strategists feel that this does not constitute monopoly, that the newspaper still faces competitors such as radio, TV, and direct mail. But chances are that an antitrust-minded plaintiff will move against a dominant newspaper and its shopper, not against, say, a radio or TV station or city magazine.

Second, you must plan to operate your shopper at a profit as quickly as possible. Do *not* plan to run it at a loss indefinitely, subsidizing it from the established paper. That can be construed as intending a low-cost operation to ensure low ad rates that unfairly undercut a competitor's rates. And that is predatory pricing, an illegal tactic. Unfortunately, courts have not clarified how long a newspaper could reasonably subsidize start-up costs of a new shopper before being guilty of predatory pricing.

Third, be certain advertisers are entirely free to buy space in either the dominant paper or its companion shopper and are not forced or coerced unfairly to buy in one publication to obtain space in the other. Such forced combination buys are illegal "tie-ins." It *is* legal to offer an advertiser a discount to buy in both— but the discount must reflect the newspaper's cost saving when, for example, it uses the same ad mechanical in both publications. Obviously, antitrust cases often revolve around the definition of "reasonable" cost savings.

Fourth, be extremely careful in setting shopper ad rates. When there is even a whiff of a potential antitrust action in the air, let legal counsel assist.

Cost Allocation and Rate Setting Are Crucial

Antitrust actions involving shoppers focus on ad strategies and rates. A villain in the piece can be predatory pricing—selling advertising below cost with the intent of driving competitors from the market and eventually monopolizing a market to obtain abnormally high profits in the future.

In many antitrust cases revolving around

this principle, a key is determining what a newspaper's true costs in operating its shopper are. Accountants use different approaches in determining this. Whatever the approach, your shopper must be allocated a fair, equitable portion of *fixed costs* plus *variable costs*. That is, the shopper should be charged a fair portion of, say, building expense and administrative overhead as well as cost of newsprint, labor, and other variables that go into shopper operations. Courts have not established precise cost allocation guidelines. But you must make sure that you allocate costs fairly and equitably to the shopper and intend that it produce a profit. Obviously, these are areas where it is unsettling to be at the mercy of lay jurors—after all, what is fair and equitable cost allocation in a highly complex newspaper operation? And what is a reasonable time for a newspaper to expect its shopper to turn a profit? At this point in any trial, plaintiff might ask the jury to consider the newspaper's overall profit picture, its reputation in the community—an appeal to emotion, not law.

You must be sure that your newspaper is not discriminatory in pricing, secretive or arbitrary in ad-rate implementation, or coercive. The risk of attracting an antitrust lawsuit—and losing—increases significantly with such tactics. A few hints:

- Combination rates granting advertisers discounts for using both newspaper and shopper cannot be so heavily biased for such "combo" buying that they constitute coercion or an illegal tying arrangement.

- Off-card selling—departing from a published rate card—can be highly dangerous if it grants more favorable treatment to one advertiser than to others. That's price discrimination. Insist that salespeople avoid secret or arbitrary deals. Publish a rate card and stick to it with all advertisers.

- Discount for frequency or volume of advertising, long a fixture of newspaper pol-

icy, has come under scrutiny by the Federal Trade Commission. Get an antitrust expert to look over your discount policies.

Launching and operating shoppers, then, is legally tricky if your newspaper is dominant in your market. Dominant papers simply must accept that they have to operate under restrictions—self-imposed or otherwise—that other competitors do not face. It is a price of success and all employees must be aware of it. It can be helpful in any later lawsuit to demonstrate that your awareness included establishing an antitrust compliance program. This should be a formal, documented effort proving that top management committed itself to fair and legal competition in the marketplace and that reasonable moves were made to inform the full staff.

IN ADVERTISING: THE LEGAL TRAPS

Legal traps await the unwary in many sectors of newspaper advertising.

You must make sure that all advertising employees are sensitive to possible problems in libel; FTC regulations covering misleading ads; lottery advertisements; liquor ads; and particularly federal, state, and local laws prohibiting ads that discriminate on the basis of race, color, religion, sex, or national origin. In 1986, Gannett's *Jackson (Miss.) Clarion-Ledger* and *Daily News*, 68,000 morning circulation and 37,000 evening circulation, respectively, settled a U.S. Justice Department complaint by signing a consent decree permanently enjoining the papers from using words such as "white male," "female only," or "gentleman" in advertisements. There can also be problems in publishing ads that make false or fraudulent claims, that promote illegal activity, or that encourage activities harmful to health and safety.

It is impractical to retain legal counsel to clear each of the thousands of ads a newspaper publishes. But each employee should be trained to recognize those occasional ads that must be viewed by supervisors and possibly the paper's attorney before publication.

Beware: Three Danger Areas

First, all employees should understand that the newspaper can be as legally responsible for ad copy published as for news or editorials.

Second, a newspaper has the right to refuse an ad, but the circumstances under which that is done and how it is done can be extremely important.

Third, in some cases, merely accepting an ad handed over the counter or telephoned in can constitute a contractual agreement to publish, even though the ad taker may have private reservations and intends to submit the copy for higher review.

Libel and invasion of privacy considerations, discussed earlier as they relate to news, apply fully to ad copy. It was an *advertisement* that triggered the lengthy, costly *Times* v. *Sullivan* case (see the first box in this chapter). Advertising employees must be included in your libel training program.

Be certain that rate cards, contracts, and classified ad pages carry disclaimers of financial responsibility for ad copy or photographs that libel or invade privacy. Contracts should make advertisers and ad agencies responsible for indemnifying the paper and holding it harmless for an ad's contents. Your attorney should draft

the language, of course, but see the box for an example.

A newspaper's right to refuse an ad is founded in the First Amendment and the right of a company to decline to enter a contract. However, that right is not unconditional. Antitrust law, for example, prohibits the paper from conspiring with a third party to refuse ads from another. It is illegal to agree with your largest food store advertiser that you will reject ads to drive an upstart fruit store operator out of business. Also, a new problem arises out of a Rhode Island case, *Home Placement Service* v. *Providence Journal Company.* It appears that antitrust law can limit a newspaper's right to reject advertising that might compete with its own advertising business if the newspaper has a clear monopoly position in its market. In this case, the *Providence (R.I.) Journal* declined ads from a home rental agency, saying readers complained about that kind of advertising. The agency claimed the *Journal* so dominated the advertising scene that to be excluded from its pages was harmful. Issues are far from clarified, but papers strongly dominating their advertising marketplaces must be careful.

Once you alert employees to types of copy that, for legal reasons, will not be published, you must make sure that no dangerous copy is accepted under terms that constitute a contract. To accept copy but then not publish it can invite lawsuit for breach of contract. This is troublesome particularly in classified, because many

INDEMNIFICATION CLAUSE A MUST

All rate cards and advertising contracts must carry language under which advertisers and ad agencies agree to indemnify the paper for legal problems arising from published ad copy. The Macon (Ga.) Telegraph and News *uses this:*

Advertiser and advertising agency will indemnify and hold harmless *Telegraph and News,* its officers, agents, employees and contractors, for all contents supplied to publisher, including text, representations and illustrations of advertisements printed, and for any claims arising from contents including, but not limited to, defamation, invasion of privacy, copyright infringement, plagiarism, and in the case of a pre-printed insert, deficient postage.

ads are telephoned in or casually accepted for cash over the counter. If not handled properly, both techniques can constitute a contract to publish. There are two steps to take.

First, publish daily in the classified section an appropriate disclaimer. The *Schenectady (N.Y.) Gazette* uses this:

> The *Schenectady Gazette* reserves the right not to accept an advertiser's order. Only publication of an advertisement shall constitute final acceptance of the advertiser's order.

This gives supervisors time to read and, if necessary, reject any dangerous ad even though the ad was taken by telephone.

Second, drill employees in proper techniques of taking ads. The International Newspaper Advertising and Marketing Executives' Association recommends these steps if an ad taker senses copy is unacceptable:

- Tell the customer the ad must be reviewed by a supervisor *before* it can be accepted.

- *Do not* give the customer a reason or respond to questions. What is said at this point may be pivotal in any later lawsuit.

- *Do* give the customer a copy of the rate card (which contains standards of acceptability).[5]

Beware of Other Problem Areas

Liquor advertising is banned in two states, Oklahoma and Mississippi, and it is a controversial subject. Some press groups, including ANPA, argue that such bans abridge commercial free speech rights. In cases from both states in 1984, the U.S. Supreme Court declined to address First Amendment issues. Rising public opinion against drunk drivers could bring pressure for restrictions on liquor advertising, now $1 billion annually ($100 million for newspapers).

You must make sure that all employees know the dangers in lottery advertising. State lotteries have been exempted, but postal regulations forbid mail delivery of newspapers advertising other lotteries.

The FTC could attempt to make newspapers responsible for ensuring compliance with the law regarding truth in lending. At present, lending institutions, not newspapers, are responsible for ensuring that their advertising reflects lending terms available to consumers, specifies annual interest rates, and sets forth all major terms of a loan.[6] But FTC officials are known to want newspapers to ensure compliance.

Generally, the advertiser, not the newspaper, is responsible under federal law for ad content. However, you must guard against ads that blatantly promote illegal activity or are false, fraudulent, or misleading.

Local counsel must be consulted on local and state laws concerning ads that discriminate because of race, color, religion, sex, or national origin. Laws vary widely and are complex. Under federal laws, the Equal Employment Opportunity Commission could move against your newspaper if ads discriminate in employment or housing matters.

IN CIRCULATION: ANTITRUST BREEDING GROUND

In circulation operations, you must avoid antitrust difficulties in three areas particularly: relationships with distributors, price setting, and assignment of circulation routes or territories.

Sounds as if it covers all of circulation? Correct. Circulation is a breeding ground for antitrust problems. Antitrust suits often follow marketplace changes that draw new competitors, particularly shoppers, into a field occupied by an established daily or weekly. Others arise from

[5] "How to Refuse An Ad . . . Reminders For Your Ad-Takers," *INAME News*, June 1984, p. 13.

[6] "FTC Eyes Housing Ads For Financial Data," *presstime*, March 1984, p. 36.

newspapers' efforts to gain control of the ultimate pricing, sale, and delivery of their own products. And many papers have simply become large, financially successful businesses that constitute attractive targets for antitrust action.

In the currently litigious climate, you must consult counsel on important circulation strategies.

Take Care with Distributors

Most newspapers—90 percent, according to the International Circulation Managers' Association—use adult or teenage independent-contract distributors who buy newspapers and put together their own distribution schemes.[7]

Out of that arise major operational problems: Some papers face subscriber discontent over faulty delivery handled by independent distributors. Some distributors aggressively sell new subscriptions, some don't. They set their own retail prices, which sometimes vary within the same general area. Some set prices higher than the paper's "suggested retail price," seeking higher profit by delivering fewer papers at higher prices, and that can contradict the newspaper's strategy of seeking greater circulation. Distributors establish their own routes and territories; sometimes the results fit the paper's overall circulation and advertising strategies and sometimes they don't. In extreme cases, management virtually loses control over its own product. Once lost, control of pricing and sale of the paper can be difficult to regain.

Any attempt to force independent-contract distributors to do things the newspaper's way can significantly increase exposure to antitrust charges. Courts have long held that in certain circumstances a newspaper's effort to control retail prices that independent distributors charge subscribers can be an antitrust violation per se. A price agreement between a newspaper and a distributor can be construed as a "vertical agree-

ment" to fix prices, which is prohibited by Section 1 of the Sherman Act. ("Horizontal" agreement—say, conspiracy between two distributors in adjacent territories to fix prices—also is prohibited.) If you use independent-contract distributors, you must restrict yourself to issuing "suggested" retail prices, and be careful how you do that. There will be the temptation to subtly, indirectly force distributors to toe a price line or try to set mandatory upper and lower price ranges. Resist the temptation. It is dangerous.

You must seek expert legal counsel if you want to establish territorial boundaries for your independent-contract distributors. Dividing a market between them can be illegal under Section 1 of the Sherman Act if it tends to lessen competition. Under some circumstances, particularly if competition is *increased*, a vertical agreement between newspaper and distributor on territorial boundaries may be acceptable. But don't make a move without counsel's approval. Note that prohibited division of a market can include not only cutting it up along territorial boundaries but also by types of products to be sold within the market or types of subscribers or purchasers to be approached.

Obviously, if you use independent-contract carriers, you should at least study switching to another system. But changing can create problems. First, there are operational problems of terminating arrangements that may be decades old. Choices for a new system are an employee carrier force, under which you are free to set retail prices and fix territories, or an agent system, under which you *hire* independent individuals or companies to deliver papers. Note the distinction: an agent does not purchase papers for resale, thus you can control pricing as well as territorial and other operational factors.

Second, independent-contract carriers sometimes sue a newspaper that terminates their contracts, demanding compensation for routes or territories. Courts generally have not found routes to be tangible property for which compensation is due. But suits have demanded tens

---

[7] C. David Rambo, "Distribution & The Law," *presstime*, October 1983, p. 4.

of thousands of dollars and are costly to defend against; you should seek counsel before risking suit by terminating agreements.

Third, your newspaper could be vulnerable to FTC action if competition is lessened in any way by terminating agreements with independent contractors and taking over their territories. The FTC shows growing interest in monitoring this area.

Other Problem Areas

Other potentially troublesome areas in circulation to watch:

- Antitrust laws on tie-in arrangements can prohibit forcing a distributor to purchase one product to get another—for example, a morning paper to obtain the afternoon paper if the papers are separate products and competition would be lessened. Courts generally hold that separate editions of the same newspaper are not separate products. This issue arose when one paper was charged with illegally tying its Saturday edition to the Monday-Friday editions; the issue was decided in the paper's favor. A suit brought in Maine by three subscribers charged a paper with illegally tying its Sunday edition to the weekday editions. Many daily papers "force" their Sunday editions, meaning, in newspaper parlance, that they automatically include it in a subscription for the daily paper. This could be legally delicate in the future.

- Refusal to deal with, say, an uncooperative independent-contract distributor can be prohibited if the newspaper has consulted third parties—subscribers or other distributors, for example—and if courts find the newspaper has illegal objectives. This can arise if a newspaper refuses to deal with a distributor who will not follow "suggested" pricing, for example, or who refuses to handle both morning and afternoon news-

papers. Generally, however, a newspaper is free, unilaterally, to refuse to deal with a buyer of any kind.

- News racks and vending machines can create problems because some municipalities try to limit their numbers and locations for esthetic reasons or, more importantly, tax them to raise new revenue. Absent larger legal issues, local counsel should handle such incidents on a case-by-case basis.

- Sampling or free distribution of a newspaper as an inducement to subscribe occasionally ends up in court. Some courts hold that, under certain circumstances, intense sampling in the same area for, say, five to ten weeks is excessive; two weeks has been held to be usual. The issue in longer sampling is whether a newspaper is unfairly undercutting competition by giving away papers.

IN POSTAL LAW: WORDY COMPLEXITY

Thousands of words are used in regulations governing first-, second-, third-, and fourth-class mail. Second class is the primary vehicle used to mail most paid-circulation newspapers. Regulations frequently change.

So your first mission is to stay current by maintaining effective relations with the local postmaster. Second, you must watch ANPA and other trade groups for early signals of shifts in regulations that affect newspapers. Papers relying heavily on mail delivery should obtain the *Domestic Mail Manual* and subscribe to the *Postal Bulletin*, which announces manual changes. A "Book and Pamphlet Order Form" is contained in Publication 113, which may be obtained from the local post office. Order both the manual and bulletin from the Superintendent of Documents, U.S. Government Printing Office, Washington,

DC 20402. Improper use of the mail can increase your newspaper's costs tremendously or even jeopardize its mailing permit.

The Rate Controversy

The hottest controversy over postal regulations stems from newspaper competition with direct mail. Because this involves both the costs of your newspaper and those of your competitors, you must be alert to its implications. Watch these factors:

Relatively low second-class rates and expeditious delivery are available to newspapers (and other publications) that are issued at least four times annually at stated intervals (daily, weekly, monthly, etc.), are formed of printed sheets (not stenciled or mimeographed), and are sold for more than a nominal price. To qualify, newspapers must have a list of subscribers more than half of whom pay ("the 51 percent rule") and must disseminate information of a public character. The newspapers must not contain more than 75 percent advertising in more than half their issues in any single year and must meet certain other Postal Service requirements. Second-class rates for newspapers meeting those specifications are calculated from factors including weight, distance, and number of pieces mailed. Since colonial days, when Congress decided for the public good to encourage the dissemination of information through the mail, second-class rates have been lower than those for other classes.

With the recent expansion of direct-mail competition, there has been explosive growth in third-class mail, the category used by most direct-mail companies. Some newspaper strategists say the postal service tries to increase its own revenues by creating specially favorable conditions for third-class users. A joint Postal Task Force is operated by ANPA, the Newspaper Advertising Bureau, and the National Newspaper Association to counterattack. Otto Silha, then chairman of both Cowles Media and the task force, described his view as follows:

During the late 1970s, the U.S. Postal Service, a government protected and subsidized agency, began aggressive [third class] pricing practices which effectively changed the rules of the game. . . . never before have we seen a situation where a government agency has embarked on a policy which will affect advertising lineage of newspapers of every size. Hundreds of millions of advertising dollars, just like the ducks in fall, are migrating from newspapers to mailboxes in many markets."[8]

Task-force research indicates that third class is 34 percent of mail delivered by the postal service but yields only 15 percent of its revenue; First class represents 54 percent of volume and 60 percent of revenue. Silha says the Postal Service keeps third-class rates low so competitors, including newspapers, won't take over the delivery of advertising circulars, which constitute much of direct mail's business. Silha says direct mailers paid, in 1984, 8 cents for a delivery via third class that would, by weight, have cost 64 cents by first class mail.[9]

The Postal Service claims that third class, as required by federal law, covers its own costs. Postmaster General William F. Bolger, speaking to a publishers' convention, said:

. . . now, I'm not going to deny that advertising mailers are out to "eat your lunch." The Third Class mailing industry in this country is dynamic, innovative and aggressive. It is at the top of its game. And if newspapers do not rise to its challenge, if you do not offer equally attractive and innovative advertising services . . . then the mailers will eat your lunch. What I do deny—categorically—is that the Postal Service has somehow engaged in pedatory pricing of Third Class mailers, that we cross-subsidize Third Class mail at the expense of First Class mail.[10]

---

[8] Otto Silha, "The Impact of 'Junk Mail' on Postal Rates and the Newspaper Business," speech to International Newspaper Advertising and Marketing Executives' annual conferences, New Orleans, Jan. 29, 1984.
[9] Ibid.
[10] William F. Bolger, "The Post Office Point of View," speech to American Newspaper Publishers' Association, Montreal, May 1, 1984.

Check Controlled-Circulation Rates

If you are launching free-circulation papers—or competing against them—you should investigate controlled-circulation mail rates. This is a special rate category established for newspapers without sufficient paid circulation to qualify for second-class rates.

Controlled-circulation rates give a free-circulation paper the enormous cost advantage of second-class rates, which are substantially lower in general than third-class rates, plus what postal regulations describe as "newspaper treatment"—that is, faster delivery. For example, the *San Diego (Calif.) Citizen*, a free-circulation paper, says it cost, in 1982, $4,185.27 to mail 23,000 copies of its publication under controlled-circulation rates and that it would have cost $8,366.70 under third class. [11]

To qualify for controlled-circulation rates, a publication must be issued at least four times annually at regular intervals. Each issue must contain at least 25 percent nonadvertising content and have at least twenty-four pages. It cannot be published primarily to promote the main business of an individual or company. It must be able to prove to postal officials that more than 50 percent of its recipient households want to receive it (many establish this through return mail cards enclosed in the newspaper or recorded telephone surveys).

Other Postal Issues to Watch

"Red-tag" handling in post offices gives newspapers and weekly magazines special fast delivery because of their timely content. You should make sure that your newspaper is, in fact, receiving it. Since 1984, all publications mailed second class, not just dailies and weeklies, get red-tag treatment and you must be certain that delivery of your paper isn't delayed by the increased volume. Have a copy of your paper mailed to your home as a cross-check on delivery delays.

If you are launching a newspaper and newly requesting a second class postal permit, you must mail via third class until the Postal Service approves the request. In the interim, be sure that the local postmaster records your third-class costs on Form 3503. When the second-class permit is in hand (the process can take months), you are due a refund on the difference between your actual third-class costs and what second-class postage would have been. If no Form 3503 is kept, the refund may be impossible to collect. When the second-class permit is issued, be sure your newspaper conforms to postal regulations by publishing each day, somewhere in its first five pages, this information: date of issue, frequency of publication, consecutive issue number, subscription price, name/address of office, and the statement, "Second class postage paid at (city, state, zip code)." If mailed from other offices, the statement should add, "and additional mailing offices." The name and publication number must be carried on the front page of each issue, along with the number of sections in the issue. Each section, in turn, must carry on its front page the publication's name. Annually, on or before October 1, a newspaper using second-class mail must file a statement of ownership and circulation. Forms for this are obtained from the local postmaster.

Throughout, your primary concern must be to protect the newspaper's second-class permit and rates. Special problems can arise from the insertion and delivery in the newspaper of advertising supplements—material that might otherwise be mailed third class. Postal regulations specify in great detail the types of material that may be carried as supplements, how they are to be labeled, and the rates that can be charged. Carrying unacceptable material as a supplement can result in higher third-class rates being charged for the entire paper. Sit down with the local postmaster and get guarantees that your newspaper's approach is correct. If things cannot be worked out, there are appeal

---

[11] Andrew Radolf, "USPS 50% Requester Rule Seen Helping Free Papers," *Editor & Publisher*, Sept. 11, 1982, p. 11.

avenues on all subjects, including classification of mail, rates, and cancellation of privilege.

IN MANAGING THE HUMAN ELEMENT: A MYRIAD OF LAWS

Yet another legally complex responsibility awaits you in labor matters. There are three broad areas of concern: discrimination in hiring and employment, terms and conditions of employment, and regulation of workplace environment and health and safety.

Many federal, state and, often, local laws are important to you as a manager in these and other labor matters. There is aggressive government intervention to be concerned about. Also, more than ever before, individual employees are willing, if not eager, to sue for real or imagined wrongs on the job. Close cooperation with legal counsel is necessary to establish programs to ensure that the newspaper conforms to the law and, if trouble occurs, that it defends itself properly.

Root out Discrimination

As discussed in Chapter 5, there is enormous legal (and societal) pressure on newspapers, like all businesses, to eliminate discrimination on the basis of color, race, sex, religion, national origin, or age. The Equal Employment Opportunity Commission (EEOC) additionally requires you take affirmative action in hiring and promoting women, blacks, and other minorities. The EEOC's basic task is enforcement of Title VII of the Civil Rights Act of 1964, the seminal legislation for federal involvement.

You should take affirmative action that not only ensures conformity with law but also strengthens your paper operationally by including in the workforce and promoting to upper management qualified individuals of merit and skill from all sectors of the newspaper's environment. Top management must be directly and enthusiastically involved. A written statement of policy should be issued to all employees and made a permanent part of the newspaper's public stance. To ensure accountability, a senior manager should be assigned responsibility for making the program work. Specific goals should be set for recruiting and training minorities. Periodic monitoring of progress should be part of the program.

Cleanse Hiring Practices

Charges of discrimination often arise from interviews of prospective employees and from hiring practices. If twenty persons apply for a single vacancy, nineteen are disappointed, perhaps hurt or angrily thinking they were discriminated against. This, then, is one of those particularly sensitive links in the management chain where careful handling is needed.

EEOC guidelines require that your selection process not only be nondiscriminatory but avoid the "adverse impact" of screening out individuals by establishing standards not tightly tied to job performance. That is, requiring a college degree for a forklift operator's job could draw trouble. With counsel's assistance, you should review your entire hiring process. Some pointers:[12]

- Put the hiring process in the hands of experts who are sensitive to the human factors involved as well as disciplined in the law's requirements. Those who interview, particularly, must be personally committed to your affirmative action program.

- Be sure that advertisements or announcements of job openings conform to EEOC guidelines on nondiscrimination. Avoid language seeking, for example, "young" applicants. Age discrimination suits are increasing in number.

---

[12] "EEOC Charges—What to Do Before You Call the Lawyer," a special SNPA *Labor Bulletin*, Jan. 10, 1984.

- Examine all form letters, applications, tests, job specifications, or other documents used in the hiring process and eliminate language that might be discriminatory or have "adverse impact."

- Be sure application forms state they will be void after a specified period. Inform all applicants new forms must be submitted by anyone desiring consideration after the specified period that ends in, say, thirty or sixty days.

- Be sure your system and employees who direct it treat people professionally and whenever possible, gently. The lawsuit is a club for an angry employee. Let counsel establish procedures for informing unsuccessful applicants they won't be hired; you make sure that however the response is cloaked in legalisms, the unsuccessful are let down gently.

Check Pay, Terms, and Conditions

You must also examine terms and conditions of employment to ensure that nondiscriminatory and affirmative action procedures continue in the workplace. Here are some areas to watch.

Pay scales and job assignments must be nondiscriminatory. That means *no* disparities based on race, sex, color, religion, national origin, or age in any sector—overtime, fringe benefits, vacation, and so on. Much litigation stems from alleged discrimination between male and female, black and white employees. Be certain that differences in work conditions or treatment are not founded in race or sex. There is controversy over the "comparable worth" theory, which holds that comparable wages must be paid for different jobs if the skills used, responsibility required, and effort put forth are similar. The issue sometimes arises when women working as, say, secretaries feel underpaid in relation to, for example, truck drivers. The U.S. Civil Rights Commission is on record against

the theory, and it hasn't been raised often in the newspaper industry, but be aware of the controversy.

There must, of course, be no sexual harassment in the workplace. Yesteryear's crude, offensive "macho" remark to a woman employee today can be all of that—and decidedly illegal as well.

Training opportunities must be made available to employees on a nondiscriminatory basis. On-job performance must be monitored and appraised with equality. Promotion possibilities should be opened without regard to race, sex, color, religion, national origin, or sex. Discipline or discharge must be handled similarly.

Here are some general guidelines:

- Taking affirmative action is not only the right thing to do but also makes business sense. Better that you implement progressive personnel policies conforming to society's expectations and the law than wait for visits from unfriendly EEOC investigators or lawyers representing disgruntled employees. Look on affirmative action with enthusiasm as a modern management tool you can turn to good advantage.

- An affirmative action program is only as effective as your front-line supervisors. If they are not enthusiastically implementing the program, it can collapse or, worse, create conditions that cause lengthy, expensive, and damaging lawsuits. Monitor their implementation of your policies.

- Don't get so enthusiastic that you become trapped in reverse discrimination. Don't open so many rich opportunities for one group of employees that you unwittingly discriminate against another. The same balance and standards for all are an absolute must.

- Keep EEOC matters private; don't draw fire. ANPA and other major press associations provide background and even legal counsel on EEOC questions. No need to go directly to EEOC. They might not know you are there. If you are threatened with a lawsuit, talking about it might inspire others to sue. Certainly, if you settle a suit out of court with a check, keep that quiet.

- Remember: Nothing is off the record anymore, not a casual remark in the cafeteria, not a hurriedly typed memo slipped into a forgotten file. In a lawsuit, anything on paper—and a lot more—can be dredged up.

Watch Other Labor-Legal Areas

EEOC is not your only legal concern in labor policy. The federal Fair Labor Standards Act, enforced by the U.S. Labor Department, sets stringent regulations for minimum-wage and overtime payment. Work above forty hours in one week must be compensated at the rate of 1½ times base pay. The labor department's Wage and Hour Division will act against papers that don't properly compensate employees for overtime worked. Beware the editor who works reporters overtime but, to keep the newsroom budget in shape, quietly discourages them from claiming overtime pay. The Wage and Hour Division can sue for reimbursement plus hefty damages and penalties. The overtime issue has long been troublesome with journalists who work irregular hours. Under "Belo" contracts, newspapers are permitted to reach individual agreements with employees and to gain certain exemptions from wage and hour laws. These contracts, initiated by Belo Corp., owner of the *Dallas Morning News*, involve newspapers and employees who work varying hours agreeing on certain compensation arrangements which include overtime pay. The overtime issue surfaced in 1986 when the 21,500-circulation *Concord (N.H.) Monitor*, charged with not paying appropriate overtime, went into U.S. District

Court to argue reporters, photographers and non-supervisory editors should be considered "professionals" exempt from overtime laws. The issue is far from clarified. Seek counsel's help on overtime policy.

Also beware of child labor laws. You may be in trouble if a well-meaning fifteen-year-old carrier jumps on a forklift to move bundles in the mailroom. The Fair Labor Standards Act prohibits that and closely regulates employment of persons under age sixteen. Carriers are exempt from the act's regulations on pay and its child labor provisions provided that they deliver the paper exclusively to the final consumer. Any other kind of work can be a serious violation of state and federal laws.

The Employee Retirement Income Security Act of 1974 (ERISA) regulates benefit plans and some pension plans. It does not require the establishment of programs but lays down voluminous guidelines for those papers that do.

The Occupational Safety and Health Act of 1970 opened newspaper plants to an aggressive new government agency determined to improve the job-related safety and health of workers. Armed with warrants, if necessary, OSHA inspectors can check a plant for unhealthy, unsafe conditions. Penalties up to $10,000 can be meted out for violation. States also set safety standards. In 1981, 61 newspapers were inspected by OSHA; in 1982, there were 48 (compared with 68,577 work sites of all kinds inspected in 1982). The Labor Department reported 19,400 job-related injuries at daily papers in 1982, or one for every twenty-two newspaper employees that year.[13]

New technology—particularly the switch from hot metal to cold type—removed many dangerous jobs from newspaper production. But OSHA demonstrates concern over noise levels, particularly in pressrooms, and dangers from fast presses. OSHA regulations require employ-

---

[13] "Special Report," *presstime*, March 1984, p. 15.

ers to record injuries and illnesses among the workforce. Details are available in the Compliance Operations Manual, OSHA No. 2006, obtainable from the Superintendent of Documents, Government Printing Office, Washington, DC 20402.

IN COPYRIGHT: BEWARE SCOOPING THE HOLDER

Copyright protection is available automatically with publication of the paper. Two additional steps should be taken:

First, publish on the front page each day the statement, "Copyright (c) (year) The Daily Herald." Sending two copies of the newspaper via second-class mail within three months to the Library of Congress, Washington, DC 20559 fulfills the requirement.

Second, the copyright should be registered. Only with registration will a paper be able to sue for copyright infringement. Registration, for a nominal fee, is accomplished through the United States Copyright Office, Registrar of Copyrights, Library of Congress, Washington, DC 20559.

The Copyright Act gives an author exclusive right to control publication and distribution of a work. Under federal law, the "fair use" doctrine grants an important exception: copyrighted material may be used under certain conditions for "criticism, comment, news reporting, teaching, scholarship or research. . . ."

Until 1985, newspapers widely reprinted brief excerpts of copyrighted material (up to 300 words was a rule of thumb) and claimed "fair use" protection. In 1985, however, the U.S. Supreme Court held that *The Nation* magazine had infringed on former President Gerald R. Ford's copyright on his memoirs with unauthorized publication of quotations from his book before it was published. The ruling strengthens the copyright holder's right to first publication. Newspapers and others may be in legal jeopardy if they "scoop" the copyright holder—if they publish material and then claim a First Amendment right on the grounds that it was newsworthy.

SUMMARY

Every manager should be keenly aware of the litigious environment in which the newspaper operates today. Lawsuits against newspapers are proliferating. Huge judgments are sought; simply paying defense costs can be financially destabilizing.

The most dangerous legal threats come in libel, antitrust, and Equal Employment Opportunity violations. Newspapers also face legal difficulties in advertising and circulation operations.

Legal counsel must ensure that the paper's policies conform to the law. Detailed libel instruction must be given to both newsroom and ad staffs. Most libel stems from sloppy reporting; root it out. Libel manuals must be on all news desks; seminars in libel should be given by the paper's lawyer.

Antitrust violations are potentially dangerous. Suits often follow the introduction of new competitors, such as shoppers, into a market occupied by an established daily or weekly. Management must be sure that legal counsel helps plan any significant move in the marketplace under such conditions. Advertising and circulation departments must be certain that their operations do not include activities prohibited under antitrust law. In *all* matters even remotely smacking of legal difficulties, call in the lawyers. Law as it affects newspapers is extraordinarily complicated, and it is getting more so every day.

RECOMMENDED READING

ANPA regularly flags important legal developments with articles in *presstime* and announcements by its vice president/general counsel. *Washington Journalism Review* is similarly close to legal events affecting newspapers. *Newspaper Research Journal* is a fine source, particularly on First Amendment and freedom of information issues. On postal affairs, note *INAME News*. Among daily newspapers, the *New York Times* and *Baltimore Sun* are strong on U.S. Supreme Court coverage and developments in Washington concerning the press. Columnist Gerald A. Smith in *INAME News* is strong on legal developments in advertising. The Southern Newspaper Publishers' Association's *Labor Bulletin*, issued weekly, is alertly current on legal developments in human resources. Note also ANPA's *Free Press and Fair Trial* and periodic surveys of libel and privacy legal developments in the states, available from the Libel Defense Resource Center, 708 Third Ave., New York, NY 10017.

Also note an excellent section on antitrust law in Robert Ballow, *The Newspaper: Everything You Need to Know to Make It in the Newspaper Business*, Englewood Cliffs, N.J., Prentice-Hall, 1981; and Robert Macklin, *Newspaper Circulation Management Training*, Newspaper Center, Reston, Va., International Circulation Managers Association, 1979.

THOSE EXTRA DIMENSIONS: ACQUISITIONS, WEEKLIES, PUBLIC TRUST

PART III

The three chapters of Part III explore what we choose to call the "extra dimensions" of managerial activity.

First is acquisition of newspaper properties. In the expectation that some readers by now feel entrepreneurial stirrings, we'll approach the subject from the buyer's (not the seller's) viewpoint. We'll also discuss how newspaper groups diversify and become media conglomerates.

Second, we will delve into weekly newspapers, starting with a case study of acquisition and operation. If you do aspire to ownership, you will probably start in weeklies. Even if you don't so aspire, you may start a management career on a weekly. Hence this book's interest in that area of newspaper operations.

Third, we will look at the newspaper's public trust and managerial ethics. It's a subject large enough for a book in itself, and we cannot get deeply into it. But good business practice and mounting societal pressures require each aspiring manager to start, now, wrestling with the personal and corporate problems of conscience that are likely to arise.

Now, on to newspaper acquisitions.

CHAPTER
THIRTEEN

Acquisitions, Diversification, and Group Ownership

Harte-Hanks Communications acquires newspapers and other communications properties and diversifies into new fields to create what President Robert Marbut terms a "totally integrated communications company."

Helen Copley shifts and maneuvers her Copley Newspapers to achieve corporate "balance."

Chairman Warren Phillips of Dow Jones launches new information services to strengthen his company's extremely profitable "multiple use of the same resources." [1]

Reaching for greater profit, searching for streamlined corporate "balance" or, simply put, ego-driven to play in a bigger league, many American communications managers are leading their newspaper-based companies into expansion and diversification. It is a heady business that promises enormous rewards for the successful and lucky—and their shareholders. But the imprudent, unlucky managers and *their* shareholders can suffer costly failure on the expansion and diversification trail. Students of newspaper management should grasp the fundamentals of acquisition and diversification strategy. It is part of nearly every career in communications management today and, of course, is the path to private ownership for aspiring entrepreneurs.

---

[1] Robert Marbut, Helen Copley, Warren Phillips, letters to the author, March 3, 31, and 18, 1983, respectively.

Helen Copley strives for corporate "balance" in Copley Newspapers. (Courtesy of Copley Newspapers)

WHY THEY BUY AND SELL

After witnessing—and participating in—the sometimes frenetic expansion by U.S. communications companies in the 1970s and early 1980s, the author is convinced that a major motivation in it all is the dynamic, acquisitive nature of the men and women who lead these companies.

Paul Miller and Al Neuharth enjoyed being powerful chairmen of Gannett and transforming it from a small, upstate New York newspaper company into (in 1986) a $2.2 billion nationwide media conglomerate. Combative, hard-driving Alvah Chapman sought challenge in taking Knight-Ridder from $86.6 million revenue in 1961, when he became president, to (in 1986) over $1.7 billion. Otis Chandler, heir to an enormous

Los Angeles Times fortune, could have lazed away his days on a surfboard in sunny Southern California. Instead, he sought new records in building Times Mirror Corp. to (in 1986) over $3 billion revenue. These executives strive for personal gratification plus higher salaries, private jets, and other "perks" that reward those who builds profitable companies. But companies don't finance risky expansion to feed any executive's ego. There must be solid business rationale—and in the communications industry there is.

Why They Expand: For Profit and Protection

As manager of the newspaper, your *business* responsibility is to enhance shareholder investment, whether you act for a single private owner or thousands of shareholders in a public company. Expanding the company, broadening its revenue base, and improving its profits are your goals. With that in mind, this is why managers seek acquisitions and diversification:

- To achieve geographic spread and protect the company from vulnerable reliance on a single local or regional economy. Newspaper companies based solely on midwestern smokestack markets were hard hit in the recession of the late 1970s and early 1980s; companies whose markets included relatively prosperous Sun Belt towns weathered those harsh years more successfully.

- To build market diversification and reduce reliance on single industries. Newspaper companies operating solely in, say, auto-manufacturing cities or steel towns were hit hard in the recession, no matter where those cities were—Sun Belt or Midwest. As auto and steel towns slid into recession, so did newspapers living off them. Balance the economic and demographic character of your markets.

- To build product diversification and lessen reliance on a single medium. Many newspapers diversify into broadcasting for this reason. In 1985, 113 TV and radio stations and cable companies were bought or sold by the top 100 media companies. Of the top 20 (in total revenue), 18 operate in broadcast, cable TV, or both as well as print. Product diversification is also accomplished with weekly or free-circulation papers, magazines, direct mail. Such diversification permits reusing for additional profit an existing product. For example, the *New York Times* pays more than six hundred reporters and editors to handle more than 1.5 million words daily but uses only 200,000 in the paper itself. Is there profitable use for the 1.3 million dumped? That question drives many diversification efforts.

- To achieve more profitable use of existing staff and technical facilities. A weekly newspaper manager could seek increased profits by acquiring nearby weeklies and printing them in a central printing facility that otherwise would stand mostly idle. Dow Jones maximizes profit by using copy from, say, a single foreign correspondent in the *Wall Street Journal* (in Asian, European plus U.S. editions), twenty-one community papers of its Ottaway Newspapers subsidiary, its Dow Jones New Service (the businessman's "Ticker"), and other supplemental services carefully built in decades of diversification.

- To leapfrog beyond the limitations of a single newspaper market. However expertly a newspaper market is exploited, its population and economic base offer only so much expansion. New markets offer additional expansion room.

- To grow and simultaneously lower tax bills. Tax laws create highly favorable conditions for companies buying newspapers. In 1970–86, before tax reform, $1 spent to acquire a newspaper could generate 25 to 45 cents in tax savings for the buyer (thus newspapers were often more valuable to buyer than seller).[2]

There are, then, solid business reasons for expansion and diversification. But it takes two to make a deal, and if newspaper ownership is so attractive, why do owners sell?

Why They Sell: Taxes and Prices

Newspaper owners sell for many reasons. Some long for sunny retirement or falter before the cost and effort of taking their papers into new

---

[2] Elise Burroughs, "Newspapers on the Block," *presstime*, November 1983, p. 4; also see Jeffrey Good, "Fugitives From A Chain Gang," *Washington Journalism Review*, May 1982, p. 34.

technology or competition. Others, their heirs uninterested in publishing, are lured by high prices—3 to 5 times one year's gross revenue or 30 to 40 times annual earnings are not unusual for dailies in growing markets; many weeklies sell for 1.1 to 1.5 times gross plus value of real estate. (In other businesses, 10 to 12 times earnings often is a handsome price multiple). But many (in the author's experience, most) sales are forced by inheritance-tax laws preventing the orderly transition of a newspaper to a succeeding generation. Contrary to widespread belief, it is tax law, not the seller's greed or insatiable, grasping newspaper groups, that generally forces once-independent dailies and weeklies into media conglomerates. Whether you are a young person trying to get started as an owner or an acquisition-minded manager, learn to spot tax imperatives that signal available targets.

There follows a hypothetical example of the tax realities that spurred the frenetic acquisition activity of the 1970s and 1980s, a period in which scores of privately owned newspapers moved into group ownership.

A privately owned daily with annual gross revenue of, say, $10 million could often take 20 percent or $2 million—sometimes much more— down to pretax profit. About half that went for income taxes, leaving $1 million. At three times annual gross revenue—a conservative multiple for this newspaper—the price would be $30 million (a multiple of thirty times earnings also yields a $30 million price, of course). Federal inheritance tax is levied by the IRS against the paper's *fair market value* (what a willing buyer would pay a willing seller). At the maximum estate tax of 63 percent, heirs to this $30 million property faced $18.9 million taxes. Unless they had $18.9 million cash, the heirs had to borrow to pay taxes. At 14 percent interest, it costs $2,646,000 in first-year *interest* alone to borrow $18.9 million. But no accounting legerdemain would pay $2,646,000 interest annually from a newspaper with $2 million pretax profit. Another way of stating the heirs' problem: the $18.9

million estate tax would, at current levels, consume profits for nearly twenty years. These stunning facts in hand, a buyer could gain polite hearing from owners if they were planning their estates—or their heirs if they hadn't planned. On this, today's huge newspaper groups largely were built. Sale was often the only option open to owners, and that will continue. The Economic Recovery Tax Act lowered maximum estate tax to 50 percent after 1986—but even at that level, the heirs in our hypothetical example still would face $15 million in taxes.

On the buyer's side, another tax consideration surfaces. Simply put, the federal tax on excessive retained earnings is high. Many newspaper companies are very profitable and must distribute a great deal of money or spend it to avoid heavy taxes. The result is often a donnybrook, with cash-rich rival companies bidding newspaper prices above what seem reasonable levels. But it's either spend money to expand or pay it to Uncle Sam.

For both seller and buyer, an understanding of tax law can spell the difference between business success and failure. Let's look at other factors to consider when you set forth on the acquisition trail.

HOW TO BUY: AN ACQUISITION CHECKLIST

Let's assume that you are a youthful entrepreneur or a manager involved for the first time in a corporate acquisition. Each managerial challenge in newspapering can be unique, particularly in acquisition work, but there are general guidelines to follow.

First Audit Your Resources

First, obviously, determine how big a buy you or your company can afford. A common error is not looking beyond the purchase price to the operating funds you may need while you get the new acquisition on its own profitable feet. There is no formula to determine affordability, particularly because an important factor is the degree of risk the acquirer is willing to run. Determine affordability based on the *worst possible* scenario. That should include possible rising interest rates (if you are borrowing money for the purchase) or an economic downturn that could cut ad revenue.

Second, decide precisely what type new property you seek. If you are just out of college or if your company's entire experience is with 15,000-circulation newspapers, don't bid for the New York *Daily News*. Successful expansion turns on objective analysis of your own personal or corporate strengths *and* weaknesses, including financing and operating experience. Carefully pick a league to play in—then stick to it.

Third, if capable management talent does not come with the new property, do you have talent to send in? Can you operate it alone? If not, beware. First-rate management talent is scarce. A newly acquired property can falter quickly. Employees can get restive; advertisers can wander away, community distrust of you as an "outsider" can grow. From first day, top-flight management talent on the job is necessary.

Fourth, in what area of the country can you best operate? Don't buy a 10,000-circulation paper in Maine while operating another in New Mexico; you must minimize travel time and costs plus the administrative nightmares of operating widely separated properties.

Fifth, do you have the time, money and talent to get the new acquisition going? Inevitably, new properties have more operating problems than expected, and it takes more management time and talent to run a sour, faltering newspaper, even a small one, than a successful one.

Sixth, simply, would the new acquisition "fit" your existing operation? One Sun Belt company sent an executive to the Dakotas to inspect a possible acquisition. He arrived in a blizzard, climbed back aboard the same plane and, without ever seeing the newspaper, re-turned to the sunny South and said, "That one is not for us." It was probably a wise decision. If it doesn't *feel* right, the odds are it won't fit.

Once you understand the type acquisition you should seek, you face the problem of finding one to buy. Finding them is an art. As his era's most successful acquirer, Paul Miller of Gannett knew not only publishers' first names but their wives' names and golf handicaps as well. Paraphrasing his fellow Oklahoman, Will Rogers, Miller said he never met a publisher he didn't like. Asked what he would pay for a newspaper, he always responded, in public, "Whatever the owner asks"—a line certain to attract sellers. Miller was highly visible. He served many industry groups and for years was chairman of the Associated Press, which gave him frequent contact with publishers. Miller's personal approach, backed by deep understanding of newspaper operations and tax law, engineered dozens of acquisitions for Gannett and launched it toward becoming the nation's largest group. His style set the tone for most acquisition work. With many attractive dailies already group-owned, the "universe" of available papers is small. Competition is fierce; many large, reputable companies are ready with cash. Brokers can sometimes spot potential acquisitions but are expensive (fees usually are 5 percent of the first million dollars of purchase price, 4 percent of the second, 3 percent of the third, and negotiated above that). Generally, then, it is knowing and being known plus the personal touch, principal to principal, that is crucial in acquisitions. Luck can play a role, too. J. M. McClelland, Jr., heard at a cocktail party that two weeklies were for sale near Seattle. He moved quickly, bought both—and merged them into what is now the highly successful *Bellevue (Wash.) Journal-American*, a 28,000-circulation daily (which he sold in 1986). But was McClelland truly *lucky* or was he, like Paul Miller, just getting around, being visible and listening?[3]

---

[3] J. M. McClelland Jr., letter to author, March 17, 1983.

Now Research Market and Product

Before you open serious talks with the owner, carefully research the newspaper, market, and competition. Know all three as well as any outsider can. Using research outlined in Chapter 3, study the market's economic strength—its demographic and psychographic characteristics. Talk with bankers, chamber of commerce officials, and others. Study the newspaper's circulation and advertising history, its competitive status.

Even publishers of remote country weeklies know the value of newspaper properties. You will probably pay a handsome price, so *your research should concentrate on the growth potential of the paper and its market*. Will you be able to pay the cost of acquisition? Based on external research, rough but educated guesses can be made about growth potential. With millions of dollars often involved, however, this is not the time for guessing. You must obtain financial statements from the owner. A few pointers:

- Don't trust financial statements that are not audited by a reputable outside accounting firm which vouches for their accuracy (and be careful even then.) Look for written assurance in the statements by certified public accountants that they examined the financials "in accordance with generally accepted auditing standards" and that the statements "present fairly" the company's financial position "in conformity with generally accepted accounting principles applied on a consistent basis during the period. . . ." Unaudited statements often are unreliable.

- At minimum, obtain a balance sheet and profit-and-loss statement for the immediately preceding three years plus interim results for current year to date. You can't project trends accurately with less.

- Make analyzing the statements a team effort. Your chief financial adviser must search out accounting esoterica that can disguise

a company's true condition. You must search for ways to increase revenue and decrease expenses. If you're a beginner without a staff, go outside and hire, if only on a consultant basis, the expertise you need.

Analyze the Owner's Balance Sheet

Let's examine a balance sheet adapted from the actual operations of a small newspaper company as if you were thinking of acquiring it (or arriving to take over its management for the owner). Perhaps you will want to refresh your memory on terms discussed in Chapter 4.

Some things to note (see Table 13.1):

- *Current assets* (cash or assets that can be turned into cash within one year) come with the newspaper unless specifically exempted in a sales contract and are key in determining what price you can afford. Nearly $500,000 worth would be in a deal for Valley Publishing predicated on its Dec. 31, 1985, balance sheet.

- *Total accounts receivable* (what the paper is owed) minus reserve for bad debts can help you determine the paper's track record in collecting debt. Frankly, reserve for Valley Publishing's doubtful accounts looks low, and some of those receivables should probably be written off as uncollectable. Guideline: if accounts receivable are more than 1½ months of annual business, you, as new owner, might have trouble collecting. In your forthcoming price negotiations with the owner, don't "buy" accounts receivables you cannot collect.

- *Inventories*, particularly in newsprint, should be valued on the balance sheet by the more conservative approach of cost or current market value, whichever is lower. Watch that you're not buying old, useless newsprint. Determine number of days of operation for which newsprint and ink exist. Sufficient?

Table 13.1

Valley Publishing Co.
Balance Sheets
Dec. 31, 1985, 1984, 1983

Assets	1985	1984	1983
Current assets			
Cash	43,780	37,534	45,132
Accounts receivable, net of allowance for doubtful accounts of $17,780, $18,380, $6,506 in 1985, 1984, 1983 respectively	377,838	439,312	391,574
Other receivables	—	4,860	19,440
Inventories	53,422	35,904	47,410
Prepaid expenses	12,608	16,468	7,102
	487,648	534,078	510,658
Fixed assets, at cost	1,592,678	1,547,248	1,540,922
Less: accumulated depreciation	1,195,976	1,152,612	1,102,032
	396,702	394,636	438,890
Other assets			
Goodwill	388,750	401,670	422,634
	1,273,100	1,330,384	1,372,182

Liabilities and Stockholders' Equity

	1985	1984	1983
Current liabilities			
Bank note payable	11,000	30,000	—
Accounts payable	144,752	201,802	109,886
Deferred subscriptions	13,180	13,180	13,180
Accrued wages	25,210	26,664	22,576
Payroll taxes payable	6,170	7,062	4,190
Sales tax payable	792	488	354
Estimated corporation income tax liability	12,862	—	220
Current portion of long-term debt	164,884	144,210	111,600
	378,850	423,406	262,006
Long-term debt, net of current portion	750,002	881,172	1,014,531
Stockholders' equity			
Capital stock	73,954	73,954	73,954
Retained earnings (deficit)	24,530	18,358	(14,195)
Net income (loss) for years ended December 31	45,764	(66,506)	35,886
	70,294	(48,148)	21,691
	144,248	25,806	95,645
	1,273,100	1,330,384	1,372,182

- *Fixed assets*, such as plant and equipment, should be valued at cost minus depreciation (their decline in useful value due to usage or obsolescence). Most widely accepted is "straight-line" calculation of depreciation. That is, equipment that cost $20,000 and is expected to last five years should be valued after one year at $20,000 minus $4,000, or $16,000; after two years, at $12,000, and so forth. So, look for *net fixed assets*—cost of assets less depreciation. Ask the owner for a *depreciation schedule*. It will list each piece of equipment. Unless you are an equipment expert, hire one to examine major items, such as presses. Failure of a $500,000 press six months after acquisition can create havoc with your expense projections.

- *Prepayments* for such things as insurance or equipment leases often constitute assets of considerable value. Note them carefully.

- *Intangibles* such as goodwill are important in newspaper acquisition. Goodwill is the difference between the net value of the newspaper's tangible assets and its total worth due to reputation in the marketplace, customer loyalty, and so on. It will play a major role in the price eventually set for the paper.

In studying *liabilities* on the balance sheet, note the following:

- Total *current liabilities* of $378,850 will fall due within the coming year.

- *Accounts payable*, or amounts the paper owes creditors, total $144,752.

- *Notes payable*, including promissory notes, are of particular concern. Interest paid on notes is often high for short-term money. Unless you specify otherwise, you will be paying off those notes.

- *Accrued expenses payable*, such as wages owed employees, pension contributions,

and so on, can be a significant liability for you to undertake.

- *Long-term liabilities*, or debts due after one year, such as mortgages, must be studied. Unless specifically exempted, you will be assuming those debts. What is the interest rate on them?

- *Retained earnings* are profits not distributed to shareholders as dividends. They are normally invested in various assets of the company and not held as cash.

Here are some particularly important balance-sheet indicators:

- *Working capital* (total current liabilities less total current assets) shows what will be left if current debts are paid and thus signals how flexible the company will be in expanding and operating to its marketplace potential. This can indicate whether you, as the new owner, will have to transfuse cash.

- The *current ratio* (current assets to current liabilities) determines whether a company has sufficient working capital. Many managers feel comfortable only with about $2.50 current assets for $1 current liabilities.

- *Quick assets* are available for meeting current liabilities immediately. They include cash and easily convertible securities (but not, for example, newsprint, which must be sold). Some financial officers say $1.30 or so in quick assets for $1 in current liabilities is about right.

- *Shareholder equity* is the company's net worth after liabilities are subtracted from assets. It is what owners would receive were the company liquidated. It will be a factor when you get around to negotiating price.

In sum, the balance sheet presents the newspaper's financial picture on a specific date but doesn't reveal much about its operating profitability. For that you must turn to the profit-and-loss statement.

Analyze the Profit-and-Loss Statement

Whether you should buy and, if so, at what price can be decided only after determining how much the newspaper makes (or loses). The paper obviously must be profitable enough to cover acquisition costs. Even for groups that can subsidize a loser for a while, the paper must at least promise profitability within an acceptable period. Below (Table 13.2) is a P&L statement adapted from the small newspaper whose balance sheet we studied. For space reasons, we'll limit our analysis to results over a two-year period. When you actually start buying newspapers or managing them, however, always look at the most recent *three* years plus interim results for the current year.

On the *sales or revenue side* of the P&L, look for:

- *Advertising revenue*, which must be broken down into local, preprint, national (general), classified, and legal. If it isn't (and for space reasons it isn't here), ask for a detailed "schedule of newspaper and commercial printing sales" that provides year-by-year results in each category. Steady revenue growth throughout the period is a good sign. Match past performance with your analysis of the newspaper, its competition, and its market, then estimate how revenues can be increased with your superior management and marketing effort.

- *Circulation revenue* must also be viewed over a three-year period. If revenue increased, was it from higher circulation or price hikes? You might be able to increase revenue substantially through carefully staged price increases if the old owner did not institute regular increases.

- *Printing and miscellaneous revenue* should be analyzed carefully. Experience indicates

that job printing revenue is uncertain, often built by the former owner through personal contacts. As much as 50 percent or more likely will disappear when he leaves.

Turning to expenses, you won't find sufficient detail on the P&L. You'll need further conversations with the seller. In those talks and on the P&L, look for the following:

- *Costs* should show growth consistent with inflation and newspaper operating conditions. Lengthy periods of no growth may mean that the owner has not raised wages and that you will face demands for huge increases. Conversely, large year-to-year jumps may signal inefficient administration and opportunities for you to trim costs. Circulation and editorial expense must be matched with your understanding of the owner's operating style, the paper's journalistic quality, and your strategy for improving it. As owner, you may be forced to increase spending in these sectors to improve market acceptance of the paper.

- *Administrative expenses* must be dissected dollar by dollar. They may yield your greatest savings after taking over. Plan on replacing the often inordinately high salary the owner pays himself or herself with an appropriate salary for yourself or your publisher. Deduct private cars, country club memberships, and other perks owners often let the company pay for. They're all in "administrative expense," often one of the largest cost categories on small- or medium-size privately owned newspapers.

- *Operating income* (net revenue or sales minus all operating costs) is a prime indicator of how efficiently a paper is being run and, importantly, what you will be able to do with it.

- *Conversion ratio* of net revenue or sales to operating income is a common measurement of operating efficiency. High conver-

Table 13.2

Valley Publishing Co.
Profit & Loss Statement
For Years Ended Dec. 31, 1984/85

	1985	1984	Increase (Decrease)
Sales			
Newspaper advertising			
Display	1,116,930	885,108	231,822
Classified	171,160	157,888	13,272
National	88,892	109,080	(20,188)
Circulation			
Subscriptions	206,638	223,740	(17,102)
Single-copy sales	151,370	147,954	3,416
Commercial printing and composition	1,098,828	1,034,410	64,148
	2,833,818	2,558,180	275,638
Less discounts allowed	(24,550)	(28,042)	3,492
	2,809,268	2,530,138	279,130
Cost of sales	2,200,632	1,996,956	203,676
Gross profit	608,636	533,182	75,454
Operating expenses	622,734	564,876	57,858
Operating income (loss)	(14,098)	(31,694)	17,596
Other income			
Rental income	45,096	46,228	(1,132)
Sale of used plates	5,342	4,562	780
Bad debts recovered	19,714	20,030	316
Interest income	3,182	4,990	(1,808)
Miscellaneous income	644	1,406	(762)
Insurance dividend	12,958	5,326	7,632
Other deductions	86,936	82,542	4,394
Writeoff goodwill resulting from discontinuance of "Northside Shopper"		58,712	(58,712)
Noncompete covenant to former owner	32,616	32,616	
	32,616	91,328	(58,712)
Net income (loss) before income taxes	40,222	(40,480)	80,702
Provision for state franchise tax	4,336	2,166	2,170
Net income (loss)	35,886	42,646	78,532

sion ratios—some reach 40 percent or more—may mean that the paper is starved for resources and isn't properly serving the reader, advertiser, or community. Buying such a paper may confront you with formidable rebuilding in news quality and advertiser service. Of course, a low conversion ratio sometimes means gross inefficiencies that you can eliminate—and still improve the paper. That, the happiest of all conditions, permits you to raise journalistic quality and still increase profits.

- *Total income* (operating profit plus dividends or interest from company investments, etc.) is important. Many independently owned papers have substantial income from "other" sources.

- *Net income* is all income minus all expenses, federal income tax, and any interest paid to bondholders.

- *Cash flow* (net profit plus depreciation) should be followed through to *how funds were used*—for dividends to owners, investment in plant and equipment, or whatever. Total cash flow minus total funds used yields *working capital*, and charting this over three years will show whether the paper's financial health is improving.

- *Footnotes* are integral to any financial statement. Search them carefully for extraordinary factors. For example, a one-time sale of real estate or equipment, reported in footnotes, could pump up profit in any given year and make the paper look stronger than it really is.

In sum, the balance sheet and P&L indicate even to the uninitiated that Valley Publishing Co. is not highly profitable. For its size and track record, Valley Publishing's accounts receivables are too high; longterm debt is heavy. On the P&L, there is growth in display advertising 1984–85, but national is down—and there is no legal. Is the paper on the outs with

the local government jurisdictions that award contracts for legal advertising? Note also the extremely large contribution to total sales of commercial printing and composition. As we have seen, this is a highly competitive sector of newspaper operations, and a new owner of Valley Publishing should not count on carrying forward that revenue. On an operating basis, the paper is losing money ($14,098 in 1985). It shows net profit of $35,886 in 1985 only because it had $86,936 in "other" and "miscellaneous" income. Note also that Valley Publishing discontinued *Northside Shopper* in 1984. Clearly, not all is well.

However, though crucial to any acquisition analysis, financial statements tell only part of the story. It may be, for example, that Valley Publishing's owner is discouraged by an inability to improve the paper's profitability and thus is open to a low price offer. *If* you can see ways of improving profitability, buying what may appear to be a faltering paper could prove to be a good deal. So let us assume that you find positive factors in the market and the newspaper itself and are encouraged to continue negotiations.

Other Areas to Probe

Determine precise ownership details. Is the company a *sole proprietorship*, with all business assets owned by a single individual? If so, your strategy must be to construct an offer attractive in that owner's individual tax situation. If the company is a *partnership*, be sure that the person you are negotiating with can actually deliver the company in a sale. (Is there a recalcitrant partner waiting in the background to kill your deal or jack up the price?) Also, note that owners in a partnership generally report net income or losses from the newspaper on their individual tax returns. So, to construct a tax-attractive offer, you must know each partner's overall tax situation. If it is organized as a *corporation*, the newspaper is taxed separately as a business entity. Some small newspapers are

Subchapter S corporations, not taxed as separate entities; shareholders report on their individual returns any pro rata income, losses, or credits from the corporation.

In negotiating for any company, be certain the principal can deliver 80 percent of the company's stock. You need at least 80 percent to consolidate the new operation with your existing company for tax purposes. Consolidation can be crucial, for if the newspaper has been operating at a loss or is projected to for a couple years, you can write off those losses against your profitable operations elsewhere (and that, in fact, is yet another tax reason for communications groups to acquire losers: the acquired financial losses can be written off against the mother company's profits).

Get details on *retirement programs, employment contracts*, and any similar commitments you will assume with ownership. If ten top executives have lifetime job contracts at fat salaries, your operating flexibility will be constricted, to say the least. *Union contracts, news service contracts*, and all other *contractual obligations* should be investigated carefully. You may have to operate under those contracts.

Watch for *pending lawsuits* or threats of lawsuits. Under certain purchase terms you will accept responsibility for them. To be safe, insist on the seller warranting in the sales contract that no lawsuits or threats of lawsuits exist and, additionally, that he or she will be responsible for any that develop out of conditions arising before your ownership.

Don't accept the present owner's revenue and cost budgeting or market projections. Even honest sellers put forward optimistic views. *Let the buyer beware.*

Buy Stock or Assets

Now you are close to a decision. Your financial adviser is integral to the next steps. And, again, if you don't have one, hire one—if only for this task. It's essential.

Begin this way: Decide whether to buy the stock of the newspaper company or its assets. If you buy stock, you get the entire company, including liabilities (some of which may be hidden or unknown at time of sale). If you are uneasy about liabilities, buy assets, not stock.

Your negotiating strategy must, or course, be based on your own best interests. But be prepared to bend. If you are willing to structure an offer to meet the seller's tax needs, you have the best chance of succeeding. Remember, to the seller it is after-tax dollars *received* that counts.

Now that you have studied market, product, competition, and (in the financial statements) the owner's track record and reputation, you must project how the paper will perform under *your* ownership. You must estimate how much you can increase revenue and reduce costs in years ahead. Watch those "big ticket" items— retail, classified, and circulation revenue and, in expense, personnel and newsprint. Error in any can invalidate your analysis. This is tricky business, for you must estimate how the overall economy will develop in years ahead—a difficult task indeed. Also, project your future capital expenditures. Your expert's inspection of presses and other equipment will provide guidelines on what equipment you might have to buy, when, and at what cost.

If all signals still are "go," next decide how much you will offer for the paper and how to structure your offer. Structure can dramatically influence your true cost in the purchase price.

Structuring Your Offer

There are many ways to structure your offer. Here are two that are popular among acquiring companies: 100 percent cash, or some cash down with the balance paid over a number of years. (Publicly owned companies, of course, can offer a third option, swap of their own stock for the newspaper's. This is often attractive to owners who can defer tax on sale proceeds until they dispose of the newly acquired stock.)

For most buyers and sellers, cash down

plus notes over ten years for unpaid balance is attractive. For sellers, payment stretch-out can keep taxes lower. For buyers, inflation can mean paying down the road in cheaper dollars earned by the newspaper itself. During the wild inflation of the 1970s, many groups rapidly acquired newspapers even at inflated prices with reasonable assurance that they would prove profitable in the end.

The interest rate you agree to pay on notes is crucial. There are two concerns: First, a shrewd seller will trap you early in negotiations with discussions that get inordinately high interest rates on the table. Early loose talk will haunt you later on. Second, beware of paying banks adjustable or "floating" interest rates if you borrow to make the acquisition. They can rise sharply over a ten year stretch-out and increase significantly your cost of acquisition. A 1 percent increase on several million dollars over ten years means real money.

Also crucial: How much of the total consideration to seller will you offer in purchase price and how much in consultancy and noncompete convenant? To explain: you need assurance that once you buy the paper the owner will not reenter the market and compete against you. The owner knows the market, has personal contacts, and could damage you. So you should offer payment over a number of years (try for ten) if the owner contractually agrees not to compete against you and, additionally, agrees to offer advice and assistance after you assume ownership.

Another important reason you should seek a noncompete covenant: payments under it are tax-deductible business expenses. This reduces considerably your cost of acquiring the paper. For the seller, a "noncompete" is often attractive because payments are received over a period of years and may be taxed at lower rates. Caution: if too much of the total consideration is paid in noncompete, the IRS can rule that the covenant represents buyer-seller evasion of taxes and it can therefore impose higher taxes. Allocating no more than 29 percent of total consideration

to noncompete is about right, but *seek expert tax counsel on where exactly to peg your offer.*

You must also decide how much to pay down. Seller will decide based on their tax brackets. For buyers, of course, the smaller the down payment, the better.

Now we have researched Valley Publishing and want to get our thinking straight on whether it is an attractive acquisition target.

1. Let's say we project that we can increase revenues 15 percent in the first year and 11 percent annually thereafter. The paper is in a growing market and its sales staff is poorly led; we can send in professional sales trainers and show the staff how to exploit sales potential better.

2. Let's say we project we can reduce costs substantially in the first year because the owner—and his wife—are paying themselves handsomely and both drive company cars. We can eliminate those plus other high costs and serve as publisher at a $190,000 reduction in first-year costs. We think we can hold payroll increases to 8 percent annually thereafter; newsprint and circulation costs will grow at 10 percent; and all other costs will increase 8 percent annually.

3. Capital expenditures will average $10,000 annually for our first five years, $20,000 for the next five (the press is in good shape and a new electronic editing system has been installed recently).

4. We will depreciate fixed assets straight-line over ten years.

5. Our parent company will counsel the new paper on operational procedures and provide other assistance, so we will charge the paper an annual management fee. For the new paper, that's a tax-deductible business expense; for us, it's a tax-favorable way of getting money up to headquarters. Around 4 percent of the new

paper's annual gross revenue is about right.

6. The day we take over, we'll draw off $43,780 in cash and securities that the paper has in the bank.

7. Now, we're still worried about that commercial printing revenue. To be safe, let's discount 50 percent or $549,414 of it from the $2,809,268 in 1985 sales. Thus we come up with an "adjusted" figure of $2,259,854 for 1985 sales, and we will base our offer on that. Obviously, Valley Publishing and its market are not "hot"; there is growth but not enough to warrant an offer of three to four times sales that some groups pay for rapidly growing papers in strong Sun Belt markets. Let us say our research indicates that two times adjusted sales is correct. That yields a figure of $4,519,708, which we will offer as *total consideration.*

8. We will structure our offer this way:

- Of the total, 24 percent or $1,084,729 will be in noncompete; 14 percent or $151,862 to owner's wife because she was assistant publisher. Her noncompete and owner's $932,867 will be paid in equal annual installments over ten years (no interest will be paid because a noncompete is for services rendered, not a note payable).

- With 24 percent of total consideration allocated to noncompetes, we must plan how to pay the remaining $3,434,979. We'll allocate 29 percent or $996,143 to *down payment* and pay the rest over ten years in equal annual installments. We'll offer 10 percent annual interest on unpaid balances.

Now sit back and think. It is here, in the author's experience, that you may have convinced yourself the acquisition is a good deal and be emotionally committed to proceeding—and damn the cost. So, let your financial adviser

calmly and objectively "run out" the projection to determine if the acquisition will be viable financially.

This involves projecting ten years ahead with all the research and estimates made so far. Revenue and expense in years ahead, interest to be paid on any money borrowed for the purchase, payments to former owners, tax implications—all go into calculating how long to *payback*, or how many years it will take to recover acquisition costs and establish the paper's profitability. No industrywide formula exists for what is an acceptable payback period. Some groups require new acquisitions to "turn positive"—make contributions to profit—in two to three years; others, particularly private owners who need not justify deals to shareholders, accept payback of even ten years. But let's assume payback for Valley Publishing works out at 6.3 years and that is acceptable.

Now—but only now—are we ready to talk with the owner about money and terms.

HOW TO NEGOTIATE A DEAL: GUIDELINES

Acquisition lore has it that one group successfully negotiated a daily newspaper acquisition, from start to finish, in thirty minutes. Often, however, they take years. So plan your negotiations carefully.

Open Negotiations Cautiously

Here are some guidelines for negotiating an acquisition:

- Be patient. Newspapers are not widget factories to be bought and sold coldly. Many owners feel strong loyalty to their papers and communities. They want to know you and how you operate—how you will treat the paper. Before talking sale, give the owner time to become comfortable with you.

- Before talking money and terms, determine if the owner is truly ready to sell. Some owners will lead you through costly and time-consuming discussions simply because they (1) love to negotiate and (2) want to determine their paper's market value.

- Try to gain the owner's commitment to negotiate exclusively with you. The owner may take your offer to your competitor, who will bid up your price, but try for agreement that you won't be used that way. You don't want the owner revealing your negotiating strategy and pricing technique; your competitor would beat you with that knowledge if you met again on the acquisition circuit.

- Open with an offer (1) high enough to capture owner's attention but (2) low enough to give yourself upward negotiating room. Don't *ever* open with your "best" offer. Be prepared to prove, with your own balance sheet or banker's references, your ability to pay for the acquisition. The owner may demand security for unpaid notes, perhaps that you pledge back the newspaper stock if you default. He may ask for your personal endorsement of the notes. Beware: That means your personal assets—home, car— are in the deal, along with your company's assets.

- Present a package offer and require package acceptance. Don't agree, for example, on amount of down payment and leave open the interest rate on unpaid balances. You cannot agree to one without knowing your cost in the other.

In negotiations, each conversation, even over coffee, can be a serious probe into the other side's thinking. Listen carefully. A seemingly innocuous comment by the seller might signal where negotiations are headed. Be careful what you say. The seller is listening for signals, too, and your most offhand comment can go on the record.

Contract terms are often negotiated orally, almost informally, long before either side pushes forward a sheet of paper. So don't mention over coffee 12 percent interest on unpaid balances and expect to later write a contract offering 10 percent. That, simply put, is bad faith and can ruin your deal. A formal *sales contract* will be signed at the *closing* when actual transfer of ownership takes place. It must be highly detailed to preclude any misunderstanding, and that makes it an unwieldly document in your direct negotiations with seller. It's much better to lay before the seller a shorter yet precise and binding *offer to purchase*.

A Purchase-Offer Checklist

The purchase offer is just that—your signed offer to buy the paper under certain terms and conditions. You can be committed once you present it to the seller, so your attorney must be consulted on its language. Let's outline a purchase offer.

1. State precisely what you offer to purchase—i.e., "100 percent of the stock of Valley Publishing, Inc., which publishes *The Valley Daily News.*"

2. Definitely state the price—$3,434,979 (noncompetes are handled in a separate document) and how it will be paid (29 percent down with remainder paid in equal annual installments over ten years). Notes on the unpaid amount will carry 10 percent simple (not compound) interest. Notes will be subordinated to any bank debt you already have. That means your bank gets paid before Valley Publishing does in a financial crunch. Your bank will insist on this; seller will argue against it. But subordination is the rule with most acquiring groups.

3. State seller's responsibility for any undisclosed or unknown liabilities that arise later from conditions under seller's own-

ership. Specify that the cost of any such liabilities will be deducted from your future payments to seller.

4. Peg the entire deal, its terms and conditions, to that balance sheet and profit-and-loss statement delivered to you earlier by the seller. Remember, a company's financial condition changes hourly. Nothing prevents the seller from drawing off that $43,780 in cash and securities *after* you get the balance sheet—unless you make seller warrant in this purchase offer that you are getting a company whose current financial condition is as good as or better than represented on the balance sheet. Include language committing the seller to deliver a company with current assets not less than—and current liabilities no greater than—those on the balance sheet (seller will press, of course, for upward adjustment of price if liabilities are lower or assets higher at closing).

5. Include language in which the seller warrants as true the facts about the newspaper delivered in negotiations. Seller should warrant accuracy of *circulation figures;* details of any *union contracts, employment agreements,* or *pending lawsuits;* that all *financial statements* accurately and fairly represent the company's financial condition; and that the newspaper's *equipment* is in good operating condition and comes in the deal.

6. Language should assign to the seller any liabilities you aren't assuming. That should include all taxes prior to closing; any broker, legal, or accounting fees incurred by the seller; and unpaid vacation pay or advertising discounts earned before closing.

7. Hold the seller to operating the paper normally between signing of purchase offer and closing. That is, seller should not rush back to the office and celebrate by giving the entire staff raises. You will have to pay those increases unless the agreement prohibits them.

8. Be sure the language requires all shareholders to sign. You may not get 100 percent of stock unless they do.

A Noncompete Checklist

Along with the seller's signed acceptance of your purchase offer, you must obtain signed agreement to the consultancy and noncompete covenant to be executed at closing (with Valley Publishing, of course, we'll need noncompete agreements from both husband and wife). The elements are as follows:

1. Define what the owner will *not* do. Don't exclude the owner simply from "newspaper publishing" in Valley Publishing's home county. The owner should agree "not to compete in, finance, or support any advertising-related activity," not just publishing. Exclude the owner from competing in all counties contiguous to the home county or any other area you think appropriate.

2. Specify what the owner *will* do under the consultancy. That can include smoothing community and staff relations during transition to your ownership, meeting with advertisers, or performing other tasks both of you agree would help ensure the newspaper's efficient, profitable operation.

3. Specify the payments you will make for services rendered. For Valley Publishing's owner, that will be $932,867 over ten years, or $93,286 annually. That's high, so assign real duties to the owner and make sure they are performed. Otherwise, the IRS might challenge the covenant as disguised purchase price and not a separate contract for services rendered.

4. Sometimes, the buyer retains the owner under an *employment contract* to continue

as publisher. That contract would be separate, with consultancy/noncompete beginning on termination of employment. But that's academic for Valley Publishing's owner. He's going fishing.

Congratulations. Subject to closing and signing the actual sales agreement, you have bought a newspaper.

THE FINAL WORRY: DID YOU PAY TOO MUCH?

Now, it's only human to worry that you may have paid too much and that you won't be able to make your new property pay for itself. Well, prices paid for newspapers may seem outrageously high. But there is more discerning method than unthinking madness in what acquiring groups are doing.

First, truly high prices are being paid mostly for papers in markets whose booming economies promise extraordinary growth; papers in lesser markets draw lower prices. Second, high-paying groups are expertly sniffing out inefficiently run newspapers, where their superior management skills can achieve a dramatic financial management turnaround by reducing costs and increasing revenue. Third, tax law sometimes makes an acquisition, at a price within reason, a valid move for a cash-rich buyer.

Wall Street feels that high prices are often justified because newspapers regularly outperform many other types of U.S. firms in earnings. Investors reward this by placing relatively high valuations on communications companies. C. Patrick O'Donnell, Jr., a newspaperman-turned-analyst, identifies some primary reasons:

1. Most local dailies have no head-on newspaper competition and their strong franchises permit them to raise ad rates "opportunistically."

2. It is difficult and expensive to launch a new newspaper in a market already oc-

cupied by a daily, and this creates high barriers that discourage potential competitors.

3. New technology and marketing innovation permit high profits by holding down costs and making new products possible.

4. Advertising spending grows faster than the gross national product and has done so since 1975.[4]

Prosperous Sun Belt markets draw the most attention from acquisition-minded groups. Gannett paid $54 million or eighty-three times earnings for the *Shreveport Times* in sunny Louisiana; Hearst paid $35 million or thirty-five times earnings for two papers, the *Midland Reporter-Telegram* and *Plainview Herald*, in rapidly expanding Texas markets.

Prices of five times gross revenue are paid, yet Times Mirror, though loaded with cash, paid only 2.51 times gross revenue for the 128,000-circulation *Allentown (Pa.) Call-Chronicle* ($108 million, with $42 million down, $66 million in five, ten, and fifteen-year notes at 10 percent interest). Why so comparatively little for such a journalistically fine paper? Because Allentown is one of those aging northeast U.S. cities that aren't growing; Pennsylvania is projected to lose 5.6 percent population in the period 1980–2000. Rupert Murdoch paid Hearst Corp. for the venerable *Boston Herald American* just $1 million plus up to $7 million of any future profits. Hearst walked away with less in hand than many country publishers get for small rural dailies. Boston isn't growing; Massachusetts is losing population. And the *Herald American* (now the *Herald*) was a high-cost relic, heavily unionized and tottering far behind the market leader, the *Boston Globe*. Murdoch avoided heavy up-front financial exposure but assumed the high risk of substantial continuing losses, confident he could

---

[4] Patrick O'Donnell, Jr., *The Valuation of Publishing and Information Company Stocks*, a booklet, New York, Donaldson, Lufkin & Jenrette, 1984.

turn the paper around operationally. In agreeing to high prices, groups bet that they can quickly increase revenue and decrease costs. Many succeed, but it takes guts to bet millions of dollars that you will. The bet is really that many privately owned newspapers are inefficiently run. Groups often find that private owners don't exploit full revenue potential and that costs, particularly wages, are out of control. When they spot such inefficiencies, groups move quickly and willingly pay thirty times or more earnings, knowing that the price multiple drops if efficient management increases earnings (once earnings double of course, the price multiple drops from thirty to fifteen times earnings).

In sum, your acquisition price may look, in retrospect, stunningly high. But if you do your homework properly, acquisitions can work out handsomely for you. They did for Gannett, Harte-Hanks, Knight-Ridder, and others in the past fifteen years.

GROUP OWNERSHIP: BIG AND GETTING BIGGER

In the not distant past, the U.S. newspaper industry was dominated by individual owners.

Some were egocentric, colorful personalities who sought personal power as much as profit. Many felt accountable to no one; all would have shuddered at opening their financial books or managerial methods to public scrutiny. Some were inefficient managers, other strong. The journalistic quality of some papers was excellent, in others it was poor. Whatever their managerial approach, owners put their personal stamps on newspapers.

Today, of all the old families, only Hearst, Newhouse, and Scripps own private companies counted among the nation's largest. The industry is dominated by huge media conglomerates; most of the largest are publicly traded, owned by thousands of shareholders, and operated from glass executive suites open not only to public but also to regulatory scrutiny (by the Federal

Communications Commission, if they own broadcast properties, and also by the Securities and Exchange Commission and others). Most companies, private or public, are managed by professional, profit-oriented marketing experts. Yet, groups produce some of the finest journalism this county has ever seen.

Today, more than 70 percent of all dailies (and nearly 80 percent of all Sunday papers) are group-owned. More than 80 percent of all daily circulation and nearly 90 percent of Sunday's is controlled by groups.[5]

Some media critics fear such concentration of media ownership is inherently bad in a democracy. It's a highly subjective, complex question, of course, but for managers of the 1990s, it raises the threat that, good or bad, ownership concentration could create a societal demand for stronger government regulation of the press. Some critics are particularly disturbed because a few groups own large numbers of papers. Gannett owns (in 1987) 93 daily papers and a few corporate executives—or, indeed Chairman Al Neuharth alone—can make decisions affecting them all. The Canadian-based Thomson Group owns 88 in the United States (and scores elsewhere in the world); Knight-Ridder owns 28, The New York Times Co., 26. There are memories of power misused in an earlier era, when imperious owners turned front pages into personal ideological showcases. A case could probably be made that many abuses of ownership power that today so frighten some critics in fact occurred in those "good old days," and that it is memory of abuse, not current abuse, that is worrisome. Perhaps the present-day situation isn't so bleak.

The Alternative—Big Government

Any analysis of ownership concentration must dig behind the statistics and consider the following facts:

---

[5] ANPA.

1. Group ownership will continue to grow. For tax and other business reasons already outlined in this chapter, it is inevitable. The alternative is regulatory intervention by government, an infringement of the First Amendment that is fraught with dangers and should be unthinkable even to the press's harshest critics.

2. Statistics depict the situation as worse than it is. For example, of 149 groups, 53 percent or 79 own 4 or fewer papers; many are individually or family-owned (analyst John Morton regards all but 25 of the nation's groups as "basically family operations").[6] Groups have headquarters throughout the country, in towns small and large, and are widely diverse in character. Any potential danger arising from ownership concentration would probably come not so much from the number of papers that are group-owned as from circulation controlled by groups. The 79 small groups control just 9.5 percent of total U.S. daily circulation; the 6 largest groups alone control well over 26 percent.

3. By any objective standards, groups publish many of the nation's finest papers. Knight-Ridder, the New York Times Co., Times Mirror, the Washington Post Co., the Tribune Co., Belo, Dow Jones—all are groups and all spend millions on outstanding journalism. They have the financing and journalistic talent to achieve excellence; some newspapers they now own lacked both of these assets under private ownership and, in the "good old days," were sorry rags indeed.

4. Perhaps the strongest insurance against group misuse of ownership power is, simply, that it is bad for business to interfere with local editorial autonomy. If for none

other than marketing reasons, most groups want their papers to assume local flavor, reflecting the news needs of local readers and editorializing on local matters. And group managers are aware that critics *perceive* a problem to exist, so many lean over backward to avoid even a suggestion of interference.

A far greater danger than that of some modern-day press baron pulling editorial strings from group headquarters is the unthinking pursuit of ever-greater profit, which can starve a local newspaper's newsroom for the resources needed to serve its community properly. The "bottom line" syndrome can lead to cost controls so stringent that high-quality journalism becomes impossible. And, that is a real possibility in any group whose "personality" changes as it diversifies far afield from its newspaper base and as it promotes managers skilled in direct-mail advertising, high finance, baseball, or country music—but not, always, news.

Corporate Personalities Change with Diversification

Gannett, Times Mirror, Knight-Ridder, the New York Times Co., the Washington Post Co., and Belo all share two corporate characteristics: first, all sprang from newspaper origins and, second, none today is a "newspaper" company. The corporate personalities of leading U.S. communications companies are changing rapidly as they diversify to widen their revenue base, enter new fields in search of greater profits, and hire nonnewspaper executives who can show them how to accomplish that. Signs of the times:

- Gannett, which grew from a handful of small upstate New York dailies, now has operating divisions for radio-television, Gannett News Service, Gannett Satellite Information Network, Gannett Marketing, outdoor advertising, Louis Harris & Associates (research), and television program

---

[6] Margaret Genovese, "Small Family Groups Still Outnumber The Giants," *presstime*, November 1983, p. 47.

production in addition to divisions for daily and nondaily papers. Is Gannett a "newspaper" company?

- Times Mirror's board of directors in 1986 included Otis Chandler, as chairman, and two other current or former executives of the newspaper company. But twelve other directors included three private investors, the chairman of American Airlines, executives of law and accounting firms, the chairman of an insurance company, a foundation director, and one university official. Times Mirror policy obviously is not set by news executives.

- A New York Times Co. annual report pictured Chairman Arthur Ochs Sulzberger with twelve "top company executives." Not one full-time editor was present among these specialists in law, forest products, cable TV, finance, broadcasting, personnel, magazines, and newspaper business operations.

- When Kay Graham sought a new president for the Washington Post Co. she employed an executive search firm that described the job as involving primarily "assets redeployment"—that is, shedding losers and buying winners—and requiring strong financial background. Newspaper experience was not required. Richard D. Simmons, a lawyer serving as executive vice president of Dun & Bradstreet Corp., was hired (and the company flourished under his direction).

- Belo transformed itself in one day in 1984 from primarily a newspaper company (the *Dallas Morning News* and six small dailies) to a predominately broadcast company. Belo bought six TV stations for $606 million—a price nearly three times the newspaper company's total revenues. Why the heavy emphasis on broadcasting? Because of profits found there. A fledgling broadcast

division was already contributing 60 percent of Belo's profits, even though newspapers brought in two-thirds of its revenue.

Hallmarks of Success

Sometimes, unwise acquisition or diversification leads a company into deep trouble. Recent expansion indicates there is no single path to success. But the successful *do* display certain corporate characteristics. Most apparent is that successful, growing companies are led by strong-willed individuals with a clear vision of where their companies must go, and who build skilled management teams to get there.

A second commonality among the successful is that they initially stick closely to a narrow operating base where they have proven managerial skills. Today's top groups (see Table 13.3) are multidimensional companies with many interests, but their original impetus for expansion—including all-important financing—came from newspapers. Of the top 20 media companies (measured in gross revenues), 13 grew out of newspaper operations or are heavily newspaper-oriented, 5 are mostly broadcast, and 2 are primarily magazine publishers (see Table 13.4).

Expansionist newspaper companies generally demonstrate that they *know* the newspaper business. It is not clear, however, that they can operate profitably far afield in, say, electronic home delivery, where Knight-Ridder and Times Mirror lost tens of millions of dollars. Washington Post Co., whose prizes and profits prove its success in newspapering, now seeks new triumphs in cellular radio and other equally dissimilar areas. The outcome is far from certain. Will Tribune Co., owner of successful newspapers, flourish in baseball, having bought the Chicago Cubs (in 1981 for $21 million to provide programming for Tribune Co.'s WGN-TV in Chicago)? Will Oklahoma Publishing Co., parent of the *Oklahoma City Times* and *Daily Oklahoman*, win in country music as owner of Nashville's

Table 13.3   Top 20 Media Companies 1985 Revenue (millions)

Company	Newspaper	Magazine	Broadcast	Cable	Other
1. Capital Cities/ABC	$ 405	$ 210	$3,094	$ 132	
2. CBS		385	2,785		
3. Time Inc.		1,482		1,370	
4. RCA (NBC)			2,648		
5. Times Mirror	1,620	144	129	279	
6. Gannett	1,680		265		$ 208
7. Advance (Newhouse)	1,350	510		170	
8. Dun & Bradstreet		406			1,312
9. Tribune Co.	1,357		273	53	
10. Knight-Ridder	1,534		65		80
11. Hearst	740	569	224	7	
12. New York Times Co.	1,109	217	42	26	
13. Cox	644		261	421	
14. Westinghouse			539	530	
15. Washington Post Co.	556	326	155		
16. McGraw-Hill		676			272
17. Dow Jones	844	32			102
18. Scripps Howard	702	50	135	14	
19. Kohlberg Kravis Roberts & Co.			278	491	
20. Triangle	72	648			

Source: Advertising Age.

Table 13.4   Newspaper Revenue Leaders—(1985 total dollars in millions)

Company	Newspaper Revenue	Newspaper Revenue Percent of Media Revenue	Largest Paper	Circulation
1. Gannett	$1,680	78	USA Today	1,168,222
2. Times Mirror	1,620	74.6	Los Angeles Times	1,088,155
3. Knight-Ridder	1,534	91.3	Detroit Free Press	645,266
4. Tribune Co.	1,357	80.6	New York Daily News	1,275,268
5. Advance	1,350	66.5	Cleveland Plain Dealer	454,042
6. New York Times Co.	1,109	79.5	New York Times	1,035,426
7. Dow Jones	844	86.3	Wall Street Journal	1,985,559
8. Hearst	740	48.1	L.A. Herald Examiner	245,291
9. Scripps Howard	702	77.9	Rocky Mountain News	320,441
10. Cox	644	48.6	Atlanta Constitution	251,042

Source: Advertising Age; circulations as of March 31, 1986.

Grand Ole Opry? Gannett, truly expert in small-town journalism, has learned that publishing a national newspaper is a new business. Its *USA Today* lost hundreds of millions of dollars before turning, in May 1987, its first monthly profit of $1.1 million.

A third common characteristic among successful expansionists is a willingness to take risks in diversification, then kill off losers and adjust internally to emphasize profitable sectors. Knight-Ridder took less than one year to decide that *All Sports*, a seven-day sports daily, wouldn't turn the corner financially (it was losing an estimated $250,000 monthly) and killed the paper. The New York Times Co. sold its educational services, which never did well, and expanded in magazines, which did. Dow Jones, amazingly innovative in spin-off services using existing staff, learned the hard way not to stick too long with losers. It carried the weekly *National Observer* for years at a cost of millions of dollars before killing it. *Book Digest* and other subsequent diversifications that faltered were given less time by Dow Jones's leadership to become profitable. Harte-Hanks, evolving from newspaper origins, projects that by 1994 newspapers will contribute only 43 percent of its operating revenues. Consumer direct marketing is expected to contribute 42 percent, and TV, 15 percent (the radio division was sold in 1984).[7]

Many Must Continue Expanding

For some companies, particularly those that are publicly owned, the imperatives remain strong for continued expansion. Knight-Ridder is an example of why.

From 1974 to 1984, growth of the company's stock prices and dividends gave stockholders annual average yield of 22 percent.[8] Shareholders will expect similar results in the years ahead. Like many publicly owned companies, Knight-Ridder achieved much growth through newly

acquired properties. It will have difficulty maintaining momentum through operating gains (increased advertising and circulation revenue) at existing properties. Acquisitions or new ventures, and big ones, will be needed.

Additionally, Knight-Ridder, doing what it does best, concentrated so heavily in newspapers that it grew dangerously unbalanced: More than 90 percent of its total revenue comes from newspapers. Knight-Ridder management is strongly optimistic about the future of newspapers. But in this era of rapid changes in communications, it is too heavily based on a single medium. It lacks the balance achieved through diversification by, among others, Harte-Hanks or the Washington Post Co. and, in a sense, is thus vulnerable.

For Knight-Ridder or any other large company, however, achieving significant growth through acquisitions or corporate balance through diversification will be much more difficult in years ahead.

First, the number of suitable newspaper targets is limited. Nearly three decades of intensive acquisition work leave relatively few highly attractive papers still privately owned. Many still available would make relatively minor incremental additions to any acquiring group's bottom line. A $2 billion media conglomerate adds little with a 15,000-circulation daily.

Second, supply and demand has driven newspaper prices to high levels. In search of sizable and profitable acquisitions, groups will devour groups. Between 1978 and 1984, twenty groups were acquired or merged into other groups. That trend will continue and the top 100 companies in the country, in terms of revenue, will inevitably propose marriage to each other or, if that doesn't work, launch takeover raids.

And that brings up an important factor in all this: the shareholder. The shareholder wants corporate expansion but no cut in dividends, bold management but no risk. The shareholder is clearly a conservative element in the formulation of corporate strategy. And the sharehold-

---

[7] Prospectus, Harte-Hanks Communications, San Antonio, Inc., Aug. 3, 1984, p. 19.
[8] *Second Quarter Report to Shareholders*, Miami, Fla., Knight-Ridder Newspapers, Inc., 1984, p. 2.

er's presence, interests, and demands exert pressure on every publicly owned company's management. Not even managers like the powerful Neuharth, with a track record of delivering more than (in 1986) seventy consecutive quarters of increased dividends, can ignore shareholders or risk their ire by jeopardizing future dividends with risky new ventures. It's just one more complication in what promises to be an increasingly difficult time ahead for group managers.

SUMMARY

Groups acquire newspapers and diversify operations in search of new profit, to reduce dependence on a single regional economy or type of market, and to achieve corporate "balance" through product diversification. But many expansionist companies are motivated also by (1) dynamic, acquisitive leaders who, simply put, want to build larger companies and (2) tax laws that create highly favorable conditions for reinvesting profits.

For sellers, tax laws are key in the sale of independent newspapers to groups. Inheritance taxes often make it prohibitively expensive for families to pass ownership to succeeding generations.

A buyer's preacquisition homework must include deciding precisely how big an acquisition can be afforded, what type of property can be profitably operated if acquired, and where it should be located for most efficient management. Analysis of the target paper, its market, and its competitors must follow. Financial reports for at least the preceding three years must be studied and projections made on cost of acquisition and when the new property will "turn positive," or start producing profit. The buyer's offer to purchase must be structured carefully to meet the seller's tax needs and deliver maximum after-tax dollars.

Though they may appear to pay astronomical prices for newspapers, groups generally pay top prices only for those in strong markets.

Groups are also expert at finding ways to increase profits and thus achieve a dramatically fast financial turnaround. Groups now own more than 70 percent of all daily papers in the country and nearly 80 percent of the Sunday papers; importantly, they control more than 80 percent of total daily circulation and nearly 90 percent of Sunday circulation. Whatever the real or perceived social evil inherent in group expansion, it will inevitably continue.

Concurrent with continued expansion are rapid changes in the corporate personalities of many leading media groups. Companies that started with only newspapers now are widely diversified conglomerates whose executive suites and board rooms are increasingly occupied by lawyers, accountants, and executives who are highly skilled in many specialities but not always in news.

RECOMMENDED READING

Another look at *How to Read a Financial Report* by Merrill Lynch Pierce Fenner & Smith Inc., One Liberty Plaza, 165 Broadway, New York, NY 10080, would be wise for any nonaccountant reader setting forth on the acquisition trail. Acquisition developments and publicly owned newspaper groups are covered superbly by John Morton, analyst for Lynch, Jones & Ryan, 1037 Thirtieth Street, N.W., Washington, DC 20007, in his *Newspaper Newsletter*. Each June, *Advertising Age* devotes an issue to 100 leading media companies, describing the operations and finances of each. In October, *Forbes* publishes capsule looks at owners of media fortunes in its edition titled "The Richest People in America." For publicly owned companies, readers may obtain annual reports and 10-K reports from secretaries of the respective corporations or from the Securities & Exchange Commission, Washington, DC. For a critical view, see Norman Isaacs, *Untended Gates: The Mismanaged Press*, New York, Columbia University Press, 1986.

CHAPTER FOURTEEN

The "New" Weekly Newspaper Industry

If it's quick experience in many dimensions of management you want, a weekly newspaper gives you the best opportunities. In weekly publishing, a manager "does it all." If it's ownership you want, the weekly field certainly offers the best chances for entrepreneurship early in your career and at *relatively* low cost (relatively, mind you; there is no cheap entry into newspaper ownership).

In this chapter, we'll first look at the status of the weekly newspaper industry, which is changing rapidly. Then, we will use a detailed case study to trace one young man's entry into weekly newspaper ownership and operations. Put yourself in his place as we look at how he did it, primarily through "leverage," the use of borrowed funds. There is room for others in his type of business.

THE NEW LOOK

An unmistakable "new look" is developing in the oldest of newspaper industries, weekly publishing, where it all began for American newspapers back in colonial days. A quick rundown:

- There is strong growth in weekly circulation, readership, and advertising. The number of paid circulation weeklies hit 7,600 in 1987. Their circulation was over 47.5 million (compared to paid daily circulation of nearly 63 million; see Table 14.1 for a growth history). With an effective "shelf life" of five or six days in most households, some weeklies draw as many as 4 readers per copy (compared with 2.5 or so for most dailies). Calculating weeklies' ad revenue is difficult, but the Newspaper Advertising Bureau estimated in 1985 it was at $1.5 billion annually for both paid weeklies and free circulation shoppers. Between them, paid and free weeklies produced ad revenue probably equivalent to 11 to 13 percent of total paid daily ad revenue.

- In suburban areas, weeklies flourish in the shadow of some of the nation's strongest, most effective dailies. Suburban Newspapers of America (111 E. Wacker Dr., Chicago IL 60601), a trade organization, esti-

mates that 25 percent of all weeklies are now in urban or suburban areas and account for 40 to 45 percent of total weekly circulation. Emphasizing detailed local coverage, these weeklies offer readers a news dimension unmatchable by large dailies, which must provide panoramic coverage of world, national, and state news. For advertisers, many weeklies offer the kind of deep household penetration and readership that few dailies can promise. In some markets, weekly competition has been near fatal for dailies. (See box for an example of how they strangled one daily.)

- In rural areas, "ye olde country editors" of lore, independent owners struggling with a single ill-equipped, underfinanced weekly based on a narrow (and perhaps shrinking) market, are disappearing. Replacing them are publishers who achieve economies of scale by putting together groups of weeklies and using a single administrative facility under one roof for all production, sales, and news functions. Almost half of U.S. weeklies are owned by groups of two or more papers.

- Distribution strategies based on free circulation are gaining popularity among weekly managers. Particularly in suburban areas,

Table 14.1 U.S. Weekly Newspapers 1960–1986

	Total Weekly Newspapers	Average Circulation	Total Weekly Circulation (millions)
1960	8,174	2,566	20.9
1965	8,061	3,106	25.0
1970	7,612	3,660	27.8
1975	7,612	4,715	35.8
1980	7,954	5,324	42.3
1985	7,704	6,359	48.9
1987	7,600	6,262	47.5

Source: American Newspaper Publishers' Association.

METROS VS. SUBURBANS

Of all metro vs. suburban newspaper battles, none was so clearly dominated by suburban weeklies as the fight for the greater St. Louis market. Weeklies encircling St. Louis and its sister city, East St. Louis, Illinois, contributed to the decline of the Newhouse Group's *St. Louis Globe Democrat* (which was sold in 1984, then closed in 1986), forcing the *St. Louis Post-Dispatch* into emergency steps for survival.

The weeklies' winning formula was strictly local news content plus local advertising. As early as 1976, there was solid evidence that local ads as well as news were important reader attractions and that the weeklies' combined market strength was reaching extraordinary dimensions. A survey by U.S. Suburban Press, Inc., an association of weeklies, found the market served by 37 free-distribution and 9 paid circulation weeklies, all but 5 published once weekly (those 5 were published twice weekly). At stake was a market with 1,025,000 persons 18 or older that for decades had been prime circulation territory for both metros.

The survey results are instructive for any manager trying to position a weekly in a suburban market: the weeklies had high readership. Of all adults surveyed, 60 percent reported reading the most recent issue of their local suburban paper; 72 percent had read one or more in the previous four weeks. These reading patterns were highly attractive to advertisers.

HAD READ	ALL ADULTS	MEN	WOMEN
Local community news	75%	76%	74%
Food store ads	77	61	90
Other store ads	72	69	75
Classified ads	60	59	60

Importantly for advertisers, readers often took action after reading ads.

ACTION TAKEN	ALL ADULTS	MEN	WOMEN
Visited store	79%	77%	81%
Planned shopping list	69	60	76
Cut coupon	76	65	86
Mentioned news or ad to others	59	56	64

The weeklies offered another strength to advertisers—readers whose earnings profiles matched those of the market as a whole: 27 percent of the total population had an annual income of $20,000 or more; the weeklies reported that 28 percent of an average issue's readership earned $20,000 or more. Of those with less than $20,000 annually, the weeklies were found to deliver 43 percent—precisely the percentage of total population in that earning category.

Source: Englewood Cliffs, N.J., U.S. Suburban Press, Inc., 1976.

where advertisers seek TMC of large, demographically attractive populations, free-circulation weeklies are certain to expand.

- Competitive patterns are shifting rapidly, forcing weekly managers to adopt modern, efficient management techniques to survive. No longer can managers of small-town weeklies assume that Main Street is their exclusive preserve. Free-circulation shoppers, relatively inexpensive to launch and operate, battle for the local retailer's ad dollar. So do local radio stations, another low-budget medium. Suburban weeklies also face zoned editions of metros focusing on market slices and offering Main Street attractively low ad rates.

Generally, however, weeklies—particularly those clustered in single-facility operations—are flourishing. Let's take a closer look at "Main Street" journalism.

BUYING AND OPERATING WEEKLIES: A CASE STUDY

Following college, Richard Sanford tried his hand in the hotel business, working for somebody else. But he quickly returned to the profession of his father and grandfather—weekly newspaper publishing—where, as he now explains, he can do his own thing. At age thirty-four, after seven years as an understudy learning the family business, Sanford used a $60,000 personal nest egg to parlay his father's small weekly in upstate New York into a group of four weeklies with an annual gross revenue (in 1985) of over $1.5 million. The weeklies are supporting his family and him, albeit modestly, *and* paying off debt to former owners and the bank that backed his expansion. Within twelve years of purchase, unless disaster intervenes, Sanford will own outright a company that, even without further acquisitions, should gross $2.5 to $3 million annually and be worth about that if he wants to sell. He will then be forty-six.

Sanford's story illustrates how weekly newspapers offer young entrepreneurs promising opportunities to build their own companies. For those lacking strong financial backing, weeklies may offer the *only* reasonable opportunity for relatively low-cost entry into newspaper ownership.

How to Purchase A Weekly: The Lessons

There are lessons in the successes and failures of Richard Sanford's acquisition strategy. Here,

as developed through interviews with Sanford, are some.[1]

After the University of Denver and that brief fling in the hotel business, Sanford joined his father's 5,000-circulation once-weekly *Margaretville (N.Y.) Catskill Mountain News* (a paper his grandfather bought in 1903 with a promissory note for less than $1,000). Sanford started as a one-man ad sales force. Then came conversion to offset printing and Sanford became as technically expert "about what we were doing as everyone else in the shop. I continued selling advertising, began doing some writing, and also began doing most of the darkroom work. . . ."

Lesson one. Few weekly papers can afford compartmentalized specialists. If you plan a career in weekly publishing, learn it all, preferably with the security of being on somebody's payroll.

With offset, the *News* for the first time didn't have its own press. Sanford contracted with Ryder Newspapers, a weekly group with headquarters in Cobleskill, N.Y., 50 miles north of Margaretville, to print the *News*. But that was expensive. Sanford calculates he paid Ryder a 60 percent markup on newsprint. He also felt uneasy depending on outside printing, since "in the late 1970s there were newsprint shortages. . . . I knew very well that if it came down to a question of whose paper got printed during a shortage, it wasn't going to be the Ryder papers that got left in the lurch. . . . I was at the mercy of a competing newspaper to get the *News* printed. . . ." Sanford discussed the joint purchase of a press with two neighboring publishers and decided as a courtesy to inform the president of Ryder Newspapers, Charles Ryder. Sanford recalls, "His immediate response was, 'If you want a press so damn bad, why don't you buy mine?' " Thus, "in a backhanded way," came Sanford's chance to buy Ryder's five weeklies, grossing $800,000 annually.

---

[1] This extensive series of interviews with Richard Sanford was conducted during 1983–85.

Lesson two. Circulate, talk to people, investigate multiple solutions to a single problem. Make your own luck. Sanford certainly tried to do that, but his first mistake was a big one.

> I immediately put the press purchase on hold and began to think about the Ryder deal. There seemed a slew of good reasons to see if I could put it together. I had grown very tired of walking up and down Main Street in Margaretville in three generations of my family's footsteps. *That was the worst reason.* I was looking for a new challenge . . . I was also looking for a way to expand my territory rather than see it encroached upon from all sides . . . I was scared to death (Ryder) would fall into the hands of someone who would be aggressive and threaten the *News* from the north. There also was the psychological disadvantage of being in the newspaper business without the ability to print your own newspaper. . . .

So, young Dick Sanford was bitten—badly—by the acquisition bug. He convinced himself to buy Ryder without thoroughly researching the project.

Lesson three. Stay cool. Research the market, the competition, the target company and its potential, and your available resources before committing, even in your own mind, to a course of action. Sanford's second mistake was bigger:

> My grandmother died in 1976 and left me $60,000 which was burning a hole in my pocket. I had been searching for a way to leverage it into something meaningful and into something I also had some control over. I resolved that if I could close the Ryder deal with that $60,000 I was going to move ahead. Although I was able to do it, that resolve was actually a liability as I made it the major goal in my negotiations. In my ignorance I quickly agreed with Charlie Ryder that the company was worth a year's gross sales. . . . I was so eager to close the deal I blindfolded myself to a host of problems the Ryder group had. I wanted those newspapers and I wanted to spend my $60,000.

Lesson four. Seller's asking price is simply the starting point for negotiations; never agree to any price without your own thorough analysis. Sanford:

> I also placed too much faith in the law firm my father had used for years. Our analysis of the company books consisted of nothing more than a cash flow analysis to see if we were capable of servicing [paying] the purchase debt. In the end I got a bill for $16,000 from the lawyer for having done not much more than a cash flow analysis and the real estate closing. I was a babe in the woods.

Lesson five. You must take two partners into any acquisition analysis (or other major business deal). They are a lawyer to advise you on the law but, as importantly, also an accountant to help you judge the financial soundness of the deal. Negotiate their fees in advance.

To Sanford, cash flow (net profit plus depreciation) looked good—"and that was all I cared about"—because Charles Ryder and his co-owner sister each drew $30,000 annually in salary and there was $25,000 after-tax profit on sales of $800,000. Eliminate $60,000 in salaries and add in that profit, Sanford thought, and there will be almost enough to pay off the debt after acquisition. And:

> Inflation was roaring in the solid double digits in the late '70s. . . . I was hoping that inflation would service most of the debt . . . and I reasoned that in a year or two we could get the gross sales up to a point where the debt service would be only a minor annoyance . . . my ego also got involved. I wanted to do this project and that was all there was to it. . . .

Lesson six. Don't bet, as Sanford did, on any external variable, such as inflation, that is beyond your control. And unless you have thoroughly analyzed how you will increase sales (or reduce expenses) after acquisition, don't factor that into your projections either.

After assuming ownership, Sanford quickly

found that the purchase price of $800,000 was too high:

> There was over $100,000 in gross that was worthless. It came from [Ryder] papers in Delhi and Worcester that were losing their shirts. All of the gross that came from the commercial printing business in Stamford was worthless. The work was so underpriced that sometimes the selling price barely covered the cost of [paper] stock. The purchase price was too high. . . .

Lesson seven. Price multiples of 1 to 1.5 times annual gross revenues are standard for weekly papers. But the quality of that revenue is a paramount consideration. Revenue that yields no profit must not be in the gross figure on which the price is predicated. Commercial printing revenue, highly competitive in pricing and subject to wide variables in cost, is particularly suspect. Automatically discount 50 percent of it in any price discussion.

Then, a development almost killed the deal: "We were about set to close the deal on May 1, 1979, when a group of Ryder Newspapers people came to me on the sly and told me there was going to be a union organizing attempt. . . . it scared me silly and I went to Charlie and told him that all bets were off until after the (union) election." The union was eventually beaten and the deal proceeded.

Lesson eight. A company's condition can change between your agreement to purchase and the actual closing. If there is substantive change, move quickly, as Sanford did. Don't get so committed that you must proceed in a materially changed situation.

Once the deal was back on track, Sanford negotiated the payment terms wisely:

- $468,000, or 58.5 percent of $800,000 total consideration, went for purchase of the company's stock. Of that, $32,000, or 6.8 percent, was paid in cash down, with the remainder to be paid over twelve years— better than usual stretch-out, from Sanford's view. He agreed to pay 9 percent annual interest on unpaid balances, 1.5 to 2.5 percent under prevailing levels, and that was an excellent move.

- $140,000, or 17.5 percent, went for real estate. Of that, $28,000, or 20 percent, was in cash down, with the remainder financed over fifteen years through a local bank at 12 ¾ percent mortgage interest.

- $192,000, or 24 percent over twelve years, went for noncompete consultancy payments, which are tax-deductible business expenses for Sanford (as are all his interest costs). This, too, was a wise move by Sanford.

For twelve years from date of purchase, Sanford's *annual* payments are $94,224. (Broken down, this is $63,912 to the Ryders for stock; $16,008 to them for noncompete/consultancy; $14,304 on the bank mortgage.) He then must pay $14,304 annually for three more years to finish off the mortgage. Sanford's total projected cost for Ryder Newspapers—including principal and interest—is $1,173, 600.

Lesson nine. Payment structure is extremely important. Sanford gains the maximum tax deduction benefit from noncompete/consultancy payments. That 9 percent interest on unpaid balances to the Ryders is excellent; he will renegotiate that bank loan to lower the 12 ¾ percent mortgage. The twelve year stretch-out payment to the Ryders (contrasted with the one-time up-front cash payment) means it is likely that inflation will indeed cover part of his debt service. The dollars he pays the Ryders in the final year, 1992, will be somewhat cheaper than the dollars he committed to pay at the closing on January 2, 1980.

In sum, Sanford is happy:

I still think it wasn't a bad deal although I would dearly love to have a chance to do it over again today knowing what I didn't know then. . . . I got tremendous leverage, over which I had full control, on my $60,000; our business territory expanded tremendously; a competing newspaper was eliminated; we got back in the newspaper printing business; my income potential took a huge leap and we seemed to have the damaging effects of [what at the time was] double-digit inflation working to our advantage. It also got me out of those footsteps and provided me with an opportunity to make it on my own.

How to Organize and "Tune" a Weekly

After buying Ryder Newspapers, Sanford began an internal reorganization designed to achieve a corporate configuration that many rural and small-town weekly publishing companies could adopt in the future. Sanford's vision is a centrally located administrative, sales, news, and production facility serving his four weeklies in a market stretching nearly 75 miles north and south across small towns and rolling hills of central upstate New York. He can now move 25 to 30 miles west before meeting serious daily competition (Dow Jones/ Ottaway has a daily in Oneonta, N.Y., and Gannett has one in Utica). To the east, Sanford meets dailies from Albany (Hearst) and Schenectady and Amsterdam (both independently owned). Weeklies and shoppers operate in his market, but most are small. (See Figure 14.1 for a map of his market.) Sanford's papers are listed in Table 14.2.

Additionally, Sanford prints under contract the *Cooperstown Freeman's Journal*, a Ryder paper he bought but sold because its profit potential was limited (a good move; Sanford got rid of a loser and concentrated on his winners). He sells advertising with a five-newspaper com-

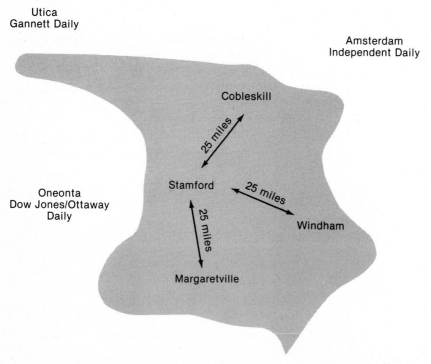

Figure 14.1   The Market of the Catskill Mountain Publishing Corporation

Table 14.2   Sanford's Papers

	Circulation	Publication Day	Number of Employees
Margaretville			
Catskill Mountain News	5,000	Thursday	11
Stamford			
Mirror Recorder			
(site of press)	3,100	Tuesday	13
Cobleskill			
Times-Journal	7,050	Wednesday	16
Windham			
Journal	2,800	Thursday	3
Total	17,950		43

bination rate that includes the *Freeman's Journal*, a paper of 4,455 circulation published on Tuesdays.

Although Sanford has a centrally located press at the *Stamford Mirror Recorder*, he must do prepress composition work at each of his three other points. "I would ultimately like to get all of our manufacturing under one roof," he says.

> The triplication of processes that we go through is awful and is a major drain on our financial resources. We maintain three typesetting systems with the resultant labor costs; we run three darkrooms; we operate two commercial printing shops [Cobleskill and Margaretville], and we do a host of other things three times. It is very expensive. None of our current buildings is capable of holding a consolidated operation, which means building. At this time we do not have the financial ability to go to the credit markets and borrow what would be needed to get under one roof. My best guess is that it would cost at least $500,000 and we simply are incapable of doing it at this time.

Sanford, however, *is* able to consolidate some operations for efficiency:

- He hired an experienced sales manager, Bob Evans, who coordinates all sales efforts from Cobleskill headquarters. In twelve months, Evans replaced the entire sales force and moved it from a combination salary/commission to full commission. In twenty-four months, he lowered the sales costs of display advertising from 21 to 17 percent of gross revenue. Gross sales increased by 50 percent.

- Sanford put Editor Jim Poole in charge of two papers, the *Cobleskill Times-Journal* and *Stamford Mirror Recorder*. Poole will take over news coverage for the company's two other papers when their editors retire.

Of forty-three full-time employees, then, two managers, both showing unusual skill and high energy, occupy key spots in Sanford's centralized concept. They are paid city scale wages so that Albany and Schenectady papers won't hire them away. As we shall see later, this helps push Sanford's personnel costs too high for an operation the size of his. But he counts that as a cost of doing business, the only way to retain key employees who are good enough to be attractive to larger papers.

Other consolidation steps:

- All four papers are mailed from Stamford, where they are printed. Previously, pre-press production materials from the other papers were trucked to Stamford, then the printed papers were trucked back. For Cobleskill, that meant all employees spent four hours minimum once weekly doing unskilled labor. Now, cheaper part-time workers handle the chore.

- Bookkeeping for the papers is consolidated in Stamford.

- All commercial printing for the two papers in the market's southern tier—Stamford and Margaretville—is handled in Margaretville.

In sum, weekly companies that are unable to finance the big jump into centralization can often achieve economies with small yet meaningful steps. Sanford is well on the way to reducing costs substantially and, just as importantly, instituting efficiencies that redirect staff time into more rewarding channels. The major economies of centralization, however, must await significant improvement in his financial position.

To improve the company's financial position, Sanford spends his days tuning its opera-tions. He reports spending restless nights won-dering how to better exploit his sprawling market's potential. No detail can be too minor for Sanford, no cost reduction too insignificant, no ad sale too small. Such is the life of a weekly's owner and publisher. Sanford's tuning process paid off immediately in improvement almost across the board. Table 14.3 shows Sanford's gains in sales.

Revenue Sectors to Watch

There are too many variables in weekly markets, competition, and individual newspaper opera-tions to permit sweeping conclusions about the sales patterns Sanford has established. However, Sanford's tuning process is clearly moving trend lines in the right direction. His 15.6 percent increase in total 1982–83 sales is excellent. The 33 percent increase in display advertising, the single most important revenue category for this type operation, is outstanding.

But there are disturbing elements: Too much of his revenue, 39.04 percent, depends on commercial and web printing plus composi-tion work Sanford does for a nearby weekly. The relatively low cost of new composition equipment is spurring the proliferation of com-mercial printing operations in upstate New York

Table 14.3 Gains in Sales

	Percent of 1983 Sales	Percent Change 1982–83
Display advertising	39.27%	+ 33.0%
Classified advertising	6.04	+ 14.5
Legal advertising	3.11	− 16.1
Subscription sales	7.24	+ 0.4
Newsstand sales	5.30	+ 7.2
Commercial printing	21.37	+ 20.9
Web printing	16.44	− 5.9
Contract composition	1.23	+ 68.5
Total sales		+ 15.6

(and elsewhere; there are 53,000 in the country). This will eventually drive down prices, making it more difficult to obtain printing work and do it at a profit. Sanford is much more strongly positioned competitively against other newspapers in his market than against commercial printers. His long-range strategy should be to shift emphasis accordingly. Sanford's corporate balance will improve if he can increase advertising revenue to, say, a minimum 55 percent of total revenue from the current 48.42 percent.

Sanford's classified-ad revenue is too low for newspapers the size and character of his. Classified's contribution to total revenue should be closer to 10 percent; the current 6.04 percent reflects competition from many free-circulation shoppers. Some offer free classified ads to obtain "reader material" and make their profit from retail ads.

The proportion of total revenue Sanford derives from circulation, 12.54 percent, is close to what many weeklies get. But it is disturbing on two counts: First, too much, 5.3 percent, comes from single-copy newsstand sales. Sanford must sell more subscriptions, which guarantee revenue over longer periods and prove to advertisers that the papers (and their ads) are getting into consumers' homes. Second, San-

ford's readers, like most across the country, are simply not carrying large enough share of total costs; like most publishers, Sanford has increased ad rates more frequently than subscription or single-copy rates.

Allocating Your Time and Resources

As a manager, you must decide carefully where to spend your time and resources for best results, concentrating particularly on maximizing revenue and holding costs to minimum levels. Let's look at Sanford's strategy.

Although he visits all four newspapers regularly, Sanford concentrates on his winners, spending the most time—often four out of five days—at the *Cobleskill Times-Journal*, directing the company's affairs from an office there. His fifth day is spent operating from the *Margaretville Catskill Mountain News*. Table 14.4 shows why.

As must all managers, Sanford watches cost control closely. He is having considerable success and would fare even better but for two factors: First, inefficiencies are inherent in operating four far-flung newspapers as nearly independent entities, as Sanford must until he can centralize. No matter how sharp his pencil,

Table 14.4 Revenue Contributions by Sanford's Papers

Division	Contribution to 1983 Gross (including commercial printing)	Percent Change, 1982–83
Cobleskill Times-Journal	40.81%	+25.2%
Margaretville Catskill Mountain News	22.36	+35.5
Stamford Mirror Recorder	12.76	−0.8
Windham Journal	7.63	+7.7
Web Printing	16.44	−5.9

Sanford faces irreducible minimums in some costs until he gets more operations under one roof. Second, payroll costs are too high for his type operation. Sanford's office and plant salaries (not including his own) were 57 percent of total cost of sales; they should be 40 to 42 percent for optimum profitability and no more than 45 to 47 percent under any circumstances.

In part, Sanford's disproportionately high payroll is inherent in his decentralized operation; also, his key executives must be paid city wages to keep them from moving to bigger papers nearby. It is payroll, then, where Sanford slipped badly in cost control. Salaries increased 15.1 percent in 1982–83. That year, with inflation slowing, many companies across the country limited employee raises to 3 to 5 percent and held their total payroll increase under 10 percent. There may be a special factor: Sanford is a pleasant man, deeply committed to building a stable company with a loyal staff. He may be granting inordinately high wage increases (15.1 percent annually) in an effort to accomplish that. Clearly, however, he must put a stop to that, otherwise his future profits will suffer.

In attacking his second-largest cost category, newsprint, Sanford has had greater success. Newsprint and stock for job printing are 18.2 percent of total cost of sales, well within acceptable parameters for his type operation. And he reduced those costs 2.54 percent in 1982–1983. Sanford also reduced postage costs by 9.12 percent. They now constitute 3.62 percent of total cost of sales, a bit high but acceptable for a paper distributing heavily by mail. Cost-control successes include reducing news reporting expense 18.1 percent and holding photos, features, and engraving to a 5.83 percent increase.

However, Sanford's total cost of sales in 1983 rose 10.1 percent. That was due mostly to those increased payroll costs, but his administrative expense was also up 10.2 percent. Holding increases to those levels would have won Sanford applause in many publicly owned, diversified communications companies. In 1982–1983, comparable cost increases included 12.1 percent for Harte-Hanks, 17 percent for Gannett, 11 percent for the New York Times Co., 12.8 percent for Dow Jones. Within the context of Sanford's operating and ownership situation, however, he should aim at holding cost increases well below his 1982–83 range.

In sum, if you plan a career in weekly publishing, note that cost control is the top priority. For Richard Sanford, it is particularly important. His company's revenue is increasing nicely; if he can contain costs, he will bring even closer that day when his acquisition and operating strategy pays off in a big way.

The Bottom Line of It All

What, then, is the bottom line for Richard Sanford?

First, he is modest in being merely "happy" with the Ryder acquisition. Leveraging $60,000 into ownership of a company with $800,000 gross revenue is a remarkable feat. With imagination and old-fashioned entrepreneurial guts, Sanford leapfrogged ahead professionally.

Second, his daily tuning of revenue and expense is pulling Sanford nicely through his early years of ownership, when money is tight. His net profit is low—just 1.27 percent of revenue in 1983—but he is handily paying off his debt to the former owners while allowing himself an acceptable if modest salary. Of course, he must work hard; no lengthy Caribbean vacations for Richard Sanford.

Third, given continued revenue growth and cost containment, Sanford should be ready soon to finance centralization of his four-paper operations. Getting everything under one roof will boost profitability.

Fourth, Sanford will be ready for further expansion in a few years. He should look for nearby weeklies that could fit into his centralization concept. And he should consider adding a free-circulation shopper to help fight off shoppers already active in his backyard.

Fifth, in 1992, twelve years from the date

of the Ryder acquisition, he should own the company outright. He can then consider (1) selling at what should be a handsome price, (2) taking out as personal compensation the $94,224 now being paid annually to the former owners and the bank, or (3) use what then will be a substantial cash flow to leverage even larger acquisitions.

Richard Sanford's bottom line, in sum, looks good. Now, could *you* do the same as Sanford?

HOW TO FIND AN OPENING AND EXPLOIT IT

Despite moves into weekly publishing by some large daily newspaper groups, opportunities exist there for beginning entrepreneurs who want to follow in Richard Sanford's footsteps.

First, many weeklies are too small and require too much management time for groups to operate profitably. A group's cost of maintaining a publisher in a town like Cobleskill, New York, can easily range from $30,000 to $40,000 annually *if* capable talent can be persuaded to go to such a small town. A group's management fee of 4 percent of total revenue would pull $56,000 annually out of Sanford's operation. If owned by a group, his company could not operate effectively, pay off acquisition debt, *and* provide $86,000 to $96,000 annually for the publisher's salary and management fee. Most groups won't acquire a weekly unless it has $600,000 or so annual gross from advertising and circulation alone. Groups favor larger weeklies that can be expanded into dailies, because even small dailies often provide a pretax operating profit of 15 to 25 percent or more of total revenue—considerably better than many weeklies.[2]

Second, individual ownership opportunities are opened by the relatively low cost of entry into weekly publishing. A mere $60,000 leveraged Sanford into ownership; more than one owner starts small—perhaps with a sparsely furnished storefront office and a contract for getting composition and printing done by an outside firm so a press need not be purchased initially.

Third, population shifts or sudden market growth, particularly in suburbs, can open opportunities for individual entrepreneurs who are shrewd enough to see a possibility and willing to start small, then operate on a thin margin until they can prosper with their developing market.

None of this means that traditional "mom and pop" newspapers will flourish if that term connotes amateurish management by an inexperienced husband-and-wife team in a market that is simply too small to support a newspaper. Regardless of size, weekly newspapers must be expertly managed to flourish.

Robert Tribble, a highly successful weekly publisher in Manchester, Georgia, says the key for the owner of any small weekly is to expand quickly to achieve economy of scale. Tribble says:

> On today's market, it is most nearly impossible to earn a living of any sort on an eight-page weekly with no commercial printing income. Put three of these small-town eight-page weeklies together in the same production shop and you have a 24-pager—and you can earn a living on this if you are any sort of manager at all. To be able to do this, the weeklies almost have to be in adjoining counties in order to establish an advertising base in larger cities, and to offer pickup (combination) ad rates from one publication to the other. . . . 1,400 paid circulation doesn't sound too good [to a prospective advertiser] but 3 × 1,400 doesn't sound too bad, either.[3]

Tribble began in weekly management in 1960 as ad manager for the *Manchester (Ga.)*

[2] For fuller discussion, see B. E. Wright and John M. Lavine, *The Constant Dollar Newspaper*, Chicago, Inland Daily Press Association, 1982. This is a financial analysis covering a "typical" 20,000-circulation newspaper.

[3] Robert Tribble, publisher, Tri-County Newspaper, Inc., in Manchester, Ga., letter to author.

Mercury. He now owns eleven weeklies as small as 975 paid circulation. His largest market is a town with 6,500 population; the smallest has 1,200. A recipe for starvation? Far from it. Tribble's Tri-County Newspapers, Inc., has pumped those eleven weeklies up to a total 27,000 paid circulation. His fifty-five full-time employees publish an average of 200 pages weekly, and Tri-County is nicely profitable.

Tribble is quick to praise the cost-efficiencies of offset printing and centralized operations:

> Our small operation in Manchester acts as the publishing house for seven weekly newspapers, all printed for counties adjoining each other in the west-central Georgia area. I believe that if it had not been for the coming of the offset, it would not be economical for at least three of these newspapers to be published today.

His centralized operation makes it profitable (and thus possible) for Tribble to publish papers for areas that cannot support a locally produced newspaper. For example, he prints in Manchester a paper for Stewart County, 62 miles away, but does not station one full-time employee in that county.

Based on an analysis of Georgia's weekly newspapers that he directed for the Georgia Press Association, Tribble is convinced weeklies of 3,000 to 5,000 circulation offer optimum profit potential. Papers this size, he says, have

> the best balance in terms of costs and profits. . . . there are certain fixed costs in the newspaper industry that are not related directly to circulation. Basic equipment, overhead and personnel costs must be paid, regardless of the size paper. . . . it could be that these size papers have overcome the basic cost of doing business, yet they are not so large as to have greatly increased costs with more employees, equipment, postage, paper, etc. . . .[4]

Note how tentatively even an experienced owner like Tribble draws a profile of a profitable weekly. No form of publishing is as highly individualistic as weekly publishing, and it is difficult to draw precise conclusions, but let's look at one effort.

How to Spot a Profitable Weekly

A broad profile of what is probably the most profitable form of weekly publishing nationwide emerges from a survey by the National Newspaper Association (NNA), composed mainly of weeklies.[5] Clearly, highest profit is to be made in low-cost markets, not necessarily those that yield high revenue.

For example, responses to NNA's survey from 129 companies representing 165 weeklies show higher-than-average gross revenue reported by weeklies that have their own press, publish more than once weekly, are in suburban areas, have competition for advertising from papers of like character, publish a shopper, and operate a job shop. However, papers with *lowest expenses and highest profit margins* have these characteristics: they are published more than once weekly, their markets are nonsuburban, they publish a free-circulation shopper and operate a job printing shop, and they have no direct competition of like nature. Newspapers with those characteristics averaged pretax profit 12.3 percent of total revenue. *All* weeklies averaged 8.24 percent.

Let's look at the most profitable weekly paper:

- Publishing more than once weekly means a newspaper has a market with strong advertiser support. It can also mean the paper is shrewdly managed for efficient use

---

[4] *Local Rate Study of Georgia Weekly Newspapers,* Atlanta, Georgia Press Association, 1982.

[5] *Annual Weekly Newspaper Cost & Revenue Survey 1979,* Washington, D.C., National Newspaper Association, 1979.

of resources. Any once-weekly is terribly inefficient: it maintains for once-weekly publication a building, press, and corporate structure capable of supporting publication two or more times weekly or even daily. In publishing more than once weekly, a manager often can achieve an extra margin of efficiency that adds dramatically to profitability.

- Publishing in rural areas can mean costs considerably lower than those in cities or suburban areas. Rent, wages, building costs, transportation—all are higher near large cities.

- Publishing a free-circulation shopper permits multiple use of an existing corporate structure for this often highly profitable form of publishing. Expansion to twice-weekly publishing is increasingly popular, with the paid paper serving the market once weekly, as always, and the free-circulation shopper, issued on another day, defending against outside shopper competition.

- Operating a commercial printing shop is the weekly publisher's traditional means of using an existing corporate structure more efficiently. A key to profitability is securing relatively long-term contracts for, say, printing other weeklies and shifting away from reliance on highly competitive, transient small printing jobs.

- Publishing without competition of like nature, final characteristic of the "most profitable" profile, will be difficult in years ahead. In weekly (as in daily) newspaper strategy, direct competition from another newspaper of like size and characteristics is only one worry. Radio, shoppers, direct mail—all are competing in small-town markets against weekly papers.

How to Evaluate Your Performance

At times, managing can be a lonely task. You may have few opportunities to compare your results against those of other managers and, because two markets or competitive situations are never precisely the same, matching your weekly's performance against another is difficult.

Limited operating guidelines can be drawn, however, from the NNA survey *if* the student of weekly publishing is mindful that it represents just 129 companies publishing in 41 states, randomly responding from an industry (in 1987) of 7,600 weeklies. Second, understand who the respondents are: they average $416,065 annual revenue ($309,379 for the 78 percent who contract outside for printing, about $900,000 for the 22 percent printing in house); 85 percent publish just one newspaper, fewer than 5 percent publish four or more; only 24 percent publish more than once weekly; 89 percent are nonsuburban papers; 31 percent publish a shopper; 67 percent do commercial printing; and 73 percent have direct competition for advertising. With these caveats in mind, let's look at what the NNA found in its study of 1978 operating results. Table 14.6 provides fuller details, but Table 14.5 shows what the survey found in revenue and expense patterns for weeklies that (1) had their printing done by outside firms or (2) printed in house on their own presses.

NNA findings translate into the operating ratios shown in Table 14.7.

As these wide-ranging ratios show, there is really no norm for weekly newspaper operation. Weeklies operate in many different rural, suburban, and inner-city markets, and this defeats efforts to construct market profiles against which you, as a beginning entrepreneur, can realistically judge whether the market you select is capable of supporting a weekly. As a result, there are many valiant but doomed efforts to publish in markets that are simply not strong enough for profitable operation.

Market research, then, is extremely important before launching a weekly. Even more

Table 14.5   Revenue and Expense Patterns

Percent of Revenue	Weeklies Printing Outside	Weeklies Printing in House
Advertising	76.3%	53.0%
Circulation	12.0	7.2
Miscellaneous	1.9	.6
Commercial printing	8.7	36.8
Other	1.1	1.4
Total	100.0%	100.0%
Percent of Expense		
Payroll/other comp.	42.7%	40.7%
Printing	21.4	22.4
Depreciation/leases	4.3	5.4
Operating costs	20.4	19.7
Other	3.6	2.6
Total	92.4%	90.8%
Pretax profit	7.6	9.2

so than dailies, weeklies are often inextricably tied to the economic fortunes of a single small town and, sometimes, a single industry or handful of retailers in that town. Even minor economic dislocations are felt immediately by a weekly, so pick your market carefully. (See box for an example of one sector in weekly publishing, the ethnic paper, that is suffering dramatically because of market changes.)

The diversity of the weekly industry also makes it difficult to construct models with widespread application in amount of capital investment needed for a weekly or, as we have seen, what its operating patterns—its cost to revenue ratios—should be. Unless a beginning entrepreneur is very careful, that can mean struggling with an undercapitalized newspaper or blindly trying to reinvent the wheel to achieve what Georgia's Robert Tribble calls the crucial "balance" between costs and revenue. It's no way to achieve fame or fortune. State press associations can often assist new entrepreneurs judge local conditions. A wider view is available through the National Newspaper Association, 1627 K Street, N.W., Washington, DC 20006.

The Weekly's Basic Strength and Weakness

If the weekly newspaper's expenses are high, its operating margins thin, and its market invaded by competitors, how is its continued success explained? In major part, this rests on its local news content.

All across America there are thousands of small towns and villages whose residents will never be named on the front page of the *New York Times;* whose high school football teams will never be shown on ABC's *Wide World of Sports;* and whose births, weddings, and deaths are of no real interest anywhere else in the world. But in local weekly newspapers, those names, teams, and vital statistics are big news. They are the community newspaper's strength, and in market after market they are exclusive to the newspaper. Radio, TV, outdoor advertis-

Table 14.6   NNA Figures on Operating Patterns of 129 Weekly Newspapers (average annual revenue: $416,065)

Revenue	Average	Range
Advertising		
Local	50.56%	50.73%–69.96%
National	2.08	1.11–3.43
Classified	8.54	3.70–10.54
Legal	2.34	1.70–4.93
Preprinted inserts	3.04	1.42–4.71
Total ad revenue	66.56	68.96–86.43
Circulation	10.02	7.61–13.67
Miscellaneous	1.36	.30–2.98
Total newspaper/shopper	77.94	81.56–99.91
Commercial web printing	15.05	2.49–22.88
Commercial job printing	5.82	4.31–16.05
Total printing	20.87	5.26–23.38
Other	1.19	.20–1.96
Total	100.00%	
Expense		
Payroll		
News/editorial	7.86	5.82–12.24
Advertising	7.72	4.50–9.79
Pre-press	6.58	5.01–9.80
Camera/plate making	1.28	.85–2.68
Press	1.99	.76–4.77
Mailing/circulation	2.83	1.30–3.72
Administrative	8.18	6.48–13.77
Job shop	1.51	1.60–6.33
Total payroll	37.95	33.36–45.24
Other compensation	3.93	2.65–5.29
Printing	21.79	14.08–23.60
Depreciation/lease payments	4.79	3.01–7.04
Telephone	1.01	.66–1.32
Second Class Postage	2.15	1.31–3.05
Other operating expense	16.96	8.08–22.44
Total operating expense	20.11	11.50–25.95
Interest	1.05	.84–3.09
Amortization of goodwill	.61	.27–5.26
Miscellaneous	1.52	.60–3.76
Total expense	91.75	83.46–96.62
Pretax profit	8.24	3.37%–16.53%

Table 14.7   NNA Findings on Weeklies' Operating Ratios

	Average	Range
Circulation penetration of home county households	43.6%	12.96%–87.48%
Advertising revenue as percentage of home county's retail sales	0.29	0.04–0.56
Ad content as percentage of total space		
Newspaper	55.57	46.44–60.71
Shopper	79.23	63.03–90.92

ing, direct mail—none of the competitors for ad dollars seriously challenge the newspaper in local news coverage. As a weekly publisher, you would be wise to remember that. Harried as you may be by other pressing business matters, you must devote sufficient time and resources to local news coverage.

Nationwide trends are not comforting. The NNA found that the news and editorial payroll on the average weekly is just 7.86 percent of its total expense. For NNA's average paper grossing $416,065 annually, that means about $30,000 annually for *all* news and editorial payroll expense. That won't hire many experienced reporters or writers. To succeed over the long haul, a weekly's manager must realize that local news doesn't come over a wire or in a cheap feature packet mailed from a distant syndicate. Local news is collected on local streets and local fields by staff reporters and correspondents. Giving that effort appropriate support is key.

In exploiting full ad revenue potential, the

THE SHRINKING ETHNIC WEEKLY INDUSTRY

Ethnic newspapers in foreign languages were once important in U.S. weekly publishing. But their numbers are diminishing rapidly.

The Center for Migration Studies in Staten Island, New York, reports that there were 794 ethnic newspapers and periodicals nationwide in 1884; 1,163 in 1900; 1,323 in 1917; 1,092 in 1940, and 960 in 1975. Since 1975, reliable statistics were not kept because of the large number of mergers, failures, and launchings of new ethnic periodicals.

Ethnic publications flourished during the great waves of immigration in the late 1800s and early 1900s. Their numbers shrank as immigration subsided and as second-generation Americans dropped "old country" languages in favor of English.

However, Spanish-language dailies as well as weeklies grew strong in the 1970s and 1980s with influx of Hispanics into many large cities. Three dailies, each with about 60,000 circulation, are particularly successful: Knight-Ridder's *Miami Herald* capitalizes on the many Hispanics in its market by publishing the *El Miami Herald* in Spanish. Gannett Co. serves New York City Hispanics with *El Diario,* a Spanish-language daily sold widely in single-sales outlets. And in Los Angeles, the independently owned *La Opinion* is published seven days a week.

In Dallas, the *Morning News* aims a monthly tabloid of about 40,000 circulation at Hispanics in its market. This paper, *The Texican,* is mostly in English.

An Italian-language paper that is highly successful as a daily is *Il Progresso,* published in Emerson, New Jersey. It claims about 55,000 circulation.

Ethnic dailies are one example of newspapers designed for a particular market.

weekly industry faces many obstacles. The industry's very diversity is among them. Few weeklies offer audited circulation figures, so neither individual papers nor the industry as a whole can prove their value to advertisers. Lack of mechanical standardization makes it difficult for large advertisers to put together significant blocs of weekly circulation for a single campaign. The standard advertising unit (SAU) system, widely accepted by dailies, has yet to find universal acceptance among weeklies. Weeklies often lack strong, professional sales representation. Most have none at the national level. Some weeklies cannot attract advertisers, who complain that their circulation duplicates the circulation of dailies. This is true particularly for inner-city and suburban weeklies, which, in many households, represent a "second buy" with dailies. However, the greatest single ob-

stacle to weeklies in wooing advertisers is their relatively high CPMs (or cost per thousand readers). In many markets, daily papers and other media deliver larger audiences at lower CPMs than do weeklies. The Georgia Press Association found that its weekly members had CPMs from $57 to $216. Relevant CPMs for dailies with over 10,000 circulation were $30 to $55 for national ads, lower for local retail ads. The Georgia study also found that the smaller the weekly, the higher its CPMs (they averaged $182 for papers under 2,499 circulation, $62 for those over 5,000).

SUMMARY

Unless they are strongly financed, beginning entrepreneurs will probably find that the weekly newspaper offers the only reasonable opportunity for quick ownership. Dailies sometimes sell for five times gross annual revenues, but it is possible to leverage limited capital into weekly ownership at price multiples of 1 to 1.5 times gross and then, through hard work and smart management, to "tune" the newspaper for profitable operation.

It is a rapidly changing weekly industry in which this is being done. U.S. paid-circulation weeklies—there were 7,600 in 1987—have dramatically increased circulation to over 47.5 million (compared with nearly 63 million daily circulation).

In suburban areas, weeklies are flourishing under the shadow of large dailies, which testifies to the popular appeal of their local news and advertising. In rural areas, there is a trend toward the creation of small groups that own two or more weeklies and operate in a centralized facility. The best preparation for a weekly career is to learn all operations, since few weeklies can afford specialization.

Weekly newspapers are so diverse in the types of markets they serve, the character of their management, and many other variables that few comparative operating profiles are available. But the most profitable weeklies publish more than once weekly in nonsuburban markets without direct competition and also issue a free-circulation shopper and operate a commercial printing shop. This type paper might not have the highest gross revenues, but studies indicate that it does have the lowest costs and highest profit margins.

Major industrywide problems include general lack of audited circulation among weeklies as well as the absence of mechanical standardization. Both are increasingly demanded by advertisers. Many weeklies also lack strong, professional advertising sales forces. But the largest problem is ad rates that are too high, in cost per thousand readers, relative to rates charged by other media.

RECOMMENDED READING

Weekly newspaper affairs are reported by *Publisher's Auxiliary*. Three trade groups specialize in weeklies: National Newspaper Association, 1627 K St., N.W., Suite 400, Washington, DC 20006-1790; Suburban Newspapers of America, 111 E. Wacker Drive, Chicago, IL 60601, and, for black papers, National Newspaper Publishers' Association, 970 National Press Building, Washington, DC 20045.

Also note D. Early Newsom, ed., *The Newspaper*, Englewood Cliffs, N.J., Prentice-Hall, 1981, and, by editors of the *Harvard Post*, *How to Produce a Small Newspaper*, Boston, Harvard Common Press, 1983. Both offer much to students of community newspapers.

CHAPTER FIFTEEN

Public Trust and Manager Ethics

The study of management you have pursued in this book necessarily focuses on the *business* aspects of newspapering. But no manager can forget that this is a business with unique historic and societal responsibilities to do much more than simply make a profit and keep shareholders happy.

A newspaper's responsibilities are to inform and enlighten, create a marketplace of ideas, foster public discussion, and facilitate the democratic consensus that has guided this nation since days of the Founding Fathers. A newspaper must guard the public's First Amendment rights and its need to know, serving as surrogate of the governed in their relationship with those who govern.

Free-circulation shoppers filled only with advertising don't assign watchdog reporters to the county courthouse. Direct-mail companies don't investigate bureaucratic inefficiencies in Washington. Radio and TV, with notable exceptions, race to entertain but lag in questioning and probing to defend the people's right to know. Cable TV doesn't walk patrol.

No, much of this heavy responsibility falls to newspapers. But newspaper managers should rejoice in that. For by accepting the public trust with sincere, professional dedication, newspapers can meet their historic imperatives *and* secure for themselves a meaningful and prosperous future.

That, of course, is a thesis difficult to prove. The *costs* of faithfully serving readers, advertisers, and community are stiff and immediate. They can be calculated with precision. *Benefits* often are intangible and sometimes real over only the long run. For example, adding another county courthouse reporter will cost a paper, say, $20,000 annually in salary plus perhaps $7,500 in related costs—somewhere around $27,500 to hire just one reporter to shine light in dark corners over there. Assigning a single foreign correspondent to, say, Hong Kong can cost $200,000 annually. How many extra subscriptions will be sold with better courthouse coverage? Are readers really interested in Hong Kong and can that $200,000 be translated into advertising revenue? Don't some papers skimp on news coverage, rejecting any larger societal responsibility and still do well financially? Conversely, haven't some fine papers, strong in news coverage and courageous in editorial stands, failed in recent years? The answer, of course, is yes. There is *strong evidence* that a paper's faithful, long-term pursuit of excellence and unswerving discharge of public trust will help assure financial success. But there is no *proof.*

So, we may ask, is this an area of newspaper management where the dollars-and-cents cost/benefit approach extolled in this book comes up lacking? Is this an area for instinctive acceptance of the proposition that a newspaper has a greater responsibility than simply seeking ever-improved profits? The author suggests that the answer is yes; that practicing high-quality, principled journalism is a newspaper's *duty* and that to reject that duty is to commit treason against higher ideals. Such ideals must be related, however, to the everyday reality that the newspaper has to show a profit. One depends on the other. An ill-managed newspaper that cuts newsroom staff becomes a mockery; a newspaper that fails financially fails totally. Young, aspiring managers must, early in their careers, sort all that out and construct an ethical approach relating higher ideals to daily reality.

As a first-line supervisor, your task will be to demonstrate for every employee your personal commitment to ethical, socially responsible journalism and business methods. As a member of top management—an owner, perhaps—you will set the tone for the newspaper's ethical stance. If top management is not committed, the staff will not be.

In days past, managers often created a shareholder-oriented newspaper dedicated to profit with little regard for societal responsibilities much beyond sponsoring the local Soap Box Derby each year. True, many newsrooms took the wider view that *journalistically* a newspaper had deeper responsibilities. But as *businesses,* many newspapers were run in a much narrower way.

Enlightened self-interest is a necessity in the managerial duties. In addition, boards of directors must be reconstituted to reflect more accurately the social and ethnic composition of newspaper marketplaces. Companies must structure a modern outlook on questions of social responsibility and ethics. These questions arise in all sectors of management.

DEFINING JOURNALISTIC ETHICS

When the *Washington Post* investigated the Nixon administration during Watergate, then publisher Katharine Graham had widespread backing among press peers plus significant (but far from unanimous) public support. So did Arthur Ochs Sulzberger when he and his *New York Times* editors defied the same powerful Nixon administration and published the previously secret Pentagon Papers, with their revealing insights into U.S. conduct of the Vietnam War. With dramatic boldness and the public spotlight full on them, both publishers made decisions that gained their newspapers secure places in U.S. journalism history.

For you as a manager, the tests of ethical resolve, the crises of professional conscience, probably won't come with such historic clarity. And in meeting them, you may stand alone; the world may not take note, may not care. The test, for example, may be the town's leading citizen pleading (demanding?) that his name, heretofore unblemished, be withheld from tomorrow's "Court Notes" column, where *all* arrests for drunk driving are normally recorded. He *is* a nice fellow; what's the harm? It may be the chamber of commerce suggesting that your newspaper back off its investigation of local toxic waste dumps. It's bad for business and, after all, what is bad for business *is* bad for the newspaper. Or the test may be the leading advertiser in town subtly hinting at an off-card rebate, just a quiet little deal recognizing his importance to the paper. He *is* important, and who is to know? Your test may be an urge you feel to invest privately in a controversial real estate development your newspaper supports editorially.

Thus, in various forms and guises, often innocent in appearance and cloaked in good intentions, ethical challenges sneak up on today's newspaper manager. As a manager, you must do more than take steps to ensure that the paper avoids unethical conflicts of interest. You must ensure that it avoids even the *appearance* of an ethical lapse.

There is legitimate concern that reducing ethical principles to a comprehensive, written code is dangerous in this litigious area. Some lawyers say a paper could be vulnerable in a libel suit if, for example, its coverage of a story provably strayed from its own written guidelines. Would not that in itself be damaging evidence of error or malice? Or, some editors say, widespread voluntary adoption of a written code could lead to demands by government and others that the code be used for regulation—or licensing—of the press. But absent written, enforceable codes, who watches the watchdog?

With each edition, a newspaper subjects itself to scrutiny anew. Day after day, reporters and editors put their best and worst on full public display and risk economic retaliation in the marketplace. The critics number nearly 63 million—those who buy daily papers every day; more than 47.5 million judge weeklies each week. Their ability to stop buying tomorrow is a powerful incentive for you to serve them well.

So the watchdog is watched in a very real sense by millions of other watchdogs. Yet, there is no formal, disciplined, or truly effective critique of the press from any widely respected groups outside the industry itself. In large measure, this stems from the reluctance—outright refusal, mostly—of newspaper editors and managers to cooperate in establishing formal watchdog groups or listening seriously to those that spring up independently. Submitting to reader judgments daily is sufficient for many editors; others are unimpressed with the professional quality of outside criticism or sense that much of it comes, tainted, from highly partisan groups. Probably most important, there is fear that submitting voluntarily to even informal judgment by outsiders inevitably will lead to formal licensing or other infringements on First Amendment rights.

The National News Council, funded in 1973 by the Twentieth Century Fund, tried for a decade to establish effective monitoring procedures with press cooperation. It failed from lack of media support. Accuracy in Media, with conservative principles and backing, spends more than $1.5 million annually to critique the press, but it is regarded by many editors as highly partisan. Journalism schools generally lack effective links with newspapers in this regard. Much academic research and commentary never finds its way into newspaper strategy. Journalism reviews come and go, with only two—*Columbia Journalism Review* and *Washington Journalism Review*—winning much credence among editors and publishers. Effective critiques come from the Associated Press Managing Editors' Association and the American Society of Newspaper Editors, but those insider groups are not perceived by the public as truly dispassionate critics. Nevertheless, both groups contribute mightily to raising ethical and operating standards throughout the industry.

In critiquing themselves, some papers toy with creating internal watchdogs—ombudsmen—and letting them represent the public by reporting on ethical questions arising out of daily operations. But only thirty to thirty-five papers today employ full-time ombudsmen. Even fewer papers assign significant staff resources to cover journalism or the business of journalism as a news story. Among those that do are the *New York Times*, *Washington Post*, *Los Angeles Times*, *Newsday*, and *Wall Street Journal*.

In sum, it is only in the marketplace, in the daily decision as to whether or not to buy, that there is any external and effective watch on the watchdog. However, whether ethical principles are enunciated orally or in writing, newspapers are shaping internal standards of conduct in advertising, the publisher's office, and news. Let's look at each sector.

ETHICS IN ADVERTISING

Ethical, principled methods are the foundation of a newspaper's credibility in advertising. Not only for reasons of right or wrong must a manager fashion credibility in advertising; it is imperative for business reasons.

Says Robert P. Smith of the *New York Times*:

The character of a newspaper is determined not only by its news and editorial content, but also by the advertising it publishes. Those that accept inaccurate, misleading, deceptive, or offensive advertising, or that tolerate slipshod performance by advertisers can run the risk of demeaning their most valuable asset—their credibility. That's just plain bad business.[1]

At that writing, in 1984, Smith had directed the *Times*'s Advertising Acceptability Department for eleven years. Reporting only to the publisher (not the advertising director), Smith is responsible for ensuring that advertising is not illegal or in violation of *Times* policy.

The *Times* has a detailed code of acceptability for advertising. Smith says it is

nothing more than an accumulation of value judgments—decisions, made on a case-by-case basis, where certain types of advertisements were found to be contrary to the best interests of the *Times* and its readers. . . . Our decisions in this area are sometimes arbitrary and subjective. We don't deny that. But these decisions, arbitrary or not, must be made if we are to protect the character of our own product. There is no alternative. Either we accept everything that is submitted to us or we're selective. We don't hesitate to be selective.[2]

Among unacceptable ads are those for x-rated movies, mail-order weapons, bust developers, devices to cure serious illness, escort services, speed radar detection devices, and fur products made from endangered species.

The *Dallas Morning News*, like many papers, publishes its code in general terms in its rate card, disclaiming responsibility for ad copy that is legally actionable:

The *Dallas Morning News* reserves the right to reject or revise any copy which it considers not in the public interest, either because said copy is not in keeping with usual newspaper advertising

[1] Robert P. Smith, "Advertising Acceptability Policies Protect Newspaper's Credibility," *INAME News*, June 1984, p. 11.
[2] Ibid.

acceptability standards or for any other reason deemed material by the publisher. . . . advertising set to resemble news matter must carry the word "Advertisement" at the top of the advertisement. Newspaper news department headline type cannot be used in reader ads.

The *St. Joseph (Mo.) Gazette and News-Press*, a morning-afternoon combination of 82,000 total circulation, provides employees with a detailed manual outlining advertising acceptability standards. Among ads refused are those for questionable business opportunities, palmistry, and lonely hearts clubs.

Managers Must Take the Lead

A selective approach to advertising won't work unless management is strongly committed to it, for rejecting advertising means rejecting money. The St. Joseph papers estimate that rejected ads total less than 1 percent of annual ad revenues.[3] That doesn't seem like much, but rejecting 1 percent of the, say, $80 million or $90 million ad revenue that a large metro daily enjoys could mean, of course, turning away $800,000 to $900,000.

All ad takers should be taught to spot questionable ads and send them to the individual charged with reading for acceptability. Many newspapers guard against ads that might cause financial loss to readers or harm their health or that disparage individuals or other businesses. At the *Detroit News*, Mary Mirasole, classified ad manager, urges her staff to use "good common sense" in screening ads. She gives particular attention to ads such as those placed by single persons seeking companionship.[4]

Delicate Areas to Watch

Most newspapers refuse to vouch for goods or services offered in advertising. How could any paper check the credentials of all advertisers? And yet, if a newspaper takes pains to present accurate, believable *news* to readers, does it not have the same responsibility toward readers of *advertising?*

In Florida, some newspapers check whether advertisers of home-improvement services are licensed for competency. The *St. Petersburg Times and Evening Independent* started this when two of its reporters discovered that 25 percent of advertisers of roofing, plumbing, and electrical services in a *Times* special supplement were not properly licensed. The *Miami Herald* requires such advertisers to show a county occupational license, which is granted only if an applicant is certified in his or her field.[5]

Advocacy advertising can be dangerous and should get full scrutiny in an acceptable program. A full-page ad attributing anti-Israel sentiment to six relief organizations appeared in 1982 in the *New York Times, Chicago Tribune, Washington Post*, and *Atlanta Journal* and *Constitution*. It was a bogus ad and neither the newspapers nor the ad agency that placed it with them had checked out its originators.

Opinions differ on whether advertising from extremist political groups should be accepted. Some newspapers reject it; not Smith of the *New York Times:*

> We've published opinion advertisements representing a wide range of public discourse—from the John Birch Society to the Communist Party. In our view, the First Amendment does not only guarantee a newspaper's right to disseminate news or publish editorials and commercial messages, but it also guarantees the public's right to enter into open discussion in the realm of ideas.[6]

Liquor and cigarette advertising, a major source of revenue for newspapers, is highly controversial. Cigarette advertising must, by law, carry statements of the health hazards of

---

[3] "Missouri Paper Organizes Convenient Manual for Ad Codes," *INAME News*, June 1984, p. 13.
[4] C. David Rambo, "Newspapers Ponder Advertising Codes," *presstime*, August 1984, p. 43.
[5] "St. Petersburg Papers Start Checking Advertisers for Necessary Licenses," *SNPA Advertising Bulletin*, Jan. 10, 1983, p. 1.
[6] Robert P. Smith, *INAME News*, op. cit.

smoking. The American Newspaper Publishers' Association (ANPA), among others, argues that First Amendment issues will be raised if stronger warnings are required. ANPA says that would result in

> substantial expansion of governmental control over the commercial speech of advertisers and, indirectly, over the newspapers printing that speech. . . . Congress should proceed with extreme sensitivity when it considers regulating speech as a method of regulating the use and sale of an entirely legal product.

ANPA also objected to a ban by the state of Oklahoma on liquor advertising on cable TV. The Oklahoma ban, later overturned by the U.S. Supreme Court, abridged commercial free speech and had serious First Amendment implications, ANPA said. Legal questions aside, it is quite possible that societal pressures, particularly against cigarette advertising, will increase.

Another controversial subject is advertorials, which are ads designed to resemble news stories. Their purpose is to mislead readers into believing they are reading news when in fact they are reading advertising. Advertorials are regarded as highly successful by some ad agency executives. Pieter Verbeck, executive creative director of Ogilvy & Mather Partners, says people are *five times* more likely to read editorial than ad matter, "so the idea of advertorials is probably a pretty good one." Says Robert O'Donnell, president of O'Donnell Organization: "They're attractive because they look like news. . . . no law says advertising has to look like advertising."[7] For the newspaper, advertorials blur the line between news and advertising and in the long run can harm credibility of both news and ad content. Consequently, many papers have devised signals to readers that they hold an ad, not news, in their hands. The *New York Times* publishes a notice that

preparation of an ad supplement "did not involve the *Times* reporting or editing staff." The *Wall Street Journal* runs advertorials with body and headline type that is noticeably different in style from that used for *Journal* news copy. Many papers insist on a clear "advertisement" slug atop each advertorial. If readers can peruse an advertorial and not be aware that it is advertising, the newspaper has not met its ethical responsibility.

In sum, the best thing you as a manager can do for advertisers is to establish your newspaper's credibility as a principled source of believable news and information that attracts and holds readers. Any advertising practice interfering with that is not in the long-term interests of either newspaper or advertiser.

Advertorials—advertisements designed to resemble news stories—are a successful but highly controversial form of advertising.

---

[7] Stuart J. Elliott, "Advertorials: Straddling A Fine Line in Print," *Advertising Age*, April 30, 1984, p. 3.

ETHICS IN THE MANAGER'S SUITE

It was none other than Katherine Graham, heroine of free press resistance to Nixon pressure during Watergate, who was lobbying hard at the White House and in the halls of Congress in the early 1980s. She was making the rounds on behalf of ANPA, the industry's leading trade group of more than 1,300 U.S. daily newspapers. The mission was to keep the American Telephone & Telegraph Company (AT&T) out of electronic publishing.

ANPA hastened to say it was not what it appeared to be—an attempt to use political persuasion to knock out potential competition; rather, it really was an effort to defend the First Amendment, to prevent AT&T from using its enormous resources to publish its own news and advertising and transmit it over AT&Ts wires and perhaps gain monopoly control over the free flow of information.

It all sounded disingenuous to Sen. Robert Packwood (R-Ore.) when he was visited by a group of publishers led by Mrs. Graham, then chairman of ANPA as well as the Washington Post Co. Packwood opined that what really worried publishers was that AT&T might offer electronic "Yellow Pages" and thus destroy newspaper advertising. Responded Mrs. Graham: "You're damn right it is." So much for defense of the First Amendment.

Scott Low, publisher of the *Quincy (Mass.) Patriot-Ledger*, present at the meeting, later said, "It was a disaster, a complete disaster." To some members of Congress, he said, " . . . we come on as fat-cat heavies trying to protect our turf." All this was reported in elaborate detail by the *Wall Street Journal* in a front-page article headlined, "Newspaper Publishers Lobby To Keep AT&T From Role They Covet." The article also reported that Warren Phillips, *Journal* publisher, helped draft an ANPA statement on the issue.[8]

Some publishers disassociate themselves from newspaper-industry lobbying that is so nakedly motivated by self-interest. Said Barry Bingham, then publisher of the *Louisville Courier-Journal:* "I break ranks with the publishers' group when they say in the name of the First Amendment they're going to abbreviate Bell's right to publish."[9]

ANPA's efforts spread far beyond Washington, providing background material for editorials in many newspapers. The *Wall Street Journal* reported that only about half the editorials told readers outright of newspapers' commercial stake in the issue.[10] It was a very public and, to some, embarrassing example of how ethical considerations are not limited to the newsroom or advertising department. Publishers must establish standards of conduct for their own office and in that be no less demanding, no less conscientious. For it is performance in the publisher's office that will set the ethical "tone" for the entire newspaper. The publisher's code must look outward, to the newspaper's external relationships and its public image, as well as inward, to internal operating procedures.

The Basic Dilemma

In looking outward, the publisher's basic dilemma is that the newspaper is both an observer-critic of society and an integral part of it, a recorder of news but also a maker of news, an instrument claiming special legal and societal status as watchdog surrogate of the people but also a business out to make a profit. To illustrate these complex ethical implications in simplistic terms:

- Should a publisher lobby with government for special privilege while knowing full well that the newspaper is feared for its political clout?

---

[8] Margaret Garrard Warner, "Newspaper Publishers Lobby to Keep AT&T From Role They Covet," *Wall Street Journal*, July 9, 1982, p. 1.

[9] Ibid.
[10] Ibid.

- Should a publisher join, say, the chamber of commerce or otherwise engage in "boosterism" of public activities the newspaper must cover?

- Should publishers claim special status and First Amendment rights for their companies that, though once newspaper-oriented, are now widely diversified business conglomerates?

These are real-life, not hypothetical questions.

Areas Where Interests Conflict

Direct-mail executives say that newspapers try to drive them out of business by lobbying against favorable postal rates for third-class direct-mail materials. Jack Valentine, president of Advo-Systems, the nation's largest direct-mail firm, told an ANPA convention: "People are not being fooled by canned editorials about junk mail and subsidized rates. . . . you really are only seeking higher rates in order to protect your monopolies in local print advertising."[11] Newspapers, through ANPA, argue against postal subsidy for direct mail. But newspapers and other second-class publications, of course, enjoy favorable postal rates and post office treatment.

Inheritance taxes are burdensome, particularly for newspaper families because of the substantial increase in the newspapers' market value (on which taxes are based). Families that pass along farms, gas stations, or other businesses must also pay inheritance taxes. Yet some newspaper families have suggested special exemptions for newspapers.

Newspapers receive exemptions from certain child labor laws so teenage carriers can deliver papers and from certain minimum wage regulations and social security payments cov-

---

[11] Andrew Radolf, "Detached Labeler Fights Back," *Editor & Publisher*, June 16, 1984, p. 9; also see, "Valentine, ANPA Trying to Kill Advo," *presstime*, June 1984, p. 35.

ering adult carriers. The industry lobbies strongly for the continuation of this.

Newspapers often win special status for news racks and coin boxes on streets and in public places. Attempts by municipal authorities to tax or license them draw vigorous attack on First Amendment grounds.

Special-interest legislation exempts some newspapers from antitrust laws and permits them to form joint operating agreements. Only the newspaper industry enjoys exemption in that form.

Increased diversification of newspaper-based companies into wider fields in search of profit adds complex dimensions to the discussion of corporate ethics. Times Mirror Co., publisher of the *Los Angeles Times* and other papers, obviously should shelter beneath the First Amendment umbrella. But how to distinguish *that* Times Mirror Co. from the Times Mirror Co. that manufactures newsprint, plywood, and other forest products? Harte-Hanks, leading supporter of ANPA's efforts to exclude AT&T from the electronic information business on First Amendment grounds, is itself in the electronic information business as an operator of cable TV systems. Gannett, Knight-Ridder, New York Times Co.—along with many other "newspaper" companies—are also in that business. Should the press's special legal and societal status embolden a profit-oriented company like Gannett to argue, as it did, that the First Amendment prohibits New York City's Metropolitan Transportation Authority from charging fees for newspaper vending machines in train stations?

Diversification has grown to such an extent that some newspapers own companies that their reporters cover. *Chicago Tribune* baseball writers cover the Chicago Cubs, owned by the Chicago Tribune's parent Tribune Co. The *New York Times* and *Washington Post*, which, like many companies, own TV stations, assign reporters to cover the television industry and the Federal Communications Commission (which regulates it). Thomson Newspapers' parent has huge holdings in oil production, a subject covered on many Thomson business news pages. Many companies invest in—and cover the news from—cellular radio, entertainment, real estate, and other industries.

None of this is to suggest there is flagrant misuse of the press's political clout or its First Amendment status. Neither is it meant to imply that a newspaper should not enter the marketplace in vigorous defense of its own business interests. It *is* meant to suggest that the next generation of newspaper managers will face new, complex questions in constructing an ethical relationship between their newspapers and the society within which they operate.

Some ethical questions have been around for a very long time. That doesn't make them any easier to solve. Consider, for example, boosterism—a newspaper backing local community and industry with chamber-of-commerce fervor, or a publisher joining local business or professional groups and serving charitable organizations. If the publisher isn't careful, that can mean that the newspaper drops its role as a dispassionate observer and becomes an advocate *or* that the public perceives the newspaper as having joined forces with certain groups. Pressures for boosterism are enormous, particularly in small-daily and weekly journalism where the publisher is known to all in town ("I go to church with those folks," one weekly editor says). The question, of course, is whether boosterism leaves the newspaper free to report what is wrong in town and editorialize on how it should be fixed. If the *publisher* is on the United Way advisory board, is the *editorial writer* really free to comment on how money is raised and spent?

It is hoped, of course, that publisher and newspaper will find ways to be constructively involved in their community and still maintain journalistic and editorial independence—and if straddling both those responsibilities is not possible, to opt for the historic role of reporting as facts dictate and commenting editorially as conscience orders. Those that so opt can expect

problems occasionally. Witness the *Fort Worth Star-Telegram*, which published articles on safety problems with Huey and Cobra helicopters manufactured by Bell Helicopter. Bell, which has a plant in Forth Worth, publicly attacked the series and banned *Star-Telegram* employees from servicing newspaper coin boxes in the plant. The company's union organized a campaign against the paper and 1,200 subscriptions were canceled. The army grounded 600 Hueys and ordered new parts for 4,500 other helicopters; the *Star Telegram* won a Pulitzer Prize for the series.[12]

The question of whether newspapers should endorse political candidates (a very old controversy) assumes new ethical overtones as many editorial pages strive for a centrist, objective position. Centrists argue that a newspaper must present all sides of controversies and comment editorially on issues—but avoid endorsements and thus leave the decision to voters. Papers that are alone in a market often feel greater responsibility to represent all shades of opinion. *USA Today* declared that it would not endorse candidates because it is "the only general-interest national daily. . . . our mission is to inform, to enlighten, to provide debate, but not to dictate. We seek neither to be king-makers nor king-breakers."[13] To some, that is an ethical lapse, a failure to provide leadership, waffling rather than taking a stand. Endorsements, of course, may not change voters' minds. Franklin Delano Roosevelt won the presidency four times despite thousands of unfavorable editorials. But whether endorsements change minds is irrelevant; the issue is newspaper leadership in the community. *USA Today* asked Senator Robert Dole (R-Kan.) whether papers should endorse candidates. Dole said: "Yes. Newspapers choose up sides in everything else. If they can speak out on every public issue from fruit flies to

[12]Jonathan Friendly, "Paper Assailed For Exposing Faulty Army Copters," *New York Times*, Aug. 5, 1984, p. 30.
[13] "We Say You Should Pick Your President," *USA Today*, Sept. 21, 1984, p. 109.

traffic stoplights they can spare a little space for the most important issue of all—the presidential race."[14] There is deep meaning in that: editorial pages that take stands on fruit flies, which will create no enemies for a newspaper, but which bob and weave on a presidential election, a subject that will, have trivialized their historic role and failed their ethical responsibility.

ETHICS IN THE NEWSROOM

Newspapers have never been without critics. But, like many institutions in modern society, newspapers are coming under attacks that are more numerous and serious than ever. It is the newsroom, of course, that each day places its efforts before the public and thus receives the brunt of criticism. And it is in the newsroom that you will find managers indulging in very heavy self-criticism and analysis on ethical issues. There is no rulebook of ethics. Newspapers have come up with a few general guidelines, but even they are far from unanimously accepted. For an aspiring manager, the importance of what follows is not that we provide *answers* but that, perhaps, we sketch some *questions* that you should start asking yourself as you firm up your own approach to ethical issues.

Invasion of Privacy

This is a troublesome area for many newsroom managers who attempt to balance respect for the individual's right to privacy against the newspaper's duty to inform the public about matters of significance. A general subscription to both seemingly conflicting principles is as far as any ethical code can go. There must be case-by-case decisions on where to draw the line between desire to shield the innocent from the glare of unwanted publicity and the professional

commitment to shine the public's spotlight in truly important dark corners.

Few ethical problems create so many gray areas. For example, Richard V. Allen's resignation as President Reagan's national security advisor was a matter of public interest. But was it in the public interest for a reporter on "stake-out" on Allen's front lawn to climb a tree so as to peer into his bedroom to see if he was home? A woman held hostage by her estranged husband in Florida was involved in news of public significance. But was it in the public interest to publish a photograph of her—nearly naked—fleeing her home? These and similar incidents draw public criticism and send many editors into agonizing reappraisal of the privacy issue. But most stop short of any definitive policy statement, aiming instead at sensitizing their staffs to weigh the individual's right to privacy against the public's right to know—and, in a close call, to come down on the side of serving that larger constituency, the public, with full disclosure.

Free Press and Fair Trial

Six members of the Black Liberation Army and Weather Underground were arrested in 1982 on charges of robbing a Brink's armored truck in Rockland County, New York, and killing a guard and two policemen. The *Rockland (N.Y.) Journal-News*, a 45,000-circulation Gannett paper, covered the story in depth. In two months, seventy-six articles were published, many on the front page. This intensity of coverage was determined by public concern, says Editor Barry Hoffman. "The interest was there already. The newspaper's role is reflecting the attitudes of people who live in Rockland County. I don't see that we molded anything that wasn't there already."[15] Defense attorneys saw it as a conflict between the First Amendment guarantee of a

---

[14] Robert Dole, "Papers Have Opinions, So Why Not Endorse?" *USA Today*, Sept. 21, 1984, p. 10a.

[15] Jonathan Friendly, "Rockland Editor Defends Newspaper's Role in Brink's Case Publicity," *New York Times*, Dec. 20, 1982, p. B3.

free press and the Sixth Amendment guarantee of a fair trial. An appeals court agreed and ordered the trial moved to another county. The court said it did not question the *Journal-News*'s right to publish but that "intensive, localized, continuing and prejudicial publicity" at least intensified "a deep and abiding resentment in Rockland County against the defendants."

Many editors argue that the Sixth Amendment guarantees trial by *unbiased* jurors—not jurors totally ignorant of the case—and that there need be no conflict with the First Amendment. Nevertheless, extensive coverage that tends to convict a defendant in the public eye before trial bothers many jurists and news executives alike. On this issue, there will surely be increased tension between the press and the courts.

Covering or Making the News

Just as geese fly north each spring, so do news stories. A typical one might come from a bass-fishing lake in the Deep South, reporting that a renowned left-hander, possessor of the world's best-ever fastball, won't report to baseball training camp until his salary is increased. Back come reports from team headquarters that the salary demand is outrageous, that the holdout can continue fishing until the lake freezes over. Thus starts the bargaining—and the press injects itself into the process as a vehicle for the public exchange of demands and counterdemands. Is that reporting or *making* the news?

Do political reporters report or make news by carrying charges and countercharges from candidate to opponent and back again? When a business news writer initiates an interview and develops news that moves stock prices, is that reporter making or reporting news? Business reporting creates ethical problems with increasing frequency. The problems stem not so much from those occasions when reporters betray the trust of their newspapers (and public) by trading and profiting on inside information before sharing it with their readers. As spectacularly uneth-

ical (and perhaps illegal) as such practices are, these betrayals are clear violations of trust and punishable by discharge. The code—written or unwritten—is clear on that. Rather, problems arise in gray areas, such as the following.

- Business-world rumor can be self-serving and can cause profound marketplace changes. A rumor of a corporate takeover attempt, for example, can boost or depress stock prices in minutes. Yet business news sections regularly publish rumors (often upgraded to "industry reports"). Should they? If the answer is no, how does that square with the press's responsibility to dig out the news, wherever it is, and publish it?

- Should business writers, like political candidates, disclose their personal finances? Should they avoid any suspicion of insider trading by refusing to handle a story about a company in which they have invested? Some publications require reporters to inform management of their holdings and to step aside from stories that would involve potential conflicts of interest. None requires reporters to inform the reading public.

- Some business stories can be self-fulfilling. Reporting a withdrawal run on a bank, for example, can create panic. Yet newspapers have a responsibility to inform readers of developments affecting their lives, and many editors agree that this might have to include shouting "financial fire" outside the bank. But it is a heavy responsibility that causes grave ethical concerns for many business-news editors and their publishers. Here is one newsman who didn't hesitate: Normally, the Federal Reserve Board's economic forecasts are held tightly confidential, for even a slight public hint of how the "Fed" views the future can move markets dramatically. But on October 28, 1982, Owen Ullmann of the Associated Press learned what the Fed was privately projecting for 1983. AP wires carried Ullmann's story, which was quickly interpreted by Wall Street as meaning the Fed was "gloomy" about the year ahead. The Dow Jones Industrial average of stock prices fell 15 points. Says Ullmann:

The incident raises a journalistic question I had never considered before: Should we consider the potential impact one of our market news stories might have on the financial markets before moving the report on the wire? I would answer "definitely not." Our criteria should be whether the story is newsworthy and the information accurate to the best of our knowledge. The potential impact should be as far removed from our thoughts as it was from mine that late October day.[16]

Personal Involvement in the News

There is, obviously, life outside the newsroom and editors and reporters must live it. Can you as a manager dictate *how* they should live it? To greater or lesser degree, many managers say yes. Examples:

- A reporter wins election to a school board. Even if that reporter doesn't cover education news, has the reporter changed hats and become an activist? Importantly, has this created doubt about the newspaper's objectivity? The *Knoxville (Tenn.) News-Sentinel* answered yes to both questions and fired a reporter newly elected to the school board of Alcoa, Tennessee.

- Should a newspaper move to avoid appearance of conflict of interest involving even spouses of staff members? The *Seattle Times* did. It told its managing editor he would lose his job if his wife became the mayor's press secretary. She declined the job.

In some cases, newspaper people *become the news*, as do reporters and columnists who use fame achieved through newspaper publication to command huge fees for lectures. Washington columnists sometimes earn $10,000 or more for a single speech, and some—including George Will, William Safire, Carl Rowan, and others—become national "personalities." Columnist Will was the center of one celebrated flap over outside activity. It was revealed that he had helped Ronald Reagan's staff prepare for debates with President Carter. The *New York Daily News* promptly dropped Will's column, saying that he had violated journalistic ethics (the *News* later reinstated the column). Other papers said Will was a declared conservative who was paid to express his views, and that they saw no ethical problem. Many managers prohibit employees from taking outside employment that might create conflict of interest. ANPA examined 115 labor agreements with the Newspaper Guild and found that 66 required employer permission for outside work; 87 prohibited working for a competitor; and 81 prohibited work that exploits the employee's position with the company or which could embarrass the company.

Newspapers must prohibit conduct that casts doubt on the paper's objectivity. Accepting gifts from news sources or participants in the news must be prohibited, and so must free press tours. "Junkets" are out.

Cooperation with Authorities

Press cooperation with police or other authorities causes grave ethical dilemmas—as when, for example, lives are at stake and the press, like any citizen, is asked to help save them. A *New York Daily News* reporter served as intermediary between police and a prisoner holding hostages in a Brooklyn hospital. An AP reporter was the link between Washington, D.C., police and a man threatening to blow up the Washington Monument.

At risk to themselves, other reporters have

---

[16] Owen Ullmann, "Should Reporter Consider Impact of Stories?", *AP Log*, Nov. 8, 1982, p. 1.

played similar roles. Should they? Should reporters step out of observer ranks and become participants? Can a press that participates in the news-making process hope to be impartial or to be perceived by its reading public as impartial?

There is a long history of press cooperation with police in certain crime situations. News organizations, for example, knew that the wife of a former ambassador to El Salvador had been kidnapped in Washington in 1983, but they withheld the news at FBI request. When she was freed, the story was published. Newspapers often cooperate by withholding precise details of tactics used by antiterrorist police to enter skyjacked airlines to free hostages. They do so to prevent future terrorists from benefiting. But such *cooperation* is quite different from *participation* as a prime mover. And while the former is generally deemed acceptable—indeed, necessary—by many newspapers, the latter often is not.

The question of press cooperation arises frequently in matters of national security. There has long been an adversarial relationship between many reporters and government. Tension flared when reporters were excluded from the U.S. invasion of Grenada in 1983. Uneasy accommodation followed, with the Pentagon agreeing to carry pool reporters to represent the entire press corps on any future operations, consistent that is, with mission security and troop safety. The controversy over reporting on Grenada and, earlier, Vietnam is multifaceted and includes charges that reporters were unpatriotic. Reporters have known and held military secrets in every U.S. war in this century, and there is no documented case of the press causing failure of a mission or death of U.S. servicemen. However, reporting has sometimes been embarrassing politically to the government, and that is a major factor in the adversarial relationship.

Sometimes, ethical problems arising from cooperation with authorities are easily resolved: it is possible for a newspaper to discharge its obligation to readers by alerting them, for ex-

ample, that a murderer is on the loose and simultaneously accede to police requests not to publish exact details of his gory methods that might inspire "copycat" criminals. Generally, however, questions of cooperation with authorities defy such easy answers. Each case requires careful consideration in light of what role the press plays: Is it simply an objective, dispassionate observer whose mission is to serve that broadest of constituencies, the public, or is it an observer that on occasion must become a participant? On the firing line, when events are moving rapidly, the judgment is often difficult to make.

Sources: Revealing and Protecting Them

Major ethical problems often surround news sources. A newspaper is obligated to tell readers the source of news stories and, importantly, the motives the source has in revealing news. It is unfair to ask readers repeatedly to take on blind faith news attributed to "officials" or "sources who declined to be identified." However, sources not granted anonymity sometimes won't reveal important stories—and *that* isn't in the public interest. So, sparingly, grudgingly, quote anonymous sources selectively when there is real need. A source should be granted anonymity only after much deep thought and agreement between reporter, editor, and publisher that the secrecy pledge will be kept. For it might mean jail for somebody on the staff if a judge demands that the source be revealed.

Many editors prohibit secret tape recording of sources, hidden cameras, or other "undercover" reportorial techniques. Secret taping, illegal in many states, smacks of dishonesty and fraud. A newspaper's strength is built on being a forthright, open, and honorable journal of news, information, and opinion.

How to Say You're Sorry

Despite rigid editing safeguards and eternal copy-desk vigilance, the hoax, the lie, and the distortion have penetrated the pages of many newspapers. What to do when that happens? Come clean. Level with readers. Disclose all. *Explain* what happened and, yes, you might even say you're sorry. Some newspapers avoid candid explanations. A "damage control" syndrome calls for quiet internal investigation, private remedial efforts, and, at most, guarded discussion with peers at professional meetings of editors. Too often, readers are left in the dark—not that something went wrong; that's obvious. Rather, too often readers don't know *why* it went wrong or what the newspaper is doing to prevent recurrence. And that carries the stench of cover-up. Probably nothing is more damaging to a newspaper's credibility.

Not much is done for credibility, either, with a coy dismissal of error—"Oops, our slip is showing." And how should readers take the incomplete, unhelpful "The *Bugle* stands by its story"? Refreshingly, some newspapers practice candid full disclosure:

- The *New York Times* published a story plus editorial explaining how it was hoaxed by a freelance writer on a story about Cambodia. Said the *Times*, in part:

When a newspaper uses precious front-page space, as the *Times* did yesterday, to expose a lie in its own columns, it is trying to do much more than confess a procedural lapse. The point is to reaffirm a compact with the reader: that what is printed has been honestly gathered and labeled; that any credible challenge will be rigorously examined, and that serious error will get prompt and conspicuous notice.[17]

- When Eastern Airlines objected to inaccuracies in a *Wall Street Journal* story, the *Journal* published a lengthy letter from an Eastern official clarifying the facts, and attached an editor's note acknowledging

error. "The *Journal* stands corrected . . .", it said.[18]

Many newspapers address possible reader perceptions of unfairness and imbalance even when major error is not involved. Examples:

- When it became clear from reader reaction that a *Milwaukee Journal* story on home buying, carried in an inside section, was misleading, the *Journal* published on its *front* page an article explaining how the story was reported, where its facts came from, and why, under later examination, it appeared that, yes, the story was partly misleading. Key to the *Journal*'s treatment was precise dollars-and-cents detail on exactly what was misleading.[19]

- In what he calls "an annual column of confession," *New York Times* columnist Tom Wicker looks back at a year of his reporting and acknowledges even minor errors of fact and judgment. Of leveling thus with the reader, he says the following: "while it may be good neither for the soul nor the digestion, [it] is necessary to clear the record and answer the mail."[20]

Clear the record. Be accountable. That is what the press forces every day from the institutions and individuals that it covers. And that is what the press must do with its readers. It's the ethical thing to do.

In sum, a considered, principled approach to ethics is essential for any newspaper manager today. Whether that approach should be codified in writing is arguable. But written or oral, ethical guidelines must be laid down and the entire

---

[17] "A Lie in the *Times*," editorial, *New York Times*, Feb. 23, 1982, p. A22.

[18] "Eastern Airlines on *Journal* Article," letter to editor, *Wall Street Journal*, July 20, 1982, p. 24.
[19] Russell Austin, "Advice to Delay Buying Home Was Not Meant For All," *Milwaukee Journal*, Feb. 22, 1982, p. 1.
[20] Tom Wicker, "Excuse It, Please," *New York Times*, Dec. 31, 1982, p. A19.

staff must be sensitized to the newspaper's responsibility to operate within them. An aspiring manager will do well to construct his or her personal code of ethics around two goals of any newspaper—to search out the truth and serve the reader.

SUMMARY

Newspapers have historic responsibilities beyond making shareholders happy. They must inform, enlighten, lead opinion, and serve as the people's surrogates. That is a heavy burden, but no other medium is as well equipped to do it.

Compelling ethical issues in newsrooms today include balancing the individual's right to privacy and the public's right to be informed, free press vs. fair trial, the press's tendency to make news, not simply report it. Many newspapers insist that staff members' outside work or activities not jeopardize the paper's objectivity or public perception of its objectivity.

In advertising, many newspapers establish standards of acceptability and reject ads that fail certain ethical tests. This involves subjective judgments on whether ads are likely to cause financial loss to readers, to injure their health, or otherwise to be contrary to the best interests of the newspaper and its readers. Advertorials—ads made up to look like news copy—are met increasingly with disfavor because they blur distinctions between news and advertising. That damages the newspaper's credibility, which harms advertiser interests as well.

Ethical concerns in the publisher's suite range from lobbying at the White House in the newspaper industry's own naked self-interest to whether an individual paper should endorse political candidates.

For ethical questions, there are no rulebook answers. The burden for each aspiring manager is to begin, now, working out where he or she stands on compelling issues of the day.

RECOMMENDED READING

Extensive research in ethics is published on a continuing basis by APME, ASNE, and the Society of Professional Journalists/Sigma Delta Chi. Note particularly the latter's annual *Journalism Ethics Report*. ASNE's *Newspaper Credibility: 206 Practical Approaches to Heighten Reader Trust*, April 1986, is very helpful. The *Newspaper Research Journal* is active in covering newspaper accountability and media credibility. Also note *The Adversary Press*, Modern Media Institute, 801 Third Street South, St. Petersburg, FL 33701. On social responsibility of business, note W. Jack Duncan, *Management*, New York, Random House, 1983; J. W. McGuire, *Business and Society*, New York, McGraw-Hill, 1963.

Name Index

Subject Index

About the Author

CONRAD C. FINK recalls that his first management job, as Associated Press night city editor in Chicago, posed severe challenges. He was young, inexperienced, had no management training, was given limited resources—yet had to perform immediately with efficiency and speed. "And that," he says, "is how it was subsequently with each new management job. There were no rule books, no guidelines. I was simply thrown into increasing responsibility without adequate background. *Strategic Newspaper Management* is written to give the next generation of aspiring managers a headstart on how to handle the responsibilities that will come their way." In learning management on the job, Fink traveled the world for twenty-five years as an AP foreign correspondent and manager and as an executive in newspaper and broadcast operations. As AP vice president in New York City, Fink worked closely with managers of newspapers throughout the United States. As a media manager and acquisition executive, he studied the finances and management of more than 100 newspapers. In 1982, Fink launched a new career at the University of Georgia's Henry W. Grady School of Journalism and Mass Communication where he has been cited for superior teaching of newspaper management and strategy and advanced reporting. He also is a consultant in newspaper management and acquisitions.